murach's
ASP.NET 3.5
web programming with
C# 2008

TRAINING & REFERENCE

murach's
ASP.NET 3.5
web programming with
C# 2008

Anne Boehm

Joel Murach

MIKE MURACH & ASSOCIATES, INC.

1-800-221-5528 • (559) 440-9071 • Fax: (559) 440-0963
murachbooks@murach.com • www.murach.com

Author:	Anne Boehm
	Joel Murach
Writer:	Ray Harris
Editor:	Mike Murach
Cover Design:	Zylka Design
Production:	Tom Murach
	Cynthia Vasquez

Books for .NET 3.5 developers

Murach's C# 2008
Murach's ADO.NET 3.5, LINQ, and the Entity Framework with C# 2008
Murach's ASP.NET 3.5 Web Programming with C# 2008

Murach's Visual Basic 2008
Murach's ADO.NET 3.5, LINQ, and the Entity Framework with VB 2008
Murach's ASP.NET 3.5 Web Programming with VB 2008

Books for application developers using SQL

Murach's SQL Server 2008 for Developers
Murach's Oracle SQL and PL/SQL

Books for web developers

Murach's Java SE 6
Murach's JavaScript and DOM Scripting
Murach's Java Servlets and JSP (2nd Edition)

Books for IBM mainframe programmers

Murach's OS/390 and z/OS JCL
Murach's Mainframe COBOL
Murach's CICS for the COBOL Programmer
DB2 for the COBOL Programmer, Part 1

For more on Murach books,
please visit us at www.murach.com

10 9 8 7 6 5 4 3
ISBN: 978-1-890774-48-6

Contents

Introduction   xix

Section 1   The essence of ASP.NET web programming

Chapter 1   An introduction to ASP.NET web programming   3
Chapter 2   How to develop a one-page web application   31
Chapter 3   How to develop a multi-page web application   73
Chapter 4   How to test and debug an ASP.NET application   121

Section 2   Basic ASP.NET skills

Chapter 5   A crash course in HTML   161
Chapter 6   How to work with server controls   201
Chapter 7   How to use the validation controls   245
Chapter 8   How to manage state   271
Chapter 9   How to use master pages   299
Chapter 10   How to use site navigation   323
Chapter 11   How to use themes   341

Section 3   ASP.NET database programming

Chapter 12   An introduction to database programming   365
Chapter 13   How to use SQL data sources   391
Chapter 14   How to use the GridView control   427
Chapter 15   How to use the DetailsView and FormView controls   465
Chapter 16   How to use the ListView and DataPager controls   505
Chapter 17   How to use object data sources   545
Chapter 18   How to use LINQ data sources   589

Section 4   Professional ASP.NET skills

Chapter 19   How to secure a web site   617
Chapter 20   How to authenticate and authorize users   639
Chapter 21   How to use profiles to personalize a web site   685
Chapter 22   How to use the MultiView and Wizard controls   717
Chapter 23   How to use email, custom error pages, and back-button control   743
Chapter 24   How to use web parts to build portals   773
Chapter 25   How to use AJAX   805
Chapter 26   How to configure and deploy ASP.NET applications   839

Section 5   Developing reusable code

Chapter 27   How to develop user controls   861
Chapter 28   How to develop custom server controls   883
Chapter 29   An introduction to web services   925

Reference aids

Appendix A   How to install and use the software and downloadable files   941
Appendix B   How to work with web applications using IIS under Windows XP   957
Appendix C   How to work with web applications using IIS under Windows Vista   965
Index   973

Expanded contents

Section 1 The essence of ASP.NET web programming

Chapter 1 An introduction to ASP.NET web programming

An introduction to web applications 4
Two pages of a Shopping Cart application 4
The hardware and software components for web applications 6
How static web pages work 8
How dynamic web pages work 10
How state is handled in ASP.NET applications 12

An introduction to ASP.NET application development 14
The software you need 14
The components of the .NET Framework 16
Three environments for developing ASP.NET applications 18

A quick preview of how an ASP.NET application works 20
The files used by the Shopping Cart application 20
The aspx code for the Order form 22
The C# code for the Order form 24
How an ASP.NET application is compiled and run 26

Chapter 2 How to develop a one-page web application

How to work with ASP.NET web sites 32
How to start a new web site 32
How to work with the Visual Studio IDE 34
How to add folders and files to a web site 36
How to open or close an existing web site 38

How to use Design view to build a web form 40
The design of the Future Value form 40
How to use flow layout 42
How to add a table to a form 44
How to add text to the cells of a table 44
How to add server controls to a form 46
How to set the properties of the controls 46
Common properties for web server controls 48

How to work in Source and Split views 50
How to use Source view to modify the design 50
How to use Split view to work with the design 52
The aspx code for the Future Value form 54

How to add validation controls to a form 56
An introduction to the validation controls 56
How to use the required field validator 58
How to use the range validator 58

How to add code to a form 60
How to use the Code Editor 60
How to use page and control events 62
The C# code for the Future Value form 64

How to test a web application 66
How to run a web site with the built-in development server 66
How to review the HTML that's sent to the browser 68

Chapter 3   How to develop a multi-page web application

The Shopping Cart application **74**
The Order page 74
The Cart page 76
The files and folders used by the Shopping Cart application 78
How to add a class to a web site 80

Six skills for working with multiple web forms **82**
How to add a web form to a web site 82
How to rename a web form 84
How to change the starting web form 84
How to redirect or transfer to another page 86
How to use cross-page posting 88
How to code absolute and relative URLs 90

How to create and use data sources **92**
How to create an Access data source 92
How to configure an Access data source 94
How to bind a drop-down list to a data source 96
How to use C# code to get data from a data source 98

How to use session state **100**
How session state works 100
How to work with data in session state 102

The code for the Shopping Cart application **104**
The code for the Product and CartItem classes 104
The aspx code for the Order page 104
The C# code for the Order page 108
The aspx code for the Cart page 112
The C# code for the Cart page 112

Chapter 4   How to test and debug an ASP.NET application

How to create ASP.NET web sites that run under IIS **122**
How to create a local IIS web site 122
How to create a remote IIS web site 124
How to create an FTP web site 126

How to test an ASP.NET application **128**
How to test an application with the default browser.................................. 128
How to test an application with a browser other than the default 130
How to test a file-system web site with IIS 132
How to test an application from outside of Visual Studio 134
How to use the Exception Assistant 136

How to use the debugger **138**
How to use breakpoints 138
How to use tracepoints 140
How to work in break mode 142
How to control the execution of an application 144
How to use the Autos, Locals, and Watch windows to monitor variables 146
How to use the Immediate window to work with values 148

How to use the Trace feature **150**
How to enable the Trace feature 150
How to interpret Trace output 150
How to create custom trace messages 152

How to write information directly to the HTTP output stream **154**

Section 2 Basic ASP.NET skills

Chapter 5   A crash couse in HTML

An introduction to HTML **162**
Basic rules for coding HTML elements 162
How to work with HTML using Visual Studio 164
How web server controls are rendered 166

How to code HTML documents **168**
The basic structure of an HTML document 168
The Page directive 170
The Doctype declaration 170
How to code basic text formatting elements 172
How to code links to other HTML pages 174

How to use styles **176**
How to use inline styles 176
How to use the Span element to apply styles 178
How to use an internal style sheet 180
How to use classes in a style sheet 182
How to add and modify style rules 184
How to use an external style sheet 186
Visual Studio features for working with external style sheets 188
How to use the Apply Styles window to work with styles 190
How to use the CSS Properties window to work with styles 192

How to code tables **194**
How to create a table 194
Common table attributes and style properties 196
How to use a table to control the layout of a page 198

Chapter 6   How to work with server controls

An introduction to server controls **202**
Types of server controls 202
The web server controls presented in this chapter 204
Two ways to handle control events 206
How to use access keys with web server controls 208
How to set the focus on a web server control 208
How to set the default button control 208

How to work with button controls **210**
How to work with buttons, link buttons, and image buttons 210
How to use the e argument of an image button control 212
How to use the Command event 214

How to work with text boxes, labels, check boxes, and radio buttons .. 216
How to work with text boxes and labels 216
How to work with check boxes and radio buttons 218
C# code for working with these controls 220

How to work with list controls **222**
Basic skills for working with list boxes and drop-down lists 222
Properties for working with list boxes, drop-down lists, and list items 224
Members for working with list item collections 226
How to use the ListItem Collection Editor 228
How to work with radio button lists and check box lists 230
How to work with bulleted lists and numbered lists 232

How to use other web server controls **234**
How to get the information you need for using a control 234
How to use the image control 236
How to use the hyperlink control 236
How to use the file upload control 238
How to use the image map control 240
How to use the calendar control 242

Chapter 7   How to use the validation controls

An introduction to the validation controls **246**
How to use the validation controls 246
Common validator properties 248
How ASP.NET processes validation controls 250

How to use the basic validation controls **252**
How to use the required field validator 252
How to use the compare validator 254
How to use the range validator 256

Validation techniques **258**
How to use the validation summary control 258
How to use validation groups 260

How to use the advanced validation controls **262**
How to use the regular expression validator 262
How to create your own regular expressions 264
How to use a custom validator 266
A validation routine that validates credit card numbers 268

Chapter 8   How to manage state

How to use view state **272**
How to work with view state 272
How to use view state for your own data 274

How to use session state **276**
How to work with session state 276
When to save and retrieve session state items 278
Options for storing session state data 280
Options for tracking session IDs 280
How to set session state options 282

How to use application state **284**
How application state works 284
How to work with application state data 286
How to work with application events 288

How to use cookies and URL encoding **290**
How to create cookies 290
How to work with cookies 292
How to enable or disable cookies 294
How to use URL encoding 296

Chapter 9   How to use master pages

How to create master pages **300**
An introduction to master pages 300
How to create a master page 302
The aspx code for a new master page 304
The aspx code for the Halloween Store master page 306
The code-behind file for the master page 306

How to create and develop content pages **310**
How to create a content page 310
How to add content to a page 312
The aspx code for the Order content page 314

How to nest master pages **316**
How to create nested master pages 316
How to add content to a child master page 316

How to access master page controls from a content page **318**
How to expose a master page control as a public property 318
How to access a public property of the master page from a content page 320

Chapter 10   How to use site navigation

An introduction to site navigation **324**
An introduction to the navigation controls 324
How to create a web.sitemap file 326
The web.sitemap file for the Navigation application 328

How to use the site navigation controls **330**
How to use the TreeView control 330
How to create a SiteMapDataSource control 332
How to use the Menu control 334
How to use the SiteMapPath control 336
A master page for the Navigation application 338

Chapter 11   How to use themes

An introduction to themes **342**
A page before and after a theme has been applied 342
How themes work 344
How to make an existing theme available to an application 346
How to apply a theme to an application 346

How to create your own themes **348**
How to use cascading style sheets 348
How to use skins 350
Another way to store skins 352
How to use images 354

More skills for working with themes **356**
How to apply a theme to a page 356
How to apply a skin to a control 356
How to remove a theme from an application 358
How to remove a theme from a page 358
How to remove a theme from a control 358
How to use style sheet themes 360

Section 3   ASP.NET database programming

Chapter 12   An introduction to database programming

An introduction to relational databases **366**
How a table is organized 366
How the tables in a database are related 368
How the columns in a table are defined 370
The design of the Halloween database 372

How to use SQL to work with the data in a relational database **374**
How to query a single table 374
How to join data from two or more tables 376
How to add, update, and delete data in a table 378

An introduction to ADO.NET 3.5 .... **380**
How the basic ADO.NET components work 380
Concurrency and the disconnected data architecture 382
How to work with data without using a data adapter 384

An introduction to the ADO.NET 3.5 classes **386**
The SqlConnection class 386
The SqlCommand class 386
The SqlParameter class 388
The SqlDataReader class 388
The SqlDataAdapter class 388

Chapter 13   How to use SQL data sources

How to create a SQL data source **392**
A Product List application that uses two SQL data sources 392
How to create a SqlDataSource control 394
How to define the connection 396
How to save the connection string in the web.config file 398
How to configure the Select statement 400
How to create a Where clause 402
How select parameters work 404

How to use the Query Builder **406**
How to create a Select statement with the Query Builder 406
How to define the parameters 408

How to use the DataList control **410**
How the DataList control works 410
How to define the templates for a data list 412
How to format a data list 414

How to use data binding **416**
How to bind a list control to a data source 416
How to bind the controls in a template 418
The aspx file for the Product List application 420

How to use the advanced features of a SQL data source **422**
How to create a data source that can update the database 422
How to change the data source mode 424
How to use caching 424

Chapter 14   How to use the GridView control

How to customize the GridView control **428**
How the GridView control works 428
How to define the fields in a GridView control 430
Elements used to create and format fields 432
How to enable sorting 434
How to enable paging 436
How to customize paging 438

A list application that uses a GridView control **440**
The Product List application 440
The aspx file 442

How to update GridView data **444**
How to work with command fields 444
How to use events raised by the GridView control 446
How to insert a row in a GridView control 448

A maintenance application that uses a GridView control **450**
The Category Maintenance application 450
The aspx file 452
The code-behind file 456

How to work with template fields **458**
How to create template fields 458
The template version of the Category Maintenance application 460
The aspx code for the template version 460

Chapter 15   How to use the DetailsView and FormView controls

How to use the DetailsView control **466**
An introduction to the DetailsView control 466
Attributes and child elements for the DetailsView control 468
How to define the fields in a DetailsView control 468
How to enable paging 470
How to create a Master/Detail page 472

How to update DetailsView data **474**
An introduction to command buttons 474
How to add command buttons 476
How to use events raised by the DetailsView control 478
How to fix the optimistic concurrency bug 480
How to create template fields 482

The Product Maintenance application **484**
The operation of the application 484
The aspx file 484
The code-behind file 488

How to use the FormView control **492**
An introduction to the FormView control 492
How to work with the Item template 494
How to work with the EditItem and InsertItem templates 496

A Shopping Cart application that uses a FormView control **498**
The operation of the application 498
The aspx file for the Order page 500
The code-behind file for the Order page 500

Chapter 16   How to use the ListView and DataPager controls

How to use the ListView control **506**
An introduction to the ListView control 506
How to configure a ListView control 508
How to work with the Layout template 510
How to work with the Item template 512
How to provide for sorting 514
How to provide for paging 516
How to customize paging 518

A list application that uses a ListView control **520**
The Product List application 520
The aspx file 522

How to group ListView data **526**
How to define the templates for a group 526
A Product List application that uses groups 528
The aspx file for the grouped Product List application 528

How to update ListView data **532**
How to use buttons to perform update operations 532
How to work with the EditItem and InsertItem templates 534
How to use events raised by the ListView control 534

A maintenance application that uses a ListView control **536**
The Category Maintenance application 536
The aspx file 538
The code-behind file 538

Chapter 17   How to use object data sources

An introduction to object data sources **546**
How 3-layer applications work in ASP.NET 546
How to use the ObjectDataSource control 548
How to configure an ObjectDataSource control 550
How to work with bound controls 550

A Product List application **552**
The aspx file 554
The ProductDB class 556

How to create a data access class **558**
How to design a data access class 558
How to create a select method 560
How to create update, delete, and insert methods 562
How to use attributes to mark a data access class 564

A Category Maintenance application **566**
The design 566
The aspx file 566
The code-behind file 570
The CategoryDB class 572

How to use business objects with object data sources **576**
How to create methods that use business objects 576
The aspx file for a Category Maintenance application that uses business objects 578
The Category business class 580
A CategoryDB class that uses business objects 580

How to use paging with object data sources **584**
How to create an ObjectDataSource control that provides for paging 584
How to create a data access class that provides for paging 586

Chapter 18   How to use LINQ data sources

An introduction to LINQ **590**
How LINQ works 590
How to use LINQ with SQL Server databases 592

How to use the Object Relational Designer **594**
How to create an object model 594
How to create entity classes 596

How to use the LinqDataSource control **598**
An introduction to the LinqDataSource control 598
How to configure a LinqDataSource control 600
A Product List application 602
The aspx file for the Product List application 604

How to update data 606
How to configure a LINQ data source for updates 606
How to use optimistic concurrency 606

How to group data 608
How to configure groups 608
An Invoices By Date application that uses groups 610
The aspx file for the Invoices By Date application 610

Section 4 Professional ASP.NET skills

Chapter 19 How to secure a web site

An introduction to SSL 618
How secure connections work 618
How digital secure certificates work... 620
How to determine if a digital secure certificate is installed on your server 620

How to get and use a digital secure certificate 622
How to get a digital secure certificate 622
How to get a trial certificate for testing 624
How to use the IIS Certificate Wizard 626
How to work with certificates using IIS 7.0 628

How to use a secure connection 630
How to request a secure connection 630
How to force a page to use a secure connection 632

A Halloween Store application that uses SSL 634
The operation of the Halloween Store application 634
The code for the Halloween Store application 634

Chapter 20 How to authenticate and authorize users

An introduction to authentication 640
Three types of authentication 640
How forms-based authentication works 642

How to set up authentication and authorization 644
How to start the Web Site Administration Tool 644
How to enable forms-based authentication... 646
How to create and manage roles 648
How to create and manage users 650
How to create and manage access rules 652
How to modify the membership and role provider 654

How to use the login controls 656
How to use the Login control 656
How to use the LoginStatus and LoginName controls 658
How to use the CreateUserWizard control 660
How to use the PasswordRecovery control... 662
How to use the ChangePassword control 664
How to use the LoginView control 666

The Authentication application 668
The pages 668
The directory structure 672
The access rules 672
The web.config files.. 674

How to use code to work with authentication **676**
How to use the Membership class 676
How to use the MembershipUser class 678
How to use the FormsAuthentication class 680
How to use the Roles class 682

Chapter 21   How to use profiles to personalize a web site

An introduction to profiles **686**
Profiles compared with session state 686
An overview of how profiles work 688
How the default profile provider works 690

How to use profiles with authenticated users **692**
How to define profile properties 692
How to specify data types 694
How to group profile properties 696
How to specify default values 698
How to specify read-only properties 698
How to use custom types 700

How to use profiles with anonymous users **702**
How to enable anonymous identification 702
How to allow anonymous users to access profile properties 702
How to migrate data from anonymous to authenticated users 704

The Cart Profile application **706**
The pages 706
The code 710

Chapter 22   How to use the MultiView and Wizard controls

How to use the MultiView control **718**
How the MultiView control works 718
How to add views 720
How to add controls to a view 722
How to navigate between views with commands 724
How to access the data stored in a MultiView control 726
Properties and events of the MultiView and View controls 728

How to use the Wizard control **730**
How the Wizard control works 730
How to add or remove steps 732
How to add a Cancel button 734
How to add a completion step 736
Properties and events of the Wizard and WizardStep controls 738
How to use templates and styles with a Wizard control 740

Chapter 23   How to use email, custom error pages, and back-button control

How to send email **744**
An introduction to email 744
How to configure the SMTP service in IIS 746
How to create an email message 748
How to send an email message 750
How to add an attachment to an email message 752
How to create an HTML message 754

How to use custom error handling **756**

An introduction to custom error handling 756

How to get and use the Exception object for an error 758

How to code methods that redirect to a custom error page 760

The code for a custom error page 762

How to handle HTTP errors with the web.config file 764

How to handle the back-button problem **766**

An introduction to the back-button problem 766

How to disable browser page caching 768

How to use timestamps to avoid the back-button problem 770

Chapter 24   How to use web parts to build portals

An introduction to the portal framework **774**

A portal that uses web parts 774

How user configurations are stored 778

SharePoint and ASP.NET 778

Types of controls that can be used as web parts 780

How to use web parts **782**

How to create a page that uses web parts 782

How to add a user control to a web part zone 786

How to let the user move web parts between zones 790

How to let the user add web parts to a zone 792

How to let the user edit the properties of a web part 794

How to apply formatting to web parts 798

How to write code that works with web parts **800**

Classes for working with web parts 800

How to develop and use a custom WebPart control 802

Chapter 25   How to use AJAX

An introduction to AJAX **806**

AJAX concepts 806

How AJAX works 808

An introduction to ASP.NET AJAX **810**

How ASP.NET AJAX works 810

The Microsoft AJAX Library 812

The ASP.NET AJAX server controls 814

The ASP.NET AJAX Control Toolkit 816

How to use the ASP.NET AJAX server controls **818**

How to use the ScriptManager control 818

How to use the ScriptManagerProxy control 820

How to use the UpdatePanel control 822

How to use the Timer control 824

How to use the UpdateProgress control 826

An application that uses AJAX **828**

The Shout Box application 828

The ShoutItem class 830

The ShoutItemList class 830

The aspx file 832

The css file 832

The code-behind file 836

Chapter 26 How to configure and deploy ASP.NET applications

How to configure an ASP.NET application **840**
How to use the Web Site Administration Tool 840
How to use the IIS Management Console with Windows XP 842
How to use the IIS Management Console with Windows Vista 844

How to deploy an ASP.NET application **846**
Three ways to deploy an ASP.NET application 846
How to use the Copy Web Site command for XCopy deployment 848
How to use the Publish Web Site command for precompiled deployment 850
How to use the aspnet_compiler command for precompiled deployment 852
How to create a Web Setup project 854
How to create and use a Setup program 856

Section 5 Developing reusable code

Chapter 27 How to develop user controls

An introduction to user controls **862**
A web page that contains three user controls 862
A procedure for creating and using user controls 862

How to create user controls **864**
How to add a user control to a project 864
How to design a user control 864
How to code a user control 866
How to expose properties, methods, and events 868

How to use user controls **872**
How to add a user control to a web form 872
The aspx code that's generated when you add a user control to a form 874
How to write code that works with properties, methods, and events 876

The ProductDisplay user control **878**
The design 878
The ascx file 878
The code-behind file 878

Chapter 28 How to develop custom server controls

An overview of custom server controls **884**
An introduction to custom server controls 884
How custom server controls compare with user controls 886
Three types of custom server controls 888

How to create a rendered control **890**
The default class for a custom server control 890
How to override the Render or RenderContents method for a custom control 892
The design of the DaysUntil control 894
The code for the DaysUntil control 894

How to create and test a web control library **898**
Step 1: Create a web control library 898
Step 2: Create the custom server controls 898
Step 3: Build the web control library 898
Step 4: Add the library to a web site 900
Step 5: Test the controls 900

Additional programming techniques for custom controls **902**
How to use the HtmlTextWriter class to render HTML 902
How to use designer attributes 904
How to raise events in a custom control 906

How to create a superclassed control **908**
How to code a superclassed control 908
The design of the CaptionedBox control 908
The code for the CaptionedBox control 910

How to create a composite control **914**
How to code a composite control 914
The design of the DateDDL control 916
The code for the DateDDL control 916

Chapter 29   An introduction to web services

Basic concepts and terms **926**
What web services are used for 926
How web services work 926

How to create a web service **928**
How to start a web service web site 928
How to add a web service 928
How to develop the code for a web service 930
The code for the DaysUntilDates web service 932
How to test a web service 934

How to consume a web service **936**
How to add a web reference 936
How to use a web service 938

Introduction

As we see it, Microsoft's ASP.NET 3.5 has the potential to help you develop web applications faster and better than ever before. If, for example, you've been using a previous version of ASP.NET for developing web applications, you'll soon see that ASP.NET 3.5 has many new and improved features. And if you've been using Java servlets and JSP for developing web applications, you'll see that ASP.NET offers many features that just aren't available on the Java platforms.

Whether or not you're new to web programming, though, this book will get you off to a fast start. In fact, by the end of chapter 4, you'll know how to use Visual Studio to develop and test multi-page database applications. *No other ASP.NET book gets you started that fast.*

On the other hand, this is much more than a beginning book. By the time you're done, you'll have all the skills you need for developing e-commerce web applications at a professional level. You'll also find that this book does double duty as the best on-the-job reference book that money can buy. *No other ASP.NET 3.5 book teaches you so much or so thoroughly.*

What this book does

To be more specific about what this book presents, here is a brief description of each of its five sections:

- Section 1 is designed to get you off to a fast start. So the first three chapters show you how to use Visual Studio and ASP.NET to design and code both one-page and multi-page web applications that get data from a database. Then, chapter 4 shows you how to test and debug your web applications. At that point, you're ready to write some serious web applications of your own, and you're ready for rapid progress in the sections that follow.

- Section 2 presents the other skills that you're likely to use in every ASP.NET application that you develop. That includes the essential HTML skills, how to use the server and validation controls, and more about managing the state of an application than what's covered in section 1. Then, the last three chapters in this section present features that make it easier for you to develop professional-looking applications: master pages, site navigation, and themes.

- In section 3, you'll learn how to use the data access features of ASP.NET 3.5. That includes using data sources, which can dramatically reduce the amount of data access code that you need for an application. It includes some bound controls that are designed to work with data sources, including the new ListView and DataPager controls. It includes object data sources, which make it easier for you to separate presentation code from data access code. And it includes the new LINQ data sources, which let you take advantage of the new Language-Integrated Query (LINQ) feature of C# for accessing data from a variety of sources. This is powerful stuff, so you're going to want to read this section from start to finish.

- Section 4 completes the set of skills that you need for developing professional e-commerce web applications. Here, you'll learn how to secure data transmissions between client and server, authenticate and authorize users, use profiles to personalize your applications, use email within your applications, and much more, including how to use the new AJAX features of ASP.NET. Then, the last chapter in this section shows you the best ways to configure and deploy your applications.

- Last, section 5 shows you how to develop user controls, custom server controls, and web services. Those are three different ways that you can write code once and reuse it in more than one web page or application. And these techniques are commonly used in large development shops.

To get the most from this book, we recommend that you start by reading the first section from start to finish. But after that, you can skip to any of the other sections to get the information that you need, whenever you need it. Since this book has been carefully designed to work that way, you won't miss anything by skipping around.

Why you'll learn faster and better with this book

Like all our books, this one has features that you won't find in competing books. That's why we believe you'll learn faster and better with our book than with any other. Here are just three of those features.

- To make sure that you learn ASP.NET as quickly and easily as possible, all of its features are presented in the context of complete applications. These applications include the web forms, the aspx code, and the C# code. As we see it, the best way to learn is to study applications like these, even though you won't find them in most competing books.

- Unlike many ASP.NET books, this one shows you how to get the most from Visual Studio 2008 as you develop your applications. Because we've found that this IDE is one of the keys to development productivity, we're surprised that most books still ignore or neglect it.

- If you page through this book, you'll see that all of the information is presented in "paired pages," with the essential syntax, guidelines, and examples on the right page and the perspective and extra explanation on the left page. This not only helps you learn faster by reading less, but is also the best reference format that you'll find anywhere. That's why this book works so well for both training and reference.

What software you need

To develop ASP.NET 3.5 applications, you can use any of the full editions of Visual Studio 2008, including the Standard Edition, Professional Edition, or Team System. All of these editions come with everything you need, including the Visual Studio development environment, version 3.5 of the Microsoft .NET Framework, C# 2008 and Visual Basic 2008, a built-in web server that's ideal for testing ASP.NET applications, and a scaled-back version of SQL Server called SQL Server Express.

You can also use the Visual Web Developer 2008 Express Edition plus SQL Server Express to develop ASP.NET 3.5 applications. Together, they provide all of the items listed above, and both can be downloaded from Microsoft's web site for free.

Keep in mind, though, that Web Developer 2008 is a scaled-back version of the full editions. That's why you'll find that some of its user interfaces are simpler than the ones in this book, which are all based on the Professional Edition. You'll also find that a few of the features in this book aren't available with Web Developer 2008. Nevertheless, Web Developer 2008 is a terrific product for learning how to develop ASP.NET 3.5 applications. And both the applications and skills that you develop will work with any of the full editions.

How our downloadable files make learning easier

To help you get the most from this book, you can download the source code and databases for all of the applications presented in this book. Then, you can test and review these applications on your own to see exactly how they work. And you can copy and paste the code that you want to use in your own applications.

The download also includes the applications and files you'll need to do the exercises at the end of chapters 1 through 4. And it includes the solutions for the exercises for chapters 2 and 3. That way, you can compare your own solutions to ours. For more information about downloading and installing all the files for this book, please see appendix A.

2 companion books that will enhance your skills

As you read this book, you may discover that your C# skills aren't as strong as they ought to be. In that case, we recommend that you get a copy of *Murach's C# 2008*. It will get you up-to-speed with the language. It will show you how to work with the most useful .NET classes. And as a bonus, it will show you how to develop Windows Forms applications.

Another book that you may be interested in is *Murach's SQL Server 2005 for Developers*. To start, it shows you how to write SQL statements in all their variations so you can code the right statements for your data sources. This often gives you the option of having Microsoft SQL Server do more so your applications do less. Beyond that, this book shows you how to design and implement databases and how to use advanced features like stored procedures.

Last, please check our web site periodically for new books. In particular, we will soon be publishing a book on SQL Server 2008. Before too long, we also intend to publish ADO.NET 3.5 books in both C# and Visual Basic editions.

Support materials for trainers and instructors

If you're a corporate trainer or a college instructor who would like to use this book for a course, we offer an Instructor's CD that includes: (1) a complete set of PowerPoint slides that you can use to review and reinforce the content of the book; (2) instructional objectives that describe the skills a student should have upon completion of each chapter; (3) test banks that measure mastery of those skills; (4) the solutions to the exercises in this book; (5) projects that the students start from scratch; (6) solutions to those projects; and (7) the source code and database for the book applications.

To learn more about this Instructor's CD and to find out how to get it, please go to our web site at www.murach.com and click on the Trainers link or the Instructors link. Or, if you prefer, you can call Kelly at 1-800-221-5528 or send an email to kelly@murach.com.

Please let us know how this book works for you

When we started this book, our main goal was to teach you the new features of ASP.NET 3.5 along with the old features that you still need to know to master ASP.NET programming. Whenever possible, we've integrated these new features with the old to help you become a proficient ASP.NET 3.5 programmer as quickly and easily as possible. Otherwise, we've presented the new features in separate chapters so you can read them whenever the need or interest arises.

Now that we're done, we hope that we've succeeded. So, if you have any comments about our book, we would appreciate hearing from you. If you like our book, please tell a friend. And good luck with your web programming.

A special welcome goes to our newest employee, Ray Harris, who wrote the AJAX chapter for this book. You can expect many books from him on new and exciting topics in the near future.

Anne Boehm, Author
anne@murach.com

Joel Murach, Author
joelmurach@yahoo.com

Section 1

The essence of ASP.NET web programming

This section presents the essential skills for designing, coding, and testing ASP.NET web applications. After chapter 1 introduces you to the concepts and terms that you need to know for web programming, chapters 2 and 3 teach you the essential skills for designing web forms and writing the C# code that makes them work. Then, chapter 4 shows you how to use the many features for testing and debugging ASP.NET applications.

When you finish all four chapters, you'll be able to develop real-world applications of your own. You'll have a solid understanding of how ASP.NET works. And you'll be ready to learn all of the other ASP.NET features and techniques that are presented in the rest of this book.

1

An introduction to ASP.NET web programming

This chapter introduces you to the basic concepts of web programming and ASP.NET. Here, you'll learn how web applications work and what software you need for developing ASP.NET web applications. You'll also see how the HTML code for a web form is coordinated with the C# code that makes the web form work the way you want it to. When you finish this chapter, you'll have the background you need for developing web applications of your own.

An introduction to web applications **4**
Two pages of a Shopping Cart application 4
The hardware and software components for web applications 6
How static web pages work 8
How dynamic web pages work 10
How state is handled in ASP.NET applications 12
An introduction to ASP.NET application development **14**
The software you need 14
The components of the .NET Framework 16
Three environments for developing ASP.NET applications 18
A quick preview of how an ASP.NET application works ... **20**
The files used by the Shopping Cart application 20
The aspx code for the Order form 22
The C# code for the Order form 24
How an ASP.NET application is compiled and run 26
Perspective **28**

An introduction to web applications

A *web application* consists of a set of *web pages* that are generated in response to user requests. The Internet has many different types of web applications, such as search engines, online stores, auctions, news sites, discussion groups, games, and so on.

Two pages of a Shopping Cart application

Figure 1-1 shows two pages of a simple web application. In this case, the application is for an online store that lets users purchase a variety of Halloween products, including costumes, masks, and decorations. You'll see parts of this application throughout the book, so it's worth taking the time to become familiar with it in this chapter.

The first web page in this figure is used to display information about the various products that are available from the Halloween store. To select a product, you use the drop-down list that's below the banner at the top of the page. Then, the page displays information about the product including a picture, short and long descriptions, and the product's price.

If you enter a quantity in the text box near the bottom of the page and click the Add to Cart button, the second page in this figure is displayed. This page lists the contents of your shopping cart and provides several buttons that let you remove items from the cart, clear the cart entirely, return to the previous page to continue shopping, or proceed to a checkout page.

Of course, the complete Halloween Superstore application also contains other pages. For example, if you click the Check Out button on the second page, you're taken to a page that lets you enter the information necessary to complete a purchase.

An important point to notice about these pages is that they both contain controls that let the user interact with the page, like the drop-down list and buttons on the Order page. A page that contains controls like these is called a *web form*, and an ASP.NET application consists of one web form for each page in the application.

The Order page of a Shopping Cart application

The Cart page of a Shopping Cart application

Figure 1-1   Two pages of a Shopping Cart application

The hardware and software components for web applications

Figure 1-2 shows the basic hardware and software components that are required for a web application. To start, a web application is a type of *client/ server application*, which means that the functions of the application are split between a *client* computer and a *server* computer. The client and server computers are connected to one another via the Internet, and they communicate with each other using *HTTP*, or *Hypertext Transfer Protocol*.

To access a web application, you use a *web browser* that runs on a client computer. By far the most popular web browser is Microsoft's Internet Explorer, but two alternatives are Mozilla Firefox and Opera.

The web application itself is stored on the server computer. This computer runs *web server* software that enables it to send web pages to web browsers. Although many web servers are available, the two most popular are Microsoft's *Internet Information Services* (or *IIS*) and The Apache Software Foundation's *Apache HTTP Server*, which is usually just called *Apache*. For ASP.NET applications, though, the server typically runs IIS. (Although Apache can be configured to run ASP.NET applications, it doesn't support all of the features of ASP.NET.)

Because most web applications work with data that's stored in a database, most server computers also run a *database management system* (or *DBMS*). Two popular database management systems for ASP.NET development are Microsoft SQL Server and Oracle. Note, however, that the database server software doesn't have to run on the same server computer as the web server software. In fact, a separate database server is often used to improve an application's overall performance.

Although this figure shows the client and server computers connected via the Internet, this isn't the only way a client can connect to a server in a web application. If the client and the server are on the same *local area network* (or *LAN*), they can connect via an *intranet*. Since an intranet uses the same protocols as the Internet, a web application works the same on an intranet as it does on the Internet.

Components of a web application

Client computer

Internet

Server computer

Web browser

Web server
Database management system

Description

- Web applications are a type of *client/server application*. In that type of application, a user at a *client* computer accesses an application at a *server* computer. In a web application, the client and server computers are connected via the Internet or via an *intranet* (a local area network).

- In a web application, the user works with a *web browser* at the client computer. The web browser provides the user interface for the application. The most popular web browser is Microsoft's Internet Explorer, but other web browsers like Mozilla Firefox and Opera may also be used.

- The application runs on the server computer under the control of *web server* software. For ASP.NET web applications, the server typically runs Microsoft's web server, called *Internet Information Services*, or *IIS*.

- For most web applications, the server computer also runs a *database management system*, or *DBMS*, such as Microsoft's SQL Server. The DBMS provides access to information stored in a database. To improve performance on larger applications, the DBMS can be run on a separate server computer.

- The user interface for a web application is implemented as a series of *web pages* that are displayed in the web browser. Each web page is defined by a *web form* using *HTML*, or *Hypertext Markup Language*, which is a standardized set of markup tags.

- The web browser and web server exchange information using *HTTP*, or *Hypertext Transfer Protocol*.

Figure 1-2   The hardware and software components for web applications

How static web pages work

Many of the web pages on the Internet are *static web pages* that don't change in response to user input. These pages are *HTML documents* that are defined by *HTML*, or *Hypertext Markup Language*.

Figure 1-3 shows how a web server handles static web pages. The process begins when a user at a web browser requests a web page. This can occur when the user enters a web address, called a *URL (Uniform Resource Locator)*, into the browser's address box or when the user clicks a link that leads to another page.

In either case, the web browser uses HTTP to send an *HTTP request* to the web server. The HTTP request includes information such as the name and address of the web page being requested, the address of the browser making the request, and the address of the web server that will process the request.

When the web server receives an HTTP request from a browser, the server retrieves the requested HTML file from disk and sends the file back to the browser in the form of an *HTTP response*. The HTTP response includes the HTML document that the user requested along with the addresses of the browser and the web server.

When the browser receives the HTTP response, it formats and displays the HTML document. Then, the user can view the content. If the user requests another page, either by clicking a link or typing another web address in the browser's address box, the process begins again.

Figure 1-3 also shows the components of a URL. The first component is the protocol, in this case, HTTP. In most cases, you can omit the protocol and HTTP is assumed.

The second component is the *domain name*, which identifies your web site. The URL in this figure, for example, includes the domain name for our web site, www.murach.com. The browser uses the domain name to identify the server that's hosting the web site.

After the domain name, you specify the path where the file resides on the server. Notice that front slashes are used to separate the components of a path in a URL. After the path, you specify the name of the file you want to display in the browser. In this case, the file is a static web page named index.htm.

How a web server processes static web pages

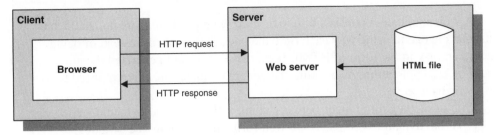

The components of an HTTP URL

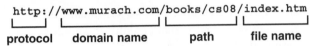

protocol   domain name   path   file name

Description

- A *static web page* is an HTML document that is the same each time it's viewed. In other words, a static web page doesn't change in response to user input. Everyone who views a static web page sees exactly the same content.

- Static web pages are usually simple HTML files that are stored on the web server. When a browser requests a static web page, the web server retrieves the file from disk and sends it back to the browser. Static web pages usually have a file extension of .htm or .html.

- A web browser requests a page from a web server by sending the server an HTTP message known as an *HTTP request*. The HTTP request includes, among other things, the name of the HTML file being requested and the Internet addresses of both the browser and the web server.

- A user working with a browser can initiate an HTTP request in several ways. One way is to type the address of a web page, called a *URL*, or *Uniform Resource Locator*, into the browser's address area and then press the Enter key. Another way is to click a link that refers to a web page.

- A web server replies to an HTTP request by sending a message known as an *HTTP response* back to the browser. The HTTP response contains the addresses of the browser and the server as well as the HTML document that's being returned.

Figure 1-3   How static web pages work

How dynamic web pages work

A web application consists of one or more web pages that are not static, but that can change in some way each time the page is displayed. Instead of being stored on disk in the form of HTML files, these pages are generated dynamically by the application. As a result, the generated pages are often referred to as *dynamic web pages*.

One of the key differences between static web pages and dynamic web pages is that dynamic web pages are web forms that contain one or more *server controls*, such as labels, text boxes, and buttons. Users work with these controls to interact with the application.

Figure 1-4 shows the basic processing for a dynamic web page. To start, the browser sends an HTTP request to the web server (IIS) that contains the address of the web page being requested, along with the information that the user entered into the form. When IIS receives this request, it determines that it's a request for a web form rather than for a static web page. As a result, the web server passes the request on to the *application server* (ASP.NET) for processing. ASP.NET, in turn, manages the execution of the web form that's requested.

To determine if the request is for a static page or a dynamic page, the web server looks up the extension of the requested page in a list of *application mappings*. These mappings indicate what program a file extension is associated with. For example, a static web page typically has an extension of htm or html, while a dynamic ASP.NET page has an extension of aspx. As a result, when the web server receives an HTTP request for an aspx file, it passes this request to ASP.NET, which processes the web form for that page.

When the web form is executed, it processes the information the user entered and generates an HTML document. If, for example, the web form displays data from a database, it queries the database to get the requested information. Then, it generates a page with that information, which is returned by ASP.NET to the web server. The web server, in turn, sends the page back to the browser in the form of an HTTP response, and the browser displays the page. This entire process that begins with the browser requesting a web page and ends with the page being sent back to the client is called a *round trip*.

When a user clicks on a control to start an HTTP request, it is called "posting back to the server," which is referred to as a *postback*. In the Order form in figure 1-1, for example, the user starts a postback by selecting an item in the drop-down list or by clicking on the Add to Cart button. Then, the web form for the Order page is processed using the new values that the user has entered into the page.

Incidentally, the application server for ASP.NET 3.5 can handle requests for web forms that were developed by ASP.NET 2.0 as well as requests for forms that were developed by ASP.NET 3.5. That means that your old 2.0 web forms can run right along with your new 3.5 forms, which means that you don't have to convert your old applications to ASP.NET 3.5. Then, you can maintain your old web forms with ASP.NET 2.0 and develop your new web forms with 3.5.

How a web server processes dynamic pages

The URL for an ASP.NET web page

`http://www.microsoft.com/express/product/default.aspx`

Description

- A *dynamic web page* is an HTML document that's generated by a web form. Often, the web page changes according to information that's sent to the web form by the browser.

- When a web server receives a request for a dynamic web page, it looks up the extension of the requested file in a list of *application mappings* to find out which application server should process the request. If the file extension is aspx, the request is passed on to ASP.NET for processing.

- When the *application server* receives a request, it runs the specified web form. Then, the web form generates an HTML document and returns it to the application server, which passes it back to the web server and from there to the browser.

- The browser doesn't know or care whether the HTML was retrieved from a static HTML file or generated dynamically by a web form. Either way, the browser simply displays the HTML that was returned as a result of the request.

- After the page is displayed, the user can interact with it using its controls. Some of those controls let the user *post* the page *back* to the server, which is called a *postback*. Then, the page is processed again using the data the user entered.

- The process that begins with the user requesting a web page and ends with the server sending a response back to the client is called a *round trip*.

- If you omit the file name from the URL when you use your browser to request a page, IIS will look for a file with one of four names by default: Default.htm, Default.asp, index.htm, and iisstart.asp. (If you're using IIS 7.0, it will also look for a file with the name index.html or default.aspx.) If you want another page to be displayed by default, you can add the name of that page to this list. See appendix B (Windows XP) or C (Windows Vista) for more information.

Figure 1-4   How dynamic web pages work

How state is handled in ASP.NET applications

Although it isn't apparent in the previous figure, an application ends after it generates a web page. That means that the current status of any data maintained by the application, such as variables or control properties, is lost. In other words, HTTP doesn't maintain the *state* of the application. This is illustrated in figure 1-5.

Here, you can see that a browser on a client requests a page from a web server. After the server processes the request and returns the page to the browser, it drops the connection. Then, if the browser makes additional requests, the server has no way to associate the browser with its previous requests. Because of that, HTTP is known as a *stateless protocol*.

Although HTTP doesn't maintain state, ASP.NET provides several ways to do that, as summarized in this figure. First, you can use *view state* to maintain the values of server control properties. For example, you can use view state to preserve the Text properties of label controls that are changed as a web form is processed or to maintain a list of items in a drop-down list. Because ASP.NET implements view state by default, you don't need to write any special code to use it.

Second, you can use *session state* to maintain data between executions of an application. To make this work, ASP.NET creates a *session state object* that is kept on the server whenever a user starts a new session. This session state object contains a unique *session ID*, and this ID is sent back and forth between the server and the browser each time the user requests a page. Then, when the server receives a new request from a user, it can retrieve the right session state object for that user. In the code for your web forms, you can add data items to the session state object so their previous values are available each time a web form is executed.

Third, you can use an *application state object* to save *application state* data, which applies to all of the users of an application. For example, you can use application state to maintain global counters or to maintain a list of the users who are currently logged on to an application.

Fourth, you can use the *profile* feature to keep track of user data. Although a profile is similar to a session state object, it persists between user sessions because it is stored in a database. When you use profiles, for example, you can keep track of the last three products that a user looked at in his last session. Then, when the user starts a new session, you can display those products in a "Recently viewed items" list.

Why state is difficult to track in web applications

Concepts

- *State* refers to the current status of the properties, variables, and other data maintained by an application for a single user. The application must maintain a separate state for each user currently accessing the application.

- HTTP is a *stateless protocol*. That means that it doesn't keep track of state between round trips. Once a browser makes a request and receives a response, the application terminates and its state is lost.

Four ASP.NET features for maintaining state

- ASP.NET uses *view state* to maintain the value of form control properties that the application changes between executions of the application. Since view state is implemented by default, no special coding is required.

- When a user starts a new session, ASP.NET creates a *session state object* that contains a *session ID*. This ID is passed from the server to the browser and back to the server so the server can associate the browser with an existing session. To maintain *session state*, you can add program values to the session state object.

- When an application begins, ASP.NET creates an *application state object*. To maintain *application state*, you can add program values to the application state object. These values are available to all users of the application until the application ends.

- ASP.NET can also maintain a *profile* for each user of an application. Because profiles are stored in a database, the profile data is maintained from one user session to another. This makes it easier to personalize an application.

Figure 1-5   How state is handled in ASP.NET applications

An introduction to ASP.NET application development

In the three topics that follow, you'll find out what software you need for developing ASP.NET web applications, what the components of the .NET Framework are, and what development environments you can work in.

The software you need

The first table in figure 1-6 summarizes both the client and the server software that you need for developing ASP.NET applications. On your own PC, you need an operating system like Windows XP or Windows Vista, the Microsoft .NET Framework 3.5, and a browser like Microsoft Internet Explorer. You also need Visual Studio 2008 if you want to get the benefits from using that Integrated Development Environment (IDE).

If you're using a server for your development, it will need a server operating system like Windows Server 2003 or later, Microsoft .NET Framework 3.5, and Internet Information Services. If you're going to develop applications from a remote computer, it will also need FrontPage Server Extensions. And if you're going to develop applications for the Internet, it will need an FTP server. In appendix A, you can get information about installing the software for both client and server.

Because most ASP.NET applications require database access, you also need a database server such as Microsoft SQL Server. For development work on your own PC, you can use SQL Server 2005 Express Edition, which is a scaled-back version of SQL Server that comes with Visual Studio 2008. But you'll probably need SQL Server itself on the server for a production application.

If you're developing production applications, you should also download and install other web browsers on your PC including Mozilla Firefox and Opera. That way, you can test your applications with a variety of popular browsers.

The second table in this figure shows that Visual Studio 2008 is available in several editions. Most professional developers will work with either the Standard Edition or the Professional Edition. But large development teams may use the Team System edition, which includes features designed for specialized development roles such as architects, developers, and testers.

A free alternative is Visual Web Developer 2008 Express Edition. This product is designed for individual developers, students, and hobbyists, and most of the features in this book will work with this edition.

The third table in this figure lists some of the most important new features of ASP.NET 3.5. Because each of these features is presented in detail later in this book, I won't describe them here. But this table should show you that ASP.NET 3.5 provides some new features that you may want to use in your new applications.

Software requirements for ASP.NET 3.5 application development

Client	Server
Windows XP or later	Windows Server 2003 or later
Microsoft .NET Framework 3.5	Microsoft .NET Framework 3.5
A browser like Internet Explorer (6.0 or later)	Internet Information Services 6.0 or later
Visual Studio 2008	Microsoft SQL Server or equivalent database
	FrontPage Server Extensions (for remote development only)

Visual Studio 2008 Editions

Edition	Description
Visual Studio 2008 Standard Edition	Supports Windows and Web development using Visual Basic, C#, and C++.
Visual Studio 2008 Professional Edition	Same as Standard Edition with several additional features such as additional deployment options and integration with SQL Server 2005.
Visual Studio 2008 Team System	The top-of-the-line version of Visual Studio, with special features added to support large development teams.
Visual Web Developer 2008 Express Edition	Free downloadable edition for web development in Visual Basic or C#

New programming features for ASP.NET 3.5

Feature	Chapter	Description
Nested master pages	9	Lets you define the overall look of a web site with one master page and then define the look of individual portions of the web site with other master pages that refer to the main master page.
ListView control	16	Lets you display, sort, insert, update, and delete the data in a bound data source. Provides a highly-customizable interface.
DataPager control	16	Adds paging capabilities to the ListView control. The DataPager control is displayed separately from the control it's used to page.
LINQ data source control	18	Provides for using LINQ (Language-Integrated Query) to query and update a variety of data sources.
AJAX	25	Provides for developing web pages that are more responsive to the user and reduce the load on the web server.

Figure 1-6   The software you need for developing ASP.NET 3.5 applications

The components of the .NET Framework

Because you should have a basic understanding of what the *.NET Framework* does as you develop applications, figure 1-7 summarizes its major components. As you can see, this framework is divided into two main components, the .NET Framework Class Library and the Common Language Runtime, and these components provide a common set of services for applications written in .NET languages like Visual Basic or C#.

The *.NET Framework Class Library* consists of *classes* that provide many of the functions that you need for developing .NET applications. For instance, the ASP.NET classes are used for developing ASP.NET web applications, and the Windows Forms classes are used for developing standard Windows applications. The other .NET classes let you work with databases, manage security, access files, and perform many other functions.

Although it's not apparent in this figure, the classes in the .NET Framework Class Library are organized in a hierarchical structure. Within this structure, related classes are organized into groups called *namespaces*. Each namespace contains the classes used to support a particular function. For example, the System.Web namespace contains the classes used to create ASP.NET web applications, and the System.Data namespace contains the classes used to access data.

The *Common Language Runtime*, or *CLR*, provides the services that are needed for executing any application that's developed with one of the .NET languages. This is possible because all of the .NET languages compile to a common *Intermediate Language* (or *IL*). The CLR also provides the *Common Type System* that defines the data types that are used by all the .NET languages. That way, you can use the same data types regardless of what .NET language you're using to develop your application.

To run an ASP.NET application, the web server must have the .NET Framework installed. However, the client computers that access the web server don't need the .NET Framework. Instead, the client computers can run any client operating system with a modern web browser.

The .NET Framework

Description

- .NET applications work by using services of the *.NET Framework*. The .NET Framework, in turn, accesses the operating system and computer hardware.
- The .NET Framework consists of two main components: the .NET Framework Class Library and the Common Language Runtime.
- The *.NET Framework Class Library* provides pre-written code in the form of *classes* that are available to all of the .NET programming languages. These classes are organized into groups called *namespaces*. The classes that support ASP.NET web programs are stored in the System.Web namespace.
- The *Common Language Runtime*, or *CLR*, manages the execution of .NET programs by coordinating essential functions such as memory management, code execution, security, and other services.
- The *Common Type System* is a component of the CLR that ensures that all .NET applications use the same data types regardless of what programming languages are used to develop the applications.
- All .NET programs are compiled into *Microsoft Intermediate Language* (*MSIL*) or just *Intermediate Language* (*IL*), which is stored on disk in an assembly. This assembly is then run by the CLR.

Figure 1-7   The components of the .NET Framework

Three environments for developing ASP.NET applications

Figure 1-8 shows three common ways to set up a development environment for coding and testing ASP.NET applications. As you'll see, each setup has its advantages and disadvantages. The environment you choose will depend on your development needs and on the resources that are available to you.

The simplest development environment is a *standalone environment*. In this case, a single computer serves as both the client and the server. Because of that, it must run an operating system that supports ASP.NET development, and it must have the .NET Framework and Visual Studio 2008 installed. Because Visual Studio 2008 comes with its own *development server* for local testing, you don't have to install IIS when you use a standalone environment. Also, since Visual Studio comes with SQL Server 2005 Express Edition (or just *SQL Server Express*), you don't have to install a separate database product.

The second development environment works with separate client and server computers that are connected via a local area network. Here, the client computer has Windows, the .NET Framework, and Visual Studio 2008 installed, while the server runs Windows Server with the .NET Framework, IIS, and *FrontPage Server Extensions* (*FPSE*). FPSE provides the services that Visual Studio 2008 uses to communicate with a web site on a remote computer. In addition, the server uses SQL Server to handle database access. With this environment, more than one programmer can work on the same application, but all of the programmers are located at the same site.

With the third development environment, the client computers are connected to the server via the Internet rather than a LAN. This makes it possible to work with a web site that's hosted on another server. This environment requires an *FTP server*, which is used to copy the files in a web site between the client computer and the server. The FTP server uses *File Transfer Protocol* (*FTP*) to perform the copy operations, and IIS can be configured to act as an FTP server as well as a web server. So if a web site is hosted on a server that you have access to, you can configure the server so remote users can access it using FTP.

Standalone development

Windows XP or later
.NET Framework 3.5
Visual Studio 2008
Optional: IIS, SQL Server

Local area network development

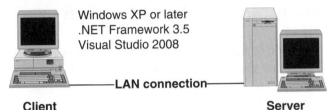

Windows XP or later
.NET Framework 3.5
Visual Studio 2008

———LAN connection———

Windows Server 2003 or later
.NET Framework
IIS 6.0 or later
SQL Server
FrontPage Server Extensions

Client   **Server**

Internet development

Windows XP or later
.NET Framework 3.5
Visual Studio 2008

Internet
connection

Windows Server 2003 or later
.NET Framework
IIS 6.0 or later
FTP server
SQL Server

Client   **Server**

Description

- When you use standalone development, a single computer serves as both the client and the server. Because Visual Studio comes with a scaled-back web server called the ASP.NET Development Server (or just *development server*), you don't need to use IIS for testing web applications on your own PC. However, you do need to use IIS to test certain features of web applications.

- When you use a *local area network* (*LAN*), a client computer communicates with a server computer over the LAN. With this setup, two or more programmers at the same site can work on the same application. This setup requires that *FrontPage Server Extensions* (*FPSE*) be installed on the server.

- When you use Internet development, a client computer communicates with a server computer over the Internet. With this setup, programmers at different locations can work on the same application. This setup requires an *FTP server* on the server. The FTP server uses *File Transfer Protocol* (*FTP*) to transfer files between the client computer and the server.

Figure 1-8   Three environments for developing ASP.NET applications

A quick preview of how an ASP.NET application works

With that as background, you're ready to learn more about how an ASP.NET application works. That's why this topic presents a quick preview of how the Order form in the Shopping Cart application works.

The files used by the Shopping Cart application

Figure 1-9 presents the Order form of the Shopping Cart application as it appears in the Web Forms Designer that you use when you develop web forms with Visual Studio 2008. In chapter 2, you'll learn how to use this Designer, but for now just try to get the big picture of how this form works.

If you look at the Designer window in the middle of the IDE, you can see the table that's used for this form as well as the label controls that are used to display the data for each product. You can also see that the smart tag menu for the drop-down list has been used to enable the AutoPostBack property. This means that the Order form will be posted back to the web server when the user selects an item from the drop-down list.

If you look at the Solution Explorer to the right of the Designer window, you can see the folders and files that this application requires. For now, though, just focus on the six code files that are summarized in the table in this figure. The first two files in this table, which are in the App_Code folder, are two files that represent *business classes* named CartItem and Product. Both of these files have cs as the extension, which means that they're C# files.

The next four files in the table are for the two web forms, Cart and Order, with two files for each form. The files with aspx as the extension (Cart.aspx and Order.aspx) contain the code that represents the design of the form. This code consists of standard HTML code plus asp tags that define the server controls used on the forms. We refer to this as *aspx code*, because the files that contain the code have the aspx extension.

The other two files, which have aspx.cs as the extension, contain the C# code that controls the operation of the forms. These are called *code-behind files* because they provide the code behind the web forms. For instance, the Order.aspx.cs file is the code-behind file for the Order form.

Before I go on, you should realize that it isn't necessary to store the aspx and C# code for a web form in separate files. Instead, ASP.NET lets you combine this code into a single aspx file. However, storing the aspx and C# code in separate files can simplify application development because it lets you separate the presentation elements for a page from its C# coding. This also makes it possible for HTML designers to work on the aspx files for an application, and then have C# programmers develop the code for the code-behind files.

The Order form in Design view

The aspx and C# files in the Shopping Cart application

Folder	File	Description
App_Code	CartItem.cs	A class that represents an item in the shopping cart.
App_Code	Product.cs	A class that represents a product.
(root)	Cart.aspx	The aspx file for the Cart page.
(root)	Cart.aspx.cs	The code-behind file for the Cart page.
(root)	Order.aspx	The aspx file for the Order page.
(root)	Order.aspx.cs	The code-behind file for the Order page.

Description

- For each web form in an application, ASP.NET 3.5 keeps two files. The file with the aspx extension holds the HTML code and the asp tags for the server controls. The file with the aspx.cs extension is the *code-behind file* that contains the C# code for the form.

- If an ASP.NET 3.5 application requires other classes like *business classes*, they are kept in the App_Code folder.

Figure 1-9   The files used by the Shopping Cart application

The aspx code for the Order form

To give you some idea of how aspx code works, figure 1-10 shows some of the aspx code for the Order form. All of this code is generated by Visual Studio as you use the Web Forms Designer to design a form, so you don't have to code it. But you still should have a general understanding of how this code works.

The first set of tags for each web form defines a *page directive* that provides four *attributes*. Here, the Language attribute says that the language is C#, the CodeFile attribute says that the code-behind file is named Order.aspx.cs, and the Inherits attribute specifies the class named Order. In figure 1-12, you'll see how the Order.aspx class inherits the Order class.

The second set of tags defines a DOCTYPE declaration, which tells the browser what version of HTML the HTML document uses. You can ignore this declaration for now, because you'll learn more about it in chapter 5.

The Html tags mark the beginning and end of the HTML document, and the Head tags define the heading for the document. Here, the Title tags define the title that is displayed in the title bar of the browser when the page is run. In addition, the Style tags define the styles used by the page. As you'll learn in chapter 5, this is just one way to define styles.

The content of the web page itself is defined within the Div tags, which are within the Body and Form tags. Notice that the first Form tag includes a Runat attribute that's assigned a value of "server." That indicates that the form will be processed on the server by ASP.NET. This attribute is required for all ASP.NET web forms and all web server controls.

The asp tags within the Div tags define the web server controls that appear on the page. Since these controls include the Runat attribute with a value of "server," they will be processed on the server by ASP.NET. The last phase of this processing is *rendering* the controls, which means that the asp code is converted to standard HTML so the page can be displayed by a browser.

If you look at the asp code for the drop-down list, you can see that the AutoPostBack attribute has been set to True. That means that a postback will occur whenever the user selects an item from that list. Note that a postback will also occur whenever the user clicks the Add to Cart button. However, the AutoPostBack attribute isn't required for this control because performing a postback is the default operation of a button.

Although the asp code for the Add to Cart button doesn't include an AutoPostBack attribute, it does include an OnClick attribute. This attribute names the event handler that's executed when the user clicks the button and the form is posted back to the server.

Another attribute that you should notice is the PostBackUrl attribute for the last button in the aspx code. This attribute provides the path for the Cart.aspx file, which means that the Cart form will be requested when this button is clicked. That's one way to switch from one form to another as an application is run, and you'll see another in the next figure.

Although this has been a quick introduction to the aspx code for a web form, you should begin to see how this code defines a web page. In the next two chapters, though, you'll learn more about this code. And just in case you need it, chapter 5 presents a crash course in HTML.

The aspx file for the Order form (Order.aspx)

```
<%@ Page Language="C#" AutoEventWireup="true"  CodeFile="Order.aspx.cs"
Inherits="Order" %>

<!DOCTYPE html PUBLIC "-//W3C//DTD XHTML 1.0 Transitional//EN" "http://www.w3.org/TR/
xhtml1/DTD/xhtml1-transitional.dtd">

<html xmlns="http://www.w3.org/1999/xhtml" >
<head id="Head1" runat="server">
    <title>Chapter 3: Shopping Cart</title>
    <style type="text/css">
        .style1 {
            width: 250px;
        }
        .style2 {
            width: 20px;
        }
    </style>
</head>
<body>
    <form id="form1" runat="server">
    <div>
        <asp:Image ID="Image1" runat="server"
            ImageUrl="~/Images/banner.jpg" /><br /><br />
        <asp:Label ID="Label1" runat="server"
            Text="Please select a product:"></asp:Label> 
        <asp:DropDownList ID="ddlProducts" runat="server"
            DataSourceID="AccessDataSource1" DataTextField="Name"
            DataValueField="ProductID" Width="150px" AutoPostBack="True">
        </asp:DropDownList>
        <asp:AccessDataSource ID="AccessDataSource1" runat="server"
            DataFile="~/App_Data/Halloween.mdb"
            SelectCommand="SELECT [ProductID], [Name], [ShortDescription],
                [LongDescription], [ImageFile], [UnitPrice]
                FROM [Products] ORDER BY [Name]">
        </asp:AccessDataSource><br />
        <table>
            <tr>
                <td class="style1"><asp:Label ID="lblName" runat="server"
                        style="font-weight: 700; font-size: larger"></asp:Label>
                </td>
                <td class="style2" rowspan="4"></td>
                <td rowspan="4" valign="top">
                    <asp:Image ID="imgProduct" runat="server" Height="200px" />
                </td>
            </tr>
            <tr>
                .
                .   (Code for 3 more rows of a table)
                .
        </table><br />
        <asp:Label ID="Label3" runat="server" Text="Quantity:"
            Width="80px"></asp:Label>
        <asp:TextBox ID="txtQuantity" runat="server" Width="80px"></asp:TextBox>
        <asp:Button ID="btnAdd" runat="server" Text="Add to Cart"
            OnClick="btnAdd_Click" /> 
        <asp:Button ID="btnCart" runat="server" CausesValidation="False"
            PostBackUrl="~/Cart.aspx" Text="Go to Cart" />
    </div>
    </form>
</body>
</html>
```

Figure 1-10   The aspx code for the Order form

The C# code for the Order form

To give you some idea of how the C# code for a form works, figure 1-11 presents the code-behind file for the Order form. Here, I've highlighted the code that's specific to ASP.NET, and all of the other code is standard C# code. Note that to get this code to fit on the page, I didn't code many of the braces that mark the beginning and end of blocks of code on separate lines. However, we recommend you do this to make your code easier to read.

The first group of highlighted statements consists of using statements that are generated automatically when you start a web form. These statements make available the classes that you'll use as you develop the form.

The next highlighted line of code contains the declaration for the class, which has the same name as the form. Because this declaration includes the partial keyword, this is a partial class that must be combined with another partial class when it's compiled. The class declaration also indicates that the class inherits the System.Web.UI.Page class, which is the .NET class that provides all of the basic functionality of ASP.NET pages.

Each time the page is requested, ASP.NET initializes it and raises the Load event, which is handled by the Page_Load event handler. This event handler uses the IsPostBack property of the page to determine whether the page is being posted back to the server from the same page. If this property isn't True, the DataBind method of the drop-down list is used to bind the products that are retrieved from a database to the list. You will often see the IsPostBack property used like this in a Page_Load event handler.

The btnAdd_Click event handler is executed when the user clicks the Add to Cart button on the Order page, which starts a postback. After this event handler adds the selected item to the cart, it uses the Redirect method of the Response property of the page to transfer to the Cart page. This is a second way to switch from one page to another.

The GetCart method, which is called by the AddToCart method, uses the Session property of the page to refer to the session state object. Here, if the session state object doesn't already contain a cart, a new sorted list is added to it. Then, the new or existing sorted list in the session state object is returned to the AddToCart method, and this method updates the cart. Note that because the cart is stored in the session state object, the Cart page will also have access to it.

One coding point worth noting is that IsPostBack, Response, and Session are all properties of the page. As a result, you could refer to them like this:

```
Page.IsPostBack
```

However, since Page is the default object within a code-behind file, you can omit the Page reference.

This introduction to a code-behind file should give you some insight into the way code-behind files are coded. Keep in mind, though, that all of this code will be explained in detail in the next two chapters. For now, you just need a general idea of how events are processed, how the IsPostBack property is used, how one web page can switch to another page, and how the session state object is used.

The code-behind file for the Order form (Order.aspx.cs)

```
using System;
using System.Collections;
using System.Configuration;
using System.Data;
using System.Linq;
using System.Web;
using System.Web.Security;
using System.Web.UI;
using System.Web.UI.HtmlControls;
using System.Web.UI.WebControls;
using System.Web.UI.WebControls.WebParts;
using System.Xml.Linq;

public partial class Order : System.Web.UI.Page{
    protected void Page_Load(object sender, EventArgs e){
        if (!IsPostBack)
            ddlProducts.DataBind();
        Product p = this.GetSelectedProduct();
        lblName.Text = p.Name;
        lblShortDescription.Text = p.ShortDescription;
        lblLongDescription.Text = p.LongDescription;
        lblUnitPrice.Text = p.UnitPrice.ToString("c");
        imgProduct.ImageUrl = "Images/Products/" + p.ImageFile;
    }
    private Product GetSelectedProduct(){
        DataView productsTable = (DataView)
            AccessDataSource1.Select(DataSourceSelectArguments.Empty);
        productsTable.RowFilter =
            "ProductID = '" + ddlProducts.SelectedValue + "'";
        DataRowView row = (DataRowView) productsTable[0];
        Product p = new Product();
        p.ProductID = row["ProductID"].ToString();
        p.Name = row["Name"].ToString();
        p.ShortDescription = row["ShortDescription"].ToString();
        p.LongDescription = row["LongDescription"].ToString();
        p.UnitPrice = (decimal) row["UnitPrice"];
        p.ImageFile = row["ImageFile"].ToString();
        return p;
    }
    protected void btnAdd_Click(object sender, EventArgs e){
        if (Page.IsValid){
            CartItem item = new CartItem();
            item.Product = this.GetSelectedProduct();
            item.Quantity = Convert.ToInt32(txtQuantity.Text);
            this.AddToCart(item);
            Response.Redirect("Cart.aspx");}
    }
    private void AddToCart(CartItem item){
        SortedList cart = this.GetCart();
        Product p = this.GetSelectedProduct();
        string productID = p.ProductID;
        if (cart.ContainsKey(productID)){
            CartItem existingItem = (CartItem) cart[productID];
            existingItem.Quantity += item.Quantity;}
        else
            cart.Add(productID, item);
    }
    private SortedList GetCart(){
        if (Session["Cart"] == null)
            Session.Add("Cart", new SortedList());
        return (SortedList) Session["Cart"];
    }
}
```

Figure 1-11   The C# code for the Order form

How an ASP.NET application is compiled and run

The diagram in figure 1-12 shows what actually happens behind the scenes when a user requests a page of an ASP.NET 3.5 application. In step 1, the ASP.NET runtime reads the aspx file for the requested web page and generates a class and a partial class. The partial class contains the declarations for the form and the controls it contains and is given the same name as the partial class that's defined by the code-behind file for the page (Order in this example). In step 2, these partial classes are compiled to create a single class that provides all of the event-handling code for the page. The result is stored in a single *assembly* (dll file).

The class that's generated by the ASP.NET runtime contains the code that actually creates the ASP.NET page. This class gets its name from the aspx file for the web page plus _aspx, so its name is Order_aspx in this example. In step 3, this class is compiled and stored in another assembly. Because this class inherits the Order class, an object that is instantiated from the Order_aspx class will contain the code that creates the page, as well as the event-handling code provided by the Order class.

In step 4, after the page classes are compiled, the ASP.NET runtime calls the C# compiler to compile any class files that are in the application's App_Code folder. For the Shopping Cart application, this means that the CartItem and Product classes are compiled and the result is saved in a single assembly.

After all the files are compiled into assemblies, ASP.NET creates an instance of the page and raises the appropriate events. Then, the events are processed by the event handlers for the page and the HTML for the page is rendered. To complete the round trip, the HTML document for the page is passed back to the web server and on to the user's browser.

Please note that the first four steps are done only the first time an aspx page is accessed. That's because ASP.NET caches the assemblies that are created by these steps. Then, when the page is accessed again, the saved assemblies are reused, so the application doesn't have to be recompiled. However, ASP.NET does compare the time stamps on the source files with the time stamps on the dll files. If any of the source files have been modified since they were last compiled, ASP.NET automatically recompiles them.

How an ASP.NET application is compiled

What happens when an ASP.NET page is requested

1. The ASP.NET runtime processes the .aspx file and generates a partial class (Order) that contains the declarations for the form and its controls, and a class (Order_aspx) that contains the code that will initialize the form, instantiate the controls, and generate the HTML for the web page.

2. The C# compiler compiles the partial class that contains the control declarations with the partial class defined by the code-behind file for the form into an *assembly* (.dll) that provides the event-handling code for the requested page.

3. The C# compiler compiles the Order_aspx class, which inherits the first compiled class (Order), and saves the result as an assembly that's executed when the page is requested.

4. If necessary, the C# compiler compiles any other class files that are stored in the application's App_Code folder. These classes are saved in a single assembly.

5. ASP.NET creates an instance of the page from the page's final assembly. Then, ASP.NET raises the appropriate events, which are processed by the event handlers for the page, and the page generates the HTML that's passed back to IIS for the response.

Description

- The first four steps of this process are done only the first time the aspx page is requested. After that, the page is processed directly from the compiled assemblies.

- For the Default page, the name of the code-behind class is _Default.

Figure 1-12   How an ASP.NET 3.5 application is compiled and run

Perspective

Now that you've read this chapter, you should have a general understanding of how ASP.NET applications work and what software you need for developing these applications. With that as background, you're ready to learn how to develop ASP.NET applications of your own. And that's what you'll learn to do in the next two chapters.

Terms

web application
web page
web form
client/server application
client
server
HTTP (Hypertext Transfer Protocol)
web browser
web server
IIS (Internet Information Services)
DBMS (database management system)
LAN (local area network)
intranet
static web page
HTML document
HTML (Hypertext Markup Language)
URL (Uniform Resource Locator)
HTTP request
HTTP response
domain name
dynamic web page
server control
application server
application mapping
round trip
postback
state
stateless protocol
view state

session state
session state object
session ID
application state
application state object
profile
.NET Framework
.NET Framework Class Library
class
namespace
CLR (Common Language Runtime)
IL (Intermediate Language)
MSIL (Microsoft Intermediate
    Language)
Common Type System
standalone environment
development server
SQL Server Express
FPSE (FrontPage Server Extensions)
FTP (File Transfer Protocol)
FTP server
business class
aspx code
code-behind file
page directive
attribute
render
assembly

About the book's applications

You can download all of the applications that are presented in this book from our web site (www.murach.com). Then, you can run the applications, review all of their code, and experiment with them on your own system. For more information about downloading and running these applications, please read appendix A.

About the exercises

If you're new to ASP.NET web programming, we recommend that you practice what you've learned after you finish each chapter in the first section of this book. To help you do that, we provide exercises for each of these chapters. Most of these exercises use directories and files that you can download from our web site. Before you start the exercises, then, you'll need to install these directories and files. When you do, they'll be placed in a directory named ASP.NET 3.5 C# on your C drive.

By the time you complete section 1, you should be ready to start building applications of your own. Because of that, we don't include exercises for the remaining chapters. Instead, as you go through each chapter, you can use the techniques that are illustrated on your own application. When you're done, you can compare your application with the one you've downloaded.

Exercise 1-1   Use your web browser to run Internet applications

1. Open your web browser and type in this URL:

    `http://www.microsoft.com`

    Then, search for information about Visual Web Developer 2008 Express Edition. This of course is the site that you can use to download Visual Web Developer 2008 Express and SQL Server Express for free. As you move from page to page, note that some are static html pages and others are dynamic aspx pages.

2. Type this URL into your web browser:

    `http://www.discountasp.net`

    Then, click on some of the links on the home page, and note which pages are static and which are dynamic.

Exercise 1-2   Use your web browser to run the Shopping Cart application on your PC

In this exercise, you'll use your web browser to run the Shopping Cart application that's illustrated in this chapter. This assumes that you've already installed IIS, Visual Studio 2008, and the files for these exercises as described in appendix A. When you get this application running, you'll know that you've got IIS and the application set up correctly on your PC. Note that if you're using Windows XP Home Edition or Windows Vista Home Basic or Starter Edition, you won't be able to do this exercise because these editions don't come with IIS.

Create a virtual directory for the Shopping Cart application

1. If you're using Windows XP, use the procedure in figure B-1 of appendix B to create an IIS virtual directory named Ch01Cart under the Default Web Site node for the application in C:\ASP.NET 3.5 C#\Ch01Cart. If you're using Windows Vista, use the procedure in figure C-1 of appendix C to create an IIS application named Ch01Cart under the Default Web Site node for the application in C:\ASP.NET 3.5 C#\Ch01Cart.

Run the Shopping Cart application

2. Open your web browser, and type in the following URL, which uses the virtual directory as the path:

    `http://localhost/Ch01Cart/Order.aspx`

    This should start the Shopping Cart application that's shown in figure 1-1. If it doesn't, you need to make sure that IIS is installed, that the exercise files are installed, and that you did step 1 correctly. If you're using Windows Vista and you get an "insufficient permissions" error, you may also need to add permissions for two groups as described on page 966 of appendix C.

3. Select a product from the drop-down list on the Order page that's displayed. Note that this starts a postback that returns the Order page with the data and image for the product that was selected.

4. Enter a quantity and click the Add to Cart button to display the Cart page. Then, click the Continue Shopping button to return to the Order page.

5. Continue to experiment with this application until you understand how it works. Then, click the Close button in the upper right corner of the browser window to end the application.

2

How to develop a one-page web application

In the last chapter, you were introduced to the basic concepts of web programming and ASP.NET. Now, this chapter shows you how to develop a one-page web application using Visual Studio 2008. If you've used Visual Studio to develop Windows applications, you'll soon see that you develop web applications in much the same way. As a result, you should be able to move quickly through this chapter.

How to work with ASP.NET web sites **32**
How to start a new web site 32
How to work with the Visual Studio IDE 34
How to add folders and files to a web site 36
How to open or close an existing web site 38

How to use Design view to build a web form **40**
The design of the Future Value form 40
How to use flow layout 42
How to add a table to a form 44
How to add text to the cells of a table 44
How to add server controls to a form 46
How to set the properties of the controls 46
Common properties for web server controls 48

How to work in Source and Split views **50**
How to use Source view to modify the design 50
How to use Split view to work with the design 52
The aspx code for the Future Value form 54

How to add validation controls to a form **56**
An introduction to the validation controls 56
How to use the required field validator 58
How to use the range validator 58

How to add code to a form **60**
How to use the Code Editor... 60
How to use page and control events 62
The C# code for the Future Value form 64

How to test a web application **66**
How to run a web site with the built-in development server 66
How to review the HTML that's sent to the browser 68

Perspective **70**

How to work with ASP.NET web sites

This chapter starts by presenting some basic skills for working with
ASP.NET web sites. Once you're comfortable with those skills, you'll be ready
to learn how to build your first ASP.NET application.

How to start a new web site

In Visual Studio 2008, a web application is called a *web site*, and figure 2-1
shows the dialog box for starting a new web site. After you open the New Web
Site dialog box, you select the language you want to use for the web site and
you specify the location where the web site will be created.

The Location drop-down list gives you three options for specifying the
location of the web site. The simplest method is to create a *file-system web site*.
This type of web site can exist in any folder on your local hard disk, or in a
folder on a shared network drive. You can run a file-system web site using either
Visual Studio's built-in development server or IIS. You'll learn how to do that
later in this chapter.

You use the HTTP option to create a web site that runs under IIS on your
local computer or on a computer that can be accessed over a local area network.
To use this option, you must specify the IIS server where you want to create the
web site. In addition, you must select or create the IIS directory that will contain
the files for the web site, or you must select or create a virtual directory for the
web site.

The third option, FTP, lets you create a web site on a remote server by
uploading it to that server using FTP. To create this type of web site, you must
specify at least the name of the FTP server and the folder where the web site
resides. You'll learn more about how to use the HTTP and FTP options in
chapter 4.

In addition to the language and location, Visual Studio 2008 lets you choose
a *target framework* for a web site. By default, .NET Framework 3.5 is used,
which is usually what you want. Then, you can use the features that this framework provides within your web applications. If you'll be deploying the application to a server that doesn't have .NET Framework 3.5, however, you may want
to target .NET Framework 2.0 or 3.0 instead. Then, you can be sure that you'll
use only the features that these frameworks provide.

By default, Visual Studio 2008 creates a solution file for your web site in
My Documents\Visual Studio 2008\Projects. This solution file is stored in this
folder regardless of the location of the web site itself. To change the location
where solutions are stored by default, choose Tools→Options. Then, expand the
Projects and Solutions node, select the General category, and enter the location
in the Visual Studio Projects Location text box.

In the dialog box in this example, I'm starting a new file-system web site
named Ch02FutureValue in the ASP.NET 3.5 web sites folder on my own PC.
Then, when I click the OK button, Visual Studio creates the folder named

The New Web Site dialog box

Three location options for ASP.NET web sites

Option	Description
File System	A web site created in a folder on your local computer or in a shared folder on a network. You can run the web site directly from the built-in development server or create an IIS virtual directory for the folder and run the application under IIS.
HTTP	A web site created under the control of an IIS web server. The IIS server can be on your local computer or on a computer that's available over a local area network.
FTP	A web site created on a remote hosting server.

Description

- To create a new ASP.NET 3.5 web application, called a *web site,* you use the File→New Web Site command.

- A *web project* is a project that's used for the development of a web site. In practice, web sites are often referred to as web projects, and vice versa. However, ASP.NET 3.5 web sites don't use project files. Instead, they use web.config files to store project information.

- When you start a new web site, Visual Studio creates a solution file for the web site in the default location for solution files, which is normally My Documents\Visual Studio 2008\Projects.

- By default, the web sites you create target .NET Framework 3.5 so you can use the features it provides. If you want to target a different version of the .NET Framework, you can select the version from the drop-down list in the upper right corner of the dialog box.

- Visual Studio 2008 provides for a new type of web project, called a *web application project*. With this type of project, you can create web applications that are similar in structure to applications created using Visual Studio 2003.

Figure 2-1   How to start a new web site

Ch02FutureValue and puts the starting files for the web site in that folder. It also creates a solution file in the default folder for those files.

The folders and files that are used for developing a web site can be referred to as a *web project*. So in practice, web sites are often referred to as web projects, and vice versa. It's important to note, however, that ASP.NET 3.5 web sites don't use project files to store project information. Instead, they use web.config files.

How to work with the Visual Studio IDE

When you start a new web site, ASP.NET provides the starting folders and files for the site, including two files for the first *web form* of the site. The file named Default.aspx contains the HTML and asp code that defines the form, and the file named Default.aspx.cs contains the C# code that determines how the form works. Then, Visual Studio displays the aspx file for the web form as shown in figure 2-2.

If you've used Visual Studio for building Windows applications, you should already be familiar with the *Toolbox*, *Solution Explorer*, and *Properties window*, as well as the Standard toolbar. They work much the same for web applications as they do for Windows applications. The Solution Explorer, for example, shows the folders and files of the web site. In this example, the Solution Explorer shows one folder named App_Data, plus the two files for the default web form and the web.config file.

To design a web form, you use the *Web Forms Designer* that's in the center of this Integrated Development Environment (IDE). When you start a new web site, this Designer is displayed in *Source view*, which shows the starting HTML code for the first (or only) web form of the application. Normally, though, you'll do most of the design in *Design view*, which you can switch to by clicking on the Design button at the bottom of the Designer window. With Visual Studio 2008, you can also work in *Split view*, which lets you see both Source view and Design view at the same time.

If you have your environment settings set to Web Developer, you'll notice that different toolbars are enabled depending on what view you're working in. In Source view, for example, the Standard and HTML Source Editing toolbars are enabled, and in Design view, the Standard and Formatting toolbars are enabled. This is typical of the way the Visual Studio IDE works. By the way, to change the environment settings, you use the Tools→Import and Export Settings command.

As you go through the various phases of building a web site, you may want to close, hide, or size the windows that are displayed. You'll see some examples of this as you progress through this chapter, and this figure presents several techniques that you can use for working with the windows.

After you've designed a web form, you'll need to switch to the Code Editor, which replaces the Web Forms Designer in the center of the screen. Then, you can write the C# code in the code-behind file for the form. One way to switch to

The starting screen for a new web site

How to work with views and windows

- To change the Web Forms Designer from one view to another, click on the Design, Split, or Source button.
- To close a window, click on the close button in the upper right corner. To redisplay it, select it from the View menu.
- To hide a window, click on its Auto Hide button. Then, the window is displayed as a tab at the side of the screen, and you can display it by moving the mouse pointer over the tab. To restore the window, display it and click on the Auto Hide button again.
- To size a window, place the mouse pointer over one of its boundaries and drag it.

Description

- When you start a new web site, the primary window in the Visual Studio IDE is the Web Forms Designer window, or just *Web Forms Designer*. The three supporting windows are the *Toolbox*, the *Solution Explorer*, and the *Properties window*.
- You use the Web Forms Designer to design a *web form*. Later, to write the C# code for the form, you use the Code Editor as shown in figure 2-15.
- Visual Studio often provides several different ways to accomplish the same task. In this book, we'll try to show you the techniques that work the best.

Figure 2-2   How to work with the Visual Studio IDE

the Code Editor is to double-click on the code-behind file in the Solution Explorer. If, for example, you double-click on the file named Default.aspx.cs, you'll switch to the Code Editor and the starting code for that file will be displayed. Later in this chapter, you'll learn other ways to switch between the Web Forms Designer and the Code Editor.

As you work with Visual Studio, you'll see that it commonly provides several ways to do the same task. Some, of course, are more efficient than others, and we'll try to show you the best techniques as you progress through this book. Often, though, how you work is a matter of personal preference, so we encourage you to review and experiment with the toolbar buttons, the buttons at the top of the Solution Explorer, the tabs at the top of the Web Forms Designer or Code Editor, the shortcut menus that you get by right-clicking on an object, and so on.

How to add folders and files to a web site

Right after you start a new web site, it often makes sense to add any other folders and existing files that the application is going to require. To do that, you can use the shortcut menus for the project or its folders in the Solution Explorer as shown in figure 2-3. As you can see, this menu provides a New Folder command as well as an Add Existing Item command.

For the Future Value application, I first added a folder named Images. To do that, I right-clicked on the project at the top of the Solution Explorer, chose the New Folder command, and entered the name for the folder. Then, I added an existing image file named MurachLogo.jpg to the Images folder. To do that, I right-clicked on the folder, chose Add Existing Item, and then selected the file from the dialog box that was displayed.

Those are the only other folders and files that I needed for the Future Value application, but often you'll need others. For instance, the application in the next chapter requires two existing business classes, an Access database, and a number of image files.

The Future Value project as a new folder is being added

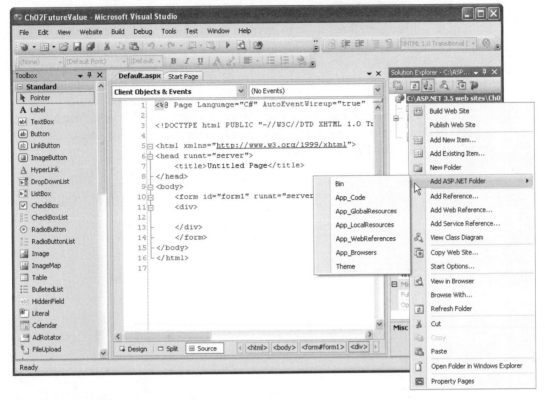

How to add a folder to a web site

- To add a standard folder, right-click on the project or folder you want to add the folder to in the Solution Explorer and choose New Folder. Then, type a name for the folder and press Enter.
- To add a special ASP.NET folder, right-click on the project in the Solution Explorer and choose Add ASP.NET Folder. Then, select the folder from the list that's displayed.

How to add an existing item to a web site

- In the Solution Explorer, right-click on the project or on the folder that you want to add an existing item to. Then, select Add Existing Item and respond to the resulting dialog box.

Description

- When you create a new web form, Visual Studio generates the starting HTML for the form and displays it in Source view of the Web Forms Designer.
- Before you start designing the first web form of the application, you can use the Solution Explorer to add any other folders or files to the web site.

Figure 2-3   How to add folders and files to a web site

How to open or close an existing web site

Figure 2-4 presents three ways to open an existing web site. The Open Project and Recent Projects commands are the easiest to use, but the Open Web Site command provides more flexibility. In the Open Web Site dialog box, you can use the icons on the left to identify the type of web site that you're opening so you can open a web site directly from the web server on which it resides.

To close a project, you use the Close Project command. After you close a project for the first time, you'll be able to find it in the list of projects that you see when you use the Recent Projects command.

The Open Web Site dialog box

Three ways to open a web site

- Use the File→Open Project command.
- Use the File→Recent Projects command.
- Use the File→Open Web Site command.

How to use the Open Web Site dialog box

- To open a file-system web site, select File System on the left side of the dialog box, then use the File System tree to locate the web site.
- If a web site is managed by IIS on your own computer, you can open it by using the File System tree. Or, if you prefer, you can click Local IIS and select the web site from a list of sites available from IIS.
- The other icons on the left of the Open Web Site dialog box let you open web sites from an FTP site or from a remote IIS site.

How to close a project

- Use the File→Close Project command.

Note

- The Recent Projects list and the Open Project and Open Web Site commands are also available from the Start page.

Figure 2-4   How to open or close an existing web site

How to use Design view to build a web form

Now that you know how to start, open, and close a web site, you're ready to learn how to build a web form. To start, I'll show you the web form that you're going to build. Then, I'll show you how to build it.

The design of the Future Value form

Figure 2-5 presents the design of a Future Value web form that calculates the future value of a fixed monthly investment. This form has enough features to give you a realistic idea of what's involved in the development of a form, but it's so simple that you won't be overwhelmed by detail. In this case, the entire application consists of this single form.

If you study the form, you can see that it contains six *web server controls*. These controls are derived from ASP.NET classes, and they have special features that make them suitable for web applications. This form contains one *drop-down list*, two *text boxes*, one *label*, and two *buttons*. These controls are analogous to the ones that you use for Windows applications.

When you click on a button in a web form, it automatically starts a postback to the server. When you click the Calculate button, for example, the application calculates the future value based on the values in the drop-down list and two text boxes. The result is displayed in the label when the form is returned to the browser. When you click on the Clear button, the text boxes and label are cleared and the value in the drop-down list is reset to 50.

In contrast to the web server controls, the image at the top of this page (the Murach logo) is defined by a standard HTML element. Because you can't refer to standard HTML elements in code, you won't typically use them in web applications. Like the element in this application, though, they can occasionally be useful.

The arrangement of the web server controls on this web form is done through an HTML table. Above the table, a heading has been entered and formatted. In the first column of the first four rows of the table, text has been entered that describes the data in the second column. The fifth row of the table contains no text or controls. And the six row contains the two buttons.

In the rest of this chapter, you'll learn how to build this web form, how to validate the data the user enters in the form, and how to write the code for its code-behind file. Then, you'll learn how to test a web application. At the end of this chapter, you'll find exercises that will walk you through the development of this Future Value application and help you experiment with other features of Visual Studio.

Throughout this chapter, please note that the term *page* is sometimes used to refer to a web form. That's because a web form represents a page that's sent to a browser.

The Future Value web form in a browser

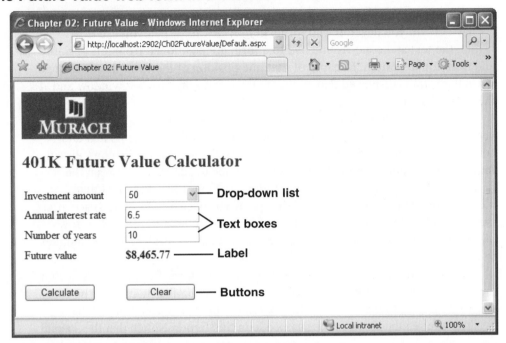

The six web server controls used by the Future Value form

- The *drop-down list* can be used to select a monthly investment value ranging from 50 to 500.
- The two *text boxes* are used to enter values for the annual interest rate and the number of years that the monthly payments will be made.
- The *label* is used to display the future value that is calculated.
- The Calculate and Clear *buttons* are used to post the form back to the server and initiate the processing that needs to be done.

Description

- Besides the *web server controls*, the Future Value form uses a standard HTML element to display the image at the top of the form, and it uses text to display the heading below the image. It also uses an HTML table to align the text and web server controls below the image and heading.
- When the user clicks on the Calculate button, the future value is calculated based on the three user entries and the results are displayed in the label control.
- When the user clicks on the Clear button, the two text boxes and the label are cleared and the drop-down list is reset to a value of 50.
- To end the application, the user can click the Close button in the upper right corner of the browser window.

Figure 2-5   The design of the Future Value form

How to use flow layout

By default, you develop web forms in *flow layout*. When you use flow layout, the text and controls you add to a form are positioned from left to right and from top to bottom. Because of that, the position of the controls can change when the form is displayed depending on the size of the browser window and the resolution of the display.

To understand how flow layout works, figure 2-6 shows the beginning of a version of the Future Value form that doesn't use a table to align its text and controls. To create this form, I started by typing the text for the heading directly into the form. Then, I pressed the Enter key twice to add space between the heading and the text and controls that follow it. Next, I typed the text that identifies the first control, I pressed the space bar twice to add some space after the text, and I added a drop-down list. When I added the drop-down list, it was placed immediately to the right of the text and spaces. I used similar techniques to enter the remaining text and text box.

Finally, I formatted the heading at the top of the form. To do that, I selected the text and then used the controls in the Formatting toolbar to change the font size to "x-large", to make the heading bold, and to change its color to blue.

You can see the result in the aspx code in this figure. Notice that the special code   was inserted for each space between the text and the controls that follow. In addition, a Br element is inserted for each line break. To apply the formatting to the heading, a Span element is used with a Class attribute that names a style class. Although you can't see it here, this style class is defined within the Head element for the page, and it specifies the font size, color, and weight.

The beginning of the Future Value form created using flow layout

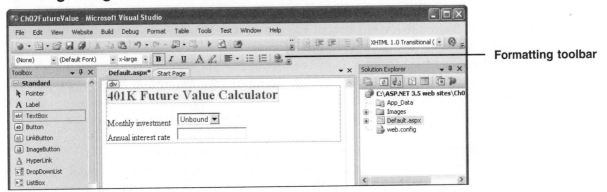

Formatting toolbar

The aspx code for the Future Value form

```
<form id="form1" runat="server">
<div>
    <span class="style1">401K Future Value Calculator</span><br />
    <br />
    Monthly investment  
    <asp:DropDownList ID="DropDownList1" runat="server">
    </asp:DropDownList>
    <br />
    Annual interest rate  
    <asp:TextBox ID="TextBox1" runat="server"></asp:TextBox>
</div>
</form>
```

How to use flow layout

- When you add controls to a form in *flow layout*, they will appear one after the other, from left to right and from top to bottom. Flow layout is the default for web forms in Visual Studio 2008.

- To make it easier to work with a form in Design view, Visual Studio 2008 places a border around the area defined by the Div tags.

- To insert a space after a control, use the space bar. The special code   is inserted into the aspx file.

- To insert a line break after a control, press Enter. A <br /> tag is inserted into the aspx file.

- To insert literal text, type it directly into the Designer window. Then, you can use the controls in the Formatting toolbar and the commands in the Format menu to change the font or font size; apply bold, italics, or underlining; or apply foreground or background color.

- When you apply formatting to literal text, Visual Studio creates a style class and applies that class to the text. Then, you can apply the same class to other literal text. See chapter 5 for more information.

- To align text and controls when you use flow layout, you normally use tables as described in the next figure.

Figure 2-6   How to use flow layout

How to add a table to a form

Because you're limited to what you can do with spaces and line breaks, you'll frequently use tables to format a form in flow layout. Figure 2-7 shows how to add a table to a form. In this case, a table of six rows and two columns has already been added to the form, but the Insert Table dialog box is displayed to show what the settings are for that table. Usually, you can keep the dialog box entries that simple, because you can easily adjust the table once it's on the form.

The easiest way to resize a row or column is to drag it by its border. To change the width of a column, drag it by its right border. To change the height of a row, drag it by its bottom border. You can also change the height and width of the entire table by selecting the table and then dragging it by its handles. Note that when you make this type of change, Visual Studio creates style classes just like it does when you format text. Then, these classes are applied to the appropriate elements of the table.

You can also format a table in Design view by selecting one or more rows or columns and then using the commands in the Table menu or the shortcut menu that's displayed when you right-click the selection. These commands let you add, delete, or resize rows or columns. They also let you merge the cells in a row or column. If, for example, you want a control in one row to span two columns, you can merge the cells in that row.

How to add text to the cells of a table

In figure 2-7, you can see that text has been entered into the cells in the first four rows of the first column of the table. To do that, you just type the text into the cells. Then, you can format the text by selecting it and using the controls in the Formatting toolbar or the commands in the Format menu. If, for example, you want to bold the four text entries, you can select the four cells that contain the text and click on the Bold button.

The Future Value form with a table that has been inserted into it

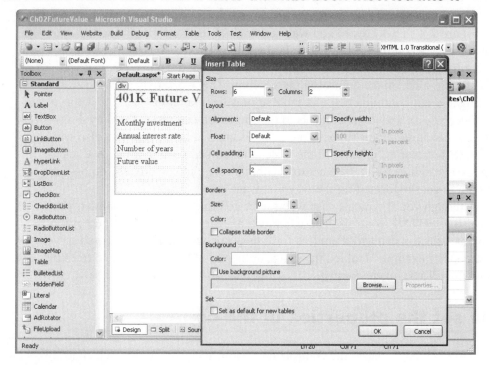

How to add a table to a form

- Use the Table→Insert Table command to display the Insert Table dialog box. Then, set the number of rows and columns that you want in the table, set any other options that you want, and click OK.

How to format a table after it has been added to a form

- To resize a row, drag it by its bottom border. To resize a column, drag it by its right border. To resize the entire table, select the table and then drag its handles.
- Select rows or columns and then use the commands in the Table menu or the shortcut menu to add, delete, resize, or merge the rows or columns.
- Some of the formatting that you apply to tables, rows, and columns is saved in style classes. Then, you can apply the same formatting to other tables, rows, and columns.

How to add and format text

- To add text to a table, type the text into the cells of the table.
- To format the text in a table, select the text, and then use the controls in the Formatting toolbar or the commands in the Format menu to apply the formatting.

Description

- To control the alignment of the text and controls on a web form in flow layout, you can use tables.

Figure 2-7   How to add a table to a form and text to a table

How to add server controls to a form

Figure 2-8 shows how to add web server controls to a form. To do that, you can just drag a control from the Standard group of the Toolbox and drop it on the form. Or, you can move the cursor where you want a control inserted and then double-click on the control in the Toolbox. This works whether you're placing a control within a cell of a table or outside of a table.

Once you've added the controls to the form, you can resize them by dragging the handles on their sides. If the controls are in a table, you may also want to resize the columns or rows of the table at this time. Keep in mind that you can resize a cell as well as the control within a cell, and sometimes you have to do both to get the formatting the way you want it.

Although you'll typically use web server controls on your web forms, you can also use HTML controls. These controls appear in the HTML group of the Toolbox, and you can add them to a form the same way that you add web server controls. For example, I added the image at the top of the Future Value form by using the HTML Image control.

How to set the properties of the controls

After you have placed the controls on a form, you need to set each control's properties so the control looks and works the way you want it to when the form is displayed. To set those properties, you work in the Properties window as shown in figure 2-8. To display the properties for a specific control, just click on it in Design view.

In the Properties window, you select a property by clicking it. Then, a brief description of that property is displayed in the pane at the bottom of the window. To change a property setting, you change the entry to the right of the property name by typing a new value or choosing a new value from a drop-down list. In some cases, a button with an ellipsis (...) on it will appear when you click on a property. In that case, you can click this button to display a dialog box that helps you set the property.

Some properties are displayed in groups. In that case, a plus sign appears next to the group name. This is illustrated by the Font property in this figure. To display the properties in a group, just click the plus sign next to the group name.

To display properties alphabetically or by category, you can click the appropriate button at the top of the Properties window. At first, you may want to display the properties by category so you have an idea of what the different properties do. Once you become more familiar with the properties, though, you may be able to find the ones you're looking for faster if you display them alphabetically.

As you work with properties, you'll find that most are set the way you want them by default. In addition, some properties such as Height and Width are set interactively as you size and position the controls in Design view. As a result, you usually only need to change a few properties for each control. The only

The Future Value form after six web server controls have been added to it

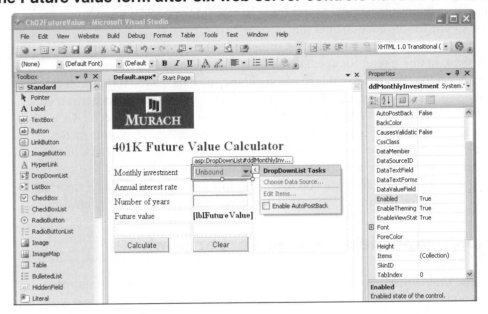

How to add a web server control to a web form

- Drag the control from the Standard group in the Toolbox to the form or to a cell in a table on the form. Or, move the cursor to where you want the control, and then double-click on the control in the Toolbox.

How to set the properties for a control

- Select a control by clicking on it, and all of its properties are displayed in the Properties window. Then, you can select a property in this window and set its value. When you select a property, a brief description is displayed in the pane at the bottom of the window.

- To change the Height and Width properties, you can drag one of the handles on a control. This also changes the Height and Width in the Properties window.

- You can use the first two buttons at the top of the Properties window to sort the properties by category or alphabetically.

- You can use the plus and minus signs that are displayed in the Properties window to expand and collapse the list of properties.

- Many web server controls have a *smart tag menu* that provides options for performing common tasks and setting common properties. To display a smart tag menu, click the Smart Tag icon in the upper right of the control.

Note

- The image on this form was created by using an HTML Image control.

Figure 2-8   How to add web server controls to a form and set their properties property that I set for the drop-down list, for example, is the ID property. This property contains the name that you'll use to refer to the control when you write the C# code for the code-behind file.

Another way to set properties for some controls is to use the control's *smart tag menu*. In this figure, for example, you can see the smart tag menu for the drop-down list. You can use this menu to choose the data source for the control, which sets the DataSourceID, DataTextField, and DataValueField properties; edit the items in the list, which modifies the collection of items that's accessed through the Items property; and enable or disable the automatic posting of the page when a value is selected from the list, which sets the AutoPostBack property. Because smart tag menus help you set common properties, they're displayed automatically when you drag a control to a form. You can also display a smart tag menu by clicking the Smart Tag icon in the upper right corner of the control.

Common properties for web server controls

The first table in figure 2-9 presents the properties for web server controls that you're most likely to use as you develop web forms. If you've worked with Windows controls, you'll notice that many of the properties of the web server controls provide similar functionality. For example, you use the ID property to name a control that you need to refer to in code, and you can use the Text property to determine what's displayed in or on the control. However, the AutoPostBack, CausesValidation, EnableViewState, and Runat properties are unique to web server controls. Since you already know the purpose of the Runat property, I'll focus on the other three properties here.

The AutoPostBack property determines whether the page is posted back to the server when the user changes the value of the control. Note that this property is only available with certain controls, such as check boxes, drop-down lists, and radio buttons. Also note that this property isn't available with button controls. That's because button controls always either post a page back to the server or display another page.

The CausesValidation property is available for button controls and determines whether the validation controls are activated when the user clicks the button. This lets you check for valid data before the page is posted back to the server. You'll learn more about validation controls a few figures from now.

The EnableViewState property determines whether a server control retains its property settings from one posting to the next. For that to happen, the EnableViewState property for both the form and the control must be set to True. Since that's normally the way you want this property set, True is the default.

The second table in this figure lists four more properties that are commonly used with drop-down lists and list boxes. However, you don't need to set these at design time. Instead, you use them when you write the C# code for the code-behind file. For instance, you use the Items collection to add, insert, and remove ListItem objects. And you use the SelectedValue property to retrieve the value of the currently selected item. You'll learn more about these properties when you review the code-behind file for the Future Value form.

Common web server control properties

Property	Description
AutoPostBack	Determines whether the page is posted back to the server when the value of the control changes. Available with controls such as a check box, drop-down list, radio button, or text box. The default value is False.
CausesValidation	Determines whether the validation that's done by the validation controls occurs when you click on the button, link button, or image button. The default value is True. (You'll learn how to use two common validation controls later in this chapter.)
EnableViewState	Determines whether the control maintains its view state between HTTP requests. The default value is True.
Enabled	Determines whether the control is functional. The default value is True.
Height	The height of the control.
ID	The name that's used to refer to the control.
Runat	Indicates that the control will be processed on the server by ASP.NET.
TabIndex	Determines the order in which the controls on the form receive the focus when the Tab key is pressed.
Text	The text that's displayed in the control.
ToolTip	The text that's displayed when the user hovers the mouse over the control.
Visible	Determines whether a control is displayed or hidden.
Width	The width of the control.

Common properties of drop-down list and list box controls

Property	Description
Items	The collection of ListItem objects that represents the items in the control. Although you can set the values for these list items at design time, you normally use code to add, insert, and remove the items in a drop-down list or list box.
SelectedItem	The ListItem object for the currently selected item.
SelectedIndex	The index of the currently selected item. If no item is selected in a list box, the value of this property is -1.
SelectedValue	The value of the currently selected item.

Note

- When buttons are clicked, they always post back to the server. That's why they don't have AutoPostBack properties.

Figure 2-9   Common properties for web server controls

How to work in Source and Split views

As you design a form in Design view, HTML and asp tags are being generated in Source view. This is the code that's used to render the web page that's sent to the user's browser. What you see in Design view is just a visual representation of that code. In many cases, you'll need to work in Source view to get a page to look just the way you want it to. You may also want to work in Split view so you can see both Design view and Source view at the same time.

How to use Source view to modify the design

As you saw in the last chapter, HTML consists of tags. For instance, the <form> and </form> tags mark the start and end of the HTML code for a web form. And the <table> and </table> tags mark the start and end of the HTML code for a table.

In addition to the HTML tags, ASP.NET adds asp tags for the web server controls that are added to the form. In figure 2-10, you can see some of the asp tags for the Future Value form. For instance, the <asp:DropDownList> and </asp:DropDownList> tags mark the start and end of the code for a drop-down list. Within these tags, you'll find the code for the property settings of the controls. Note, however, that all of this asp code is converted to HTML before the page can be sent to a browser, because a browser can only interpret HTML.

Because the file that contains the source code for a web form has an aspx extension, we refer to the source code for a form as *aspx code*. This also indicates that the code contains both HTML and asp tags.

In case you need it, chapter 5 presents a crash course in HTML. In the meantime, though, you may be surprised to discover how easy it is to modify the design of a form by adjusting the aspx code using the *HTML Editor*.

To start, you can modify the title of the form that you'll find between the Head tags near the top of the source code. This is the title that's displayed in the title bar of the browser when the form is run (see figure 2-5). In this example, the title has been changed from "Untitled Page" to "Chapter 02: Future Value." As you will see, all of the applications in this book have titles that indicate both the chapter number and the type of application.

You can also use this technique to change the text that has been entered into a form or to change some of the settings for HTML elements. If, for example, you want to change the text in the first row of the table from "Monthly investment" to "Investment amount," you can just edit the text in Source view. And if you want to modify the color for the heading, you can do that too. As you edit, just follow the syntax of the other entries, which will be easier to do after you read chapter 5.

To change the properties of a server control, you can click in the starting asp tag to select the control. Then, you can use the Properties window just as if you were in Design view. When you change a property, the *attribute* that represents the property in the asp tag for the control is changed. You can also change the attributes directly in the source code whenever the syntax is obvious. That's often the fastest way to make an adjustment.

The design of the Future Value form in Source view

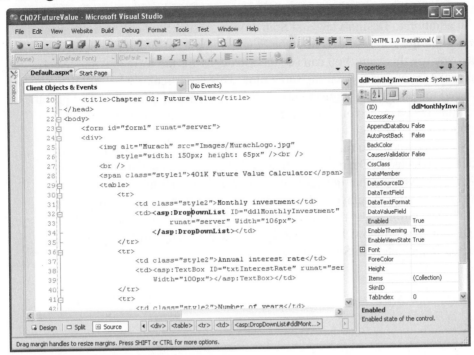

How to change the title of the form

- Change the text between the <title> and </title> tags.

How to change the HTML and text for the form

- Change the source code itself.

How to change the property settings for a control

- To select a control, move the insertion point into the asp tag for the control. Then, use the Properties window to change the property settings for the control. Or, you can modify the property settings in the source code itself.

Description

- Design view presents a visual representation of the code that you see in Source view.
- The source code includes HTML tags and asp tags. Before the form is sent to a browser, the asp tags are converted to HTML because browsers can only interpret HTML.
- The properties you set for a control appear as *attributes* in the asp tag for the control.
- We refer to the source code as *aspx code*, because the source files have aspx extensions.

Figure 2-10   How to use Source view to modify the design of a form

How to use Split view to work with the design

In addition to Design view and Source view, Visual Studio 2008 introduces Split view. Figure 2-11 shows how the Future Value form appears in Split view. When you use this view, you can see the aspx code for the form and the visual representation of that code at the same time. This is particularly helpful when you need to make minor adjustments to the appearance of a form. Then, you can check that the changes you make in Source view look the way you want them to without having to switch to Design view.

Note that when you make a change in Source view, the change isn't automatically reflected in Design view. Instead, a bar is displayed at the top of the Design view window that indicates that the two views are out of sync. In this figure, this bar was displayed when I changed the text in the first cell of the table. To synchronize the two views, you can click on this bar or anywhere in the Design view window. In contrast, if you make a change in Design view, it's reflected immediately in Source view.

The design of the Future Value form in Split view

Description

- With Visual Studio 2008, you can also use Split view to work with the design of a form.

- When you work in Split view, the top half of the designer window displays the form in Source view, and the bottom half of the window displays the form in Design view. This can make it easier to work with these two views.

- If you make a change in Design view, it's reflected immediately in Source view. If you make a change in Source view, however, a bar is displayed at the top of the Design view window that indicates that Design view is out of sync with Source view. Then, you can click this bar or anywhere in the Design view window to synchronize the views.

Figure 2-11   How to use Split view to work with the design of a form

The aspx code for the Future Value form

Figure 2-12 presents the aspx code for the Future Value form that has been developed thus far (except for the Page and Doctype directives, which you'll learn more about in chapter 5). For now, though, please note that the code for the title that's displayed in the web browser is between the <head> tags, along with the code for the style classes that are used by the form, and the code for the form design is between the <div> tags.

Within the <div> tags, I've highlighted the code for the HTML image control and the code for the six web server controls. If you study this code, you can see how the properties are set for each of these controls. For instance, you can see that I set the Width properties of the button controls to 100 pixels so they are both the same width. You can also see that I set the width of the drop-down list to 106 pixels, even though it appears to be the same width as the text boxes, which are 100 pixels wide. My point is that the sizing properties in the aspx code aren't always consistent, so you often have to fiddle with these properties to get the design the way you want it.

Before I go on, I want to point out that when you create an HTML Image control, it's generated with Alt and Src properties with no values. Then, you can set the Src property to the location and name of the image file as shown here. In addition, you can set the Alt property to the text that's displayed if for some reason the image can't be displayed.

The aspx code for the Future Value form

```
<html xmlns="http://www.w3.org/1999/xhtml">
<head runat="server">
    <title>Chapter 02: Future Value</title>
    <style type="text/css">
        .style1 {
            color: #0000FF;
            font-size: x-large;
            font-weight: bold;
        }
        .style2 {
            width: 140px;
            height: 23px;
        }
    </style>
</head>
<body>
    <form id="form1" runat="server">
    <div>
        <img alt="Murach" src="Images/MurachLogo.jpg"
            style="width: 150px; height: 65px" /><br /><br />
        <span class="style1">401K Future Value Calculator</span><br /><br />
        <table>
            <tr>
                <td class="style2">Monthly investment</td>
                <td><asp:DropDownList ID="ddlMonthlyInvestment"
                        runat="server" Width="106px"></asp:DropDownList></td>
            </tr>
            <tr>
                <td class="style2">Annual interest rate</td>
                <td><asp:TextBox ID="txtInterestRate" runat="server"
                        Width="100px">6.0</asp:TextBox></td>
            </tr>
            <tr>
                <td class="style2">Number of years</td>
                <td><asp:TextBox ID="txtYears" runat="server"
                        Width="100px">10</asp:TextBox></td>
            </tr>
            <tr>
                <td class="style2">Future value</td>
                <td><asp:Label ID="lblFutureValue" runat="server"
                        style="font-weight: 700"></asp:Label></td>
            </tr>
            <tr>
                <td class="style2"></td>
                <td></td>
            </tr>
            <tr>
                <td class="style2"><asp:Button ID="btnCalculate" runat="server"
                        onclick="btnCalculate Click"
                        Text="Calculate" Width="100px" /></td>
                <td><asp:Button ID="btnClear" runat="server"
                        OnClick="btnClear_Click" Text="Clear" Width="100px" /></td>
            </tr>
        </table>
        </div>
    </form>
</body>
</html>
```

Figure 2-12   The aspx code for the Future Value form

How to add validation controls to a form

A *validation control* is a type of ASP.NET control that's used to validate input data. The topics that follow introduce you to the validation controls and show you how to use two of the commonly used controls. Then, in chapter 7, you can learn all the skills that you need to master the use of these controls.

An introduction to the validation controls

Figure 2-13 shows the Validation group in the Toolbox. It offers five controls that can be called *validators*. These are the controls that you use to check that the user has entered valid data. You can use the last control in this group, the validation summary control, to display all the errors that have been detected by the validators on the form.

The easiest way to add a validation control to a web form is to drag it from the Toolbox. In this example, four validators have been added to the form: two required field validators and two range validators. In this case, the controls have been added below the table so ASP.NET will use flow layout to position the controls. However, these controls could have been added to a third column of the table. Although these controls aren't displayed when the form is displayed, the messages in their ErrorMessage properties are displayed if errors are detected.

In this case, the first required field validator checks to make sure that a value has been entered in the text box for the interest rate, and the first range validator checks to make sure that this value ranges from 1 to 20. Similarly, the second required field validator checks to make sure that a value has been entered in the text box for the number of years, and the second range validator checks to make sure that this value ranges from 1 to 45.

Validation tests are typically done on the client before the page is posted to the server. That way, a round trip to the server isn't required to display error messages if any invalid data is detected.

In most cases, client-side validation is done when the focus leaves an input control that has validators associated with it. That can happen when the user presses the Tab key to move to the next control or clicks another control to move the focus to that control. Validation is also done when the user clicks on a button that has its CausesValidation property set to True.

To perform client-side validation, a browser must support *Dynamic HTML*, or *DHTML*. Because most browsers in use today support DHTML, validation can usually be done on the client. However, validation is always done on the server too when a page is submitted. ASP.NET does this validation after it initializes the page.

When ASP.NET performs the validation tests on the server, it sets the IsValid property of each validator to indicate if the test was successful. In addition, after all the validators are tested, it sets the IsValid property of the page to indicate if all the input data is valid. You can test this property in the event handler for the event that causes the page to be posted to the server. You'll see how this works when you review the code-behind file for this form.

The validation controls on the Future Value form

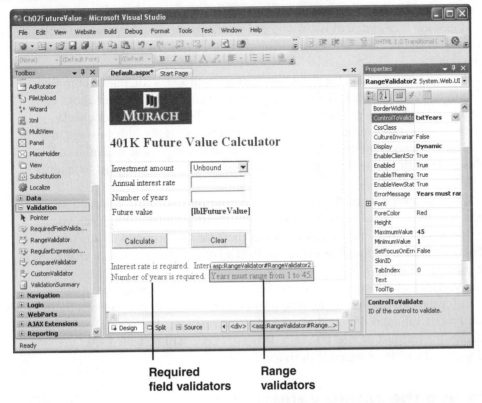

Required
field validators

Range
validators

Description

- You can use *validation controls* to test user input and produce error messages. The validation is typically performed when the focus leaves the control that's being validated and also when the user clicks on a button control whose CausesValidation property is set to True.

- Each validation control is associated with a specific server control, but you can associate one or more validation controls with a single server control.

- The validation controls work by running client-side script. Then, if the validation fails, the page isn't posted back to the server. However, the validation is also performed on the server in case the client doesn't support scripts.

- If the client doesn't support scripts, you can test whether validation has been successful on the server by testing whether the IsValid property of the page is True.

Figure 2-13   An introduction to the validation controls

How to use the required field validator

To use the *required field validator*, you set the properties shown in the table at the top of figure 2-14. These are the properties that are used by all the validators.

To start, you associate the validation control with a specific input control on the form through its ControlToValidate property. Then, when the user clicks on a button whose CausesValidation property is set to True, the validator checks whether a value has been entered into the input control. If not, the message in the ErrorMessage property is displayed. The error message is also displayed if the user clears the value in the input control and then moves the focus to another control.

When an error occurs, the Display property of the validation control determines how the message in the ErrorMessage property is displayed. When you use flow layout, Dynamic usually works the best for this property. If you use a validation summary control as explained in chapter 7, though, you can change this property to None.

If you look at the aspx code in this figure, you can see how the properties are set for the two required field validators that are shown in the previous figure. The first one validates the text box named txtInterestRate. The second one validates the text box named txtYears. This aspx code will be added after the end tag for the table in the code in figure 2-12.

How to use the range validator

The *range validator* lets you set the valid range for an input value. To use this control, you set the properties in the first table in figure 2-14, plus the properties in the second table. In particular, you set the minimum and maximum values for an input value.

For this control to work correctly, you must set the Type property to the type of data you're testing for. Because the interest rate entry can have decimal positions, for example, the Type property for the first range validator is set to Double. In contrast, because the year entry should be a whole number, the Type property for the second range validator is set to Integer. You can see how all of the properties for the two range validators are set by reviewing the aspx code.

Common validation control properties

Property	Description
ControlToValidate	The ID of the control to be validated.
Display	Determines how an error message is displayed. Specify Static to allocate space for the message in the page layout, Dynamic to have the space allocated when an error occurs, or None to display the errors in a validation summary control.
ErrorMessage	The message that's displayed in the validation control when the validation fails.

Additional properties of a range validator

Property	Description
MaximumValue	The maximum value that the control can contain.
MinimumValue	The minimum value that the control can contain.
Type	The data type to use for range checking (String, Integer, Double, Date, or Currency).

The aspx code for the validation controls on the Future Value form

```
<asp:RequiredFieldValidator ID="RequiredFieldValidator1" runat="server"
    ControlToValidate="txtInterestRate" Display="Dynamic"
    ErrorMessage="Interest rate is required.">
</asp:RequiredFieldValidator> 
<asp:RangeValidator ID="RangeValidator1" runat="server"
    ControlToValidate="txtInterestRate" Display="Dynamic"
    ErrorMessage="Interest rate must range from 1 to 20."
    MaximumValue="20" MinimumValue="1" Type="Double">
</asp:RangeValidator><br />
<asp:RequiredFieldValidator ID="RequiredFieldValidator2" runat="server"
    ControlToValidate="txtYears" Display="Dynamic"
    ErrorMessage="Number of years is required.">
</asp:RequiredFieldValidator> 
<asp:RangeValidator ID="RangeValidator2" runat="server"
    ControlToValidate="txtYears" Display="Dynamic"
    ErrorMessage="Years must range from 1 to 45."
    MaximumValue="45" MinimumValue="1" Type="Integer">
</asp:RangeValidator>
```

Description

- The *required field validator* is typically used with text box controls, but can also be used with list controls.
- The *range validator* tests whether a user entry falls within a valid range.
- If the user doesn't enter a value into the input control that a range validator is associated with, the range validation test passes. Because of that, you should also provide a required field validator if a value is required.

Figure 2-14   How to use the required field and range validators

How to add code to a form

To add the functionality required by a web form, you add C# code to its code-behind file. This code responds to the events that the user initiates on the form. This code also responds to events that occur as a form is processed.

How to use the Code Editor

To create and edit C# code, you use the *Code Editor* shown in figure 2-15. The easiest way to display the Code Editor window is to double-click the form or a control in the Web Forms Designer window. That displays the code-behind file for the form.

If you double-click the form in Design view, an *event handler* for the Load event of the page is generated. If you double-click a control, an event handler for the default event of the control is generated. If you double-click on a button control, for example, an event handler for the Click event of that control is created. Then, you can enter the code you want to be executed when the event occurs within the event handler.

To create event handlers for other control events, you can use the Events button at the top of the Properties window. When you click this button, a list of all the events for the control that's currently selected is displayed. Then, you can double-click on any event to generate an event handler for that event.

When Visual Studio generates an event handler for a control, it also adds the appropriate event attribute to the asp code for that control. In figure 2-12, for example, you saw the OnClick event attributes that were generated for the Calculate and Clear buttons on the Future Value form. This is how events are wired to event handlers in ASP.NET, and you'll learn more about it in chapter 6.

You can also code methods other than event handlers by entering code directly into the Code Editor window. When you see the complete code for the Future Value form later in this chapter, for example, you'll see that it includes a method named CalculateFutureValue. This method performs the actual future value calculation, and it's called by the event handler for the Click event of the Calculate button.

As you work with the Code Editor, you'll notice that it provides some powerful features that can help you code more quickly and accurately. One of the most useful of these features is the List Members feature provided by IntelliSense. This feature displays a list of members that are available for an object when you type the object name and a period. Then, you can highlight the member you want by clicking on it, typing the first few letters of its name, or using the arrow keys to scroll through the list. In this figure, you can see the members that are listed for a drop-down list after the first character of the member name is entered. When you press the Tab key, the member you select is inserted into your code.

A project with the Code Editor window displayed

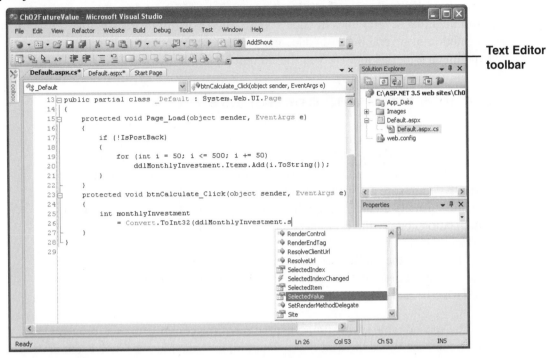

Text Editor toolbar

Three ways to open or switch to a file in the Code Editor window

- Select a web form in the Solution Explorer and click the View Code button at the top of the Solution Explorer. Double-click on a C# file (.aspx.cs or .cs) in the Solution Explorer. Or, click on a tab at the top of the Web Forms Designer (if the file is already open).

Three ways to start an event handler

- Double-click on a blank portion of a web form to start an event handler for the Load event of the page.
- Double-click on a control in the Web Forms Designer to start an event handler for the default event of that control.
- Select a control in the Web Forms Designer, click the Events button in the Properties window (the button with the lightening bolt), and double-click the event you want to create an event handler for.

Description

- The *Code Editor* includes powerful text editing features such as automatic indentation, syntax checking, and statement completion (as shown above).
- To enter a method other than an event handler, you type the method from scratch.

Figure 2-15   How to use the Code Editor

You can also use the Text Editor toolbar to work with code in the Code Editor. You can use it to perform functions such as commenting or uncommenting several lines of code at once, increasing or decreasing the indentation of several lines of code, and working with bookmarks. If you experiment with this toolbar, you should quickly see how it works.

How to use page and control events

The first table in figure 2-16 presents some of the common events for working with web pages. The Init and Load events of a page occur whenever a page is requested from the server. The Init event occurs first, and it's used by ASP.NET to restore the view state of the page and its controls. Because of that, you don't usually create an event handler for this event. Instead, you add any initialization code to the event handler for the Load event. You'll see how this works in the next figure.

In contrast, the PreRender event is raised after all the control events for the page have been processed. It's the last event to occur before a page is rendered to HTML. In later chapters, you'll see a couple of cases in which this event is useful.

The second table in this figure lists some of the common events for web server controls. When the user clicks a button, for example, the Click event of that control is raised. Then, the page is posted back to the server, the event handlers for the Init and Load events of the page are executed, if present, followed by the event handler for the Click event of the control that was clicked.

The TextChanged event occurs when the user changes the value in a text box. In most cases, you won't code an event handler for the TextChanged event. However, you might code an event handler for the CheckedChanged event that occurs when the user clicks a radio button or checks a check box. You might also code an event handler for the SelectedIndexChanged event that occurs when the user selects an item from a list.

If you want the event handler for one of these events to be executed immediately when the event occurs, you can set the AutoPostBack property of the control to True. Then, the event handler will be executed after the Init and Load event handlers for the page. Note that if you don't set the AutoPostBack property to True, the event is still raised, but the event handler isn't executed until another user action causes the page to be posted to the server. Then, the event handlers for the Init and Load events of the page are executed, followed by the event handlers for the control events in the order they were raised.

In this figure, you can see the event handler for the Click event of the Clear button on the Future Value form. This event handler resets the value in the drop-down list to 50 and resets the text boxes and label to empty strings. Note that the name for this event handler is btnClear_Click, which is the ID of the button followed by the name of the event. If you look back to the aspx code for the Future Value form in figure 2-12, you'll see that this is the same name that's referenced in the OnClick event attribute that ASP.NET adds to the control when it generates the event handler.

Common ASP.NET page events

Event	Method name	Occurs when...
Init	Page_Init	A page is requested from the server. This event is raised before the view state of the page controls has been restored.
Load	Page_Load	A page is requested from the server, after all controls have been initialized and view state has been restored. This is the event you typically use to perform initialization operations such as retrieving data and initializing form controls.
PreRender	Page_PreRender	All the control events for the page have been processed but before the HTML that will be sent back to the browser is generated.

Common ASP.NET control events

Event	Occurs when...
Click	The user clicks a button, link button, or image button.
TextChanged	The user changes the value in a text box.
CheckedChanged	The user selects a radio button in a group of radio buttons or selects or unselects a check box.
SelectedIndexChanged	The user selects an item from a list box, a drop-down list, a check box list, or a radio button list.

Code for the Click event of the btnClear button

```
protected void btnClear_Click(object sender, EventArgs e)
{
    ddlMonthlyInvestment.SelectedIndex = 0;
    txtInterestRate.Text = "";
    txtYears.Text = "";
    lblFutureValue.Text = "";
}
```

Description

- All of the events associated with an ASP.NET web page and its server controls are executed on the server. Because of that, the page must be posted back to the server to process any event for which you've coded an event handler.

- When a page is posted back to the server, the Init and Load events are always raised so any event handlers for those events are run first. Next, the event handlers for any control events that were raised are executed in the order they were raised. When these event handlers finish, the PreRender event is raised and any event handler for that event is run.

- When you generate an event handler for a control, ASP.NET adds the appropriate event attribute to the asp code for the control to wire the event to the event handler. This isn't necessary for page events because the event handlers are called automatically when the events occur.

Figure 2-16   How to use page and control events

The C# code for the Future Value form

Figure 2-17 presents the complete C# code for the code-behind file of the Future Value form. It consists of three event handlers that handle the Load event for the page and the Click events of the Calculate and Clear buttons. This code also includes a method named CalculateFutureValue that is called by the event handler for the Click event of the Calculate button.

In this code, I've highlighted the two page properties that are commonly tested in the code for web forms. The first one is the IsPostBack property that's used in the Page_Load event handler. If it is True, it means that the page is being posted back from the user. If it is False, it means that the page is being requested by the user for the first time.

As a result, the statements within the if statement in the Page_Load event handler are only executed if the page is being requested for the first time. In that case, the values 50 through 500 (in increments of 50) are added to the drop-down list. For all subsequent requests by that user, the IsPostBack property will be True so the values aren't added to the drop-down list.

The other page property that's commonly tested is the IsValid property. It's useful when the user's browser doesn't support the script for the validation controls. In that case, the application has to rely on the validation that's always done on the server. Then, if IsValid is True, it means that all of the input data is valid. But if IsValid is False, it means that one or more controls contain invalid input data so the processing shouldn't be done.

In the btnCalculate_Click event handler, you can see how the IsValid test is used. If it isn't True, the processing isn't done. But otherwise, this event handler gets the years and interest rate values from the text boxes, and it uses the SelectedValue property of the drop-down list to get the value of the selected item, which represents the monthly investment. Then, it converts the years and interest rate to monthly units. Last, it calls the CalculateFutureValue method to calculate the future value, uses the ToString method to format the future value, and puts the formatted value in the label of the form. When this event handler ends, the web form is sent back to the user's browser.

With the exception of the IsPostBack and IsValid properties, this is all standard C# code so you shouldn't have any trouble following it. But if you do, you can quickly upgrade your C# skills by getting our latest C# book.

The C# code for the Future Value form

```csharp
using System;
using System.Collections;
using System.Configuration;
using System.Data;
using System.Linq;
using System.Web;
using System.Web.Security;
using System.Web.UI;
using System.Web.UI.HtmlControls;
using System.Web.UI.WebControls;
using System.Web.UI.WebControls.WebParts;
using System.Xml.Linq;

public partial class _Default : System.Web.UI.Page
{
    protected void Page_Load(object sender, EventArgs e){
        if (!IsPostBack)
            for (int i = 50; i <= 500; i += 50)
                ddlMonthlyInvestment.Items.Add(i.ToString());
    }
    protected void btnCalculate_Click(object sender, EventArgs e){
        if (IsValid)
        {
            int monthlyInvestment
                = Convert.ToInt32(ddlMonthlyInvestment.SelectedValue);
            decimal yearlyInterestRate =
                Convert.ToDecimal(txtInterestRate.Text);
            int years = Convert.ToInt32(txtYears.Text);

            int months = years * 12;
            decimal monthlyInterestRate = yearlyInterestRate / 12 / 100;

            decimal futureValue = this.CalculateFutureValue(monthlyInvestment,
                monthlyInterestRate, months);

            lblFutureValue.Text = futureValue.ToString("c");
        }
    }
    protected decimal CalculateFutureValue(int monthlyInvestment,
    decimal monthlyInterestRate, int months){
        decimal futureValue = 0;
        for (int i = 0; i < months; i++)
        {
            futureValue = (futureValue + monthlyInvestment)
                * (1 + monthlyInterestRate);
        }
        return futureValue;
    }
    protected void btnClear_Click(object sender, EventArgs e){
        ddlMonthlyInvestment.SelectedIndex = 0;
        txtInterestRate.Text = "";
        txtYears.Text = "";
        lblFutureValue.Text = "";
    }
}
```

Figure 2-17   The C# code for the Future Value form

How to test a web application

After you design the forms and develop the code for a web application, you need to test it to be sure it works properly. Then, if you discover any errors in the application, you can debug it, correct the errors, and test it again.

In chapter 4, you'll learn all the skills you need to test and debug a web application. For now, I just want to show you how to run a web site with the built-in development server so you can test any applications that you develop for this chapter. Then, I'll show you the HTML code that's sent to the browser so you can see how that works.

How to run a web site with the built-in development server

When you run a file-system web site by using one of the techniques in figure 2-18, Visual Studio 2008 compiles the application. If the application compiles without errors, Visual Studio automatically launches the built-in ASP.NET Development Server and displays the starting page of the web site in your default browser. Then, you can test the application to make sure that it works the way you want it to.

However, if any errors are detected as part of the compilation, Visual Studio opens the Error List window and displays the errors. These can consist of errors that have to be corrected as well as warning messages. In this figure, three error and two warning messages are displayed in the Error List window.

To fix an error, you can double-click on it in the Error List window. This moves the cursor to the line of code that caused the error in the Code Editor. By moving from the Error List window to the Code Editor for all of the messages, you should be able to find the coding problems and fix them.

As you're testing an application with the development server, exceptions may occur. If an exception isn't handled by the application, ASP.NET switches to the Code Editor window and highlights the statement that caused the exception. In this case, you can end the application by clicking on the Stop Debugging button in the Debug toolbar or using the Debug→Stop Debugging command. Then, you can fix the problem and test again.

In chapter 4, you'll learn all of the debugging skills that you'll need for more complex applications. For simple applications, though, you should be able to get by with just the skills you have right now.

An ASP.NET project with the Error List window displayed

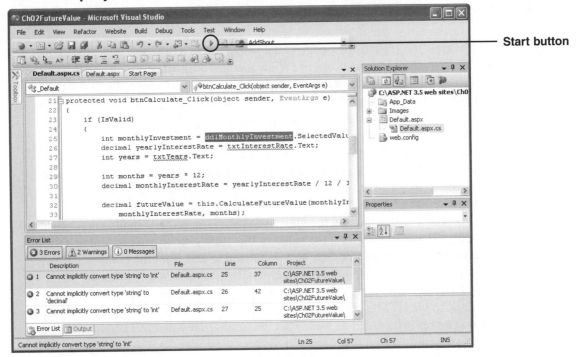

Start button

How to run an application

- Click on the Start button in the Standard toolbar or press F5. Then, the project is compiled and the starting page is displayed in your default browser.

- The first time you run an ASP.NET application, a dialog box will appear asking whether you want to create a new web.config file with debugging enabled. Click the OK button to proceed.

How to stop an application

- Click the Close button in the upper right corner of the browser. Or, if an exception occurs, click the Stop Debugging button in the Debug toolbar or press Shift+F5.

How to fix build errors

- If any errors are detected when the project is compiled, an Error List window is opened and a list of errors is displayed along with information about each error. To display the source code that caused an error, double-click on the error in the Error List window.

- After you've fixed all of the errors, run the application again, and repeat this process if necessary. Note, however, that you don't have to fix the warnings.

Figure 2-18   How to run a web site with the built-in development server

How to review the HTML that's sent to the browser

To view the HTML for a page that's displayed in a browser, you can use the Source command in your browser's View menu. To illustrate, figure 2-19 presents the HTML that's sent back to the browser after I selected a new value from the drop-down list, entered new values into the text boxes, and clicked the Calculate button. Although you'll rarely need to view this code, it does give you a better idea of what's going on behind the scenes.

First, you'll see that this code doesn't include any asp tags. That's because these tags are rendered to standard HTML so the controls they represent can be displayed in the browser. For instance, the asp tag for the drop-down list in the first row of the table has been converted to an HTML select tag.

Second, you can see that the view state data is stored in a hidden input field named _VIEWSTATE. Here, the value of this field is encrypted so you can't read it. Because the data in view state is passed to and from the browser automatically, you don't have to handle the passing of this data in your code.

Third, you can see that the data that I selected from the drop-down list is included in the HTML. Although you can't see it, the data that was entered into the text boxes is included as well. This illustrates that you don't need view state to save the information that's entered by the user. Instead, view state is used to maintain the state of properties that have been set by code. For example, it's used to maintain the values that are loaded into the drop-down list the first time the user requests the form.

Keep in mind that this HTML is generated automatically by ASP.NET, so you don't have to worry about it. You just develop the application by using Visual Studio in the way I've just described, and the rest of the work is done for you.

The HTML for the Future Value form after a post back

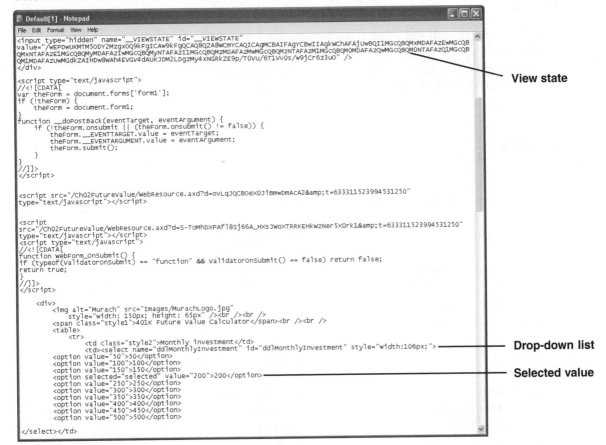

Description

- To view the HTML for a page, use the View→Source command in the browser's menu.

- The HTML that the browser receives consists entirely of standard HTML tags because all of the asp tags are converted to standard HTML when the page is rendered.

- View state data is stored in a hidden input field within the HTML. This data is encrypted so you can't read it.

- If the page contains validation controls and client scripting is enabled for those controls, the HTML for the page contains script to perform the validation on the client if the client supports DHTML.

- Values that the user enters into a page are returned to the browser as part of the HTML for the page.

Figure 2-19   How to review the HTML that's sent to the browser

Perspective

The purpose of this chapter has been to teach you the basic skills for creating one-page ASP.NET applications with Visual Studio. If you've already used Visual Studio and C# to develop Windows applications, you shouldn't have any trouble mastering these skills. You just need to get used to HTML and the properties and events for web server controls and validation controls.

Terms

web site	label
file-system web site	button
target framework	flow layout
web project	HTML control
project	smart tag menu
Web Forms Designer	HTML Editor
Toolbox	attribute
Solution Explorer	aspx code
Properties window	validation control
web form	validator
Source view	required field validator
Design view	range validator
Split view	Dynamic HTML (DHTML)
web server control	Code Editor
drop-down list	event handler
text box	smart tag

Exercise 2-1   Build the Future Value application

This exercise guides you through the development of the Future Value application that's presented in this chapter.

Start, close, and open the application

1. Start a new file-system web site as shown in figure 2-1 named FutureValue in the C:\ASP.NET 3.5 C# directory.

2. Add a folder named Images to your project and add the Murach logo to it, as shown in figure 2-3. You can find the logo in the C:\ASP.NET 3.5 C#\Ch01Cart directory.

3. Close the web site using the technique in figure 2-4, and reopen it using one of the three techniques in that figure. Then, switch to Design view.

Use Design view to build the form

4   Drag the logo from the Images folder in the Solution Explorer to the top of the web form. When the Accessibility Properties dialog box is displayed, enter "Murach" for the alternate text but leave the long description blank. Then, use the techniques in figure 2-6 to enter and format the text for the heading in figure 2-5.

5.   Use the techniques in figure 2-7 to add and format a table that provides for the six rows shown in figure 2-5. Then, add the text shown in figure 2-5 to the first four rows in the first column of the table.

6.   Use the techniques in figure 2-8 to add the drop-down list, text boxes, label, and buttons shown in figure 2-5 to the table. Then, adjust the size of the columns, rows, and controls, so the table looks the way it does in figure 2-5.

7.   Use the techniques of figure 2-8 and the summary in figure 2-9 to set the properties of the controls so they look like the ones in figure 2-5.

Use Source view to modify the aspx code

8.   Switch to Source view, and change the title of the form to Future Value using the technique of figure 2-10.

9.   Press F5 to run the application. When the dialog box asks whether you want to add a new web.config file with debugging enabled, click the OK button. Now, test to see what works by clicking on the controls. Also, check to make sure that the web form looks the way it's supposed to when it's displayed in the default browser.

10.   To end the application, click the Close button in the upper right corner of the browser. Then, switch to Split view, adjust the design of the form as necessary, and test it again.

Add the validation controls

11.   Add the validation controls for the interest rate and years text boxes as shown in figures 2-13 and 2-14.

12.   Press F5 to run the application. Then, test the validators by leaving fields blank or entering invalid data. The validation will be done when the focus leaves a text box or when you click on a button.

13.   To end the application, click the browser's Close button. Then, fix any problems and test again. If, for example, validation is done when you click the Clear button, you can fix that by setting its CausesValidation property to False.

Add the C# code and test as you go

14.   Use one of the techniques in figure 2-15 to open the Code Editor for the form. Then, use the tab at the top of the window to switch to Design view.

15.   Double-click on a blank portion of the form to switch to the Code Editor and start an event handler for the Load event. Next, write the code for this event handler, which should be like the code in figure 2-17. Then, press F5 to compile and test this event handler. If any errors are detected as you enter code or when the application is compiled, use the techniques in figure 2-18 to fix them.

16. Switch back to Design view, and double-click on the Clear button to start an event handler for the Click event of that button. Next, write the code for this event handler, which should be like the code in figure 2-17. Then, compile and test this event handler, and fix any errors.

17. Write the CalculateFutureValue method from scratch as shown in figure 2-17.

18. Switch back to Design view, and double-click on the Calculate button to start an event handler for the Click event of that button. Next, write the code for this event handler, which should use the CalculateFutureValue method and be like the code in figure 2-17. Then, compile and test, and fix any errors.

Do more testing and experimenting

19. Set the EnableViewState property of the drop-down list to False, and test the application to see what happens. When an exception occurs, click the Stop Debugging button in the Debugging toolbar. Then, reset the property.

20. Set the EnableClientScript property for the validators of the first text box to False so this validation will only be done on the server. Then, test the application to make sure that the validation still works.

21. Run the application again, and use the technique in figure 2-19 to review the HTML that's sent to the browser. When you're through, close the project.

3

How to develop a multi-page web application

In the last chapter, you learned how to develop a simple, one-page web application. Now, you'll learn how to develop a multi-page application, which requires several new skills. You'll also learn how to get the data for a web form from a database.

The Shopping Cart application **74**
The Order page 74
The Cart page 76
The files and folders used by the Shopping Cart application 78
How to add a class to a web site 80
Six skills for working with multiple web forms **82**
How to add a web form to a web site 82
How to rename a web form 84
How to change the starting web form 84
How to redirect or transfer to another page 86
How to use cross-page posting 88
How to code absolute and relative URLs 90
How to create and use data sources **92**
How to create an Access data source 92
How to configure an Access data source 94
How to bind a drop-down list to a data source 96
How to use C# code to get data from a data source 98
How to use session state **100**
How session state works 100
How to work with data in session state 102
The code for the Shopping Cart application **104**
The code for the Product and CartItem classes 104
The aspx code for the Order page 104
The C# code for the Order page 108
The aspx code for the Cart page 112
The C# code for the Cart page 112
Perspective **116**

The Shopping Cart application

To illustrate the skills that you're going to learn, this chapter presents two pages of a Shopping Cart application. This application gets product data from a database, stores data in session state, and uses two business classes. So even though this is a simple application, it isn't trivial.

In the four topics that follow, you'll be introduced to the two web forms and the folders and files that this application requires. Then, you'll learn how to add the two business classes to this project.

The Order page

Figure 3-1 presents the first page of the Shopping Cart application. This page, named Order.aspx, includes a drop-down list from which the user can select a product. The products are retrieved from an Access database via an AccessDataSource control. Since the drop-down list is bound to the data source, the product names are displayed automatically.

Although it isn't apparent in this figure, the product data is retrieved from an Access database named Halloween.mdb. This database includes a table named Products. The Products table has these columns: ProductID, Name, ShortDescription, LongDescription, CategoryID, ImageFile, UnitPrice, and OnHand. All of these columns except CategoryID and OnHand are used by this application.

The AutoPostBack property of the drop-down list is set to True. That way, when the user selects a product, the page is posted back to the server. Then, the code for the page retrieves the data for the selected product from the data source, which has retrieved the data for all of the products from the Access database. The data for the selected product is displayed in several labels. In addition, the ImageUrl property of an Image control is set to the value of the ImageFile column so the product image is displayed in that control.

Once a product is selected, the user can enter a quantity and click the Add to Cart button. However, if the user clicks the Add to Cart button without entering a valid quantity, an error message is displayed. To accomplish that, two validation controls are included on the page. A required field validator makes sure that the user enters a quantity, and a range validator makes sure that the quantity is an integer that ranges from 1 to 500.

If the user enters a valid quantity, a sorted list that contains the user's shopping cart is updated with the product information. If the product isn't already in the shopping cart, a new item is added to the sorted list. But if the product already exists in the shopping cart, the quantity entered is added to the quantity for the product that's in the shopping cart. Because the shopping cart must be retrieved and updated each time a product is added or updated, the sorted list that represents the shopping cart is saved in session state.

The design of the Order page

Description

- The Order page of this application accepts an order for any items in the online store.
- To order an item, the user selects the product from the drop-down list, enters a quantity in the text box, and clicks the Add to Cart button.
- When the user clicks the Add to Cart button, the selected product is added to the shopping cart. If the product is already in the shopping cart, the quantity is added to the quantity in the existing shopping cart item. Then, the Cart page is displayed.
- The product information is retrieved from an Access database by an AccessDataSource control that's bound to the drop-down list.
- The AutoPostBack property of the drop-down list is set to True so the page is posted when the user selects a product. Then, the information for the selected product is displayed.
- The shopping cart information is stored in a SortedList object. This sorted list is saved in session state so it can be retrieved and updated each time a product is ordered.
- Validation controls ensure that the user enters a positive integer for the quantity that ranges from 1 to 500.

Figure 3-1   The Order page of the Shopping Cart application

The Cart page

After the user selects a product from the Order page, enters a quantity, and clicks the Add to Cart button, the Cart page in figure 3-2 is displayed. This page lists all the items currently in the shopping cart in a list box. To do that, it must retrieve the shopping cart from session state.

To work with the items in the shopping cart, the user can use the two buttons to the right of the list box. To remove an item from the shopping cart, the user can select the item and click the Remove Item button. Or, to remove all the items from the shopping cart, the user can click the Empty Cart button.

If the user wants to add items to the shopping cart, he can click the Continue Shopping button to return to the Order page. Alternatively, the user can click the Check Out button to complete the order. However, the check out function hasn't yet been implemented in this version of the Shopping Cart application. So if the user clicks the Check Out button, a message is displayed to indicate that the check out feature isn't implemented. In a complete application, of course, clicking this button would cause additional pages to be displayed to complete the order.

Like most applications, there are several different ways to implement a shopping cart in ASP.NET. For instance, one design decision is how to save the shopping cart data. For this application, I decided to save the shopping cart data in session state. As an alternative, though, you could save the shopping cart data in a database table. Or, you could use ASP.NET's profile feature to save the data. Each approach has its advantages and disadvantages.

A second design decision for a shopping cart application is what type of ASP.NET control to use when you display the shopping cart. To keep this application simple, I used a list box. However, you can create a more advanced shopping cart by using the GridView control that's presented in chapter 14. With this control, you can display the shopping cart data in neatly arranged columns and include buttons or other controls in each row to let the user delete or modify the cart items.

The design of the Cart page

Description

- The Cart page displays the items in the shopping cart in a list box control. To load the list box, it uses the shopping cart information that's saved in session state by the Order page.

- The user can select any item in the shopping cart and then click the Remove Item button to remove the item from the cart. If the user checks the Remove Item button without selecting an item, a message is displayed that asks the user to select the item to be removed. To remove all the items from the cart, the user can click the Empty Cart button.

- After reviewing the cart, the user can click the Continue Shopping button to return to the Order page and order additional products.

- If the user clicks the Check Out button, a message is displayed that indicates that the check out function hasn't been implemented yet.

Figure 3-2   The Cart page of the Shopping Cart application

The files and folders used by the Shopping Cart application

Figure 3-3 summarizes the files and folders used by the Shopping Cart application. By default, Visual Studio 2008 places new web page files and their related code-behind files in the application's root folder, but other files used by the application are placed in special folders. The first table in this figure lists the most commonly used special folders. Besides these folders, though, you can also create your own folders. For example, it's common to create an Images folder to store any image files used by the application.

The App_Code, App_Data, App_Themes, and Bin folders are used for certain types of files required by the application. For instance, class files (other than the class files for web pages) are stored in the App_Code folder, and any database files used by the application are stored in the App_Data folder. In contrast, the App_Themes folder is used to store any theme data, which you'll learn more about in chapter 11. And the Bin folder is used to store any compiled assemblies, such as class libraries, that are used by the application.

Note that the special folders aren't available to the application through normal means. For example, you can't store an image file in the App_Data folder and then refer to it in the ImageUrl attribute of an Image control. The only exception is that you can refer to the App_Data folder in a connection string for an Access database.

The second table in this figure lists the specific files and folders that make up the Shopping Cart application. As you can see, the App_Code folder contains two class files named CartItem.cs and Product.cs that define the CartItem and Product classes required by the application. And the App_Data folder contains an Access database named Halloween.mdb, plus an .ldb file that stores the record locking information for that file.

The Shopping Cart application also includes a folder named Images. This folder includes just one image file, banner.jpg, which provides the banner that's displayed at the top of each page. However, this folder also includes a subfolder named Products, which includes a separate image file for each product in the Products table of the database. Because the Products table includes a column named ImageFile that provides the file name for each product's image, the application can display the correct image for each product.

Finally, the root folder for the application contains two files for each of the application's web pages: one for the page itself, the other for the code-behind file. For example, the Cart.aspx file contains the aspx code that defines the Cart page, and the Cart.aspx.cs file is the code-behind file that contains the C# code for the Cart page.

Please note that the root folder also contains a web.config file. This file is added the first time you run an application with debugging.

The Solution Explorer for the Shopping Cart application

Special folders used in ASP.NET 3.5 applications

Folder	Description
App_Code	Non-page class files that are compiled together to create a single assembly.
App_Data	Database files used by the application.
App_Themes	Themes used by the application.
Bin	Compiled code used by the application.

Files in the Shopping Cart application

Folder	File	Description
App_Code	CartItem.cs	A class that represents an item in the shopping cart.
App_Code	Product.cs	A class that represents a product.
App_Data	Halloween.mdb	The Access database file that contains the Halloween database.
App_Data	Halloween.ldb	The locking file associated with the Halloween.mdb database file.
Images	Banner.jpg	An image file that displays the banner used at the top of each page.
Images\Products	(multiple)	Contains an image file for each product in the database.
(root)	Cart.aspx	The aspx file for the Cart page.
(root)	Cart.aspx.cs	The code-behind file for the Cart page.
(root)	Order.aspx	The aspx file for the Order page.
(root)	Order.aspx.cs	The code-behind file for the Order page.
(root)	web.config	The application configuration file.

Description

- The Images folder is a custom folder that I created to hold the image files used by this application. The Products subfolder contains the image files for the products in the Products table of the Halloween database.

Figure 3-3   The files and folders used by the Shopping Cart application

How to add a class to a web site

As you just saw in the previous figure, the Shopping Cart application requires two business classes named Product and CartItem. To use these classes with the web site, you can use the techniques presented in figure 3-4.

To add a new class to the web site, you use the Add New Item dialog box shown in this figure. From this dialog box, you select the Class template, enter the name for the class, and then click the Add button. When you do, Visual Studio will generate the new class declaration along with an empty constructor. Then, you can complete the class by coding its properties and methods.

Before you create a new class, you'll typically add the special App_Code folder to the web site so that you can add the class directly to this folder. However, you can also add a new class without first adding the App_Code folder. To do that, just select Add New Item from the shortcut menu for the project. Then, when you click the Add button to add the class, Visual Studio will display a dialog box that indicates that the class should be placed in an App_Code folder and asks if you want to place the class in that folder. If you click the Yes button in this dialog box, Visual Studio will create the App_Code folder and place the new class in it.

To add an existing class to a web site, you use the Add Existing Item command as described in this figure. Then, the class file that you select is copied to your web site.

If the existing class you want to use is stored in a *class library*, you can use that class by adding a reference to the class library to your web site as described in this figure. One of the advantages of using class libraries is that the source code is stored in a single location. Then, if you need to modify a class, you can just modify the code in the class library and it will be available to any web sites that use that library. In contrast, if you copy a class to each web site that uses it, you have to modify the code in each web site.

The dialog box for adding a new class to the App_Code folder

Two ways to open the Add New Item dialog box

- Right-click the App_Code folder in the Solution Explorer if it already exists, and then choose Add New Item from the shortcut menu.

- Click on the App_Code folder in the Solution Explorer to select it, and then choose the Website→Add New Item command.

How to add a new class to a web site

- From the Add New Item dialog box, select the Class template, name the class, and click the Add button. Visual Studio will create the class with a class block and an empty constructor.

- If you try to add a class directly to the project instead of to the App_Code folder, Visual Studio will warn you that the class should be placed in the App_Code folder and ask you if you'd like to place the class in this folder. If you click the Yes button, Visual Studio will create the App_Code folder if necessary and place the class in this folder.

How to add an existing class to a web site

- To add a class from another project to a web site, right-click the App_Code folder in the Solution Explorer and select Add Existing Item. Then, locate the class file you want to add, select it, and click the Add button. The file is copied to your project.

How to use a class that's part of a class library

- Right-click the project in the Solution Explorer and select Add Reference from the shortcut menu. Click the Browse tab in the dialog box that's displayed, and then locate and select the dll file for the class library you want to use. The class library is added to the project's Bin folder, which is created if it doesn't already exist. To use the classes in the class library without qualification, add a using statement for the class library.

Figure 3-4   How to add a class to a web site

Six skills for working with multiple web forms

To create a multi-page web site, you need to learn some new skills like how to add a new web form to a web site, how to rename a web form, how to change the starting page for a web site, and how to transfer from one form to another.

How to add a web form to a web site

To add a new web form to a web site, you use the Add New Item dialog box shown in figure 3-5. From this dialog box, you select the Web Form template. Then, you enter the name you want to use for the new form and click the Add button to add it to your web site along with the code-behind file.

When you add a new web form, be sure that the language setting is Visual C# and that the Place Code in Separate File box is checked. These settings are easy to overlook, but difficult to change manually if they're set wrong when you create the page.

To add an existing web form from another web site, you can use the second procedure in this figure. You might want to do that if you need to create a form that's similar to a form in another web site. When you add the aspx file for a form, the code-behind file is added too. Then, you can modify the aspx and C# code so the form works the way you want it to in your new web site.

The Add New Item dialog box for adding a new web form

Two ways to open the Add New Item dialog box

- Right-click the project in the Solution Explorer, and then choose Add New Item from the shortcut menu.
- Click on the project in the Solution Explorer to select it, and then choose the Website→Add New Item command.

How to add a new web form to a project

- From the Add New Item dialog box, select the Web Form template, name the form, check the Place Code in Separate File box, and click the Add button.

How to add an existing web form to a project

- In the Solution Explorer, right-click the project and choose Add Existing Item. Then, locate the form you want to add, select it, and click the Add button.

Description

- If there's a form in another application that is like one that you're going to develop, you can copy that form into your web site. That copies both the web form and the code-behind file. Then, you can modify the aspx code and C# code so the form works the way you want it to.

Figure 3-5   How to add a web form to a web site

How to rename a web form

When you add a web form to a web site, the form file is given the name you specify in the Add New Item dialog box. In addition, the partial class that contains the C# code for the form is given the same name, which is usually what you want. In some cases, though, you may need to rename the form file or the form class. In particular, you'll want to rename the default form so its name is more descriptive. Figure 3-6 shows you how.

When you change the name of a form file, you might think that Visual Studio would change the name of the class that contains the C# code for the form to the same name. However, it doesn't. To do that, you have to open the Code Editor window for the form and change the name on the class declaration.

When you change the name of a form file, the CodeFile attribute in the Page directive for the page is changed automatically. However, if you change the name of a class, the Inherits attribute in the Page directive is not changed. Because of that, you'll have to change this attribute manually when you change the name of a class.

How to change the starting web form

If a web site consists of a single form, that form is displayed by default when you run the application. When you add forms to a web site, however, the current form—the one that's selected in the Solution Explorer—is displayed when you run the application. Or, if a form isn't currently selected, the form named Default.aspx is displayed. If the web site doesn't contain a form named Default, a directory listing of the application is displayed.

To make sure that the correct page is displayed when you run an application, you should set the start page for the application. To do that, just right-click on the form in the Solution Explorer and select the Set As Start Page command from the shortcut menu. Note that this only sets the start page that Visual Studio uses when you run an application. It doesn't set the page IIS displays by default when you run the application from a browser outside of Visual Studio. To do that, you have to use IIS. See appendix B (Windows XP) or appendix C (Windows Vista) for more information.

A web form file being renamed in the Solution Explorer window

Two ways to rename a web form

- Right-click the form in the Solution Explorer, and then select the Rename command from the shortcut menu. Then, change the name directly in the Solution Explorer window.
- Click on the form in the Solution Explorer to select it. Then, click on it again and change the name directly in the Solution Explorer window.

How to rename the class that contains the C# code for a web form

- Display the code for the form in the Code Editor window. Then, change the name that's used for the form on the class declaration.
- Display the aspx code for the form, and then change the name in the Inherits attribute of the Page directive to the name of the class.

How to change the starting web form for a web site

- Right-click on the web form that you want to use as the starting form in the Solution Explorer. Then, choose Set As Start Page from the shortcut menu.

Note

- In most cases, you'll give a web form an appropriate name when you add it to the project. Since the form that's added by default when you create a web site is named Default, however, you will often want to change this name so it's more descriptive.

Figure 3-6   How to rename a web form and change the starting web form

How to redirect or transfer to another page

When you develop an application with two or more pages, you'll need to know how to display one page from another page. When the user clicks the Add to Cart button on the Order page of the Shopping Cart application, for example, the Cart page should be displayed. Similarly, when the user clicks the Continue Shopping button on the Cart page, the Order page should be displayed. Two ways to do that are presented in figure 3-7.

When you use the Transfer method of the HttpServerUtility class, ASP.NET immediately terminates the execution of the current page. Then, it loads and executes the page specified on the Transfer method and returns it to the browser. The drawback to using this method is that when the new page is sent to the browser, the browser has no way of knowing that the application returned a different page. As a result, the URL for the original page is still displayed in the browser's address box. This can be confusing to the user and prevents the user from bookmarking the page.

The Redirect method of the HttpResponse class works somewhat differently. When this method is executed, it sends a special message called an *HTTP redirect message* back to the browser. This message causes the browser to send a new HTTP request to the server to request the new page. Then, the server processes the page and sends it back to the browser.

Note that because of the way the Redirect method works, it requires an extra round trip to the browser. If this extra round trip will cause a performance problem, you may want to use the Transfer method instead. For most applications, however, the user friendliness of the Redirect method outweighs the small performance gain you get when you use the Transfer method.

The Transfer method of the HttpServerUtility class

Method	Description
Transfer(URL)	Terminates the execution of the current page and transfers control to the page at the specified URL.

The Redirect method of the HttpResponse class

Method	Description
Redirect(URL)	Redirects the client to the specified URL and terminates the execution of the current page.

Code that transfers control to another page

```
Server.Transfer("Cart.aspx")
```

Code that redirects the client to another page

```
Response.Redirect("Cart.aspx")
```

Description

- The Transfer method is a member of the HttpServerUtility class, which contains helper methods for processing web requests. To refer to this class, you use the Server property of the page.

- The Redirect method is a member of the HttpResponse class, which contains information about the response. To refer to this class, you use the Response property of the page.

- Both the Transfer and Redirect methods cause the page specified by the URL to be displayed in the browser. See figure 3-9 for more information on coding URLs.

- When you use the Transfer method, the current page is terminated and a new page is processed in its place. This processing is efficient because it takes place on the server. However, the browser isn't updated to reflect the address of the new page.

- When you use the Redirect method, the server sends a special message called an *HTTP redirect message* to the browser. When the browser receives this message, it sends an HTTP request to the server to request the new page. The server then processes the new page and sends it back to the browser. Because this involves a round trip to the browser, it's less efficient than the Transfer method.

- In general, you should use the Redirect method to display another web page. You should use the Transfer method only if the application's performance is critical.

Figure 3-7   How to redirect or transfer to another page

How to use cross-page posting

A third way to transfer to a different web page is to use *cross-page posting* as described in figure 3-8. To use cross-page posting, you specify the URL of another page in the PostBackUrl property of a button control. Then, when the user clicks the button, an HTTP Post message that contains the URL specified by the PostBackUrl property is sent back to the server. As a result, the page with that URL is loaded and executed instead of the page that was originally displayed.

For example, the Go to Cart button on the Order page uses cross-page posting to go to the Cart page. As a result, the PostBackUrl property of this button is set to Cart.aspx as shown in this figure. Then, when the user clicks the Go to Cart button, ASP.NET loads and executes the Cart.aspx page instead of the Order.aspx page.

Notice that the URL in the PostBackUrl property of this control starts with a tilde (~) operator. This operator is added automatically when you set the PostBackUrl property from the Properties window, and you'll learn more about it in the next topic.

If the user enters data into one or more controls on a page that uses cross-page posting, you can use the PreviousPage property to retrieve the data entered by the user. As the code example in this figure shows, you should first check to make sure that the PreviousPage property refers to a valid object. If this property doesn't refer to a valid object, it means that either the page isn't being loaded as the result of a cross-page posting, or the request came from another web site. In either case, no previous page is available.

If the PreviousPage property refers to a valid object, you can use the FindControl method to find a control on the previous page. Then, you can cast the control to a text box (if the control is a text box). Finally, you can use the Text property to retrieve the data that the text box contains.

Because of the extra programming required to retrieve data entered by the user, cross-page posting is best used when no user input needs to be processed. For instance, since no data needs to be processed when the user clicks the Go to Cart button, I used cross-page posting instead of Response.Redirect or Server.Transfer. However, I used Response.Redirect for the Add to Cart button on the Order page so I could easily retrieve the selected product and the quantity entered by the user.

The PostBackUrl property of the Button control

Property	Description
PostBackUrl	Specifies the URL of the page that should be requested when the user clicks the button.

Members of the Page class used with cross-page posting

Property	Description
PreviousPage	Returns a Page object that represents the previous page.
Method	**Description**
FindControl(id)	Returns a Control object with the specified id. If the control is a text box, you can cast the Control object to TextBox, then use the Text property to access the data entered by the user.

The aspx code for a button that posts to a different page

```
<asp:Button ID="btnCart" runat="server" Text="Go to Cart"
    CausesValidation="False" PostBackUrl="~/Cart.aspx" />
```

Code that retrieves data from the previous page

```
protected void Page_Load(object sender, EventArgs e)
{
    if (PreviousPage != null)
    {
        TextBox txtQuantity
            = (TextBox) PreviousPage.FindControl("txtQuantity");
        lblQuantity.Text = txtQuantity.Text;
    }
}
```

Description

- *Cross-page posting* lets you use the PostBackUrl property of a button to specify the page that should be requested when the user clicks the button.

- When you post back to another page, the previous page is available via the PreviousPage property. Then, you can use the FindControl method to retrieve data entered by the user.

- In general, cross-page posting is more efficient than the Server.Transfer and Response.Redirect methods. However, cross-page posting makes it more difficult to retrieve data from the original page.

- If you don't need to retrieve data from the original page, cross-page posting is clearly better than the Server.Transfer and Response.Redirect methods.

Figure 3-8   How to use cross-page posting

How to code absolute and relative URLs

In chapter 1, you learned about the basic components of a URL. The URLs you saw in that chapter were all *absolute URLs*. An absolute URL includes the domain name of the web site. When coded within a Transfer or Redirect method, an absolute URL lets you display a page at another web site. For example, the first two statements in figure 3-9 display a page at the web site with the domain name www.murach.com. The first statement displays a page named Default.aspx in the root directory of the web site. The second statement displays a page named Search.aspx in the Books directory of the web site.

To display a page within the same web site, you can use a *relative URL*. This type of URL specifies the location of the page relative to the directory that contains the current page. This is illustrated by the third and fourth statements in this figure. The third statement displays a page that's stored in the same directory as the current page. The fourth statement displays a page in the Login subdirectory of the directory that contains the current page.

The next two statements show how you can use a relative URL to navigate up the directory structure from the current directory. To navigate up one directory, you code two periods followed by a slash as shown in the fifth statement. To navigate up two directories, you code two periods and a slash followed by two more periods and a slash as shown in the sixth statement. To navigate up additional directories, you code two periods and a slash for each directory.

To navigate to the root directory for the host, you code a slash as shown in the seventh statement. You can also navigate to a directory within the root directory by coding the path for that directory following the slash as shown in the eighth statement.

In addition to coding URLs on Transfer and Redirect methods, you can code them for the attributes of some server controls. This is illustrated in the last two examples in this figure. The next to last example shows how you might set the PostBackUrl attribute of a button control. And the last example shows how you might set the ImageUrl attribute of an image control.

Notice that both of these URLs start with a tilde (~) operator. This operator causes the URL to be based on the root directory of the web site. For example, the Cart.aspx file in the first URL is located directly in the root directory, and the banner.jpg file in the second URL is located in the Images subdirectory of the root directory.

Although I could have used relative URLs in these examples, it's easier to maintain URLs that use the tilde operator when you move pages or files from one folder to another. That's because it's easier to maintain a URL that's relative to the root directory of the web site than it is to maintain a URL that's relative to another page. So I recommend you use the tilde operator whenever you code a URL for an attribute of a server control.

Examples of absolute and relative URLs

Statements that use absolute URLs

```
Response.Redirect("http://www.murach.com/Default.aspx")
Response.Redirect("http://www.murach.com/Books/Search.aspx")
```

Statements that use relative URLs that are based on the current directory

```
Response.Redirect("Checkout.aspx")
Response.Redirect("Login/Register.aspx")
```

Statements that use relative URLs that navigate up the directory structure

```
Response.Redirect("../Register.aspx")
Response.Redirect("../../Register.aspx")
Response.Redirect("/Register.aspx")
Response.Redirect("/Login/Register.aspx")
```

Server control attributes that use URLs that are based on the root directory of the current web site

```
PostBackUrl="~/Cart.aspx"
ImageUrl="~/Images/banner.jpg"
```

Description

- When you code an *absolute URL*, you code the complete URL including the domain name for the site. Absolute URLs let you display pages at other web sites.

- When you code a *relative URL*, you base it on the current directory, which is the directory that contains the current page.

- To go to the root directory for the host, you code a slash. Then, you can code one or more directories after the slash.

- To go up one level from the current directory, you code two periods and a slash. To go up two levels, you code two periods and a slash followed by two more periods and a slash. And so on.

- If you're specifying a URL for the attribute of a server control, you can use the web application root operator (~) to base the URL on the root of the web site.

Figure 3-9   How to code absolute and relative URLs

How to create and use data sources

To connect to a database and work with its data, you can use an ASP.NET control called a *data source*. To illustrate how this works, the following topics show you how to create a data source that connects to a Microsoft Access database and bind it to a drop-down list. Keep in mind, though, that there's much more to working with data sources than these topics let on. That's why section 3 of this book is devoted to the use of data sources and databases.

How to create an Access data source

ASP.NET 3.5 provides several data source controls in the Data group of the Toolbox. The simplest of these controls is AccessDataSource, which is designed to retrieve data from a Microsoft Access database file. Figure 3-10 shows how to create this type of data source.

Before you can use an Access data source, though, you must first create an Access database and add it to the App_Data folder of the web site. As I've mentioned before, the Shopping Cart application for this chapter uses a database named Halloween.mdb.

To create an AccessDataSource control, open the Data group of the Toolbox, drag the AccessDataSource control, and drop it onto the form. Since the data source isn't displayed on the page when the application is run, it doesn't matter where you drop the data source on the page. However, if the data source is going to be bound to a server control, it makes sense to place it near that control.

When you drop the Access data source on the page, a smart tag menu will appear. Then, choose the Configure Data Source command to bring up the first page of the Configure Data Source wizard, which is shown in this figure. From this dialog box, select the Access database file you want to use for the data source.

Once you've selected the database file for the data source, you must configure the data source as described in the next figure. Then, you can bind it to the drop-down list as described in figure 3-12.

The Configure Data Source dialog box

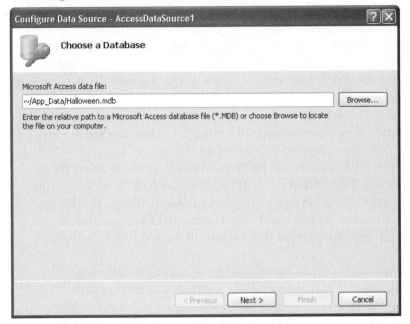

How to create an Access data source

1. In the Web Forms Designer, open the Data group of the Toolbox and drag the AccessDataSource control to the form.

2. Select Configure Data Source from the smart tag menu of the data source control to display the Configure Data Source dialog box.

3. Identify the Access database that you want to use in the App_Data folder and click Next. Then, complete the Configure Data Source wizard as described in the next figure.

Description

- Before you can create an Access *data source*, you must add the Access database file to the App_Data folder.

- The Shopping Cart application uses an AccessDataSource control to provide the list of products that's displayed in the drop-down list. This control reads data from a Microsoft Access database file.

- Although data source controls are visible in the Web Forms Designer, they don't render any HTML to the browser. As a result, they aren't visible when the application runs.

Figure 3-10   How to create an Access data source

How to configure an Access data source

Figure 3-11 shows how to configure an Access data source using the Configure Data Source wizard. After the first page of this wizard lets you select the Access database file you want to use (as in the previous figure), the second page that's shown in this figure lets you specify the query that retrieves data from the database.

To create a query, you can code a SQL Select statement. Or, you can choose columns from a single table or view and let the wizard generate the Select statement for you. For now, we'll use the second technique.

To select columns from a table, use the Name drop-down list to select the table you want to select the columns from. Then, check each of the columns you want to retrieve in the Columns list. In this figure, I chose the Products table and selected six of the columns. As you check the columns, the Configuration wizard creates a SQL Select statement that's shown in the text box at the bottom of the dialog box.

The buttons to the right of the Columns list let you specify additional options for selecting data. If you want to select just rows that meet certain criteria, click the WHERE button, then specify the criteria you want. Or, if you want to specify a sort order, click the ORDER BY button, then choose the columns you want the data sorted by. In this figure, I used this button to specify that the data should be sorted on the Name column, so the Select statement includes an Order By clause.

When you've finished specifying the data you want the data source to retrieve, click Next. This takes you to a page that includes a Test Query button. If you click this button, the Wizard immediately retrieves the data that you have specified. You can then look over this data to make sure it's what you expected. If it isn't, click the Back button and adjust the query as needed.

The Configure Data Source wizard

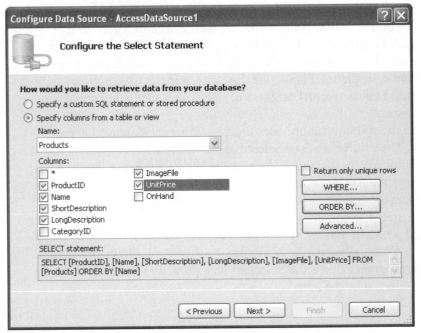

The aspx code for an Access data source control

```
<asp:AccessDataSource ID="AccessDataSource1" runat="server"
    DataFile="~/App_Data/Halloween.mdb"
    SelectCommand="SELECT [ProductID], [Name], [ShortDescription],
        [LongDescription], [ImageFile], [UnitPrice]
        FROM [Products] ORDER BY [Name]">
</asp:AccessDataSource>
```

Description

- The Configure Data Source wizard lets you create a query using SQL. You can specify the Select statement for the query directly, or you can let the wizard construct the Select statement from your specifications.

- You can click the WHERE button to specify one or more conditions that will be used to select the records.

- You can click the ORDER BY button to specify a sort order for the records.

- You can click the Advanced button to include Insert, Update, and Delete statements for the data source.

Figure 3-11   How to configure an Access data source

How to bind a drop-down list to a data source

Once you've created a data source, you can bind a drop-down list to it as shown in figure 3-12. To start, select the Choose Data Source command from the smart tag menu for the drop-down list. Then, when the Data Source Configuration Wizard is displayed, choose the data source in the first drop-down list. In this figure, I chose AccessDataSource1, the data source that I created in the previous figures.

Next, select the column that provides the data you want displayed in the drop-down list. The column that you select here is used for the drop-down list's DataTextField property. In this figure, I chose the Name column so the drop-down list displays the name of each product in the data source.

Finally, select the column that you want to use as the value of the item selected by the user. The column you select here is used for the list's DataValueField property, and the value of that column can be retrieved by using the list's SelectedValue property. In this figure, I selected the ProductID column. As a result, the program can use the SelectedValue property to determine the ID of the product selected by the user.

The Data Source Configuration Wizard dialog box

The aspx code for a drop-down list that's bound to a data source

```
<asp:DropDownList ID="ddlProducts" Runat="server" Width="150px"
    AutoPostBack="True"
    DataSourceID="AccessDataSource1"
    DataTextField="Name"
    DataValueField="ProductID" >
</asp:DropDownList>
```

Attributes for binding a drop-down list

Attribute	Description
DataSourceID	The ID of the data source that the drop-down list should be bound to.
DataTextField	The name of the data source field that should be displayed in the drop-down list.
DataValueField	The name of the data source field whose value should be returned by the SelectedValue property of the drop-down list.

Description

- You can bind a drop-down list to a data source so the list automatically displays data retrieved by the data source.
- You can use the Data Source Configuration Wizard dialog box to configure the data binding for a drop-down list. To display this dialog box, select the Choose Data Source command from the list's smart tag menu.
- Alternatively, you can use the Properties window or edit the aspx code directly to set the data binding attributes for a drop-down list.

Figure 3-12   How to bind a drop-down list to a data source

How to use C# code to get data from a data source

For the Shopping Cart application to work, it must retrieve the data for the product selected by the user from the drop-down list. Although there are several ways to do that, none of them are easy. One way is to create a second data source that queries the database again to retrieve the data for the selected product, and then use a special type of ASP.NET server control called a DetailsView control that is bound to this second data source. You'll learn how to do that in section 3.

A simpler way, though, is to write code that retrieves the product data from the existing Access data source. That's the technique that the Shopping Cart application uses. However, to make this work, you must contend with the classes, methods, and properties that are summarized in figure 3-13.

The example in this figure shows how to retrieve data from a row that matches the ProductID value returned by the SelectedValue property of the drop-down list. First, you use the Select method of the AccessDataSource class with the Empty argument to retrieve all of the rows from the underlying Access database. Then, because the return type of this method is IEnumerable, you must cast the returned object to a DataView object so you can use the methods of that class.

Once you have the rows in a DataView object, you can use the RowFilter property to filter the rows so only the row selected by the user is available. To do that, you build a simple *filter expression* that lists the column name and value. For example, ProductID='jar01' filters the data view so only the row whose ProductID column contains jar01 is included.

Once you've filtered the DataView object so only the selected row is available, you can use two indexes to retrieve the data for a column. The first index identifies the only row that has been selected, so its value is 0, and this row is returned as a DataRowView object. Then, you can specify the index of the column you want to retrieve from the row, either as a string that provides the column name or as the index position of the column. In this example, column names are used for the columns that need to be retrieved. (Although using an index value is a little more efficient, specifying the column name makes the code more understandable.)

Once you establish the row and column index for each value, all that remains is to cast this value to the appropriate type. In this example, all of the columns except the UnitPrice column are cast to strings using their ToString methods. The UnitPrice column is cast to a decimal type.

Please note that all six of the values that are retrieved are stored in the Product object that's instantiated by the fourth statement in this example. If you want to review the code for this class, you can look ahead to figure 3-16.

The Select method of the AccessDataSource class

Method	Description
`Select(selectOptions)`	Returns an IEnumerable object that contains the rows retrieved from the underlying Access database. To get all the rows, the selectOptions parameter should be DataSourceSelectArguments.Empty.

Members of the DataView class for retrieving rows

Property	Description
`RowFilter`	A string that is used to filter the rows retrieved from the Access database.

Indexer	Description
`[index]`	Returns a DataRowView object for the row at the specified index position.

Members of the DataRowView class for retrieving columns

Indexer	Description
`[index]`	Returns the value of the column at the specified index position as an object.
`[name]`	Returns the value of the column with the specified name as an object.

Code that gets product information for the selected product

```
DataView productsTable = (DataView)
    AccessDataSource1.Select(DataSourceSelectArguments.Empty);
productsTable.RowFilter =
    "ProductID = '" + ddlProducts.SelectedValue + "'";
DataRowView row = (DataRowView) productsTable[0];
Product p = new Product();
p.ProductID = row["ProductID"].ToString();
p.Name = row["Name"].ToString();
p.ShortDescription = row["ShortDescription"].ToString();
p.LongDescription = row["LongDescription"].ToString();
p.UnitPrice = (decimal) row["UnitPrice"];
p.ImageFile = row["ImageFile"].ToString();
```

Description

- The Select method of the AccessDataSource class returns a DataView object that contains the rows retrieved from the Access database. Because the return type of this method is IEnumerable, you must convert the returned object to a DataView object.

- The RowFilter property of the DataView class lets you filter rows in the data view based on a criteria string.

- You can use the indexer of the DataView class to return a specific row as a DataRowView object. Then, you can use the indexer of the DataRowView class to return the value of a specified column. The indexer for the column can be an integer that represents the column's position in the row or a string that represents the name of the column.

Figure 3-13   How to use C# code to get data from a data source

How to use session state

In chapter 1, you learned that HTTP is a stateless protocol. You also learned that ASP.NET uses *session state* to keep track of each user session and that you can use session state to maintain program values across executions of an application. Now, you'll learn more about how session state works and how you use it.

How session state works

Figure 3-14 shows how session state solves the problem of state management for ASP.NET applications. As you can see, session state tracks individual user sessions by creating a *session state object* for each user's session. This object contains a session ID that uniquely identifies the session. This session ID is passed back to the browser along with the HTTP response. Then, if the browser makes another request, the session ID is included in the request so ASP.NET can identify the session. ASP.NET then matches the session with the session state object that was previously saved.

By default, ASP.NET sends the session ID to the browser as a *cookie*. Then, when the browser sends another request to the server, it automatically includes the cookie that contains the session ID with the request. In chapter 8, you'll learn more about how cookies work. You'll also learn how URL encoding works and how ASP.NET can use it to maintain session state with browsers that don't support cookies.

Although ASP.NET automatically uses session state to track user sessions, you can also use it to store your own data across executions of an application. This figure lists three typical reasons for doing that. First, you can use session state to maintain information about the user. After a user logs in to an application, for example, you can use the login information to retrieve information about the user from a file or a database. Then, you can store that information in the session state object so it's available each time the application is executed.

Second, you can use session state to save objects that the user is working with. For example, consider a maintenance application that lets the user change customer records. In that case, you can save the customer record that's currently being modified in the session state object so it's available the next time the application is executed.

Third, you can use session state to keep track of the operation a user is currently performing. If a maintenance application lets the user add or change customer records, for example, you can save an item in the session state object that indicates if the user is currently adding or changing a record. That way, the application can determine how to proceed each time it's executed.

How ASP.NET maintains the state of a session

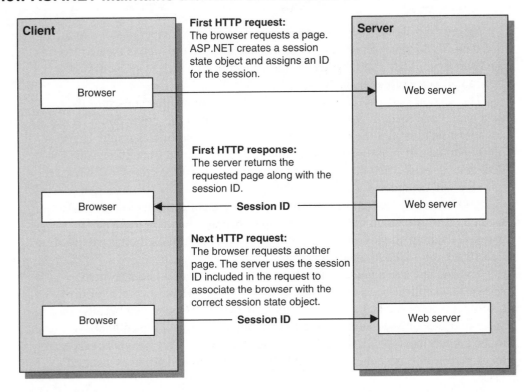

First HTTP request:
The browser requests a page. ASP.NET creates a session state object and assigns an ID for the session.

First HTTP response:
The server returns the requested page along with the session ID.

Next HTTP request:
The browser requests another page. The server uses the session ID included in the request to associate the browser with the correct session state object.

Description

- ASP.NET uses *session state* to track the state of each user of an application. To do that, it creates a *session state object*.

- The session state object includes a session ID that's sent back to the browser as a *cookie*. Then, the browser automatically returns the session ID cookie to the server with each request so the server can associate the browser with an existing session state object.

- If you want your application to work on browsers that don't support cookies, you can configure ASP.NET to encode the session ID in the URL for each page of the application. For more information, see chapter 8.

- You can use the session state object to store and retrieve items across executions of an application.

Typical uses for session state

- **To keep information about the user**, such as the user's name or whether the user has registered.

- **To save objects the user is working with**, such as a shopping cart or a customer record.

- **To keep track of pending operations**, such as what steps the user has completed while placing an order.

Figure 3-14   How session state works

How to work with data in session state

Figure 3-15 shows how you can use the session state object to store application data. To do that, you use the members of this object, which is created from the HttpSessionState class. To access this object from a web form, you use the Session property of the page.

The session state object contains a collection of items that consist of the item names and their values. One way to add an item to this collection is to use an index that identifies the item by name as shown in the first example. Here, an object named cart is assigned to a session state item named Cart. If the Cart item doesn't exist when this statement is executed, it will be created. Otherwise, its value will be updated.

Another way to add an item to the session state collection is to use the Add method, as illustrated in the second example. Just as when you use a name index, if the item already exists, it's updated when the Add method is executed. Otherwise, it's added to the collection.

You can also use a name index to retrieve the value of an item from the session state collection as shown in the third example. Here, the value of the Cart item is retrieved and assigned to the cart variable. Notice that because the value of a session state item is stored as an Object type, you typically convert it to the appropriate type. In this example, the value of the Cart item is converted to a sorted list because the cart variable it's assigned to is defined as a sorted list.

Because the session state object uses valuable server memory, you should avoid using it to store large items. Or, if you must store large items in session state, you should remove the items as soon as you're done with them. To do that, you use the Remove method as illustrated in the fourth example in this figure.

The first four examples in this figure use the Session property of the page to access the session state object. Because Session is a property of the System.Web.UI.Page class, however, you can only use this property from a class that inherits the System.Web.UI.Page class. In other words, you can only use it from a code-behind file for a page. To access session state from a class that doesn't inherit the System.Web.UI.Page class, such as a database or business class, you use the Session property of the HttpContext object for the current request. To get this HttpContext object, you use the Current property of the HttpContext class as illustrated in the last example in this figure.

Common members of the HttpSessionState class

Property	Description
SessionID	The unique ID of the session.
Count	The number of items in the session state collection.

Indexer	Description
[name]	The value of the session state item with the specified name.

Method	Description
Add(name, value)	Adds an item to the session state collection.
Clear()	Removes all items from the session state collection.
Remove(name)	Removes the item with the specified name from the session state collection.

A statement that adds or updates a session state item

```
Session["Cart"] = cart;
```

Another way to add or update a session state item

```
Session.Add("Cart", cart);
```

A statement that retrieves the value of a session state item

```
SortedList cart = (SortedList) Session["Cart"];
```

A statement that removes an item from session state

```
Session.Remove("Cart");
```

A statement that retrieves the value of a session state item from a class that doesn't inherit System.Web.UI.Page

```
SortedList cart = (SortedList) HttpContext.Current.Session["Cart"];
```

Description

- The session state object is created from the HttpSessionState class, which defines a collection of session state items.

- To access the session state object from the code-behind file for a web form, use the Session property of the page.

- To access the session state object from a class other than the code-behind file for a web form, use the Current property of the HttpContext class to get the HttpContext object for the current request. This object contains information about the HTTP request. Then, use the Session property of the HttpContext class to get the session state object.

- By default, session state objects are maintained in server memory. As a result, you should avoid storing large items in session state.

Figure 3-15   How to work with data in session state

The code for the Shopping Cart application

Now that you've learned the basic skills for developing a multi-form application, you're ready to see all the aspx and C# code for the Shopping Cart application. Because you should be able to follow it without much trouble, I'll keep the descriptions to a minimum.

The code for the Product and CartItem classes

Figure 3-16 shows the C# code for the Product and CartItem classes. The Product class, which represents a product, has public fields for each of the columns in the Products table except CategoryID and OnHand.

The CartItem class, which represents one item in the shopping cart, has two public fields that hold the Product object and quantity for each item. In addition, the Display method returns a string that formats this data so it can be displayed in one line of the list box on the Cart page.

The aspx code for the Order page

Figure 3-17 shows the aspx code for the Order page, which is shown in its rendered form in figure 3-1. Since all of the code for this page is generated by the Web Forms Designer, you don't have to code any of it. To make it easier to follow this code, I highlighted the start tag and ID attribute for each of the server controls that appear on this page.

The first group of four controls defines an image that's used for the banner, a label with the text "Please select a product:", a drop-down list named ddlProducts, and the Access data source that the drop-down list is bound to. Here, the AutoPostBack attribute for the drop-down list is set to True so the page will be posted back to the server when the user selects a product. In addition, the DataSourceID, DataTextField, and DataValueField attributes specify how the drop-down list is bound to the Access data source.

The second group of server controls displays product information using several labels and an image control. A table is used to manage the layout of these controls so the image can be displayed to the right of the labels.

The third group of server controls defines a label with the text "Quantity:" followed by a text box named txtQuantity. Then, two validator controls provide data validation for the text box. Notice that both specify txtQuantity in the ControlToValidate attribute and Dynamic in the Display attribute. The range validator also provides MaximumValue, MinimumValue, and Type attributes, which specify that the quantity must be an integer in the range from 1 to 500.

The last group of controls for this page contains the two buttons. Here, the btnCart button uses the PostBackUrl attribute to indicate that when the user clicks the button, the Cart.aspx page should be requested rather than the Order.aspx page. Since the CausesValidation attribute is set to False, the validation controls for the txtQuantity text box won't be executed when this button is clicked.

The code for the Product class

```
using System;
using System.Configuration;
using System.Data;
using System.Linq;
using System.Web;
using System.Web.Security;
using System.Web.UI;
using System.Web.UI.HtmlControls;
using System.Web.UI.WebControls;
using System.Web.UI.WebControls.WebParts;
using System.Xml.Linq;

/// <summary>
/// Summary description for Product
/// </summary>
public class Product{
    public string ProductID;
    public string Name;
    public string ShortDescription;
    public string LongDescription;
    public decimal UnitPrice;
    public string ImageFile;
}
```

The code for the CartItem class

```
using System;
using System.Configuration;
using System.Data;
using System.Linq;
using System.Web;
using System.Web.Security;
using System.Web.UI;
using System.Web.UI.HtmlControls;
using System.Web.UI.WebControls;
using System.Web.UI.WebControls.WebParts;
using System.Xml.Linq;

/// <summary>
/// Summary description for CartItem
/// </summary>
public class CartItem{
    public Product Product;
    public int Quantity;

    public string Display(){
        string displayString =
            Product.Name + " (" + Quantity.ToString()
            + " at " + Product.UnitPrice.ToString("c") + " each)";
        return displayString;
    }
}
```

Description

- The Product class represents a product.

- The CartItem class represents a product that the user has added to the shopping cart plus the quantity ordered.

- For simplicity, these classes are defined with public fields. In a production application, they'd most likely be defined with private fields that are accessible through properties.

Figure 3-16   The code for the Product and CartItem classes

The aspx file for the Order page (Order.aspx)   Page 1

```
<%@ Page Language="C#" AutoEventWireup="true"  CodeFile="Order.aspx.cs"
Inherits="Order" %>

<!DOCTYPE html PUBLIC "-//W3C//DTD XHTML 1.0 Transitional//EN"
"http://www.w3.org/TR/xhtml1/DTD/xhtml1-transitional.dtd">

<html xmlns="http://www.w3.org/1999/xhtml" >
<head id="Head1" runat="server">
    <title>Chapter 3: Shopping Cart</title>
    <style type="text/css">
        .style1
        {
            width: 250px;
        }
        .style2
        {
            width: 20px;
        }
    </style>
</head>
<body>
    <form id="form1" runat="server">
    <div>
        <asp:Image ID="Image1" runat="server"
            ImageUrl="~/Images/banner.jpg" /><br /><br />
        <asp:Label ID="Label1" runat="server"
            Text="Please select a product:"></asp:Label> 
        <asp:DropDownList ID="ddlProducts" runat="server"
            DataSourceID="AccessDataSource1" DataTextField="Name"
            DataValueField="ProductID" Width="150px" AutoPostBack="True">
        </asp:DropDownList>
        <asp:AccessDataSource ID="AccessDataSource1" runat="server"
            DataFile="~/App_Data/Halloween.mdb"
            SelectCommand="SELECT [ProductID], [Name], [ShortDescription],
                [LongDescription], [ImageFile], [UnitPrice]
                FROM [Products] ORDER BY [Name]">
        </asp:AccessDataSource><br />
        <table>
            <tr>
                <td class="style1">
                    <asp:Label ID="lblName" runat="server"
                        style="font-weight: 700; font-size: larger">
                    </asp:Label>
                </td>
                <td class="style2" rowspan="4"></td>
                <td rowspan="4" valign="top">
                    <asp:Image ID="imgProduct" runat="server" Height="200px" />
                </td>
            </tr>
```

Description

- The Order.aspx page displays a drop-down list that is bound to an Access data source.

- A table is used to specify the layout of the label and image controls that display information about the product selected by the user.

Figure 3-17   The aspx code for the Order page (part 1 of 2)

The aspx file for the Order page (Order.aspx)   **Page 2**

```
                <tr>
                    <td class="style1">
                        <asp:Label ID="lblShortDescription" runat="server">
                        </asp:Label>
                    </td>
                </tr>
                <tr>
                    <td class="style1">
                        <asp:Label ID="lblLongDescription" runat="server">
                        </asp:Label>
                    </td>
                </tr>
                <tr>
                    <td class="style1">
                        <asp:Label ID="lblUnitPrice" runat="server"
                            style="font-weight: 700; font-size: larger">
                        </asp:Label>
                        <asp:Label ID="Label2" runat="server" Text="each"
                            style="font-weight: 700; font-size: larger">
                        </asp:Label>
                    </td>
                </tr>
            </table>
            <br />
            <asp:Label ID="Label3" runat="server" Text="Quantity:"
                Width="80px"></asp:Label>
            <asp:TextBox ID="txtQuantity" runat="server" Width="80px">
            </asp:TextBox>
            <asp:RequiredFieldValidator ID="RequiredFieldValidator1"
                runat="server" ControlToValidate="txtQuantity" Display="Dynamic"
                ErrorMessage="Quantity is a required field.">
            </asp:RequiredFieldValidator>
            <asp:RangeValidator ID="RangeValidator1" runat="server"
                ControlToValidate="txtQuantity" Display="Dynamic"
                ErrorMessage="Quantity must range from 1 to 500."
                MaximumValue="500" MinimumValue="1" Type="Integer">
            </asp:RangeValidator><br /><br />
            <asp:Button ID="btnAdd" runat="server" Text="Add to Cart"
                OnClick="btnAdd_Click" /> 
            <asp:Button ID="btnCart" runat="server" CausesValidation="False"
                PostBackUrl="~/Cart.aspx" Text="Go to Cart" />
        </div>
        </form>
</body>
</html>
```

Description

- The txtQuantity text box lets the user enter the order quantity of the selected item. A RequiredFieldValidator and a RangeValidator are used to ensure that the user enters valid data in this text box.

- The OnClick attribute of the btnAdd button indicates that an event handler named btnAdd_Click will be executed when this button is clicked.

- The btnCart button uses cross-page posting to post to the Cart.aspx page.

Figure 3-17   The aspx code for the Order page (part 2 of 2)

The C# code for the Order page

Figure 3-18 presents the code for the Order page's code-behind file, Order.aspx.cs. This code starts by declaring a class-level variable that will hold a Product object that represents the item that the user has selected from the drop-down list. This variable is assigned a Product object by the second statement in the Page_Load event handler, which gets the Product object by calling the GetSelectedProduct method.

The Page_Load event handler starts by calling the DataBind method of the drop-down list if the page is being loaded for the first time (IsPostBack isn't True). This method binds the drop-down list to the Access data source, which causes the data specified in the SelectCommand property of the data source to be retrieved. Then, this event handler calls the GetSelectedProduct method, which gets the data for the selected product from the Access data source and returns a Product object. That object is stored in the selectedProduct variable, which is available to all of the other methods in this class. Finally, the Page_Load event handler formats the labels and the image control to display the data for the selected product. At that point, the Order page is sent back to the user's browser.

For many applications, you don't need to call the DataBind method in the Page_Load event handler when you use data binding. Instead, you let ASP.NET automatically bind any data-bound controls. Unfortunately, this automatic data binding doesn't occur until after the Page_Load event handler has been executed. In this case, because the GetSelectedProduct method won't work unless the drop-down list has already been bound, I had to call the DataBind method to force the data binding to occur earlier than it normally would.

The code-behind file for the Order page (Order.aspx.cs)   Page 1

```
using System;
using System.Collections;
using System.Configuration;
using System.Data;
using System.Linq;
using System.Web;
using System.Web.Security;
using System.Web.UI;
using System.Web.UI.HtmlControls;
using System.Web.UI.WebControls;
using System.Web.UI.WebControls.WebParts;
using System.Xml.Linq;

public partial class Order : System.Web.UI.Page
{
    private Product selectedProduct;

    protected void Page_Load(object sender, EventArgs e){
        if (!IsPostBack)
            ddlProducts.DataBind();

        selectedProduct = this.GetSelectedProduct();
        lblName.Text = selectedProduct.Name;
        lblShortDescription.Text = selectedProduct.ShortDescription;
        lblLongDescription.Text = selectedProduct.LongDescription;
        lblUnitPrice.Text = selectedProduct.UnitPrice.ToString("c");
        imgProduct.ImageUrl = "Images/Products/" + selectedProduct.ImageFile;
    }

    private Product GetSelectedProduct(){
        DataView productsTable = (DataView)
            AccessDataSource1.Select(DataSourceSelectArguments.Empty);
        productsTable.RowFilter =
            "ProductID = '" + ddlProducts.SelectedValue + "'";
        DataRowView row = (DataRowView) productsTable[0];

        Product p = new Product();
        p.ProductID = row["ProductID"].ToString();
        p.Name = row["Name"].ToString();
        p.ShortDescription = row["ShortDescription"].ToString();
        p.LongDescription = row["LongDescription"].ToString();
        p.UnitPrice = (decimal) row["UnitPrice"];
        p.ImageFile = row["ImageFile"].ToString();
        return p;
    }
}
```

Description

- The Page_Load event handler binds the drop-down list if the page is not being posted back to itself. Then, it calls the GetSelectedProduct method to get a Product object for the selected product. Finally, it sets the label and image controls to display the information for the selected product.

- The GetSelectedProduct method extracts the data for the selected product from the data source. Then, it uses this data to create a Product object.

Figure 3-18   The C# code for the Order page (part 1 of 2)

If the user clicks the Add to Cart button, the btnAdd_Click event handler is executed. It starts by creating a new instance of the CartItem class named item. Next, it sets the item's Product field to the Product object that's stored in the selectedProduct variable, and it sets the Quantity field to the value entered by the user. Then, it calls the AddToCart method to add the CartItem object to the user's shopping cart, which is a SortedList object. Finally, it uses Response.Redirect to go to the Cart.aspx page.

The AddToCart method declares a SortedList variable named cart and calls the GetCart method to retrieve the shopping cart from Session state. If you look at the GetCart method, you'll see that it first checks to see if a Session state item named "Cart" is equal to null. If it is, which means that a cart hasn't yet been created for the current user, a new shopping cart is created and added to Session state. Then, the GetCart method returns the shopping cart to the AddToCart method as a SortedList object.

After the shopping cart list has been returned, the AddToCart method determines whether the list already contains an entry for the selected product. To do that, it uses the ContainsKey method of the SortedList class to look for a cart entry with the product ID of the product. If an entry is found with this product ID, the quantity the user entered is added to the existing quantity for this item. Otherwise, the Add method for the SortedList object that represents the shopping cart is used to add the cart item to the shopping cart with the product's ID as the key.

The code-behind file for the Order page (Order.aspx.cs)   **Page 2**

```
protected void btnAdd_Click(object sender, EventArgs e){
    if (Page.IsValid)
    {
        CartItem item = new CartItem();
        item.Product = selectedProduct;
        item.Quantity = Convert.ToInt32(txtQuantity.Text);
        this.AddToCart(item);
        Response.Redirect("Cart.aspx");
    }
}

private void AddToCart(CartItem item){
    SortedList cart = this.GetCart();
    string productID = selectedProduct.ProductID;
    if (cart.ContainsKey(productID))
    {
        CartItem existingItem = (CartItem) cart[productID];
        existingItem.Quantity += item.Quantity;
    }
    else
        cart.Add(productID, item);
}

private SortedList GetCart(){
    if (Session["Cart"] == null)
        Session.Add("Cart", new SortedList());
    return (SortedList) Session["Cart"];
}
}
```

Description

- The btnAdd_Click event handler is called when the user clicks the Add button. It creates a CartItem object, and then calls the AddToCart method to add the item to the shopping cart.

- The AddToCart method calls the GetCart method to get the shopping cart from session state. Then, it checks to see if the shopping cart already contains an item for the selected product. If so, the item's quantity is incremented. If not, the CartItem object is added to the shopping cart.

- The GetCart method retrieves the shopping cart from session state. If session state doesn't contain a cart, a cart is created and added to session state.

Figure 3-18   The C# code for the Order page (part 2 of 2)

The aspx code for the Cart page

Figure 3-19 shows the aspx code for the second page of the Shopping Cart application, Cart.aspx, which is rendered in figure 3-2. Once again, I've highlighted the start of each tag that defines a server control.

Here, the shopping cart is displayed in a ListBox control within an HTML table that allows the Remove and Empty buttons to be displayed to the right of the list box. The Continue button uses the PostBackUrl attribute to return to the Order.aspx page. And the lblMessage label is used to display messages to the user. Like the Order page, this page also contains an image control that defines the image that's displayed in the banner.

The C# code for the Cart page

Figure 3-20 presents the code-behind file for the Cart page. This code starts by declaring a class-level variable that will hold the SortedList object for the shopping cart. Then, each time the page is loaded, the Page_Load event handler calls the GetCart method to retrieve the shopping cart from session state and store it in this variable.

If the page is being loaded for the first time, the Page_Load event handler also calls the DisplayCart method. This method starts by clearing the list box that will display the shopping cart items. Then, it uses a foreach loop to add an item to the list box for each item in the shopping cart list.

To understand this loop, remember that each item in a sorted list is a DictionaryEntry object that consists of a key and a value. Here, the key is the product ID, the value is a CartItem object, and the first line in the body of the loop uses the Value property to retrieve the CartItem object for that entry. However, because the Value property returns an Object type, it must be explicitly cast to CartItem to assign the value to the item variable.

If the user clicks the Remove Item button, the btnRemove_Click event handler is executed. This event handler begins by making sure that the cart contains at least one item and that an item in the shopping cart list box is selected. If so, the selected item is deleted from the shopping cart. Then, the DisplayCart method is called to add the cart items to the list box again, but without the deleted item.

If the user clicks the Empty Cart button, the btnEmpty_Click event handler is executed. This event handler clears the shopping cart and the shopping cart list box. Please note, though, that instead of clearing the list box by calling the Items.Clear method, this event handler could call the DisplayCart method. Similarly, the btnRemove_Click event handler could use the Items.Remove method of the list box to remove the item at the selected index instead of calling the DisplayCart method. This just shows that there is usually more than one way that methods like these can be coded.

Note that there is no event handler for the Click event of the Continue Shopping button. That's because this button uses the PostBackUrl attribute to post directly to the Order.aspx page. As a result, the Cart page isn't executed if the user clicks the Continue Shopping button.

The aspx file for the Cart page (Cart.aspx)

```
<%@ Page Language="C#" AutoEventWireup="true" CodeFile="Cart.aspx.cs"
Inherits="Cart" %>

<!DOCTYPE html PUBLIC "-//W3C//DTD XHTML 1.0 Transitional//EN"
"http://www.w3.org/TR/xhtml1/DTD/xhtml1-transitional.dtd">

<html xmlns="http://www.w3.org/1999/xhtml">
<head runat="server">
    <title>Chapter 3: Shopping Cart</title>
    <style type="text/css">
        .style1 {
            width: 286px;
            height: 153px;
        }
        .style2 {
            height: 153px;
        }
    </style>
</head>
<body>
    <form id="form1" runat="server">
    <div>
        <asp:Image ID="Image1" runat="server"
            ImageUrl="~/Images/banner.jpg" /><br /><br />
        Your shopping cart:<br />
        <table cellpadding="0" cellspacing="0">
            <tr>
                <td class="style1">
                    <asp:ListBox ID="lstCart" runat="server"
                        Height="135px" Width="267px"></asp:ListBox></td>
                <td class="style2">
                    <asp:Button ID="btnRemove" runat="server"
                        Text="Remove Item" Width="100px"
                        OnClick="btnRemove_Click" /><br /><br />
                    <asp:Button ID="btnEmpty" runat="server" Text="Empty Cart"
                        Width="100px" OnClick="btnEmpty_Click" /></td>
            </tr>
        </table><br />
        <asp:Button ID="btnContinue" runat="server"
            PostBackUrl="~/Order.aspx" Text="Continue Shopping" /> 
        <asp:Button ID="btnCheckOut" runat="server"
            Text="Check Out" OnClick="btnCheckOut_Click" /><br /><br />
        <asp:Label ID="lblMessage" runat="server" ForeColor="Red">
            EnableViewState="False"></asp:Label>
    </div>
    </form>
</body>
</html>
```

Description

- The Cart.aspx page uses a list box to display the shopping cart.
- The btnContinue button uses cross-page posting to post to the Order.aspx page. The other buttons post back to the Cart page, where the event handler specified by the OnClick attribute of the button is executed.

Figure 3-19   The aspx code for the Cart page

The code-behind file for the Cart page (Cart.aspx.cs)   Page 1

```
using System;
using System.Collections;
using System.Configuration;
using System.Data;
using System.Linq;
using System.Web;
using System.Web.Security;
using System.Web.UI;
using System.Web.UI.HtmlControls;
using System.Web.UI.WebControls;
using System.Web.UI.WebControls.WebParts;
using System.Xml.Linq;

public partial class Cart : System.Web.UI.Page
{
    private SortedList cart;

    protected void Page_Load(object sender, EventArgs e){
        this.GetCart();
        if (!IsPostBack)
            this.DisplayCart();
    }

    private void GetCart(){
        if (Session["Cart"] == null)
            Session.Add("Cart", new SortedList());
        cart = (SortedList) Session["Cart"];
    }

    private void DisplayCart(){
        lstCart.Items.Clear();
        CartItem item;
        foreach (DictionaryEntry entry in cart)
        {
            item = (CartItem) entry.Value;
            lstCart.Items.Add(item.Display());
        }
    }
}
```

Description

- Each time the page is loaded, the Page_Load event handler calls the GetCart method to get the shopping cart, which is a SortedList object, from session state. This object is then stored in the SortedList variable named cart.

- The GetCart method retrieves the SortedList object for the shopping cart from session state. But if session state doesn't contain a cart, a cart is created and added to session state.

- If IsPostBack is False in the Page_Load event handler, it calls the DisplayCart method to add the shopping cart items to the list box.

- The DisplayCart method retrieves each CartItem object from the shopping cart using the Value property of the DictionaryEntry object that represents the item in the sorted list that contains the cart. Then, it calls the Display method of that object to format it for display, and it adds the formatted string to the list box.

Figure 3-20   The C# code for the Cart page (part 1 of 2)

The code-behind file for the Cart page (Cart.aspx.cs) Page 2

```csharp
protected void btnRemove_Click(object sender, EventArgs e){
    if (cart.Count > 0)
    {
        if (lstCart.SelectedIndex > -1)
        {
            cart.RemoveAt(lstCart.SelectedIndex);
            this.DisplayCart();
        }
        else
        {
            lblMessage.Text =
                "Please select the item you want to remove.";
        }
    }
}

protected void btnEmpty_Click(object sender, EventArgs e){
    cart.Clear();
    lstCart.Items.Clear();
}

protected void btnCheckOut_Click(object sender, EventArgs e){
    lblMessage.Text = "Sorry, that function hasn't been implemented yet.";
}

}
```

Description

- The btnRemove_Click event handler is called when the user clicks the Remove Item button. If an item is selected, it removes that item and then calls the DisplayCart method to redisplay the shopping cart. If an item isn't selected, it displays a message asking the user to select an item.

- The btnEmpty_Cart event handler is called when the user clicks the Empty Cart item. It clears the sorted list for the shopping cart as well as the list box.

- The btnCheckOut_Click event handler is called when the user clicks the Check Out button. It displays a message to indicate that the check out function hasn't been implemented yet.

- There isn't an event handler for the Click event of the Continue Shopping button because it uses cross-page posting to go to the Order page.

Figure 3-20   The C# code for the Cart page (part 2 of 2)

Perspective

The purpose of this chapter has been to get you started with the development of multi-page web applications. Now, if this chapter has worked, you should be able to develop simple multi-page applications of your own. Yes, there's a lot more to learn, but you should be off to a good start.

Frankly, though, much of the C# code in the Shopping Cart application is difficult, even in a simple application like this one. So if your experience with C# is limited, you may have trouble understanding some of the code. And you may have trouble writing the same type of code for your new applications.

If that's the case, we recommend that you get our latest C# book. It will quickly get you up to speed with the C# language. It will show you how to use dozens of the .NET classes, like the SortedList class. It will show you how to develop Windows applications. It is a terrific on-the-job reference. And it is the perfect companion to this book, which assumes that you already know C#.

Terms

HTTP redirect message
cross-page posting
absolute URL
relative URL
data source
session state
session state object
cookie

Exercise 3-1   Build the Shopping Cart application

This exercise guides you through the process of building a Shopping Cart application similar to the one that's presented in this chapter. This is good practice if you're relatively new to Visual Studio and ASP.NET 3.5, and you'll learn a lot by doing it. To help you get started fast, the images, database, and classes needed by the application are provided for you.

Start the web site

1. Start a new file-system web site named Ch03Cart that's stored in the C:\ASP.NET 3.5 C# directory.

2. By default, this web site already contains a special folder named App_Data. However, this folder doesn't contain any data yet. Add the existing Access database named Halloween.mdb to this folder. You can find this file in the C:\ASP.NET 3.5 C#\Ch01Cart\App_Data directory.

3. Add a folder named App_Code as described in figure 2-3.

4. Add an existing class named Product to the App_Code folder as described in figure 3-4. You can find the file for this class in the App_Code folder of the C:\ASP.NET 3.5 C#\Ch01Cart directory. Then, open this class in the Code Editor and review its code. This code should be similar to the code shown in figure 3-16.

Build a simple Order page

5. Open the form named Default in the Web Forms Designer.

6. Add the Products drop-down list that lets the user select the product, along with the text that identifies it. Next, add an Access data source and configure it to get product data from the Halloween database as described in figures 3-10 and 3-11. Then, bind the combo box to the data source as described in figure 3-12.

7. Add the labels that are used to display the product's name, short description, long description, and unit price. Make sure to set the ID property for these labels appropriately. For example, use lblName for the label that will display the product's name. When you're done, the page should look something like this:

8. Run the application to see how the drop-down list works. At this point, you should be able to select a product from the list, but it won't change the text that's displayed by the labels.

9. Switch to the Code Editor and enter the code that displays the product that's selected in the combo box. To do that, you can code an event handler for the Load event of the page, and you can use a method named GetSelectedProduct as shown in part 1 of figure 3-18.

10. Set the AutoPostBack property of the Products drop-down list to True. Then, run the application and test the code. At this point, when you select a product from the list, the appropriate data for the product should be displayed on the page (but no image is displayed for the product yet).

Build a simple Cart page

11. Add an existing class named CartItem to the App_Code folder as described in figure 3-4. You can find the file for this class in the C:\ASP.NET 3.5 C#\Ch01Cart\App_Code directory. Then, open this class in the Code Editor and review its code. This code should be similar to the code shown in figure 3-16.

12. Add a second web form to the project named Cart as described in figure 3-5.

13. Rename the first web form from Default to Order as described in figure 3-6. Then, set this web form as the starting page as described in figure 3-6.

14. Add text and controls to the Cart page so it looks like the page shown in figure 3-2 without the image control at the top of the page. To help you align the controls, you can use a table. Make sure to set the ID property of the controls appropriately.

15. Set the PostBackUrl property of the Continue Shopping button so it displays the Order page.

16. Switch to Design view for the Order page and add the Add to Cart and Go to Cart buttons. Then, set the PostBackUrl property of the Go to Cart button so it displays the Cart page.

17. Run the application and use the Go to Cart and Continue Shopping buttons to switch between the two pages.

Modify the Cart and Order pages so the cart can store items

18. In the Order page, add code to the Click event of the Add to Cart button so that it adds the selected product. To do that, you can use methods named AddToCart and GetCart as shown in part 2 of figure 3-18. However, since there isn't a text box for the quantity, you can assume that the quantity is always 1. Note that these methods store the cart, which is implemented as a SortedList object, in session state. (You may need to add a using statement for the System.Collections namespace for this to work correctly.)

19. In the Cart page, add the code that displays the cart items in the list box. To do that, you can code an event handler for the Load event of the page, and you can use methods named GetCart and DisplayCart as shown in part 1 of figure 3-20. Note that these methods retrieve the cart from session state. When you add this code, don't forget to declare the Cart variable outside of any methods.

20. Run the application and test this code. At this point, when you select a product and click the Add to Cart button, the application should add the item to the cart and display it in the Cart page. If the cart already contains the item, it should increase the quantity of the item by 1.

Modify the Cart page so it can remove items from the cart

21. In the Cart page, add the code that removes the selected item from the cart. To do that, you can code an event handler for the Click event of the Remove Item button as shown in part 2 of figure 3-20 but without the else block that displays an error message.

22. In the Cart page, add the code that clears all items from the cart. To do that, you can code an event handler for the Click event of the Empty Cart button as shown in part 2 of figure 3-20.

23. Run the application and test this code. At this point, you should be able to use the Remove Item and Empty Cart buttons to remove items from the cart.

Exercise 3-2   Add another page to the Shopping Cart application

In this exercise, you'll add a third page to the Shopping Cart application that you developed in exercise 3-1. That will give you another chance to work with session state data.

Add a CheckOut page

1. Add a new form named CheckOut to your web site. This form should accept the first name, last name, and email address of the customer. In addition, it should have three required field validators (one for each text box) and two buttons that can be used to continue shopping or to cancel the order. Here's how this form should look in Design view:

2. Add a new class named Customer to the App_Code folder. This class should define a customer that has a first name, last name, and email address.

3. Switch to the Cart page and add an event handler for the Click event of the Check Out button that displays the CheckOut page. This code should use the Redirect method of the HttpResponse class to transfer control.

4. Switch back to the CheckOut page and add an event handler for the Load event of the page. This event handler should check for a Customer object in session state and then display the customer information in the text boxes if this object exists.

5. Code an event handler for the Click event of the Continue Shopping button. This event handler should create a Customer object, save that object in session state, and then display the Order page.

6. Code an event handler for the Click event of the Cancel Order button. This event handler should remove the customer and cart data from session state and display the Order page. In addition, change the CausesValidation property of this button so that validation isn't performed when it's clicked.

7. Run the application and test the CheckOut page. To do that, add one or more products to the cart and then click the Check Out button on the Cart page to display the CheckOut page. Click the Continue Shopping button to be sure that the validators on this page work properly. Then, enter customer information in

the text boxes and click the Continue Shopping button again. Add another item to the cart and click the Check Out button again. This time, the customer information should be displayed on the CheckOut page. Now, click the Cancel Order button to return to the Order page. Then, click the Go to Cart button to see that there isn't anything in the cart, and click the Check Out button to see that no customer information is displayed. If you encounter any problems, fix them.

Exercise 3-3   Add images and formatting to the Shopping Cart application

In this exercise, you'll add images to the Shopping Cart application that you developed in exercises 3-1 and 3-2. That will give you a chance to work with a more complicated table and to format the text in that table.

Add images to the application

1. Add a folder named Images to your web site. Then, add the file named banner.jpg to this folder. You can find this file in the C:\ASP.NET 3.5 C#\Ch01Cart\Images directory.

2. Within the Images folder, add a subfolder named Products. Then, add the jpg files for each product to this subfolder. You can find these files in the C:\ASP.NET 3.5 C#\ Ch01Cart\Images\Products directory.

3. Add the banner.jpg file to the top of all the pages in the Shopping Cart application.

Modify the Order page so it displays the images

4. Add a table and formatting to the Order page so it looks similar to the Order page shown in figure 3-1, but without the Quantity text box.

5. Add an Image control to the right column of the table, and set the ID property to imgProduct.

6. Add code to the Order page to display the image for the selected product in the Image control. To do that, you can set the ImageUrl property of the Image control to the location of the image file relative to the page appended with the ImageFile property of the Product object for the selected product. Note that this works because the ImageFile property contains a string with the name of the image file.

7. Run the application and test the Order page. When it loads, it should display an image for the product that's displayed in the combo box. When you select a new product, it should display that product in the Image control.

4

How to test and debug an ASP.NET application

If you've done much programming, you know that testing and debugging are often the most difficult and time-consuming phase of program development. Fortunately, Visual Studio includes an integrated debugger that can help you locate and correct even the most obscure bugs. And ASP.NET includes a Trace feature that displays useful information as your ASP.NET pages execute.

In this chapter, you'll learn how to use both of these powerful debugging tools. But first, you'll learn how to create web sites that run under IIS so that you can test them with that web server, and you'll learn how to test an application to determine if it works properly.

How to create ASP.NET web sites that run under IIS 122
How to create a local IIS web site 122
How to create a remote IIS web site 124
How to create an FTP web site 126

How to test an ASP.NET application 128
How to test an application with the default browser 128
How to test an application with a browser other than the default 130
How to test a file-system web site with IIS 132
How to test an application from outside of Visual Studio 134
How to use the Exception Assistant 136

How to use the debugger 138
How to use breakpoints 138
How to use tracepoints 140
How to work in break mode 142
How to control the execution of an application 144
How to use the Autos, Locals, and Watch windows to monitor variables .. 146
How to use the Immediate window to work with values 148

How to use the Trace feature 150
How to enable the Trace feature 150
How to interpret Trace output 150
How to create custom trace messages 152

**How to write information directly to the HTTP output
stream 154**

Perspective 156

How to create ASP.NET web sites that run under IIS

In chapter 2, you learned how to create a file-system web site that runs under the ASP.NET Development Server. If you have access to an IIS web server, though, you may want to create a web site that runs under IIS so you can test the web site in that environment. Or, you may want to create and test a file-system web site with the ASP.NET Development Server first, and then test it under IIS later.

How to create a local IIS web site

A local IIS web site is a web site that resides on your local computer. To create a local IIS web site, then, you must have IIS installed on your computer. Please see appendix A for information on how to install IIS.

Figure 4-1 illustrates how you create a local IIS web site. To start, you select HTTP for the location option in the New Web Site dialog box (see the next figure). Then, you typically click the Browse button to display the Choose Location dialog box shown in this figure.

In the Choose Location dialog box, you can click the Local IIS button at the left side of the dialog box to display the IIS web server. Then, you can select the directory where you want to create your web site. In this case, I selected the ASPNET2008 directory. Then, I clicked the Create New Web Application button to create a new web site named Ch03Cart in that directory.

When you use this technique, the files for the web site are stored within the directory you create. If that's not what you want, you can create a *virtual directory* that points to the directory where the files for the web site will be stored. To do that, just click the Create New Virtual Directory button in the Choose Location dialog box. Then, a dialog box is displayed that lets you enter a name for the virtual directory and the path where the files for the web site should be stored. In the dialog box shown in this figure, for example, the virtual directory will be named Ch03Cart, and the files will be stored in a directory with the same name within the ASP.NET 3.5 web sites directory on the C drive.

In addition to using the New Virtual Directory dialog box to create a virtual directory for a new web site, you can also use it to create a virtual directory for a file-system web site you've already created. To do that, just enter the path for the existing web site in this dialog box. Then, when you click the OK button in the New Web Site dialog box, Visual Studio will warn you that there is already a web site at the location you specified. To create a virtual directory that points to the existing web site, select the Open the Existing Web Site option.

Before I go on, you should realize that you can also create a virtual directory for a file-system web site using the IIS Management Console. If you're interested, you can learn how to do that in appendix B (Windows XP) or appendix C (Windows Vista). Unless you need to change the default permissions for a virtual directory, though, I recommend that you create the virtual directory from within Visual Studio.

The dialog box for selecting a local IIS web site

The dialog box for creating a virtual directory

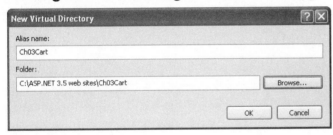

Description

- To create a web site that will run under IIS on your local computer, select HTTP for the location option in the New Web Site dialog box. Then, enter the path of the IIS directory where you want to create the web site, or click the Browse button to display the Choose Location dialog box.

- From the Choose Location dialog box, click the Local IIS button and expand the Default Web Site node. Then, select the directory where you want to create the web site from the default web site and click the Open button, or create a new directory or virtual directory.

- To create a new IIS directory for a web site, click the Create New Web Application button and then enter the name of the directory. The files for the web site will be stored in this directory.

- To create a *virtual directory* for the web site, click the Create New Virtual Directory button to display the New Virtual Directory dialog box. Enter a name for the directory and the path where you want to store the files for the web site. If the path you specify already contains a web site, you can open that web site from the virtual directory.

Figure 4-1   How to create a local IIS web site

How to create a remote IIS web site

A remote web site is similar to a local web site except that a remote web site resides on a computer that you have access to over a LAN. To create this type of web site, FrontPage Server Extensions must be installed on the remote computer. Then, you can just select the HTTP location option and enter the location of the web site as shown in figure 4-2. Here, a web site named Ch03Cart is being created in a directory named ASPNET2008 on a server named mma1.

Although you use the same techniques to work with a remote web site as you use to work with a local web site, you should realize that the permissions for a remote web site may not be set the way you want. For example, suppose you create a web site that writes to a text file that's stored in the App_Data folder of the site. To do that, the web site must have write permissions on that folder. By default, though, a remote web site is given only read permissions. Because of that, you'll need to have the system administrator assign the appropriate permissions to the web site.

The dialog box for creating a remote IIS web site

Description

- To create a remote web site, select HTTP from the Location drop-down list. Then, enter the URL of the web site you want to create.

- If you want to use a version of the .NET Framework other than 3.5, select that version from the drop-down list in the upper right corner of the dialog box.

- You can also create a remote web site by clicking the Browse button and then using the Choose Location dialog box that's displayed for a remote site. However, this dialog box doesn't provide any additional options.

- By default, a web application that you create on a remote server doesn't have the permissions needed to change files in the web site at runtime. If an application needs to change a file, then, you'll need to contact the system administrator about giving it the appropriate permissions.

- Visual Studio communicates with a web site on a remote server using HTTP and FrontPage Server Extensions. Because of that, FPSE must be installed on the remote server. For information on how to install FPSE, see appendix A.

Figure 4-2   How to create a remote IIS web site

How to create an FTP web site

An FTP web site is a web site that resides on a remote computer and that supports FTP file transfers. In most cases, FTP web sites are hosted on a server that you have access to over the Internet. In that case, the web site may already be set up for you. If not, you can use the Choose Location dialog box shown in figure 4-3 to create a new web site.

To display this dialog box, select FTP for the location option from the New Web Site dialog box, and click the Browse button. Then, enter the name of the server where you want to create the site and the path to the directory where the files for the web site will be stored. Note that except for the final directory, all the directories in the directory path must already exist. In this example, that means that the Murach directory must already exist. That's because this directory maps to a *virtual root* that must be set up on the server. The virtual root works much like an IIS virtual directory. However, it points to the location where files are transferred to and from the server.

In addition to the server name and directory path, you can specify the port that Visual Studio should use to send commands to the server, you can specify whether the connection to the server is established using active or passive mode, and you can specify whether you're logged in as an anonymous user or an authenticated user. In most cases, you'll leave the port set at 21. However, you may need to change the Passive Mode and Anonymous Login options.

By default, Visual Studio uses *passive mode* to establish a connection with the FTP server. To understand how passive mode works, you need to realize that two ports are required to use FTP: one to transmit commands and one to transmit data. In passive mode, Visual Studio establishes the connections for both the command port and the data port.

In contrast, with *active mode*, Visual Studio connects to the server using the command port and then passes the address of the data port to be used to the server. Then, the server connects to Visual Studio using the data port. If the client is behind a firewall, however, the server probably won't be able to connect to it. In that case, you'll need to use passive mode. If the client isn't behind a firewall and you want to use active mode, just deselect the Passive Mode option.

In some cases, an FTP server will require that you provide a user name and password to connect to the server. Then, you'll need to remove the check mark from the Anonymous Login option and enter the required information in the Username and Password text boxes that become available. Note that because this information is saved until you end Visual Studio, you only need to enter it the first time you connect to the server during a Visual Studio session.

After you enter the required information into the Choose Location dialog box, you click the Open button to return to the New Web Site dialog box. When you do, the location will look something like this:

```
ftp://Murach/Ch03Cart
```

Then, you can just click the OK button to create the web site.

The dialog box for creating an FTP web site

Description

- To create a new FTP web site, select FTP from the Location drop-down list in the New Web Site dialog box. Then, click the Browse button to display the Choose Location dialog box shown above.

- Enter the name of the server and the directory where you want to create the web site. You can typically leave the port set at 21.

- Visual Studio can use either *active mode* or *passive mode* to establish connections to the FTP server. Passive mode is the default, which is usually necessary if the client is behind a firewall. If the client isn't behind a firewall, you can use active mode by deselecting the Passive Mode option.

- By default, Visual Studio logs you in to the FTP server as an anonymous user. However, some FTP servers require you to provide a user name and password. In that case, you can deselect the Anonymous Login option and then enter your user name and password. The user name and password are saved until you end the Visual Studio session.

- If you try to create a new FTP web site by entering a URL in the New Web Site dialog box, Visual Studio will display a dialog box that lets you specify whether you want to use passive mode and whether you want to log in as an anonymous user.

- IIS can be configured to act as an FTP server as well as a web server. For more information, please see appendix A.

Figure 4-3   How to create an FTP web site

How to test an ASP.NET application

To test an ASP.NET application, you typically start by running it from within Visual Studio so that you can locate and correct any errors you encounter. This initial testing uses the default browser and, if you're working with a file-system web site, the ASP.NET Development Server. Next, you test the application with other web browsers to make sure it works with them, and you test a file-system web site under IIS. Finally, you run the application from outside of Visual Studio to be sure it will work correctly in a production environment.

You'll learn the techniques for performing all of these types of testing in the topics that follow. In addition, you'll learn how to use the Exception Assistant that's displayed if an error occurs while you're testing an application.

How to test an application with the default browser

Unless you've changed it, Visual Studio uses Internet Explorer as its default browser. Figure 4-4 presents six different ways you can run a web application with the default browser. Three of these techniques start the debugger so you can use its features to debug any problems that might arise. The other three techniques do not start the debugger.

The first time you run a web application using one of the first three techniques, Visual Studio displays a dialog box indicating that debugging isn't enabled in the web.config file. From this dialog box, you can choose to add a new web.config file with debugging enabled, or you can choose to run the application without debugging. In most cases, you'll add a new web.config file with debugging enabled so that you can use the debugger with your application.

Before I go on, you should realize that before you can run an application with debugging on a remote server, a program called the *Remote Debug Monitor* must be installed and running on the server. For information on how to set up this program, see the help topic "How to: Set Up Remote Debugging."

All of the techniques listed in this figure except the View in Browser command start the application and display the application's designated start page. However, the View in Browser command displays the selected page. For example, if you right-click the Cart page and choose View in Browser, the Cart page will be displayed. This command is most appropriate for making sure that the pages of an application look the way you want them to.

At this point, you should realize that the type of web site you're developing determines the web server that's used to run the application. For example, if you're developing a file-system web site, the ASP.NET Development Server is used to run the application. In that case, the URL for the page that's displayed identifies the server as "localhost:" followed by a number that's assigned by the development server. In contrast, if you're developing an IIS web site, IIS is used to run the application. Then, the server is identified as just "localhost" for a local web site or by its actual name for a remote or FTP web site.

The Order page displayed in the default browser

Three ways to run an application with debugging

- Click the Start Debugging button in the Standard toolbar
- Press F5
- Choose the Debug→Start Debugging command

Three ways to run an application without debugging

- Press Ctrl+F5
- Choose Debug→Start Without Debugging
- Right-click a page in the Solution Explorer and choose View in Browser.

Three ways to stop an application that's run with debugging

- Press Shift+F5
- Click the Stop Debugging button in the Debug toolbar
- Choose Debug→Stop Debugging

Description

- If you run an application with debugging, you can use Visual Studio's built-in debugger to find and correct program errors.
- By default, an application is run using Internet Explorer. See figure 4-5 for information on using a different browser. To end the application, close the browser.

Figure 4-4   How to test an application with the default browser

You should also realize that you can't just run an FTP application from its FTP location. That's because this location is used only to transfer files to and from the server. Instead, a *browse location* must be set up for the web site. A browse location is simply an IIS virtual directory that points to the directory that stores the files for the web site. Then, to access and run the web site, you enter the HTTP URL for the virtual directory. The first time you run an FTP web site, you will be asked to enter this URL. Because the URL is stored as part of the web site, you won't need to enter it again.

How to test an application with a browser other than the default

Once you've thoroughly tested your application with Internet Explorer, you'll want to test it with other browsers to make sure it works as expected. Figure 4-5 describes two ways to do that. First, you can right-click the starting page for the application in the Solution Explorer and choose the Browse With command. This displays a Browse With dialog box like the one shown in this figure. From this dialog box, you can choose the browser you want to use and then click the Browse button.

Notice that the list of browsers in the Browse With dialog box includes the Internal Web Browser. If you choose this browser, the page is displayed in a Browse window within Visual Studio. You can test the application from this browser just as you would from any other browser. Then, when you're done with the browse operation, just close the Browse window.

You can also test an application with another browser by making that browser the default browser. To do that, right-click any page in the Solution Explorer and choose Browse With. Next, select the browser you want to designate as your default browser and click the Set As Default button. Then, click the Cancel button to close the Browse With dialog box. You can then use any of the techniques listed in figure 4-4 to start the application in the browser you selected. Note that setting a browser as the default is the only way to use the debugger with the browser. That's because the Browse With command runs an application without debugging.

Sometimes, the browser you want to test an application with doesn't appear in the Browse With dialog box even though it's installed on your computer. In most cases, that's because you installed the browser after installing Visual Studio. Then, you can add the browser by clicking the Add button in the Browse With dialog box to display the Add Program dialog box. This dialog box lets you locate the executable file for the browser you want to add and enter a "friendly" name that's used for the browser in the Browse With dialog box.

The Browse With dialog box

Two ways to test an application with a browser other than the default

- Right-click the starting page for the application in the Solution Explorer and choose Browse With from the shortcut menu. In the Browse With dialog box that's displayed, select the browser you want to use and click the Browse button.
- Select the browser you want to use in the Browse With dialog box and then click the Set as Default button to make that browser the default. The next time you run the application, it will be displayed in the browser you selected.

Description

- It's important to test an ASP.NET application in any browsers that might be used to run the application.
- If a browser isn't included in the list of available browsers, you can add it to the list by clicking the Add button in the Browse With dialog box and then using the Add Program dialog box that's displayed to add the desired browser.
- If you select the Internal Web Browser option, the page is displayed in a Browse window within Visual Studio. To end the browse operation from this window, just close the window.
- You'll need to change the default browser if you want to use the debugger with another browser, since the Browse With command starts the application without debugging.

Figure 4-5   How to test an application with a browser other than the default

How to test a file-system web site with IIS

When you run a file-system web site, it runs under the ASP.NET Development Server by default. Because this server has limitations, however, you'll want to be sure to test a file-system web site under IIS as well as under the development server. Figure 4-6 describes how you do that.

To start, you need to create a virtual directory for the web site as described in figure 4-1. Then, if you open the web site from this virtual directory, it will automatically run under IIS. Alternatively, you can open the file-system web site directly and change its start options so the URL you specify is used to start the application. In this figure, for example, you can see that the Use Custom Server option has been selected and the URL for the web site's virtual directory has been entered in the Base URL text box.

This figure also lists the limitations of the ASP.NET Development Server. The most significant of these limitations is that it always runs under the current user's security context, but your own user account probably has stronger security privileges than the account IIS runs ASP.NET applications under. As a result, when you move the application to a production web server, you may have to contend with security issues that weren't apparent when you tested with the development server, especially if you access files or databases located in folders outside of the application's folder structure.

The dialog box for specifying a web server

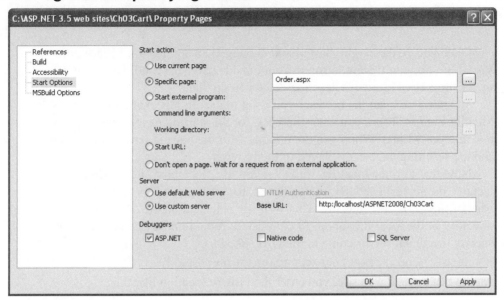

How to test a file-system web site with IIS

- Create a virtual directory for the web site as described in figure 4-1.
- Open the web site from its virtual directory, or open the file-system web site and then use the Property Pages dialog box shown above to specify the URL for the virtual directory.
- Run the application using one of the techniques in figure 4-4.

Limitations of the ASP.NET Development Server

- Can serve pages only to the local computer.
- Runs in current user's security context, so it doesn't accurately test security issues.
- Does not include an SMTP server, so it can't be used to test email applications.
- Uses a randomly chosen port rather than the standard HTTP port 80.

Description

- By default, a file-system web site is run using the ASP.NET Development Server. To run a file-system web site using IIS, you can use one of the techniques above.
- To open the Property Pages dialog box, right-click the project in the Solution Explorer and select Property Pages from the shortcut menu. Then, to change the server that's used to run the web site, click the Start Options node, select the Use Custom Server option, and enter the URL of the virtual directory for the web site.

Figure 4-6   How to test a file-system web site with IIS

How to test an application from outside of Visual Studio

Once you've thoroughly tested and debugged an application from within Visual Studio, you'll want to run it from outside of Visual Studio to make sure it works properly. Figure 4-7 describes how you do that.

To start, you open the browser you want to use. In this example, I used Mozilla Firefox. Then, you enter the URL for the starting page of the application and press Enter. When you do, a request for the page is sent to the server and the resulting page is displayed in the browser.

Note that to run a local IIS web site, you use "localhost" in the URL to identify the server. The URL in this figure, for example, refers to the Order.aspx page of the Ch03Cart web site. This web site is located in the ASPNET2008 directory of the local IIS server. In contrast, to run a remote IIS web site, you specify the actual server name in the URL like this:

```
http://mma1/ASPNET2008/Ch03Cart/Order.aspx
```

And to run an FTP web site, you enter the browse location like this:

```
http://Murach/Ch03Cart/Order.aspx
```

If you haven't already tested an application from within Visual Studio in each browser that might be used to run the application, you should do that from outside Visual Studio. In addition, if the application retrieves and updates data in a database, you'll want to test it simultaneously in two browser windows. To understand why, you need to realize that after an application retrieves data from a database, it closes the connection to the database. Because of that, two or more users can retrieve the same data at the same time. This is called *concurrency*, and it can cause *concurrency errors* when the data is updated.

In section 3 of this book, you'll learn more about concurrency and how you avoid concurrency errors. For now, you should just realize that you'll need to test your applications to be sure that they handle concurrency problems.

The Order page displayed in a Mozilla Firefox browser outside of Visual Studio

Description

- You can run any IIS application from outside of Visual Studio. To do that, open the browser you want to use, enter the URL for the starting page of the application as shown above, and press Enter.

- When you run an application from outside of Visual Studio, you can run it in two or more browser windows simultaneously. That way, you can be sure that the application provides for any *concurrency errors* that can occur.

- If you want to use the debugger while testing for concurrency errors, you can run one instance of the application from within Visual Studio with debugging, and you can run another instance from outside of Visual Studio.

Figure 4-7   How to test an application from outside of Visual Studio

How to use the Exception Assistant

As you test an ASP.NET application, you may encounter runtime errors that prevent an application from executing. When that happens, an exception is thrown. In many cases, the application anticipates these exceptions and provides code to catch them and process them appropriately. If an exception is not caught, however, the application enters *break mode* and the *Exception Assistant* displays a dialog box like the one shown in figure 4-8.

As you can see, the Exception Assistant dialog box indicates the type of exception that occurred and points to the statement that caused the error. In many cases, this information is enough to determine what caused the error and what should be done to correct it. For example, the Exception Assistant dialog box in this figure indicates that an input string value was not in the correct format. The problem was encountered in this line of code for the Order page:

```
item.Quantity = Convert.ToInt32(txtQuantity.Text);
```

Based on that information, you can assume that the Text property of the txtQuantity control contains a value that can't be converted to an integer, since the Quantity property of the item object is declared as an integer. This could happen if the application didn't check that the user entered an integer value into this control. (To allow this error to occur, I disabled the range validator for the Quantity text box on the Order page.)

Many of the exceptions you'll encounter will be system exceptions like the one shown here. These exceptions apply to general system operations such as arithmetic operations and the execution of methods. If your applications use ADO.NET, you can also encounter ADO.NET and data provider exceptions. If the connection string for a database is invalid, for example, a data provider exception will occur. And if you try to add a row to a data table with a key that already exists, an ADO.NET error will occur.

In some cases, you won't be able to determine the cause of an error just by analyzing the information in the Exception Assistant dialog box. Then, to get more information about the possible cause of an exception, you can use the list of troubleshooting tips in this dialog box. The items in this list are links that display additional information in a Help window. You can also use the other links in this dialog box to search for more help online, to display the content of the exception object, and to copy the details of the exception to the clipboard.

If you still can't determine the cause of an error, you can use the Visual Studio debugger to help you locate the problem. You'll learn how to do that next.

An Exception Assistant dialog box

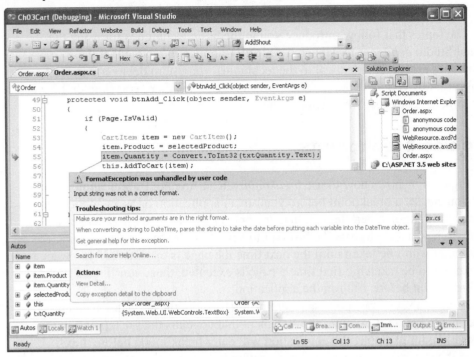

Description

- If an uncaught exception occurs in an ASP.NET application, the application enters *break mode* and the *Exception Assistant* displays a dialog box like the one shown above.

- The Exception Assistant provides the name and description of the exception, and it points to the statement in the program that caused the error. It also includes a list of troubleshooting tips. You can click on these tips to display additional information in a Help window.

- The information provided by the Exception Assistant is often all you need to determine the cause of an error. If not, you can close this window and then use the debugging techniques presented in this chapter to determine the cause.

- If you continue program execution after an exception occurs, ASP.NET terminates the application and sends a Server Error page to the browser. This page is also displayed if you run an application without debugging. It provides the name of the application, a description of the exception, and the line in the program that caused the error. It also includes a *stack trace* that indicates the processing that led up to the error.

Figure 4-8   How to use the Exception Assistant

How to use the debugger

The topics that follow introduce you to the basic techniques for using the Visual Studio *debugger* to debug an ASP.NET application. Note that these techniques are almost identical to the techniques you use to debug a Windows application. If you've debugged Windows applications, then, you shouldn't have any trouble debugging web applications.

How to use breakpoints

Figure 4-9 shows how to use *breakpoints* in an ASP.NET application. Note that you can set a breakpoint before you run an application or as an application is executing. Remember, though, that an application ends after it generates a page. So if you switch from the browser to Visual Studio to set a breakpoint, the breakpoint won't be taken until the next time the page is executed. If you want a breakpoint to be taken the first time a page is executed, then, you'll need to set the breakpoint before you run the application.

After you set a breakpoint and run the application, the application enters break mode before it executes the statement that contains the breakpoint. In this illustration, for example, the application will enter break mode before it executes the statement that caused the exception in figure 4-8 to occur. Then, you can use the debugging features described in the topics that follow to debug the application.

In some cases, you may want to set more than one breakpoint. You can do that either before you begin the execution of the application or while the application is in break mode. Then, when you run the application, it will stop at the first breakpoint. And when you continue execution, the application will execute up to the next breakpoint.

Once you set a breakpoint, it remains active until you remove it. In fact, it remains active even after you close the project. If you want to remove a breakpoint, you can use one of the techniques presented in this figure.

You can also work with breakpoints from the *Breakpoints window*. To disable a breakpoint, for example, you can remove the check mark in front of the breakpoint. Then, the breakpoint isn't taken until you enable it again. You can also move to a breakpoint in the Code Editor window by selecting the breakpoint in the Breakpoints window and then clicking on the Go To Source Code button at the top of this window, or by right-clicking the breakpoint in the Breakpoints window and choosing Go To Source Code from the shortcut menu.

The Order page with a breakpoint

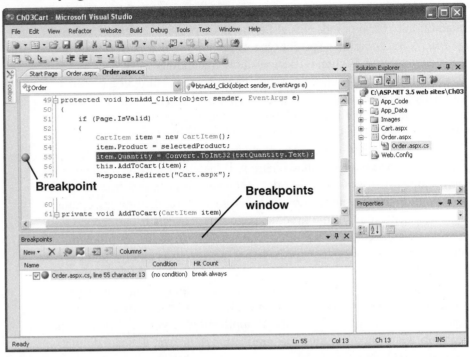

How to set and clear breakpoints

- To set a *breakpoint*, click in the margin indicator bar to the left of the statement where you want the break to occur. The statement will be highlighted and a breakpoint indicator (a large dot) will appear in the margin. You can set a breakpoint before you run an application or while you're debugging the application.

- To remove a breakpoint, click the breakpoint indicator. To remove all breakpoints at once, use the Debug→Delete All Breakpoints command.

- To disable all breakpoints, use the Debug→Disable All Breakpoints command. You can later enable the breakpoints by using the Debug→Enable All Breakpoints command.

Description

- When ASP.NET encounters a breakpoint, it enters break mode before it executes the statement on which the breakpoint is set. From break mode, you can use the debugger to determine the cause of an error.

- The current breakpoints are listed in the *Breakpoints window* (Debug→Windows→ Breakpoints). You can use the toolbar at the top of this window to work with the breakpoints, and you can use the check box next to a breakpoint to enable or disable the breakpoint.

- You can't set breakpoints on blank lines or comments.

Figure 4-9   How to use breakpoints

How to use tracepoints

In addition to breakpoints, Visual Studio 2008 provides a feature called *tracepoints*. A tracepoint is a special type of breakpoint that performs an action when it's encountered. Figure 4-10 shows how tracepoints work.

To set a tracepoint, you use the When Breakpoint Is Hit dialog box to indicate what you want to do when the tracepoint is encountered or "hit." In most cases, you'll use the Print a Message option to display a message in the *Output window*. As indicated in this dialog box, the message can include variable values and other expressions as well as special keywords.

For example, the message shown here will include the value of the SelectedValue property of the ddlProducts control. You can see the output from this tracepoint in the Output window in this figure. Here, the first tracepoint message was displayed the first time the page was requested. The second message was displayed when a product was selected from the drop-down list. And the third message was displayed when a quantity was entered and the Add to Cart button was clicked.

Notice that the Output window is also used to display Visual Studio messages like the first one shown in this figure. Because of that, this window is displayed automatically when you run an application. If you ever close it and want to reopen it without running the application, however, you can do that using the View→Output command.

To run a macro when a tracepoint is encountered, you select the Run a Macro option. Then, the drop-down list becomes available and you can select the macro you want to run from this list.

By default, program execution continues after the tracepoint action is performed. If that's not what you want, you can remove the check mark from the Continue Execution option. Then, the program will enter break mode when the tracepoint action is complete.

After you set a tracepoint on a statement, the statement will be highlighted and a breakpoint indicator will appear in the margin. If program execution will continue after the tracepoint action is performed, the indicator will appear as a large diamond. If the program will enter break mode, however, the same indicator is used as for a standard breakpoint.

The Order page with a tracepoint and the dialog box used to set it

Output from the tracepoint in the Output window

Description

- A *tracepoint* is a special type of breakpoint that lets you perform an action. When ASP.NET encounters a tracepoint, it performs the specified action and then continues execution if the Continue Execution option is selected or enters break mode if it isn't.

- You typically use tracepoints to print messages to the *Output window*. A message can include text, values, and special keywords. You can also use tracepoints to run macros.

- To set a tracepoint, right-click on the statement where you want it set and choose Breakpoint→Insert Tracepoint. Then, complete the When Breakpoint Is Hit dialog box and click OK. You can also convert an existing breakpoint to a tracepoint by right-clicking on its indicator and choosing When Hit.

- If program execution will continue after the tracepoint action is performed, the tracepoint will be marked with a large diamond as shown above. Otherwise, it will be marked just like any other breakpoint.

Figure 4-10   How to use tracepoints

How to work in break mode

Figure 4-11 shows the Order page in break mode. In this mode, the next statement to be executed is highlighted. Then, you can use the debugging information that's available to try to determine the cause of an exception or a logical error.

For example, you can place the mouse pointer over a variable, property, or expression to display its current value in a *data tip*. You can also display the values of the members of an array, structure, or object. To do that, place the mouse pointer over the array, structure, or object to display its data tip, and then point to the plus sign in that data tip. In this figure, for example, you can see the current values of the members of the Product object named selectedProduct.

You can also use a data tip to change the value of a variable or property. To do that, just right-click the data tip and then choose Edit Value from the shortcut menu. When you do, the value that's displayed will become editable so you can enter a new value.

You can also see the values of other properties and variables in the Autos window near the bottom left of the Visual Studio window. You'll learn more about the Autos window and some of the other debugging windows in a minute.

In addition to changing the values of variables and properties while in break mode, you can also make changes to the C# code. To do that, you use a Visual Studio feature called Edit and Continue. This feature lets you make changes to most statements within the methods of an application, and some statements outside the methods, in the Code Editor. Then, when you continue program execution using one of the techniques presented in this figure, the new code is compiled and debugging continues with the new code.

The Shopping Cart application in break mode

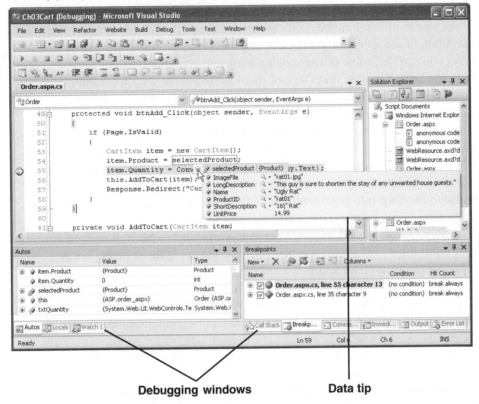

Debugging windows   **Data tip**

Description

- When you enter break mode, the debugger highlights the next statement to be executed.
- You can use the debugging windows and the buttons in the Debug menu and toolbar to control the execution of the program and determine the cause of an exception.
- To display the value of a variable or property in a *data tip,* position the mouse pointer over the variable or property in the Code Editor window. To display a data tip for an expression, highlight the expression and then point to it. The expression must not contain a method call.
- To display the members of an array, structure, or object in a data tip, position the mouse pointer over it to display its data tip, and then point to the plus sign in the data tip.
- To change the value of a variable in a data tip, right-click the data tip, choose Edit Value, and then enter the new value.
- You can also make changes to your code in break mode. These changes are applied when you continue program execution.
- To continue program execution, press F5 or click the Continue button in the Standard or Debug toolbar. For more options about controlling program execution, see figure 4-12.

Figure 4-11   How to work in break mode

How to control the execution of an application

Once you're in break mode, you can use a variety of commands to control the execution of the application. These commands are summarized in figure 4-12. As you can see, most of these commands are available from the Debug menu or the Debug toolbar, but three of them are available only from the shortcut menu for the Code Editor window. You can also use shortcut keys to start some of these commands.

To execute the statements of an application one at a time, you use the Step Into command. When you use this command, the application executes the next statement, then returns to break mode so you can check the values of properties and variables and perform other debugging functions. The Step Over command is similar to the Step Into command, but it executes the statements in called methods without interruption (they are "stepped over").

The Step Out command executes the remaining statements in a method without interruption. When the method finishes, the application enters break mode before the next statement in the calling method is executed.

To skip over code that you know is working properly, you can use the Run To Cursor or Set Next Statement command. You can also use the Set Next Statement command to rerun lines of code that were executed before an exception occurred. And if you've been working in the Code Editor window and have forgotten where the next statement to be executed is, you can use the Show Next Statement command to move to it.

If your application gets caught in a processing loop so it keeps executing indefinitely without generating a page, you can force it into break mode by choosing the Debug→Break All command. This command lets you enter break mode any time during the execution of an application.

Commands in the Debug menu and toolbar

Command	Toolbar	Keyboard	Function
Start/Continue	▶	F5	Start or continue execution of the application.
Break All	❚❚	Ctrl+Alt+Break	Stop execution and enter break mode.
Stop Debugging	■	Shift+F5	Stop debugging and end execution of the application.
Restart	↻	Ctrl+Shift+F5	Restart the entire application.
Show Next Statement	⇨		Display the next statement to be executed.
Step Into	⤵	F11	Execute one statement at a time.
Step Over	⤳	F10	Execute one statement at a time except for called methods.
Step Out	⤴	Shift+F11	Execute the remaining lines in the current method.

Commands in the Code Editor window's shortcut menu

Command	Function
Run to Cursor	Execute the application until it reaches the statement that contains the insertion point.
Set Next Statement	Set the statement that contains the insertion point as the next statement to be executed.
Show Next Statement	Move the insertion point to the next statement that will be executed.

Description

- Once the application enters break mode, you can use the Step Into, Step Over, Step Out, and Run To Cursor commands to execute one or more statements and return to break mode.

- To alter the normal execution sequence of the application, you can use the Set Next Statement command. Just place the insertion point in the statement you want to execute next, issue this command, and click the Continue button to continue application execution.

- To stop an application that's caught in a loop, switch to the Visual Studio window and use the Debug→Break All command.

Figure 4-12   How to control the execution of an application

How to use the Autos, Locals, and Watch windows to monitor variables

If you need to see the values of several application variables or properties, you can do that using the Autos, Locals, or Watch windows. By default, these windows are displayed in the lower left corner of the IDE when an application enters break mode. If they're not displayed, you can display them by selecting the appropriate command from the Debug→Windows menu. Note that you can display up to four separate Watch windows.

The content of the Autos, Locals, and Watch windows is illustrated in figure 4-13. The difference between the Autos and Locals windows is in the amount of information they display and the scope of that information.

The *Locals window* displays information about the variables within the scope of the current method. If the code in a form is currently executing, this window also includes information about the form and all of the controls on the form.

The *Autos window* also displays information about the form and all of its controls if a form is currently executing. In addition, it displays the variables, properties, and constants used in the current statement, the three statements before that statement, and the three statements after that statement. Although the information in this window can be more limited than the information shown in the Locals window, the Autos window helps you focus on the variables that are relevant to the current statement.

Unlike the Autos and Locals windows, the *Watch windows* let you choose the values that are displayed. The Watch window shown in this figure, for example, displays the Text property of the txtQuantity and lblUnitPrice controls, the Quantity property of the item object, and the UnitPrice property of the Product object that's stored in the item object. The Watch windows also let you watch the values of expressions you specify. Note that an expression doesn't have to exist in the application for you to add it to a Watch window.

To add an item to a Watch window, you can type it directly into the Name column. Alternatively, if the item appears in the Code Editor window, you can highlight it in that window and then drag it to a Watch window. You can also highlight the item in the Code Editor or a data tip and then right-click on it and select the Add Watch command to add it to the Watch window that's currently displayed.

Besides displaying the values of variables and properties, you can use the Autos, Locals, and Watch windows to change these values. To do that, you simply double-click on the value you want to change and enter a new value. Then, you can continue debugging or continue the execution of the application.

The Autos window

The Locals window

A Watch window

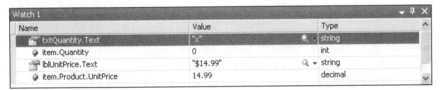

Description

- The *Autos window* displays information about variables, properties, and constants in the current statement and the three statements before and after the current statement.

- The *Locals window* displays information about the variables within the scope of the current method.

- The *Watch windows* let you view the values of variables and expressions you specify, called *watch expressions*. You can display up to four Watch windows.

- To add a watch expression, type a variable name or expression into the Name column, highlight a variable or expression in the Code Editor window and drag it to the Watch window, or right-click on a variable, highlighted expression, or data tip in the Code Editor window and choose Add Watch.

- To delete a row from a Watch window, right-click the row and choose Delete Watch. To delete all the rows in a Watch window, right-click the window and choose Select All to select the rows, then right-click and choose Delete Watch.

- To display any of these windows, click on its tab if it's visible or select the appropriate command from the Debug→Windows menu.

- To change the value of a property or variable from any of these windows, double-click on the value in the Value column, then type a new value and press the Enter key.

Figure 4-13   How to use the Autos, Locals, and Watch windows to monitor variables

How to use the Immediate window to work with values

The *Immediate window*, shown in figure 4-14, is useful for displaying the values of variables or properties that don't appear in the Code Editor window. To display a value, you simply type a question mark followed by the name of the variable or property. The first line of code in this figure, for example, displays the Text property of the item selected from the Products drop-down list. You can see the result in the second line of this window.

The Immediate window is also useful for executing C# statements. For example, you can execute an assignment statement to change the value of a variable or property. After I displayed the Text property of the Quantity text box, for example, I assigned a value of 1 to this property. Similarly, you can execute a user-defined method. This can be useful for testing the result of a method with different arguments. If you execute a method that returns a value, you can also preface the method name with a question mark to display the value it returns.

When you enter commands in the Immediate window, they're executed in the same context (or scope) as the application that's running. That means that you can't display the value of a variable that's out of scope. If you try to do that, the debugger displays an error message.

The commands that you enter into the Immediate window remain there until you exit from Visual Studio or explicitly delete them using the Clear All command in the shortcut menu for the window. That way, you can use standard Windows techniques to edit and reuse the same commands from one execution of an application to another without having to reenter them.

To execute a command that you've already entered in the Immediate window, just use the Up and Down arrow keys to scroll through the commands. As you scroll, the commands are displayed at the bottom of the window. Then, you can change a command if necessary and press Enter to execute it.

The Immediate window

```
Immediate Window                                            ▼ ╄ X
?ddlProducts.SelectedItem.Text
"Ugly Rat"
?txtQuantity.Text
"x"
txtQuantity.Text = "1"
"1"


◄                                                            ►
```

Description

- You can use the *Immediate window* to display and assign values from a program during execution. To display this window, click on the Immediate Window tab or use the Debug→Windows→Immediate command.

- To display a value in the Immediate window, enter a question mark followed by the expression whose value you want to display. Then, press the Enter key.

- To assign a different value to a variable, property, or object, enter an assignment statement in the Immediate window. Then, press the Enter key.

- To execute a user-defined method from the Immediate window, enter its name and any arguments it requires. Then, press the Enter key. If you want to display the value that's returned by a method, precede the method call with a question mark.

- To reissue a command, use the Up and Down arrow keys to scroll through the commands until you find the one you want. Then, modify the command if necessary and press the Enter key to execute it.

- To remove all commands and output from the Immediate window, use the Clear All command in the shortcut menu for the window.

Figure 4-14   How to use the Immediate window to work with values

How to use the Trace feature

The *Trace feature* is an ASP.NET feature that displays some useful information that you can't get by using the debugger. Because the debugger works so well, you probably won't need to use the Trace feature very much, but you should at least be aware of the information that it can provide.

How to enable the Trace feature

To use the Trace feature, you must first enable tracing. To do that, you add a Trace attribute to the Page directive for the page, and you assign a value of True to this attribute. Then, when you run the page, trace information will be displayed at the end of the page output, as shown in figure 4-15.

When you enable the Trace feature, it is enabled only for the current page, which is usually what you want. To enable tracing for another page, you must modify the Page directive for that page too. Once this feature has been enabled for a page, ASP.NET adds trace output to the page whenever the page is requested.

How to interpret Trace output

In figure 4-15, you can see the start of the output for the Cart page after the user added an item to the shopping cart. After the request details, the trace information provides a list of trace messages that are generated as the application executes. Here, ASP.NET automatically adds Begin and End messages when major page events such as PreInit, Init, and InitComplete occur. If you scroll down to see all of these trace messages, you can see the variety of events that are raised during the life cycle of a page.

After the trace messages, you'll find information about the controls used by the page, the items in the session state object, the cookies that were included with the HTTP request, the HTTP request headers, and the server variables. In this figure, for example, you can see the session state and cookies data for the Cart page of the Shopping Cart application. In this case, an item named Cart has been added to the session state object. And a cookie named ASP.NET_SessionId is used to keep track of the user's session ID so the user's session state object can be retrieved.

The beginning of the trace output for the Cart page

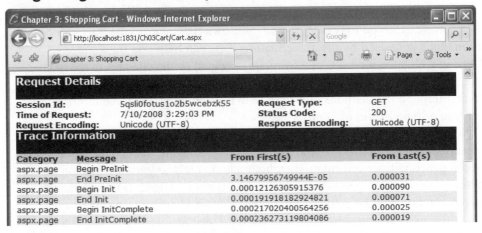

The session and cookies information for the Cart page

A Page directive that enables tracing for the Cart page

```
<%@ Page Language="C#" AutoEventWireup="true" CodeFile="Cart.aspx.cs"
Inherits="Cart" Trace="true" %>
```

Description

- The ASP.NET *Trace feature* traces the execution of a page and displays trace information and other information at the bottom of that page.

- To activate the trace feature for a page, you add a Trace attribute to the Page directive at the top of the aspx file for the page and set its value to True as shown above.

- The trace information is divided into several tables that provide specific types of trace information. For example, the Trace Information table provides information about how the page request was processed, and the Session State table provides information about the items currently stored in session state.

Figure 4-15   How to enable the Trace feature and interpret Trace output

How to create custom trace messages

In some cases, you may want to add your own messages to the trace information that's generated by the Trace feature. This can help you track the sequence in which the methods of a form are executed or the changes in the data as the methods are executed. Although you can also do this type of tracking by stepping through the methods of a form with the debugger, the trace information gives you a static listing of your messages.

Note, however, that you can also create this type of listing using tracepoints as described earlier in this chapter. The advantage to using tracepoints is that you can generate trace information without adding code to your application. In addition, this output is generated only when you run an application with debugging. In contrast, you have to add program code to add custom trace messages, and the trace output is generated whenever the Trace feature is enabled. Because of that, you may not want to create custom trace messages. But I've included it here in case you do.

To add messages to the trace information, you use the Write or Warn method of the TraceContext object. This is summarized in figure 4-16. The only difference between these two methods is that messages created with the Warn method appear in red. Notice that to refer to the TraceContext object, you use the Trace property of the page.

When you code a Write or Warn method, you can include both a category and a message or just a message. If you include just a message, the category column in the trace output is left blank. If you include a category, however, it appears as shown in this figure. In most cases, you'll include a category because it makes it easy to see the sequence in which the methods were executed.

If you want to determine whether tracing is enabled before executing a Write or Warn method, you can use the IsEnabled property of the TraceContext object as shown in the example in this figure. Normally, though, you won't check the IsEnabled property because trace statements are executed only if tracing is enabled.

Common members of the TraceContext class

Property	Description
`IsEnabled`	True if tracing is enabled for the page.

Method	Description
`Write(message)`	Writes a message to the trace output.
`Write(category, message)`	Writes a message to the trace output with the specified category.
`Warn(message)`	Writes a message in red type to the trace output.
`Warn(category, message)`	Writes a message in red type to the trace output with the specified category.

Code that writes a custom trace message

```
if (Trace.IsEnabled)
    Trace.Write("Page_Load", "Binding products drop-down list.");
```

A portion of a trace that includes a custom message

Trace Information

Category	Message	From First(s)	From Last(s)
aspx.page	Begin PreInit		
aspx.page	End PreInit	3.1736160340272E-05	0.000032
aspx.page	Begin Init	5.82994994736955E-05	0.000027
aspx.page	End Init	0.000106556608164522	0.000048
aspx.page	Begin InitComplete	0.000127874445948172	0.000021
aspx.page	End InitComplete	0.000147114634128877	0.000019
aspx.page	Begin PreLoad	0.000165352337579572	0.000018
aspx.page	End PreLoad	0.000202724968314322	0.000037
aspx.page	Begin Load	0.000222947591530436	0.000020
Page_Load	Binding products drop-down list.	0.00170552977737678	0.001483
aspx.page	End Load	0.111980880109987	0.110275
aspx.page	Begin LoadComplete	0.112027044531804	0.000046
aspx.page	End LoadComplete	0.112050773345363	0.000024
aspx.page	Begin PreRender	0.112070151375194	0.000019
aspx.page	End PreRender	0.112191915676713	0.000122

Custom trace message

Description

- You can use the TraceContext object to write your own messages to the trace output. The TraceContext object is available through the Trace property of a page.

- Use the Write method to write a basic text message. Use the Warn method to write a message in red type.

- Trace messages are written only if tracing is enabled for the page. To determine whether tracing is enabled, you use the IsEnabled property of the TraceContext object.

Figure 4-16   How to create custom trace messages

How to write information directly to the HTTP output stream

Another way to display information as a program executes is to write it directly to the HTTP output stream. To do that, you use the Write method of the HTTP Response object as shown in figure 4-17. When you use this technique, you'll want to be sure to remove any statements you've added when you finish testing your application.

At the top of this figure, you can see a Cart page that includes output that indicates the number of items that are currently in the shopping cart. To generate this output, I added a Response.Write method to the Page_Load event handler of the page. As you can see, this event handler uses the Count property of the cart object to determine the number of items that are in the cart.

Notice that the text you include on the Write method can include HTML tags. For example, the Write method shown here includes a <br /> tag so that the item count is followed by a blank line. Also note that the output you write to the output stream is always added to the beginning of the stream. Because of that, it always appears at the top of the browser window.

The Cart page with output generated by Response.Write

A Page_Load event handler that writes to the HTTP output stream

```
protected void Page_Load(object sender, EventArgs e)
{
    this.GetCart();
    if (!IsPostBack)
    {
        this.DisplayCart();
        Response.Write("Items in cart = " + cart.Count + "<br />");
    }
}
```

Code that writes HTML output from another class

```
HttpContext.Current.Response.Write("Now updating file.<br />");
```

Description

- The Write method of the HttpResponse object provides a convenient way to write data directly to the HTTP output stream. The output can include any valid HTML.

- To access the HttpResponse object from the code-behind file for a web page, you use the Response property of the page. To access this object from a class that doesn't inherit the Page class, you use the Response property of the HttpContext object for the current request. To access this object, you use the Current property of the HttpContext class.

- The HTML output you add to the HTTP output stream using the Write method of the HttpResponse object appears at the beginning of the output stream. As a result, the output from the Write method always appears at the top of the page in the browser window.

Figure 4-17   How to write information directly to the HTTP output stream

Perspective

As you can now appreciate, Visual Studio provides a powerful set of tools for debugging ASP.NET applications. For simple applications, you can usually get the debugging done just by using breakpoints, data tips, and the Autos window. You may also need to step through critical portions of code from time to time. For complex applications, though, you may discover the need for some of the other features that are presented in this chapter. With tools like these, a difficult debugging job becomes manageable.

Terms

virtual directory	break mode	data tip
virtual root	Exception Assistant	Immediate window
active mode	stack trace	Autos window
passive mode	debugger	Locals window
Remote Debug Monitor	breakpoint	Watch window
browse location	Breakpoints window	watch expression
concurrency	tracepoint	Trace feature
concurrency error	Output window	

Exercise 4-1   Use the Visual Studio debugger

In this exercise, you'll step through the Shopping Cart application that you developed in the exercises for chapter 3. In the process, you'll set breakpoints, use the Locals window, and use buttons in the Debug toolbar for controlling program execution.

1. Open the Shopping Cart application, display the code for the Order page, and set a breakpoint on the statement in the Load event handler that calls the GetSelectedProduct method.

2. Run the application in the default browser. When the application enters break mode, point to the IsPostBack property to display its value in a data tip.

3. Press the F11 key to execute the next statement. Notice that this statement is in the GetSelectedProduct method. Press the F11 key two more times to see that only one statement is executed each time.

4. Click the Step Out button in the Debug toolbar to skip over the remaining statements in the GetSelectedProduct method. This should return you to the Load event handler.

5. Click the Continue button in the Debug toolbar. This should execute the remaining statements in the Load event handler and display the Order page.

6. Select another product from the combo box. This should cause the application to enter break mode again and stop on the statement that calls the GetSelectedProduct method.

7. Press the F10 key to execute the Step Over command. This should step over all statements in the GetSelectedProduct method and enter break mode before the next statement in the Load event handler is executed.

8. Point to the Text property of the labels to display these values. Then, point to the properties of the selected product to see the values that are stored in this object. Step through the statements that assign the product properties to the Text property of the labels and note how the values in the Text property change.

9. Note the values that are displayed in the Locals window. Click the plus sign next to the form object (this) to expand it and review the information that's available. When you're done, click the minus sign to collapse the information for this object.

10. Remove the breakpoint from the Load event handler.

11. Set another breakpoint on the statement in the GetSelectedProduct method that sets the value of the selected product's name, continue execution of the application, and select another product. When the application enters break mode again, notice the variables that are now displayed in the Locals window. That should include all of the variables that are in scope.

12. Display a Watch window. Add the Name column of the DataViewRow object to this window by dragging it from the Code Editor window. In the Watch window, it should look something like this:

    ```
    row["Name"]
    ```

    Then, enter an expression into the Watch 1 window that displays the Count property of the DataView object. In the Watch window, it should look something like this:

    ```
    productsTable.Count
    ```

    Note the value of the Count property. It should be 1.

13. Enter the same expression into the Immediate window, preceded by a question mark. Press the Enter key to see the value that's displayed. It should be 1.

14. Use the Immediate window to assign a new value to the Name column of the DataViewRow object. Check the value of this property in the Locals window and note that the new value is displayed in the Locals window.

15. Press F5 to continue program execution. This should display the Order page. Note that the Name value that you set in the previous step is displayed on the Order page.

16. Select another product from the combo box. This should cause the application to enter break mode again.

17. Click the Stop Debugging button in the Debug toolbar to end the application. Note that the breakpoint remains in the Code Editor even after you have stopped debugging.

Exercise 4-2   Use the Trace feature

In this exercise, you'll use the Trace feature of ASP.NET to display trace output on the Cart page of the Shopping Cart application that you created in the exercises for chapter 3.

1. If it's not already open, open the Shopping Cart application.

2. Display the Cart page in the Web Forms Designer and switch to Source view. Then, enable tracing for the page by adding a Trace attribute to the Page directive as shown in figure 4-15.

3. Run the application and notice that the trace output is displayed below the controls on the Cart page.

4. View the trace information. In particular, review the Session state information. When you're done, end the application.

5. Add a custom trace message to the GetCart method that indicates whether this method has created a new cart. Use "GetCart" as the category for this message. If you need help, you can refer to figure 4-16.

6. Add a custom trace message to the Page_Load event handler that indicates that the cart has been successfully retrieved from session state. Use "Page_Load" as the category for this message.

7. Run the application and click the Go to Cart button to see what messages are displayed. Continue shopping, add an item to the cart, and see what messages are displayed this time.

8. End the application. Then, close and save the project.

Exercise 4-3   Test the Shopping Cart application with IIS and other browsers

In this exercise, you'll create a local IIS site for the Shopping Cart application that you created in exercise 3-1, and you'll test this application using other browsers besides Microsoft's Internet Explorer.

1. If IIS isn't installed on your system, install it as described in figure A-2 (Windows XP) or figure A-3 (Windows Vista) of appendix A.

2. Create a local IIS site for the Shopping Cart application as described in figure 4-1. In the Choose Location dialog box, click the Local IIS button and then select the Default Web Site node. Next, click the Create New Virtual Directory button and enter Ch03Cart as the alias that points to the web site in the C:\ASP.NET 3.5 C#\Ch03Cart directory. This is the web site that you created in the exercises for chapter 3.

3. In the Web Site Already Exists dialog box, select the "Open the existing web site" option.

4. Test the application with the default browser as described in figure 4-4. To get this to work properly, you may need to set the Order page as the start page. You can tell that the web site is using IIS instead of the Web Development server because no port is specified in the URL.

5. If another browser, such as Mozilla Firefox, is available to you, test the Shopping Cart application with that browser as described in figure 4-5. When you're done, end the application and close the project.

6. Launch a browser from outside of Visual Studio and run the Shopping Cart application as described in figure 4-7. When you're done, close the browser.

Section 2

Basic ASP.NET skills

The seven chapters in this section expand upon the essentials that you learned in section 1. To start, chapter 5 presents the essential HTML skills that you will need as an ASP.NET programmer. Then, chapter 6 shows you how to work with the server controls that can be used for developing web pages; chapter 7 shows you how to work with the validation controls; and chapter 8 presents the several ways that you can manage the state of an application or form.

The next three chapters present features of ASP.NET that make it easier to develop professional-looking web sites. Chapter 9 shows you how to use master pages to create pages with common elements; chapter 10 shows you how to use site navigation to make it easy for users to navigate through your site; and chapter 11 shows you how to use themes to customize the formatting that's applied to the elements on a page.

To a large extent, each of the chapters in this section is an independent unit. As a result, you don't have to read these chapters in sequence. If, for example, you want to know more about state management after you finish section 1, you can go directly to chapter 8. Eventually, though, you're going to want to read all seven chapters. So unless you have a compelling reason to skip around, you may as well read the chapters in sequence.

5

A crash course in HTML

When you add ASP.NET controls to a form in Design view, Visual Studio generates the HTML that will be used to render the web page. Although you could work exclusively in Design view, it sometimes makes sense to work directly with the HTML for a form in Source view. In addition, you may occasionally need to include HTML within the C# coding for a form. To be sure that you have the skills you need to do that, this chapter presents a crash course in HTML.

If you already know how to code HTML, you should be able to go through this chapter quickly. However, you won't want to skip this chapter altogether, because it presents some skills that are specific to Visual Studio.

An introduction to HTML 162
Basic rules for coding HTML elements 162
How to work with HTML using Visual Studio 164
How web server controls are rendered 166

How to code HTML documents 168
The basic structure of an HTML document 168
The Page directive 170
The Doctype declaration 170
How to code basic text formatting elements 172
How to code links to other HTML pages 174

How to use styles 176
How to use inline styles 176
How to use the Span element to apply styles 178
How to use an internal style sheet 180
How to use classes in a style sheet 182
How to add and modify style rules 184
How to use an external style sheet 186
Visual Studio features for working with external style sheets ... 188
How to use the Apply Styles window to work with styles 190
How to use the CSS Properties window to work with styles 192

How to code tables 194
How to create a table 194
Common table attributes and style properties 196
How to use a table to control the layout of a page 198

Perspective 200

An introduction to HTML

HTML documents consist of *HTML elements* that define the content and appearance of the page when it's viewed in a web browser. In the topics that follow, you'll learn the basic rules for coding HTML elements, you'll learn how to work with HTML using Visual Studio, and you'll see how some of the basic web server controls are rendered to HTML.

Basic rules for coding HTML elements

Figure 5-1 presents the basic rules for coding HTML elements. To start, each HTML element is coded within a *tag* that starts with an opening bracket (<) and ends with a closing bracket (>). For example, <title>, </h1>, and <hr style="color: Red" /> are all examples of HTML tags.

Most HTML elements are made up of three parts. First, a *start tag* marks the start of the element. The start tag consists of the element name (such as title or h1) plus one or more optional *attributes* that provide additional information for the tag. After the start tag is the *content*, which is the text or other data that makes up the element. After the content is the *end tag* that marks the end of the element. The end tag consists of a slash followed by the element's name. This is illustrated by the three lines of code in the first example in this figure.

It's important to realize that the content of an element can contain other elements. For example, consider this HTML code:

```
<h1>This is a <b>bold</b>heading</h1>
```

Here, the H1 element contains the text "This is a bold heading." Within this text, the B element indicates that the word "bold" should be boldfaced. You'll learn about these and other formatting elements later in this chapter.

Not all HTML elements have content and end tags. For example, the line of code in the second example in this figure includes two elements without content or end tags. The first element, <br /> inserts a line break, and the second element, <hr />, inserts a horizontal rule. Notice that the text in this line of code isn't enclosed in tags. That's because, like the <br /> and <hr /> tags, it is content for another tag that's coded at a higher level in the document. You'll learn more about that later.

Notice that all of the tags shown in this figure are lowercase. This will be a requirement of the new XHTML version 1.0 standards. Although ASP.NET web pages currently use XHTML version 1.0 Transitional, which allows uppercase tags, you'll want to use lowercase tags so that you won't need to change your HTML in the future.

Notice also that the <br /> and <hr /> tags include a slash before the closing bracket. Although these slashes were optional in earlier HTML standards, they will be required with XHTML version 1.0. As a result, you'll want to use them so you won't need to change your HTML in the future.

You can also code *comments* within an HTML document as shown in the third example in this figure. That way, you can document sections of code that

Three HTML elements with start tags, content, and end tags

```
<title>Murach's Halloween Superstore</title>
<h1>About Us</h1>
<b>Choose a product:</b>
```

Two elements that have no content or end tags

```
A red line appears below.<br /><hr style="color: Red" />
```

A comment

```
<!-- This text will be ignored. -->
```

A line that has three consecutive spaces

```
Last name:   Wilson
```

Elements and tags

- An *HTML document* includes *HTML elements* that specify the content and appearance of the page when viewed in a web browser.
- Most HTML elements have three parts: a start tag, content, and an end tag. Each *tag* is coded within a set of brackets (< >).
- An element's *start tag* includes the name of the element. The *end tag* includes the element name preceded by a slash. And the *content* includes everything that appears between the start and end tags.
- Some HTML elements have no content or end tag. For example, the <br /> element, which forces a line break, and the <hr /> element, which inserts a horizontal rule, consist of just a start tag.
- You should use lowercase letters for all your tags.

Attributes

- *Attributes* can appear within a start tag to supply optional values. For example, you can use the Color attribute within an <hr /> element to specify the color of the rule.
- All attribute values should be enclosed in quotation marks.
- Use spaces to separate attributes from one another.

Comments and white space

- A *comment* is text that appears between the <!-- and --> characters. Web browsers ignore comments, so you can use them to document sections of your HTML code that might otherwise be confusing.
- *White space*, such as tabs, line returns, and consecutive spaces, is ignored by browsers. As a result, you can use space to indent lines of code and line breaks to separate elements from one another. Used properly, white space can make your HTML code easier to read.
- To force the browser to display two or more consecutive spaces, use the special code   for each space.

Figure 5-1   Basic rules for coding HTML elements

might be confusing. In addition, you can use spaces, indentation, and blank lines to make your code easier to read. This is called *white space*, and web browsers ignore it. If you want to include space within a line that the web browser doesn't ignore, you can use the special code   as shown in the last example of figure 5-1.

How to work with HTML using Visual Studio

In chapter 2, you learned how to create a simple web form by dragging ASP.NET controls onto the design surface of the Web Forms Designer. You also learned some basic skills for modifying the design of a form from Source view using the HTML Editor. Now, figure 5-2 reviews some of these skills and presents some additional skills for working in Source view.

When you display a web form in Source view, you'll notice that Visual Studio uses different colors to identify various items of information. For example, element names are displayed in maroon, attribute names are displayed in red, and attribute values are displayed in blue. Visual Studio also makes syntax errors easy to locate by underlining them with a red wavy line.

Visual Studio also provides tools that help you enter and edit HTML code. One of the most useful is the statement completion feature provided by IntelliSense. With this feature, a list of the available elements is displayed when you enter the opening bracket for a start tag. Then, you can select the element you want to add from this list and press the Tab key to add the element name to your document.

After you enter an element name followed by a space, Visual Studio displays a list of the available attributes for that element. In this figure, for example, you can see the list of attributes that's displayed for a Td element. To add an attribute, you just select it from the list and press the Tab key. Then, you can type an equal sign and enter a value for the attribute. When you enter a value, be sure to enclose it in quotation marks or you'll get a syntax error. To enter additional attributes, type a space to redisplay the list. When you're finished entering the attributes for an element, you enter its closing bracket. Then, the end tag for that element, if it has one, is added automatically.

As you make changes in Source view, you'll frequently want to check the results of those changes in Design view. One way to do that is to switch back and forth between these two views. Another way is to use the new Split view you learned about in chapter 2, which lets you see both Design view and Source view at the same time.

A web page in Source view with a completion list displayed

Description

- To edit the HTML for a web page in Visual Studio, display the page in Source view by clicking on the Source button at the bottom of the Web Forms Designer window.

- Visual Studio uses distinctive colors to identify various items in Source view. In addition, it highlights syntax errors with a red wavy underline so they're easy to locate.

- When you enter the opening bracket (<) for a start tag, Visual Studio displays a list of the available elements. To select an element, type one or more letters of the element or scroll to the element, and then press the Tab key.

- When you enter the name of an HTML element followed by a space, Visual Studio displays a list of the attributes you can use with that element. To select an attribute, type one or more letters of the attribute or scroll to the attribute, and then press the Tab key.

- When you enter the closing bracket (>) for a start tag, Visual Studio automatically adds the end tag.

- You can also add or modify element attributes using the Properties window. To do that, move the insertion point into the tag for the element to display its attributes in the Properties window and then change the attribute values as appropriate.

- You can use Visual Studio's drag-and-drop feature to add server controls to a form in Source view. To do that, just drag the control from the Toolbox to the location where you want it to appear in the HTML document.

Figure 5-2   How to work with HTML using Visual Studio

How web server controls are rendered

Before a web page can be displayed in a browser, any web server controls it contains must be rendered to standard HTML. To help you understand how this works, figure 5-3 lists some common web server controls and describes the HTML elements they're rendered to.

If you review the HTML elements that are used to implement the controls in this figure, you can see that the same element can be used to implement more than one control. For example, the text box, button, and image button controls are all implemented by an Input element. The difference in how these controls appear and act depends on how their attributes are set. In this case, the Type attribute indicates the type of input control that's rendered. The Type attribute of a text box, for example, is set to "text," the Type attribute of a button is set to "submit," and the Type attribute of an image button is set to "image." Because of that, the browser handles each of these controls differently.

To give you a better idea of how web server controls are rendered, this figure also shows the aspx code for four web server controls along with the HTML code that's rendered for those controls. If you compare the aspx and HTML code, you should quickly see how it's related. Of course, the HTML that's generated for a control depends on how you set its attributes. You'll learn more about the attributes that you can set for various web server controls in the next chapter.

Some common web server controls and how they're rendered

Name	HTML element	Additional information
Label	\<span\>	The \<span\> element is typically used to apply special formatting to the text it encloses.
TextBox	\<input\>	The type="text" attribute identifies this element as a text box.
Button	\<input\>	The type="submit" attribute identifies this element as a button.
ImageButton	\<input\>	The type="image" attribute identifies this element as an image button.
LinkButton	\<a\>	This control is rendered as an Anchor element that posts the page back to the server.
HyperLink	\<a\>	This control is rendered as an Anchor element that links to a URL.
ListBox	\<select\>	Each item in the list is defined by an \<option\> element within the \<select\> element.
DropDownList	\<select\>	Each item in the list is defined by an \<option\> element within the \<select\> element.
Image	\<img\>	Displays the specified image.

The aspx code for four web server controls

```
<asp:Label ID="lblName" runat="server" Font-Bold="True" Font-Size="Larger"
    Text="Murach Books"></asp:Label>

<asp:TextBox ID="txtSearch" runat="server" Width="248px"></asp:TextBox>

<asp:Button ID="btnSearch" runat="server" Text="Search"
    OnClick="btnSearch_Click" />

<asp:ListBox ID="lstBooks" runat="server">
    <asp:ListItem Value="ACS8">ASP.NET 3.5 with C# 2008</asp:ListItem>
    <asp:ListItem Value="CS08">C# 2008</asp:ListItem>
    <asp:ListItem Value="SQL5">SQL Server 2005</asp:ListItem>
</asp:ListBox>
```

How the four web server controls are rendered in HTML

```
<span id="lblName" style="font-size:Larger;font-weight:bold;">Murach
Books</span>

<input name="txtSearch" type="text" id="txtSearch" style="width:248px;"/>

<input type="submit" name="btnSearch" value="Search"
onclick="javascript:WebForm_DoPostBackWithOptions(new
WebForm_PostBackOptions(&quot;btnCart&quot;, &quot;&quot;, false,
&quot;&quot;, &quot;Cart.aspx&quot;, false, false))" id="btnSearch" />

<select size="4" name="lstBooks" id="lstBooks">
    <option value="ACS8">ASP.NET 3.5 with C# 2008</option>
    <option value="CS08">C# 2008</option>
    <option value="SQL5">SQL Server 2005</option>
</select>
```

Description

- All of the web server controls are *rendered* as standard HTML that can be interpreted by a browser.
- To view the HTML that's rendered for a web page, choose the View→Source command from the browser window. The HTML will be displayed in a separate Notepad window.

Figure 5-3   How web server controls are rendered

How to code HTML documents

Every HTML document for a web form must be structured in a certain way for it to be interpreted properly by ASP.NET. In the topics that follow, you'll learn about the basic structure of an HTML document. You'll also learn how to code some of the common elements that appear within an HTML document.

The basic structure of an HTML document

Figure 5-4 shows the HTML that's generated for a new ASP.NET web page. This HTML illustrates the overall structure of an HTML document. Because the elements that make up this structure are generated for you automatically, you don't have to worry about coding them yourself.

The first two elements are an ASP.NET Page directive and an HTML Doctype declaration. The Page directive supplies the information ASP.NET needs to process the web form, and the Doctype declaration provides information the browser needs to display the page. You'll learn about both of these elements in the next figure.

After the Page directive and the Doctype declaration is an Html element. This element, known as the *root element*, contains all of the document's remaining elements. Prior to the XHTML version 1.0 standards, the start and end tags for the Html element were optional. As a result, you'll sometimes see HTML documents without the <html> and </html> tags.

Within the html section, an HTML document contains two additional sections: a document head and a document body. The document head, defined by a Head element, contains various information about the document. As shown here, one element it contains by default is the Title element. The value of this element determines what's displayed in the title bar of the browser window. Later in this chapter, you'll learn about two additional elements that you can add to the Head element.

The document body, defined by a Body element, contains the HTML content that's displayed when the document is viewed in a browser. For a web form, the document body typically consists of just a single Div element within a Form element. As you've seen in previous chapters, the Div element contains all of the asp and HTML elements for the form. You can use the Div element to apply formatting to all of the elements it contains. Although you can code more than one Div element within a Form element to apply different formatting to different parts of the form, that's unusual.

Because the Head and Body elements are contained within an Html element, the Html element is called a *parent element* and the Head and Body elements are called *child elements*. The Body element is also a parent element because it contains a Form element. And the Form element is a parent element because it contains a Div element. This hierarchy of elements becomes particularly important when you're working with styles, as you'll see later in this chapter.

The HTML generated for a new ASP.NET web page

```
<%@ Page Language="C#" AutoEventWireup="true" CodeFile="Cart.aspx.cs"
Inherits="Cart" %>

<!DOCTYPE html PUBLIC "-//W3C//DTD XHTML 1.0 Transitional//EN"
"http://www.w3.org/TR/xhtml1/DTD/xhtml1-transitional.dtd">

<html xmlns="http://www.w3.org/1999/xhtml" >
<head runat="server">
    <title>Untitled Page</title>
</head>
<body>
    <form id="form1" runat="server">
    <div>

    </div>
    </form>
</body>
</html>
```

HTML elements generated for a new page

Element	Start tag	End tag	Description
Page directive	<%@ Page ...>		Identifies various options applied to the web page. See figure 5-5 for details.
Doctype declaration	<!DOCTYPE ...>		Identifies the type of HTML document. See figure 5-5 for details.
Html element	<html>	</html>	Marks the beginning and end of an HTML document.
Head element	<head>	</head>	Marks the beginning and end of the document head.
Title element	<title>	</title>	Provides the title for the page.
Body element	<body>	</body>	Marks the beginning and end of the document body.
Form element	<form>	</form>	Marks the beginning and end of the form.
Div element	<div>	</div>	Marks the beginning and end of a division within the form.

Description

- The Html element contains the content of the document. This element is called the *root element* because it contains all the other elements in the document. Within this element, you code the Head and Body elements.
- The Body element contains the Form element that defines the form.
- The Form element contains a Div element that's used to provide formatting that applies to the entire page. Any elements you add to the page in the Web Forms Designer are inserted within the Div element.
- An element that's contained within another element is called a *child element*. The element that contains a child element is called the child's *parent element*.

Figure 5-4   The basic structure of an HTML document for an ASP.NET web page

The Page directive

Figure 5-5 shows the Page directive that appears at the beginning of all ASP.NET pages. Notice that the Page directive begins with the characters <%@ and ends with the characters %>. These special sequences of characters form a *directive block*. Because directive blocks aren't a part of standard HTML, they aren't included in the final HTML that's sent to the browser when the page is displayed. Instead, directive blocks are processed by ASP.NET when the page is compiled.

As you can see in this figure, the Page directive has several attributes. The first attribute, Language, specifies the programming language that's used for the page's code. For C# projects, the value of this attribute is C#.

The next attribute is AutoEventWireup. For C# web forms created in Visual Studio, this attribute is set to True. That causes the event handlers for page events such as Init and Load to be executed automatically when the events occur. For this to work, you must name the event handlers appropriately. For example, the event handlers for the Init and Load events must be named Page_Init and Page_Load.

The CodeFile and Inherits attributes work together to link the ASP.NET web page to the code-behind file. First, the CodeFile attribute provides the name of the code-behind file. Visual Studio uses this attribute to associate the partial class it generates for the page at runtime (the class that contains the control declarations) with the file that contains the C# code for the page. Then, the Inherits attribute provides the name of the compiled class that the page inherits at runtime. This is the name that's specified on the class declaration within the code-behind file.

Another attribute you can include in the Page directive is Trace. You learned about this attribute in chapter 4. It determines whether or not trace information that you can use for debugging is displayed on the web page.

The Doctype declaration

Figure 5-5 also shows the Doctype declaration. This declaration is used by a web browser to determine which version of HTML the document uses. The Doctype declaration generated by Visual Studio 2008 specifies XHTML version 1.0 Transitional, which includes certain HTML elements that are expected to be phased out in the future. If you use these elements, error or warning messages are displayed in the Error List window.

A typical Page directive

```
<%@ Page Language="C#" AutoEventWireup="true" CodeFile="Cart.aspx.cs"
Inherits="Cart" %>
```

Common attributes of the Page directive

Attribute	Description
Language	Specifies the language used to implement the processing for the page. For C# applications, this attribute is set to C#.
AutoEventWireup	Indicates that the event handlers for the page will be called automatically when the events occur for the page.
CodeFile	Specifies the name of the code-behind file. This file defines the partial class that is compiled with the partial class that ASP.NET generates from the page at runtime.
Inherits	Specifies the name of the compiled class (dll) that the page inherits at runtime. This name is typically the same as the name of the partial class defined in the CodeFile attribute.
Trace	Indicates whether tracing is enabled. The default is False.

A typical Doctype declaration

```
<!DOCTYPE html PUBLIC "-//W3C//DTD XHTML 1.0 Transitional//EN"
"http://www.w3.org/TR/xhtml1/DTD/xhtml1-transitional.dtd">
```

Description

- The Page directive is processed by ASP.NET when the page is compiled. It isn't included in the output that's sent to the browser.
- The Doctype declaration specifies that the root element of the document—that is, the first element after the Doctype declaration—is an HTML element.
- The Public attribute of the Doctype declaration and the string that follows it specify the version of HTML that the document complies with.

Figure 5-5   The Page directive and the Doctype declaration

How to code basic text formatting elements

As you know, a web form can contain literal text in addition to server controls. To format literal text like this, you can use the elements shown in figure 5-6.

To use the elements shown in this figure, you enclose the text you want to format in the start and end tags for the element. The exception is the Br tag, which is used to insert a line break. Since this tag doesn't have an end tag, it can be referred to as a *self-closing tag*.

The first three elements listed in this figure are the H1, H2, and H3 heading elements. (Although HTML actually has six levels of headings, it's unlikely that you'll use more than three.) The heading elements are designed to create headings with various formats. For instance, all three of the headings shown in the output in this figure are formatted using H2 elements.

The next two elements, P and Br, let you format paragraphs and force line endings. When you use the P element to create standard text paragraphs, the web browser determines where to break lines based on the width of the browser window and the size of the text. If you want to force a line ending at a particular spot, you need to use a Br element. For instance, the paragraph that describes the P element in this figure is formatted using the P element. Because of that, the text flows to the right side of the browser window. In contrast, the paragraph that describes the Br element contains a Br element that forces a line break.

The last two elements let you create bold or italic text. These elements are typically used within P elements or literal text to format all or part of the text. For instance, the last paragraph shown in the output in this figure illustrates how individual words can be formatted within literal text.

Before I go on, you should realize that the basic appearance of the text in an HTML document is determined by the browser. Because of that, headings and body text may appear differently in one browser than they do in another. Later in this chapter, though, you'll learn how to use styles to control the overall appearance of the elements in a document.

Basic HTML formatting elements

Element	Start tag	End tag	Description
H1	<h1>	</h1>	Level-1 heading
H2	<h2>	</h2>	Level-2 heading
H3	<h3>	</h3>	Level-3 heading
P	<p>	</p>	Standard paragraph
Br	 		Line break
B	<b>	</b>	Bold
I	<i>	</i>	Italic

HTML that uses some basic formatting elements

```
<h2>The P element</h2>
<p>The P element marks a standard paragraph. Note that the
web browser determines where the individual lines within the
paragraph will break.</p>
<h2>The Br element</h2>
In contrast, the Br element lets you force a<br />
line break wherever you wish.
<h2>The B and I elements</h2>
This is <b>bold</b>.  This is <i>italic</i>.
```

The HTML viewed in a browser window

The P element

The P element marks a standard paragraph. Note that the web browser determines where the individual lines within the paragraph will break.

The Br element

In contrast, the Br element lets you force a
line break wherever you wish.

The B and I elements

This is **bold**. This is *italic*.

Description

- The default appearance of heading and body text is determined by the browser. However, you can also use styles to determine the default formatting for various elements.

- The P element formats text as a standard paragraph. The browser determines where line endings occur for the text within the paragraph. If you want to force a line break at a specific location within a paragraph, use the Br element.

Figure 5-6   How to code basic text formatting elements

How to code links to other HTML pages

Most web applications consist of a series of web pages. In chapter 3, you learned how you can display one web page from another by using the Redirect method of the HttpResponse object, the Transfer method of the HttpServerUtility object, or cross-page posting. Another way to display a different page is to code an Anchor, or A, element, often called a link.

Figure 5-7 shows how to use the Anchor element. As you can see, this element typically consists of just the start and end tags, an Href attribute that specifies the URL of the page you want to link to, and the text that's displayed by the browser to identify the link. When viewed in a browser, the text within the Anchor element is usually underlined. In addition, the mouse pointer typically changes to a hand when hovered over the text for the link. Then, when the user clicks on the link, the browser requests the page specified by the Href attribute.

When you code an Href attribute in an Anchor element, you can use either a relative URL or an absolute URL. For instance, the first Anchor element in this figure uses a relative URL to display the Register page in the Login subdirectory of the directory that contains the current page. The second Anchor element uses an absolute URL to display the Index page on the www.murach.com web site.

In the next chapter, you'll learn how to use the hyperlink control to link to another web page. Because this control provides the same functionality as the Anchor element, you'll typically use it in your web forms instead of Anchor elements. However, Anchor elements can be useful in some situations. In particular, they're useful for creating menus in code.

Examples of Anchor elements

An anchor element that uses a relative URL

```
<a href="Login/Register.aspx">Register as a new user</a>
```

An anchor element that uses an absolute URL

```
<a href="http://www.murach.com/Index.aspx">View Murach's web site</a>
```

The Anchor elements viewed in a browser

Register as a new user

View Murach's web site

The Anchor element

Start tag	End tag	Description
<a>	</a>	Defines a link to another URL. When the user clicks on the text that's displayed by the element, the browser requests the page that's identified by the Href attribute of the element.

One attribute of an Anchor element

Attribute	Description
href	The URL for the page to be displayed.

Description

- You can code both relative and absolute URLs in the Href attribute. See figure 3-9 in chapter 3 for the details on coding these URLs.
- Because ASP.NET provides a Hyperlink control, you may not use the Anchor element often. However, you may want to assign a series of Anchor elements that are created in code to the Text property of a label or other control to create a menu.

Figure 5-7   How to code links to other HTML pages

How to use styles

With early versions of HTML, the appearance of the HTML elements in a page was determined almost entirely by the browser where the page was displayed. With newer versions of HTML, however, you can use a feature called *cascading style sheets*, or *CSS*, to provide better control over the appearance of your web pages. Like the basic formatting elements you learned about earlier in this chapter, you're most likely to use styles to format the literal text you add to a form. Then, you can use a feature of ASP.NET called skins to apply formatting to the web server controls. As you'll learn in chapter 11, you can store style sheets and skins together in themes.

In the topics that follow, you'll learn about three types of CSS styles: inline styles, internal styles, and external styles. With *inline styles*, you specify style formatting directly in an HTML element. With *internal styles*, you store formatting information in the Style element of the document so you can apply it anywhere in the page. And with *external styles,* you store formatting information in a separate file so you can apply it to all of the pages in a site. When you develop ASP.NET applications, you'll probably work with all three types of styles from time to time. However, you should avoid using inline styles whenever possible because they make a web site more difficult to maintain.

How to use inline styles

To use inline styles, you include a Style attribute in the element you want to format. Within this attribute, you specify one or more individual *style properties* that control various style settings. Some of the most common style properties are listed in figure 5-8.

The HTML in this figure illustrates how you can use the Style attribute. Here, the style properties for the H1 element specify that the text it contains should be displayed in a bold, 16-point, white, Arial font against a blue background. Similarly, the style properties for the H2 element specify that the text it contains should be displayed in an italic, 14-point, Times New Roman font.

The three P elements in this figure show how you can use the Text-align property to align text on a page. The first element aligns the text at the left margin, the second element centers the text between the margins, and the third element aligns the text at the right margin. All three of these elements also specify the Courier New font, which is a mono-spaced font. This figure illustrates how these elements and the two heading elements appear in a browser window.

Notice that the syntax for specifying style properties is different from the syntax you use for HTML attributes. Instead of an equals sign, you separate a style name from its value with a colon. And to separate items, you use semicolons.

You should also notice that the Font-family property in each of the Style attributes specifies a specific font plus a generic font style. For example, the

Common properties of the Style attribute

Property	Description
Font-family	A comma-separated list of font names, such as Arial, Times New Roman, and Courier New, and generic font styles, such as serif, sans-serif, and monospace.
Font-size	A specific number of points, a point size relative to the parent element's font size, or a keyword such as small, medium, or large.
Font-style	A keyword that determines how the text is slanted. Possible values are normal, italic, and oblique.
Font-weight	A keyword or number that determines the boldness of the font. Possible values are normal, bold, bolder, lighter, 100, 200...800, and 900. Bolder and lighter are relative to the parent element.
Background-color	A color name, such as red, blue, or yellow, or a color value, such as #0000FF, that controls the background color of an element.
Color	A color name or value that controls the foreground color of an element.
Text-align	A keyword that determines the alignment of the text in a P element relative to the page margins. Possible values are left, right, center, or justify.

HTML that uses inline styles

```
<h1 style="font-weight: bold; font-size: 16pt; color: White; font-family:
    Arial, Sans-Serif; background-color: Blue">The Halloween Store</h1>
<h2 style="font-size: 14pt; font-style: italic; font-family:
    Times New Roman, Serif">The Halloween Store</h2>
<p style="font-size: 10pt; font-family: Courier New, Monospace;
    text-align: left">This text is left-justified and mono-spaced.</p>
<p style="font-size: 10pt; font-family: Courier New, Monospace;
    text-align: center">This text is centered and mono-spaced.</p>
<p style="font-size: 10pt; font-family: Courier New, Monospace;
    text-align: right">This text is right-justified and mono-spaced.</p>
```

The HTML viewed in a browser window

Description

- You can use the Style attribute to create an *inline style* that affects the appearance of a single element in an HTML document and any child elements it contains. If you specify a style for a child element, it overrides the style specified by the parent element.

- Within the Style attribute, you specify one or more *style properties*, such as Font-size and Font-family. The name of each property is separated from its value by a colon, and the properties are separated from one another with semicolons.

Figure 5-8   How to use inline styles

Font-family property for the H1 element specifies Arial and Sans-Serif. That way, if the Arial font isn't installed on the computer where the page is displayed, the text will be displayed in the default sans-serif font. When you code the Font-family property, you can specify as many different fonts as you want, and the first one that's available will be used. In case none of the fonts you specify are available, however, you should always end the list with a generic font style.

Although it's not illustrated in this figure, you should realize that if an element contains child elements, the style properties for the parent element are also applied to the child elements. For example, if you wanted to display most of the text in the body of a document in 10-point Arial, you could add a Style attribute to the Body element with the appropriate style properties. Then, if you wanted to display a child element within the Body element in a different font, you could add a Style attribute to that element to override the style properties in the Body element.

How to use the Span element to apply styles

When you use inline styles, the style properties you specify apply to the entire element. If you want to apply a style to just a portion of an element, though, you can do that using a Span element. Figure 5-9 illustrates how this works.

The first example in this figure shows how you can use the Span element to format a portion of literal text. Similarly, the second example shows how you can format a portion of the text that's displayed for an Anchor element. If you look at how the literal text and Anchor element appear in a browser, you shouldn't have any trouble understanding how the Span element works.

Before I go on, you should realize that when you format literal text using the Formatting toolbar or the Format menu, Visual Studio creates a style class that defines that formatting instead of creating an inline style. As you saw in the Future Value application of chapter 2, this style class is stored in the Style element of the document, and its name consists of the word "style" appended with a number. For example, the first style class that's created is named style1, the second class is named style2, and so on. Then, a Span element is used to apply that style class to the selected text as illustrated in the third example in this figure. Here, a style class named style1 has been applied to the literal text. Although you can't see the definition of the style class in this figure, you can see how the text is formatted in the browser. You'll learn more about working with style classes later in this chapter.

Examples of Span elements

A Span element used to format a portion of literal text

```
This is the <span style="background-color: Blue; color: White">selected
</span> item.
```

A Span element used to format text that's displayed for an Anchor element

```
<a href="inlinestyles.aspx">Click here for a list of
    <span style="font-weight: bold; font-size: large; color: Red">
    Drastically Reduced</span> items</a>
```

A Span element that uses an automatically-generated style class to format text

```
<span class="style1">401K Future Value Calculator</span>
```

The elements viewed in a browser

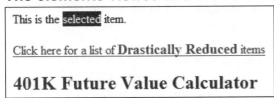

This is the ▆selected▆ item.

Click here for a list of **Drastically Reduced** items

401K Future Value Calculator

The Span element

Start tag	End tag	Description
<span>	</span>	Delimits HTML content.

Two attributes of a Span element

Attribute	Description
Style	Specifies one or more style properties that affect the appearance of the text within the Span element.
Class	Specifies one or more style classes that define the style rules to be applied to the text within the Span element.

Description

- The Span element delimits content within an HTML document. It's typically used to apply styles to all or part of the text within another element.
- When you format selections of text using the controls on the Formatting toolbar, Visual Studio often inserts a Span element to apply the formatting you select.
- See figure 5-8 for some common properties of the Style attribute.
- See figure 5-11 for more information on creating and using style classes.

Figure 5-9   How to use the Span element to apply styles

How to use an internal style sheet

An *internal style sheet* contains a set of *style rules* that are defined within an HTML document. Each style rule specifies a list of style properties that can be applied to one or more HTML elements. The code at the top of figure 5-10 illustrates how this works.

To start, you should notice that the style rules are coded within a Style element, which in turn is coded within the Head element for the document. A single attribute, Type, is specified for this element. This attribute specifies the language that the style sheet is written in, and it's required.

The first two style rules in this style sheet are associated with specific HTML elements. This type of style rule, called an *element-based style*, is applied automatically any time you use the specified element in the document. For example, the first style rule is applied to the Body element of this document, and the second style rule is applied to the H1 element.

The third style rule defines a *style class* named Title that can be applied to any HTML element. To apply a style class, you name the class on the Class attribute for the element. In the previous figure, for example, you saw an automatically-generated style class that was applied using a Span element. In this figure, I applied the Title style class to a P element.

Note that because both the H1 and Title style rules are applied to child elements of the Body element, the style properties they specify override the style properties specified by the Body style rule. The browser output shown in this figure should help you understand how this works. Here, only the last line of text is formatted according to the Body style rule.

The code for an HTML document that uses internal styles

```
<head runat="server">
    <title>Chapter 5: Internal Style Sheet</title>
    <style type="text/css">
        body {font-family: Times New Roman, Serif; font-size: 11 pt;}
        h1 {font-family: Arial, Helvetica, Sans-Serif;
            font-size: 14px; font-weight: bold; color: Blue;}
        .Title {font-family: Arial, Sans-Serif; font-size: 30pt;
                color: Blue; font-weight: bold; font-style: italic;}
    </style>
</head>
<body>
    <form id="form1" runat="server">
    <div>
        <p class="Title">Halloween Superstore</p>
        <h1>Halloween Supplies for the Discerning Haunter</h1>
        This is standard body text.
    </div>
    </form>
</body>
```

The elements viewed in a browser

Halloween Superstore

Halloween Supplies for the Discerning Haunter

This is standard body text.

The Style element

Tag	Description
<style>	Defines a style sheet for the page.

One attribute of a Style element

Attribute	Description
Type	The CSS language that the style sheet is written in.

Description

- An *internal style sheet* contains *style rules* that specify a list of style properties.
- A style rule can be defined for a specific HTML element, in which case the style is applied automatically whenever an element of the specified type appears in the document.
- A style rule can also define a *style class*, which is applied when the class name is specified on the Class attribute for an element.
- An internal style sheet is coded in the Style element, which must be coded within the Head element for the page.

Figure 5-10   How to use an internal style sheet

How to use classes in a style sheet

You've already seen one way to use style classes in a style sheet. Now, figure 5-11 presents some additional ways to use style classes. Keep in mind as you review this information that you're more likely to use style classes with Visual Studio 2008 than with previous versions of Visual Studio. That's because Visual Studio 2008 creates style classes automatically when you format text. In addition, it provides a variety of tools for working with style classes. You'll learn about two of those tools later in this chapter.

With *regular classes*, you can define more than one style rule for the same element. In addition, you can define a generic style rule that can be applied to any element. The first set of examples in this figure illustrates how this works.

The first statement shows how to define a style rule for a class that can be used only with a specific element. To do that, you code the element name, followed by a period and the class name you want to use for the class. Then, you code the style properties just as you would for any other style. To apply a style class to an element, you name the class on the Class attribute for that element as illustrated in the second statement.

The third statement shows how to define a style rule for a class that can be used with any element. To do that, you simply omit the element name from the beginning of the style rule. Then, you can apply the class to any element using its Class attribute. You've already seen several examples like this in this book.

In addition to the regular classes you define, HTML also provides for *pseudo-classes*. The names of these classes are predefined and, in some cases, can be applied only to specific elements. The Link and Visited classes, for example, can only be applied to an A element, as indicated by the first table in this figure. You can use these classes to specify the style for an A element based on its state. If the user hasn't clicked on the link defined by the element, it's displayed with the style specified by the Link class. Otherwise, it's displayed with the style specified by the Visited class.

Unlike the pseudo-classes you use for A elements, you can apply the Hover, Active, and Focus classes, called *dynamic pseudo-classes*, to any element. In this case, the class that's used is based on a user action. If the user points to the element with the mouse, for example, the element is displayed with the style specified by the Hover class. And if the user moves the focus to the element, it's displayed with the style specified by the Focus class.

The last three style rules in this figure illustrate how you might use pseudo-classes with an A element. Here, the first style rule defines the basic formatting for the element: 9-point Arial. Then, the second style rule specifies that after the user clicks on the link defined by the element, it should be displayed in blue. Finally, if the user points to the link, it should be displayed in bold.

How to use regular classes

A style rule that can be used only with the specified element

```
p.ProductList {font-size: x-large; font-family: Arial, Sans-Serif}
```

An element that uses the style rule

```
<p class="ProductList">Ugly Rat</p>
```

A style rule for a generic class

```
.ProductList {font-size: x-large; font-family: Arial, Sans-Serif}
```

Pseudo-classes for the Anchor element

Tag	Class	Description
\<a\>	Link	The style that's applied to links that haven't been visited by the user.
\<a\>	Visited	The style that's applied to links that have been visited by the user.

Dynamic pseudo-classes

Class	Description
Hover	The style that's applied while the user points to an element with a pointing device (usually the mouse).
Active	The style that's applied while an element is being activated by the user.
Focus	The style that's applied while an element has the focus.

Style rules that include a pseudo-class and a dynamic pseudo-class

```
a {font-family: Arial, Sans-Serif; font-size: 9pt}
a:visited {color: Blue}
a:hover {font-weight: bold}
```

Description

- You can use style classes to define styles that can be used with any element, or to define two or more styles for the same element. You can define your own *regular classes* or use predefined *pseudo-classes*.

- To define a regular class that can be used only with a specified element, code the name of the element, followed by a period, followed by the class name and style properties. To define a generic class that can be used with any element, omit the element name.

- To use a regular class, name it on the Class attribute of the element you want to apply it to.

- To define a pseudo-class, code the name of the element, followed by a colon, followed by the class name and the style properties. The styles defined by these classes are applied automatically when the specified condition occurs.

- The pseudo-classes you're most likely to use are the ones for the Anchor element and the *dynamic pseudo-classes* shown above. You can use the dynamic pseudo-classes with any element. The style rules for dynamic pseudo-classes must always be coded after any other style rules.

Figure 5-11   How to use classes in a style sheet

How to add and modify style rules

To simplify the task of creating style rules, you can use the New Style dialog box shown in figure 5-12. This dialog box lets you create element-based styles as well as style classes. It also lets you select whether a style is defined in the current page or in a new or existing style sheet. In this case, the Style Sheet selections refer to external style sheets, which you'll learn about in the next figure.

As you can see in this figure, the New Style dialog box separates the style properties into several categories. To display a specific category, you simply click on the category name in the list at the left side of the dialog box. In this figure, for example, you can see the properties in the Font category, which are the ones you'll use most often.

Note here that the font color for the style rule that's being created is specified as a color value rather than a color name. This value is generated automatically when you drop down the Color list and then select a color from the available palettes. Although you can also enter a color name in the Color box, you'll typically use color values because they provide a wider range of colors.

As you select style properties, a preview of the style and the style attributes are shown at the bottom of the dialog box. When the style looks the way you want it to, you can click the OK button to create it. If you selected one or more elements or text before you displayed the New Style dialog box, you can also apply the new style to those elements or that text when you create it. To do that, just select the Apply option in the upper right portion of the dialog box.

To modify an existing style, you can use the Modify Style dialog box. This dialog box is similar to the New Style dialog box, but it doesn't include the options at the top of the New Style dialog box. So you can only use it to change the attributes for a style.

The New Style dialog box

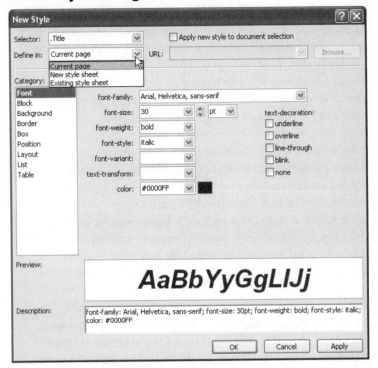

Description

- You can use the New Style dialog box to generate style rules for you. To display the New Style dialog box, choose the Format➔New Style command.

- The Selector drop-down list lets you select an element that you want the style to apply to or enter the name of the style class you want to create.

- The Define In drop-down list lets you determine whether the style is added to the current page (an internal style sheet) or a new or existing external style sheet. See figure 5-13 for information on external style sheets.

- The Category list at the left side of the New Style dialog box lets you display different categories of style settings.

- If you want to apply the style you create to one or more elements or literal text, select those elements or text before you display the New Style dialog box. Then, select the Apply New Style To Document Selection option.

- To display the Modify Style dialog box, select the elements or literal text whose style you want to modify. Then, click the ellipsis button that appears when you click the Style property in the Properties window. This dialog box lets you change all the categories of attributes that are available from the New Style dialog box.

Figure 5-12   How to add and modify style rules

How to use an external style sheet

Although an internal style sheet provides a convenient way of formatting the elements in a document, you'll typically use an external style sheet to define the basic formatting for a document. That way, you can use the same styles for each document you create in a web site without having to define the styles in each page. Then, if you need to add or modify a style for a specific document, you can do that by creating a style rule in an internal style sheet or by using an inline style.

Figure 5-13 shows how to use an external style sheet. Like an internal style sheet, an *external style sheet* contains a set of style rules. Unlike an internal style sheet, the style rules for an external style sheet are stored in a separate file. In this case, the style rules are stored in a file named Murach.css.

To use an external style sheet, a page must include a Link element in its document head. In the next figure, you'll learn two techniques you can use to generate a Link element from Visual Studio. For now, you just need to understand the three attributes presented in this figure in case you want to code the Link element yourself.

The first attribute, Href, specifies the URL of the style sheet you want to use. The Link element in this figure, for example, specifies the Murach.css style sheet. The second attribute, Rel, indicates that the link is for a style sheet. And the third attribute, Type, indicates the MIME type of the link. The *MIME* type is used by a browser for applications that send email. Because of that, you won't need to code this attribute for most applications. However, it's included automatically when you generate a Link element from Visual Studio.

The code for the Murach.css style sheet

```
body {font-family: 'Times New Roman', Times, serif; font-size: 11pt;}

.H1 {font-family: Arial, Helvetica, sans-serif; font-size: 30pt;
     font-weight: bold; color: #0000FF;}
.H2 {font-family: Arial, Helvetica, sans-serif;
     font-size: 14pt; color: #0000FF;}
.H3 {font-family: Arial, Helvetica, sans-serif;
     font-size: 12pt; color: #0000FF;}

a {font-family: Arial, Helvetica, sans-serif; font-size: 9pt;}
```

The code in an HTML document that links to the style sheet

```
<head>
    <title>Chapter 5: Shopping Cart</title>
    <link href="Murach.css" rel="stylesheet" type="text/css" />
</head>
```

The Link element

Tag	Description
<link>	Defines the link to an external style sheet.

Attributes of the Link element

Attribute	Description
Href	The URL of the document to be linked. For a style sheet, the document must have a file extension of *css*.
Rel	The relationship between the Link element and the URL specified in the Href attribute. For a style sheet, supply a value of stylesheet.
Type	The MIME (Multipurpose Internet Mail Extension) type of the Link element. For a style sheet, supply a value of text/css. Required only for email applications.

Description

- An *external style sheet* contains style rules just like an internal style sheet, but those styles are stored in a separate file.
- To link an HTML document to an external style sheet, you include a Link element that identifies the style sheet within the document's Head element.

Figure 5-13   How to use an external style sheet

Visual Studio features for working with external style sheets

Although you can create an external style sheet using any text editor, Visual Studio provides some features that make it easy to create and work with external style sheets. These features are described in figure 5-14. To create a new style sheet, for example, you can use the Style Sheet template in the Add New Item dialog box. When you use this template, a style sheet with an empty Body style is created.

To work with an existing style sheet, you display it in a Text Editor window. Then, you can add a style rule using the Add Style Rule dialog box shown in this figure. As you can see, this dialog box lets you define a style rule for an element, for a class, or for an element with a specified ID. (ID is an attribute you can use to uniquely identify an element.) Note that if you create a style rule for a class, a generic class is defined by default. To define a class for a specific element, check the Optional Element option and then select the element from the drop-down list. A preview of the style rule appears near the lower right corner of the dialog box. Then, you can click the add button (>) to create the style rule. When you're done creating style rules, you can click the OK button to add the style rules to the style sheet.

When you add a new style rule, Visual Studio creates the rule without any style properties. After I added the style rule shown in this figure, for example, this code was added to the style sheet:

```
p.ProductList
{
}
```

Then, you can add properties to the style rule using the Modify Style dialog box you learned about in figure 5-12. To display the Modify Style dialog box, click anywhere in the style rule and choose the Styles→Build Style command.

You should also notice the CSS Outline window that's displayed at the left side of the Visual Studio window when a style sheet is displayed. This window displays the style rules defined by the style sheet in a tree structure. You can use this tree to navigate to a specific style rule by expanding the folder that contains that rule and then clicking on the rule.

An external style sheet in Visual Studio

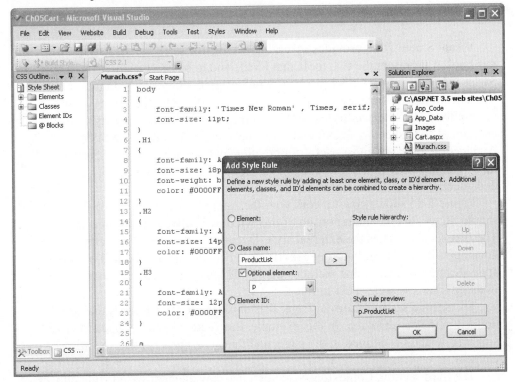

Discussion

- To create an external style sheet, choose the Web Site→Add New Item command. Then, select the Style Sheet template from the list of available templates, type the name you want to use for the new style sheet, and click Add.

- To edit an existing style sheet, double-click on it in the Solution Explorer to display it in a Text Editor window.

- To link a page to a style sheet, display the page in the Web Forms Designer. Then, choose the Format→Attach Style Sheet command and select the style sheet from the Select Style Sheet dialog box that's displayed.

- You can also link a page to a style sheet by displaying the page in Source view and then dragging the style sheet from the Solution Explorer to the Head element for the page.

- To add a style rule to a style sheet, use the Add Style Rule dialog box. To display this dialog box, open the style sheet in an editor window, then choose Styles→Add Style Rule.

- You can also use the New Style dialog box to create a new style sheet or to add a style rule to an existing style sheet (see figure 5-12).

- To modify a style rule, click anywhere in the rule and choose the Styles→Build Style command to display the Modify Style dialog box.

- You can use the CSS Outline window (View→Document Outline) that's displayed at the left side of the Visual Studio window to navigate to the style rule you want.

Figure 5-14   Visual Studio features for working with external style sheets

How to use the Apply Styles window to work with styles

Visual Studio 2008 provides several new tools for working with styles. In this book, I'll present the two tools that I've found to be most useful: The Apply Styles window and the CSS Properties window. Two other tools you may want to use from time to time are the Manage Styles window and the Style Application toolbar. The Manage Styles window is most useful for moving styles from an internal style sheet to an external style sheet and vice versa. The Style Application toolbar is most useful for creating and modifying styles. For more information on how to use these tools, please see the Visual Studio documentation.

Figure 5-15 shows how to work with the Apply Styles window. To start, you should notice that the main portion of this window is divided into three sections. The first section names the external style sheet that's attached to the current document, if any, and it lists any generic style classes that are defined in that style sheet. In this case, that includes the H1, H2, and H3 style classes you saw in the Murach.css style sheet in figure 5-13.

The second section, Current Page, lists any generic style classes that are defined in the current page. In this example, this section is empty because a single style class is defined in the page, and that style class is for a specific element.

The third section, Contextual Selectors, lists any element-based style classes that can be applied to the current selection, along with any element-based styles that have been applied. In this figure, the selection consists of literal text that's part of a P element. Because of that, the p.Center style that's defined in the current page is included in this section. Notice that the heading above this style indicates where it's defined. Also notice that an outline appears around the p.Center item, which indicates that this style has been applied to the selected text.

In addition to the three sections shown here, the Apply Styles window can also include an Inline Style section. If this section is displayed, it simply indicates that the current selection is formatted with an inline style.

As its name implies, the Apply Styles window is most useful for applying styles to a document. To apply a style, you just select the elements or text you want to apply it to and then click on the style in the Apply Styles window. Before you do that, though, you may want to be sure that the style you're applying is defined with the correct attributes. To do that, just point to the style in the Apply Styles window to display the definition of the style as shown here.

In addition to applying styles, you can use the Apply Styles window to create a new style, attach a style sheet, and remove styles from a selection. You can also use the drop-down list for an individual style to perform a number of functions. If you take a few minutes to experiment with this window, you will quickly see how useful it can be.

The Apply Styles window

Description

- The Apply Styles window is a new feature of Visual Studio 2008 that lets you work with the style classes defined in both internal and external style sheets. To display this window, use the View→Apply Styles command.

- To view the style properties for a style class, just point to the class in the Apply Styles window.

- To apply a style class to an element or literal text, select the element or text and then click on the style class in the Apply Styles window.

- The list of style classes is divided into several sections, including the classes that are available from an external style sheet (listed under the name of the style sheet), the classes that are defined in the current page (listed under Current Page), and the element-based classes that can applied to the current selection (listed under Contextual Selectors).

- Element-based styles are also listed in the Apply Styles window if an element with that style is selected. You can't apply element-based styles from this window, though.

- You can use the drop-down list for a style class to perform a variety of functions, including applying the style, going to the code for the style, selecting all elements that the style is applied to, creating a new style from the existing style, modifying the style, and deleting the style.

- You can use the two links at the top of the Apply Styles window to create a new style and to attach a style sheet to the current document. You can use the Options button to control what styles are displayed in the window.

Figure 5-15   How to use the Apply Styles window to work with styles

How to use the CSS Properties window to work with styles

Figure 5-16 presents the CSS Properties window. Although you can use this window to create new inline styles and style classes, it's most useful for working with the styles that have already been applied to a document. So that's what I'll focus on in this topic.

The CSS Properties window is divided into two panes. The Applied Rules pane at the top of the window lists the styles that have been applied to the current element. If you look at the Design view portion of the screen in this figure, for example, you'll see that the cursor is in the second line of literal text. If you review the code in Source view, you'll see that the Span element that contains this text is formatted with the H2 class that's defined by the Murach.css style sheet. In addition, the P element that contains the Span element is formatted with the Center class that's defined by the page. Finally, the Body element that contains the P element is formatted with the Body style that's defined in the style sheet. So all three of these styles—Body, p.Center, and .H2—are listed in the Applied Rules pane in the order that they're applied.

When you select an element in Design view, all the attributes defined by that style are listed in the CSS Properties pane. In this figure, for example, you can see the attributes for the H2 style. Then, you can change these attributes any way you want and the changes will be recorded in the style rule. That means that the changes you make will be applied to any element that's formatted with the selected style.

You can also change the attributes for any styles higher up in the hierarchy than the style that's applied to the current element. To do that, just select the style in the Applied Rules pane to display the style properties in the CSS Properties pane. Note that if a property of a style is overridden by another style that's applied to the current element, a red line will appear through the property name. If you selected the Body style in this example, for instance, the CSS Properties window would indicate that the Color, Font-Family, and Font-size properties are all overridden. In this case, they're overridden by the H2 style.

To make it easier to work with the style properties for an element, you can use the buttons at the top of the CSS Properties window. By default, the third button, Show Set Properties On Top, is selected, which is usually what you want. If you want to list the properties by category or alphabetically, however, you can click one of the first two buttons. And if you want to display only the properties that have been applied to the current element, you can click the Summary button.

The CSS Properties window

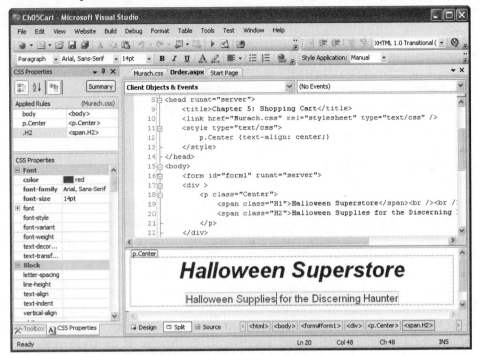

Description

- The CSS Properties window is another new feature of Visual Studio 2008 for working with styles. It's most useful for reviewing and modifying the styles that have been applied to a page. To display this window, use the View→CSS Properties command.

- The Applied Rules pane of the CSS Properties window lists the styles that have been applied to the currently selected element in the order in which they're applied. It also indicates if the style is an inline style or a style rule that's stored in an internal or external style sheet.

- The CSS Properties pane of the CSS Properties window lists the style properties that have been applied to the currently selected element. If you select a style rule from the Applied Rules pane, a red line will appear through any properties of that style that are overridden by another style.

- To modify a style, select an element with that style in Design view, select the style in the Applied Rules pane, and then change its properties in the CSS Properties pane.

- You can use the buttons at the top of the CSS Properties window to sort the list of properties by category, alphabetically, or by the properties that have been applied. You can click the Summary button to display only the properties that are applied to the currently selected element.

- You can also use the CSS Properties window to create new inline styles and style classes for the page. However, this is usually more easily done using other techniques.

Figure 5-16   How to use the CSS Properties window to work with styles

How to code tables

HTML *tables* present content in grids of *rows* and *columns*. You can use tables to present tabular information in a way that resembles a spreadsheet. You can also use tables as a way to control the overall layout of page elements such as titles, banners, navigation bars, and content areas. You learned the basic skills for creating tables in chapter 2. Now, you'll learn more about the HTML you can use to code tables.

How to create a table

Figure 5-17 presents the basic HTML elements you use to create a table. To start, you use a Table element to identify the start and end of the table. Within the Table element, you use one or more Tr elements to define each row of the table. (Tr stands for Table Row.) Then, within each Tr element, you use one or more Td elements to create each *cell*. (Td stands for Table Data.)

The code shown in this figure defines a table that contains three rows, each with two cells. Below the code, you can see how the table is displayed in a browser. Tables are frequently used to align form content like this.

Notice that the HTML shown here doesn't specify the size of the table or its cells. Because of that, the sizes will change dynamically depending on the data in each cell. If that's not what you want, you can use some of the formatting attributes you'll learn about in the next figure to control the table and cell sizes.

In this example, the first cell in each row contains literal text, and the second cell in each row contains a text box. You should realize, however, that a cell can store any type of data, including other tables. In fact, it's common for a web page to consist of tables nested within other tables.

The HTML elements for working with tables

Element	Start tag	End tag	Description
Table	<table>	</table>	Defines the start and end of a table.
Tr	<tr>	</tr>	Defines the start and end of a row.
Td	<td>	</td>	Defines the start and end of a cell within a row.

The HTML code for a table

```
<p>Please enter the following information:</p>
<table cellspacing="5" cellpadding="5" border="1">
  <tr>
    <td align="right">First name:</td>
    <td><asp:TextBox id="txtFirstName" runat="server"></asp:TextBox></td>
  </tr>
  <tr>
    <td align="right">Last name:</td>
    <td><asp:TextBox id="txtLastName" runat="server"></asp:TextBox></td>
  </tr>
  <tr>
    <td align="right">Email address:</td>
    <td><asp:TextBox id="txtEmail" runat="server"></asp:TextBox></td>
  </tr>
</table>
```

The table displayed in a browser

Please enter the following information:

First name:	
Last name:	
Email address:	

Description

- A *table* consists of *rows* and *columns*. The intersection of a row and column is a *cell* that can hold content, such as text, images, controls, or even other tables.

- By default, the height and width of the cells in a table change dynamically depending on their content. However, you can specify static cell sizes as well as other table formatting options using the attributes and style properties presented in figure 5-18.

- Tables are often used to align form content and to control the overall layout of a page.

Figure 5-17   How to create a table

Common table attributes and style properties

Figure 5-18 presents some of the attributes you can use with Table, Tr, and Td elements. To control the border that's displayed around a table and between the cells in a table, for example, you set the Border attribute of the table. Notice that to hide the border, you can set this attribute to 0. To control the amount of space between the cells in a table, you set the Cellspacing attribute of the table. And to control the amount of space between the border and the contents of a cell, you set the Cellpadding attribute of the table.

Two of the attributes shown in this figure, Colspan and Rowspan, are essential when working with complicated table layouts. These attributes let you create cells that span two or more columns or rows. You'll see an example of a table that uses the Colspan attribute in the next figure.

This figure also shows some of the style properties you can use with table elements. You can use the Height and Width properties to set an absolute height or width for the table or for individual rows or cells. These properties are especially useful when you use a table to control page layout. Then, you'll want the total height and width of the table to be less than the total number of pixels for your target resolution. If you design a web site to be viewed best in a 1024x768 pixel window, for example, that usually means coding tables with widths less than 1004 pixels and heights less than 748 pixels. That leaves an extra 20 pixels for the horizontal and vertical scroll bars. Note that the width of a table includes the width of all of the cells plus the spacing between the cells.

Common attributes of the Table element

Attribute	Description
Border	Specifies the visual border of the table. To turn the border off, specify a value of 0. To specify the width of the border in pixels, specify a value of 1 or greater.
Cellspacing	Specifies the number of pixels between cells.
Cellpadding	Specifies the number of pixels between the contents of a cell and the edge of the cell.

Common attribute of the Tr element

Attribute	Description
Valign	Specifies the vertical alignment of the contents of the row. Acceptable values include Top, Bottom, and Middle.

Common attributes of the Td element

Attribute	Description
Align	Specifies the horizontal alignment of the contents of the cell. Acceptable values include Left, Right, and Center.
Colspan	Specifies the number of columns that the cell will span. This attribute is used to create wide cells that span two or more columns.
Rowspan	Specifies the number of rows that the cell will span. This attribute is used to create tall cells that span two or more rows.
Valign	Specifies the vertical alignment of the contents of the cell. Acceptable values include Top, Bottom, and Middle. This value overrides any alignment you specify for the row.

Common style properties for table elements

Property	Description
Height	The height of the element. To specify the height in pixels, use a number such as 60px. To specify the height as a percent of the parent element, use a number followed by the percent sign such as 20%. The height of the parent element must be specified explicitly.
Width	The width of the element. This works like the height property except that you don't have to specify the width of the parent element explicitly if you specify the width of the child element as a percent. You can also specify the width of a table using the Width attribute.
Background-color	The background color for the element. The background color of a row overrides the background color of the table, and the background color of a cell overrides the background color of the row.

Figure 5-18   Common table attributes and style properties

How to use a table to control the layout of a page

Figure 5-19 shows how to use a table to arrange a page that consists of three areas. A banner area is displayed at the top of the page, a navigation area is displayed at the left side of the page, and a content area occupies the rest of the page. This table consists of two rows. The first one consists of a single cell that contains the banner area. The second one consists of two cells that contain the navigation and content area.

The key to the HTML for this table is the Colspan attribute in the first Td element. It causes the cell in the first row to span both of the columns in that row. Also notice that the Border and Cellspacing attributes of the table are set to 0 so the cells will appear right next to each other. In addition, each cell has a different background color so you can see the area that it occupies. Although this is a relatively simple layout, it should help you begin to see how you can use tables to divide a page into distinct areas.

A table that defines a simple page layout

```
<table style="width: 750px" border="0" cellspacing="0">
    <tr style="height: 75px">
        <td colspan="2" style="background-color: Gray">
            Banner area
        </td>
    </tr>
    <tr style="height: 400px">
        <td style="width: 150px; background-color: Silver" valign="top">
            Navigation area
        </td>
        <td style="width: 600px; background-color: White" valign="top">
            Content area
        </td>
    </tr>
</table>
```

The table viewed in a browser

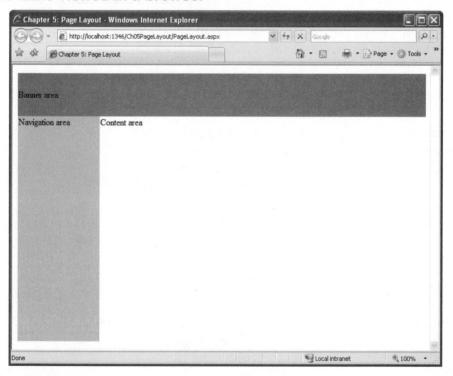

Description

- The Colspan attribute for the cell that makes up the banner area is set to 2 so that it spans both of the columns in the table.

- The Border attribute for the table is set to zero so no border appears around the table or between the cells in the table, and the Cellspacing attribute for the table is set to zero so there is no space between the cells in the table.

- Each cell is defined with a different color so you can see how the layout appears when displayed in the browser.

Figure 5-19   How to use a table to control the layout of a page

Perspective

The goal of this chapter has been to teach you the HTML essentials that you need for ASP.NET programming. So at this point, you should feel qualified to modify the HTML that's generated by Visual Studio so each form looks just the way you want it to. In some cases, you may even find that it's easier to use HTML for creating an element like a table from scratch than it is to use the features of Visual Studio for generating the HTML.

Above all, you should now be able to understand most of the HTML that's generated for a form. You should also understand much of the code that actually gets sent to the browser. Then, to complete your understanding of the code that gets generated for the controls of a form, the next chapter tells you more about asp elements.

Of course, there's a lot more to HTML than what's presented in this chapter. So if you want to learn more about HTML, you can get a book that's dedicated entirely to that topic. When you use Visual Studio to develop your forms, though, that shouldn't be necessary.

Terms

HTML document
HTML element
tag
start tag
end tag
content
attribute
comment
white space
render a control
root element
child element
parent element
directive block
self-closing tag
cascading style sheets (CSS)
inline style

internal style
external style
style property
internal style sheet
style rule
element-based style
style class
regular class
pseudo-class
dynamic pseudo-class
external style sheet
MIME (Multipurpose Internet Mail Extension)
table
row
column
cell

6

How to work with server controls

So far in this book, you've learned the basic skills for working with some of the most common server controls: labels, text boxes, buttons, drop-down lists, and list boxes. Now, this chapter presents some additional skills for working with these controls. It also presents the skills for working with other common controls, like check boxes and radio buttons, and some advanced controls, like the file upload and image map controls. When you complete this chapter, you'll be able to create ASP.NET web forms that use any of the server controls.

An introduction to server controls **202**
Types of server controls 202
The web server controls presented in this chapter 204
How to handle control events 206
How to use access keys with web server controls 208
How to set the focus on a web server control 208
How to set the default button control 208

How to work with button controls **210**
How to work with buttons, link buttons, and image buttons 210
How to use the e argument of an image button control 212
How to use the Command event 214

How to work with text boxes, labels, check boxes, and radio buttons **216**
How to work with text boxes and labels 216
How to work with check boxes and radio buttons 218
C# code for working with these controls 220

How to work with list controls **222**
Basic skills for working with list boxes and drop-down lists 222
Properties for working with list boxes, drop-down lists, and list items 224
Members for working with list item collections 226
How to use the ListItem Collection Editor 228
How to work with radio button lists and check box lists 230
How to work with bulleted lists and numbered lists 232

How to use other web server controls **234**
How to get the information you need for using a control 234
How to use the image control 236
How to use the hyperlink control 236
How to use the file upload control 238
How to use the image map control 240
How to use the calendar control 242

Perspective **244**

An introduction to server controls

In chapter 2, you learned how to add server controls to a web form and set control properties. Now, you'll learn about the different types of server controls and how you use them. You'll also see a summary of the web server controls that are presented in this chapter, you'll learn how to handle control events, and you'll learn three additional techniques ASP.NET provides for working with web server controls.

Types of server controls

Figure 6-1 describes the eight different types of server controls that you can use in your ASP.NET applications. These eight categories correspond to the groups in the Visual Studio Toolbox. For example, you'll find the standard controls in the Standard group of the Toolbox.

The controls you'll use most often are the standard controls, the data controls, and the validation controls. You'll learn how to use many of the standard controls in this chapter. Then, in chapter 7, you'll learn how to use the validation controls. And you'll learn how to use the data controls in chapters 13 through 18.

You'll use the next four types of controls only for special situations. For example, you can use the navigation controls to provide menus and path maps that let users navigate to various pages within your web site. You can use the login controls to manage access to your site. You can use the web part controls to build pages that users can customize. And you can use the AJAX extension controls to design pages where only parts of a page are updated during a postback. You'll learn about these types of controls in later chapters.

Together, the first seven types of controls are typically referred to as *web server controls*. As you know, a web server control is implemented by a class that you can use to work with the control from a web application that runs on a web server. In contrast, you can't work with the HTML controls from a web application. That's because these controls map directly to standard HTML elements. For example, the Text control maps directly to an Input element that has its Type attribute set to "Text".

If you want to work with an HTML control from a web application, you can convert it to a server control. To do that, just select the Run As Server Control command from the shortcut menu for the control. This adds a Runat attribute with the value "Server" to the HTML element. This attribute indicates that the element should be processed on the server. Then, you can work with the control using standard object-oriented techniques. Since *HTML server controls* don't provide the same functionality as the web server controls, however, you won't use them often.

Standard

- Commonly used user input controls such as labels, text boxes, and drop-down lists
- Many can be bound to a data source
- The MultiView and Wizard controls will be described in chapter 22

Data

- Databound user-interface controls that display data via a data source control
- Data source controls that access data from a variety of databases, XML data sources, and business objects
- Described in chapters 13 through 18

Validation

- Used to validate user input
- Work by running client-side script
- Can handle most validation requirements
- Described in chapter 7

Navigation

- Controls that provide menus and path maps for navigating a web site
- Described in chapter 10

Login

- Controls that provide user authentication
- Described in chapter 20

WebParts

- Controls that let you create a page from user-selectable components
- Described in chapter 24

AJAX Extensions

- Controls that provide for updating selected parts of a page during a postback
- Described in chapter 25

HTML

- Standard HTML controls that can be converted to HTML server controls
- Not commonly used in ASP.NET applications

Description

- The Toolbox contains several groups that contain more than 90 different controls. The headings in this figure correspond to the names of the groups in the Toolbox.

Figure 6-1   Types of server controls

The web server controls presented in this chapter

Figure 6-2 summarizes the web server controls that you'll learn about in this chapter. You'll find all of these controls in the Standard group of the Toolbox.

If you've developed Windows applications, you'll notice that many of these controls have Windows counterparts and operate similarly to the Windows controls. Because of that, you shouldn't have much difficulty learning how to use most of these controls. As you'll see in this chapter, however, some of the techniques you use to work with these controls are different from the techniques you use to work with their Windows counterparts. In addition, some of the functionality they provide is different. So you'll want to be sure to read about each control even if you're familiar with Windows controls.

Also, you should realize that there are other standard controls besides the ones shown in this figure. In fact, the Standard group of the Toolbox provides 28 different web server controls. You'll learn about a couple of the controls that aren't listed here in later chapters. And, later in this chapter, you'll learn how to use the Visual Studio documentation to get information about the other controls so you can use them too.

The web server controls presented in this chapter

Control	Name	Suggested prefix	Description
A	Label	lbl	Displays descriptive information.
abl	TextBox	txt	Lets the user enter or modify a text value.
ab	Button	btn	Submits a page for processing.
ab	LinkButton	lbtn	Submits a page for processing.
	ImageButton	ibtn	Submits a page for processing.
A	HyperLink	hlnk	Lets the user move to another page in the application.
	DropDownList	ddl	Lets the user choose an item from a list that drops down from the control.
	ListBox	lst	Lets the user choose one or more items from a list.
	CheckBox	chk	Turns an option on or off.
	CheckBoxList	cbl	Turns options in a list of options on or off.
	RadioButton	rdo	Turns an option on or off. Only one radio button in a group can be on.
	RadioButtonList	rbl	Turns an option in a list of options on or off. Only one radio button in the list can be on.
	Image	img	Displays an image.
	ImageMap	imap	Displays an image with one or more clickable areas that submit the page for processing when clicked.
	BulletedList	blst	Displays a bulleted or numbered list.
	Calendar	cln	Displays a calendar and lets the user select one or more dates.
	FileUpload	upl	Displays a text box and a button that lets the user browse for a file to be uploaded.

Description

- The button, image button, and link button controls all provide the same functionality. They differ only in how they appear on the form.
- The check box list and radio button list controls serve as containers for a collection of check box or radio button items. They're typically used to create a list of check boxes or radio buttons that are bound to a data source. If you need more control over the layout of the check boxes or radio buttons, though, you can use individual controls.

Figure 6-2   The web server controls presented in this chapter

How to handle control events

Like other objects, server controls have events that are fired when certain actions are performed on them. When you click on a button control, for example, the Click event is fired. If your application needs to respond to an event, you code a method called an *event handler* as shown in figure 6-3.

When you generate an event handler from Visual Studio, an event attribute that names the event handler is added to the asp code for the control. Then, you enter the code you want to be executed when that event occurs within the event handler. This is illustrated by the first example in this figure. Here, the OnClick attribute of a button named btnCancel indicates that an event handler named btnCancel_Click will be executed when the Click event of the control is raised.

You can also use a single event handler to handle more than one event. To do that, you name the event handler on the appropriate event attribute of each control as illustrated in the second example. Here, the event handler will handle the Click event of two buttons named btnPrevious and btnNext. Notice in this example that I changed the name of the event handler to indicate that it processes more than one event.

This figure also lists some of the most common control events and their associated attributes. As I present each of the web server controls in this chapter, I'll illustrate how you can use these events.

Code that handles a Click event using the OnClick attribute

The asp tag for a button control

```
<asp:Button id="btnCancel" runat="server" Text="Cancel Order"
    OnClick="btnCancel_Click" />
```

The event handler for the Click event of the control

```
protected void btnCancel_Click(object sender, EventArgs e)
{
    Session.Remove("Cart");
    Response.Redirect("Order.aspx");
}
```

The asp tags for two button controls that use the same event handler

```
<asp:Button id="btnPrevious" runat="server" Text="Previous"
    OnClick="NavigationButtons_Click" />
<asp:Button id="btnNext" runat="server" Text="Next"
    OnClick="NavigationButtons_Click" />
```

Common control events

Event	Attribute	Controls
Click	OnClick	Button, image button, link button, image map
Command	OnCommand	Button, image button, link button
TextChanged	OnTextChanged	Text box
SelectedIndexChanged	OnSelectedIndexChanged	Drop-down list, list box, radio button list, check box list
CheckedChanged	OnCheckedChanged	Check box, radio button

Description

- An *event handler* is a method that's called when a specified event occurs. An event handler must be declared with Public or Protected scope.

- To wire an event to an event handler, you name the handler in the appropriate event attribute of the control. For example, you use the OnClick attribute to name the event handler that's executed when the user clicks a control.

- A single event handler can be used to handle more than one event. To do that, you name the handler on each event attribute of each control you want it to handle.

Figure 6-3   How to handle control events

How to use access keys with web server controls

Most Windows applications use *access keys* (also called *accelerator keys*) that let the user select controls by using keyboard shortcuts. If, for example, you designate F as the access key for an input field that accepts a customer's first name, the user can move the focus directly to this field by pressing Alt+F.

As figure 6-4 shows, ASP.NET lets you create access keys for web applications too. To create an access key, you simply add the AccessKey attribute to the control you want to create the keyboard shortcut for. Since the AccessKey attribute is defined by the System.Web.UI.WebControls.WebControl class, you can use it with any web control.

When you use access keys with text boxes and other controls that are identified by literal text, it's common to underline the access key in the literal text. To do that, you can use a Span element with the Text-decoration property set to underline. This is illustrated by the text that identifies the two text boxes in this figure.

If you use a label to identify a control instead of literal text, you can assign the access key to the label and then underline the appropriate letter of the label. In this case, you should also code the AssociatedControlID attribute to specify the control that should receive the focus when the user uses the access key.

Unfortunately, ASP.NET doesn't provide a way to underline the access key in a button control. That's because buttons are rendered using the <input type="submit"> HTML element, which doesn't provide a way to format the text displayed by the button. You can still specify an access key, though, as illustrated by the aspx code in this figure.

How to set the focus on a web server control

ASP.NET provides two features that let you set the focus to a specific control on a form. First, you can use the DefaultFocus attribute of the form to determine which control receives the focus when the page is first displayed. In figure 6-4, for example, this attribute is set to the txtName control.

Second, you can move the focus to a control at runtime. To do that, you use the Focus method of the control. The statement shown in this figure, for example, moves the focus to the txtEmail control.

How to set the default button control

ASP.NET also lets you set the button that's activated by default when you press the Enter key. To do that, you set the DefaultButton attribute of the form. In the example in this figure, this attribute is set to the btnNext button. Because of that, the form is posted back to the server when the Enter key is pressed, and the event handler for the Click event of the Next button is executed.

A form that uses access keys and default focus and button attributes

```
Please enter your contact information:

Name:  [                    ]
Email: [                    ]

[ Previous ]  [ Next ]
```

The aspx code for the form

```
<form id="form1" runat="server" defaultfocus="txtName" defaultbutton="btnNext">
<div>
    Please enter your contact information:<br /><br />
    <table>
        <tr>
            <td style="width: 75px"><span style="text-decoration:
                underline">N</span>ame:</td>
            <td style="width: 100px">
                <asp:TextBox ID="txtName" runat="server"
                    AccessKey="N"></asp:TextBox></td></tr>
        <tr>
            <td style="width: 75px"><span style="text-decoration:
                underline">E</span>mail:</td>
            <td style="width: 100px">
                <asp:TextBox ID="txtEmail" runat="server"
                    AccessKey="E"></asp:TextBox></td></tr></table><br />
    <asp:Button ID="btnPrevious" runat="server" AccessKey="P"
        Text="Previous" OnClick="btnPrevious_Click" /> 
    <asp:Button ID="btnNext" runat="server" AccessKey="N" Text="Next"
        OnClick="btnNext_Click" /><br />
</div>
</form>
```

A statement that moves the focus to a control

```
txtEmail.Focus();
```

Description

- You can use the AccessKey attribute on a web server control to specify a keyboard shortcut for the control. To use the keyboard shortcut, the user holds down the Alt key and presses the *access key* to move the focus to the control.

- If you use literal text to identify another control, you can identify the access key used by that control by underlining the appropriate letter in the literal text as shown above.

- If you use a label to identify another control, you can set the AccessKey attribute for the label and then set the AssociatedControlID attribute to the other control. When the user presses the access key for the label, the focus will be moved to the associated control.

- You can set the control that receives the focus when a form is first displayed using the DefaultFocus attribute of the form. To move the focus to a control at runtime, use the Focus method of the control.

- You can set the button that causes a form to be posted back when you press the Enter key using the DefaultButton attribute of the form.

Figure 6-4   How to use access keys and set form defaults

How to work with button controls

Most web forms have at least one button control that the user can click to submit the form to the server for processing, commonly called a *submit button*. In the topics that follow, you'll learn how to use all three types of button controls that ASP.NET provides: buttons, link buttons, and image buttons.

How to work with buttons, link buttons, and image buttons

Figure 6-5 presents the three types of button controls. These controls differ only in how they appear to the user. This is illustrated by the three buttons shown at the top of this figure. As you can see, a *button* displays text within a rectangular area. A *link button* displays text that looks like a hyperlink. And an *image button* displays an image.

This figure also presents the asp tags for the three buttons that are illustrated. For the button and link button, the Text attribute provides the text that's displayed for the control. For the image button, the ImageUrl attribute provides the URL address of the image that's displayed on the button. In some cases, though, a browser may not be able to display the image. Because of that, you should also code the AlternateText attribute so it provides the text that's displayed if the browser isn't able to display the image.

When a user clicks one of the button controls, ASP.NET raises two events: Click and Command. You can see an event handler for the Click event of a button control in this figure. Notice that this event handler receives two arguments. The sender argument represents the control that was clicked. Because this argument has a type of Object, you'll need to convert it to a button control if you want to access the properties and methods of the control. You might want to do that, for example, if you code an event handler that handles the processing for more than one button. Then, you can use the Id property of the control to determine which button was clicked. An easier way to do that, however, is to use the Command event. You'll see how to use this event in figure 6-7.

The second argument that's passed to the event handler of a Click event, e, contains event-specific information. You're most likely to use this argument with an image button control to determine where the user clicked on the image. You'll learn more about that in the next figure.

Of course, the Click and Command event handlers are executed only if the page posts back to itself. If a value is specified for the PostBackUrl attribute, however, the page at the specified URL is executed and displayed. This is the cross-page posting feature you learned about in chapter 3.

Incidentally, from this point on in this chapter and this book, the figures will often present the asp elements for the controls that are used. By studying the code for these controls, you can quickly see how their attributes are set. Please keep in mind, though, that you usually add a control to a form by using the Designer, and you set the properties for a control by using the Properties window. Then, the code for the asp element in the aspx file is generated automatically.

A button, a link button, and an image button in a browser

The asp tags for the three buttons

```
<asp:Button ID="btnAdd" runat="server" Text="Add to Cart"
    OnClick="btnAdd_Click" />
    
<asp:LinkButton ID="lbtnCheckOut" runat="server"
    PostBackUrl="~/CheckOut1.aspx">Check Out</asp:LinkButton>
    
<asp:ImageButton ID="ibtnCart" runat="server" AlternateText="Cart"
    ImageUrl="~/Images/cart.gif" Height="60px" Width="68px"
    PostBackUrl="~/Cart.aspx" />
```

Common button attributes

Attribute	Description
Text	(Button and LinkButton controls only) The text displayed by the button. For a LinkButton control, the text can be coded as content between the start and end tags or as the value of the Text attribute.
ImageUrl	(ImageButton control only) The image to be displayed for the button.
AlternateText	(ImageButton control only) The text to be displayed if the browser can't display the image.
CausesValidation	Determines whether page validation occurs when you click the button. The default is True.
CommandName	A string value that's passed to the Command event when a user clicks the button.
CommandArgument	A string value that's passed to the Command event when a user clicks the button.
PostBackUrl	The URL of the page that should be requested when the user clicks the button.

An event handler for the Click event of a button control

```
protected void btnAccept_Click(object sender, EventArgs e)
{
    this.AddInvoice();
    Response.Redirect("Confirmation.aspx");
}
```

Description

- When a user clicks a *button*, *link button*, or *image button*, the page specified in the PostBackUrl attribute is loaded and executed. If this attribute isn't included, the page is posted back to the server and the Click and Command events are raised. You can code event handlers for either or both of these events.

- Two arguments are passed to the Click event handler: sender and e. Sender is the control that the user clicked, and e contains event-specific information. You can use the e argument with the image button control to determine where the user clicked in the image. See figure 6-6 for more information.

- See figure 6-7 for information on coding an event handler for the Command event.

Figure 6-5   How to work with buttons, link buttons, and image buttons

How to use the e argument of an image button control

In some cases, the processing that's performed when the user clicks on an image button will depend on where within the button the user clicks. To illustrate, consider the image button shown at the top of figure 6-6 that represents four navigation buttons. (This image uses the standard icons for First (<<), Previous (<), Next (>), and Last (>>)). This image button could be used to let the user navigate through pages in a section of your web site or to different rows of a data table.

To process an image button like this, you can use the X and Y properties of the e argument that's passed to the Click event handler of the button. These properties indicate the x and y coordinates where the user clicked. The event handler shown in this figure illustrates how this works.

In this example, an if statement is used to determine the value of the X property. If it's between 0 and 23, it indicates that the user clicked the << icon. Then, the event handler executes the GoToFirstRow method. If it's between 24 and 47, it indicates that the user clicked the < icon, and the GoToPreviousRow method is executed. If it's between 48 and 71, it indicates that the user clicked the > icon, and the GoToNextRow method is executed. Last, if it's between 72 and 95, it indicates that the user clicked the >> icon, and the GoToLastRow method is executed. Notice that it's not necessary to check the y coordinate in this example. That's because all of the icons have the same y-coordinate range.

An image used for an image button control

The asp tag for the control

```
<asp:ImageButton ID="ibtnNavigate" runat="server"
    ImageUrl="~/Images/navbuttons.gif" Height="24px" Width="96px"
    OnClick="ibtnNavigate_Click" />
```

An event handler for the Click event of the control

```
protected void ibtnNavigate_Click(object sender, ImageClickEventArgs e)
{
    if (e.X >= 0 & e.X <= 23)
        this.GoToFirstRow();
    else if (e.X >= 24 & e.X <= 47)
        this.GoToPreviousRow();
    else if (e.X >= 48 & e.X <= 71)
        this.GoToNextRow();
    else if (e.X >= 72 & e.X <= 95)
        this.GoToLastRow();
}
```

Properties of the ImageClickEventArgs class

Property	Description
X	An integer that represents the x coordinate where the user clicked the image button.
Y	An integer that represents the y coordinate where the user clicked the image button.

Description

- When the user clicks an ImageButton control, ASP.NET calls the Click event handler for the control and passes the x and y coordinates where the user clicked the image as properties of the e argument.
- You can use the X and Y properties to determine the processing that's performed when the user clicks on a particular part of an image.

Figure 6-6   How to use the e argument of an image button control

How to use the Command event

Figure 6-7 shows how you can use the Command event to process a group of button controls using a single event handler. Like the Click event, this event receives both a sender argument and an e argument. In this case, the e argument represents a CommandEventArgs object.

The two properties of the CommandEventArgs class are shown in this figure. You can use these properties to get the CommandName and CommandArgument properties of a control. When you create a button control, you can set the CommandName and CommandArgument properties to any string value. Then, you can examine them in the Command event handler to determine how the application should respond when the user clicks the button.

The examples in this figure illustrate how this works. The first example shows the asp tags for four button controls. Notice that a different CommandName value is assigned to each one. However, the same event handler is named on the OnCommand attributes. That way, the same event handler will handle the Command event of all four controls. Although you can also assign CommandArgument values to each control, that's not necessary here.

The second example shows an event handler that processes the Command event of all four controls. To do that, it uses a switch statement to test the value of the CommandName property of the e argument. Since this value indicates the control that was clicked, it can be used to determine which method to call based on the button that was clicked. This is another way to do the processing you saw in figure 6-6 that used an image button control.

Four button controls that use the CommandName attribute

```
<asp:Button ID="btnFirst" runat="server" Text="<<" Width="25px"
    CommandName="First" OnCommand="NavigationButtons_Command" />
<asp:Button ID="btnPrevious" runat="server" Text="<" Width="25px"
    CommandName="Previous" OnCommand="NavigationButtons_Command" />
<asp:Button ID="btnNext" runat="server" Text=">" Width="25px"
    CommandName="Next" OnCommand="NavigationButtons_Command" />
<asp:Button ID="btnLast" runat="server" Text=">>" Width="25px"
    CommandName="Last" OnCommand="NavigationButtons_Command" />
```

An event handler for the Command events of the buttons

```
protected void NavigationButtons_Command(object sender, CommandEventArgs e)
{
    switch (e.CommandName)
    {
        case "First":
            this.GoToFirstRow();
            break;
        case "Previous":
            this.GoToPreviousRow();
            break;
        case "Next":
            this.GoToNextRow();
            break;
        case "Last":
            this.GoToLastRow();
            break;
    }
}
```

Properties of the CommandEventArgs class

Property	Description
CommandName	The value specified in the CommandName property for the control that generated the Command event.
CommandArgument	The value specified in the CommandArgument property for the control that generated the Command event.

Description

- The Command event is raised whenever a user clicks a button control. It's useful as an alternative to the Click event when you want to code a single event handler for a group of buttons that perform related functions.

- The e argument that's passed to a Command event handler is a CommandEventArgs object. This object includes properties that let you retrieve the values of the CommandName and CommandArgument properties of the control. You can use these values to determine which control raised the Command event.

Note

- If you code an event handler for both the Click event and the Command event, the Click event handler will be executed first.

Figure 6-7   How to use the Command event

How to work with text boxes, labels, check boxes, and radio buttons

Two controls you'll use frequently as you develop web forms are text boxes and labels. As you know, text boxes let you accept input from the user, and labels let you display information to the user. Since you already know the basic skills for working with these controls, the topic that follows presents some additional skills. After that, you'll learn how to use check boxes and radio buttons to let users select from one or more options.

How to work with text boxes and labels

At the top of figure 6-8, you can see part of a web page that contains a *text box* and a *label*. Unlike the text boxes you've seen up to this point, the text box shown here lets the user enter multiple lines of text. To accomplish that, the TextMode attribute of the text box is changed from its default of SingleLine to MultiLine. In addition, to indicate the number of lines that can be displayed in the text box at one time, the Rows attribute is set to 5. You can see these attributes in the asp tag for this control.

Another attribute you can use with a multi-line text box is Wrap. By default, this attribute is set to True, which means that text wraps automatically when it reaches the end of the text box. If you set this attribute to False, the user must press the Enter key to start a new line of text.

In addition to SingleLine and MultiLine, you can set the TextMode attribute to Password. Then, the characters the user enters are masked so they aren't displayed. Because ASP.NET provides a Login control that you can use to accept a user name and password from the user, you're not likely to use a text box to accept a password.

Although most text boxes are used to accept data from the user, you may occasionally need to restrict the user from entering data into a text box. To do that, you can set the ReadOnly attribute of the control to True. Then, the user can see the text in the control but can't change it.

You can use the MaxLength attribute to specify the maximum number of characters that can be entered into a text box. This is particularly useful if the data the user enters will be stored in a column of a database table. Then, you can limit the entry to the number of characters that are allowed for that column.

Although the width of a text box is set automatically as you size it in Design view, you can also set the width using the Columns attribute. This attribute specifies the width of the text box in characters. Note, however, that the width is approximate because it's based on the average width of a character for the font that's used.

The label control in this figure is also different from the ones you have seen so far in that it consists of two lines of text. To accomplish that, the text that's assigned to the Text property of the label includes HTML. You'll see the code that assigns this value in just a minute.

A text box and a label displayed in a browser

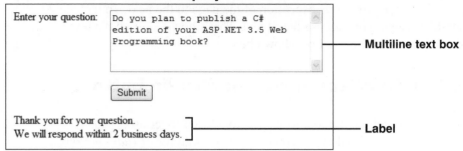

Multiline text box

Label

The asp tag for the text box

```
<asp:TextBox ID="txtQuestion" runat="server" Rows="5" TextMode="MultiLine"
    Width="296px"></asp:TextBox>
```

Common text box attributes

Attribute	Description
TextMode	The type of text box. SingleLine creates a standard text box, MultiLine creates a text box that accepts more than one line of text, and Password causes the characters that are entered to be masked. The default is SingleLine.
Text	The text content of the text box.
MaxLength	The maximum number of characters that can be entered into the text box.
Wrap	Determines whether or not text wraps automatically when it reaches the end of a multi-line text box. The default is True.
ReadOnly	Determines whether the user can change the text in the text box. The default value is False, which means that the text can be changed.
Columns	The width of the text box in characters. The actual width is determined based on the font that's used for the text entry.
Rows	The height of a multi-line text box in lines. The default value is 0, which sets the height to a single line.

The asp tag for the label

```
<asp:Label ID="lblConfirm" runat="server"></asp:Label>
```

Common label attribute

Attribute	Description
Text	The text displayed by the label.

Description

- *Text box controls* are typically used to accept input from the user. A text box can accept one or more lines of text depending on the setting of the TextMode attribute.

- *Label controls* provide an easy way to display text that can change from one execution of an ASP.NET page to the next. To display text that doesn't change, you typically use literal text.

Figure 6-8   How to work with text boxes and labels

Before I go on, I want to remind you that you typically use labels only to display text that changes from one execution of the page to the next. To include text that doesn't change, you can use literal text. That's how I entered the text "Enter your question:" in the example shown here.

How to work with check boxes and radio buttons

In addition to entering text into a form, you may want to let users select from one or more options. To do that, you can use *check boxes* or *radio buttons*. The main difference between these two types of controls is that radio buttons in groups are mutually exclusive and check boxes operate independently. In other words, if the user selects one radio button in a group, all of the other radio buttons in the same group are automatically turned off. In contrast, when a user selects a check box, it has no effect on other check boxes.

Figure 6-9 presents part of a web page that includes four check box controls and a group of two radio button controls. The first check box lets the user indicate if he wants to be added to a mailing list. The other check boxes let the user select what he wants to be contacted about. The radio buttons let the user select how he wants to be contacted.

To create a group of radio buttons, you simply specify the same name for the GroupName attribute of each radio button in the group. If you want to create two or more groups of radio buttons on a single form, just use a different group name for each group. Note that if you don't specify a group name for a radio button, that button won't be a part of any group. Instead, it will be processed independently of any other radio buttons on the form.

If you've developed Windows applications, you'll realize that this is in contrast to how Windows radio buttons work. In a Windows application, any radio buttons on a form that aren't specifically included in a group are treated as part of the same group. As a result, if a form has only one group of radio buttons, you can let them default to the same group. Since the Web Server radio button controls don't work that way, however, you'll almost always specify a group name for them.

To determine whether or not a radio button or check box is selected when it's first displayed, you use the Checked attribute. If you look at the aspx code for the check boxes and radio buttons shown in this figure, for example, you'll see that the Checked attributes of the first check box and the first radio button are set to True. When the web page is first displayed, then, these options will be selected as shown. Note that since only one radio button in a group can be selected, you should only set the Checked attribute to True for one button. If you set this property to True for more than one button in a group, the last one will be selected.

Four check boxes and two radio buttons displayed in a browser

The aspx code for the check boxes and radio buttons

```
<asp:CheckBox ID="chkMail" runat="server" Checked="True"
    Text="Add me to your mailing list" /><br /><br />

Contact me about:<br />

<asp:CheckBox ID="chkSpecial" runat="server"
    Text="Special offers" /><br />
<asp:CheckBox ID="chkNew" runat="server"
    Text="New products" /><br />
<asp:CheckBox ID="chkRelated" runat="server"
    Text="Related products" /><br /><br />

Contact me by:<br />

<asp:RadioButton ID="rdoEmail" runat="server"
    Checked="True" GroupName="Contact" Text="Email" /> 
<asp:RadioButton ID="rdoPostal" runat="server"
    GroupName="Contact" Text="Postal mail" />
```

Common check box and radio button attributes

Attribute	Description
Text	The text that's displayed next to the check box or radio button.
Checked	Indicates whether the check box or radio button is selected. The default is False.
GroupName	The name of the group that the control belongs to (radio buttons only).

Description

- A *check box* displays a single option that the user can either check or uncheck. *Radio buttons* present a group of options from which the user can select just one option. All of the radio buttons in a group should have the same group name.

- If you want a check box or radio button to be selected when it's initially displayed, set its Checked attribute to True. If you set the Checked attribute of more than one radio button in the same group to True, only the last one will be selected.

Figure 6-9   How to work with check boxes and radio buttons

C# code for working with these controls

The examples in figure 6-10 show how you can work with text boxes, labels, check boxes, and radio buttons in code. First, to retrieve the value the user enters into a text box, you use the Text property. In the example shown here, the Text property is assigned to a string variable. Note, however, that if the text box contains numeric data, you can convert it to the appropriate data type and then assign it to a variable with that data type. To be sure the user enters the correct data type, you can use validation controls as shown in the next chapter.

To assign a value to a label, you use the Text property of the label as shown in the second example in this figure. Notice here that the first line of text ends with an HTML tag for a line break (<br />). That way, the text will be displayed on two lines as you saw in figure 6-8.

The third and fourth examples in this figure show two ways you can process check boxes and radio buttons. First, you can process these controls in the event handler for the Click event of the form's submit button. Then, you just use if statements to test the Checked properties of the check boxes and radio buttons.

You can also process check boxes and radio buttons by writing event handlers for their CheckedChanged events. For a check box, this event is raised whenever the checked status of the control changes. Then, you can use an if statement to test the Checked property of the control just as you do in the event handler for the Click event of a submit button.

The CheckedChanged event works a bit differently for a radio button. Instead of being raised any time the status of the control changes, it's raised only when the status changes to checked. Because of that, there's no need to test the Checked property within the event handler for the CheckedChanged event.

In addition to the check box and radio button controls shown here, ASP.NET provides check box list and radio button list controls. These controls can simplify the task of creating groups of controls. You'll learn about these controls and the other list controls next.

Code that retrieves the text entered by the user in figure 6-8

```
string question = txtQuestion.Text;
```

Code that changes the Text property of the label in figure 6-8

```
lblConfirm.Text = "Thank you for your question.<br />"
                + "We will respond within 2 business days.";
```

Code that processes the first check box and radio button in figure 6-9

```
protected void btnContinue_Click(object sender, EventArgs e)
{
    if (chkMail.Checked)
        customer.Mail = true;
    else
        customer.Mail = false;
    if (rdoEmail.Checked)
        customer.MailType = "Email";
    else
        customer.MailType = "Postal";
}
```

Another way to process the check box and radio buttons

```
protected void chkMail_CheckedChanged(object sender, EventArgs e)
{
    if (chkMail.Checked)
        customer.Mail = true;
    else
        customer.Mail = false;
}

protected void rdoEmail_CheckedChanged(object sender, EventArgs e)
{
    customer.MailType = "Email";
}

protected void rdoPostal_CheckedChanged(object sender, EventArgs e)
{
    customer.MailType = "Postal";
}
```

Description

- To determine whether a check box or radio button is selected, you test its Checked property.
- For a check box, the CheckedChanged event is raised whenever the checked status of the control changes. For a radio button, this event is raised only when the status of the control changes to checked.

Figure 6-10   C# code for working with these controls

How to work with list controls

ASP.NET provides several controls that are designed to present lists of information. You'll learn about all five of those controls here: the drop-down list, list box, radio button list, check box list, and bulleted list.

Basic skills for working with list boxes and drop-down lists

Figure 6-11 presents the basic skills for working with *list boxes* and *drop-down lists*. The list box shown here lets the user select from one of four colors. List boxes are typically used in cases like this where there are a small number of items to select from. In contrast, drop-down lists are typically used with larger lists so they don't take up as much space on the page. The drop-down list in this figure, for example, displays a list of the days of the week.

The asp tags for the list box and drop-down list are also shown in this figure. Here, you can see that the ListBox element has four ListItem elements that correspond to the four colors in the list. Similarly, the DropDownList element has seven ListItem elements that correspond to the days of the week. The easiest way to add elements like these to a list is to use the ListItem Collection Editor. You'll see how to do that in figure 6-14.

You can also add items to a list using C# code. In that case, the aspx code for the form won't include ListItem elements like those shown here. Instead, ASP.NET will generate the elements when the page is rendered. You'll learn two ways to add items to a list in figure 6-13.

A list box displayed in a browser

The asp tag for the list box

```
<asp:ListBox ID="lstColor" runat="server">
    <asp:ListItem Value="Black" Selected="True">Black</asp:ListItem>
    <asp:ListItem Value="Red">Red</asp:ListItem>
    <asp:ListItem Value="Blue">Blue</asp:ListItem>
    <asp:ListItem Value="Green">Green</asp:ListItem>
</asp:ListBox>
```

A drop-down list displayed in a browser

The asp tag for the drop-down list

```
<asp:DropDownList id="ddlDay" runat="server">
    <asp:ListItem Value="1">Sunday</asp:ListItem>
    <asp:ListItem Value="2">Monday</asp:ListItem>
    <asp:ListItem Value="3">Tuesday</asp:ListItem>
    <asp:ListItem Value="4">Wednesday</asp:ListItem>
    <asp:ListItem Value="5">Thursday</asp:ListItem>
    <asp:ListItem Value="6">Friday</asp:ListItem>
    <asp:ListItem Value="7">Saturday</asp:ListItem>
</asp:DropDownList>
```

Description

- *List boxes* and *drop-down lists* typically contain one or more list items. You can load list items by using C# code or the ListItem Collection Editor. See figures 6-13 and 6-14 for details.

- A list box lets a user choose one or more items from a list of items. A drop-down list lets a user choose an item from a drop-down list of items.

Figure 6-11   Basic skills for working with list boxes and drop-down lists

Properties for working with list boxes, drop-down lists, and list items

Figure 6-12 presents some common properties for working with list boxes and drop-down lists. As you just saw, these controls contain ListItem objects that define the items in the list. These objects are stored in a collection that you can refer to using the Items property of the control. You'll see examples that use this property in the next figure.

In addition to using the Items property to work with the items in a list, you can get the selected item using the SelectedItem property of the control, you can get or set the index of the selected item using the SelectedIndex property, and you can get or set the value of the selected item using the SelectedValue property. By default, the SelectedIndex property of a drop-down list is set to zero, which means that the first item is selected. In contrast, the SelectedIndex property of a list box is set to -1 by default, which means that none of the items in the list are selected. Then, you can check if the user has selected an item using code like this:

```
if (lstColor.SelectedIndex > -1) ...
```

You can also select an item by setting the SelectedIndex property to the appropriate index value. And you can clear the selection from a list box by setting this property to -1. Finally, you can select an item by setting the SelectedValue property to the appropriate value.

The Rows and SelectionMode properties apply only to list box controls. The Rows property determines how many items are displayed at one time. The SelectionMode property determines whether the user can select more than one item from the list. Note that when multiple selections are allowed, the SelectedItem property gets the first selected item, the SelectedIndex property gets the index of the first selected item, and the SelectedValue property gets the value of the first selected item.

To work with an item in a drop-down list or list box, you use the properties shown in this figure. The Text property specifies the text that's displayed for the item. The Value property specifies a value that's associated with the item. And the Selected property indicates whether the item is selected.

This figure also shows three examples for working with a drop-down list or list box. In the first example, the SelectedValue property of a drop-down list is assigned to an int variable. Note that because the SelectedValue property contains a string, it is converted to an integer.

The second example uses the SelectedItem property to retrieve the ListItem object for the selected item. Then, it uses the Text property of the ListItem object to get the text that's displayed for the selected item.

The third example is an event handler for the SelectedIndexChanged event of the drop-down list. This event occurs any time the item that's selected changes between posts to the server. If you want the page to post immediately when the user selects an item, you should set the AutoPostBack property to True.

Common properties of list box and drop-down list controls

Property	Description
Items	The collection of ListItem objects that represents the items in the control. This property returns an object of type ListItemCollection.
Rows	The number of items that are displayed in a list box at one time. If the list contains more rows than can be displayed, a scroll bar is added automatically.
SelectedItem	The ListItem object for the currently selected item, or the ListItem object for the item with the lowest index if more than one item is selected in a list box.
SelectedIndex	The index of the currently selected item, or the index of the first selected item if more than one item is selected in a list box. If no item is selected in a list box, the value of this property is -1.
SelectedValue	The value of the currently selected item, or the value of the first selected item if more than one item is selected in a list box. If no item is selected in a list box, the value of this property is an empty string ("").
SelectionMode	Indicates whether a list box allows single selections (Single) or multiple selections (Multiple).

Common properties of list item objects

Property	Description
Text	The text that's displayed for the list item.
Value	A string value associated with the list item.
Selected	Indicates whether the item is selected.

Code that retrieves the value of a selected item in a drop-down list

```
int dayNumber = Convert.ToInt32(ddlDay.SelectedValue);
```

Code that retrieves the text for a selected item in a drop-down list

```
string dayName = ddlDay.SelectedItem.Text;
```

Code that uses the SelectedIndexChanged event of a drop-down list

```
protected void ddlDay_SelectedIndexChanged(object sender, EventArgs e)
{
    int dayNumber = Convert.ToInt32(ddlDay.SelectedValue);
}
```

Description

- To work with the items in a drop-down list or list box, you use the Items property of the control. This property returns a ListItemCollection object that contains all of the items in the list.
- The SelectedIndexChanged event is raised when the user selects a different item from a drop-down list or list box.

Figure 6-12   Properties for working with drop-down lists, list boxes, and list items

Members for working with list item collections

Figure 6-13 presents some common members for working with a collection of list item objects. To get a count of the number of items in the collection, for example, you use the Count property. And to get a specific item, you use an index.

All but two of the methods shown here let you add and remove items in the collection. The method you're most likely to use is Add, which adds an item to the end of the collection. The examples in this figure show two different ways you can use this method.

The first example contains the code that's used to load the colors into the list box you saw in figure 6-11. Here, the Add method is used to add an item with the specified string value. When you code the Add method this way, the value you specify is assigned to both the Text and Value properties of the item.

If you want to assign different values to the Text and Value properties of an item, you use the technique shown in the second example. Here, a new list item object is created with two string values. The first one contains a string that's stored in the Text property, and the second one contains a string that's stored in the Value property. Then, the Add method is used to add the new item to the list item collection of the drop-down list you saw in figure 6-11.

Notice in both of these examples that the Items property is used to refer to the collection of list item objects for the control. You can also use the SelectedIndex property of a control to refer to an item at a specific index. For example, you could use a statement like this to remove the selected item from a drop-down list:

```
ddlDay.Items.RemoveAt(ddlDay.SelectedIndex)
```

The last two methods let you locate a list item based on the value of its Text or Value property. These methods are useful when you need to access a list item and you don't know its index value.

Common members of list item collection objects

Property	Description
`Count`	The number of items in the collection.

Indexer	Description
`[index]`	A ListItem object that represents the item at the specified index.

Method	Description
`Add(string)`	Adds a new item to the end of the collection, and assigns the specified string value to both the Text and Value properties of the item.
`Add(ListItem)`	Adds the specified list item to the end of the collection.
`Insert(index, string)`	Inserts an item at the specified index location in the collection, and assigns the specified string value to the Text property of the item.
`Insert(index, ListItem)`	Inserts the specified list item at the specified index location in the collection.
`Remove(string)`	Removes from the collection the item whose Text property is equal to the specified string value.
`Remove(ListItem)`	Removes the specified list item from the collection.
`RemoveAt(index)`	Removes the item at the specified index location from the collection.
`Clear()`	Removes all the items from the collection.
`FindByValue(string)`	Returns the list item whose Value property has the specified value.
`FindByText(string)`	Returns the list item whose Text property has the specified value.

Code that loads items into a list box using strings

```
lstColor.Items.Add("Black");
lstColor.Items.Add("Red");
lstColor.Items.Add("Blue");
lstColor.Items.Add("Green");
```

Code that loads items into a drop-down list using ListItem objects

```
ddlDay.Items.Add(new ListItem("Sunday", "1"));
ddlDay.Items.Add(new ListItem("Monday", "2"));
ddlDay.Items.Add(new ListItem("Tuesday", "3"));
ddlDay.Items.Add(new ListItem("Wednesday", "4"));
ddlDay.Items.Add(new ListItem("Thursday", "5"));
ddlDay.Items.Add(new ListItem("Friday", "6"));
ddlDay.Items.Add(new ListItem("Saturday", "7"));
```

Description

- The ListItemCollection object is a collection of ListItem objects. Each ListItem object represents one item in the list.
- Items in a ListItemCollection object are numbered from 0. So the index for the first item in the list is 0, the index for the second item is 1, and so on.
- When you load items into a list box using strings, both the Text and Value properties of the list item are set to the string value you specify. To set the Text and Value properties of a list item to different values, you must create a list item object and then add that item to the collection.

Figure 6-13   Members for working with list item collections

How to use the ListItem Collection Editor

In the last figure, you saw how to use the Add method of a list item collection to load items into a drop-down list or list box control. If the items are static, however, you might want to use the ListItem Collection Editor to load them instead. Figure 6-14 shows you how to use this editor.

When you first display the ListItem Collection Editor, the list is empty. Then, you can use the Add button below the Members list to add items to the list. When you do, the item appears in the Members list and its properties appear in the Properties list. The first property lets you disable a list item so that it doesn't appear in the list. The other three properties are the same properties you learned about in figure 6-12. Note, however, that when you set the Text property, the Value property defaults to the same value. If that's not what you want, you can change this value.

The ListItem Collection Editor dialog box

Description

- You can use the ListItem Collection Editor to add items to a drop-down list or list box. You'll typically use it to create a static list of items. Each item you add generates an <asp:ListItem> tag in the aspx file.

- To display the Collection Editor dialog box, select Edit Items from the smart tag menu, or select the control and then click the ellipsis button that appears when you select the Items property in the Properties window.

- To add an item to the list, click the Add button and then enter the properties for the item in the Properties list. The item appears in the Members list.

- By default, the ListItem Collection Editor sets the Value property of a list item to the value you specify for the Text property.

- To remove an item, select it in the Members list and then click the Remove button.

- You can use the up and down arrow buttons to the right of the Members list to move the selected item up or down in the list.

Figure 6-14   How to use the ListItem Collection Editor

How to work with radio button lists and check box lists

Earlier in this chapter, you learned how to use radio buttons and check boxes. But ASP.NET also provides *radio button lists* and *check box lists* that you can use to create lists of radio buttons or check boxes. Figure 6-15 shows you how to use these controls.

As you can see from the asp tags for the check box list and radio button list, each control consists of a collection of ListItem objects. You can refer to this collection through the Items property of the control just as you can for drop-down lists and list boxes. These controls also have SelectedItem, SelectedIndex, and SelectedValue properties just like drop-down lists and list boxes.

Just like a group of radio buttons, only one item in a radio button list can be selected at one time. Then, you can use the SelectedValue property to get or set the value of the selected item, and you can use the SelectedIndex property to get or set the index of the selected item. This is illustrated by the first statement in this figure, which uses the SelectedValue property to get the value of the selected item. Note that this is much simpler than the code you use to get the value of the selected radio button in a group.

Like a list box, you can select more than one item in a check box list. Because of that, you'll usually determine whether an item in the list is selected using the Selected property of the item. This is illustrated in the second example in this figure. Here, the Items property of a check box list is used to get the item at index 0. Then, the Selected property of that item is used to determine if the item is selected. Notice here that you can't refer to individual check boxes by name when you use a check box list. Because of that, your code may not be as readable as it is when you use individual check box controls. That's why I recommend that you use check box lists only when they provide a distinct advantage over using individual controls.

To determine the layout of the items in a radio button or check box list, you use the attributes shown in this figure. The RepeatLayout attribute determines whether ASP.NET aligns the buttons or check boxes in a list using tables or HTML flow. I recommend that you use tables since they're more precise.

The RepeatDirection attribute determines whether the controls are listed horizontally or vertically. For the radio button list in this figure, I set this attribute to Horizontal. In contrast, I left this attribute at its default of Vertical for the check box list.

The RepeatColumns attribute specifies the number of columns in the radio button or check box list. By default, the items are displayed in a single column. If a list contains more than just a few items, however, you may want to display the items in two or more columns to save space. The four check boxes in the list shown in this figure, for example, are displayed in two columns.

A check box list and a radio button list displayed in a browser

Check box list

Radio button list

The asp tag for the check box list

```
<asp:CheckBoxList id="cblContact" runat="server" Width="305px"
    RepeatColumns="2">
    <asp:ListItem Value="Special">Special offers</asp:ListItem>
    <asp:ListItem Value="New">New products</asp:ListItem>
    <asp:ListItem Value="Related">Related products</asp:ListItem>
    <asp:ListItem Value="Events">Local events</asp:ListItem>
</asp:CheckBoxList>
```

The asp tag for the radio button list

```
<asp:RadioButtonList id="rblMail" runat="server" Width="346px"
    RepeatDirection="Horizontal">
    <asp:ListItem Value="Email">Email</asp:ListItem>
    <asp:ListItem Value="Postal">Postal mail</asp:ListItem>
    <asp:ListItem Value="Both" Selected="True">Both</asp:ListItem>
</asp:RadioButtonList>
```

Attributes for formatting radio button and check box lists

Attribute	Description
RepeatLayout	Specifies whether ASP.NET should use table tags (Table) or normal HTML flow (Flow) to format the list when it renders the control. The default is Table.
RepeatDirection	Specifies the direction in which the controls should be repeated. The available values are Horizontal and Vertical. The default is Vertical.
RepeatColumns	Specifies the number of columns to use when repeating the controls. The default is 0.

A statement that gets the value of the selected item in a radio button list

```
customer.MailType = rblMail.SelectedValue;
```

A statement that checks if the first item in a check box list is selected

```
if (cblContact.Items[0].Selected)...
```

Description

- A *radio button list* presents a list of mutually exclusive options. A *check box list* presents a list of independent options. These controls contain a collection of ListItem objects that you refer to through the Items property of the control.

- These controls also have SelectedItem, SelectedIndex, and SelectedValue properties. These properties work just like they do for drop-down list and list box controls. See figure 6-12 for more information.

Figure 6-15   How to work with radio button lists and check box lists

How to work with bulleted lists and numbered lists

Figure 6-16 shows how to work with the bulleted list control. In spite of its name, this control can be used to create both *bulleted lists* and *numbered lists*. The type of list that's created depends on the value of the BulletStyle attribute.

Like the other list controls presented in this chapter, a bulleted list control contains a collection of ListItem objects. In this figure, for example, you can see the aspx code for the list items contained in the two controls shown at the top of this figure. Because the BulletStyle attribute of the first control is set to Disc, it's displayed as a bulleted list. In contrast, the BulletStyle attribute of the second control is set to Numbered, so it's displayed as a numbered list.

Unlike the other list controls, the bulleted list control is typically used only to display a list. In other words, it's not used to let the user make a selection. That's the case if the DisplayMode attribute is set to Text. If this attribute is set to Hyperlink, however, the user can click on the link to display the page at the URL specified by the Value attribute of the list item. This is illustrated by the numbered list in this figure.

If the DisplayMode attribute is set to LinkButton, the page is posted back to the server when the user clicks a link. Then, you can respond to the user clicking the link by coding an event handler for the Click event of the bulleted list control. Within that event handler, you can use the Selected property of a list item to determine if the item was clicked. This is illustrated by the statement in this figure. Alternatively, you can use the value of the e argument's Index property to determine which list item the user clicked.

A bulleted list and a numbered list displayed in a browser

Materials you will need:

- Styrofoam panel
- Gray and black latex paint
- Stone texture paint
- Rotary tool

Select a project type:

1. Costumes
2. Static props
3. Animated props

Common attributes of the bulleted list control

Attribute	Description
BulletStyle	Specifies the bullet style. For a bulleted list, allowable values are Disc, Circle, Square, or CustomImage. For a numbered list, allowable values are Numbered, LowerAlpha, UpperAlpha, LowerRoman, or UpperRoman.
BulletImageUrl	Specifies the URL of the image used to display the bullets if the BulletStyle attribute is set to CustomImage.
FirstBulletNumber	Specifies the starting number if numbers are displayed.
DisplayMode	Specifies how the text for each item should be displayed. Allowable values are Text, HyperLink, or LinkButton. Text is the default.

The aspx code for the bulleted list shown above

```
<asp:BulletedList ID="BulletedList1" runat="server" BulletStyle="Disc">
    <asp:ListItem>Styrofoam panel</asp:ListItem>
    <asp:ListItem>Gray and black latex paint</asp:ListItem>
    <asp:ListItem>Stone texture paint</asp:ListItem>
    <asp:ListItem>Rotary tool</asp:ListItem>
</asp:BulletedList>
```

The aspx code for the numbered list shown above

```
<asp:BulletedList ID="BulletedList2" runat="server" BulletStyle="Numbered"
    DisplayMode="HyperLink">
    <asp:ListItem Value="Costumes.aspx">Costumes</asp:ListItem>
    <asp:ListItem Value="StaticProps.aspx">Static props</asp:ListItem>
    <asp:ListItem Value="AnimatedProps.aspx">Animated props</asp:ListItem>
</asp:BulletedList>
```

A statement that checks if the first link button in a bulleted list was clicked

```
if (blstCategories.Items[0].Selected)...
```

Description

- The bulleted list control creates *bulleted lists* or *numbered lists*. This control contains a collection of ListItem objects that you refer to through the Items property of the control.

- If you set the DisplayMode attribute to Hyperlink, you can set the Value attribute of each ListItem object to the URL of the page you want to display when the link is clicked.

- If you set the DisplayMode attribute to LinkButton, you can use the Click event of the bulleted list to respond to the user clicking one of the links.

- Unlike the other list controls, the bulleted list control doesn't have SelectedItem, SelectedIndex, and SelectedValue properties.

Figure 6-16   How to work with bulleted lists and numbered lists

How to use other web server controls

As you learned earlier, ASP.NET provides many other controls besides those you've already seen in this chapter. So in the remaining topics of this chapter, I'll present several of those controls. But first, I want to show you how to get information about using a control that you haven't used before. You can also use this technique to get additional information about controls you have used.

How to get the information you need for using a control

The easiest way to get information about a web server control is to use the Help documentation that comes with Visual Studio. To access this documentation, you can use the commands in the Help menu. The one I've found to be most useful is the Index command. When you select this command, a Help window like the one in figure 6-17 is displayed.

The Index tab in the left pane of this window lets you enter the text you want to look for in the Look For text box. To look for information on a control, for example, you can enter the name of the control. You can also filter the information that's displayed using the drop-down list at the top of the Index tab.

In this figure, I filtered the list so that only information related to developing web applications is displayed. Then, I entered "Calendar" and selected the "about Calendar control" topic under the "Calendar control [Web Forms]" heading. When I did that, some basic information about the Calendar control was displayed in the right pane of the window. This is usually a good place to start when you're learning how to use a control that you haven't used before.

Once you have a basic idea of how a control works, you can display other topics that describe specific features or functions of the control. You can do that by using the links that are available within a topic or by selecting topics from the Index tab.

Although you can typically find all the information you need using the Index command, you may occasionally need to use other Help features. To access these features, you can use the other commands in the Help menu, or you can use the buttons in the Help window's Standard toolbar if that window is already displayed. If you want to find out how to perform a specific task, for example, you can click the How Do I button and then select from the predefined tasks that are displayed. Or, if you want to search for specific information, you can click the Search button. This opens another tab that lets you enter search text and criteria. If you experiment with these and other Help features, you'll quickly get a feel for how they work.

Some of the Help documentation for the calendar control

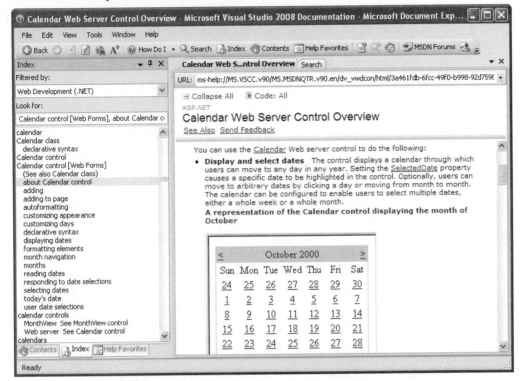

Description

- Visual Studio 2008 provides an abundance of information on the web server controls. The easiest way to display this information is to use the Help→Index command.

- To start, you can review the information about the basic function, usage, and appearance of the control. To do that, just enter the name of the control in the Look For text box and then select the appropriate topic.

- Most controls include an "About" topic like the one shown above that provides basic information about the control along with links to related topics. In addition, you'll find topics that describe specific features of the control.

- Once you display the Help documentation, you can use the buttons in the toolbar to switch to a different view of the documentation.

Figure 6-17   How to get the information you need for using a control

How to use the image control

Figure 6-18 shows part of a web page that includes an *image control* that displays a graphic image. In this case, the graphic image is stored in a *JPEG* file. JPEG is a graphics format commonly used for photographs and scanned images. Graphic images are also frequently stored in *GIF* files. GIF files are typically used for small images such as button images and icons.

You can also see some common attributes of an image control in this figure. The most important attribute is ImageUrl, which specifies the URL of the image file. As you can see in the asp tag for the image in this figure, the image file is located in the Images folder of the web site.

If you need to change the image that's displayed in an image control when a page is executed, you can do that by assigning a different value to the ImageUrl property. This is illustrated in the C# code example in this figure. Here, a URL that refers to an image named cat01.jpg in the Images\Products directory of the web site is assigned to the ImageUrl property of a control named imgProduct.

If you know that some browsers won't be able to display an image, you should also set the AlternateText attribute. Then, the text you specify will be displayed in place of the image if the image can't be displayed. If, for example, the image in this figure can't be displayed, the text "Murach Books" will be displayed instead.

The ImageAlign attribute determines how the image is aligned relative to the web page or other elements on the page. If you set this attribute to Left, for example, the image is aligned at the left side of the page and any text on the page will wrap around the right side of the image. For more information on the available alignment options, see the topic on this attribute in online help.

The last two attributes, Width and Height, let you control the size of the displayed image. If you leave both of these attributes at their defaults, ASP.NET will display the image at its original size. If you specify just one of these attributes, ASP.NET will automatically set the other attribute so that the proportions of the original image are maintained. If you set both attributes, the image will be distorted if necessary to fit the dimensions you specify. Because of that, you'll usually set just one of these attributes.

How to use the hyperlink control

The web page in figure 6-18 also includes a *hyperlink control*. This control navigates to the web page specified in the NavigateUrl attribute when the user clicks the control. If you want to display text for a hyperlink control, you set the Text attribute or code the text as content between the start and end tags. Either way, the text appears with an underline as shown in this figure. Alternatively, you can display an image for this control. To do that, you set the ImageUrl attribute to the URL of an image you want to display.

An image control and a hyperlink control displayed in a browser

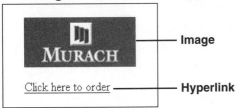
— Image

Click here to order — — Hyperlink

The asp tag for the image control

```
<asp:Image ID="Image1" runat="server" ImageUrl="~/Images/MurachLogo.jpg"
    AlternateText="Murach Books" />
```

Code that sets the URL of an image control

```
imgProduct.ImageUrl = "Images/Products/cat01.jpg";
```

Common image attributes

Attribute	Description
ImageUrl	The absolute or relative URL of the image.
AlternateText	The text that's used in place of the image if the browser can't display the image.
ImageAlign	The alignment of the image relative to the web page or other elements on the page.
Width	The width of the image.
Height	The height of the image.

The asp tag for the hyperlink control

```
<asp:HyperLink ID="HyperLink1" runat="server"
    NavigateUrl="http://www.murach.com">Click here to order
</asp:HyperLink>
```

Common hyperlink attributes

Attribute	Description
NavigateUrl	The absolute or relative URL of the page that's displayed when the control is clicked.
Text	The text that's displayed for the control.
ImageUrl	The absolute or relative URL of the image that's displayed for the control.

Description

- An *image control* displays a graphic image, typically in *GIF* (*Graphic Interchange Format*) or *JPEG* (*Joint Photographic Experts Group*) format.
- If you don't specify the Height or Width attributes of an image control, the image will be displayed at full size.
- A *hyperlink control* navigates to another web page when the user clicks the control. You can display either text or an image for the control.

Figure 6-18   How to use the image and hyperlink controls

How to use the file upload control

The *file upload control*, shown in figure 6-19, is designed for applications that let the user upload files to the web site. This control displays a text box that lets the user enter the path for the file to be uploaded, plus a Browse button that displays a dialog box that lets the user locate and select the file.

To upload the selected file, you must also provide a separate control that results in a postback, like the Upload button in this figure. When the user clicks this button, the page is posted and the file selected by the user is sent to the server along with the HTTP request.

The first example in this figure shows the aspx code that declares the file upload control and the Upload button shown at the top of this figure. Note here that the file upload control doesn't include an attribute that specifies where the file should be saved on the server. That's because the file upload control doesn't automatically save the uploaded file. Instead, you must write code that calls the SaveAs method of this control. The second example in this figure shows how to write this code.

Before you call the SaveAs method, you should test the HasFile property to make sure the user has selected a file. If the user has selected a valid file and it was successfully uploaded to the server, the HasFile property will be True. Then, you can use the FileName property to get the name of the selected file, and you can combine the file name with the path where you want the file saved. In this figure, the file is stored in the C:\Uploads directory.

To illustrate the use of the PostedFile.ContentLength property, the event handler in this figure uses this property to determine the size of the uploaded file. Then, if this value exceeds the limit set by the sizeLimit variable, the file isn't saved. Instead, an error message is displayed.

A file upload control displayed in a browser

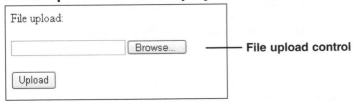

File upload control

The aspx code used to implement the file upload

```
File upload:<br /><br />
<asp:FileUpload ID="FileUpload1" runat="server" /><br /><br />
<asp:Button ID="btnUpload" runat="server" Text="Upload"
    OnClick="btnUpload_Click" /><br /><br />
<asp:Label ID="lblMessage" runat="server"></asp:Label>
```

The Click event handler for the Upload button

```
protected void btnUpload_Click(object sender, EventArgs e)
{
    int sizeLimit = 5242880;    // 5,242,880 is 5MB
    if (FileUpload1.HasFile)
    {
        if (FileUpload1.PostedFile.ContentLength <= sizeLimit)
        {
            string path = "C:\\uploads\\" + FileUpload1.FileName;
            FileUpload1.SaveAs(path);
            lblMessage.Text = "File uploaded to " + path;
        }
        else
            lblMessage.Text = "File exceeds size limit.";
    }
}
```

Properties and methods of the FileUpload class

Property	Description
HasFile	If True, the user has selected a file to upload.
FileName	The name of the file to be uploaded.
PostedFile	The HttpPostedFile object that represents the file that was posted. You can use this object's ContentLength property to determine the size of the posted file.

Method	Description
SaveAs(string)	Saves the posted file to the specified path.

Description

- The *file upload control* displays a text box and a button that lets the user browse the client computer's file system to locate a file to be uploaded.

- Because the file upload control doesn't provide a button to upload the file, you must provide a button or other control to post the page. Then, in the button's Click event handler, you must call the SaveAs method of the file upload control to save the file on the server.

- To use the SaveAs method, the user must have write access to the specified directory.

Figure 6-19   How to use the file upload control

How to use the image map control

An *image map* is an image that has several clickable regions, called *hot spots*. Figure 6-20 shows how the *image map control* provides a simple way to create image maps in ASP.NET.

The image map control lets you create three types of hot spots: rectangles, circles, and polygons. The example in this figure displays a map of California with two polygon hot spots: one for Northern California, the other for Southern California. Each hot spot is defined by a PolygonHotSpot element, and the polygon shapes are defined on the Coordinates attribute using a list of x and y coordinates that indicate the corners of the hot spot.

You use similar techniques to define rectangle and circle hot spots. To create a rectangle hot spot, you specify the locations of its sides using the Top, Bottom, Left, and Right attributes. To create a circle hot spot, you specify the x and y coordinates of its midpoint and the length of its radius using the X, Y, and Radius attributes.

Unfortunately, Visual Studio doesn't provide a convenient point-and-click editor to define hot spots. As a result, you'll need to use a separate graphics program to determine the x and y coordinates for the map's hot spots, particularly for a polygon hot spot. Once you've determined those coordinates, you can return to Visual Studio to create the hot spot elements for the image map.

The HotSpotMode attribute of an image map indicates whether the page will link to another page (Navigate) or be posted back to the server (PostBack) when the user clicks a hot spot. If you set this attribute to Navigate, you should set the NavigateUrl attribute of each hot spot to the URL of the page you want to be displayed when the hot spot is clicked. If you set this attribute to PostBack, you should set the PostBackValue attribute of each hot spot to the value you want to be passed to the Click event handler of the image map when the hot spot is clicked. Then, you can use the PostBackValue attribute of the e argument in the Click event handler to determine which hot spot was clicked. This is illustrated in the code example in this figure.

Note that you can also specify the HotSpotMode attribute for each hot spot rather than for the whole image map. That way, you can perform a postback when some hot spots are clicked and link to other pages when other hot spots are clicked.

The California.gif image

The aspx code for the image map control

```
<asp:ImageMap ID="imapCA" runat="server" ImageUrl="~/Images/California.GIF"
    HotSpotMode="PostBack" OnClick="imapCA_Click">
    <asp:PolygonHotSpot Coordinates="76, 228, 177, 158, 121, 111,
        121, 3, 0, 3, 0, 83, 76, 228" PostBackValue="North" />
    <asp:PolygonHotSpot Coordinates="76, 229, 177, 159, 301, 275,
        296, 347, 215, 358, 111, 295, 76, 229" PostBackValue="South" />
</asp:ImageMap>
```

The Click event handler for the image map

```
protected void imapCA_Click(object sender, ImageMapEventArgs e)
{
    string region;
    if (e.PostBackValue.Equals("North"))
        region = "NorthernCalifornia";
    else
        region = "SouthernCalifornia";
}
```

Common image map attributes

Attribute	Description
ImageUrl	The URL of the image to be displayed.
HotSpotMode	Sets the behavior for the hot spots. PostBack causes the page to be posted and Navigate links to a different page. This attribute can also be specified for individual hot spot elements.

Description

- The *image map control* lets you display an *image map* with one or more *hot spots*. The page either posts back or links to another page when the user clicks a hot spot.
- To post the page back when the user clicks a hot spot, set the HotSpotMode attribute to PostBack, and set the PostBackValue attribute of the hot spot to the value you want passed to the Click event handler.
- To link to another page when the user clicks a hot spot, set the HotSpotMode attribute to Navigate and specify the URL of the page in the NavigateUrl attribute of the hot spot.
- To create a CircleHotSpot element, use the X, Y, and Radius attributes. To create a RectangleHotSpot element, use the Top, Bottom, Left, and Right attributes. To create a PolygonHotSpot element, use the Coordinates attribute.

Figure 6-20　How to use the image map control

How to use the calendar control

The *calendar control* provides an easy way for a user to select a date. Although this control can be used for more sophisticated purposes, this is its most common use. Figure 6-21 shows how you use this control.

The web page at the top of this figure illustrates one way to implement a calendar control. To start, the web page displays two drop-down lists that let the user select a month and day, plus an image button. If the user clicks the image button, the calendar control is displayed and the image button is hidden. Then, the user can use the controls at the top of the calendar to move to the previous or next month if necessary. Finally, when the user selects a date from the calendar, the drop-down lists are set to the selected month and day, the image button is displayed again, and the calendar is hidden.

By default, the calendar control lets the user select a single date. However, you can also let the user select an entire week or month by setting the SelectionMode property to the appropriate value. If you want the user to select entire weeks, set this property to DayWeek. If you want the user to select entire months, set it to DayWeekMonth. If you just want to display a calendar and not let the user make selections, you can set this property to None.

If you review the aspx code for the calendar control in this figure, you'll see that most of the attributes are used to apply styles to the calendar. For example, the BorderStyle and BorderColor attributes display a solid black border around the calendar. The attributes in the TodayDayStyle and TitleStyle elements cause the current date and the month heading to be displayed in white bold text on a blue background. And the ForeColor attribute in the NextPrevStyle element causes the symbols for going to the previous and next page to be displayed in white. In addition, the Visible attribute that's used for this control causes the control to be hidden when the page is first displayed.

When the user selects a date from the calendar, the SelectionChanged event is raised and the page is posted to the server. Then, you can use the SelectedDate property of the control within the event handler for this event to determine what date was selected. The event handler shown in this figure, for example, uses this property to select the appropriate values in the drop-down lists so they display the selected date.

If a calendar control lets the user select an entire week or month, you can use the SelectedDates property to retrieve the dates in the week or month the user selects. This property contains a collection of the selected dates, and you can use standard properties to work with this collection. For example, if you want to know how many dates were selected, you can use the Count property of this collection.

A web page with an image button that displays a calendar

The web page with the calendar displayed

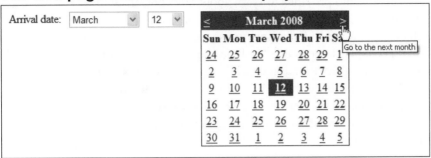

The aspx code for the calendar control

```
<asp:Calendar ID="clnArrival" runat="server" Visible="False"
    OnSelectionChanged="clnArrival_SelectionChanged"
    BorderColor="Black" BorderStyle="Solid">
    <TodayDayStyle BackColor="Blue" Font-Bold="True" ForeColor="White" />
    <TitleStyle BackColor="Blue" Font-Bold="True" ForeColor="White" />
    <NextPrevStyle ForeColor="White" />
</asp:Calendar>
```

The SelectionChanged event handler for the calendar control

```
protected void clnArrival_SelectionChanged(object sender, EventArgs e)
{
    ddlMonth.SelectedValue = clnArrival.SelectedDate.Month.ToString();
    ddlDay.SelectedValue = clnArrival.SelectedDate.Day.ToString();
    clnArrival.Visible = false;
    ibtnCalendar.Visible = true;
}
```

Common properties of the Calendar class

Property	Description
SelectionMode	Specifies the type of selection that can be made. Acceptable values are Day, DayWeek, DayWeekMonth, and None.
SelectedDate	The currently selected date if a single date was selected, or the first selected date if multiple dates were selected.
SelectedDates	A collection that contains all of the selected dates in sequence. To determine the number of dates that were selected, use the Count property of this collection.

Description

- The *calendar control* is typically used to provide users with an easy way of selecting a date. Entire weeks and months can also be selected.
- When the user makes a selection from a calendar control, the SelectionChanged event is raised and the page is posted to the server.

Figure 6-21   How to use the calendar control

Perspective

In this chapter, you've learned how to use 17 of the standard web server controls that ASP.NET provides. In addition, you've learned how to use the Help documentation that Visual Studio provides to learn about any control. With that as background, you should be able to use any of the server controls.

Keep in mind, though, that you'll learn how to use many of the controls that weren't presented in this chapter later in this book. In the next chapter, for example, you'll learn how to use the validation controls. And in chapters 13 through 18, you'll learn how to use the data controls. If a control is presented in this book, then, you'll want to read about it here before you go to the Help documentation. Then, you can use the Help documentation to learn about any aspects of these controls that we may not present.

Terms

web server control
HTML server control
event handler
access key
accelerator key
submit button
button
link button
image button
text box
label
check box
radio button
list box
drop-down list
radio button list
check box list
bulleted list
numbered list
image control
JPEG (Joint Photographic Experts Group)
GIF (Graphic Interchange Format)
hyperlink control
file upload control
image map
image map control
hot spot
calendar control

7

How to use the validation controls

In chapter 2, you learned the basic skills for using two of the validation controls: the required field validator and the range validator. Now, you'll learn more about using those controls as well as how to use the other validation controls. As you'll see, you can use the validation controls to perform the data validation required by most web forms.

An introduction to the validation controls **246**
How to use the validation controls 246
Common validator properties 248
How ASP.NET processes validation controls 250

How to use the basic validation controls **252**
How to use the required field validator 252
How to use the compare validator 254
How to use the range validator 256

Validation techniques **258**
How to use the validation summary control 258
How to use validation groups 260

How to use the advanced validation controls **262**
How to use the regular expression validator 262
How to create your own regular expressions 264
How to use a custom validator 266
A validation routine that validates credit card numbers 268

Perspective **270**

An introduction to the validation controls

ASP.NET provides six *validation controls* that you can use to validate the data on a web form. You'll learn the basic skills for using these controls in the topics that follow.

How to use the validation controls

Figure 7-1 summarizes the validation controls that are available with ASP.NET. As you learned in chapter 2, the first five controls are called *validators*. These are the controls that you use to check that the user has entered valid data into the input controls on a web form. In contrast, you use the validation summary control to display a summary of all the errors on a page.

This figure also illustrates how the validation controls appear in the Web Forms Designer. Here, you can see the Order form for the application that was presented in chapter 3. This form uses two validation controls. The first one is a required field validator that checks that the user entered a value into the Quantity text box, and the second one is a range validator that checks that the user entered an integer that ranges from 1 to 500.

Notice in this example that the required field validator appears directly to the right of the text box, and the range validator appears to the right of the required field validator. As you will see later in this chapter, though, these validators are defined so the error message will be displayed directly to the right of the text box no matter which validator detects the error.

Validation controls on an Order form

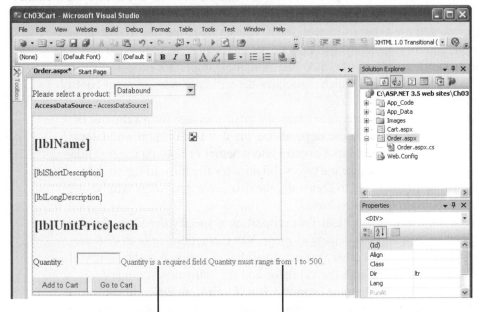

Required field validator   Range validator

The validation controls provided by ASP.NET

Control	Name	Description
	RequiredFieldValidator	Checks that an entry has been made.
	CompareValidator	Checks an entry against a constant value or the value of another control. Can also be used to check for a specific data type.
	RangeValidator	Checks that an entry is within a specified range.
	RegularExpressionValidator	Checks that an entry matches a pattern that's defined by a regular expression.
	CustomValidator	Checks an entry using validation code that you write yourself.
	ValidationSummary	Displays a summary of error messages from the other validation controls.

Description

- You can use the *validation controls* with any of the web server or HTML server input controls.
- Each *validator* is associated with a single input control, but you can associate two or more validators with the same input control.

Figure 7-1   How to use the validation controls

Common validator properties

After you add a validator to a web form, you set its properties to determine which input control it validates and how errors are displayed. Figure 7-2 presents the properties that you use to do that. The most important property is the ControlToValidate property, which associates the validator with an input control on the page.

The Display property determines how the error message for a validator is displayed. The option you choose depends on whether two or more validators are associated with the same input control and whether or not you use a validation summary control. Because the two validators for the form in figure 7-1 have the Display property set to Dynamic, the active error message will be displayed to the right of the text box.

You use the ErrorMessage and Text properties to specify messages that are displayed when the validator detects an error. You can set one or both of these properties depending on whether you use a validation summary control. If you want the same message in both the validator and the validation summary control, just set the ErrorMessage property. But if you want different messages, set the ErrorMessage property to the message you want in the validation summary control and the Text property to the message you want in the validator.

If the Enabled property of a validator is set to True, the validation test for the validator is performed. But if you want to skip the validation that's done by a validator, you can set this property to False. In contrast, the EnableClientScript property determines whether the client-side script for the validation is generated. If this property is set to False, the validation is only done on the server.

When ASP.NET performs the validation test specified by a validator, it sets the IsValid property of the validator to indicate whether or not the data is valid. Then, you can refer to this property in your C# code to test the result of the validation. In most cases, though, you won't test the result of individual validators. Instead, you'll test that all of the validators on the page passed their validation tests by checking the IsValid property of the page.

Common validator properties

Property	Description
ControlToValidate	The ID of the control to be validated.
Display	Determines how the error message is to be displayed. Specify Static to allocate space for the message in the page layout, Dynamic to have space allocated only when an error occurs, or None to display errors only in a validation summary control. The default is Static.
ErrorMessage	The message that's displayed in the validator and/or the validation summary control when the validation fails. To display one message in the validation summary and another in the validator, use the Text property for the validator message.
Text	The message that's displayed in the validator when you use the ErrorMessage property to display a message in the validation summary control.
Enabled	Indicates whether the validation control is enabled.
EnableClientScript	Indicates whether the validation will be done on the client.
ValidationGroup	Indicates which group the validation control is part of (see figure 7-8).
IsValid	Indicates whether the control specified in the ControlToValidate property passed the validation.

Description

- You typically set the Display property to Dynamic if you use two or more validators to validate the same control. Then, the validators that pass their validation tests don't take up space on the page.

- You can also format the error messages that are displayed by including HTML in the values you assign to the ErrorMessage and Text properties.

- In addition to the properties above, validators have properties that affect the appearance of the message that's displayed. For example, the ForeColor property is set to Red by default so the message is displayed in red.

- Each validator has an IsValid property that indicates whether its validation was successful. You typically use this property in the C# code-behind files only if you initiate validation manually using the Page.Validate method.

Figure 7-2   Common validator properties

How ASP.NET processes validation controls

To refresh your memory about how validation controls work, figure 7-3 summarizes the key points. To start, you should realize that the validation tests are typically done on the client before the page is posted to the server. That way, a round trip to the server isn't required to display error messages if any invalid data is detected.

In most cases, client-side validation is done when the focus leaves an input control that has validators associated with it. That can happen when the user presses the Tab key to move to the next control or clicks another control to move the focus to that control.

However, the required field validator works a bit differently. When you use this validator, the validation isn't done until the user clicks a button whose CausesValidation property is set to True. The exception is if the user enters a value into an input control and then tries to clear the value. In that case, an error will be detected when the focus leaves the control.

To perform client-side validation, a browser must support *Dynamic HTML*, or *DHTML*. Because most browsers today support DHTML, validation can usually be done on the client. In case the browser doesn't support DHTML, though, validation is always done on the server when a page is submitted. ASP.NET does this validation after it initializes the page.

When ASP.NET performs the validation tests on the server, it sets the IsValid property of each validator to indicate if the test was successful. In addition, it sets the IsValid property of the page to indicate whether all the input data is valid. You usually should test this property in the event handler for the event that caused the page to be posted to the server.

At the top of this figure, for example, you can see how this property is tested in the event handler for the Click event for the Add to Cart button in figure 7-1. You usually do this in case validation wasn't done on the client. That's especially true if the operations within the method perform critical tasks such as updating the database. If the validation is done on the client, of course, the page won't be posted if one or more controls contain invalid data so the IsValid test will always be True.

If you want to bypass client-side validation and just perform the validation on the server, you can set the EnableClientScript property of the validation controls to False. Then, the scripts that are typically used to perform the validation on the client aren't generated, and validation is done only on the server. This is useful in some applications.

Typical code for processing a page that contains validation controls

```
protected void btnAdd_Click(object sender, EventArgs e)
{
    if (Page.IsValid)
    {
        CartItem item = new CartItem();
        item.Product = selectedProduct;
        item.Quantity = Convert.ToInt32(txtQuantity.Text);
        this.AddToCart(item);
        Response.Redirect("Cart.aspx");
    }
}
```

Description

- If a browser supports *DHTML* (*Dynamic HTML*), the validation controls do their validation on the client using client-side script. That way, the validation is performed and error messages are displayed without the page being posted to the server.

- Validation is always done on the server too, right after the page is initialized, so the validation is done whether or not the browser supports DHTML. Although most browsers support DHTML, your code should still check that a page is valid in case a browser doesn't support DHTML.

- Validation is performed on the server when you click a button whose CausesValidation property is set to True. To create a button that doesn't initiate validation, you can set this property to False.

- Validation is performed on the client when the focus leaves the input control. The exception is a required field validator, which performs its validation only when you click a button whose CausesValidation property is set to True or when you enter a value into a control and then clear and leave the control.

- If a validation control indicates invalid data, the IsValid property of that control is set to False and the IsValid property of the page is set to False. These properties can be tested in your C# code.

- If you want to perform validation only on the server, you can set the EnableClientScript properties of the validation controls to False. Then, no client-side scripts are generated for validating the data.

Figure 7-3   How ASP.NET processes validation controls

How to use the basic validation controls

In the topics that follow, you'll learn about the three validation controls you'll use most often as you develop web applications. These are the required field validator, the compare validator, and the range validator.

How to use the required field validator

Figure 7-4 shows how to use the *required field validator*. This validator checks that the user entered a value into an input control. If the user doesn't enter a value, the validator's error message is displayed.

The three examples in this figure illustrate how you can use the required field validator. In the first example, this validator is used to check for a required entry in a text box. To do that, its ControlToValidate property is set to the ID property of the text box. Then, if the user doesn't enter anything into the text box, the text in the ErrorMessage property is displayed.

The second and third examples show how you can use the InitialValue property of the required field validator to check that the user changed the initial value of a control. By default, this property is set to an empty string, which is what you want if the input control is empty. If you specify an initial value for an input control, however, you'll want to set the InitialValue property of the required field validator to that value.

In the second example, this technique is used with a text box. Here, the initial value indicates the format for a date entry. If the user doesn't change this value, the validation test will fail.

The third example uses the InitialValue property with a list box. Here, the InitialValue property is set to None, which is the value of the first item in the list. That way, if the user doesn't select another item, the validation test will fail. You can also use this technique with a drop-down list or a radio button list.

Additional property of the required field validator

Property	Description
InitialValue	The initial value of the control that's validated. If this value isn't changed, the validation fails. The default is an empty string.

A required field validator that checks for a required entry

```
<asp:TextBox ID="txtName" runat="server"></asp:TextBox> 
<asp:RequiredFieldValidator ID="RequiredFieldValidator1" runat="server"
    ControlToValidate="txtName"
    ErrorMessage="You must enter a name.">
</asp:RequiredFieldValidator>
```

A required field validator that checks that an initial value is changed

```
<asp:TextBox ID="txtBirthDate" runat="server" Width="159px">mm/dd/yyyy
</asp:TextBox> 
<asp:RequiredFieldValidator ID="RequiredFieldValidator2" runat="server"
    ControlToValidate="txtBirthDate"
    InitialValue="mm/dd/yyyy"
    ErrorMessage="You must enter a birth date.">
</asp:RequiredFieldValidator>
```

A required field validator that forces an option to be chosen from a list box

```
<asp:ListBox ID="lstCardType" runat="server" Width="292px">
    <asp:ListItem Selected="True" Value="None">
        --Select a credit card--</asp:ListItem>
    <asp:ListItem Value="Visa">Visa</asp:ListItem>
    <asp:ListItem Value="MC">MasterCard</asp:ListItem>
    <asp:ListItem Value="AmEx">American Express</asp:ListItem>
</asp:ListBox> 
<asp:RequiredFieldValidator ID="RequiredFieldValidator3" runat="server"
    ControlToValidate="lstCardType"
    InitialValue="None"
    ErrorMessage="You must select a credit card type.">
</asp:RequiredFieldValidator>
```

How the input controls are initially displayed in a browser

Description

- The *required field validator* checks that the user entered data into an input control. It's typically used with text box controls, but can also be used with list controls.

Figure 7-4 How to use the required field validator

How to use the compare validator

Figure 7-5 shows how you use the *compare validator*. This validator lets you compare the value entered into an input control with a constant value or the value of another control. You can also use the compare validator to make sure that the value is a particular data type.

To define a compare validator, you use the four additional properties shown in this figure. To compare the input data with a constant value, you specify the value in the ValueToCompare property. Then, you set the Operator property to indicate the type of comparison you want to perform, and you set the Type property to the type of data you're comparing. The first example illustrates how this works. Here, the value entered into a text box is tested to be sure that it's an integer that's greater than zero. Then, if the user enters a value that isn't an integer, or if the user enters an integer that isn't greater than zero, the error message will be displayed.

To test for just a data type, you set the Type property to the type of data you're testing for, and you set the Operator property to DataTypeCheck. This is illustrated by the second example. Here, the value entered into a text box is tested to be sure that it's an integer.

The third example shows how to compare the value of an input control with the value of another control. To do that, you set the Operator and Type properties just as you do when you compare an input value with a constant. Instead of setting the ValueToCompare property, however, you set the ControlToCompare property to the ID of the control whose value you want to compare. This example tests that a date that's entered into one text box is after the date entered into another text box.

When you begin working with compare validators, you'll find that if the user doesn't enter a value into a control, the compare validator associated with that control will pass its validation test. Because of that, you must use a required field validator along with the compare validator if you want to be sure that the user enters a value into the input control.

You should also realize that if you compare the value of a control against the value of another control, the validation test will pass if the user doesn't enter a value into the other control or the value of the other control can't be converted to the correct type. To avoid that problem, you'll want to be sure that the other control is also validated properly.

Additional properties of the compare validator

Property	Description
ValueToCompare	The value that the control specified in the ControlToValidate property should be compared to.
Operator	The type of comparison to perform (Equal, NotEqual, GreaterThan, GreaterThanEqual, LessThan, LessThanEqual, or DataTypeCheck).
Type	The data type to use for the comparison (String, Integer, Double, Date, or Currency).
ControlToCompare	The ID of the control that the value of the control specified in the ControlToValidate property should be compared to.

A compare validator that checks for a value greater than zero

```
<asp:TextBox ID="txtQuantity" runat="server"></asp:TextBox> 
<asp:CompareValidator ID="CompareValidator1" runat="server"
    ControlToValidate="txtQuantity" Type="Integer"
    Operator="GreaterThan" ValueToCompare="0"
    ErrorMessage="Quantity must be greater than zero.">
</asp:CompareValidator>
```

A compare validator that checks for an integer value

```
<asp:TextBox id="txtQuantity" runat="server"></asp:TextBox> 
<asp:CompareValidator ID="CompareValidator2" runat="server"
    ControlToValidate="txtQuantity"
    Operator="DataTypeCheck" Type="Integer"
    ErrorMessage="Quantity must be an integer.">
</asp:CompareValidator>
```

A compare validator that compares the values of two text boxes

```
<asp:TextBox ID="txtStartDate" runat="server"></asp:TextBox><br /><br />
<asp:TextBox ID="txtEndDate" runat="server"></asp:TextBox> 

<asp:CompareValidator
    ID="CompareValidator3" runat="server"
    ControlToValidate="txtEndDate"
    Operator="GreaterThan" Type="Date"
    ControlToCompare="txtStartDate"
    ErrorMessage="End Date must be greater than Start Date.">
</asp:CompareValidator>
```

Description

- The *compare validator* compares the value entered into a control with a constant value or with the value entered into another control. You can also use the compare validator to check that the user entered a specific data type.

Figure 7-5 How to use the compare validator

How to use the range validator

The *range validator*, shown in figure 7-6, validates user input by making sure that it falls within a given range of values. To specify the valid range, you set the MinimumValue and MaximumValue properties. You must also set the Type property to the type of data you're checking. The first example in this figure, for instance, checks that the user enters an integer between 1 and 14 into a text box.

The second example in this figure shows how you can set the range for a range validator at runtime. Here, you can see that the MinimumValue and MaximumValue properties aren't set when the range validator is declared. Instead, they're set when the page is loaded for the first time. In this case, the MinimumValue property is set to the current date, and the MaximumValue property is set to 30 days after the current date.

Like the compare validator, you should realize that the range validator will pass its validation test if the user doesn't enter anything into the associated control. Because of that, you'll need to use a required field validator along with the range validator if the user must enter a value.

Additional properties of the range validator

Property	Description
MinimumValue	The minimum value allowed for the control.
MaximumValue	The maximum value allowed for the control.
Type	The data type to use for the comparison (String, Integer, Double, Date, or Currency).

A range validator that checks for a numeric range

```
<asp:TextBox ID="txtDays" runat="server"></asp:TextBox> 
<asp:RangeValidator ID="RangeValidator1" runat="server"
    ControlToValidate="txtDays" Type="Integer"
    MinimumValue="1" MaximumValue="14"
    ErrorMessage="Days must be between 1 and 14.">
</asp:RangeValidator>
```

How to set a range at runtime

A range validator that checks a date range that's set at runtime

```
<asp:TextBox ID="txtArrival" runat="server">01/01/08</asp:TextBox> 
<asp:RangeValidator ID="valArrival" runat="server"
    ControlToValidate="txtArrival" Type="Date"
    ErrorMessage="You must arrive within 30 days.">
</asp:RangeValidator>
```

Code that sets the minimum and maximum values when the page is loaded

```
protected void Page_Load(object sender, EventArgs e)
{
    if (!IsPostBack)
    {
        valArrival.MinimumValue = DateTime.Today.ToShortDateString();
        valArrival.MaximumValue
            = DateTime.Today.AddDays(30).ToShortDateString();
    }
}
```

Description

- The *range validator* checks that the user enters a value that falls within the range specified by the MinimumValue and MaximumValue properties. These properties can be set when the range validator is created or when the page is loaded.

- If the user enters a value that can't be converted to the correct data type, the validation fails.

- If the user doesn't enter a value into the associated input control, the range validator passes its validation test. As a result, you should also provide a required field validator if a value is required.

Figure 7-6   How to use the range validator

Validation techniques

Now that you're familiar with the basic validation controls, you're ready to learn some additional techniques for validating data. First, you'll learn how to use the validation summary control to display a summary of all the errors on a page. Then, you'll learn how to use validation groups.

How to use the validation summary control

The *validation summary control* lets you summarize all the errors on a page. The summary can be a simple message like "There were errors on the page," or a more elaborate message that includes information about each error. The summary can be displayed directly on the page, or, if validation is being performed on the client, in a separate message box.

Figure 7-7 shows how to use the validation summary control. The most difficult part of using this control is determining how to code the Text and ErrorMessage properties of a validator so the error messages are displayed the way you want. To display the same message in both the validator and the validation summary control, for example, you set the ErrorMessage property to that message.

To display different messages, you set the ErrorMessage property to the message you want to display in the validation summary control, and you set the Text property to the message you want to display in the validator. This technique is illustrated in the example in this figure. Here, the Text properties of two required field validators are set to "*" so those indicators appear next to the controls in error, and the ErrorMessage properties are set to more descriptive error messages. Notice that, unlike the ErrorMessage property, the Text property isn't stored in an attribute of the validator. Instead, it's stored as content between the opening and closing tags for the validator.

If you don't want to display individual error messages in the validation summary control, just set the HeaderText property of the control to the generic message you want to display. Then, leave the ErrorMessage property of each validator blank. Otherwise, you can set the HeaderText property to a value like the one shown in this figure, or you can leave it at its default so that no heading is displayed. Also, to display an error message in the validation summary control but not in a validator, set the Display property of the validator to None.

By default, the error messages displayed by a validation summary control are formatted as a bulleted list as shown in this figure. However, you can also display the errors in a simple list or paragraph format by setting the DisplayMode property accordingly. In addition, you can display the error messages in a message box rather than on the web page by setting the ShowMessageBox property to True and the ShowSummary property to False.

Properties of the validation summary control

Property	Description
DisplayMode	Specifies how the error messages from the validation controls are to be displayed. The available values are BulletList, List, or SingleParagraph. The default is BulletList.
HeaderText	The text that's displayed before the list of error messages.
ShowSummary	A Boolean value that determines whether the validation summary should be displayed on the web page. The default is True.
ShowMessageBox	A Boolean value that determines whether the validation summary should be displayed in a message box (client-side validation only). The default is False.

Two validators and a validation summary control that's displayed on the web page

```
<asp:RequiredFieldValidator ID="RequiredFieldValidator1" runat="server"
    ControlToValidate="lstCardType" InitialValue="None"
    ErrorMessage="You must select a credit card type."
    Display="Dynamic">*</asp:RequiredFieldValidator>

<asp:RequiredFieldValidator ID="RequiredFieldValidator2" runat="server"
    ControlToValidate="txtCardNumber"
    ErrorMessage="You must enter a credit card number."
    Display="Dynamic">*</asp:RequiredFieldValidator>

<asp:ValidationSummary ID="ValidationSummary1" runat="server"
    HeaderText="Please correct the following errors:"/>
```

How the controls appear on the web page

Validator messages   **Validation summary control**

Description

- The *validation summary control* displays a summary of the error messages that were generated by the page's validators. The summary can be displayed on the web page or in a separate message box.
- The error messages displayed in the validation summary control come from the ErrorMessage property of the page's validators. If you want to display a different message in the validator, set the Text property of the validator.
- If you don't want to display an error message in the validator, set its Display property to None.

Figure 7-7   How to use the validation summary control

How to use validation groups

The *validation group* feature of ASP.NET lets you group validation controls and specify which group should be validated when a page is posted. Figure 7-8 shows how to use these groups.

To illustrate, the web page in this figure provides for a bill-to address and an optional ship-to address, with a check box to indicate whether the ship-to address is the same as the bill-to address. Then, if the check box is checked, the ship-to address isn't required. As a result, the validators for the ship-to fields shouldn't be executed. To implement this type of validation, you can use two validation groups: one for the bill-to fields, the other for the ship-to fields.

The first example in this figure shows just one of the ship-to address text boxes and a validator that's assigned to a validation group named ShipTo. For the purpose of this example, though, you can assume that the other ship-to fields also have validators assigned to the ShipTo group. And you can assume that the bill-to fields have validators assigned to a group named BillTo.

The second example shows the button that submits the page. Here, the button specifies BillTo as its validation group so the bill-to text fields will be validated when the user posts the form, but the ship-to fields won't be.

The third example shows how you can invoke the ShipTo validators in your C# code if the check box is left unchecked. Here, the Validate method of the Page class is executed with the name of the validation group as its argument, which causes the Validate method of each validator in the ShipTo group to be executed. As a result, the ship-to fields will be validated on the server, but only if the check box isn't checked.

Unfortunately, the fact that validators are executed with client-side script whenever that's possible can complicate the way validation groups work. If, for example, the user leaves the check box unchecked, only the bill-to validations will be executed. That's because those validators are executed on the client side when the user clicks the button. But when they detect that required data is missing, they display their error messages and stop the page from being posted. As a result, the code that calls the validators for the ship-to fields is never executed. (The only way around this limitation is to write your own client-side validation script to validate the ship-to fields if the check box is unchecked.)

Note that any validation controls that don't specify the ValidationGroup attribute are considered part of the *default group*. The validators in this group are executed only when the page is posted with a button or other control that causes validation but doesn't specify a validation group, or when the Page.Validate method is called without specifying a validation group.

Attributes that cause group validation when a button is clicked

Attribute	Description
CausesValidation	Specifies whether validation should be performed when the user clicks the button.
ValidationGroup	Specifies the name of the group to be validated if CausesValidation is True.

A web page that accepts a bill-to and a ship-to address

Bill-to address

Name: George Constantine

Address: 2050 N. Main Street

City, state, zip: Ann Arbor | MI | 48103

Ship-to address ☑ Ship to same address

Name:

Address:

City, state, zip:

Continue

A text box with a validator that specifies a validation group

```
<asp:TextBox ID="txtShipToName" runat="server" />
<asp:RequiredFieldValidator ID="RequiredFieldValidator1" runat="server"
    ControlToValidate="txtShipToName"
    ErrorMessage="You must enter a ship-to name."
    ValidationGroup="ShipTo"></asp:RequiredFieldValidator>
```

A button that specifies a validation group

```
<asp:Button ID="btnContinue" runat="server" Text="Continue"
    ValidationGroup="BillTo" OnClick="btnContinue_Click" />
```

C# code that conditionally validates the ShipTo group

```
if (!chkShipToSameAsBillTo.Checked)
    Page.Validate("ShipTo");
```

Description

- A *validation group* is a group of validators that are run when a page is posted.
- To group validators, set the ValidationGroup attribute for each validator. Then, use the ValidationGroup attribute for each control that causes a postback (such as a button or a list box) to specify which group should be executed.
- You can use C# code to force the execution of a specific validation group by using the Page.Validate method with the validation group name as the argument.
- Any validators that don't specify the ValidationGroup attribute are part of the *default group*. This group is executed when started by a button or control that doesn't specify a validation group or when the Page.Validate method is used without an argument.

Figure 7-8   How to use validation groups

How to use the advanced validation controls

Besides the validation controls you've already learned about, ASP.NET provides two controls that provide advanced functionality. The regular expression validator lets you match data to a pattern you specify, and the custom validator lets you create your own validation routines.

How to use the regular expression validator

A *regular expression* is a string made up of special pattern-matching symbols. You can use regular expressions with the *regular expression validator* to make sure that an input control's data matches a particular pattern, such as a zip code, phone number, or email address. Figure 7-9 shows how to use the regular expression validator.

As you can see, the ValidationExpression property specifies the regular expression the input data must match. For instance, the code for the first regular expression validator in this figure specifies that the input data must contain five decimal digits (\d{5}). And the regular expression for the second validator specifies that the input data must be in the format of a U.S. phone number.

In the next topic, you'll learn how to create your own regular expressions. However, you should know that Visual Studio provides several standard expressions you can choose from. These expressions define patterns for validating phone numbers and postal codes for the U.S., France, Germany, Japan, and China; Social Security numbers for the U.S. and China; and Internet email addresses and URLs.

To use a standard expression, you simply select it from the Regular Expression Editor dialog box. You can also create a custom expression that's based on a standard expression by selecting the standard expression so its definition appears in the text box at the bottom of the Regular Expression Editor dialog box. Then, you can edit the regular expression any way you'd like.

An additional property of the regular expression validator

Property	Description
ValidationExpression	A string that specifies a regular expression. The regular expression defines a pattern that the input data must match to be valid.

A regular expression validator that validates five-digit numbers

```
<asp:TextBox ID="txtZipCode" runat="server"></asp:TextBox> 
<asp:RegularExpressionValidator ID="RegularExpressionValidator1"
    runat="server" ControlToValidate="txtZipCode"
    ValidationExpression="\d{5}"
    ErrorMessage="Must be a five-digit U.S. zip code.">
</asp:RegularExpressionValidator>
```

A regular expression validator that validates U.S. phone numbers

```
<asp:TextBox ID="txtPhone" runat="server"></asp:TextBox> 
<asp:RegularExpressionValidator ID="RegularExpressionValidator2"
    runat="server" ControlToValidate="txtPhone"
    ValidationExpression="((\(\d{3}\) ?)|(\d{3}-))?\d{3}-\d{4}"
    ErrorMessage="Must be a valid U.S. phone number.">
</asp:RegularExpressionValidator>
```

The Regular Expression Editor dialog box

Description

- The *regular expression validator* matches the input entered by the user with the pattern supplied by the ValidationExpression property. If the input doesn't match the pattern, the validation fails.

- The string you specify for the ValidationExpression property must use *regular expression* notation. For more information, see the next figure.

- ASP.NET provides several standard regular expressions that you can access using the Regular Expression Editor. To display its dialog box, select the validation control, select the ValidationExpression property in the Properties window, and click its ellipsis button.

- You can also use the Regular Expression Editor to create a custom expression that's based on a standard expression. To do that, select the standard expression and then edit it in the Validation Expression text box.

Figure 7-9   How to use the regular expression validator

How to create your own regular expressions

Figure 7-10 presents the basic elements of regular expressions. Although the .NET Framework provides many other elements that you can use in regular expressions, you can create expressions of considerable complexity using just the ones shown here. In fact, all of the standard expressions provided by ASP.NET use only these elements.

To start, you can specify any ordinary character, such as a letter or a decimal digit. If a character must be an A, for example, you just include that character in the expression. To include a character other than an ordinary character, you must precede it with a backslash. For example, \(specifies that the character must be a left parenthesis, \] specifies that the character must be a right bracket, and \\ specifies that the character must be a backslash. A backslash that's used in this way is called an *escape character*.

You can also specify a *character class*, which consists of a set of characters. For example, \d indicates that the character must be a decimal digit, \w indicates that the character must be a *word character*, and \s indicates that the character must be a *whitespace character*. The uppercase versions of these elements—\D, \W, and \S—match any character that is not a decimal digit, word character, or whitespace character.

To create a list of possible characters, you enclose them in brackets. For example, [abc] specifies that the character must be the letter a, b, or c, and [a-z] specifies that the character must be a lowercase letter. One fairly common construct is [a-zA-Z], which specifies that the character must be a lowercase or uppercase letter.

You can also use *quantifiers* to indicate how many of the preceding element the input data must contain. To specify an exact number, you just code it in brackets. For example, \d{5} specifies that the input data must be a five-digit number. You can also specify a minimum number and a maximum number of characters. For example, \w{6,20} specifies that the input data must contain from six to twenty word characters. You can also omit the maximum number to require just a minimum number of characters. For example, \w{6,} specifies that the input data must contain at least 6 word characters. You can also use the *, ?, and + quantifiers to specify zero or more, zero or one, or one or more characters.

If the input data can match one or more patterns, you can use the vertical bar to separate elements. For example, \w+|s{1} means that the input data must contain one or more word characters or a single whitespace character.

To create groups of elements, you use parentheses. Then, you can apply quantifiers to the entire group or you can separate groups with a vertical bar. For example, (AB)|(SB) specifies that the input characters must be either AB or SB. And (\d{3}-)? specifies that the input characters must contain zero or one occurrence of a three-digit number followed by a hyphen.

To help you understand how you can use each of these elements, this figure presents several examples. If you study them, you'll see the complex patterns that you can provide using these basic elements.

Common regular expression elements

Element	Description
Ordinary character	Matches any character other than ., $, ^, [, {, (, |,), *, +, ?, or \.
\	Matches the character that follows.
\d	Matches any decimal digit (0-9).
\D	Matches any character other than a decimal digit.
\w	Matches any word character (a-z, A-Z, and 0-9).
\W	Matches any character other than a word character.
\s	Matches any white space character (space, tab, new line, etc.).
\S	Matches any character other than a whitespace character.
[abcd]	Matches any character included between the brackets.
[^abcd]	Matches any character that is not included between the brackets.
[a-z]	Matches any characters in the indicated range.
{n}	Matches exactly n occurrences of the preceding element or group.
{n,}	Matches at least n occurrences of the preceding element or group.
{n,m}	Matches at least n but no more than m occurrences of the preceding element or group.
*	Matches zero or more occurrences of the preceding element.
?	Matches zero or one occurrence of the preceding element.
+	Matches one or more occurrences of the preceding element.
		Matches any of the elements separated by the vertical bar.
( )	Groups the elements that appear between the parentheses.

Examples of regular expressions

Expression	Example	Description
\d{3}	289	A three digit number.
\w{8,20}	Frankenstein	At least eight but no more than twenty word characters.
\d{2}-\d{4}	10-3944	A two-digit number followed by a hyphen and a four-digit number.
\w{1,8}.\w{1,3}	freddy.jpg	Up to eight letters or numbers, followed by a period and up to three letters or numbers.
(AB)|(SB)-\d{1,5}	SB-3276	The letters AB or SB, followed by a hyphen and a one- to five-digit number.
\d{5}(-\d{4})?	93711-2765	A five-digit number, optionally followed by a hyphen and a four-digit number.
\w*\d\w*	arm01	A text entry that contains at least one numeral.
[xyz]\d{3}	x023	The letter x, y, or z, followed by a three-digit number.

Notes

- A regular expression can include elements other than those shown above. For more information, see the *Regular Expression Language Elements* topic in help.
- The standard regular expressions use only the elements shown above.

Figure 7-10   How to create your own regular expressions

How to use a custom validator

If none of the other validators provide the data validation your program requires, you can use a *custom validator*. Then, you can code your own validation routine that's executed when the page is submitted to the server. This technique is frequently used to validate input data that requires a database lookup.

Figure 7-11 shows how you use a custom validator. In this example, a custom validator is used to check that a value entered by the user is a valid product code in a table of products. To do that, the program includes an event handler for the ServerValidate event of the custom validator. This event occurs whenever validation is performed on the server.

When the ServerValidate event occurs, the event handler receives an argument named args that you can use to validate the data the user entered. The Value property of this argument contains the input value. Then, the event handler can perform the tests that are necessary to determine if this value is valid. If it is valid, the event handler assigns a True value to the IsValid property of the args argument so the validator passes its test. If it isn't valid, the event handler can assign a False value to the IsValid property of this argument so the validator doesn't pass its test. This causes the error message specified by the validator to be displayed.

In this figure, for example, the event handler calls the CheckProductCode method of the HalloweenDB class. Although you haven't seen this class or method before, all you need to know is that it checks the product code by looking it up in a database. If the product code exists, this method returns a value of True. Otherwise, it returns a value of False. In either case, the returned value is assigned to the IsValid property of the args argument.

Properties of the ServerValidateEventArgs class

Property	Description
Value	The text string to be validated.
IsValid	A Boolean property that you set to True if the value passes the validation test or to False otherwise.

Aspx code for a text box and a custom validator

```
<asp:TextBox ID="txtProductCode" runat="server"></asp:TextBox> 
<asp:CustomValidator id="valProductCode" runat="server"
    ControlToValidate="txtProductCode"
    ErrorMessage="Product code must be in database."
    OnServerValidate="valProductCode_ServerValidate">
</asp:CustomValidator>
```

C# code for the custom validator

```
protected void valProductCode_ServerValidate(object source,
    ServerValidateEventArgs args)
{
    args.IsValid = HalloweenDB.CheckProductCode(args.Value);
}
```

Description

- You can use a *custom validator* to validate input data using the validation tests you specify.

- You code the validation tests within an event handler for the ServerValidate event of the custom validator. This event is raised whenever validation is performed on the server. Because of that, the form must be submitted before the validation can be done.

- You can use the properties of the args argument that's passed to the ServerValidate event handler to test the input data (args.value) and indicate whether the data passed the validation test (args.IsValid). If you set the IsValid property of the args argument to False, the error message you specified for the custom validator is displayed.

- If the user doesn't enter a value into the associated input control, the custom validator doesn't perform its validation test. As a result, you should also provide a required field validator if a value is required.

Figure 7-11   How to use a custom validator

A validation routine that validates credit card numbers

To give you a better idea of what you can do with a custom validator, figure 7-12 shows the C# code for a custom validator that validates credit card numbers. To do that, it checks that the credit card number meets a mod-10 algorithm that all credit card numbers adhere to. This test often catches simple typographic errors before taking the time to actually authorize the card. Please note that this test doesn't establish that an account with the specified number exists or that credit is available on the account. It merely establishes that the number meets the required mod-10 algorithm.

To validate a credit card number, the event handler for the ServerValidate event calls a method named ValidateCreditCard and passes the card number to it. After this method declares three variables, it removes any spaces in the card number by using the Replace method of the String class. Then, it uses a for loop to store the digits in the credit card in reverse order in the reversedCardNumber variable. Next, it uses another for loop to double the digits in even-numbered positions. To determine if a digit is in an even-numbered position, it uses the modulus operator (%) to divide the position by 2 to see if there's a remainder. If not, it multiplies the number in that position by 2 and then concatenates it to the variable named digits. (Note that because the Substring method that gets the number returns a string, the string is converted to an integer before it's multiplied.) Otherwise, it just concatenates the number.

After the digits in the even-numbered positions have been multiplied, the method uses another for loop to add up all the digits. (Again, the result of the Substring method is converted to an integer.) The modulus operator is then used to determine if the result is evenly divisible by 10. If so, the credit card number is valid and a true value is returned to the calling method. Otherwise, a false value is returned and the error message associated with the custom validator is displayed.

C# code for a credit card validator

```
protected void valCreditCardNumber_ServerValidate(object source,
    ServerValidateEventArgs args)
{
    args.IsValid = ValidateCreditCard(args.Value);
}

private bool ValidateCreditCard(string cardNumber)
{
    int digitSum = 0;
    string digits = "";
    string reversedCardNumber = "";
    //Remove spaces and reverse string
    cardNumber = cardNumber.Replace(" ", null);
    for (int i = cardNumber.Length - 1; i >= 0; i--)
        reversedCardNumber += cardNumber[i];
    //Double the digits in even-numbered positions
    for (int i = 0; i < reversedCardNumber.Length; i++)
    {
        if ((i + 1) % 2 == 0)
            digits += Convert.ToInt32(reversedCardNumber.Substring(i, 1))
                    * 2;
        else
            digits += reversedCardNumber.Substring(i, 1);
    }
    //Add the digits
    for (int i = 0; i < digits.Length; i++)
        digitSum += Convert.ToInt32(digits.Substring(i, 1));
    //Check that the sum is divisible by 10
    if ((digitSum % 10) == 0)
        return true;
    else
        return false;
}
```

What the mod 10 validation algorithm does

1. Removes any spaces from the number.
2. Reverses the digits in the number.
3. Doubles the digits in even-numbered positions. If the original digit is 5 or greater, this will insert an additional digit into the number.
4. Adds up the individual digits.
5. Divides the result by 10. If the remainder is 0, the credit card number is valid.

Description

- This code can be used along with a custom validator to ensure that the user enters a credit card number that passes a standard mod-10 algorithm. If the card number passes this test, the program usually continues by checking that the account is valid and that the customer has available credit.

- The ServerValidate event handler for the custom validator calls a method named ValidateCreditCard and passes the credit card number entered by the user. This method returns a bool value that indicates whether the credit card is valid.

Figure 7-12   A validation routine that validates credit card numbers

Perspective

Now that you've completed this chapter, you should be able to create web forms that provide for most of the data validation that your applications will require. Keep in mind, though, that after you add validators to a form, you need to test them thoroughly to be sure that they detect all invalid entries. Although that can be time-consuming, particularly if you use regular expression validators that require complicated expressions or custom validators that require complicated validation routines, it's an essential part of developing professional web applications.

Terms

validation control
validator
DHTML (Dynamic HTML)
required field validator
compare validator
range validator
validation summary control
validation group
default group
regular expression validator
regular expression
escape character
character class
word character
whitespace character
quantifier
custom validator

8

How to manage state

In chapters 2 and 3, you were introduced to the way that view state and session state are used. Now you'll learn more about using these states, and you'll also learn how to use application state. Beyond that, you'll learn how to use cookies and URL encoding to pass data between the server and the client. Because HTTP is a stateless protocol, these are essential skills for every web developer.

How to use view state **272**
How to work with view state 272
How to use view state for your own data 274

How to use session state **276**
How to work with session state 276
When to save and retrieve session state items 278
Options for storing session state data 280
Options for tracking session IDs 280
How to set session state options 282

How to use application state **284**
How application state works 284
How to work with application state data 286
How to work with application events 288

How to use cookies and URL encoding **290**
How to create cookies 290
How to work with cookies 292
How to enable or disable cookies 294
How to use URL encoding 296

Perspective **298**

How to use view state

For the most part, *view state* is automatic. Because of that, you don't have to set any properties or write any code to use it. Nevertheless, you should at least understand how view state works and how to use it to your advantage. In some cases, you may even want to add your own data to view state.

How to work with view state

As the summary in figure 8-1 says, view state works by saving data in the HTML stream that's sent to the browser when a page is requested. This data is saved as a hidden input field named _VIEWSTATE. Because the field is hidden, it isn't displayed in the browser. And because the field is an input field, it's automatically sent back to the server when the user posts the page.

View state is used to retain the values of the form and control properties that you set in code. In the Future Value application of chapter 2, for example, the values in the drop-down list were set by code. As a result, these values don't need to be reset by code each time the form is posted back to the server. Instead, they're automatically reset by view state.

By default, view state is enabled for each control you add to a form, which is usually what you want. Occasionally, though, you may want to disable view state. One reason for doing that is to get a control to work the way you want it to. Another reason is to improve performance when view state gets so large that it degrades performance.

If, for example, you change the value of a control property in code, but you want the initial value of that property restored each time the page is loaded, you can turn off view state to get the page to work right. Or, if a page is never posted back to itself, you can turn off view state to improve performance. In practice, though, you probably won't turn off view state until you discover that it's creating either a programming or performance problem.

To determine the size of view state, you can enable the ASP.NET Trace feature as described in chapter 4. Then, you can scroll to the Control Tree section of the trace output to see which controls are using view state and how many bytes they're using. That way, you can tell whether it's worth the effort to turn view state off.

View state concepts

- *View state* is an ASP.NET feature that provides for retaining the values of page and control properties that change from one execution of a page to another.

- Before ASP.NET sends a page back to the client, it determines what changes the program has made to the properties of the page and its controls. These changes are encoded into a string that's assigned to the value of a hidden input field named _VIEWSTATE.

- When the page is posted back to the server, the _VIEWSTATE field is sent back to the server along with the HTTP request. Then, ASP.NET retrieves the property values from the _VIEWSTATE field and uses them to restore the page and control properties.

- ASP.NET also uses view state to save the values of the page properties it uses, such as IsPostBack.

- View state is *not* used to restore data entered by a user into a text box or any other input control unless the control responds to change events.

- If view state is enabled for a data-bound control, the control will not be rebound when the page is reposted. Instead, the control's values will be restored from view state.

Two cases when you may want to disable view state

- When restoring the control properties for a page affects the way you want the form to work, you may want to disable view state for one or more controls. Otherwise, you can modify your code so the page works without turning view state off.

- When the size of the view state field gets so large that it affects performance, you may want to disable view state for one or more controls or for an entire page.

How to disable view state

- To disable view state for a control, set the control's EnableViewState property to False.

- To disable view state for an entire page, set the EnableViewState property of the page to False. That disables view state for all the controls on the page.

How to determine the size of view state for a page

- Enable the Trace feature for the page by setting the Trace attribute of the Page directive for the page to True as described in chapter 4. Then, scroll down to the Control Tree section of the trace output to see the number of bytes of view state used by the page and its controls.

Figure 8-1   How to work with view state

How to use view state for your own data

Although view state is designed to automatically save page and control property values across round trips to the browser, you can also add your own data to view state. To do that, you store the data in a *view state object* that's created from the StateBag class as shown in figure 8-2.

Like the session state object, the view state object contains a collection of key/value pairs that represent the items saved in view state. To access this object, you use the ViewState property of the page. Then, you can use the members listed in this figure to work with the view state object.

To illustrate, the first two examples in this figure show how you can add or update a view state item named TimeStamp. The third example shows how to retrieve that item. And the last example shows how to remove it. Notice in the third example that because the value of a view state item is stored as an Object type, the item must be cast to the DateTime data type when it's retrieved.

Keep in mind that you usually use session state, not view state, to save data across round trips to the browser. Occasionally, though, it does make sense to use view state for passing small amounts of data, especially when you want to associate the data with a specific page. In chapter 23, you'll see an example of that.

Common members of the StateBag class

Property	Description
Count	The number of items in the view state collection.
Keys	A collection of keys for all of the items in the view state collection.
Values	A collection of values for all of the items in the view state collection.

Indexer	Description
[name]	The value of the view state item with the specified name. If you set the value of an item that doesn't exist, that item is created.

Method	Description
Add(name, value)	Adds an item to the view state collection. If the item you name already exists, its value is updated.
Clear()	Removes all items from the view state collection.
Remove(name)	Removes the item with the specified name from the view state collection.

A statement that adds or updates a view state item

```
ViewState.Add("TimeStamp", DateTime.Now);
```

Another way to add or update a view state item

```
ViewState["TimeStamp"] = DateTime.Now;
```

A statement that retrieves the value of a view state item

```
DateTime timeStamp = (DateTime) ViewState["TimeStamp"];
```

A statement that removes an item from view state

```
ViewState.Remove("TimeStamp");
```

Description

- View state is implemented using a *view state object* that's defined by the StateBag class. This class defines a collection of view state items.

- Although the form and control properties are automatically saved in view state, you can also save other data in view state.

- To access the view state object for a page, you use the ViewState property of the page.

Figure 8-2   How to use view state for your own data

How to use session state

In chapter 3, you learned some basic skills for using session state to save data across round trips to the browser. The topics that follow review and expand on that information.

How to work with session state

As you have learned, ASP.NET uses *session state* to track the state of each user of an application. To do that, it creates a *session state object* that contains a unique *session ID* for each user's session. This ID is passed back to the browser as part of the response and then returned to the server with the next request. ASP.NET can then use the session ID to get the session state object that's associated with the request.

To manage a user session, you can store data in the session state object, as shown in figure 8-3. Since you've already seen how session state is used in the Shopping Cart application, you shouldn't have any trouble understanding the first three examples. The first one adds or updates a session state item named EMail. The second one retrieves the value of the EMail item and stores it in a string variable. And the third one removes the EMail item from session state.

All three of these examples assume that session state is being accessed from the code-behind file of a web page. In that case, you refer to the session state object using the Session property of the page. To access session state from outside of a web page, however, you use the Session property of the HttpContext object for the current request as illustrated in the fourth example.

Common members of the HttpSessionState class

Property	Description
SessionID	The unique ID of the session.
Count	The number of items in the session state collection.

Indexer	Description
[name]	The value of the session state item with the specified name. If you set the value of an item that doesn't exist, that item is created.

Method	Description
Add(name, value)	Adds an item to the session state collection. If the item you name already exists, its value is updated.
Clear()	Removes all items from the session state collection.
Remove(name)	Removes the item with the specified name from the session state collection.

A statement that adds or updates a session state item

```
Session["EMail"] = email;
```

A statement that retrieves the value of a session state item

```
string email = Session["EMail"].ToString();
```

A statement that removes an item from session state

```
Session.Remove("EMail");
```

A statement that retrieves a session state item from a non-page class

```
string email = HttpContext.Current.Session["EMail"].ToString();
```

Description

- ASP.NET uses *session state* to track the state of each user of an application. To do that, it creates a *session state object* that contains a *session ID*. This ID is passed to the browser and then back to the server with the next request so the server can identify the session associated with that request.

- Because session state sends only the session ID to the browser, it doesn't slow response time. By default, though, session state objects are maintained in server memory so they can slow performance on the server side.

- To work with the data in session state, you use the HttpSessionState class, which defines a collection of session state items.

- To access the session state object from the code-behind file for a web form, use the Session property of the page.

- To access the session state object from a class other than a code-behind file, use the Current property of the HttpContext class to get the HttpContext object for the current request. Then, use the Session property to get the session state object.

Figure 8-3   How to work with session state

When to save and retrieve session state items

Most ASP.NET developers use session state in a consistent way. First, an application retrieves data from session state and stores it in variables. Then, the application uses these variables when it processes the user events. Finally, the application saves the updated variables back to session state so they can be retrieved the next time the page is posted back to the server.

If an item in session state is used within a single method in an application, you can retrieve, process, and save that item within that method. However, it's more common for an application to use a session state item in two or more methods. Because of that, it makes sense to retrieve the item when the application first starts and save it just before it ends. To do that, you can use the Load and PreRender events of the page as shown in figure 8-4.

The example in this figure illustrates how this works. To keep this simple, this application consists of a single page that contains a Post button that the user can click to post the page back to the server. Each time the user clicks this button, the program code updates the label on the page to indicate how many times the button has been clicked.

To implement this application, a session state item named Count is used to maintain a count of the number of times the user clicks the Post button. To start, the Page_Load event handler sets a count variable to zero if the session state item named Count hasn't been created yet. Otherwise, this event handler gets the value of the Count item from the session state object and assigns it to the count variable.

If the user clicked the Post button, the program executes the btnPost_Click event handler. This event handler adds one to the count variable and updates the label on the form to indicate how many times the button has been clicked.

Then, just before ASP.NET renders the HTML for the page, the Page_PreRender event handler is executed. This event handler saves the value of the count variable to session state so it's available the next time the user clicks the Post button. Because PreRender is a page event, it's raised each time the page is executed just like the Load event.

It's important to note that the variable that's used to store the value of the session state item in this example is a value-type variable. That means that the value is actually stored in the variable. Because of that, you have to explicitly update the session state item in the Page_PreRender event handler.

In contrast, if you use a reference-type variable such as a string or other object variable, the session state item is updated automatically when you update the variable that refers to it. That's because the variable contains a pointer to the object, not the data itself. As a result, you don't have to update the session state item explicitly. If you look back to the application in chapter 3, you'll see that the Cart item in the session state object is handled that way.

A Counter application that counts the times the user clicks the button

The code for the Counter application

```
int sessionCount;

protected void Page_Load(object sender, EventArgs e)
{
    if (Session["Count"] == null)
        sessionCount = 0;
    else
        sessionCount = Convert.ToInt32(Session["Count"]);
}

protected void btnPost_Click(object sender, EventArgs e)
{
    sessionCount++;
    lblSessionClicks.Text = "You have clicked the button "
                        + sessionCount + " times.";
}

protected void Page_PreRender(object sender, EventArgs e)
{
    Session["Count"] = sessionCount;
}
```

Description

- If a session state item is accessed from two or more event handlers, you usually code the application so it retrieves the value of that item in the Load event handler and saves the updated value back to session state in the PreRender event handler.

- Since the Load event is raised before any of the control events for the page, you can use its event handler to retrieve a session state item and store it in a class-level variable. Then, the item is available to all of the other methods.

- Since the PreRender event is raised after all the control events for the page have been processed, you can use its event handler to update the session state item.

- You only need to update a session state item explicitly if it's stored in a value-type variable. If it's stored in a reference-type variable, the session state item is updated automatically when the variable is updated.

Figure 8-4   When to save and retrieve session state items

Options for storing session state data

By default, ASP.NET stores session state data in server memory and tracks user sessions using cookies. However, as figure 8-5 shows, ASP.NET actually provides four options for storing session state data and two options for tracking session IDs. Although you typically use the default options, you should be familiar with these other options in case you ever need them.

The default for storing session state data is *in-process mode*. With this mode, session state data is stored in server memory within the same process that your ASP.NET application runs. This is the most efficient way to store session state data, but it only works for applications that are hosted on a single web server.

If your application has so many users that a single web server can't carry the load, you can deploy the application on two or more servers. When you do that, you need to store session state data in a location that can be accessed by all of the servers. Session state provides two options for doing that.

State Server mode stores session state data in server memory, but not in the same process as your application. Instead, session state is managed by the ASP.NET state service, which can be accessed by all of the servers that host the application. That's necessary because when two or more servers host an application, a different server can process the application each time it's executed. So if the session state data is stored on the server that processed the application the first time it was executed, that data won't be available if the application is processed by another server the next time it's executed.

Another way to make session state data available to two or more servers is to use *SQL Server mode*. With this mode, session state data is stored in a SQL Server database rather than in server memory. Although SQL Server mode is slower than in-process and State Server mode, it's also the most reliable. That's because if your web server goes down, the session state data will be maintained in the database. In contrast, session state data is lost if the server goes down when you're using in-process or State Server mode.

The last option for storing session state data is *custom mode*. With this mode, you create your own *session state store provider* that saves and retrieves session state data. You might use this option if you want to save session state data in a database, but your shop uses Oracle or some other database instead of Microsoft SQL Server.

Fortunately, the programming requirements for all four session state modes are identical. So you can change an application from one mode to another without changing any of the application's code. If you use the custom mode, however, you'll have to create the session state store provider.

Options for tracking session IDs

By default, ASP.NET maintains session state by sending the session ID for a user session to the browser as a cookie. Then, the cookie is returned to the server with the next request so the server can associate the browser with the

Four options for storing session state data

- *In-process mode* (the default) stores session state data in IIS server memory in the same process as the ASP.NET application. This is the session state model that's used the most, but it's suitable only when a single server is used for the application.

- *State Server mode* stores session state data in server memory under the control of a separate service called the ASP.NET state service. This service can be accessed by other IIS servers, so it can be used when an application is hosted on a web farm that consists of more than one IIS server. In that case, each request for the application can be processed by a different server, so the session state information must be available to all the servers.

- *SQL Server mode* stores session state data in a SQL Server database. Like State Server mode, SQL Server mode is used for applications that require more than one IIS server. Although this mode is slower than In-process mode and State Server mode, it's also the most reliable.

- *Custom mode* lets you write your own *session state store provider* to read and write session state data.

Two options for tracking session IDs

- By default, ASP.NET uses *cookie-based session tracking* to keep track of user sessions. However, if a browser doesn't support cookies, this doesn't work.

- With *cookieless session tracking*, the session ID is encoded as part of the URL. As a result, cookieless session state works whether or not the browser supports cookies.

Description

- The programming requirements for all four session state modes are identical, so you don't have to recode an application if you change the mode. If you use custom mode, however, you do have to create a class that implements the session state store provider.

- Cookieless session tracking introduces security risks because the session ID is visible to the user. It also limits the way URL's can be specified in Response.Redirect and Server.Transfer calls. For these reasons, most developers don't use cookieless sessions.

- You can control how session state data is stored and how session IDs are tracked by setting the attributes of the session state element in the application's web.config file. For more information, see the next figure.

- Custom mode is an advanced mode that isn't covered in this book. To learn more about how to create a session state store provider for use with custom mode, see the "Implementing a Session State Store Provider" topic in the Help documentation.

Figure 8-5   Options for storing session state data and tracking session IDs session. This is called *cookie-based session tracking*, and this is the most reliable and secure way to track sessions.

If a browser doesn't support cookies, however, session state won't work unless you switch to *cookieless session tracking*. Cookieless session tracking works by adding the session ID to the URL that's used to request the ASP.NET page. Unfortunately, because the URL is visible to the user and isn't encrypted, the use of cookieless session tracking creates a security risk.

Ideally, then, you should use cookie-based session tracking when cookies are supported and cookieless session tracking when they're not. As you can see in figure 8-6, ASP.NET lets you do just that.

How to set session state options

As you know, the first time you run an application with debugging, Visual Studio adds a web.config file to your web site. If this file hasn't already been added, however, you can add it by selecting the Website→Add New Item command and then selecting the Web Configuration File template. Then, you can add session state options to this file as shown in figure 8-6.

Although the web.config file is an XML file, you shouldn't have trouble editing it even if you aren't familiar with the details of XML syntax. To edit this file, just double-click on it in the Solution Explorer to display it in a Text Editor window. Then, add a sessionState element within the system.web element as shown in this figure. Within the sessionState element, you can code any of the attributes listed in the table in this figure. In the example shown here, I included the Mode attribute to indicate that in-process mode should be used; I included the Cookieless attribute to indicate that cookies should be used if they're supported, and URLs should be used if they're not; and I included the Timeout attribute to increase the number of minutes that the session should be maintained without activity to 30.

If you use State Server mode, you'll need to set the stateConnectionString attribute to the server name or IP address and port number of the server that hosts the ASP.NET state service. If the name of the server is mma1, for example, the stateConnectionString attribute will look like this:

```
stateConnectionString="tcpip=mma1:42424"
```

Note that the port number is always 42424.

Similarly, if you use SQL Server mode, you'll need to set the sqlConnectionString attribute to the connection string for the instance of SQL Server that contains the database that's used to store the session state data. For instance, if the SQL Server instance is Murach, the attribute might look like this:

```
sqlConnectionString="Data Source=Murach;Integrated
Security=SSPI"
```

Note that the database isn't included in the connection string, which means that the default database named ASPState is used. If you want to use a different database to store session state data, you need to include the name of the database in the connection string, and you need to include the allowCustomSqlDatabase attribute with a value of True.

Attributes of the session state element in the web.config file

Attribute	Description
Mode	The session state mode. Values can be Off, InProc, StateServer, SQLServer, or Custom. The default is InProc.
Cookieless	An HttpCookieMode value that specifies whether cookieless sessions are used. AutoDetect uses cookies if they're supported and a query string if they're not. UseUri uses a query string. The default is UseCookies.
Timeout	The number of minutes a session should be maintained without any user activity. After the specified number of minutes, the session is deleted. The default is 20.
StateConnectionString	The server name or IP address and port number (always 42424) of the server that runs the ASP.NET state service. This attribute is required when State Server mode is used.
SqlConnectionString	A connection string for the instance of SQL Server that contains the database that's used to store the session state data. If the allowCustomSqlDatabase attribute is set to True, the connection string can also include the name of the database. This attribute is required when SQL Server mode is used.
AllowCustomSqlDatabase	A Boolean value that determines if the SqlConnectionString can specify the name of the database used to store state information. The default value is False, in which case the state information is stored in a database named ASPState.
CustomProvider	The name of the custom session state store provider.

A sessionState element in the web.config file that uses in-process mode

```xml
<?xml version="1.0"?>
<configuration>
  <system.web>
    .
    .
    <sessionState mode="InProc"
      cookieless="AutoDetect"
      timeout="30"
    />
    .
    .
  </system.web>
</configuration>
```

Description

- The web.config file contains settings that affect how an ASP.NET web application operates. To change the default options for session state, you can add a sessionState element to the web.config file and then specify the attributes and values you want to use.

- Before you can use SQL Server mode, you must create the database that will be used to store session state data. For information on how to do that, see the "Session State Modes" topic in the Help documentation.

- If you specify Custom mode, you must include additional information in the web.config file to identify the session state store provider. For more information, see the "Session State Modes" topic in the Help documentation.

Figure 8-6   How to set session state options

How to use application state

In contrast to session state, which stores data for a single user session, application state lets you store data that is shared by all users of an application. In the topics that follow, you'll learn how to use application state.

How application state works

Figure 8-7 presents the concepts you need for working with *application state*. To start, an *application* is made up of all the pages, code, and other files that are located under a single directory in an IIS web server.

The first time a user requests a page that resides in an application's directory, ASP.NET initializes the application. During that process, ASP.NET creates an *application object* from the HttpApplication class. This object is represented by a special class file named global.asax, which you'll learn how to work with in figure 8-9.

The application object can be accessed by any of the application's pages. This object exists until the application ends, which normally doesn't happen until IIS shuts down. However, the application is automatically restarted each time you rebuild the application or edit the application's web.config file.

Each time ASP.NET starts an application and creates an application object, it also creates an *application state object* from the HttpApplicationState class. You can use this object to store data in server memory that can be accessed by any page that's part of the application.

One common use for application state is to store hit counters that track how many times users have retrieved specific pages. For instance, the Counter application at the top of this figure tracks the number of times all of the users of the application have clicked the Post button. This is similar to the application you saw in figure 8-4, but that application used session state to track the count for a single user.

Another common use for application state is to store application-specific data, such as discount terms and tax rates for an ordering system. Although you could retrieve this type of information from a database each time it's needed, it sometimes makes sense to retrieve it just once when the application starts and then store it in application state. That way, the data is more readily accessible as the application executes.

Finally, application state is commonly used to keep track of which users are logged on to the application. That's particularly useful for applications that provide chat rooms or message boards where you can communicate with other users. Then, the application can display a list of the users who are currently in the chat room or who are using the message board.

A Counter application that counts the number of times that all users click the button

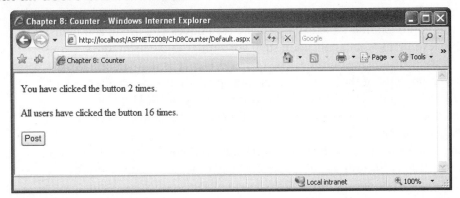

Application concepts

- An ASP.NET *application* is the collection of pages, code, and other files within a single directory on a web server. In most cases, an ASP.NET application corresponds to a single Visual Studio web project.

- An application begins when the first user requests a page that's a part of the application. Then, ASP.NET initializes the application before it processes the request for the page.

- As part of its initialization, ASP.NET creates an *application object* from the HttpApplication class. This object exists for the duration of the application. You can use the global.asax file to work with the application object, as described in figure 8-9.

- Once an application has started, it doesn't normally end until the web server is shut down. If you rebuild the application or edit the web.config file, however, the application will be restarted the next time a user requests a page that's part of the application.

Application state concepts

- If you store items in *application state*, those items are available to all users of the application.

- To provide for the use of application state, ASP.NET creates an *application state object* for each application from the HttpApplicationState class and stores this object in server memory.

Typical uses for application state

- To store hit counters and other statistical data.
- To store global application data such as discount terms and tax rates.
- To track users currently visiting the site by keeping a list of user names or other identifying data.

Figure 8-7   How application state works

How to work with application state data

Figure 8-8 presents the details for working with application state data. As you can see from the first three examples, the techniques you use to add items to and retrieve items from application state are similar to the techniques you use to work with items in session state. The main difference is that you use the Application property of the page to access the application state object from a code-behind file, and you use the Application property of the HttpContext object for the current request to access the application state object from a class other than a code-behind file.

When you're working with application state data, you'll want to lock the application state collection when you modify any of its data. This is illustrated in the last example in this figure, which increments an application state item named HitCount by one. Here, the application state collection is locked before the HitCount item is retrieved. Then, after the item is updated, the application state collection is unlocked. To minimize the length of time the application state object is locked, you should do as little processing as possible between the Lock and Unlock methods.

If you don't lock the application state collection while the count is updated, two or more users could access the count at the same time. To illustrate why that's a problem, let's assume that three users access the count item at the same time, and the starting count is 11. Then, when each of those users increment the count it becomes 12, and that's the value that each user stores in the application state collection. In this case, though, the correct count should be 14.

Common members of the HttpApplicationState class

Property	Description
Count	The number of items in the application state collection.

Indexer	Description
[name]	The value of the application state item with the specified name. If you set the value of an item that doesn't exist, that item is created.

Method	Description
Add(name, value)	Adds an item to the application state collection.
Clear()	Removes all items from the application state collection.
Remove(name)	Removes the item with the specified name from the application state collection.
Lock()	Locks the application state collection so only the current user can access it.
Unlock()	Unlocks the application state collection so other users can access it.

A statement that retrieves an item from application state

```
int applicationCount = Convert.ToInt32(Application["HitCount"]);
```

A statement that adds an item to application state

```
Application.Add("HitCount", 0);
```

A statement that retrieves the application state from a non-page class

```
int applicationCount = Convert.ToInt32
    (HttpContext.Current.Application["HitCount"]);
```

Code that locks application state while retrieving and updating an item

```
Application.Lock();
int applicationCount = Convert.ToInt32(Application["HitCount"]);
applicationCount++;
Application["HitCount"] = applicationCount;
Application.UnLock();
```

Description

- You can use the application state object to store items that are common to all users of the application.

- To access the application state object from the code-behind file for an ASP.NET web form, use the Application property of the page.

- To access the application state object from a class other than a code-behind file, use the Current property of the HttpContext class to get the HttpContext object for the current request. Then, use the Application property of this object to get the application state object.

- Before you retrieve the value of an application state item that you intend to modify, you should lock the application state object so other users can't modify the application state data at the same time. As soon as you finish modifying the application state data, you should release the application state object so other users can access it.

Figure 8-8   How to work with application state data

How to work with application events

Now that you know how to work with application state data, you may be wondering how to initialize the values of application state items. To do that, you first add a global.asax file to the project as described in figure 8-9. By default, this file contains declarations for five event handlers as shown in the example in this figure. Then, you can add code to any of these event handlers. This figure summarizes the four events you're most likely to use to work with application state data.

The example in this figure shows how you can initialize and update a session state item named HitCount that keeps track of the number of times a new session is started for an application. In this example, the Application_Start event handler retrieves the current hit count number from a database and adds an application state item named HitCount to the application state object. Similarly, the Application_End event handler saves the HitCount item to the database so it will be accurate when it's retrieved the next time the application starts. Although the HalloweenDB class that includes the methods that are used to retrieve and update the count isn't shown here, all you need to know is that the GetHitCount method retrieves the current hit count from the database as an integer value, and the UpdateHitCount method saves the integer value to the database.

The updating of the HitCount item takes place in the Session_Start event handler, which is raised whenever a new user session begins. This event handler starts by locking the application state object. Then, it increases the HitCount item by 1 and unlocks the application state object.

Four common application events

Event	Description
Application_Start	This event is raised when the first page of an application is requested by any user. It is often used to initialize the values of application state items.
Application_End	This event is raised when an application is about to terminate. It can be used to write the values of critical application state items to a database or file.
Session_Start	This event is raised when a user session begins. It can be used to initialize session state items, update application state items, or authorize user access.
Session_End	This event is raised when a user session is about to terminate. It can be used to free resources held by the user or to log the user off the application. It is raised only when in-process mode is used.

A global.asax file that creates an object in application state

```csharp
<%@ Application Language="C#" %>
<script runat="server">
    void Application_Start(object sender, EventArgs e)
    {
        // Code that runs on application startup
        Application.Add("HitCount", HalloweenDB.GetHitCount());
    }
    void Application_End(object sender, EventArgs e)
    {
        //  Code that runs on application shutdown
        HalloweenDB.UpdateHitCount(Application["HitCount"]);
    }
    void Application_Error(object sender, EventArgs e)
    {
        // Code that runs when an unhandled error occurs

    }
    void Session_Start(object sender, EventArgs e)
    {
        // Code that runs when a new session is started
        Application.Lock();
        int hitCount = Convert.ToInt32(Application["HitCount"]) + 1;
        Application["HitCount"] = hitCount;
        Application.UnLock();
    }
    void Session_End(object sender, EventArgs e)
    {
        // Code that runs when a session ends.
    }
</script>
```

Description

- To create a global.asax file, select the Website→Add New Item command, and then choose the Global Application Class template.

- The global.asax file provides event handlers for application events. The event handlers are coded within a Script element that defines a code declaration block.

- To refer to the application state object from the global.asax file, you use the Application property of the application.

Figure 8-9   How to work with application events

How to use cookies and URL encoding

Earlier in this chapter, you learned that ASP.NET uses cookies to track user sessions. Now, you'll learn how to create and use your own cookies. Then, you'll learn how to use URL encoding as an alternative to the use of cookies.

How to create cookies

A *cookie* is a name/value pair that is stored on the client's computer. For instance, the name of the first cookie in figure 8-10 is ASP.NET_SessionId, and its value is

```
jsswpu5530hcyx2w3jfa5u55
```

This is a typical session ID for a cookie that's generated by ASP.NET to keep track of a session. The other cookie examples are typical of cookies that you create yourself.

To create a cookie, you instantiate an object from the HttpCookie class. Then, you include it in the HTTP response that the server sends back to the browser, and the user's browser stores the cookie either in its own memory or in a text file on the client machine's disk.

A cookie that's stored in the browser's memory is called a *session cookie* because it exists only for that session. When the browser session ends, the contents of any session cookies are lost. Session cookies are what ASP.NET uses to track session ID's. In contrast, *persistent cookies* are written to disk, so they are maintained after the browser session ends. Whether session or persistent, though, once a cookie is sent to a browser, it's automatically returned to the server with each HTTP request.

Besides using cookies for session IDs, you can use cookies to save information that identifies each user so the users don't have to enter that information each time they visit your web site. You can also use cookies to store information that lets you personalize the web pages that are displayed for a user.

When you use cookies to store this type of information, you should keep in mind that some users may have disabled cookies on their browsers. In that case, you won't be able to save cookies on the user's computer. Unfortunately, ASP.NET doesn't provide a way for you to determine whether a user has disabled cookies. As a result, if you use cookies in an application, you may need to notify the user that cookies must be enabled to use it.

This figure also presents some properties of the HttpCookie class. Then, the first example shows how to create a session cookie. Here, both the cookie's name and value are specified on the constructor. Because the Expires property isn't set, it's given a default value of 12:00 a.m. on January 1, 0001. Because this value has already passed, the cookie is deleted when the session ends.

If you don't set the value of a cookie when you create it, you can use the Value property to set it later on. In addition, you can use the Expires property to set the expiration date for a persistent cookie. This is illustrated by the second example in this figure.

Examples of cookies

```
ASP.NET_SessionId=jsswpu5530hcyx2w3jfa5u55
EMail=Anne@Murach.com
user_ID=4993
password=opensesame
```

Two ways to create a cookie

```
New HttpCookie(name)
New HttpCookie(name, value)
```

Common properties of the HttpCookie class

Property	Description
Expires	A DateTime value that indicates when the cookie should expire.
Name	The cookie's name.
Secure	A Boolean value that indicates whether the cookie should be sent only when a secure connection is used. See chapter 19 for information on secure connections.
Value	The string value assigned to the cookie.

Code that creates a session cookie

```
HttpCookie nameCookie = new HttpCookie("UserName", userName);
```

Code that creates a persistent cookie

```
HttpCookie nameCookie = new HttpCookie("UserName");
nameCookie.Value = userName;
nameCookie.Expires = DateTime.Now.AddYears(1);
```

Description

- A *cookie* is a name/value pair that's stored in the user's browser or on the user's disk.
- A web application sends a cookie to a browser via an HTTP response. Then, each time the browser sends an HTTP request to the server, it attaches any cookies that are associated with that server.
- By default, ASP.NET uses a cookie to store the session ID for a session, but you can also create and send your own cookies to a user's browser.
- A *session cookie* is kept in the browser's memory and exists only for the duration of the browser session. A *persistent cookie* is kept on the user's disk and is retained until the cookie's expiration date.
- To create a cookie, you specify its name or its name and value. To create a persistent cookie, you must also set the Expires property to the time you want the cookie to expire.

Figure 8-10   How to create cookies

How to work with cookies

After you create a cookie, you work with it using the members of the HttpCookieCollection class shown in figure 8-11. This class defines a collection of HttpCookie objects. To refer to a cookie in a cookies collection, for example, you can use an index of the collection that refers to the cookie by name. And to add a cookie to the collection, you use the Add method of the collection.

The key to working with cookies is realizing that you must deal with two instances of the HttpCookieCollection class. The first one contains the collection of cookies that have been sent to the server from the client. You access this collection using the Cookies property of the HttpRequest object. The second one contains the collection of cookies that will be sent back to the browser. You access this collection using the Cookies property of the HttpResponse object.

To send a new cookie to the client, you create the cookie and then add it to the collection of cookies in the HttpResponse object. This is illustrated in the first example in this figure. Here, a cookie named nameCookie is created and added to the HttpResponse object.

The second example shows you how to retrieve the value of a cookie that's sent from the browser. Here, the Request property of the page is used to refer to the HttpRequest object. Then, the name indexer of the Cookies collection of the request object is used to get the cookie, and the Value property of the cookie is used to get the cookie's value.

The last example in this figure illustrates how you can delete a persistent cookie. To do that, you create a cookie with the same name as the cookie you want to delete, and you set its Expires property to a time in the past. In this example, I set the date to one second before the current time. Then, you add the cookie to the HttpResponse object so it's sent back to the browser. When the browser receives the cookie, it replaces the existing cookie with the new cookie. When the client's system detects that the cookie has expired, it deletes it.

Common members of the HttpCookieCollection class

Property	Description
Count	The number of cookies in the collection.

Indexer	Description
[name]	The cookie with the specified name.

Method	Description
Add(cookie)	Adds a cookie to the collection.
Clear()	Removes all cookies from the collection.
Remove(name)	Removes the cookie with the specified name from the collection.

A method that creates a new cookie and adds it to the HttpResponse object

```
private void AddCookie()
{
    HttpCookie nameCookie = new HttpCookie("UserName", txtUserName.Text);
    nameCookie.Expires = DateTime.Now.AddYears(1);
    Response.Cookies.Add(nameCookie);
}
```

A method that retrieves the value of a cookie from the HttpRequest object

```
protected void Page_Load(object sender, EventArgs e)
{
    if (!IsPostBack)
    {
        if (!(Request.Cookies["UserName"] == null))
            lblUserName.Text = "Welcome back "
                            + Request.Cookies["UserName"].Value
                            + ".";
    }
}
```

A method that deletes a persistent cookie

```
private void DeleteCookie()
{
    HttpCookie nameCookie = new HttpCookie("UserName");
    nameCookie.Expires = DateTime.Now.AddSeconds(-1);
    Response.Cookies.Add(nameCookie);
}
```

Description

- Cookies are managed in collections defined by the HttpCookieCollection class.

- To access the cookies collection for a request or response, use the Cookies property of the HttpRequest or HttpResponse object. To refer to these objects, use the Request and Response properties of the page.

- To delete a persistent cookie, create a cookie with the same name as the cookie you want to delete and set its Expires property to a time that has already passed. Then, when the client's system detects that the cookie has expired, it deletes it.

Figure 8-11   How to work with cookies

How to enable or disable cookies

If an application relies on the use of cookies, you'll want to be sure that cookies are enabled in your browser as you test the application. Conversely, to test an application that's intended to work even if cookies have been disabled, you'll need to disable cookies in your browser. To do that, you can use the techniques presented in figure 8-12.

If you're using Internet Explorer, you use a slider control to determine what cookies are allowed. The default setting is Medium, which enables both session and persistent cookies. To disable both types of cookies, you can select a privacy setting that blocks all cookies as shown here. Alternatively, you can use the dialog box that's displayed when you click the Advanced button to override the default settings so your browser accepts session cookies but disables persistent cookies.

This figure also describes how to enable or disable cookies if you're using Mozilla Firefox or Opera. Although these techniques are quite different from the techniques for enabling or disabling cookies with Internet Explorer, you shouldn't have any trouble understanding how to use them.

An Internet Explorer dialog box with disabled cookies

How to enable or disable cookies for Internet Explorer

1. Select the Tools➔Internet Options command.
2. Select the Privacy tab.
3. Use the slider control to set the security level to accept or block cookies.

How to enable or disable cookies for Mozilla Firefox

1. Select the Tools➔Options command.
2. Click the Privacy icon.
3. Check or uncheck the Accept Cookies From Sites option, and select an item from the Keep Until drop-down list.

How to enable or disable cookies for Opera

1. Select the Tools➔Preferences command.
2. Select the Cookies category on the Advanced tab.
3. Choose an option to determine whether cookies are accepted. You can also set options to determine if new cookies are deleted when the browser is closed and if the browser asks you before accepting cookies.

Description

- Internet Explorer also lets you enable or disable persistent cookies and session cookies separately. To do that, click the Advanced button and select from the advanced privacy settings that are displayed.

Figure 8-12   How to enable or disable cookies

How to use URL encoding

URL encoding is an alternative to the use of cookies that lets you store information in the URL after the address of the page to be displayed. This information is stored in a *query string* that's added to the end of the URL, as shown in figure 8-13. Since using query strings is a common technique, you've probably seen them used on search sites like Google (www.google.com) and shopping sites like Ebay (www.ebay.com) and Amazon (www.amazon.com).

At the top of this figure, you can see two URLs that include query strings. The first one includes a single attribute named cat, and the second one includes two attributes named cat and prod. As you can see, you add a query string by coding a question mark after the URL. Then, you code the name of the first attribute, an equal sign, and the value you want to assign to the attribute. To include another attribute, you code an ampersand (&), followed by the name and value of the attribute.

In most cases, you'll use query strings with Anchor tags or hyperlinks to pass information from one page of an application to another. This is illustrated in the second example in this figure. Here, the Href attribute of the Anchor tag indicates that it will link to a page named Product.aspx. In addition, the URL includes a query string that contains a category and a product value. The Product page can then use these values to display information for the specified product.

To retrieve the values included in a query string, you use the QueryString property of the Request object as illustrated in the third example. The two statements in this example retrieve the two values passed by the query string in the second example.

The fourth example shows that you can also use query strings in the URLs that you code for Redirect or Transfer methods. Here, the URL contains a query string with a single attribute that contains a category ID. You should also realize that you can code query strings in the PostBackUrl attribute of a button control, although you're not likely to do that.

Two URLs with query strings

```
Order.aspx?cat=costumes
Order.aspx?cat=props&prod=rat01
```

An Anchor tag with a URL that includes a query string

```
<a href="product.aspx?cat=fx&prod=fog01">Fog machine</a>
```

Statements that retrieve the values of the query string attributes

```
string categoryID = Request.QueryString["cat"];
string productID = Request.QueryString["prod"];
```

Code that uses a URL with a query string in a Redirect method

```
Response.Redirect("Order.aspx?cat=" + categoryID);
```

Description

- When you use *URL encoding*, a *query string* that consists of attribute/value pairs is added to the end of a URL.

- Query strings are frequently used in Anchor tags and hyperlinks to pass information from one page of an application to another or to display different information on the same page.

- Query strings can also be used in the URLs that are specified for Response.Redirect or Server.Transfer calls, and they can be used in the PostBackUrl property of a button control.

- When you use an Anchor tag, a hyperlink, or a Redirect or Transfer method that specifies a URL for the current page, the page is processed as if it's being requested for the first time.

- To code a query string, follow the URL with a question mark, the name of the attribute, an equal sign, and a value. To code two or more attributes, separate them with ampersands (&), and don't include any spaces in the query string.

- To retrieve the value of a query string attribute, use the QueryString property of the HttpRequest object and specify the attribute name. To refer to the HttpRequest object, use the Request property of the page.

- Different browsers impose different limits on the number of characters in a query string or on the total number of characters in a URL. Most browsers provide for a URL with at least 2000 characters, however.

Figure 8-13   How to use URL encoding

Perspective

If this chapter has succeeded, you should now be able to use view state, session state, and application state whenever they're required by your application. You should also be able to use cookies and URL encoding whenever they're appropriate for your applications. Although this chapter doesn't present a complete application that illustrates the use of all these techniques, you shouldn't have any trouble using them whenever they're called for.

As you work with these techniques, please keep in mind that they aren't exclusive of one another. In fact, you'll often use two or more of these techniques in a single application. Most web applications, for example, use both view state and session state. And many applications also use application state, cookies, and URL encoding.

You should also be aware that ASP.NET provides a feature called *profiles* that presents yet another way to manage the state of a user. This feature has some distinct advantages because it stores its data in a database that's available from one session to another. In chapter 21, you can learn how to use profiles to personalize an application.

Terms

view state
view state object
session state
session state object
session ID
in-process mode
State Server mode
SQL Server mode
custom mode
session state store provider
cookie-based session tracking
cookieless session tracking
application
application object
application state
application state object
cookie
session cookie
persistent cookie
URL encoding
query string

9

How to use master pages

As you develop the pages of a web site, you'll often find pages that require some of the same elements. For example, both the Order and Cart pages of the Shopping Cart application you saw earlier in this book have an image displayed across the top of the page. The easiest way to create pages like these that have common elements is to use a master page. In this chapter, you'll learn the most important skills for creating and working with master pages.

How to create master pages **300**
An introduction to master pages 300
How to create a master page 302
The aspx code for a new master page 304
The aspx code for the Halloween Store master page 306
The code-behind file for the master page 306

How to create and develop content pages **310**
How to create a content page 310
How to add content to a page 312
The aspx code for the Order content page 314

How to nest master pages **316**
How to create nested master pages 316
How to add content to a child master page 316

**How to access master page controls
from a content page** **318**
How to expose a master page control as a public property 318
How to access a public property of the master page from a content page . 320

Perspective **322**

How to create master pages

A *master page* is a page that provides a framework within which the content from other pages can be displayed. Master pages make it easy to include banners, navigation menus, and other elements on all of the pages in an application. In the topics that follow, you'll learn how to create master pages in your ASP.NET applications.

An introduction to master pages

Figure 9-1 shows the basics of how master pages work. As you can see, the page that's actually sent to the browser is created by combining elements from a master page and a *content page*. The content page provides the content that's unique to each page in the application, while the master page provides the elements that are common to all pages. In this example, the master page (MasterPage.master) provides a banner at the top of each page, a simple navigation menu at the side of each page, and a message that indicates how many days remain until Halloween at the bottom of each page.

In addition, the master page contains a *content placeholder* that indicates where the content from each content page should be displayed. In this example, the content page is the Order.aspx page, and its content is displayed in the content placeholder in the central portion of the master page.

Notice that the name of the content page is Order.aspx, the same as the Order page that you saw in chapter 3. In other words, when you use master pages, the individual pages of your web application become the content pages. You'll learn how to create content pages or convert existing ASP.NET pages to content pages in figure 9-6.

The Shopping Cart application with a master page

Master page (MasterPage.master)

Content page (Order.aspx)

Rendered page

Description

- A *master page* provides a framework in which the content of each page on a web site is presented. Master pages make it easy to create pages that have a consistent look.
- The pages that provide the content that's displayed in a master page are called *content pages*.
- The content of each content page is displayed in the master page's *content placeholder*.

Figure 9-1   An application that uses a master page

How to create a master page

As figure 9-2 explains, you create a master page by using the Master Page template in the Add New Item dialog box. With Visual Studio 2005, this template included a single ContentPlaceHolder control within the Form element of the page. This control marked the location on the rendered page where the content from the content page was displayed.

With Visual Studio 2008, the Master Page template includes two ContentPlaceHolder controls. The one shown in this figure is contained within the Form element of the page and serves the same purpose as the ContentPlaceHolder control provided by Visual Studio 2005. In addition, a ContentPlaceHolder control is included within the Head element of the page. You'll learn more about how both of these ContentPlaceHolder controls work in the next figure.

To develop the master page, you add elements outside of the ContentPlaceHolder controls. For example, to create the master page in figure 9-1, you add an image for a banner above the placeholder in the Form element, navigation links to the left of this placeholder, and a label to display the days remaining until Halloween below this placeholder. Typically, you'll use an HTML table to specify the layout of these elements.

Although a master page has only two content placeholders by default, you should realize that you can create additional placeholders if you need to. You might want to do that, for example, to create a page layout that has custom content in several areas. To create an additional content placeholder, you simply drag the ContentPlaceHolder control from the Standard group of the Toolbox onto the master page and give it a unique ID.

Note that an application can contain more than one master page. This allows you to create an application that has two or more sections with distinct page layouts. For example, you may want to use one master page for all of the content pages in the online shopping section of a web site, and another master page for the content pages in the customer service section.

The master pages you create can also be nested. That lets you create one master page with the elements to be used by all of the pages in a web site and nested master pages with additional elements to be used by individual sections of the web site. You'll learn more about nesting master pages later in this chapter.

A new master page in Design view

Description

- To add a master page to a project, choose the Website→Add New Item command. Then, in the Add New Item dialog box, select Master Page from the list of templates, specify the name of the master page you want to create in the Name text box (the default is MasterPage.master), and select the programming language. Then, click Add.

- The content placeholder in the Form element of the page appears as a control in the Web Forms Designer. Although you can change the position of the content placeholder, you can't edit its contents from the master page. Instead, you add content to the master page by creating content pages as described later in this chapter.

- Any elements you add to the master page outside of the content placeholder will appear on every content page that uses the master page.

- Although most master pages have just one content placeholder in the Form element, you can create more than one content placeholder if you need to. In that case, each place-holder displays a portion of the content of each content page.

- The Head element of a master page also contains a content placeholder by default. See figure 9-3 for more information.

- An application can have more than one master page, and each content page specifies which master page should be used to display the content page.

- The aspx file for a master page uses the extension .master. The code-behind file uses .master.cs.

Figure 9-2   How to create a master page

The aspx code for a new master page

The listing at the top of figure 9-3 shows the aspx code that's generated when you create a master page using the Master Page template. As you can see, this code is similar to the aspx code that's generated for a regular ASP.NET web page, with two important differences.

First, instead of a Page directive, the code begins with a Master directive. This indicates that the file contains a master page rather than a regular ASP.NET page. Second, the master page contains two ContentPlaceHolder controls. The first one, which is contained within the Head element, can be used for any element that can be coded within the Head element. In most cases, you'll use this content placeholder for a Style element that defines the internal styles for a content page. The second ContentPlaceHolder control, which is contained within the Div element, is used for the main content of the page.

Notice that the master page file is itself a well-formed HTML document with Html, Head, and Body elements. The Body element includes a Form element, which in turn includes the Div element that contains the ContentPlaceHolder control. Any elements you add to the body of the master page should appear within the Form element, but outside of the ContentPlaceHolder control. Similarly, any elements you add to the heading of the master page, such as internal styles, should appear within the Head element, but outside the ContentPlaceHolder control in the Head element.

The aspx code for a new master page

```
<%@ Master Language="C#" AutoEventWireup="true" CodeFile="MasterPage.master.cs"
Inherits="MasterPage" %>

<!DOCTYPE html PUBLIC "-//W3C//DTD XHTML 1.0 Transitional//EN" "http://
www.w3.org/TR/xhtml1/DTD/xhtml1-transitional.dtd">

<html xmlns="http://www.w3.org/1999/xhtml">
<head runat="server">
    <title>Untitled Page</title>
    <asp:ContentPlaceHolder id="head" runat="server">
    </asp:ContentPlaceHolder>
</head>
<body>
    <form id="form1" runat="server">
    <div>
        <asp:ContentPlaceHolder id="ContentPlaceHolder1" runat="server">
        </asp:ContentPlaceHolder>
    </div>

    </form>
</body>
</html>
```

Attributes of the Master page directive

Attribute	Description
Language	Specifies the language used for any code required by the page.
CodeFile	Specifies the name of the code-behind file.
Inherits	Specifies the name of the page class defined in the code-behind file.

Attributes of the ContentPlaceHolder control

Attribute	Description
ID	Specifies the name of the content placeholder.
Runat	Specifies that the control is a server-side control.

Description

- A master page must begin with a Master page directive and should include at least one ContentPlaceHolder control.
- By default, a master page contains two ContentPlaceHolder controls: one in the Head element and one in the Form element. The one in the Head element is typically used for the internal styles that are generated for a content page. The one in the Form element is used for the displayable elements of the content page.
- Any HTML or aspx elements that you add to the master page will be displayed on every page that uses the master page along with the content that's defined for the ContentPlaceHolder control in the Form element.

Figure 9-3   The aspx code for a new master page

The aspx code for the Halloween Store master page

Figure 9-4 shows the complete aspx code for the master page in figure 9-1. Although this listing fills two pages, there's nothing complex about it. So you shouldn't have any trouble understanding its elements.

To start, you should notice that the document head contains a Style element. This element contains one style for each cell of the table that's used in the body of the document. In addition, the document head contains the content place-holder that's added by default.

On page 2 of this listing, you can see the image control that's used to display the banner at the top of the page. After the banner is the table element that controls the layout of the rest of the page. The first row of this table has three cells. The first cell contains a simple navigation menu built using hyperlinks. If you look back at the style class that's applied to this cell, you'll see that it has a width of 160 pixels and a height of 400 pixels. In addition, the background color and border color for this cell is set to red. The second cell is a small (10 pixel) spacer cell that gives some space between the navigation menu and the content. And the third cell contains the content placeholder and has a width of 520 pixels.

The second row defines the footer that appears at the bottom of the page. It also has three cells, each the same width and colors as the cells in the first row. However, the height of each cell in this row is set to 25 pixels. The third cell in this row contains a label control named lblMessage. This label will be used to display the number of days that remain until Halloween.

The code-behind file for the master page

Master pages have events just like regular ASP.NET pages. So it's important to realize that most of these events are raised *after* the corresponding events for the content page are raised. For example, the Load event for the master page will be processed after the Load event for the content page. Likewise, any control events for the content page are processed before any control events for the master page. Note, however, that both the content page and the master page Load events are processed before any of the control events are processed.

Figure 9-5 shows the code-behind file for the master page in figure 9-4. This code-behind file includes a Page_Load event handler that's executed when the master page loads. As you can see, this event handler calls a method named DaysUntilHalloween, which calculates and returns the number of days remaining until October 31. Then, an appropriate message is assigned to the Text property of the lblMessage label.

The aspx code for the master page   Page 1

```
<%@ Master Language="C#" AutoEventWireup="true" CodeFile="MasterPage.master.cs"
Inherits="MasterPage" %>

<!DOCTYPE html PUBLIC "-//W3C//DTD XHTML 1.0 Transitional//EN"
"http://www.w3.org/TR/xhtml1/DTD/xhtml1-transitional.dtd">

<html xmlns="http://www.w3.org/1999/xhtml" >
<head runat="server">
    <title>Chapter 9: Master Page</title>
    <style type="text/css">
        .Row1Column1
        {
            width: 140px;
            height: 400px;
            border-color: Red;
            background-color: Red;
        }
        .Row1Column2
        {
            width: 10px;
            height: 400px;
        }
        .Row1Column3
        {
            width: 540px;
            height: 400px;
        }
        .Row2Column1
        {
            width: 140px;
            height: 25px;
            border-color: Red;
            background-color: Red;
        }
        .Row2Column2
        {
            width: 10;
            height: 25;
        }
        .Row2Column3
        {
            width: 540px;
            height: 25;
        }
    </style>
    <asp:ContentPlaceHolder id="head" runat="server">
    </asp:ContentPlaceHolder>
</head>
```

Note

- The internal styles that Visual Studio generated as I formatted the table used by the master page were renamed to make it apparent where they're applied. Here, each style is applied to a different cell of the table.

Figure 9-4   The aspx code for the Halloween Store master page (part 1 of 2)

The aspx code for the master page   **Page 2**

```
<body>
    <form id="form1" runat="server">
    <div>
        <asp:Image ID="Image1" runat="server" ImageUrl="~/Images/banner.jpg" />
        <table cellpadding="2" cellspacing="0">
            <tr>
                <td class="Row1Column1" valign="top">
                    <br />
                    <asp:HyperLink ID="HyperLink1" runat="server"
                        ForeColor="White"
                        NavigateUrl="~/Order.aspx">Home</asp:HyperLink>
                    <br />
                    <br />
                    <asp:HyperLink ID="HyperLink2" runat="server"
                        ForeColor="White" NavigateUrl="~/Cart.aspx">
                        Your Shopping Cart</asp:HyperLink>
                    <br />
                    <br />
                    <asp:HyperLink ID="HyperLink3" runat="server"
                        ForeColor="White" NavigateUrl="~/Service.aspx">
                        Customer Service</asp:HyperLink>
                    <br />
                    <br />
                    <asp:HyperLink ID="HyperLink4" runat="server"
                        ForeColor="White"
                        NavigateUrl="~/About.aspx">About Us</asp:HyperLink>
                </td>
                <td class="Row1Column2"></td>
                <td class="Row1Column3" valign="top">
                    <asp:ContentPlaceHolder id="Main" runat="server">
                    </asp:ContentPlaceHolder>
                </td>
            </tr>
            <tr>
                <td class="Row2Column1"></td>
                <td class="Row2Column2"></td>
                <td class="Row2Column3">
                    <asp:Label ID="lblMessage" runat="server"></asp:Label>
                </td>
            </tr>
        </table>
    </div>
    </form>
</body>
</html>
```

Description

- Most master pages include elements like banners and navigation controls.
- It's common to use tables to provide the layout for the elements on the master page, including the content placeholder.

Figure 9-4   The aspx code for the Halloween Store master page (part 2 of 2)

The code-behind file for the master page

```
using System;
using System.Collections;
using System.Configuration;
using System.Data;
using System.Linq;
using System.Collections;
using System.Web;
using System.Web.Security;
using System.Web.UI;
using System.Web.UI.HtmlControls;
using System.Web.UI.WebControls;
using System.Web.UI.WebControls.WebParts;
using System.Xml.Linq;

public partial class MasterPage : System.Web.UI.MasterPage
{
    protected void Page_Load(object sender, EventArgs e)
    {
        int daysUntil = DaysUntilHalloween();
        if (daysUntil == 0)
            lblMessage.Text = "Happy Halloween!";
        else if (daysUntil == 1)
            lblMessage.Text = "Tomorrow is Halloween!";
        else
            lblMessage.Text = "There are only " + daysUntil
                + " days left until Halloween!";
    }

    private int DaysUntilHalloween()
    {
        DateTime halloween = new DateTime(DateTime.Today.Year, 10, 31);
        if (DateTime.Today > halloween)
            halloween = halloween.AddYears(1);
        TimeSpan ts = halloween - DateTime.Today;
        return ts.Days;
    }
}
```

Description

- Master pages have events just like regular ASP.NET pages. For this master page, the Load event is used to display the number of days remaining until Halloween.

- Most events for the content page are raised before the corresponding events for the master page. For example, the Load event for the content page is raised before the Load event for the master page. Similarly, events for controls in the content page are raised before events for controls in the master page.

Figure 9-5   The code-behind file for the master page

How to create and develop content pages

Once you create a master page, you can create and develop the content pages for the master page. The topics that follow show how.

How to create a content page

Figure 9-6 shows how to create a content page. In short, you use the same procedure to create a content page that you use to create a regular page, but you check the Select Master Page check box. Then, you can choose the master page you want to use for the content page from the Select a Master Page dialog box that's displayed.

Alternatively, you can select the master page you want to use in the Solution Explorer and then choose the Website→Add Content Page command. This creates a content page for the selected master page. Note that when you use this technique, the content page is automatically named Default.

The code example in this figure shows the code that's generated when you create a new content page named Order for the master page shown in figure 9-4. This code is quite different from the code that's generated when you create a regular ASP.NET page. Although the Page directive includes the same information as a regular ASP.NET page, it also includes a MasterPageFile attribute that specifies the master page you selected. And the rest of the content page is also different from a normal ASP.NET page.

Before I describe the other differences, you should know that the title you specify in the Title attribute of the Page directive of a content page overrides any title you specify in the master page. That way, you can display a different title for each content page. If you want to use the same title for each content page, however, you can specify the title in the master page and then delete the Title attribute from the content pages.

Unlike normal ASP.NET pages, content pages don't include a Doctype directive or any structural HTML elements such as Html, Head, Body, or Form. That's because those elements are provided by the master page. Instead, the content page includes one ASP.NET Content element for each content placeholder in the master page. In this case, because the master page contains two placeholders, the content page contains two Content elements. As you can see, the ContentPlaceHolderID attributes of these elements identify which placeholder they're associated with. Then, you place the content of the page between the start and end tags of the Content elements.

This figure also includes a procedure for converting a regular page to a content page. You'll need to follow this procedure if you start a web site without using master pages, and later decide to use master pages. Unfortunately, though, Visual Studio doesn't provide a way to automatically do this. As a result, you'll have to manually edit each of the pages to add the MasterPageFile attribute to

The aspx code for a new page that uses the master page in figure 9-4

```
<%@ Page Language="C#" MasterPageFile="~/MasterPage.master"
AutoEventWireup="true" CodeFile="Order.aspx.cs" Inherits="Order"
Title="Untitled Page" %>

<asp:Content ID="Content1" ContentPlaceHolderID="head" Runat="Server">
</asp:Content>
<asp:Content ID="Content2" ContentPlaceHolderID="Main" Runat="Server">
</asp:Content>
```

Two ways to create a new content page

- Choose the Website→Add New Item command. Then, select the Web Form template, enter the name for the form, check the Select Master Page check box, and click Add. When the Select a Master Page dialog box appears, select the master page you want and click OK.
- Select the master page in the Solution Explorer, then choose the Website→Add Content Page command.

How to convert a regular ASP.NET page to a content page

- First, add a MasterPageFile attribute to the Page directive that specifies the URL of the master page. Next, replace the Div element that contains the actual content of the page with a Content element like the second one shown above. Then, if the Head element contains other elements used by the page, such as styles, replace the Head element with a Content element like the first one shown above. Last, delete everything that's outside the Content elements except for the Page directive.

Two other ways to specify the master page

In the web.config file

```
<system.web>
    .
    <pages masterPageFile="MasterPage.master" />
    .
</system.web>
```

In the Page_PreInit event handler

```
protected void Page_PreInit(object sender, EventArgs e)
{
    MasterPageFile = "MasterPage.master";
}
```

Description

- The Page directive in the aspx code for a content page includes a MasterPageFile attribute that specifies the name of the master page.
- The aspx code for a content page includes Content elements that indicate the IDs of the content placeholders where the content for the page should be placed. Any content you create for the page should be coded between the start and end tags for these elements.
- You can also specify the master page in the web.config file or in the Page_PreInit event handler. However, the Web Forms Designer doesn't support either of these techniques, so you won't be able to view the content page in Design view.

Figure 9-6   How to create a content page

the Page directive, remove the Doctype directive and structural HTML elements (Html, Head, Body, Form, and Div), and add one or more Content elements.

Because this conversion procedure is error prone, it pays to use master pages for all but the simplest of applications, even if each master page contains only the content placeholders. Then, when you're ready to provide a consistent look to the pages within the application, you can enhance the master pages.

This figure also shows two other ways to specify which master page is used with a content page. First, you can add a MasterPageFile attribute that specifies the master page to be used with all pages that don't specify a master file to the Pages element of the web.config file. Second, you can specify the master page at runtime by setting the MasterPageFile attribute of the page in the Page_PreInit event handler. Note, however, that the Web Forms Designer doesn't support either of these techniques. If you use them, then, you won't be able to view or edit your content pages in Design view.

How to add content to a page

Figure 9-7 shows how a content page appears in Design view. As you can see, the master page is displayed along with the Content control for the content placeholder in the Form element of the master page. However, you can't edit any of the master page elements from this view. You can only edit the content of the page by adding text to the content area or by dragging controls from the Toolbox to the content area. Later, when you switch to Source view, any elements that you've added will appear between the Content element's start and end tags.

If you work with a master page that has more than one content placeholder in the Form element, there will be a separate Content control for each placeholder. Then, you can edit the contents for each of those controls.

A content page in Design view

Description

- When you display a content page in Design view, the elements from the master page are displayed so you can see how they will affect the final appearance of the page.

- To add the content for a page, click the Content control. Then, you can type text or use the Toolbox to drag controls into the content area of the page. Any text or other elements you add will be placed between the start and end tags of the Content element in the aspx file.

- If you want to display only the master page's default content for a page, click the Smart Tag icon in the upper right corner of the content placeholder and choose Default to Master's Content. Then, you won't be able to edit the content of the placeholder. To edit the content again, choose Create Custom Content from the smart tag menu.

Figure 9-7   How to add content to a page

The aspx code for the Order content page

To help you understand how content is added to a content page, figure 9-8 presents some of the aspx code for the Order page of the Halloween Store application. As you can see, this code includes two Content controls. The first one includes a Style element that defines the internal styles that are used by the page. When the Order page is displayed, these styles will be combined with the styles defined by the master page. Note that if Visual Studio generates styles for a content page, it will automatically add a Style element with those styles to this Content element.

The second Content control contains the main content for the page. This is the same content that would normally be included in the Form element of a standard page. Because of that, you shouldn't have any trouble understanding it.

The aspx code for the content page

```
<%@ Page Language="C#" MasterPageFile="~/MasterPage.master"
AutoEventWireup="true" CodeFile="Order.aspx.cs" Inherits="Order" %>

<asp:Content ID="Content1" ContentPlaceHolderID="head" Runat="Server">
    <style type="text/css">
        .style1
        {
            width: 250px;
        }
        .style2
        {
            width: 20px;
        }
    </style>
</asp:Content>
<asp:Content ID="Content2" ContentPlaceHolderID="Main" Runat="Server">
    <br />
    <asp:Label ID="Label1" runat="server"
        Text="Please select a product:"></asp:Label> 
    <asp:DropDownList ID="ddlProducts" runat="server"
        DataSourceID="AccessDataSource1" DataTextField="Name"
        DataValueField="ProductID" Width="150px" AutoPostBack="True">
    </asp:DropDownList>
    <asp:AccessDataSource ID="AccessDataSource1" runat="server"
        DataFile="~/App_Data/Halloween.mdb"
        SelectCommand="SELECT [ProductID], [Name], [ShortDescription],
            [LongDescription], [ImageFile], [UnitPrice]
            FROM [Products] ORDER BY [Name]">
    </asp:AccessDataSource>
    <br />
    <table>
        <tr>
            <td class="style1">
                <asp:Label ID="lblName" runat="server"
                    style="font-weight: 700; font-size: larger">
                </asp:Label>
            </td>
            <td class="style2" rowspan="4">
            </td>
            <td rowspan="4" valign="top">
                <asp:Image ID="imgProduct" runat="server" Height="200px" />
            </td>
        </tr>
        .
        .
    </table>
    .
    .
    <asp:Button ID="btnAdd" runat="server" Text="Add to Cart"
        OnClick="btnAdd_Click" /> 
    <asp:Button ID="Button1" runat="server" CausesValidation="False"
        PostBackUrl="~/Cart.aspx" Text="Go to Cart" />
</asp:Content>
```

Figure 9-8   The aspx code for the Order content page

How to nest master pages

In addition to creating content pages from a master page, you can create other master pages. When you nest master pages like this, you can create a *parent master page* that contains the elements used by all the pages in a web site. Then, you can create *child master pages* that add to the contents of the parent master page and that contain the elements used by different sections of the web site.

How to create nested master pages

Unlike Visual Studio 2005, Visual Studio 2008 provides for creating *nested master pages* using the designer. To create a master page that's nested within another master page, you use a technique similar to the one in figure 9-2 for creating any master page. After you select the Master Page template and enter the name of the page, however, you check the Select Master Page check box. Then, you'll be asked to select the master page you want to use as the parent of the child master page.

The code example at the top of figure 9-9 shows the starting aspx code for a child master page. This page uses a parent master page that's similar to the one you saw in figure 9-4. The main difference is that I deleted the second row of the table that was included in this master page. As you may recall, the third column of this row contained a label that displayed the number of days until Halloween.

Note that this code is almost identical to the code for a content page. The only difference is that it starts with a Master directive instead of a Page directive. Unlike the Master directive for a parent master page, though, the Master directive for a child master page includes a MasterPageFile attribute.

How to add content to a child master page

To add content to a child master page, you add elements to the Content controls. This is illustrated in the second code example in figure 9-9. Here, I added a table with two rows and one column to the second Content control. The column in the first row contains a ContentPlaceHolder control that can be used by any content page that's created from this master page. Then, the column in the second row contains the label that was originally included on the parent master page.

The first Content control contains a Style element that defines the styles I applied to the table in the second Content control. In addition, it too contains a ContentPlaceHolder control. This control can be used by any content pages to include style and other heading information for the page.

Once you've created the parent and child master pages, you can create content pages that use either one of them. If you want a content page to include the label that indicates the number of days until Halloween, for example, you can create a page that uses the child master page. But if you don't want this label included on a content page, you can create a page that uses the parent master page.

The aspx code for a new child master page that uses a master page like the one in figure 9-4 as its parent

```
<%@ Master Language="C#" MasterPageFile="~/MasterPage.master"
    AutoEventWireup="true" CodeFile="ChildMasterPage.master.cs"
    Inherits="ChildMasterPage" %>

<asp:Content ID="Content1" ContentPlaceHolderID="head" Runat="Server">
</asp:Content>
<asp:Content ID="Content2" ContentPlaceHolderID="Main" Runat="Server">
</asp:Content>
```

The aspx code after content has been added to the page

```
<%@ Master Language="C#" MasterPageFile="~/MasterPage.master"
    AutoEventWireup="true" CodeFile="ChildMasterPage.master.cs"
    Inherits="ChildMasterPage" %>

<asp:Content ID="Content1" ContentPlaceHolderID="head" Runat="Server">
    <style type="text/css">
        .Row1 {width: 540px; height: 425px;}
        .Row2 {width: 540px; height: 25;}
    </style>
    <asp:ContentPlaceHolder ID="head" runat="server">
    </asp:ContentPlaceHolder>
</asp:Content>
<asp:Content ID="Content2" ContentPlaceHolderID="Main" Runat="Server">
        <table cellpadding="2" cellspacing="0">
            <tr class="Row1">
                <td valign="top">
                    <asp:ContentPlaceHolder ID="Main" runat="server">
                    </asp:ContentPlaceHolder>
                </td>
            </tr>
            <tr class="Row2">
                <td>
                    <asp:Label ID="lblMessage" runat="server"></asp:Label>
                </td>
            </tr>
        </table>
</asp:Content>
```

Description

- With Visual Studio 2008, you can use the designer to nest master pages. When you create *nested master pages*, the *parent master page* is typically used to provide elements for every page in the web site. Then, different *child master pages* can be used to provide additional elements for different types of pages in the web site.

- To create a child master page, use the technique in figure 9-2 for creating a master page, but check the Select Master Page check box and then select the parent master page from the dialog box that's displayed.

- To add content to a child master page, place the content between the start and end tags of the Content elements. Use ContentPlaceHolder controls to identify areas where content can be added in content pages that use the master page.

- When you use nested master pages, you can create content pages for the parent master page or any of the child master pages.

Figure 9-9   How to nest master pages

How to access master page controls from a content page

In many applications, you need to access one or more of the controls in a master page from one of the application's content pages. For example, the master page shown earlier in this chapter has a label in the footer area that normally displays the number of days remaining until Halloween. But what if you want to display other information in this label when certain content pages are displayed?

For example, when the user is shopping for products with the Order.aspx page, you may want to display the number of items currently in the shopping cart instead of the number of days left until Halloween. To do that, you can expose a master page control as a public property, and then access the property from the content page.

How to expose a master page control as a public property

The easiest way to access a control on a master page from a content page is to create a public property that provides access to the control. Figure 9-10 illustrates a code-behind file for a master page that shows you how to do that.

First, you create a public property in the master page that identifies the control you want to be able to access. In this case, the property is a Label type, and the property is named MessageLabel. Then, you code get and set accessors for the property. Here, the get accessor returns the lblMessage label, and the set accessor assigns the property value to lblMessage.

Please notice that I also added another if statement to the Page_Load event handler for the master page. Now, the lblMessage label is set to the number of days left until Halloween only if the value of the label's Text property is empty. That way, if the content page has assigned a value to this label in its Page_Load event handler, the master page's Page_Load event handler won't overwrite the value. This works because the content page's Page_Load event handler is called before the master page's Page_Load event handler.

The code-behind file for a master page that provides a public property

```
using System;
using System.Collections;
using System.Configuration;
using System.Data;
using System.Linq;
using System.Web;
using System.Web.Security;
using System.Web.UI;
using System.Web.UI.HtmlControls;
using System.Web.UI.WebControls;
using System.Web.UI.WebControls.WebParts;
using System.Xml.Linq;

public partial class MasterPage : System.Web.UI.MasterPage
{
    public Label MessageLabel
    {
        get
        {
            return lblMessage;
        }
        set
        {
            lblMessage = value;
        }
    }

    protected void Page_Load(object sender, EventArgs e)
    {
        if (lblMessage.Text == "")
        {
            int daysUntil = DaysUntilHalloween();
            if (daysUntil == 0)
                lblMessage.Text = "Happy Halloween!";
            else if (daysUntil == 1)
                lblMessage.Text = "Tomorrow is Halloween!";
            else
                lblMessage.Text = "There are only " + daysUntil
                    + " days left until Halloween!";
        }
    }

    private int DaysUntilHalloween()
    {
        DateTime halloween = new DateTime(DateTime.Today.Year, 10, 31);
        if (DateTime.Today > halloween)
            halloween = halloween.AddYears(1);
        TimeSpan ts = halloween - DateTime.Today;
        return ts.Days;
    }
}
```

Description

- A content page can access a control in the master page if you expose the control as a public property in the master page. To do that, you code a property with get and set accessors.

Figure 9-10   How to expose a master page control as a public property

How to access a public property of the master page from a content page

Figure 9-11 shows how you can access a public property in a master page from a content page. As you can see in the top part of this figure, you use the MasterType directive in the aspx file of the content page to specify the name of the type used for the master page. The value you name in this directive specifies the type of the object returned by the content page's Master property. So in this example, the Master property will return an object of type MasterPage. If you look at the class declaration in the previous figure, you'll see that MasterPage is the name of the class that defines the master page.

The second part of this figure shows two methods from the code-behind file for the Order.aspx content page. As you can see, the Page_Load event handler calls a method named DisplayCartMessage. This method determines the number of items currently in the shopping cart and sets the Text property of the label exposed by the master page's MessageLabel property accordingly. But note that no value is assigned to the message label if the shopping cart is empty. In that case, the Page_Load event handler for the master page will set the label to the number of days remaining until Halloween.

Although using the MasterType directive in the content page's aspx file makes it easier to access the properties of the master page, you should realize that this directive isn't necessary. If you don't specify the MasterType directive, the Master property will return an object of type Master. You can then cast this object to the actual type of your master page to access any properties you've created.

For example, you could use code like this to assign text to the MessageLabel property:

```
MasterPage mp = (MasterPage) this.Master;
if (cart.Count == 1)
    mp.MessageLabel.Text
        = "There is one item in your cart.";
else if (cart.Count > 1)
    mp.MessageLabel.Text
        = "There are " + cart.Count + " items in your cart.";
```

Here, the Master object is cast to MasterPage so its MessageLabel property can be accessed. The purpose of the MasterType directive is to avoid this awkward casting.

A portion of the Order.aspx page

```
<%@ Page Language="C#" MasterPageFile="~/MasterPage.master"
AutoEventWireup="true" CodeFile="Order.aspx.cs" Inherits="Order" %>

<%@ MasterType TypeName="MasterPage" %>

<asp:Content ID="Content1" ContentPlaceHolderID="Main" Runat="server">
.
.
.
</asp:Content>
```

Two methods from the code-behind file for the Order.aspx page

```
protected void Page_Load(object sender, EventArgs e)
{
    if (!IsPostBack)
    {
        ddlProducts.DataBind();
        this.DisplayCartMessage();
    }
    selectedProduct = this.GetSelectedProduct();
    lblName.Text = selectedProduct.Name;
    lblShortDescription.Text = selectedProduct.ShortDescription;
    lblLongDescription.Text = selectedProduct.LongDescription;
    lblUnitPrice.Text = selectedProduct.UnitPrice.ToString("c");
    imgProduct.ImageUrl = "Images/Products/" + selectedProduct.ImageFile;
}

private void DisplayCartMessage()
{
    SortedList cart = (SortedList)Session["Cart"];
    if (cart != null)
    {
        if (cart.Count == 1)
            this.Master.MessageLabel.Text
                = "There is one item in your cart.";
        else if (cart.Count > 1)
            this.Master.MessageLabel.Text
                = "There are " + cart.Count + " items in your cart.";
    }
}
```

Description

- The MasterType directive in an aspx file specifies the name of the master page type. If you include this directive in a content page, you can use the Master property in the code-behind file to access the exposed property of the master page.

Figure 9-11   How to access a public property of the master page from a content page

Perspective

I hope this chapter has illustrated the power of master pages. In fact, I recommend that you use master pages for all but the simplest applications, even if you start out with nothing in your master pages but placeholders. Then, when you're ready to provide a professional look to your content pages, you can enhance the master pages, which will also enhance all of your content pages.

The alternative is to convert regular content pages so they use the master pages that you develop later on. But as figure 9-6 shows, that's a time-consuming and error-prone procedure. How much better it is to think ahead.

Terms

master page
content page
content placeholder
nested master page
parent master page
child master page

10

How to use site navigation

The ASP.NET site navigation features make it easy for users to navigate to the various pages in your site. These features are valuable for both small and large web sites. This chapter shows you how to get the most from these features.

An introduction to site navigation **324**
An introduction to the navigation controls 324
How to create a web.sitemap file 326
The web.sitemap file for the Navigation application 328

How to use the site navigation controls **330**
How to use the TreeView control 330
How to create a SiteMapDataSource control 332
How to use the Menu control 334
How to use the SiteMapPath control 336
A master page for the Navigation application 338

Perspective **340**

An introduction to site navigation

ASP.NET's *site navigation* features are designed to simplify the task of creating menus and other navigation features that let users find their way around your web site. To implement that, ASP.NET provides a site map data source control and three navigation controls: TreeView, Menu, and SiteMapPath. The following topics introduce you to these controls.

An introduction to the navigation controls

Figure 10-1 shows a page from an application called the Navigation application. This application is a variation of the Halloween Store application you saw in the last chapter. It includes navigation features on the master page as well as a new page that displays a complete site map for the application. All three of the navigation controls are illustrated on this page.

The TreeView control displays the pages in a web site in a tree structure that's similar to a directory tree displayed by Windows Explorer. The user can expand or collapse a node by clicking the + or − icon that appears next to each node that has children. This control is most useful when you want to give users a complete view of the pages in a web site.

The Menu control creates dynamic menus that expand when you hover the mouse over a menu item that contains subitems. For example, if you were to hover the mouse over the Projects item in the menu in this figure, a submenu listing Costumes, Static Props, and Animated Props would appear.

The SiteMapPath control displays a list of links that lead from the web site's home page to the current page. This makes it easy for the user to quickly return to the home page or to a parent of the current page.

The TreeView and the Menu controls must be used with a SiteMapDataSource control, which binds the controls to a file named web.sitemap. This file contains XML that defines the structure of the pages that make up the web site. You'll learn how to create the web.sitemap file in the next two figures.

In most cases, you'll use either the Menu or the SiteMapPath control and possibly a TreeView control in a master page. That way, these navigation controls will be available from any page in the web site. If the site contains a large number of pages, though, you may want to use a separate Site Map page that includes a TreeView control. Then, the user can use the Site Map page to quickly locate any page within the web site.

A page with three site navigation controls

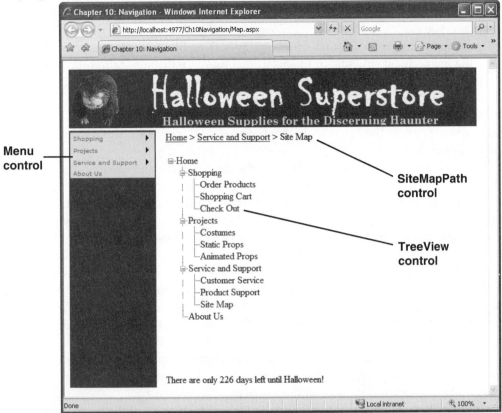

Menu control ➝

SiteMapPath control

TreeView control

ASP.NET navigation controls

Control	Description
TreeView	Provides a hierarchical view of the site's structure. The user can click the + or – icon next to a node to expand or collapse the node. Must be bound to a SiteMapDataSource control. Located in the Navigation group of the Toolbox.
Menu	Creates a horizontal or vertical menu. Must be bound to a SiteMapDataSource control. Located in the Navigation group of the Toolbox.
SiteMapPath	Displays a list of links from the application's root page (the home page) to the current page. Doesn't need to be bound to a SiteMapDataSource control. Located in the Navigation group of the Toolbox.
SiteMapDataSource	Connects a navigation control to the site hierarchy specified by the web.sitemap file. Located in the Data group of the Toolbox.

Description

- ASP.NET provides three user-interface controls and a data source control designed to let the user navigate the pages in a web site.

- The navigation structure of a web site is defined by an XML file named web.sitemap located in the application's root folder. You must create this file before you can work with the navigation controls.

Figure 10-1   An introduction to site navigation

How to create a web.sitemap file

Before you can use one of the site navigation controls, you must create a web.sitemap file in the application's root directory. This file uses XML tags to define the hierarchical structure of the pages that make up the application.

As figure 10-2 shows, you can add a web.sitemap file to an application by choosing the Website→Add New Item command and selecting Site Map from the list of templates. Then, you use the Text Editor to edit the contents of this file. The web.sitemap file can contain two types of XML elements: siteMap and siteMapNode.

The siteMap element is the root element for the XML file and should occur only once in the file. You usually don't need to modify this element.

In contrast, you need to create a siteMapNode element for each page in the web site that you want to include in the navigation controls. In the siteMapNode element, you specify the URL of the page (relative to the application's root folder); the page title that's displayed as the link in the menu, tree, or map path; and a description of the page.

To indicate the hierarchy of the pages in the site map, you nest the siteMapNode elements. The file should contain just one top-level siteMapNode element that represents the site's home page. Then, additional elements can be nested between the start and end tags for the home-page siteMapNode.

An important rule you must follow when you create the sitemap file is that each siteMapNode element must have a unique URL. That means each page in the web site can appear only once in the site map.

Another important point is that you don't have to include all of the pages in the web site in the sitemap file. Instead, you should only include those pages that you want to make available via the site's navigation controls. If, for example, the site uses a two-page checkout process, you may not want to include the second check out page in the sitemap file. That way, the user will be able to access the first checkout page from a menu or tree view control, but not the second checkout page.

The web.sitemap file created from the Site Map template

```
<?xml version="1.0" encoding="utf-8" ?>
<siteMap xmlns="http://schemas.microsoft.com/AspNet/SiteMap-File-1.0" >
    <siteMapNode url="" title=""  description="">
        <siteMapNode url="" title=""  description="" />
        <siteMapNode url="" title=""  description="" />
    </siteMapNode>
</siteMap>
```

Attributes of the siteMapNode element

Attribute	Description
Url	The URL of the page. Each siteMapNode element must specify a unique value for this attribute.
Title	The text that will appear in the menu for the page.
Description	The tool tip text for the page.

Description

- To create a web.sitemap file, choose the Website→Add New Item command, select Site Map from the list of available templates, and click Add. You can then use the Text Editor to edit the web.sitemap file.

- The web.sitemap file contains an XML-based description of the navigation hierarchy of an ASP.NET application.

- Each siteMapNode element defines a page in the web site. You can nest siteMapNode elements within other siteMapNode elements to indicate the hierarchy of pages in the web site. But you don't have to include all of the pages in your web site in the site map.

Figure 10-2   How to create a web.sitemap file

The web.sitemap file for the Navigation application

Figure 10-3 shows the complete web.sitemap file for the Navigation application. The site navigation structure defined by this file corresponds to the structure shown in the TreeView control in figure 10-1.

If you compare the siteMapNode elements in this file with the items listed in the TreeView control in figure 10-1, you should see how the nesting of the siteMapNode elements specifies the site's hierarchical structure. For example, the siteMapNode elements for the Order.aspx, Cart.aspx, and Checkout1.aspx pages are contained within the start and end elements of the siteMapNode element for the Shopping.aspx page.

In this case, not all of the pages in the Navigation application are listed in the web.sitemap file. For example, there's a second checkout page and an order confirmation page that aren't in the sitemap file. That's because users shouldn't be allowed to navigate directly to these pages.

The web.sitemap file used for the controls in figure 10-1

```xml
<?xml version="1.0" encoding="utf-8" ?>
<siteMap xmlns="http://schemas.microsoft.com/AspNet/SiteMap-File-1.0" >

    <siteMapNode url="Default.aspx" title="Home"
        description="Home page.">

        <siteMapNode url="Shopping.aspx" title="Shopping"
            description="Shop for your favorite products.">
            <siteMapNode url="Order.aspx" title="Order Products"
                description="Order a product.">
            </siteMapNode>
            <siteMapNode url="Cart.aspx" title="Shopping Cart"
                description="View your shopping cart.">
            </siteMapNode>
            <siteMapNode url="Checkout1.aspx" title="Check Out"
                description="Finalize your purchase.">
            </siteMapNode>
        </siteMapNode>

        <siteMapNode url="Projects.aspx" title="Projects"
            description="Do-it-yourself Halloween projects.">
            <siteMapNode url="Costumes.aspx" title="Costumes"
                description="Costume projects.">
            </siteMapNode>
            <siteMapNode url="StaticProps.aspx" title="Static Props"
                description="Static props.">
            </siteMapNode>
            <siteMapNode url="AnimatedProps.aspx" title="Animated Props"
                description="Animated props.">
            </siteMapNode>
        </siteMapNode>

        <siteMapNode url="Service.aspx" title="Service and Support"
            description="Customer service and product support.">
            <siteMapNode url="CustService.aspx" title="Customer Service"
                description="Customer service.">
            </siteMapNode>
            <siteMapNode url="Support.aspx" title="Product Support"
                description="Product support.">
            </siteMapNode>
            <siteMapNode url="Map.aspx" title="Site Map"
                description="A map of all the pages on this web site.">
            </siteMapNode>
        </siteMapNode>

        <siteMapNode url="About.aspx" title="About Us"
            description="All about our company.">
        </siteMapNode>

    </siteMapNode>

</siteMap>
```

Figure 10-3   The web.sitemap file for the Navigation application

How to use the site navigation controls

Once you've created the sitemap file, you're ready to use the site navigation controls. The topics that follow show you how to do that.

How to use the TreeView control

Figure 10-4 shows how to use the TreeView control, which displays the pages in a web site as a hierarchical tree. Each node on the tree is a link that represents a page in the web site. You can click any of these links to go directly to that page. You can also click the + or – icons that appear next to the nodes to expand or collapse the nodes.

The table in this figure lists the attributes you're most likely to use with the TreeView control. The ID attribute provides a name for the TreeView control, and the DataSourceID attribute specifies the ID of the data source that provides the site map data. You'll learn how to create a site map data source in the next figure.

The other attributes let you customize the appearance and behavior of the TreeView control. For example, you can use the ExpandDepth attribute to set the number of levels that are initially expanded when the TreeView is first displayed. And you can use the ShowLines attribute to include lines that graphically show the tree's hierarchical structure. The best way to learn how these attributes affect the TreeView control is to experiment with them.

A TreeView control

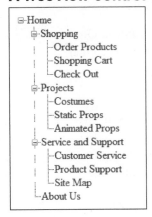

The aspx code for the TreeView control shown above

```
<asp:TreeView ID="TreeView1" runat="server"
              DataSourceID="SiteMapDataSource1"
              ShowLines="True">
</asp:TreeView>
```

Attributes of the TreeView control

Attribute	Description
ID	The ID of the control.
Runat	Must specify Server.
DataSourceID	The ID of the SiteMapDataSource control the tree should be bound to.
ExpandDepth	The number of levels to be automatically expanded when the tree is initially displayed. The default is FullyExpand.
MaxDepthDataBind	Limits the maximum depth of the tree. The default is -1, which places no limit.
NodeIndent	The number of pixels to indent each level. The default is 20.
NodeWrap	Set to True to word-wrap the text of each node. The default is False.
ShowExpandCollapse	Set to False if you want to hide the Expand/Collapse buttons. The default is True.
ShowLines	Set to True to include lines that show the hierarchical structure. The default is False.

Description

- The TreeView control is used to display the site map in a hierarchical tree.
- To display an application's navigation structure, the TreeView control must be bound to a SiteMapDataSource control as described in the next figure.

Figure 10-4   How to use the TreeView control

How to create a SiteMapDataSource control

Figure 10-5 shows two ways to create a SiteMapDataSource control. One way is to drag this control from the Data group of the Toolbox to a page. Then, you can set the properties for the control.

The other way is to click the Smart Tag icon for a TreeView or Menu control, and choose New Data Source from the menu that appears. This brings up the Data Source Configuration Wizard dialog box shown at the top of this figure. Then, you select Site Map and click OK to create a *site map data source*.

To customize the behavior of the site map data source, you can use the attributes listed in this figure. For example, the ShowStartingNode attribute determines whether the highest-level siteMapNode element in the web.sitemap file will be included in the tree or menu. Usually, you'll leave this attribute set to its default of True for TreeView controls and you'll set it to False for Menu controls.

The StartFromCurrentNode and StartingNodeUrl attributes let you bind a TreeView or Menu control to just a portion of the site map. If you specify True for the StartFromCurrentNode attribute, the tree or menu will start from the current page. As a result, only child pages of the current page will appear in the tree or menu. The StartingNodeUrl attribute lets you select any node in the site map as the starting node for the tree or menu.

The Data Source Configuration Wizard dialog box

SiteMapDataSource examples

Example 1: A default SiteMapDataSource control

```
<asp:SiteMapDataSource ID="SiteMapDataSource1" runat="server" />
```

Example 2: A SiteMapDataSource control that specifies a starting level

```
<asp:SiteMapDataSource ID="SiteMapDataSource1" runat="server"
    StartingNodeUrl="Projects.aspx" />
```

Common attributes of the SiteMapDataSource control

Attribute	Description
ID	The ID of the control.
Runat	Must specify Server.
StartingNodeUrl	The URL of the node the SiteMapDataSource control should use as its starting node.
ShowStartingNode	Set to False to omit the starting node. The default is True.
StartFromCurrentNode	Set to True to start the navigation from the current node. The default is False, which starts the navigation from the root node specified in the web.sitemap file.

Two ways to create a SiteMapDataSource control

- Drag the control from the Data group of the Toolbox to a page.
- Click the Smart Tag icon in the upper-right corner of a TreeView or Menu control, then select New Data Source in the Choose Data Source drop-down list.

Description

- You use a SiteMapDataSource control to bind a TreeView or Menu control to the navigation structure defined by the web.sitemap file.

Figure 10-5   How to create a SiteMapDataSource control

How to use the Menu control

Figure 10-6 shows how to use the Menu control, which lets you create menus that are arranged either vertically or horizontally. *Vertical menus* are usually used in a sidebar alongside the content placeholder in a master page. In contrast, *horizontal menus* typically appear beneath a banner image and above the content placeholder.

Each item in a menu can contain a submenu that appears when you hover the mouse over the item for a moment. For example, the Service and Support submenu shown in the examples in this figure doesn't appear until you hover the mouse over the Service and Support item. The part of the menu that is always displayed is called the *static menu*. Submenus that appear when you hover the mouse over a menu item are called *dynamic menus*.

Like the TreeView control, the Menu control must be bound to a site map data source. Then, the other attributes in this figure let you customize the appearance of the menu and specify which items will appear in the menu. For example, the Orientation attribute determines whether the menu is arranged vertically or horizontally. And the MaximumDynamicDisplay attribute determines how many layers of dynamic submenus should be displayed.

As you set the properties for a Menu control, you'll see that it includes many style properties that aren't listed in this figure. You can set these properties to control the formatting that's used to display the menu. Alternatively, you can automatically apply a predefined scheme to the menu by selecting Auto Format from the Menu control's smart tag menu. When you select a scheme, Visual Studio generates the style properties that apply the formatting that you selected.

A menu with vertical orientation

A menu with horizontal orientation

Typical aspx code for a Menu control

```
<asp:Menu ID="Menu1" Orientation="Horizontal" runat="server"
    DataSourceID="SiteMapDataSource1">
</asp:Menu>
```

Common attributes of the Menu control

Attribute	Description
ID	The ID of the control.
Runat	Must specify Server.
DataSourceID	The ID of the SiteMapDataSource control the menu should be bound to.
ItemWrap	If True, words in the menu items will be word-wrapped if necessary. The default is False.
MaximumDynamicDisplay	The number of levels of dynamic submenus to display.
Orientation	Horizontal or Vertical. The default is Vertical.
StaticDisplayLevels	The number of levels that should always be displayed. The default is 1.
StaticEnableDefaultPopOutImage	If True, an arrow graphic is displayed next to any menu item that has a pop-out submenu. If false, the arrow graphic is not displayed. The default is True.

Description

- The Menu control displays site navigation information in a menu. Submenus automatically appear when the user hovers the mouse over a menu item that has a submenu.

- To display an application's navigation structure, the Menu control must be bound to a SiteMapDataSource control.

- The Menu control has many formatting attributes that aren't listed in this figure. You can quickly apply a coordinated set of formatting attributes by clicking the Smart Tag icon for the Menu control and choosing Auto Format from the menu that appears. Then, you can select one of several predefined schemes for the menu.

Figure 10-6   How to use the Menu control

How to use the SiteMapPath control

Figure 10-7 shows how to use the SiteMapPath control, which creates a series of links that lead from the application's home page to the current page. These links are sometimes called *bread crumbs* because they let the user find his or her way back to the home page.

Unlike the TreeView and Menu controls, the SiteMapPath control doesn't need to be bound to a data source. Instead, it obtains the site navigation information directly from the web.sitemap file.

The attributes listed in this figure let you customize the appearance of the SiteMapPath control. In particular, you can indicate how many parent nodes to list, which direction the nodes are listed in, what text to use to separate the nodes, and whether the current page should be formatted as a link or just plain text.

Although this figure doesn't show it, the SiteMapPath control includes other style attributes that let you completely customize the appearance of the site map path. And like the Menu control, you can also use the Auto Format command to apply predefined formatting.

A SiteMapPath control

<u>Home</u> > <u>Service and Support</u> > Site Map

Aspx code for a SiteMapPath control

```
<asp:SiteMapPath ID="SiteMapPath1" runat="server">
</asp:SiteMapPath>
```

Common attributes of the SiteMapPath control

Attribute	Description
ID	The ID of the control.
Runat	Must specify Server.
ParentLevelsDisplayed	The maximum number of parent nodes to display. The default is -1, which displays all parent nodes.
PathDirection	Indicates the order in which nodes should be listed. Allowable values are RootToCurrent and CurrentToRoot. The default is RootToCurrent.
PathSeparator	The string displayed between each node of the path. The default is a greater-than sign.
RenderCurrentNodeAsLink	Set to True if you want the node that represents the current page to be rendered as a link. The default is False.

Description

- The SiteMapPath control displays a list of the links for each node in the site map from the root node to the current page.
- Unlike the TreeView and Menu controls, you don't need to bind the SiteMapPath control to a data source. Instead, it automatically uses the web.sitemap file to determine the current page's position within the web site's navigation structure.

Figure 10-7   How to use the SiteMapPath control

A master page for the Navigation application

To show you how the navigation controls work together, figure 10-8 presents the body of a master page that includes both a navigation menu and a site map path. This is the master page that was shown in figure 10-1.

This master page begins with an Image control that displays a banner at the top of the page. Then, a table is used to control the layout of the rest of the page. This table consists of two rows and three columns. The first column that's defined for the first row contains the Menu control. The second column in the first row provides ten pixels of white space. And the third column in the first row contains the SiteMapPath control, followed by two line breaks and a content placeholder. In figure 10-1, a Site Map page is displayed within the content placeholder. You can also see how the message label is defined for the second row.

Notice also that the asp:Menu element includes several style attributes and elements that specify the appearance of the menu. These attributes and elements were generated by Visual Studio when I selected a scheme for the menu.

In addition, this master page uses a code-behind file named MasterPage.master.cs. But since this code-behind file is the same as the one presented in chapter 9, it's not repeated here.

The body of the master page for the Navigation application

```
<body>
    <form id="form1" runat="server">
    <div>
        <asp:Image ID="Image1" runat="server" ImageUrl="~/Images/banner.jpg" />
        <table cellpadding="2" cellspacing="0">
            <tr>
                <td class="Row1Column1" valign="top">
                    <asp:Menu ID="Menu1" runat="server"
                        DataSourceID="SiteMapDataSource1" BackColor="#E3EAEB"
                        DynamicHorizontalOffset="2" Font-Names="Verdana"
                        Font-Size="0.8em" ForeColor="#666666"
                        StaticSubMenuIndent="10px" >
                        <StaticSelectedStyle BackColor="#1C5E55" />
                        <StaticMenuItemStyle HorizontalPadding="5px"
                            VerticalPadding="2px" />
                        <DynamicHoverStyle BackColor="#666666" Font-Bold="True"
                            ForeColor="White" />
                        <DynamicMenuStyle BackColor="#E3EAEB" />
                        <DynamicSelectedStyle BackColor="#1C5E55" />
                        <DynamicMenuItemStyle HorizontalPadding="5px"
                            VerticalPadding="2px" />
                        <StaticHoverStyle BackColor="#666666" Font-Bold="True"
                            ForeColor="White" />
                    </asp:Menu>
                    <asp:SiteMapDataSource ID="SiteMapDataSource1" runat="server"
                        ShowStartingNode="False" />
                </td>
                <td class="Row1Column2"></td>
                <td class="Row1Column3" valign="top">
                    <asp:SiteMapPath id="SiteMapPath1" runat="server">
                    </asp:SiteMapPath>
                    <br />
                    <br />
                    <asp:ContentPlaceHolder id="Main" runat="server">
                    </asp:ContentPlaceHolder>
                </td>
            </tr>
            <tr>
                <td class="Row2Column1"></td>
                <td class="Row2Column2"></td>
                <td class="Row2Column3">
                    <asp:Label ID="lblMessage" runat="server"></asp:Label>
                </td>
            </tr>
        </table>
    </div>
    </form>
</body>
```

Figure 10-8   A master page that includes navigation controls

Perspective

This should give you a pretty good idea of how useful the navigation features can be. If you experiment with them, you should quickly see that they're also easy to use.

You'll also discover that the TreeView, Menu, and SiteMapPath controls include many attributes that weren't described in this chapter. However, most of these attributes are designed to let you alter the appearance of the navigation controls, not their behavior. So once you master the basics of using these controls, you shouldn't have any trouble learning how to tweak their appearance by using the other attributes.

Terms

site navigation
site map data source
vertical menu
horizontal menu
static menu
dynamic menu
bread crumbs

11

How to use themes

When you develop a web site, you usually want to apply consistent formatting to all of its pages so the entire site has a cohesive look and feel. In addition, it's generally considered a good programming practice to separate the formatting of the web pages from the content of the web pages whenever that's possible. That way, web designers can focus on making the site look good, and programmers can focus on making the site work the way it should.

To make this easier and more flexible, ASP.NET includes a feature known as *themes* that builds upon older formatting technologies such as cascading style sheets (CSS). This feature allows you to create multiple themes for a web site, and it makes it easy to switch between themes. If you want, you can even write code that allows a user to customize a web site by choosing a preferred theme.

An introduction to themes **342**
A page before and after a theme has been applied 342
How themes work 344
How to make an existing theme available to an application 346
How to apply a theme to an application 346

How to create your own themes **348**
How to use cascading style sheets 348
How to use skins 350
Another way to store skins 352
How to use images 354

More skills for working with themes **356**
How to apply a theme to a page 356
How to apply a skin to a control 356
How to remove a theme from an application 358
How to remove a theme from a page 358
How to remove a theme from a control 358
How to use style sheet themes 360

Perspective **362**

An introduction to themes

When you work with standard HTML, it is a common practice to store the global formatting information for a web site in a file known as a *cascading style sheet (CSS)*. Then, the styles in this sheet are applied to all pages in the application unless they are overridden by individual pages or by individual elements. (To learn more about style sheets, please refer back to chapter 5.)

Although this works well for HTML elements, it can be tricky to get this to work correctly with ASP.NET server controls since this requires the programmer and web designer to understand how server controls are rendered to HTML before being returned to the browser. The solution to this problem is the use *themes*, which let you specify the formatting for both HTML elements and server controls. To start, a theme includes a cascading style sheet. In addition, a theme includes information that specifies the formatting for the ASP.NET server controls.

A page before and after a theme has been applied

Figure 11-1 shows the Order page for the Halloween Store application before and after a theme has been applied to it. If you could see these pages in color, you would clearly see the differences between them. In particular, you would see that the second page uses a different font, font color, and font size for all of the elements and controls on the page. In addition, the buttons that are defined on the second page look different than the buttons on the first page because they don't have rounded corners and do use a different background color.

This Order page includes both HTML elements and ASP.NET server controls. To start, this page includes two HTML tags that define the heading and subheading for the page like this:

```
<h1>Halloween Superstore</h1>
<h4>Halloween supplies for the discerning haunter</h4>
```

The custom formatting for these tags is stored in the cascading style sheet for the theme. Then, this page uses ASP.NET tags to define the server controls that are on the rest of the page. However, the custom formatting for these server controls isn't stored in the Order page. Instead, this formatting is stored in an external file as described in the next figure.

Before: The Order page without a theme

After: The Order page with a theme

Figure 11-1   A page before and after a theme has been applied

How themes work

Figure 11-2 gives an overview of how themes work. To start, it shows the Solution Explorer for an application that contains an App_Themes folder. This folder can contain multiple subfolders with each subfolder defining one theme.

For example, the App_Themes folder in this figure contains two folders that define themes. The first folder contains the Classic theme. To help identify this folder as a theme folder, Visual Studio adds a paintbrush to the folder icon. The second folder contains the SmokeAndGlass theme.

The SmokeAndGlass folder shows the three types of files that can be contained by a theme. First, a theme folder can contain a file for the cascading style sheet that defines the styles that define the appearance of the HTML elements. This file must have an extension of css. In addition, it typically has the same name as the theme folder, although that's not required.

Second, a theme folder can contain files for the *skins* that define the appearance of the ASP.NET server controls. A skin specifies the formatting attributes for a server control, and a file that contains skins must have an extension of skin. In addition, if the theme only has one skin file, this file typically has the same name as the theme folder, although that's not required. In fact, as you'll see later in this chapter, it's possible to store skin definitions in multiple skin files within a theme folder.

Third, a theme folder can contain the files for any images that are used by the theme. These files can be stored in the theme folder, or they can be stored in any subfolder of the theme folder. In this figure, for example, all of the GIF files that are used by the SmokeAndGlass theme are stored in the Images subfolder of the SmokeAndGlass folder.

The partial SmokeAndGlass.css file shown in this figure shows how formatting information for HTML elements is stored in a cascading style sheet. To start, the Body style sets the default formatting for any text in the body of an HTML page. This formatting includes specifying the font family, the font size, the line height relative to the font size, and the color. Then, the H1 style sets the formatting for any text within an H1 tag. This style inherits some settings such as font size from the predefined H1 style, and it inherits other settings such as font family and font color from the Body style. With a little bit of experimenting, you can typically set up a css file to get your pages to look the way you want.

The partial SmokeAndGlass.skin file shown in this figure shows how formatting information for server controls is stored in skins. In particular, this file contains one skin for each type of control that's used on the Order page shown in figure 11-1. For example, the skin for the Label control specifies the font name and font color that are used for labels. The skins for the other controls also specify font attributes, and the TextBox and Button controls specify some other attributes that control the appearance of the border and background color.

The directory structure for a theme

Part of the SmokeAndGlass.css file

```css
BODY {
    FONT-FAMILY: Verdana, Geneva, Arial, Helvetica, sans-serif;
    FONT-SIZE: 11pt;
    LINE-HEIGHT: 110%;
    COLOR : #585880;
}

H1 {
    font-family: Verdana, Geneva, Arial, Helvetica, sans-serif;
    COLOR: #585880;
    margin-top: 3px;
}
```

Part of the SmokeAndGlass.skin file

```
<asp:Label    runat="server"           ForeColor="#585880"
              Font-Names="Verdana" />

<asp:DropDownList
              runat="server"           ForeColor="#585880"
              Font-Names="Verdana" />

<asp:TextBox runat="server"        BackColor="#FFFFFF"
             BorderStyle="Solid"    Font-Names="Verdana"
             ForeColor="#585880"    BorderColor="#585880"
             BorderWidth="1pt" />

<asp:Button  runat="server"        BorderColor="#585880"
             Font-Bold="true"       BorderWidth="1pt"
             ForeColor="#585880"    BackColor="#F8F7F4" />
```

Description

- The App_Themes folder can contain multiple subfolders with each subfolder defining one *theme*.

- Each theme folder can contain a file that contains the *cascading style sheet* (CSS) that defines the appearance of the HTML elements, files that define the *skins* that control the appearance of the ASP.NET server controls, and files for any images that are used by the cascading style sheet or the skins.

Figure 11-2   How themes work

How to make an existing theme available to an application

Designing a theme that looks good isn't an easy task, even for an experienced web designer. It requires coding a cascading style sheet that defines the formatting for all of the HTML elements, coding skins that define all of the server controls, and creating any graphics that are used by the style sheets or the skins. As a result, the easiest way to get started with themes is to use an existing theme.

To obtain an existing theme, you can download the SmokeAndGlass theme that's included with the application for this chapter. This theme was included with the Beta 1 version of ASP.NET 2.0 to show how themes work, and I have made some minor modifications to it. Or, you can try to download another theme from the Internet. For example, you may be able to find a theme you like by searching the www.asp.net web site. As more developers began to create themes, the availability and quality of themes available from the Internet should improve.

Once you have a theme folder on your computer that contains the files for a theme, it's easy to make the theme available to an application. To do that, you can use Visual Studio to create the App_Themes folder. Then, you can use Windows Explorer to copy the theme folder into the App_Themes folder as described in figure 11-3. After you do that, you may need to refresh the App_Themes folder before you'll see the new folder.

How to apply a theme to an application

Once the theme has been added to the App_Themes folder, you can apply it to the entire application by editing the web.config file as shown in figure 11-3. To do that, you add a Pages element within the System.web element. Then, you code a Theme attribute within the Pages element that specifies the name of the theme.

For most applications, you'll want to apply a single theme to the entire application as shown in this figure. When you do that, you can't override the formatting that has been specified by the theme for an individual element or control. If, for example, you want to set the color for a label to red, you can't do that because that attribute has already been specified by the theme. However, if an attribute isn't specified by the theme, you can change it for a control. For example, since the SmokeAndGlass theme doesn't specify the Font-Bold attribute for labels, you can apply or remove boldfacing from individual labels.

Most of the time, this is how you want themes to work. However, if you need to apply a different theme to a page or control, if you need to remove a theme from a page or control, or if you want to change the way overriding works, you can learn how to do that later in this chapter.

How to make an existing theme available to an application

1. Create the App_Themes folder. To do that, you can right-click on the root folder, select the Add ASP.NET Folder submenu, and select the Theme item. This creates the App_Themes folder and a subfolder with a default name of Theme1. You can delete this Theme1 folder since you will be using an existing theme.

2. Copy the folder that contains the theme into the App_Themes folder. To do that, you can use Windows Explorer.

A web.config file that specifies a theme

```
<configuration>
  <system.web>
    <pages theme="SmokeAndGlass" />
  </system.web>
</configuration>
```

Description

*   You can get the SmokeAndGlass theme shown in the previous figure by downloading the applications for this book. You may also be able to download themes from the Internet.

*   To apply a theme to the current application, you can edit the web.config file for the application. Within the web.config file, you can use the Theme attribute of the Pages element to specify the name of the theme.

*   When you use the Theme attribute of the Pages element to apply a theme to a page, you can't override any of the formatting attributes specified by the theme for individual controls. However, you can change attributes that aren't specified by the theme.

*   Figures 11-8 and 11-9 show other techniques for applying and removing themes from individual pages and controls.

*   Figure 11-10 shows how to allow controls to override attributes that are specified by a theme.

Figure 11-3   How to apply a theme to the entire application

How to create your own themes

In the topics that follow, you'll learn the basic skills for creating your own themes. Even if you never need to create your own themes, you should read through these topics since they show the details of how themes work. In addition, they present skills that you can use to edit an existing theme.

How to use cascading style sheets

In chapter 5, you learned how to store cascading style sheets in an external file. You use the same techniques to create a cascading style sheet that's part of a theme, except that you store the style sheet in the theme folder. Figure 11-4 reviews the basic techniques for creating a cascading style sheet and shows the start of a style sheet named Classic.css. It also presents a simple style sheet and shows how you can use it.

The Body style in this style sheet sets the default color for any text in the body of an HTML page to navy by specifying a value of #000066. As you learned in chapter 5, it's also possible to set the Color attribute to a keyword such as Blue or Navy. However, these keywords limit the number of colors that are available. In addition, they aren't supported by all browsers. As a result, web designers typically use the #000000 format to specify colors.

The H1 and H4 styles in this figure use the Font-Size attribute to specify a font size in points. In addition, the H4 style uses the Font-Style attribute to specify that the heading should be italicized. The rest of the attributes for the H1 and H4 styles use the default settings, except that they use the Color attribute that's specified by the Body style. If you want to specify a different color, though, you can use the Color attribute of these styles to override the Color attribute of the Body style.

The style sheet in this figure also defines a style class named Highlighted that can be used to change the background color of any HTML element to light gray. To identify this class, a period is coded before the name of the class. Then, the Background-Color attribute is used to set the background to light grey.

To use the styles in a style sheet, you can code the tag as you would normally. However, to use a style class, you must specify the name of the class. To do that, you use the Class attribute for HTML tags and the CssClass attribute for ASP.NET tags.

The start of a cascading style sheet

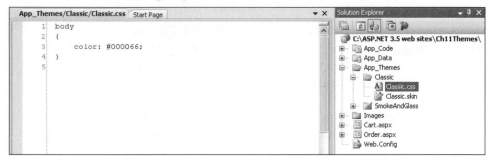

A .css file that defines three styles and one style class

```
body
{
    color: #000066;
}
h1
{
    font-size: 18pt;
}
h4
{
    font-size: 12pt;
    font-style: italic;
}
.highlighted
{
    background-color: #CCCCCC;
}
```

An HTML tag that uses a style

```
<h1>Halloween Superstore</h1>
```

An HTML tag that specifies a style class

```
<h4 class="highlighted">Halloween supplies for the discerning haunter</h4>
```

An ASP.NET tag that specifies a style class

```
<asp:Label ID="lblName" runat="server" CssClass="highlighted"></asp:Label>
```

Description

- To add a new .css file to a theme, you can right-click on the folder for the theme and select the Add New Item command. Then, you can use the Add New Item dialog box to select the Style Sheet template and enter the name for the .css file.

- When using Visual Studio to work with a css file, you can use IntelliSense to select from lists of HTML elements and attributes. You can also use the Modify Style dialog box to edit style attributes.

Figure 11-4   How to use cascading style sheets

How to use skins

Figure 11-5 shows how to create and use a file that contains skins for the controls of an application. As you would hope, this works similarly to cascading style sheets, but it allows you to define styles for ASP.NET server controls. In this figure, for example, you can see a newly created skin file named Classic.skin.

Once you create a skin file, you can add skins to the file by opening the tag, entering the name of the control, entering a RunAt attribute, and closing the tag. For example, you can begin a tag for the Label control like this:

```
<asp:Label runat="server" />
```

Then, you can set other attributes to control the formatting for the control. For example, you can change the ForeColor attribute for a Label control like this:

```
<asp:Label runat="server" ForeColor="#000066" />
```

Since this uses the standard ASP.NET syntax for setting control attributes, you shouldn't have much trouble understanding how this works.

When you use themes, you typically need to define one skin for each type of control that you use in your application. In this figure, for example, you can see the skins for the Label, TextBox, Button, and DropDownList controls. These are all the controls that are used by the Order page shown in figure 11-1. However, for a more robust application, you'd probably need to include skins for many more types of controls. Otherwise, a control that doesn't have a skin probably won't look like the rest of the controls.

The first four skins in this skin file don't include a SkinID attribute. As a result, they're the *default skins* that are used when a control of that type doesn't include a SkinID attribute. For example, the default skin for a label is applied to the Label control that's defined by the first ASP.NET tag shown in this figure.

If you need to supply multiple skins for a control, you can code a *named skin* that includes a SkinID attribute that uniquely identifies the skin. For example, the named skin in this figure provides a second skin for the Label control with a SkinID of Head1. This skin adds boldfacing to the font and sets the font size to large to make the label have the appearance of a heading. To apply this skin to a Label control, you can set the SkinID attribute of the control to Head1 as shown by the second Label control defined in this figure.

All of the skins in this figure specify the color of the font. However, this is already done by the Body style in the cascading style sheet for the Classic theme. Since all of the ASP.NET server controls are eventually rendered as HTML elements before being returned to the client, the color specified in the Body style is automatically applied to the server controls. As a result, you don't need to set the ForeColor attribute for these controls unless you want to make sure that the color specified for these server controls overrides the color that's set by the Body style.

The start of a skin file

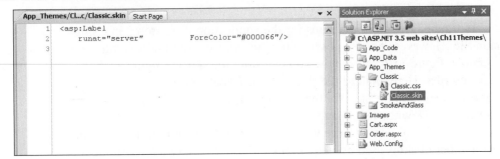

A skin file that defines four default skins and one named skin

```
<asp:Label
    runat="server"          ForeColor="#000066" />

<asp:DropDownList
    runat="server"          ForeColor="#000066" />

<asp:TextBox
    runat="server"          ForeColor="#000066"
    BorderStyle="Solid"     BorderWidth="1pt" />

<asp:Button
    runat="server"          ForeColor="#000066"
    Font-Bold="true"        BackColor="#EEEEEE"
    BorderColor="#000066"   BorderWidth="1pt" />

<%-- a named skin for labels --%>
<asp:Label
    runat="server"          ForeColor="#000066"
    Font-Bold="true"        Font-Size="large"
    SkinID="Head1" />
```

An ASP.NET tag that uses the default skin for a label

```
<asp:Label ID="Label3" runat="server" Text="Quantity:"></asp:Label>
```

An ASP.NET tag that specifies a named skin for a label

```
<asp:Label ID="lblName" runat="server" SkinID="Head1"></asp:Label>
```

Description

- To add a new skin file to a theme, you can right-click on the folder for the theme, and select the Add New Item command. Then, you can use the Add New Item dialog box to select the Skin File template and enter the name for the skin file.

- To specify a comment within a skin file, you must use the <%-- and --%> tags.

- To create a *default skin*, don't specify the SkinID attribute for the skin. Then, the skin will automatically be applied to any control of that type whose SkinID property isn't set.

- To create a *named skin*, specify the SkinID attribute for the skin. Then, you can use the SkinID attribute to apply the skin to a control of that type.

Figure 11-5   How to use skins

Another way to store skins

In figure 11-5, all of the skins for the application were stored in a single skin file. However, it's also possible to split skins up into multiple files. For example, figure 11-6 shows how you can store the skins in figure 11-5 in separate files. Here, both of the skins for the Label control are stored in a file named Label.skin, the skin for the DropDownList control is stored in a file named DropDownList.skin, and so on.

The choice of how to store your skins depends on your preferences and on the number of skins used by your application. If you have a large number of skins with multiple skins for each type of control, you may find it easier to organize and manage them by splitting them into separate files. This can make it easier to find skins and to copy them from one application to another. On the other hand, you might find that the additional skin files create a file management headache. As a result, you might prefer to keep all skins in a single file even if that file becomes very long.

A theme that uses multiple skin files

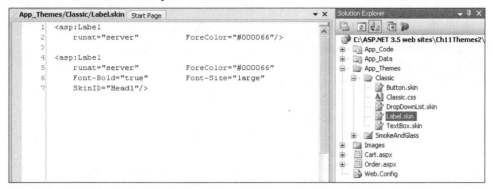

The Label.skin file

```
<asp:Label
    runat="server"          ForeColor="#000066" />

<asp:Label
    runat="server"          ForeColor="#000066"
    Font-Bold="true"        Font-Size="large"
    SkinID="Head1" />
```

The DropDownList.skin file

```
<asp:DropDownList
    runat="server"          ForeColor="#000066" />
```

The TextBox.skin file

```
<asp:TextBox
    runat="server"          ForeColor="#000066"
    BorderStyle="Solid"     BorderWidth="1pt" />
```

The Button.skin file

```
<asp:Button
    runat="server"          ForeColor="#000066"
    Font-Bold="true"        BackColor="#EEEEEE"
    BorderColor="#000066"   BorderWidth="1pt" />
```

Description

- Skins can be stored in a single file as shown in the previous figure or in separate files as shown in this figure.

Figure 11-6   Another way to store skins

How to use images

Each theme can use its own images. These images can be stored directly in the theme folder or in subfolders of the theme folder. For example, in figure 11-7, the folder for the Classic theme contains an Images subfolder that contains two gif files. Once you have added images to a theme, you can use a relative URL to refer to an image from the css and skin files as shown in figure 11-7. That way, if you switch themes, the URL will refer to the image in the new theme folder rather than the original theme folder.

The brownfadetop.gif file can be used as the background for an HTML element or a server control to create a shading effect that isn't possible using a regular colored background. This is an HTML trick that was developed by web designers to get around the limitations of plain HTML, and it's typical of the types of hacks that are often used by web designers. If you look at this image, you can see that it's very narrow. In fact, it's only 5 pixels wide and 100 pixels tall. Although it's difficult to tell from this black-and-white figure, this image contains a brown background that fades to a lighter brown as it nears the top of the image.

The Classic.css style sheet includes a style class named BrownFadeTopBack that sets the BackGround-Image property to the brownfadetop.gif file in the Images subfolder. As a result, if this style class is used to apply this image to an HTML element or server control, the image will be sized and repeated as necessary to fill the entire background for that HTML element or server control. For example, the H4 tag shown in this figure specifies the BrownFadeTopBack class. As a result, this HTML element's background is shaded accordingly.

The bullet.gif file can be used to customize controls that use bullets. For example, the skin for the BulletedList control uses the BulletImageUrl attribute to specify that this control should use the bullet.gif file stored in the Images subfolder of the current theme. In addition, this skin uses the BulletStyle attribute to specify that the bullet should use a custom image. As a result, the BulletedList control shown in this figure uses this custom bullet.gif image instead of the default bullet style, which is a small black circle.

The images for the Classic theme

The brownfadetop.gif image

A style class that uses this image

```
.brownfadetopback
{
    background-image: url(images/brownfadetop.gif);
}
```

An HTML tag that uses the image

```
<h4 class="brownfadetopback">Halloween supplies for the discerning
haunter</h4>
```

How the H4 tag appears on the page

Halloween supplies for the discerning haunter

The bullet.gif image

The skin for a BulletedList control that uses this image

```
<asp:BulletedList runat="server"
    BulletImageUrl="images/bullet.gif"
    BulletStyle="CustomImage" />
```

An ASP.NET tag that uses the image

```
<asp:BulletedList ID="BulletedList1" runat="server">
    <asp:ListItem Value="Item1">Austin Powers</asp:ListItem>
    <asp:ListItem Value="Item2">Freddy</asp:ListItem>
</asp:BulletedList>
```

How the BulletedList control appears on the page

○ Austin Powers
○ Freddy

Figure 11-7   How to use images

More skills for working with themes

Most of the time, you want to apply a single theme to all pages of an application as described in figure 11-3. However, there may be times when you want to apply a theme to individual pages or controls. For example, you may want to allow each user to select a preferred theme for a page. Conversely, there may be times when you want to remove a theme from individual pages or controls. And there may be times when you want to allow individual controls to override attributes that are specified by the theme.

How to apply a theme to a page

Figure 11-8 starts by showing how you can use the Theme attribute of the Page directive to apply a theme to a single page at design time. Then, it shows how you can use the Theme property of the Page class to apply a theme to a single page at runtime.

At runtime, you must make sure the code that applies the theme is executed before the HTML element or ASP.NET control is added to the page. To do that, you can code an event handler for the PreInit event of the Page class as shown in this figure. This event handler is executed before the Init event that adds the controls to the page. As a result, this is a good event to use to apply a theme to a page.

The code within the event handler for the PreInit event sets the Theme for the Page equal to a string for a theme that has been stored in session state. That way, if the user has selected a theme earlier in the session, the theme for this page will be changed to the theme selected by the user. However, unless you store this theme in a persistent data store, this theme will be lost when the user ends the current session.

To make the theme available for future sessions, you can use the profile feature described in chapter 21. To do that, you can configure the profile feature so it includes a Theme property that stores a string for the user's preferred theme. Then, you can use the Profile property to get the theme like this:

```
Page.Theme = Profile.Theme;
```

How to apply a skin to a control

In figure 11-5, you saw how to use the SkinID attribute to apply a named skin to a server control at design time. Now, figure 11-8 reviews this skill, and it shows how to use the SkinID property of a server control to apply a named skin at runtime. To do that, you can use the PreInit event of the page to make sure that this skin is applied before the control is added to the page. This works the same as it does for applying a theme to a page.

How to apply a theme to a page

At design time

```
<%@ Page Language="C#" Theme="SmokeAndGlass" %>
```

At runtime

```
protected void Page_PreInit(object sender, EventArgs e)
{
    Page.Theme = Session["MyTheme"].ToString();
}
```

How to apply a skin to a control

At design time

```
<asp:Label ID="lblName" runat="server" SkinID="Head1"></asp:Label>
```

At runtime

```
protected void Page_PreInit(object sender, EventArgs e)
{
    lblName.SkinID = Session["MySkinID"].ToString();
}
```

Description

- To apply a theme to a single page, you can use the Theme attribute of the Page directive or the Theme property of the Page class.
- To apply a skin to a control, you can use the SkinID attribute or property of the control.
- The code that applies a theme or skin at runtime should be coded in the event handler for the PreInit event of the Page class so the code is executed before the HTML elements and ASP.NET controls are added to the page.

Figure 11-8   How to apply themes and skins

How to remove a theme from an application

Although it isn't shown in this chapter, it's possible for a web site administrator to set a global theme that applies to all web applications running on the server. In that case, you may want to remove the global theme from all pages of your application. To do that, you can open the web.config file for your application and set the Theme attribute of the Pages element to an empty string as shown in figure 11-9.

How to remove a theme from a page

Figure 11-9 also shows how to remove a theme from a single page. At design time, you can set the Theme attribute of the Page directive to an empty string. At runtime, you can set the Theme property of the Page class to an empty string. To do that, you can use the PreInit event of the page to make sure that this theme is removed before the HTML elements and controls are added to the page. This works the same as it does for applying a theme to a page.

How to remove a theme from a control

By default, the EnableTheming property is set to True for all controls. As a result, any themes that are applied to a page are applied to all controls on the page. Typically, that's what you want. However, since you can't override an attribute that's set in a skin by setting it at the control level, you may want to remove the theme from the control so you can apply custom formatting to a control. To do that, you can set the EnableTheming attribute for the control to False as shown in figure 11-9. Then, you can use standard ASP.NET formatting techniques to format that control. In this figure, for example, the ForeColor attribute is used to change the color of a label to red.

If you need to set the EnableTheming property at runtime, you can use the PreInit event of the page to make sure that this skin is removed before the HTML elements and controls are added to the page. This works the same as it does for applying a theme to a page.

How to remove themes from the entire application

At design time

```
<system.web>
  <pages theme="" />
</system.web>
```

How to remove themes from the current page

At design time

```
<%@ Page Language="C#" Theme="" %>
```

At runtime

```
protected void Page_PreInit(object sender, EventArgs e)
{
    Page.Theme = "";
}
```

How to remove a theme from a control

At design time

```
<asp:Label ID="lblName" runat="server"
    EnableTheming="False" ForeColor="red">
</asp:Label>
```

At runtime

```
protected void Page_PreInit(object sender, EventArgs e)
{
    lblName.EnableTheming = false;
    lblName.ForeColor = System.Drawing.Color.Red;
}
```

Description

- To remove a theme from all of the pages in an application, you can set the Theme attribute of the Pages element to an empty string.

- To remove a theme from a single page, you can set the Theme attribute of the Page directive or the Theme property of the Page class to an empty string.

- To remove a theme from a control, you can set the EnableTheming attribute or property to false.

- The code that removes a theme at runtime should be coded in the event handler for the PreInit event of the Page class so the code is executed before the HTML elements and ASP.NET controls are added to the page.

Figure 11-9 How to remove themes and skins

How to use style sheet themes

When you use the Theme attribute or property to apply a theme, the theme is known as a *customization theme*. So far, all of the examples in this chapter have worked with customization themes. When you use a customization theme, you can't override any of the attributes that are set by the theme. For example, since the Classic theme sets the color of a label to blue, you can't set the color of an individual label to red unless you remove the theme from the label as shown in figure 11-9. This often isn't ideal because it also removes all other formatting that was applied by the theme.

If you want to be able to override the attributes specified by a theme, you can use the StyleSheetTheme attribute to apply the theme to all pages as shown in figure 11-10. Then, the theme is known as a *style sheet theme*, and you can override any of the attributes specified in this theme by setting them at the control level. For the most part, you can use the same skills for working with style sheet themes that you use for customization themes.

However, to apply a style sheet theme to a single page at runtime, you don't use the PreInit event. Instead, you override the StyleSheetTheme property of the page to get and set the name of the theme. Then, when a page loads, it automatically calls the StyleSheetTheme property to set the style sheet theme. In this figure, for example, the StyleSheetTheme property for the page gets the name of the style sheet theme from the session state and sets the name of the style sheet theme in the session state.

To understand how themes work, you need to understand the order in which attributes are applied. First, all attributes specified by the style sheet theme are applied. Then, the custom attributes specified for individual elements are applied, overriding the style sheet theme if necessary. Finally, the attributes specified by the customization theme are applied, overriding the custom attributes and the style sheet theme if necessary. That's why you can't override a customization theme by setting attributes for a control.

Although you won't typically apply both types of themes to an application, this figure shows you how in case you ever want to do that. Here, the SmokeAndGlass theme is applied as the style sheet theme, and the Classic theme is applied as the customization theme. As a result, if the same attribute is specified in both themes, the attribute specified in the Classic theme will override the attribute in the SmokeAndGlass theme. However, if an attribute is specified in the SmokeAndGlass theme and it isn't specified in the Classic theme, that attribute will be applied to the page unless, of course, it is overridden by a custom attribute for an element.

How to apply a style sheet theme to all pages in the application

```
<system.web>
  <pages styleSheetTheme="SmokeAndGlass" />
</system.web>
```

How to apply a style sheet theme to a single page

At design time

```
<%@ Page Language="C#" StylesheetTheme="SmokeAndGlass" %>
```

At runtime by overriding the StyleSheetTheme property in the code-behind file

```
public override string StyleSheetTheme
{
    get
    {
        return Session["MyTheme"].ToString();
    }
    set
    {
        Session["MyTheme"] = value;
    }
}
```

How to remove a style sheet theme from a single page

At design time

```
<%@ Page Language="C#" StylesheetTheme="" %>
```

The order in which themes are applied

1. Style sheet theme attributes
2. Control attributes
3. Customization theme attributes

How to apply both a customization theme and a style sheet theme

At design time

```
<%@ Page Language="C#" StylesheetTheme="SmokeAndGlass" Theme="Classic" %>
```

Description

- A *customization theme* can't be overridden by custom settings on controls. A *style sheet theme* can be overridden at the control level.
- To apply or remove a style sheet theme at design time, you can use the StyleSheetTheme attribute. This works just like the Theme attribute does for customization themes.
- To apply or remove a style sheet theme at runtime, you can override the StyleSheetTheme property of the page.

Figure 11-10   How to use style sheet themes

Perspective

In this chapter, you learned how themes work and how they can be used to separate the formatting of an application from the code of an application. In addition, you learned enough about creating a theme from scratch to realize that it isn't an easy task, even for an experienced web designer.

Now, you should have all the skills you need to work with a web designer to create a suitable theme for your application. Also, as themes become more widely used, you may be able to download an appropriate theme for your application from the Internet. Either way, once you have the theme you want, you can use the skills of this chapter to get the most from it.

Terms

theme
cascading style sheet (CSS)
skin
default skin
named skin
customization theme
style sheet theme

Section 3

ASP.NET database programming

Since most ASP.NET applications store their data in databases, this section is devoted to the essentials of database programming. When you complete it, you should be able to develop database applications that use *SQL data sources* to access and update the data in the databases that your applications use. In addition, you should have at least a general understanding of how you can use *object data sources* to develop 3-layer database applications. And you should have a general understanding of how to use a type of data source that's new to ASP.NET 3.5: the LINQ data source.

To start, chapter 12 introduces you to the concepts and terms you need to know for developing database applications. This chapter also presents an overview of the ADO.NET classes that do the database operations when you use SQL, object, or LINQ data sources. When you use SQL or LINQ data sources, though, you don't use ADO.NET directly, even though the processing is done by ADO.NET.

Then, chapter 13 shows you how to use SQL data sources and the DataList control to get data from a database. Chapter 14 shows you how to use the GridView control to create more complex applications. Chapter 15 shows you how to use the DetailsView and FormView controls. And chapter 16 shows you how to use the new ListView and DataPager controls. By using SQL data sources and the data controls, you'll be able to develop powerful applications with a minimum of code.

Next, chapter 17 shows you how to use object data sources to develop 3-layer database applications. If you already know how to use ADO.NET directly, you should be able to use object data sources when you complete this chapter. Otherwise, you will at least understand the concepts and recognize the need for learning ADO.NET.

Finally, chapter 18 shows you how to use the new LINQ data source. This data source takes advantage of the Language-Integrated Query feature of C# 2008, which provides constructs for working with data from a variety of sources. The LINQ data source along with the Language-Integrated Query feature help bridge the gap between relational data and object-oriented programming.

12

An introduction to database programming

This chapter introduces you to the basic concepts and terms that apply to database applications. In particular, it explains what a relational database is and describes how you work with it using SQL. It also presents an overview of the basic ADO.NET classes that are used to access the data in relational databases.

To illustrate these concepts and terms, this chapter presents examples that use *Microsoft SQL Server Express*. This is a scaled-back version of *Microsoft SQL Server 2005*, and SQL Server is the database you're most likely to use as you develop ASP.NET 3.5 database applications. Note, however, that the concepts and terms that you'll learn in this chapter also apply to other databases.

An introduction to relational databases 366
How a table is organized 366
How the tables in a database are related 368
How the columns in a table are defined 370
The design of the Halloween database 372

**How to use SQL to work with the data in a
relational database 374**
How to query a single table 374
How to join data from two or more tables 376
How to add, update, and delete data in a table 378

An introduction to ADO.NET 3.5 380
How the basic ADO.NET components work 380
Concurrency and the disconnected data architecture 382
How to work with data without using a data adapter 384

An introduction to the ADO.NET 3.5 classes 386
The SqlConnection class 386
The SqlCommand class 386
The SqlParameter class 388
The SqlDataReader class 388
The SqlDataAdapter class 388

Perspective 390

An introduction to relational databases

In 1970, Dr. E. F. Codd developed a model for what was then a new and revolutionary type of database called a *relational database.* This type of database eliminated some of the problems that were associated with standard files and other database designs. By using the relational model, you can reduce data redundancy, which saves disk storage and leads to efficient data retrieval. You can also view and manipulate data in a way that is both intuitive and efficient. Today, relational databases are the de facto standard for database applications.

How a table is organized

The model for a relational database states that data is stored in one or more *tables*. It also states that each table can be viewed as a two-dimensional matrix consisting of *rows* and *columns*. This is illustrated by the relational table in figure 12-1. Each row in this table contains information about a single product.

In practice, the rows and columns of a relational database table are sometimes referred to by the more traditional terms, *records* and *fields*. In fact, some software packages use one set of terms, some use the other, and some use a combination. In this book, we've used the terms *rows* and *columns* for consistency.

If a table contains one or more columns that uniquely identify each row in the table, you can define these columns as the *primary key* of the table. For instance, the primary key of the Products table in this figure is the ProductID column. Here, the primary key consists of a single column. However, a primary key can also consist of two or more columns, in which case it's called a *composite primary key*.

In addition to primary keys, some database management systems let you define additional keys that uniquely identify each row in a table. If, for example, the Name column in the Products table contains a unique name for each product, it can be defined as a *non-primary key*. In SQL Server, this is called a *unique key*, and it's implemented by defining a *unique key constraint* (also known simply as a *unique constraint*). The only difference between a unique key and a primary key is that a unique key can contain a null value and a primary key can't.

Indexes provide an efficient way to access the rows in a table based on the values in one or more columns. Because applications typically access the rows in a table by referring to their key values, an index is automatically created for each key you define. However, you can define indexes for other columns as well. If, for example, you frequently need to sort the rows in the Products table by the CategoryID column, you can set up an index for that column. Like a key, an index can include one or more columns.

The Products table in a Halloween database

Primary key   **Columns**

ProductID	Name	ShortDescription	LongDescription	CategoryID	ImageFile	UnitPrice	OnHand
arm01	Severed Arm	Bloody Severed ...	A severed arm, ...	props	arm01.jpg	19.9500	200
bl01	Black light (24")	24" black light	Create that cree...	fx	blacklight01.jpg	24.9900	200
cat01	Deranged Cat	20" Ugly Cat	This is one ugly ...	props	cat01.jpg	19.9900	45
cool01	Cool Ghoul	Cool Ghoul mask	This guy is one c...	props	cool01.jpg	69.9900	25
fog01	Fog Machine	600W Fog Machine	The perfect fog ...	fx	fog01.jpg	34.9900	100
fogj01	Fog Juice (1qt.)	1Qt bottle of Fo...	The drink your f...	fx	*NULL*	9.9900	500
frankc01	Frankenstein	Frankenstein co...	It's alive!	costumes	frank01.jpg	39.9900	100
fred01	Freddie	Freddie Krueger ...	The ultimate in ...	masks	freddy.jpg	29.9900	50
head01	Shrunken Head	Shrunken Head ...	Spikes driven thr...	props	head01.jpg	29.9900	100
head02	Severed Head	Severed Head in...	Incredibly realist...	props	head02.jpg	29.9900	100
hippie01	Hippie	Ghoulish Hippie ...	This guy did too ...	masks	hippie01.jpg	79.9900	40
jar01	JarJar	Jar Jar Binks	Meesa happy to ...	costumes	jarjar1.jpg	59.9900	25
martian01	Martian	Martian costume	Now includes an ...	costumes	martian1.jpg	69.9900	100
mum01	Mummy	Mummy mask	All wrapped up a...	masks	mummy.jpg	39.9900	30
pow01	Austin Powers	Austin Powers c...	Be the most sha...	costumes	powers1.jpg	79.9900	25
rat01	Ugly Rat	16" Rat	This guy is sure ...	props	rat01.jpg	14.9900	75
rat02	Uglier Rat	20" Rat	Yuch! This one ...	props	rat02.jpg	19.9900	50
skel01	Life Size Skeleton	Life Size Plastic ...	This blown plasti...	props	skel01.jpg	14.9500	10
skullfog01	Skull Fogger	2,800 Cubic Foo...	This fogger puts...	fx	skullfog01.jpg	39.9500	50
str01	Mini-strobe	Black mini strobe...	Perfect for creat...	fx	strobe1.jpg	13.9900	200
super01	Superman	Superman costume	Look, up in the s...	costumes	superman1.jpg	39.9900	100
tlm01	TLM	Thunder & Light...	Flash! Boom! Cr...	props	tlm1.jpg	99.9900	10
vader01	Darth Vader Mask	The legendary D...	OB1 has taught ...	masks	vader01.jpg	19.9900	100

- Rows

Concepts

- A *relational database* uses *tables* to store and manipulate data. Each table consists of one or more *records*, or *rows*, that contain the data for a single entry. Each row contains one or more *fields*, or *columns*, with each column representing a single item of data.

- Most tables contain a *primary key* that uniquely identifies each row in the table. The primary key often consists of a single column, but it can also consist of two or more columns. If a primary key uses two or more columns, it's called a *composite primary key*.

- In addition to primary keys, some database management systems let you define one or more *non-primary keys*. In SQL Server, these keys are called *unique keys*, and they're implemented using *unique key constraints*. Like a primary key, a non-primary key uniquely identifies each row in the table.

- A table can also be defined with one or more *indexes*. An index provides an efficient way to access data from a table based on the values in specific columns. An index is automatically created for a table's primary and non-primary keys.

Figure 12-1   How a table is organized

How the tables in a database are related

The tables in a relational database can be related to other tables by values in specific columns. The two tables shown in figure 12-2 illustrate this concept. Here, each row in the Categories table is related to one or more rows in the Products table. This is called a *one-to-many relationship*.

Typically, relationships exist between the primary key in one table and the *foreign key* in another table. The foreign key is simply one or more columns in a table that refer to a primary key in another table. In SQL Server, relationships can also exist between a unique key in one table and a foreign key in another table.

Although one-to-many relationships are the most common, two tables can also have a one-to-one or many-to-many relationship. If a table has a *one-to-one relationship* with another table, the data in the two tables could be stored in a single table. Because of that, one-to-one relationships are used infrequently.

In contrast, a *many-to-many relationship* is usually implemented by using an intermediate table, called a *linking table*, that has a one-to-many relationship with the two tables in the many-to-many relationship. In other words, a many-to-many relationship can usually be broken down into two one-to-many relationships.

The relationship between the Categories and Products tables

Primary key

CategoryID	ShortName	LongName
costumes	Costumes	Costumes
fx	FX	Special Effects
masks	Masks	Masks
props	Props	Props

Foreign key

ProductID	Name	ShortDescription	LongDescription	CategoryID	ImageFile	UnitPrice	OnHand
arm01	Severed Arm	Bloody Severed ...	A severed arm, ...	props	arm01.jpg	19.9500	200
bl01	Black light (24")	24" black light	Create that cree...	fx	blacklight01.jpg	24.9900	200
cat01	Deranged Cat	20" Ugly Cat	This is one ugly ...	props	cat01.jpg	19.9900	45
cool01	Cool Ghoul	Cool Ghoul mask	This guy is one c...	props	cool01.jpg	69.9900	25
fog01	Fog Machine	600W Fog Machine	The perfect fog ...	fx	fog01.jpg	34.9900	100
fogj01	Fog Juice (1qt.)	1Qt bottle of Fo...	The drink your f...	fx	*NULL*	9.9900	500
frankc01	Frankenstein	Frankenstein co...	It's alive!	costumes	frank01.jpg	39.9900	100
fred01	Freddie	Freddie Krueger ...	The ultimate in ...	masks	freddy.jpg	29.9900	50
head01	Shrunken Head	Shrunken Head ...	Spikes driven thr...	props	head01.jpg	29.9900	100
head02	Severed Head	Severed Head in...	Incredibly realist...	props	head02.jpg	29.9900	100
hippie01	Hippie	Ghoulish Hippie ...	This guy did too ...	masks	hippie01.jpg	79.9900	40
jar01	JarJar	Jar Jar Binks	Meesa happy to ...	costumes	jarjar1.jpg	59.9900	25
martian01	Martian	Martian costume	Now includes an ...	costumes	martian1.jpg	69.9900	100
mum01	Mummy	Mummy mask	All wrapped up a...	masks	mummy.jpg	39.9900	30
pow01	Austin Powers	Austin Powers c...	Be the most sha...	costumes	powers1.jpg	79.9900	25
rat01	Ugly Rat	16" Rat	This guy is sure ...	props	rat01.jpg	14.9900	75
rat02	Uglier Rat	20" Rat	Yuch! This one ...	props	rat02.jpg	19.9900	50
skel01	Life Size Skeleton	Life Size Plastic ...	This blown plasti...	props	skel01.jpg	14.9500	10
skullfog01	Skull Fogger	2,800 Cubic Foo...	This fogger puts...	fx	skullfog01.jpg	39.9500	50
str01	Mini-strobe	Black mini strobe...	Perfect for creat...	fx	strobe1.jpg	13.9900	200
super01	Superman	Superman costume	Look, up in the s...	costumes	superman1.jpg	39.9900	100
tlm01	TLM	Thunder & Light...	Flash! Boom! Cr...	props	tlm1.jpg	99.9900	10
vader01	Darth Vader Mask	The legendary D...	OB1 has taught ...	masks	vader01.jpg	19.9900	100

Concepts

- The tables in a relational database are related to each other through their key columns. For example, the CategoryID column is used to relate the Categories and Products tables above. The CategoryID column in the Products table is called a *foreign key* because it identifies a related row in the Categories table.

- Usually, a foreign key corresponds to the primary key in the related table. In SQL Server, however, a foreign key can also correspond to a unique key in the related table.

- When two tables are related via a foreign key, the table with the foreign key is referred to as the *foreign key table* and the table with the primary key is referred to as the *primary key table*.

- The relationships between the tables in a database correspond to the relationships between the entities they represent. The most common type of relationship is a *one-to-many relationship* as illustrated by the Categories and Products tables. A table can also have a *one-to-one relationship* or a *many-to-many relationship* with another table.

Figure 12-2   How the tables in a database are related

How the columns in a table are defined

When you define a column in a table, you assign properties to it as indicated by the design of the Products table in figure 12-3. The two most important properties for a column are Column Name, which provides an identifying name for the column, and Data Type, which specifies the type of information that can be stored in the column. With SQL Server, you can choose from *system data types* like the ones in this figure, and you can define your own data types that are based on the system data types. As you define each column in a table, you generally try to assign the data type that will minimize the use of disk storage because that will improve the performance of the queries later.

In addition to a data type, you must identify whether the column can store a *null value*. A null represents a value that's unknown, unavailable, or not applicable. The Products table, for example, allows nulls in its ImageFile column.

You can also assign a *default value* to each column. Then, that value is assigned to the column if another value isn't provided. If a column doesn't allow nulls and doesn't have a default value, you must supply a value for the column when you add a new row to the table. Otherwise, an error will occur.

Each table can also contain a numeric column whose value is generated automatically by the DBMS. In SQL Server, a column like this is called an *identity column*, and you establish it using the Identity, Identity Seed, and Identity Increment properties. Identity columns are often used as the primary key for a table.

A *check constraint* defines the acceptable values for a column. For example, you can define a check constraint for the Products table in this figure to make sure that the UnitPrice column is greater than zero. A check constraint like this can be defined at the column level because it refers only to the column it constrains. If the check constraint for a column needs to refer to other columns in the table, however, it can be defined at the table level.

After you define the constraints for a database, they're managed by the DBMS. If, for example, a user tries to add a row with data that violates a constraint, the DBMS sends an appropriate error code back to the application without adding the row to the database. The application can then respond to the error code.

Another alternative is to validate the data that is going to be added to a database before the program tries to add it. That way, the constraints shouldn't be needed and the program should run more efficiently. In many cases, both data validation and constraints are used. That way, the programs run more efficiently if the data validation routines work, but the constraints are there in case the data validation routines don't work or aren't coded.

The Server Explorer design view window for the Products table

Common SQL Server data types

Type	Description
bit	A value of 1 or 0 that represents a True or False value.
char, varchar, text	Any combination of letters, symbols, and numbers.
datetime, smalldatetime	Alphanumeric data that represents a date and time. Various formats are acceptable.
decimal, numeric	Numeric data that is accurate to the least significant digit. The data can contain an integer and a fractional portion.
float, real	Floating-point values that contain an approximation of a decimal value.
bigint, int, smallint, tinyint	Numeric data that contains only an integer portion.
money, smallmoney	Monetary values that are accurate to four decimal places.

Description

- The *data type* that's assigned to a column determines the type of information that can be stored in the column. Depending on the data type, the column definition can also include its length, precision, and scale.

- Each column definition also indicates whether or not the column can contain *null values*. A null value indicates that the value of the column is not known.

- A column can be defined with a *default value*. Then, that value is used for the column if another value isn't provided when a row is added to the table.

- A column can also be defined as an *identity column*. An identity column is a numeric column whose value is generated automatically when a row is added to the table.

- To restrict the values that a column can hold, you define *check constraints*. Check constraints can be defined at either the column level or the table level.

Figure 12-3   How the columns in a table are defined

The design of the Halloween database

Now that you've seen how the basic elements of a relational database work, figure 12-4 shows the design of the Halloween database that's used in the programming examples throughout this book. Although this database may seem complicated, its design is actually much simpler than most databases you'll encounter when you work on actual database applications.

The purpose of the Halloween database is to track orders placed at an online Halloween products store. To do that, the database must track not only invoices, but also products and customers.

The central table for this database is the Invoices table, which contains one row for each order placed by the company's customers. The primary key for this table is the InvoiceNumber column, which is an identity column. As a result, invoice numbers are generated automatically by SQL Server whenever new invoices are created.

The LineItems table contains the line item details for each invoice. The primary key for this table is a combination of the InvoiceNumber and ProductID columns. The InvoiceNumber column relates each line item to an invoice, and the ProductID column relates each line item to a product. As a result, each invoice can have only one line item for a given product.

The Products and Categories tables work together to store information about the products offered by the Halloween store. The Category table has just three columns: CategoryID, ShortName, and LongName. The CategoryID column is a 10-character code that uniquely identifies each category. The ShortName and LongName columns provide two different descriptions of the category that the application can use, depending on how much room is available to display the category information.

The Products table contains one row for each product. Its primary key is the ProductID column. The Name, ShortDescription, and LongDescription columns provide descriptive information about the product. The ImageFile column provides the name of a separate image file that depicts the product, if one exists. This column specifies just the name of each image file, not the complete path. In the applications in this book, the image files are stored in a directory named Images beneath the application's main directory so the application knows where to find them. If an image isn't available for a product, this column contains a null value.

Finally, the Customers table contains a row for each customer who has purchased from the Halloween Store. The primary key for this table is the customer's email address. The other columns in this table contain the customer's name, address, and phone number.

The tables that make up the Halloween database

Description

- The Categories table contains a row for each product category. Its primary key is CategoryID, a 10-character code that identifies each category.

- The Products table contains a row for each product. Its primary key is ProductID, a 10-character code that identifies each product. CategoryID is a foreign key that relates each product to a row in the Categories table.

- The Customers table contains a row for each customer. Its primary key is Email, which identifies each customer by his or her email address.

- The Invoices table contains a row for each invoice. Its primary key is InvoiceNumber, an identity column that's generated automatically when a new invoice is created. CustEmail is a foreign key that relates each invoice to a row in the Customers table.

- The LineItems table contains one row for each line item of each invoice. Its primary key is a combination of InvoiceNumber and ProductID. InvoiceNumber is a foreign key that relates each line item to an invoice, and ProductID is a foreign key that relates each line item to a product.

- The relationships between the tables in this diagram appear as links, where the endpoints indicate the type of relationship. A key indicates the "one" side of a relationship, and the infinity symbol (∞) indicates the "many" side.

Figure 12-4   The design of the Halloween database

How to use SQL to work with the data in a relational database

In the topics that follow, you'll learn about the four SQL statements that you can use to manipulate the data in a database: Select, Insert, Update, and Delete. Although you'll learn the basics of coding these statements in the topics that follow, you may want to know more than what's presented here. In that case, we recommend our book, *Murach's SQL Server 2005 for Developers*. In addition to the Select, Insert, Update, and Delete statements, that book teaches you how to code the statements you use to define the data in a database, and it teaches you how to use other features of SQL Server that the top professionals use.

Although SQL is a standard language, each DBMS is likely to have its own *SQL dialect*, which includes extensions to the standard language. So when you use SQL, you need to make sure that you're using the dialect that's supported by your DBMS. In this chapter and throughout this book, all of the SQL examples are for Microsoft SQL Server's dialect, which is called *Transact-SQL*.

How to query a single table

Figure 12-5 shows how to use a Select statement to query a single table in a database. In the syntax summary at the top of this figure, you can see that the Select clause names the columns to be retrieved and the From clause names the table that contains the columns. You can also code a Where clause that gives criteria for the rows to be selected. And you can code an Order By clause that names one or more columns that the results should be sorted by and indicates whether each column should be sorted in ascending or descending sequence.

If you study the Select statement below the syntax summary, you can see how this works. Here, the Select statement retrieves three columns from the Products table. It selects a row only if the CategoryID column for the row has a value of "Props." And it sorts the returned rows by UnitPrice, so that the least expensive products are listed first.

This figure also shows the *result table*, or *result set*, that's returned by the Select statement. A result set is a logical table that's created temporarily within the database. When an application requests data from a database, it receives a result set.

Although it's not shown here, you should realize that a result set can include columns that are calculated from other columns in the table. For example, you could create a column for the total value of each product in the Products table by multiplying the OnHand column in that table by the UnitPrice column. This type of column is called a *calculated column*, and it exists only in the results of the query.

Simplified syntax of the Select statement

```
Select column-1 [, column-2]...
From table-1
[Where selection-criteria]
[Order By column-1 [Asc|Desc] [, column-2 [Asc|Desc]]...]
```

A Select statement that retrieves and sorts selected columns and rows from the Products table

```
Select ProductID, Name, UnitPrice
From Products
Where CategoryID = 'Props'
Order By UnitPrice
```

The result set defined by the Select statement

ProductID	Name	UnitPrice
skel01	Life Size Skeleton	14.9500
rat01	Ugly Rat	14.9900
arm01	Severed Arm	19.9500
cat01	Deranged Cat	19.9900
rat02	Uglier Rat	19.9900
head01	Shrunken Head	29.9900
head02	Severed Head	29.9900
cool01	Cool Ghoul	69.9900
tlm01	TLM	99.9900

Concepts

- The result of a Select statement is a *result table*, or *result set*, like the one shown above. A result set is a logical set of rows that consists of all of the columns and rows requested by the Select statement.

- A result set can include *calculated columns* that are calculated from other columns in the table.

- To select all of the columns in a table, you can code an asterisk (*) in place of the column names. For example, this statement will select all of the columns from the Products table:

```
Select * From Products
```

Figure 12-5   How to query a single table

How to join data from two or more tables

Figure 12-6 presents the syntax of the Select statement for retrieving data from two tables. This type of operation is called a *join* because the data from the two tables is joined together into a single result set. For example, the Select statement in this figure joins data from the Categories and Products tables into a single result set.

An *inner join* is the most common type of join. When you use an inner join, rows from the two tables in the join are included in the result set only if their related columns match. These matching columns are specified in the From clause of the Select statement. In the Select statement in this figure, for example, rows from the Categories and Products tables are included only if the value of the CategoryID column in the Categories table matches the value of the CategoryID column in one or more rows in the Products table. If there aren't any products for a particular category, that category won't be included in the result set.

Although this figure shows how to join data from two tables, you should know that you can extend this syntax to join data from additional tables. If, for example, you want to include data from the LineItems table in the results shown in this figure, you can code the From clause of the Select statement like this:

```
From Categories
    Inner Join Products
        On Categories.CategoryID = Products.CategoryID
    Inner Join LineItems
        On Products.ProductID = LineItems.ProductID
```

Then, in the column list of the Select statement, you can include any of the columns in the LineItems table.

The syntax of the Select statement for joining two tables

```
Select column-list
From table-1
    [Inner] Join table-2
    On table-1.column-1 {=|<|>|<=|>=|<>} table-2.column-2
[Where selection-criteria]
[Order By column-list]
```

A Select statement that joins data from the Products and Categories tables

```
Select ShortName, ProductID, Name, UnitPrice
From Categories Inner Join Products
    On Categories.CategoryID = Products.CategoryID
Order By Categories.CategoryID
```

The result set defined by the Select statement

ShortName	ProductID	Name	UnitPrice
Costumes	frankc01	Frankenstein	39.9900
Costumes	jar01	JarJar	59.9900
Costumes	martian01	Martian	69.9900
Costumes	pow01	Austin Powers	79.9900
Costumes	super01	Superman	39.9900
FX	skullfog01	Skull Fogger	39.9500
FX	str01	Mini-strobe	13.9900
FX	bl01	Black light (24")	24.9900
FX	fog01	Fog Machine	34.9900
FX	fogj01	Fog Juice (1qt.)	9.9900
Masks	fred01	Freddie	29.9900
Masks	mum01	Mummy	39.9900
Masks	hippie01	Hippie	79.9900
Masks	vader01	Darth Vader Mask	19.9900
Props	tlm01	TLM	99.9900
Props	arm01	Severed Arm	19.9500
Props	rat01	Ugly Rat	14.9900
Props	rat02	Uglier Rat	19.9900
Props	skel01	Life Size Skeleton	14.9500
Props	head01	Shrunken Head	29.9900
Props	head02	Severed Head	29.9900
Props	cat01	Deranged Cat	19.9900
Props	cool01	Cool Ghoul	69.9900

Concepts

- A *join* lets you combine data from two or more tables into a single result set.
- The most common type of join is an *inner join*. This type of join returns rows from both tables only if their related columns match.

Figure 12-6   How to join data from two or more tables

How to add, update, and delete data in a table

Figure 12-7 presents the basic syntax of the SQL Insert, Update, and Delete statements. You use these statements to add new rows to a table, to update the data in existing rows, and to delete existing rows.

To add a single row to a table, you use an Insert statement with the syntax shown in this figure. With this syntax, you specify the name of the table you want to add the row to, the names of the columns you're supplying data for, and the values for those columns. In the example, the Insert statement adds a row to the Categories table and supplies a value for each of the three columns in that table. If a table allows nulls or provides default values for some columns, though, the Insert statement doesn't have to provide values for those columns.

To change the values of one or more columns in one or more rows, you use the Update statement. On this statement, you specify the name of the table you want to update, expressions that indicate the columns you want to change and how you want to change them, and a condition that identifies the rows you want to change. In the example, the Update statement changes the ShortName value for just the one row in the Categories table that has a CategoryID value of "food."

To delete one or more rows from a table, you use the Delete statement. On this statement, you specify the table you want to delete rows from and a condition that indicates the rows you want to delete. In the example, the Delete statement deletes just the one Categories row whose CategoryID column is "food."

How to add a single row

The syntax of the Insert statement for adding a single row

```
Insert [Into] table-name [(column-list)]
    Values (value-list)
```

A statement that adds a single row to a table

```
Insert Into Categories (CategoryID, ShortName, LongName)
    Values ('food', 'Spooky Food', 'The very best in Halloween cuisine')
```

How to update rows

The syntax of the Update statement

```
Update table-name
    Set expression-1 [, expression-2]...
    [Where selection-criteria]
```

A statement that changes the value of the ShortName column for a selected row

```
Update Categories
    Set ShortName = 'Halloween cuisine'
    Where CategoryID = 'food'
```

How to delete rows

The syntax of the Delete statement

```
Delete [From] table-name
    [Where selection-criteria]
```

A statement that deletes a specified category

```
Delete From Categories
    Where CategoryID = 'food'
```

Description

- You use the Insert, Update, and Delete statements to maintain the data in a database table.

- The Insert statement can be used to add one or more rows to a table. Although the syntax shown above is for adding just one row, there is another syntax for adding more than one row.

- The Update and Delete statements can be used for updating or deleting one or more rows in a table using the syntax shown above.

Figure 12-7   How to add, update, and delete data in a table

An introduction to ADO.NET 3.5

ADO.NET 3.5 (*ActiveX Data Objects*) is the primary data access API for the .NET Framework. It provides the classes that are used when you develop database applications. The topics that follow introduce you to the important ADO.NET concepts.

How the basic ADO.NET components work

Figure 12-8 presents the primary ADO.NET objects that are used when you develop database applications. To start, the data used by an application is stored in a *dataset* that contains one or more *data tables*. To load data into a data table, you use a *data adapter*.

The main function of the data adapter is to manage the flow of data between a dataset and a database. To do that, it uses *commands* that define the SQL statements to be issued. The command for retrieving data, for example, typically defines a Select statement. Then, the command connects to the database using a *connection* and passes the Select statement to the database. After the Select statement is executed, the result set it produces is sent back to the data adapter, which stores the results in the data table.

To update the data in a database, the data adapter uses a command that defines an Insert, Update, or Delete statement for a data table. Then, the command uses the connection to connect to the database and perform the requested operation.

Although it's not apparent in this figure, the data in a dataset is independent of the database that the data was retrieved from. In fact, the connection to the database is typically closed after the data is retrieved from the database. Then, the connection is opened again when it's needed. Because of that, the application must work with the copy of the data that's stored in the dataset. The architecture that's used to implement this type of data processing is referred to as a *disconnected data architecture*. Although this is more complicated than a connected architecture, the advantages offset the complexity.

One of the advantages of using a disconnected data architecture is improved system performance due to the use of fewer system resources for maintaining connections. Another advantage is that it works well with ASP.NET web applications, which are inherently disconnected.

The ADO.NET classes that are responsible for working directly with a database are provided by the *.NET data providers*. These data providers include the classes you use to create data adapters, commands, and connections. The .NET Framework currently includes data providers for SQL Server, Oracle, OLE DB, and ODBC. Other third-party providers are also available.

Basic ADO.NET objects

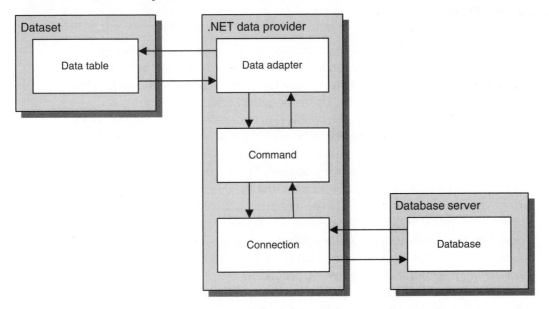

Description

- ADO.NET uses two types of objects to access the data in a database: *datasets*, which can contain one or more *data tables*, and *.NET data provider* objects, which include data adapters, commands, and connections.

- A dataset stores data from the database so it can be accessed by the application. The .NET data provider objects retrieve data from and update data in the database.

- To retrieve data from a database and store it in a data table, a *data adapter* object issues a Select statement that's stored in a *command* object. Next, the command object uses a *connection* object to connect to the database and retrieve the data. Then, the data is passed back to the data adapter, which stores the data in a table within the dataset.

- To update the data in a database based on the data in a data table, the data adapter object issues an Insert, Update, or Delete statement that's stored in a command object. Then, the command object uses a connection to connect to the database and update the data.

- The data provider remains connected to the database only long enough to retrieve or update the specified data. Then, it disconnects from the database and the application works with the data via the dataset object. This is referred to as a *disconnected data architecture.*

- All of the ADO.NET objects are implemented by classes in the System.Data namespace of the .NET Framework. However, the specific classes used to implement the connection, command, and data adapter objects depend on the .NET data provider you use.

Figure 12-8   How the basic ADO.NET components work

Concurrency and the disconnected data architecture

Although the disconnected data architecture has advantages, it also has some disadvantages. One of those is the conflict that can occur when two or more users retrieve and then try to update data in the same row of a table. This is called a *concurrency* problem. This is possible because once a program retrieves data from a database, the connection to that database is dropped. As a result, the database management system can't manage the update process.

To illustrate, consider the situation shown in figure 12-9. Here, two users are using the Products table at the same time. These users could be using the same page of a web site or different pages that have accessed the Products table. Now, suppose that user 1 modifies the unit price in the row for a product and updates the Products table in the database. Suppose too that user 2 modifies the description in the row for the same product, and then tries to update the Products table in the database. What will happen? That will depend on the *concurrency control* that's used by the programs.

When you use ADO.NET, you have two choices for concurrency control. By default, a program uses *optimistic concurrency*, which checks whether a row has been changed since it was retrieved. If it has, the update or deletion will be refused and a *concurrency exception* will be thrown. Then, the program should handle the error. For example, it could display an error message that tells the user that the row could not be updated and then retrieve the updated row so the user can make the change again.

In contrast, the *"last in wins"* technique works the way its name implies. Since no checking is done with this technique, the row that's updated by the last user overwrites any changes made to the row by a previous user. For the example above, the row updated by user 2 will overwrite changes made by user 1, which means that the description will be right but the unit price will be wrong. Since errors like this corrupt the data in a database, optimistic concurrency is used by most programs, which means that your programs have to handle the concurrency exceptions that are thrown.

If you know that concurrency will be a problem, you can use a couple of programming techniques to limit concurrency exceptions. If a program uses a dataset, one technique is to update the database frequently so other users can retrieve the current data. The program should also refresh its dataset frequently so it contains the recent changes made by other users.

Another way to avoid concurrency exceptions is to retrieve and work with just one row at a time. That way, it's less likely that two users will update the same row at the same time. In contrast, if two users retrieve the same table, they will of course retrieve the same rows. Then, if they both update the same row in the table, even though it may not be at the same time, a concurrency exception will occur when they try to update the database.

Two users who are working with copies of the same data

What happens when two users try to update the same row

- When two or more users retrieve the data in the same row of a database table at the same time, it is called *concurrency*. Because ADO.NET uses a disconnected data architecture, the database management system can't prevent this from happening.

- If two users try to update the same row in a database table at the same time, the second user's changes could overwrite the changes made by the first user. Whether or not that happens depends on the *concurrency control* that the programs use.

- By default, ADO.NET uses *optimistic concurrency*. This means that the program checks to see whether the database row that's going to be updated or deleted has been changed since it was retrieved. If it has, a *concurrency exception* occurs and the update or deletion is refused. Then, the program should handle the exception.

- If optimistic concurrency isn't in effect, the program doesn't check to see whether a row has been changed before an update or deletion takes place. Instead, the operation proceeds without throwing an exception. This is referred to as "*last in wins*" because the last update overwrites any previous update. And this can lead to errors in the database.

How to avoid concurrency errors

- For many applications, concurrency errors rarely occur. As a result, optimistic concurrency is adequate because the users will rarely have to resubmit an update or deletion that is refused.

- If concurrency is likely to be a problem, a program that uses a dataset can be designed so it updates the database and refreshes the dataset frequently. That way, concurrency errors are less likely to occur.

- Another way to avoid concurrency errors is to design a program so it retrieves and updates just one row at a time. That way, there's less chance that two users will retrieve and update the same row at the same time.

Figure 12-9   Concurrency and the disconnected data architecture

How to work with data without using a data adapter

When you want to work with two or more rows from a database at the same time, you typically use a data adapter to retrieve those rows and store them in a dataset as described earlier in this chapter. You should know, however, that you can also work with the data in a database without using a data adapter. Figure 12-10 shows you how.

As you can see, you still use command and connection objects to access the database. Instead of using a data adapter to execute the commands, though, you execute the commands directly. When you do that, you also have to provide code to handle the result of the command. If you issue a command that contains an Insert, Update, or Delete statement, for example, the result is an integer that indicates the number of rows that were affected by the operation. You can use that information to determine if the operation was successful.

If you execute a command that contains a Select statement, the result is a result set that contains the rows you requested. To read through the rows in the result set, you use a *data reader* object. Although a data reader provides an efficient way of reading the rows in a result set, you can't use it to modify those rows. In addition, it only lets you read rows in a forward direction. Once you read the next row, the previous row is unavailable. Because of that, you typically use a data reader to retrieve and work with a single database row at a time.

ADO.NET components for accessing a database directly

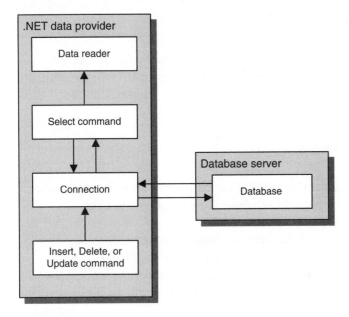

Description

- Instead of using a data adapter to execute commands to retrieve, insert, update, and delete data from a database, you can execute those commands directly.

- To retrieve data from a database, you execute a command object that contains a Select statement. Then, the command object uses a connection to connect to the database and retrieve the data. You can then read the results one row at a time using a *data reader* object.

- To insert, update, or delete data in a database, you execute a command object that contains an Insert, Update, or Delete statement. Then, the command object uses a connection to connect to the database and update the data. You can then check the value that's returned to determine if the operation was successful.

- If you use this technique in an application that maintains the data in a database, you typically work with a single row at a time. Because of that, the chance of a concurrency error is reduced.

Figure 12-10   How to work with data without using a data adapter

An introduction to the ADO.NET 3.5 classes

The topics that follow introduce you to some of the primary ADO.NET 3.5 classes. When you use SQL data sources as described in the next four chapters, though, you don't use these classes directly. Instead, they're used behind the scenes.

The SqlConnection class

Before you can access the data in a database, you have to create a connection object that defines the connection to the database. To do that, you use the SqlConnection class that's presented in figure 12-11.

The most important property of this class is ConnectionString. A *connection string* is a string that provides the information that's needed to connect to a database. That means it includes information such as the name of the database and the database server. It can also contain authentication information such as a user-id and password.

The two methods of this class that are shown in this figure let you open and close the connection. In general, you should leave a connection open only while data is being retrieved or updated. When you use a data adapter, though, the connection is opened and closed for you so you don't need to use these methods.

The SqlCommand class

To execute a SQL statement against a SQL Server database, you create a SqlCommand object that contains the statement. Figure 12-11 presents the SqlCommand class you use to create this object. Notice that the Connection property of this class associates the command with a SqlConnection object, and the CommandText property contains the SQL statement to be executed.

The CommandType property indicates how the command object should interpret the value of the CommandText property. Instead of specifying a SQL statement for the CommandText property, for example, you can specify the name of a stored procedure, which consists of one or more SQL statements that have been compiled and stored with the database.

Earlier in this chapter, you learned that you can use a data adapter to execute command objects. In addition, you can execute a command object directly by using one of the three Execute methods shown in this figure. If, for example, you use ExecuteReader for a Select statement, the results are returned as a DataReader object. If you use ExecuteScalar, only the value in the first column and row of the query results is returned.

If the command contains an Insert, Update, or Delete statement, you'll use the ExecuteNonQuery method to execute it. This method returns an integer value that indicates the number of rows that were affected by the command. If, for example, the command deletes a single row, the ExecuteNonQuery method returns 1.

Common property and methods of the SqlConnection class

Property	Description
ConnectionString	Contains information that lets you connect to a SQL Server database, including the server name, the database name, and login information.

Method	Description
Open	Opens a connection to a database.
Close	Closes a connection to a database.

Common properties and methods of the SqlCommand class

Property	Description
Connection	The SqlConnection object used to connect to the database.
CommandText	The text of the SQL statement or the name of a stored procedure.
CommandType	A constant in the CommandType enumeration that indicates whether the CommandText property contains a SQL statement (Text) or the name of a stored procedure (StoredProcedure).
Parameters	The collection of parameters used by the command.

Method	Description
ExecuteReader	Executes a query and returns the result as a SqlDataReader object.
ExecuteNonQuery	Executes the command and returns an integer representing the number of rows affected.
ExecuteScalar	Executes a query and returns the first column of the first row returned by the query.

Common properties of the SqlParameter class

Property	Description
ParameterName	The name of the parameter.
Value	The value assigned to the parameter.
SqlDbType	The SQL data type for the parameter.

Description

- A SqlConnection object is required to establish a connection to a SQL Server database.
- A SqlCommand object is used to execute a SQL command against a SQL Server database.
- A SqlParameter object is used to pass variable information to a SQL command.

Figure 12-11   The SqlConnection, SqlCommand, and SqlParameter classes

The SqlParameter class

The SqlParameter class, also shown in figure 12-11, lets you pass parameter values to a SQL command. Parameters are commonly used to limit the number of rows retrieved by a Select statement. For example, you can retrieve the Product row for a specific product by passing the ProductID as a parameter. Or, you can retrieve all of the products for a given category by passing the CategoryID as a parameter. Parameters are also commonly used to pass column values to Insert, Update, and Delete statements.

The SqlDataReader class

Figure 12-12 lists the most important properties and methods of the SqlDataReader class. You use this class to create a data reader object, which provides an efficient way to read the rows in a result set returned by a database query. In fact, when you use a data adapter to retrieve data, the data adapter uses a data reader to read through the rows in the result set and store them in a dataset.

The SqlDataAdapter class

As you have learned, the job of a data adapter is to provide a link between a database and a dataset. The four properties of the SqlDataAdapter class listed in figure 12-12, for example, identify the four SQL commands that the data adapter uses to transfer data from the database to the dataset and vice versa. The SelectCommand property identifies the command object that's used to retrieve data from the database. And the DeleteCommand, InsertCommand, and UpdateCommand properties identify the commands that are used to update the database based on changes made to the data in the dataset.

To execute the command identified by the SelectCommand property and place the data that's retrieved in a dataset, you use the Fill method. Then, the application can work with the data in the dataset without affecting the data in the database. If the application makes changes to the data in the dataset, it can use the data adapter's Update method to execute the commands identified by the DeleteCommand, InsertCommand, and UpdateCommand properties and post the changes back to the database.

Common properties and methods of the SqlDataReader class

Property	Description
Item	Accesses the column with the specified index or name from the current row. This property is coded as an indexer.
IsClosed	Gets a Boolean value that indicates if the data reader is closed.

Method	Description
Read	Reads the next row. Returns True if there are more rows. Otherwise, returns False.
Close	Closes the data reader.

Common properties and methods of the SqlDataAdapter class

Property	Description
SelectCommand	A SqlCommand object representing the Select statement used to query the database.
DeleteCommand	A SqlCommand object representing the Delete statement used to delete a row from the database.
InsertCommand	A SqlCommand object representing the Insert statement used to add a row to the database.
UpdateCommand	A SqlCommand object representing the Update statement used to update a row in the database.

Method	Description
Fill	Executes the command identified by the SelectCommand property and loads the result into a dataset object.
Update	Executes the commands identified by the DeleteCommand, InsertCommand, and UpdateCommand properties for each row in the dataset that was deleted, added, or updated.

Description

- A data reader provides read-only, forward-only access to the data in a database. Because it doesn't require the overhead of a dataset, it's more efficient than using a data adapter. However, it can't be used to update data.

- When the Fill method of a data adapter is used to retrieve data from a database, the data adapter uses a data reader to load the results into a dataset.

Figure 12-12 The SqlDataReader and SqlDataAdapter classes

Perspective

This chapter has introduced you to the basic concepts of relational databases and described how you use SQL and ADO.NET classes to work with the data in a relational database. With that as background, you're now ready to learn how to develop ASP.NET database applications.

In the next four chapters, then, you'll learn how to use SQL data sources and five of the data controls to build database applications. After that, chapter 17 will show you how to use object data sources to build 3-layer database applications, and chapter 18 will show you how to use the new LINQ data sources feature. Although you don't need to use ADO.NET directly when you use SQL or LINQ data sources, you do need to use ADO.NET directly when you use object data sources.

Terms

Microsoft SQL Server Express
Microsoft SQL Server 2005
relational database
table
record
row
field
column
primary key
composite primary key
non-primary key
unique key
unique key constraint
unique constraint
index
foreign key
foreign key table
primary key table
one-to-many relationship
one-to-one relationship
many-to-many relationship
linking table
data type
system data type
null value
default value

identity column
check constraint
SQL dialect
Transact-SQL
result table
result set
calculated column
join
inner join
ADO.NET
ActiveX Data Objects .NET
dataset
data table
.NET data provider
data adapter
command
connection
disconnected data architecture
concurrency
concurrency control
optimistic concurrency
concurrency exception
last in wins
data reader
connection string

13

How to use SQL data sources

In this chapter, you'll learn how to use the SqlDataSource control, which lets you access data from a SQL Server database with little or no programming. Along the way, you'll also learn how to use the DataList control, which lets you create lists of data.

How to create a SQL data source **392**
A Product List application that uses two SQL data sources 392
How to create a SqlDataSource control 394
How to define the connection 396
How to save the connection string in the web.config file 398
How to configure the Select statement 400
How to create a Where clause 402
How select parameters work 404

How to use the Query Builder **406**
How to create a Select statement with the Query Builder 406
How to define the parameters 408

How to use the DataList control **410**
How the DataList control works 410
How to define the templates for a data list 412
How to format a data list 414

How to use data binding **416**
How to bind a list control to a data source 416
How to bind the controls in a template 418
The aspx file for the Product List application 420

How to use the advanced features of a SQL
data source **422**
How to create a data source that can update the database 422
How to change the data source mode 424
How to use caching 424

Perspective **426**

How to create a SQL data source

In chapter 3, you learned the basics of using the AccessDataSource control to get data from an Access database. Now, in the topics that follow, you'll learn how to use a SqlDataSource control, which can be referred to as a *SQL data source,* to get data from a SQL Server database.

A Product List application that uses two SQL data sources

Figure 13-1 shows a simple one-page application that demonstrates the use of two SQL data sources. The drop-down list at the top of the page is bound to a SQL data source that gets the categories for the products that the company offers. Then, when the user selects a category from this list, the products for the selected category are retrieved from a second SQL data source, which is bound to a DataList control that's below the drop-down list. As a result, the products are displayed in the DataList control.

Since this application relies entirely on the data binding that's established in the Web Forms Designer, the code-behind file for this application contains no C# code. Although this is a simple application, even complicated applications that insert, update, and delete database data can often be written with little or no code.

That's not to say that most ASP.NET database applications are code-free. In chapters 14, 15, and 16, for example, you'll see applications that require database handling code. In particular, these applications require code to detect database errors and concurrency violations and display appropriate error messages. Also, as you'll learn in chapter 17, you can use object data sources to build 3-layer applications that require extensive amounts of database handling code.

The Product List application displayed in a web browser

Description

- The Product List application uses two SqlDataSource controls to get category and product data from a SQL Server database and display it in two bound controls.

- The drop-down list near the top of the form displays the product categories. This control is bound to the first data source control.

- The DataList control, which is bound to the second data source control, displays the data for the products that are in the category that's selected in the drop-down list.

- This application requires no C# code in the code-behind file.

Figure 13-1   The Product List application

How to create a SqlDataSource control

Figure 13-2 shows how to create a SqlDataSource control. As you will see, this process is similar to the one for creating an AccessDataSource control. To get the process started, you can drag a SqlDataSource control onto the form you're developing.

Since a data source control isn't displayed on the page when the application is run, it doesn't matter where you drop this control. But it does make sense to place it near the control that it will be bound to. Once you've got the data source control on the form, you can use its smart tag menu to run the Configure Data Source command, which brings you to the dialog box in the next figure.

You can also create a SqlDataSource control using the Choose Data Source command in the smart tag menu of a bindable control. The exact technique for doing that varies depending on the control you're binding. For a drop-down list, for example, you select the Choose Data Source command to start the Data Source Configuration Wizard. Then, you can choose New Data Source from the drop-down list in the first dialog box that's displayed and click OK. That displays the dialog box shown in this figure. From this dialog box, you can select the Database icon and click OK, which drops the data source control onto the form next to the bindable control and brings you to the dialog box in the next figure.

The technique for creating a SQL data source from a DataList control is similar. The only difference is that the Choose Data Source command in the control's smart tag menu includes a drop-down list that lets you select New Data Source. When you do that, the Data Source Configuration Wizard dialog box shown in this figure is displayed just as it is for a drop-down list.

The starting dialog box of the Data Source Configuration Wizard

Aspx code generated for a basic SqlDataSource control

```
<asp:SqlDataSource ID="SqlDataSource1" runat="server"
    ConnectionString="<%$ ConnectionStrings:HalloweenConnectionString %>"
    SelectCommand="SELECT [CategoryID], [LongName] FROM [Categories]
        ORDER BY [LongName]">
</asp:SqlDataSource>
```

Basic SqlDataSource control attributes

Attribute	Description
ID	The ID for the SqlDataSource control.
Runat	Must specify "server."
ConnectionString	The connection string. In most cases, you should use a <%$ expression to specify the name of a connection string saved in the web.config file (see figure 13-4).
ProviderName	The name of the provider used to access the database. Values can be System.Data.Odbc, System.Data.Oledb, System.Data.OracleClient, or System.Data.SqlClient. The default is System.Data.SqlClient.
SelectCommand	The SQL Select statement executed by the data source to retrieve data.

Description

- To create a SqlDataSource control, drag the control from the Data group of the Toolbox onto the form. Then, choose Configure Data Source from the control's smart tag menu and proceed from there.

- Once the SqlDataSource control has been configured, you can bind controls to it so they get their data from the SQL data source.

- You can also create a SQL data source using the Choose Data Source command in the smart tag menu of a bindable control. When you use this command, the dialog box shown above is displayed. Then, you can select the Database icon and proceed from there.

Figure 13-2   How to create a SqlDataSource control

How to define the connection

The first step in configuring a SqlDataSource control is to create the connection for the data source, as shown in figure 13-3. From this dialog box, you can select an existing connection (one you've already created for this project or for another project), or you can click the New Connection button to display the Add Connection dialog box. This dialog box helps you identify the database that you want to access and provide the information you need to access it.

In the Add Connection dialog box, you select the name of the server that contains the database you want to access, enter the information that's required to log on to the server, and select the name of the database you want to access. How you do that, though, varies depending on whether you're using the SQL Server Express Edition on your own PC or a database that resides on a database server.

If you're using SQL Server Express on your own PC, you can type localhost\sqlexpress for the server name. Alternatively, you can select the server name from the drop-down list, which will include your computer name like this: ANNEPC\SQLEXPRESS. If you will be porting your applications from one computer to another, though, it's best to use localhost. That way, you won't have to change the server name to refer to the correct computer.

For the logon information, you can click on the Use Windows Authentication option. Then, SQL Server Express will use the login name and password that you use for your computer as the name and password for the database too. As a result, you won't need to provide a separate user name and password in this dialog box. Last, you select the name of the database that you want to connect to. When you're done, you can click on the Test Connection button to be sure that the connection works.

In contrast, if you're using a database on a server computer, you need to get the connection information from the network or database administrator. That will include the server name, logon information, and database name. Once you establish a connection to a database, you can use that connection for all of the other applications that use that database.

The dialog boxes for defining a connection

Description

- The Configure Data Source dialog box asks you to identify the data connection for the database you want to use. If you've previously created a connection for that database, you can select it from the drop-down list. To see the connection string for that connection, click the + button below the drop-down list.

- To create a new connection, click the New Connection button to display the Add Connection dialog box. Then, enter the name of the database server in the Server Name text box or select it from the drop-down list. For SQL Server Express, you can use localhost\sqlexpress as the server name.

- After you enter the server name, select the authentication mode you want to use (we recommend Windows Authentication). Then, select the database you want to connect to from the Select or Enter a Database Name drop-down list.

- To be sure that the connection is configured properly, you can click the Test Connection button.

Figure 13-3   How to define the connection

How to save the connection string in the web.config file

Although you can hard-code connection strings into your programs, it's much better to store connection strings in the application's web.config file. That way, if you move the database to another server or make some other change that affects the connection string, you won't have to recompile the application. Instead, you can simply change the connection string in the web.config file.

As figure 13-4 shows, ASP.NET can store connection strings in the web.config file automatically if you check the Yes box in the next step of the wizard. That way, you don't have to manually edit the web.config file or write code to retrieve the connection string. When you select this check box, the connection string will automatically be saved with the name that you supply.

This figure also shows the entries made in the web.config file when a connection string is saved. Here, the web.config file has a connectionStrings element that contains an Add element for each connection string. In the example, the connection string is named HalloweenConnectionString. And the connection string refers to a database named Halloween on the server named localhost\sqlexpress.

Last, this figure shows how the aspx code that's generated for a data source can refer to the connection string by name. Here, the shaded portion of the example shows the value of the ConnectionString attribute. As you can see, it begins with the word ConnectionStrings followed by a colon and the name of the connection string you want to use. Note that this code is automatically generated by the Data Source Configuration Wizard, so you don't have to write it yourself.

The dialog box for saving the connection string in the web.config file

The ConnectionStrings section of the web.config file

```
<connectionStrings>
    <add name="HalloweenConnectionString"
        connectionString="Data Source=localhost\sqlexpress;
        Initial Catalog=Halloween;Integrated Security=True"
        providerName="System.Data.SqlClient" />
</connectionStrings>
```

Aspx code that refers to a connection string in the web.config file

```
<asp:SqlDataSource ID="SqlDataSource1" runat="server"
    ConnectionString="<%$ ConnectionStrings:HalloweenConnectionString %>"
    SelectCommand="SELECT [CategoryID], [LongName] FROM [Categories]
        ORDER BY [LongName]">
</asp:SqlDataSource>
```

Description

- ASP.NET applications can store connection strings in the web.config file.

- If you choose to save the connection string in the web.config file, the ConnectionString attribute of the data source control will include a special code that retrieves the connection string from the web.config file.

- If you choose not to save the connection string in the web.config file, the ConnectionString attribute of the data source control will specify the actual connection string.

- We recommend that you always save the connection string in the web.config file. Then, if the location of the database changes, you can change the connection string in the web.config file rather than in each data source that uses the connection.

Figure 13-4   How to save the connection string in the web.config file

How to configure the Select statement

Figure 13-5 shows how to configure the Select statement for a data source as you proceed through the steps of the wizard. In the first dialog box, you can specify a custom SQL statement or stored procedure, or you can choose the columns for the query from a single table or view.

To select columns from a table, use the Name drop-down list to select the table. Then, check each of the columns you want to retrieve in the Columns list box. In this figure, I chose the Products table and selected four columns: ProductID, Name, UnitPrice, and OnHand.

As you check the columns in the list box, the wizard creates a Select statement that's shown in the text box at the bottom of the dialog box. In this case, the Select statement indicates that the data source will retrieve the ProductID, Name, UnitPrice, and OnHand columns from the Products table.

The buttons to the right of the Columns list box let you specify additional options for selecting data. If, for example, you want to sort the data that's retrieved, you can click on the ORDER BY button to display a dialog box that lets you select up to three sort columns. If you want to select specific types of rows, you can click on the WHERE button to display the dialog box that's described in the next figure. And if you want to use an advanced feature, you can click on the Advanced button to display the dialog box that's described in figure 13-16.

When you finish specifying the data you want the data source to retrieve, click Next. This takes you to a page that includes a Test Query button. If you click this button, the wizard immediately retrieves the data that you specified. You can then look over this data to make sure the query retrieves the data you expected. If it doesn't, click the Back button and adjust the query as needed.

The second dialog box in this figure is the one that you use to specify a custom SQL statement or stored procedure. As you can see, this dialog box includes tabs that also let you enter Update, Insert, and Delete statements for the data source. You can also click on the Query Builder button to open the Query Builder, which lets you visually create advanced Select statements that include joins and other features. You'll learn more about the Query Builder in figure 13-8.

The dialog box for defining the Select statement

The dialog box for entering a custom Select statement

Description

- To configure the Select statement, you choose whether you want to use a custom SQL statement or specify the columns from a table or view in the database.

- If you choose to select the columns from a table or view, you can choose the table or view and columns you want retrieved. You can click the ORDER BY button to specify how the records should be sorted. And you can click the WHERE button to specify the selection criteria as shown in figure 13-6.

- If you choose to use custom SQL statements, the next dialog box lets you enter the SQL statements or click the Query Builder button to build the query as shown in figure 13-8.

Figure 13-5   How to configure the Select statement

How to create a Where clause

If you click on the WHERE button shown in the first dialog box in figure 13-5, the Add WHERE Clause dialog box in figure 13-6 is displayed. It lets you create a Where clause and parameters for the Select statement.

A Where clause is made up of one or more conditions that limit the rows retrieved by the Select statement. To create these conditions, the Add WHERE Clause dialog box lets you compare the values in the columns of a database table with several different types of data, including a literal value, the value of another control on the page, the value of a query string passed via the page's URL, a profile property (see chapter 21), or a cookie.

For example, the Select statement for the data source that's bound to the DataList control in the Product List application uses a Where clause that compares the CategoryID column in the Products table with the category selected from the drop-down list. To create this Where clause, select CategoryID in the Column drop-down list, the equals operator in the Operator drop-down list, and Control in the Source drop-down list. Next, select ddlCategory in the Control ID drop-down list. When you do, the SelectedValue property of the control is automatically selected. Then, when you click on the Add button, this condition is shown in the WHERE clause section of the dialog box.

The Add WHERE Clause dialog box

The WHERE clause section after a condition has been added

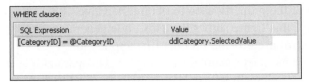

Description

- The Add WHERE Clause dialog box lets you specify a Where clause for the Select statement.

- The Where clause consists of one or more conditions that you construct by using the controls in this dialog box. To create a condition, you select the column you want to compare, the operator you want to use for the comparison, and the source of the data to use for the comparison. Then, you must click Add to add the condition to the list of Where clause conditions.

- The source of the data for the comparison can be a literal value, the value of another control on the form, a cookie, an HTML form field, a profile property, a query string in the URL for the page, or a value stored in session state.

Remember

- After you select the column, operator, and source for the comparison, be sure to click the Add button to add the condition to the generated Where clause. Otherwise, the condition won't be added to the Where clause.

Figure 13-6   How to create a Where clause

How select parameters work

When you create a Where clause as described in the previous figure, the wizard creates one or more *select parameters* that provide the values used by the Where clause. Figure 13-7 shows how these select parameters work. As you can see, each SqlDataSource control that includes select parameters is defined by a SqlDataSource element that includes a child element named SelectParameters. Then, this element contains a child element for each of the parameters used by the Select statement.

The select parameters themselves are defined by one of the elements listed in the first table. Each of these elements specifies a parameter whose value is obtained from a different type of source. For example, if the parameter's value is obtained from a form control, this *control parameter* is defined by a ControlParameter element. Similarly, the QueryStringParameter element defines a parameter whose value comes from a query string in the URL that's used for the page.

The second table in this figure lists the attributes used by the ControlParameter element to define a parameter whose value comes from a form control. As you can see, these attributes provide the name of the parameter, the SQL data type used for the parameter, the ID of the form control that provides the value, and the name of the property used to obtain the value.

The code example at the top of this figure shows the aspx code generated for the second SqlDataSource control used by the Product List application. Here, the Select statement uses one parameter named CategoryID. This parameter is defined by a ControlParameter element whose Name attribute is set to CategoryID. The SQL data type for this parameter is String, and the parameter's value is obtained from the SelectedValue property of the form control whose ID is ddlCategory.

Please note that the code in this example is generated by the Web Forms Designer when you configure the data source using the Data Source Configuration Wizard. As a result, you don't have to write this code yourself.

The aspx code for a SqlDataSource control that includes a select parameter

```
<asp:SqlDataSource
    ConnectionString="<%$ ConnectionStrings:HalloweenConnectionString %>"
    ID="SqlDataSource2" runat="server"
    SelectCommand="SELECT [ProductID], [Name], [UnitPrice], [OnHand]
        FROM [Products]
        WHERE ([CategoryID] = @CategoryID)
        ORDER BY [ProductID]">
    <SelectParameters>
        <asp:ControlParameter Name="CategoryID" Type="String"
            ControlID="ddlCategory" PropertyName="SelectedValue" />
    </SelectParameters>
</asp:SqlDataSource>
```

Elements used to define select parameters

Element	Description
SelectParameters	Contains a child element for each parameter used by the data source's Select statement.
ControlParameter	Defines a parameter that gets its value from a control on the page.
QueryStringParameter	Defines a parameter that gets its value from a query string in the URL used to request the page.
FormParameter	Defines a parameter that gets its value from an HTML form field.
SessionParameter	Defines a parameter that gets its value from an item in session state.
ProfileParameter	Defines a parameter that gets its value from a profile property.
CookieParameter	Defines a parameter that gets its value from a cookie.

The ControlParameter element

Attribute	Description
Name	The parameter name.
Type	The SQL data type of the parameter.
ControlID	The ID of the web form control that supplies the value for the parameter.
PropertyName	The name of the property from the web form control that supplies the value for the parameter.

Description

- The SelectParameters element defines the *select parameters* that are used by the Select statement of a data source. The aspx code that defines these parameters is generated automatically when you use the Add WHERE Clause dialog box to create parameters.

- A *control parameter* is a parameter whose value is obtained from another control on a web form, such as the value selected by a drop-down list. Control parameters are defined by the ControlParameter element.

- Once you understand how to use control parameters, you shouldn't have any trouble learning how to use the other types of parameters on your own.

Figure 13-7   How select parameters work

How to use the Query Builder

If you need to code a Select statement that's more complex than what the Data Source Configuration Wizard can generate and you don't want to enter your own custom statement, you can use the *Query Builder* to create the statement for you. The Query Builder provides a graphical interface that you can use to create a Select statement without even knowing the proper syntax for it. The topics that follow explain how to use the Query Builder.

How to create a Select statement with the Query Builder

To use the Query Builder, you tell the wizard that you want to specify a custom SQL statement or stored procedure in the first dialog box shown in figure 13-5. Then, when the next dialog box appears, you click the Query Builder button to display the window shown in figure 13-8.

When the Query Builder window opens, the Add Table dialog box is displayed. This dialog box, which isn't shown in this figure, lists all of the tables and views in the database that the data source is connected to. You can use this dialog box to add one or more tables to the *diagram pane* of the Query Builder window so you can use them in your query. In this figure, for example, the Products table has been added to the diagram pane.

In the *grid pane*, which appears beneath the diagram pane, you can see the columns that will be included in the query. To add columns to this pane, you just check the boxes before the column names in the diagram pane. You can also enter an expression in the Column column of the grid pane to create a calculated column, and you can enter a name in the Alias column to give the calculated column a name.

Once the columns have been added to the grid pane, you can use the Sort Type column to identify any columns that should be used to sort the returned rows and the Sort Order column to give the order of precedence for the sort if more than one column is identified. The Query Builder uses these specifications to build the Order By clause for the Select statement.

You can use the Filter column to establish the criteria to be used to select the rows that will be retrieved by the query. For the query in this figure, a parameter named @CategoryID is specified for the CategoryID column. As a result, only the products whose CategoryID field matches the value of the @CategoryID parameter will be retrieved.

The Query Builder dialog box

Description

- The *Query Builder* is displayed if you choose to enter a custom Select statement, and then click the Query Builder button in the dialog box that follows.

- The Query Builder lets you build a Select statement by choosing columns from one or more tables and views and specifying the sort order and filter criteria for each column.

- When you first start the Query Builder, a dialog box is displayed that lets you select the database tables you want to include in the query. Each table you select is displayed in the *diagram pane* at the top of the Query Builder window.

- If you add two related tables to the diagram pane, the Query Builder automatically joins the two tables by including a Join phrase in the From clause. You can also create a join by dragging a column from one table to a column in another table.

- To include a column from a table, use the check box that appears next to the column in the diagram. This adds the column to the *grid pane* that appears beneath the diagram pane. Then, you can specify any sorting or filtering requirements for the column.

- You can use a parameter in an expression in the Filter column to create a parameterized query. If you use one or more parameters in the query, the Data Source Configuration Wizard lets you specify the sources of the parameter values, as described in figure 13-9.

- As you select columns and specify sort and selection criteria, the Query Builder builds the Select statement and displays it in the *SQL pane*.

- To display the results of the query, click the Execute Query button. If the query includes parameters, you will be asked to enter the value of each parameter.

Figure 13-8   How to create a Select statement with the Query Builder

How to define the parameters

If you specify one or more parameters when you create a Select statement with the Query Builder, the next dialog box lets you define those parameters as shown in figure 13-9. Here, the list box on the left side of the dialog box lists each of the parameters you created in the Query Builder. To define the source for one of these parameters, you select the parameter in this list box. Then, you can use the controls on the right side of the dialog box to select the parameter's source.

In this example, the source of the CategoryID parameter is set to the SelectedValue property of the control named ddlCategory. When I selected the ddlCategory control, the SelectedValue property was selected by default. If you want to use a different property as the source for a parameter, however, you can click the Show Advanced Properties link to display a list of the parameter properties. Then, you can set the PropertyName property to the control property you want to use.

The dialog box for defining parameters

Parameter sources

Source	Description
Control	The parameter's value comes from a control on the page.
QueryString	The parameter's value comes from a query string in the URL used to request the page.
Form	The parameter's value comes from an HTML form field.
Session	The parameter's value comes from an item in session state.
Profile	The parameter's value comes from a profile property.
Cookie	The parameter's value comes from a cookie.

Description

- If you specify one or more parameters when you use the Query Builder to define a Select statement, the next dialog box lets you define those parameters.
- To define a parameter, you specify the source of the value for each parameter.

Figure 13-9   How to define the parameters

How to use the DataList control

A DataList control displays items from a repeating data source such as a data table. In the topics that follow, you'll learn how the DataList control works, you'll learn how to create the templates that define a DataList control, and you'll learn how to format a DataList control.

Before I present the DataList control, though, you should know that you can also create a list using the Repeater control. The Repeater control has one major drawback, however. That is, you can't define it using a visual interface. Instead, you have to enter code directly into the aspx file. Because of that, we won't present the Repeater control in this book.

How the DataList control works

Figure 13-10 shows a simple *data list* that consists of two columns of data. To create a list like this, you use the DataSourceID attribute of the DataList control to bind the control to a data source. Then, you define one or more *templates* within the control that define the content and format of the list.

In the aspx code shown in this figure, you can see that the source of data for the data list is a SQL data source control named SqlDataSource2. You can also see that a single Item template is used to create this list. This template includes two label controls that are bound to the Name and UnitPrice columns of the data source. You'll learn about the expressions you use to accomplish this binding later in this chapter.

A simple list displayed by a DataList control

```
Austin Powers $79.99
Frankenstein $39.99
JarJar $59.99
Martian $69.99
Superman $39.99
```

The asp tag for the DataList control

```
<asp:DataList ID="DataList1" runat="server" DataSourceID="SqlDataSource2">
    <ItemTemplate>
        <asp:Label ID="lblName" runat="server"
            Text='<%# Eval("Name") %>'></asp:Label>
        <asp:Label ID="lblUnitPrice" runat="server"
            Text='<%# Eval("UnitPrice", "{0:C}") %>'></asp:Label>
    </ItemTemplate>
</asp:DataList>
```

Basic attributes of the DataList control

Attribute	Description
ID	The ID for the DataList control.
Runat	Must specify "server."
DataSourceID	The ID of the data source to bind the data list to.

Description

- A *data list* displays a list of items from the data source that it's bound to. To bind a data list to a data source, use the Choose Data Source command in the control's smart tag menu.

- To define the information to be displayed in a data list, you create one or more *templates*. Visual Studio provides a designer interface you can use to create the templates as shown in the next figure.

- To display the data from a column in the data source in a data list, you add a control to a template and then bind that control. See figure 13-14 for more information.

- You can use a DataList control for edit operations as well as display operations. However, you're more likely to use the GridView, DetailsView, FormView, and ListView controls for edit operations.

Figure 13-10   How the DataList control works

How to define the templates for a data list

Figure 13-11 shows you how to define the templates for a data list. The table in this figure lists the templates you're most likely to use. Although you can also create templates that let the user select and edit items in the list, you're not likely to use a DataList control for these functions. Instead, you'll use the GridView, DetailsView, FormView, or ListView controls as described in the next three chapters.

The only template that's required for a data list is the Item template, which defines how each item in the data source is displayed. Depending on the requirements of your application, though, you may need to use one or more of the other templates as well. For example, you'll typically use a Header template to create headings that are displayed in the first row of the data list.

To define the templates for a data list, you work in *template-editing mode*. At the top of this figure, for example, you can see the Item template for a list that includes four columns. This template is displayed by default when you enter template-editing mode. To display a different template, you can use the Display drop-down list in the smart tag menu for the control. You can also display a group of related templates by selecting the group name from this list. For example, you can display both the Header and Footer templates by selecting the Header and Footer Templates item.

If a data list consists of two or more columns, you'll want to place the text and controls in each template within a table. That way, you can set the width of each column in the data list by setting the widths of the columns in the table. In addition, if you add two or more templates to a data list, you can align the columns in the templates by setting the widths of the corresponding table columns to the same values. In this illustration, for example, I set the Width attributes of the corresponding columns in the Item template and the Header template to the same values.

Before I go on, you should realize that you use templates to define the content of a data list and not its appearance. For example, you use the AlternatingItem template to display different content for every other row in a data list, not to shade or highlight every other row. To format a data list, you use styles as shown in the next figure.

The Item template in template-editing mode

A Header template

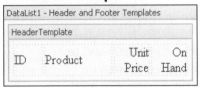

Common template elements for a data list

Element	Description
HeaderTemplate	Displayed before the first item in the data source.
FooterTemplate	Displayed after the last item in the data source.
ItemTemplate	Displayed for each item in the data source.
AlternatingItemTemplate	Displayed for alternating items in the data source.
SeparatorTemplate	Displayed between items.

Description

- The templates you define for a data list specify what content to display and what controls to use to display it. At the least, you must create an Item template that defines the items from the data source that you want to display.

- To create a template, choose Edit Templates from the smart tag menu for the control to display the control in *template-editing mode*. Then, select the template or group of templates you want to edit from the smart tag menu.

- To add text to a template, click in the template and begin typing. To add a control to a template, drag the control from the Toolbox onto the template, then use the Properties window or the control's smart tag menu to set its properties. When you're finished, choose End Template Editing from the smart tag menu.

- To line up the text and controls in two or more templates, place them in tables within the templates and set the column widths to the same values.

- When you set the data source for a DataList control, Visual Studio creates a default Item template. This template includes a text box for each column in the data source preceded by text that identifies the column.

Figure 13-11   How to define the templates for a data list

How to format a data list

To format a data list, you can use one of the techniques presented in figure 13-12. The easiest way is to use the Auto Format dialog box. This dialog box lets you select one of 17 predefined schemes that use different combinations of colors and borders for the items in the data list. To create the data list for the Product List application shown in figure 13-1, for example, I used the Black and Blue 1 scheme.

Another way to format a data list is to use the Format page of the Properties dialog box shown in this figure. This dialog box lets you set the colors, fonts, alignment, and other formatting options for the data list and each of its templates. Note that you can use this dialog box to customize an Auto Format scheme or to design your own scheme.

The Auto Format and Properties dialog boxes provide convenient ways to format a data list. However, you can also apply formatting directly from the Properties window. To do that, you use the properties in the Appearance and Style sections of this window, which are available when you display the properties by category. The properties in the Appearance section apply to the data list as a whole, and the properties in the Style section apply to the templates that make up the data list. To set the properties for the Item template, for example, you can expand the ItemStyle group, and to set the properties for the Header template, you can expand the HeaderStyle group.

This figure also presents the five style elements you're most likely to use with a data list. When you use one of the techniques in this figure to format the templates in a data list, the appropriate style elements are generated for you. In this figure, for example, you can see the HeaderStyle element that was generated when I applied the Black and Blue 1 scheme to the product list in figure 13-1. Of course, you can also format a data list by entering style elements directly into the aspx code. That's not usually necessary, however.

The Format page of the Properties dialog box

Common style elements for a data list

Element	Description
HeaderStyle	The style used for the header.
FooterStyle	The style used for the footer.
ItemStyle	The style used for each item in the data source.
AlternatingItemStyle	The style used for alternating items in the data source.
SeparatorStyle	The style for the separator.

The asp tag for a Header style

```
<HeaderStyle BackColor="Black" Font-Bold="True" ForeColor="White" />
```

Description

- You can format a data list by applying a predefined scheme, by using the Properties dialog box, by using the Properties window, or by editing the aspx code.
- To apply a scheme, choose Auto Format from the control's smart tag menu and then select the scheme you want to apply.
- To use the Properties dialog box, choose Property Builder from the control's smart tag menu and then set the properties for the data list and its templates.
- To use the Properties window to format a template, expand the style property for that template and then set its properties.

Figure 13-12   How to format a data list

How to use data binding

Once you've configured a data source control, you can bind it to a web form control to automatically display the data retrieved by the data source on the page. In the following topics, you'll learn how to bind a list control to a data source and how to bind controls defined within the templates of another control like a DataList control.

How to bind a list control to a data source

In chapter 6, you learned about the five list controls that you can use in an ASP.NET 3.5 application. Now, figure 13-13 shows you how you can bind any of these controls to a data source.

The table in this figure shows the three attributes you use to bind a list control to a data source. The DataSourceID attribute provides the ID of the data source. The DataTextField attribute provides the name of the data source field that's displayed in the list. And the DataValueField attribute provides the name of the data source field that is returned by the SelectedValue property when the user selects an item from the list.

You can set these attributes manually by using the Properties window or by directly editing the aspx code. Or, you can use the Data Source Configuration Wizard shown at the top of this figure to set these properties. To do that, display the smart tag menu for the list and select Choose Data Source. Then, use the wizard's controls to set the data source, display field, and value field.

The code example in this figure shows a drop-down list that's bound to a data source named SqlDataSource1. The field named LongName provides the values that are displayed in the drop-down list, and the field named CategoryID supplies the value that's returned by the SelectedValue property when the user selects an item from the list.

The Data Source Configuration Wizard for binding a drop-down list

List control attributes for data binding

Attribute	Description
DataSourceID	The ID of the data source to bind the list to.
DataTextField	The name of the data source field that should be displayed in the list.
DataValueField	The name of the data source field whose value should be returned by the SelectedValue property of the list.

The aspx code for a drop-down list that's bound to a SQL data source

```
<asp:DropDownList ID="ddlCategory" runat="server"
    AutoPostBack="True" Width="130px"
    DataSourceID="SqlDataSource1"
    DataTextField="LongName"
    DataValueField="CategoryID">
</asp:DropDownList>
```

Description

- You can bind any of the controls that inherit the ListControl class to a data source. That includes the list box control, the drop-down list control, the check box list control, the radio button list control, and the bulleted list control.

- You can use the Data Source Configuration Wizard to select the data source for a list control, the data field to display in the list, and the data value to return for the selected item.

- You can also use the DataTextFormatString attribute of a list control to specify a format string you want to apply to the text that's displayed in the control.

Figure 13-13   How to bind a list control to a data source

How to bind the controls in a template

Figure 13-14 shows how you can bind the controls in a template to columns of a data source. This technique can be used with any control that uses templates and specifies a data source. In the application presented in this chapter, these binding techniques are used for the DataList control.

To bind a control to a column of the data source, you use the DataBindings dialog box. From this dialog box, you can select the Field Binding option and then select the field you want to bind to from the first drop-down list. If you want to format the bound data, you can also select a format from the second drop-down list.

By default, you bind the Text property of a control so that the bound data is displayed in the control. However, you may occasionally want to bind to another property. For example, you might want to bind the Enabled or Visible property of a control to a Boolean field. To do that, you simply select the property you want to bind from the Bindable Properties list.

As you make selections in the DataBindings dialog box, Visual Studio generates an Eval method that contains the data binding expression that's used to bind the control. You can see the syntax of the Eval method in this figure along with two examples. If you compare these examples with the binding options in the DataBindings dialog, you shouldn't have any trouble understanding how this method works.

Although the drop-down lists in the DataBindings dialog box make it easy to create a data binding expression, you can also create your own custom binding expressions. To do that, you just select the Custom Binding option and then enter the binding expression in the Code Expression text box. You might want to do that, for example, if you need to apply a custom format to the data. Or, you might want to code a custom expression that uses the Bind method instead of the Eval method.

Unlike the Eval method, which only provides for displaying bound data, the Bind method provides for both displaying and updating data. This method implements a feature that was introduced with ASP.NET 2.0 called *two-way binding*. You'll see an application that uses two-way binding in the next chapter.

The DataBindings dialog box for binding a control

The syntax of the Eval and Bind methods

```
<%# {Eval|Bind}(NameString [, FormatString]) %>
```

Code examples

```
<%# Eval("Name") %>
<%# Eval("UnitPrice", "{0:C}") %>
<%# Bind("UnitPrice", "{0:C}") %>
```

Description

- To bind a control in a template, select the Edit DataBindings command from the smart tag menu for the control to display the DataBindings dialog box. Then, select the property you want to bind to (usually Text), select the Field Binding option, and select the field you want to bind to from the Bound To drop-down list.

- If you want to apply a format to the bound data, select a format from the Format drop-down list.

- As you specify the binding for a control, Visual Studio generates a data binding expression that uses the Eval method. You can see this method in the Code Expression box at the bottom of the DataBindings dialog box.

- You can also create a custom binding expression by selecting the Custom Binding option and then entering the expression in the Code Expression text box.

- The Eval method provides only for displaying data from a data source in a control. In contrast, the Bind method provides for *two-way binding*, which means that it can be used to display as well update data from a data source.

Note

- If the Field Binding option isn't enabled, you can click the Refresh Schema link and then click the OK button in the dialog box that's displayed to enable it.

Figure 13-14   How to bind the controls in a template

The aspx file for the Product List application

To show you how everything you've learned works together, figure 13-15 presents the aspx code for the Product List application of figure 13-1. To make it easier for you to follow this code, I've shaded parts of the data source controls and the controls they're bound to. Because this application relies entirely on the data binding declared in this aspx file, it doesn't require any C# code.

The first control is the drop-down list that's bound to the first SqlDataSource control, SqlDataSource1. Here, the AutoPostBack attribute for the drop-down list is set to True so the page is automatically posted back to the server when the user selects a category.

The second control is the first SqlDataSource control, which uses this Select statement to get the required data:

```
SELECT [CategoryID], [LongName] FROM [Categories]
    ORDER BY [LongName]
```

As a result, this data source gets the CategoryID and LongName columns for each row in the Categories table and sorts the result based on the LongName column. Then, these columns are used by the drop-down list that's bound to this data source.

The third control is a DataList control that's bound to the second SqlDataSource control, SqlDataSource2. The Header template for this control provides for a row of headings that are defined within a row of a table. Then, the Item template defines the table rows that display the data in the rows that are retrieved by the data source. As you can see, each column in the table contains a label whose Text attribute is bound to a column in the data source. Also notice that the columns in the Item template use the same style classes as the columns in the Header template. Although you can't see these style classes here, they simply specify the widths of the columns. Because of that, the columns in the two templates are aligned. In addition, the last two columns in each template are right aligned since they contain numeric data.

The last two elements for the DataList control define the styles for alternating items and for the header. You saw the Header style earlier in this chapter. It indicates that the header text should be displayed in a white, boldface font on a black background. The AlternatingItem style indicates that every other row in the data list should be displayed on a light gray background. Since no Item style is included, the other rows will be displayed on a white background.

The fourth control, SqlDataSource2, uses this Select statement:

```
SELECT [ProductID], [Name], [UnitPrice], [OnHand]
    FROM [Products]
    WHERE ([CategoryID] = @CategoryID)
    ORDER BY [ProductID]
```

Here, the Where clause specifies that only those rows whose CategoryID column equals the value of the CategoryID parameter should be retrieved. To make this work, the ControlParameter element specifies that the value of the CategoryID parameter is obtained from the SelectedValue property of the ddlCategory control.

The Default.aspx file

```
<body>
    <form id="form1" runat="server">
    <div>
        <asp:Image ID="Image1" runat="server"
            ImageUrl="~/Images/banner.jpg" /><br /><br />Choose a category:
        <asp:DropDownList ID="ddlCategory" runat="server" AutoPostBack="True"
            Width="130px" DataSourceID="SqlDataSource1" DataTextField="LongName"
            DataValueField="CategoryID"></asp:DropDownList>
        <asp:SqlDataSource ID="SqlDataSource1" runat="server"
            ConnectionString="<%$ ConnectionStrings:HalloweenConnectionString %>"
            SelectCommand="SELECT [CategoryID], [LongName] FROM [Categories]
                ORDER BY [LongName]"></asp:SqlDataSource><br /><br />
        <asp:DataList ID="DataList1" runat="server" DataSourceID="SqlDataSource2"
            BackColor="White" BorderColor="#999999" BorderStyle="Solid"
            BorderWidth="1px" CellPadding="3" ForeColor="Black"
            GridLines="Vertical">
            <HeaderTemplate>
                <table><tr>
                    <td class="style1">ID</td>
                    <td class="style2">Product</td>
                    <td class="style3" align="right">Unit Price</td>
                    <td class="style3" align="right">On Hand</td></tr>
                </table>
            </HeaderTemplate>
            <ItemTemplate>
                <table><tr>
                    <td class="style1">
                        <asp:Label ID="lblID" runat="server"
                            Text='<%# Eval("ProductID") %>'></asp:Label></td>
                    <td class="style2">
                        <asp:Label ID="lblName" runat="server"
                            Text='<%# Eval("Name") %>'></asp:Label></td>
                    <td class="style3" align="right">
                        <asp:Label ID="lblUnitPrice" runat="server"
                            Text='<%# Eval("UnitPrice", "{0:C}") %>'>
                        </asp:Label></td>
                    <td class="style3" align="right">
                        <asp:Label ID="lblOnHand" runat="server"
                            Text='<%# Eval("OnHand") %>'></asp:Label></td></tr>
                </table>
            </ItemTemplate>
            <AlternatingItemStyle BackColor="#CCCCCC" />
            <HeaderStyle BackColor="Black" Font-Bold="True" ForeColor="White" />
        </asp:DataList>
        <asp:SqlDataSource ID="SqlDataSource2" runat="server"
            ConnectionString="<%$ ConnectionStrings:HalloweenConnectionString %>"
            SelectCommand="SELECT [ProductID], [Name], [UnitPrice], [OnHand]
                FROM [Products]
                WHERE ([CategoryID] = @CategoryID)
                ORDER BY [ProductID]">
            <SelectParameters>
                <asp:ControlParameter Name="CategoryID" Type="String"
                    ControlID="ddlCategory" PropertyName="SelectedValue" />
            </SelectParameters>
        </asp:SqlDataSource>
    </div>
    </form>
</body>
```

Figure 13-15   The aspx file for the Product List application

How to use the advanced features of a SQL data source

The SqlDataSource control provides several advanced features that you may want to use in your applications. These features are explained in the topics that follow.

How to create a data source that can update the database

Much like ADO.NET data adapters, a SQL data source can include Insert, Update, and Delete statements that let you automatically update the underlying database based on changes made by the user to bound data controls. To automatically generate these statements, you can check the first box in the dialog box shown in figure 13-16, which is displayed when you click on the Advanced button in the first dialog box shown in figure 13-5. You can also check the box for optimistic concurrency, which enhances the generated statements so they check whether updated or deleted rows have changed since the data source retrieved the original data.

The code in this figure shows the aspx elements that are generated when you request Insert, Update, and Delete statements without using optimistic concurrency. Here, the InsertCommand, UpdateCommand, and DeleteCommand attributes provide the statements, and the InsertParameters, UpdateParameters, and DeleteParameters child elements define the parameters used by these statements. Because optimistic concurrency isn't used, these statements will update the database whether or not the data has changed since it was originally retrieved, which could lead to corrupt data.

If you check the Use Optimistic Concurrency check box, though, the update and delete commands will include Where clauses that compare the value of each column with the value originally retrieved. Because these values are passed as parameters, the generated aspx code will include additional elements that define these parameters. The SqlDataSource element will also include two additional attributes that indicate the format that should be used for the names of the parameters that will hold the original column values. Then, if the value of any column has changed since it was originally retrieved, the update or delete operation will be refused, and your application needs to provide code that handles that situation. You'll see how that works in chapter 14.

The Advanced SQL Generation Options dialog box

The aspx code for a SqlDataSource control that uses action queries

```
<asp:SqlDataSource ID="SqlDataSource1" runat="server"
    ConnectionString="<%$ ConnectionStrings:HalloweenConnectionString %>"
    SelectCommand="SELECT [CategoryID], [ShortName], [LongName]
                FROM [Categories]"
    InsertCommand="INSERT INTO [Categories] ([CategoryID], [ShortName],
                [LongName]) VALUES (@CategoryID, @ShortName, @LongName)"
    UpdateCommand="UPDATE [Categories] SET [ShortName] = @ShortName,
                [LongName] = @LongName WHERE [CategoryID] = @CategoryID">
    DeleteCommand="DELETE FROM [Categories]
                WHERE [CategoryID] = @CategoryID"

    <DeleteParameters>
        <asp:Parameter Name="CategoryID" Type="String" />
    </DeleteParameters>

    <UpdateParameters>
        <asp:Parameter Name="ShortName" Type="String" />
        <asp:Parameter Name="LongName" Type="String" />
        <asp:Parameter Name="CategoryID" Type="String" />
    </UpdateParameters>

    <InsertParameters>
        <asp:Parameter Name="CategoryID" Type="String" />
        <asp:Parameter Name="ShortName" Type="String" />
        <asp:Parameter Name="LongName" Type="String" />
    </InsertParameters>
</asp:SqlDataSource>
```

Description

- To automatically generate Insert, Update, and Delete statements for a data source, check the first box in the dialog box that you get by clicking on the Advanced button in the first dialog box in figure 13-5. To generate enhanced versions of the Update and Delete statements that use optimistic concurrency, check the second box too.

- The InsertCommand, UpdateCommand, and DeleteCommand attributes in the aspx code define the Insert, Update, and Delete statements used by a data source. If these statements require parameters, the InsertParameters, UpdateParameters, and DeleteParameters elements specify those parameters.

Figure 13-16   How to create a SQL data source that can update the database

How to change the data source mode

As you may remember from chapter 12, ADO.NET provides two basic ways to retrieve data from a database. You can either retrieve the data into a dataset, which retains a copy of the data in memory so it can be accessed multiple times and updated if necessary. Or, you can retrieve the data using a data reader, which lets you retrieve the data in forward-only, read-only fashion.

In figure 13-17, you can see how you can use the DataSourceMode attribute to set the mode for a SQL data source. If the data will be read just once and not updated, you can usually improve the application's performance by changing this attribute to DataReader mode. Otherwise, you can leave it at the default DataSet mode.

How to use caching

ASP.NET's caching feature lets you save the data retrieved by a data source in cache memory on the server. That way, the next time the data needs to be retrieved, the cached data is used instead of getting it from the database again. Since this reduces database access, it often improves an application's overall performance.

To cache the data that's retrieved by a SQL data source, you use the attributes of the data source that are presented in figure 13-17. To enable caching, you simply set the EnableCaching attribute to True. Then, you can use the CacheDuration attribute to specify how long data should be kept in the cache. If, for example, the cached data rarely changes, you can set a long cache duration value such as 30 minutes or more. Or, if the data changes frequently, you can set a short cache duration value, perhaps just a few seconds.

But what if the data in the database changes before the duration expires? In that case, the user will view data that is out of date. Sometimes, that's okay so you don't have to worry about it. Otherwise, you can minimize the chance of this happening by setting a shorter duration time.

The DataSourceMode attribute

Attribute	Description
DataSourceMode	DataSet or DataReader. The default is DataSet, but you can specify DataReader if the data source is read-only.

A SqlDataSource control that uses a data reader

```
<asp:SqlDataSource ID="SqlDataSource1" runat="server"
    ConnectionString="<%$ ConnectionStrings:HalloweenConnectionString %>"
    DataSourceMode="DataReader"
    SelectCommand="SELECT [CategoryID], [LongName]
        FROM [Categories]
        ORDER BY [LongName]"
</asp:SqlDataSource>
```

SqlDataSource attributes for caching

Attribute	Description
EnableCaching	A Boolean value that indicates whether caching is enabled for the data source. The default is False.
CacheDuration	The length of time in seconds that the cached data should be saved in cache storage.
CacheExpirationPolicy	If this attribute is set to Absolute, the cache duration timer is started the first time the data is retrieved and is not reset to zero until after the time has expired. If this attribute is set to Sliding, the cache duration timer is reset to zero each time the data is retrieved. The default is Absolute.
CacheKeyDependency	A string that provides a key value associated with the cached data. If you provide a key for the cached data, you can use the key value to programmatically expire the cached data at any time.

A SqlDataSource control that uses caching

```
<asp:SqlDataSource ID="SqlDataSource1" runat="server"
    ConnectionString="<%$ ConnectionStrings:HalloweenConnectionString %>"
    EnableCaching="True" CacheDuration="60"
    SelectCommand="SELECT [CategoryID], [LongName]
        FROM [Categories]
        ORDER BY [LongName]"
</asp:SqlDataSource>
```

Description

- The DataSourceMode attribute lets you specify that data should be retrieved using a data reader rather than being stored in a dataset. For read-only data, a data reader is usually more efficient.

- The data source caching attributes let you specify that data should be stored in cache storage for a specified period of time. For data that changes infrequently, caching can improve performance.

Figure 13-17   How to change the data source mode and use caching

Perspective

In this chapter, you've learned how to use the SqlDataSource control. However, we've only scratched the surface of what this data source can do. As you will see, the real power of a SQL data source lies in what it can do in combination with data controls like GridView, DetailsView, FormView, and ListView. As a result, all this chapter has really done is set the foundation for what you'll learn in chapters 14, 15, and 16.

I also want to point out what many developers feel is a weakness of the SQL data source control. Because this control can directly specify the SQL statements used to access and update a database, it violates one of the basic principles of good application design. That is, that the code that's used to manage the application's user interface should be separated from the code that's used to access the application's database and perform its business logic. Clearly, when you use the SqlDataSource control, the database code is mixed with the presentation code.

Fortunately, ASP.NET provides three ways to minimize or eliminate this problem. First, the SqlDataSource control can use stored procedures rather than SQL statements. That way, the SQL statements that access and update the database are placed in the database itself, separate from the presentation code.

Second, you can use ObjectDataSource controls rather than SqlDataSource controls. When you use ObjectDataSource controls, you can create and use separate database access classes, so the database access code isn't in the aspx file at all. In chapter 17, you'll learn how that works.

Third, you can use the new LinqDataSource control. When you use this control, you don't write any code for accessing the database. Instead, the SQL statements are generated and executed for you based on an object model that maps to the database. You'll learn how that works in chapter 18.

Terms

SQL data source
select parameter
control parameter
Query Builder
diagram pane
grid pane
SQL pane
data list
template
template-editing mode
two-way binding

14

How to use the GridView control

In this chapter, you'll learn how to use the GridView control. This control lets you display the data from a data source in the rows and columns of a table. It includes many advanced features, such as automatic paging and sorting. It lets you update and delete data with minimal C# code. And its appearance is fully customizable.

How to customize the GridView control **428**
How the GridView control works 428
How to define the fields in a GridView control 430
Elements used to create and format fields 432
How to enable sorting 434
How to enable paging 436
How to customize paging 438

A list application that uses a GridView control **440**
The Product List application 440
The aspx file 442

How to update GridView data **444**
How to work with command fields 444
How to use events raised by the GridView control 446
How to insert a row in a GridView control 448

A maintenance application that uses a GridView control **450**
The Category Maintenance application 450
The aspx file 452
The code-behind file 456

How to work with template fields **458**
How to create template fields 458
The template version of the Category Maintenance application 460
The aspx code for the template version 460

Perspective **464**

How to customize the GridView control

The GridView control is one of the most powerful user interface controls available in ASP.NET 3.5. It provides many options that let you customize its appearance and behavior. In the following topics, you'll learn how to define fields, customize the contents and appearance of those fields, enable sorting, and provide for custom paging.

How the GridView control works

As figure 14-1 shows, the GridView control displays data provided by a data source in a row and column format. In fact, the GridView control renders its data as an HTML table with one Tr element for each row in the data source, and one Td element for each column in the data source.

The GridView control at the top of this figure displays the data from the Categories table of the Halloween database. Here, the first three columns of the control display the data from the three columns of the table.

The other two columns of this control display buttons that the user can click to edit or delete a row. In this example, the user has clicked the Edit button for the masks row, which placed that row into edit mode. In this mode, text boxes are displayed in place of the labels for the short and long name columns, the Edit button is replaced by Update and Cancel buttons, and the Delete button is removed.

The table in this figure lists some of the basic attributes of the GridView control, and the aspx code in this figure is the code that creates the GridView control above it. By default, this control contains one column for each of the columns in the data source. These columns are defined by BoundField elements, which are coded within a Columns element. The GridView control in this figure, for example, contains a Columns element with three BoundField elements. Notice that all three BoundField elements contain ItemStyle elements that define the widths of the columns. The Columns element also contains two CommandField elements that define the button columns.

Most of the aspx code for a GridView control is created automatically by Visual Studio when you drag the control from the Toolbox onto the form and when you use the configuration wizard to configure the data source. However, you typically modify the code to customize the appearance and behavior of this control.

A GridView control that provides for updating a table

ID	Short Name	Long Name		
costumes	Costumes	Costumes	Edit	Delete
fx	FX	Special Effects	Edit	Delete
masks	Masks	Masks	Update Cancel	
props	Props	Props	Edit	Delete

The aspx code for the GridView control shown above

```
<asp:GridView ID="GridView1" runat="server" AutoGenerateColumns="False"
            DataSourceID="SqlDataSource1" DataKeyNames="CategoryID" >
    <Columns>
        <asp:BoundField DataField="CategoryID" HeaderText="ID"
                    ReadOnly="True" SortExpression="CategoryID">
            <ItemStyle Width="100px" />
        </asp:BoundField>
        <asp:BoundField DataField="ShortName" HeaderText="Short Name"
                    SortExpression="ShortName">
            <ItemStyle Width="150px" />
        </asp:BoundField>
        <asp:BoundField DataField="LongName" HeaderText="Long Name"
                    SortExpression="LongName">
            <ItemStyle Width="200px" />
        </asp:BoundField>
        <asp:CommandField ButtonType="Button" ShowEditButton="True"
                    CausesValidation="False" />
        <asp:CommandField ButtonType="Button" ShowDeleteButton="True"
                    CausesValidation="False" />
    </Columns>
</asp:GridView>
```

Basic attributes of the GridView control

Attribute	Description
ID	The ID of the control.
Runat	Must specify "server."
DataSourceID	The ID of the data source to bind to.
DataKeyNames	The names of the primary key fields separated by commas.
AutoGenerateColumns	Specifies whether the control's columns should be automatically generated.
SelectedIndex	Specifies the row to be initially selected.

Description

- The GridView control displays data from a data source in a row and column format. The data is rendered as an HTML table.

- To create a GridView control, drag the GridView icon from the Data group of the Toolbox.

- To bind a GridView control to a data source, use the smart tag menu's Choose Data Source command.

Figure 14-1   How the GridView control works

How to define the fields in a GridView control

By default, a GridView control displays one column for each column in the data source. If that's not what you want, you can choose Edit Columns from the control's smart tag menu to display the Fields dialog box shown in figure 14-2. Then, you can use this dialog box to delete fields you don't want to display, change the order of the fields, add additional fields like command buttons, and adjust the properties of the fields.

The Available Fields list box lists all of the available sources for GridView fields, while the Selected Fields list box shows the fields that have already been added to the GridView control. To add an additional field to the GridView control, select the field you want to add in the Available Fields list box and click Add. To change the properties for a field, select the field in the Selected Fields list, and use the Properties list.

The table in this figure lists some of the properties you're most likely to want to change. For example, the HeaderText property determines the text that's displayed for the field's header row, and the ItemStyle.Width property sets the width for the field.

If you want to format fields that contain numbers or dates, you can use the DataFormatString property to specify the type of formatting. For example, for a field that contains a decimal value, you can specify a string of "{0:c}" to apply standard currency formatting to the value. However, this formatting won't be applied unless you set the HtmlEncode property to False. This turns off HTML encoding, which allows the format to be applied to the data. Although HTML encoding makes your application more secure by preventing the database from returning an unsafe script to the browser, it typically isn't necessary, especially if you're confident that no unsafe scripts have been stored in your database.

Instead of defining each bound field you want to include in a GridView control, you can have the control generate the fields for you automatically. To do that, you select the Auto-generate Fields option in the Fields dialog box. Then, a field will be automatically generated for each column in the data source. Because of that, you'll want to remove any bound fields that were added to the Selected Fields list by default. If you don't, these fields will appear in the GridView control twice.

Note that if you choose to have the bound fields generated automatically, the aspx code for those fields isn't generated until runtime. That means that you can't change the appearance or behavior of these fields at design time. Because of that, you're not likely to use auto-generated fields.

The Fields dialog box

Commonly used field properties

Property	Description
DataField	For a bound field, the name of the column in the underlying data source that the field should be bound to.
DataFormatString	A format string used to format the data. For example, use {0:c} to format a decimal value as currency.
HtmlEncode	Determines if values are HTML-encoded before they're displayed in a bound field. Set this property to False if you use the DataFormatString property.
ItemStyle.Width	The width of the field.
ReadOnly	True if the field is used for display only.
NullDisplayText	The text that's displayed if the data field is null.
ConvertEmptyStringToNull	If True (the default), empty strings are treated as nulls when data is updated in the database. Set this property to False if the underlying database field doesn't allow nulls.
HeaderText	The text that's displayed in the header row for the field.
ShowHeader	True if the header should be displayed for this field.

Description

- By default, the GridView control displays one column for each column in the data source.

- To define the fields that you want to display in the GridView control, display the Fields dialog box by selecting the Edit Columns command in the control's smart tag menu.

- Another way to add a field to a GridView control is to use the Add New Column command in the smart tag menu. You'll see how to use this technique to add command buttons to a DetailsView control in the next chapter.

Figure 14-2   How to define the fields in a GridView control

Elements used to create and format fields

As figure 14-3 shows, the GridView control uses several different types of child elements to create and format its fields. The first element listed here is the Columns element, which defines the collection of columns that are displayed by the control. This element should be placed between the start and end tags for the GridView control.

Between the start and end tags for the Columns element, you can place any combination of the remaining elements listed in the first table in this figure. For example, to create a column that's bound to a column from the data source, you use the BoundField element.

The second table in this figure lists the various types of style elements you can use with a GridView control to set the formatting used for different parts of the control. Some of these elements are used as child elements of the column elements. For example, the ItemStyle element is used in the code example in this figure to set the width for the Category ID column. The other style elements in this example are used to set the foreground and background colors for different types of rows displayed by the GridView control.

Note that you don't have to create these elements yourself. Instead, these elements are created automatically when you use the Fields dialog box as described in the previous figure, when you use the Properties window to specify the styles for an element, or when you apply a scheme to the GridView control using the Auto Format command.

Column field elements

Element	Description
Columns	The columns that are displayed by a GridView control.
asp:BoundField	A field bound to a data source column.
asp:ButtonField	A field that displays a button.
asp:CheckBoxField	A field that displays a check box.
asp:CommandField	A field that contains Select, Edit, Delete, Update, or Cancel buttons.
asp:HyperlinkField	A field that displays a hyperlink.
asp:ImageField	A field that displays an image.
asp:TemplateField	Lets you create a column with custom content.

Style elements

Element	Description
RowStyle	The style used for data rows.
AlternatingRowStyle	The style used for alternating data rows.
SelectedRowStyle	The style used when the row is selected.
EditRowStyle	The style used when the row is being edited.
EmptyDataRowStyle	The style used when the data source is empty.
ItemStyle	The style used for an individual field.
HeaderStyle	The style used to format the header row.
FooterStyle	The style used to format the footer row.
PagerStyle	The style used to format the pager row.

The aspx code for a control that uses field and style elements

```
<asp:GridView ID="GridView1" runat="server" AutoGenerateColumns="False"
              DataKeyNames="CategoryID" DataSourceID="SqlDataSource1">
  <Columns>
    <asp:BoundField DataField="CategoryID" HeaderText="ID" ReadOnly="True" >
      <ItemStyle Width="100px" />
    </asp:BoundField>
    .
    .
  </Columns>
  <HeaderStyle BackColor="LightGray" ForeColor="White" Font-Bold="True" />
  <RowStyle BackColor="White" ForeColor="Black" />
  <SelectedRowStyle BackColor="Gray" ForeColor="White" Font-Bold="True" />
  <FooterStyle BackColor="LightGray" ForeColor="Blue" />
  <PagerStyle BackColor="LightGray" ForeColor="Blue"
              HorizontalAlign="Center" />
</asp:GridView>
```

Description

- The GridView control uses several child elements to define the column fields in a row and the styles used to format the data.

Figure 14-3   Elements used to create and format fields

How to enable sorting

The GridView control has a built-in ability to let the user sort the rows based on any or all of the columns displayed by the control. As figure 14-4 shows, all you have to do to enable sorting is set the AllowSorting attribute to True and provide a SortExpression attribute for each column you want to allow sorting for. When sorting is enabled for a column, the user can sort the data by clicking the column header. The first time it's clicked, the data will be sorted in ascending sequence. The second time it's clicked, the data will be sorted in descending sequence. And so on.

Note that a SortExpression attribute is automatically generated for each BoundField column that's created by default or that you create with the Fields dialog box. As a result, instead of adding SortExpression attributes for the columns you want to allow sorting for, you must remove the SortExpression attributes for the columns you don't want to allow sorting for. You can use the Fields dialog box to do that by clearing the SortExpression properties. Or, you can use the HTML Editor to delete the SortExpression attributes.

The code example in this figure allows sorting for three of the five fields displayed by the GridView control. For the first two fields, the SortExpression attribute simply duplicates the name of the data source column the field is bound to. If, for example, the user clicks the header of the ProductID column, the data is sorted on the ProductID field.

In some cases, though, you may want the sort expression to be based on two or more columns. To do that, you just use commas to separate the sort field names. In this example, the sort expression for the Category ID column is "CategoryID, Name". That way, any rows with the same Category ID will be sorted by the Name column. Note that the first time the Category ID column header is clicked, the rows will be sorted by the Name column in ascending sequence within the CategoryID column in ascending sequence. If the Category ID column header is clicked again, the category IDs will remain in ascending sequence, but the names will be sorted in descending sequence.

It's important to note that the GridView control doesn't actually do the sorting. Instead, it relies on the underlying data source to sort the data. As a result, sorting will only work if the data source provides for sorting. For a SqlDataSource or AccessDataSource, this means that you need to use the default DataSet mode.

A GridView control with sorting enabled

ID	Name	Category	Unit Price	On Hand
pow01	Austin Powers	costumes	$79.99	25
frankc01	Frankenstein	costumes	$39.99	100
jar01	JarJar	costumes	$59.99	25
martian01	Martian	costumes	$69.99	100
super01	Superman	costumes	$39.99	100
bl01	Black light (24")	fx	$24.99	200
fogj01	Fog Juice (1qt)	fx	$9.99	500
fog01	Fog Machine	fx	$34.99	100
str01	Mini-strobe	fx	$13.99	200
skullfog01	Skull Fogger	fx	$39.95	50
vader01	Darth Vader Mask	masks	$19.99	100
fred01	Freddie	masks	$29.99	50

The aspx code for the GridView control shown above

```
<asp:GridView ID="GridView1" runat="server" AllowSorting="True"
    AutoGenerateColumns="False" DataKeyNames="ProductID"
    DataSourceID="SqlDataSource1">
  <Columns>
    <asp:BoundField DataField="ProductID" HeaderText="ID"
        ReadOnly="True" SortExpression="ProductID">
      <HeaderStyle HorizontalAlign="Left" />
      <ItemStyle Width="75px" />
    </asp:BoundField>
    <asp:BoundField DataField="Name" HeaderText="Name"
        SortExpression="Name">
      <HeaderStyle HorizontalAlign="Left" />
      <ItemStyle Width="200px" />
    </asp:BoundField>
    <asp:BoundField DataField="CategoryID" HeaderText="Category"
        SortExpression="CategoryID, Name" />
    <asp:BoundField DataField="UnitPrice" DataFormatString="{0:c}"
        HtmlEncode="False" HeaderText="Unit Price">
      <ItemStyle Width="85px" HorizontalAlign="Right" />
      <HeaderStyle HorizontalAlign="Right" />
    </asp:BoundField>
    <asp:BoundField DataField="OnHand" HeaderText="On Hand">
      <ItemStyle Width="85px" HorizontalAlign="Right" />
      <HeaderStyle HorizontalAlign="Right" />
    </asp:BoundField>
  </Columns>
  <HeaderStyle BackColor="LightGray" />
</asp:GridView>
```

Description

- To enable sorting, set the AllowSorting attribute to True. Then, add a SortExpression attribute to each column you want to allow sorting for.

- For sorting to work, the DataSourceMode attribute of the data source must be set to DataSet mode (the default).

Figure 14-4   How to enable sorting

How to enable paging

Paging refers to the ability of the GridView control to display bound data one page at a time, along with paging controls that let the user select which page of data to display next. As figure 14-5 shows, the GridView control lets you enable paging simply by setting the AllowPaging attribute to True.

When you enable paging, an additional row is displayed at the bottom of the GridView control to display the paging controls. If you want, you can provide a PagerStyle element to control how this row is formatted. In the example in this figure, the PagerStyle element specifies that the background color for the pager row should be light gray and the pager controls should be horizontally centered.

Unlike sorting, the GridView control doesn't delegate the paging function to the underlying data source. Like sorting, however, paging works only for data sources that are in DataSet mode.

A GridView control with paging enabled

ID	Name	Category	Unit Price	On Hand
arm01	Severed Arm	props	$19.95	200
bl01	Black light (24")	fx	$24.99	200
cat01	Deranged Cat	props	$19.99	45
cool01	Cool Ghoul	props	$69.99	25
fog01	Fog Machine	fx	$34.99	100
fogj01	Fog Juice (1qt)	fx	$9.99	500
frankc01	Frankenstein	costumes	$39.99	100
fred01	Freddie	masks	$29.99	50
head01	Shrunken Head	props	$29.99	100
head02	Severed Head	props	$29.99	100

1 <u>2</u> <u>3</u>

The aspx code for the control shown above

```
<asp:GridView ID="GridView1" runat="server" AllowPaging="True"
    AutoGenerateColumns="False" DataKeyNames="ProductID"
    DataSourceID="SqlDataSource1">
    <Columns>
        <asp:BoundField DataField="ProductID" HeaderText="ID"
            ReadOnly="True">
            <HeaderStyle HorizontalAlign="Left" />
            <ItemStyle Width="75px" />
        </asp:BoundField>
        <asp:BoundField DataField="Name" HeaderText="Name">
            <HeaderStyle HorizontalAlign="Left" />
            <ItemStyle Width="200px" />
        </asp:BoundField>
        <asp:BoundField DataField="CategoryID" HeaderText="Category" />
        <asp:BoundField DataField="UnitPrice" DataFormatString="{0:c}"
            HtmlEncode="False" HeaderText="Unit Price">
            <ItemStyle Width="85px" HorizontalAlign="Right" />
            <HeaderStyle HorizontalAlign="Right" />
        </asp:BoundField>
        <asp:BoundField DataField="OnHand" HeaderText="On Hand">
            <ItemStyle Width="85px" HorizontalAlign="Right" />
            <HeaderStyle HorizontalAlign="Right" />
        </asp:BoundField>
    </Columns>
    <HeaderStyle BackColor="LightGray" />
    <PagerStyle BackColor="LightGray" HorizontalAlign="Center" />
</asp:GridView>
```

Description

- To enable *paging*, set the AllowPaging attribute to True. Then, add a PagerStyle element to define the appearance of the pager controls. You can also add a PagerSettings element as described in the next figure to customize the way paging works.

- For paging to work, the DataSourceMode attribute of the data source must be set to DataSet mode (the default).

Figure 14-5   How to enable paging

How to customize paging

Figure 14-6 shows how you can customize the way paging works with a GridView control. To start, the two attributes in the first table let you enable paging and specify the number of data rows that will be displayed on each page. The default setting for the second attribute is 10.

You can also customize the appearance of the pager area by including a PagerSettings element between the start and end tags of a GridView control. Then, you can use the attributes in the second table for the customization. The most important of these attributes is Mode, which determines what buttons are displayed in the pager area. If, for example, you set the mode to NextPrevious, only Next and Previous buttons will be displayed.

If you specify Numeric or NumericFirstLast for the Mode attribute, individual page numbers are displayed in the pager area so the user can go directly to any of the listed pages. You can then use the PageButtonCount attribute to specify how many of these page numbers should be displayed in the pager area. Note that if you specify NumericFirstLast, the first and last buttons are displayed only if the total number of pages exceeds the value you specify for the PageButtonCount attribute and the first or last page isn't displayed.

The remaining attributes in this table let you control the text or image that's displayed for the various buttons. By default, the values for the First, Previous, Next, and Last buttons use less-than and greater-than signs, but the example shows how you can change the text for these buttons.

Attributes of the GridView control that affect paging

Attribute	Description
AllowPaging	Set to True to enable paging.
PageSize	Specifies the number of rows to display on each page. The default is 10.

Attributes of the PagerSettings element

Attribute	Description
Mode	Controls what buttons are displayed in the pager area. You can specify NextPrevious, NextPreviousFirstLast, Numeric, or NumericFirstLast.
FirstPageText	The text to display for the first page button. The default is <<, which displays as <<.
FirstPageImageUrl	The URL of an image file used to display the first page button.
PreviousPageText	The text to display for the previous page button. The default is <, which displays as <.
PreviousPageImageUrl	The URL of an image file used to display the previous page button.
NextPageText	The text to display for the next page button. The default is >, which displays as >.
NextPageImageUrl	The URL of an image file used to display the next page button.
LastPageText	The text to display for the last page button. The default is >>, which displays as >>.
LastPageImageUrl	The URL of an image file used to display the last page button.
PageButtonCount	The number of page buttons to display if the Mode is set to Numeric or NumericFirstLast.
Position	The location of the pager area. You can specify Top, Bottom, or TopAndBottom.
Visible	Set to False to hide the pager controls.

Example

A PagerSettings element

```
<PagerSettings Mode="NextPreviousFirstLast"
               NextPageText="Next" PreviousPageText="Prev"
               FirstPageText="First" LastPageText="Last" />
```

The resulting pager area

First Prev Next Last

Description

- You can use the PageSize attribute of the GridView element to specify the number of rows to display on each page.

- You can also add a PagerSettings element to control the appearance of the pager area.

Figure 14-6   How to customize paging

A list application that uses a GridView control

Now that you've learned the basics of working with a GridView control, the following topics present the design and code for an application that uses a GridView control to list the rows of a data source. As you'll see, this application provides for sorting and paging and doesn't require a single line of C# code.

The Product List application

Figure 14-7 presents the Product List application. Here, the data from the Products table of the Halloween database is displayed in a GridView control. The data is displayed 8 rows at a time, and numeric page buttons are displayed at the bottom of the GridView control so the user can navigate from page to page. In addition, the user can sort the data by clicking the column headings for the ID, Name, and Category columns.

The Product List application

Description

- The Product List application uses a GridView control to display a list of all the products in the Products table. The GridView control is bound to a SqlDataSource control that works in DataSet mode.

- Sorting is enabled for the first three columns. That way, the user can sort the product data by ID, Name, or Category.

- Paging is enabled with 8 products displayed on each page.

- Currency formatting is applied to the Unit Price column.

Figure 14-7   The Product List application

The aspx file

Figure 14-8 shows the aspx code for this application, which is stored in the Default.aspx file. Because no C# code is needed, the code-behind file isn't shown.

Because you've already been introduced to all of the code in the aspx file, you should be able to follow it without much trouble. So I'll just point out a few highlights.

The Columns element contains five BoundField child elements that define the fields displayed by the grid. All five columns are retrieved from the SQL data source. The first three of these BoundField elements include the SortExpression attribute to allow sorting. The fourth BoundField element includes DataFormatString and HtmlEncode attributes to apply currency formatting. The ItemStyle elements for the first two fields set the width of the fields, and the ItemStyle elements for the last two fields set the alignment to right. Otherwise, the default formatting is used for the five fields.

A PagerStyle element is used to center the pager buttons in the pager area. Then, a PagerSettings element is used to specify the types of pager controls to display.

Finally, the SqlDataSource control uses this Select statement to retrieve data from the Halloween database:

```
SELECT [ProductID], [Name], [CategoryID],
    [UnitPrice], [OnHand] FROM [Products] ORDER BY [ProductID]
```

Because the DataSourceMode attribute isn't set, the default of DataSet mode is used, which means that sorting and paging can be enabled.

The Default.aspx file

```
<%@ Page Language="C#" AutoEventWireup="true" CodeFile="Default.aspx.cs"
Inherits="_Default" %>

<!DOCTYPE html PUBLIC "-//W3C//DTD XHTML 1.0 Transitional//EN"
"http://www.w3.org/TR/xhtml1/DTD/xhtml1-transitional.dtd">

<html xmlns="http://www.w3.org/1999/xhtml" >
<head runat="server">
    <title>Chapter 14: Product List</title>
</head>
<body>
    <form id="form1" runat="server">
    <div>
        <asp:Image ID="Image1" runat="server" ImageUrl="~/Images/banner.jpg" />
        <br /><br />
        <asp:GridView ID="GridView1" runat="server"
            AllowSorting="True"
            AllowPaging="True" PageSize="8"
            DataKeyNames="ProductID" DataSourceID="SqlDataSource1"
            AutoGenerateColumns="False"
            CellPadding="4" GridLines="None" ForeColor="Black">
            <Columns>
                <asp:BoundField DataField="ProductID" HeaderText="ID"
                    ReadOnly="True" SortExpression="ProductID">
                    <HeaderStyle HorizontalAlign="Left" />
                    <ItemStyle Width="75px" />
                </asp:BoundField>
                <asp:BoundField DataField="Name" HeaderText="Name"
                    SortExpression="Name">
                    <HeaderStyle HorizontalAlign="Left" />
                    <ItemStyle Width="200px" />
                </asp:BoundField>
                <asp:BoundField DataField="CategoryID" HeaderText="Category"
                    SortExpression="CategoryID, Name" />
                <asp:BoundField DataField="UnitPrice" DataFormatString="{0:c}"
                    HtmlEncode="False" HeaderText="Unit Price">
                    <ItemStyle HorizontalAlign="Right" />
                </asp:BoundField>
                <asp:BoundField DataField="OnHand" HeaderText="On Hand">
                    <ItemStyle HorizontalAlign="Right" />
                </asp:BoundField>
            </Columns>
            <HeaderStyle BackColor="Silver" Font-Bold="True" ForeColor="White" />
            <RowStyle BackColor="White" ForeColor="Black" />
            <AlternatingRowStyle BackColor="WhiteSmoke" ForeColor="Black" />
            <FooterStyle BackColor="Silver" Font-Bold="True" ForeColor="White" />
            <PagerStyle BackColor="Silver" ForeColor="Blue"
                HorizontalAlign="Center" />
            <PagerSettings Mode="NumericFirstLast" />
        </asp:GridView>
        <asp:SqlDataSource ID="SqlDataSource1" runat="server"
            ConnectionString="<%$ ConnectionStrings:HalloweenConnectionString %>"
            SelectCommand="SELECT [ProductID], [Name], [CategoryID],
                [UnitPrice], [OnHand] FROM [Products] ORDER BY [ProductID]">
        </asp:SqlDataSource>
    </div>
    </form>
</body>
</html>
```

Figure 14-8   The aspx file of the Product List application

How to update GridView data

Another impressive feature of the GridView control is its ability to update data in the underlying data source with little additional code. Before you can set that up, though, you must configure the data source with Update, Delete, and Insert statements, as described in the last chapter. Once you've done that, you can set up a GridView control so it calls the Update and Delete statements, which you'll learn how to do next.

How to work with command fields

A *command field* is a GridView column that contains one or more command buttons. Figure 14-9 shows five of the command buttons that you can include in each row of a GridView control. Please note, however, that the Update and Cancel buttons are displayed only when a user clicks the Edit button to edit a row. You can't display these buttons in separate command fields.

When the user clicks a Delete button, the GridView control calls the data source control's Delete method, which deletes the selected row from the underlying database. Then, the GridView control redisplays the data without the deleted row.

When the user clicks the Edit button, the GridView control places the selected row in *edit mode*. In this mode, the labels used to display the editable bound fields are replaced by text boxes so the user can enter changes. Also, the row is formatted using the style attributes provided by the EditRowStyle element. Finally, the Edit button itself is replaced by Update and Cancel buttons. Then, if the user clicks the Update button, the GridView control calls the data source control's Update method, which updates the underlying database. But if the user clicks Cancel, any changes made by the user are discarded and the original values are redisplayed.

The Select button lets the user select a row. Then, the selected row is displayed with the settings in the SelectedRowStyle element. Also, the SelectedIndex and SelectedRow properties are updated to reflect the selected row. The Select button is most often used in combination with a FormView or DetailsView control to create pages that show the details for an item selected from the GridView control. You'll learn how this works in chapter 15.

The two tables in this figure show the attributes of a CommandField element. For instance, you can set the ShowEditButton attribute to True to display an Edit button in a command field. And you can use the EditText attribute to set the text that's displayed on that button.

Although a single command field can display more than one button, it's common to create separate command fields for Select, Edit, and Delete buttons. It's also common to set the CausesValidation attribute of the Select and Delete buttons to False since the operations these buttons perform don't require any data validation. On the other hand, you'll usually leave the CausesValidation attribute of the Edit button set to True so that validation is performed when the user clicks the Update button. Later in this chapter, you'll learn how to use validation controls with the Edit button by creating template fields.

The Fields dialog box for working with a command field

Typical code to define command fields

```
<asp:CommandField ButtonType="Button" ShowEditButton="True"
    CausesValidation="False" />
<asp:CommandField ButtonType="Button" ShowDeleteButton="True"
    CausesValidation="False" />
```

Attributes of the CommandField element

Attribute	Description
ButtonType	Specifies the type of button displayed in the command field. Valid options are Button, Link, or Image.
CausesValidation	Specifies whether validation should be performed if the user clicks the button.
ValidationGroup	Specifies the name of the group to be validated if CausesValidation is True.

Attributes that show buttons and set the text or images they display

Button	Show	Text	Image
Cancel	ShowCancelButton	CancelText	CancelImage
Delete	ShowDeleteButton	DeleteText	DeleteImage
Edit	ShowEditButton	EditText	EditImage
Select	ShowSelectButton	SelectText	SelectImage
Update	n/a	UpdateText	UpdateImage

Description

- A *command field* adds buttons that let the user edit, delete, or select data in a GridView control.
- The CommandField element also provides for an Insert button, but the GridView control doesn't directly support insert operations.

Figure 14-9   How to work with command fields

How to use events raised by the GridView control

Although the GridView control provides many features automatically, you still must write some code to handle such things as data validation, database exceptions, and concurrency errors. As figure 14-10 shows, most of this code will be in the form of event handlers that respond to one or more of the events raised by the GridView control.

If you look at the list of events in the table in this figure, you'll see that several of them come in pairs, with one event raised before an action is taken and the other after the action completes. For example, when the user clicks the Delete button in a GridView row, two events are raised. The RowDeleting event is raised before the row is deleted, and the RowDeleted event is raised after the row has been deleted.

The most common reason to handle the before-action events is to provide data validation. For example, when the user clicks the Update button, you can handle the RowUpdating event to make sure the user has entered correct data. If not, you can set the e argument's Cancel property to True to cancel the update.

In contrast, the after-action events give you an opportunity to make sure the database operation completed successfully. In most applications, you should test for two conditions. First, you should check for any database exceptions by checking the Exception property of the e argument. If this property refers to a valid object, an exception has occurred and you can notify the user with an appropriate error message.

Second, if optimistic concurrency is used, you should check to see if a concurrency violation has occurred. To do that, you can check the AffectedRows property of the e argument. If this property is zero, which means no rows have been changed, a concurrency error has probably occurred, and you can notify the user with an appropriate error message.

When you use optimistic concurrency, remember that the Where clause in an Update or Delete statement tries to find a row that has the same values as when the row was originally retrieved. If that row can't be found, which means that another user has updated one of the columns or deleted the row, the update or delete operation never takes place so no rows are affected.

When you try to update a row, one of the most common exceptions is caused by an attempt to store a null value in a database column that doesn't allow null values. This occurs when the user doesn't enter a value in one of the columns that's being updated. In this case, you can display an appropriate error message and set the e argument's ExceptionHandled property to True to suppress further processing of the exception. You can also set the KeepInEditMode property to True to leave the GridView control in edit mode. This is illustrated by the event handler that's coded in this figure.

Events raised by the GridView control

Event	Raised when ...
RowCancelingEdit	The Cancel button of a row in edit mode is clicked.
RowDataBound	Data binding completes for a row.
RowDeleted	A row has been deleted.
RowDeleting	A row is about to be deleted.
RowEditing	A row is about to be edited.
RowUpdated	A row has been updated.
RowUpdating	A row is about to be updated.
SelectedIndexChanged	A row has been selected.
SelectedIndexChanging	A row is about to be selected.

An event handler for the RowUpdated event

```
protected void GridView1_RowUpdated(object sender,
    GridViewUpdatedEventArgs e)
{
    if (e.Exception != null)
    {
        lblError.Text = "A database error has occurred.<br /><br />" +
            "Message: " + e.Exception.Message;
        e.ExceptionHandled = true;
        e.KeepInEditMode = true;
    }
    else if (e.AffectedRows == 0)
        lblError.Text = "Another user may have updated that category." +
            "<br />Please try again.";
}
```

Description

- The GridView control raises various events that can be handled when data is updated.

- The RowUpdating and RowDeleting events are often used for data validation. You can cancel the update or delete operation by setting the e argument's Cancel property to True.

- You can handle the RowUpdated and RowDeleted events to ensure that the row was successfully updated or deleted.

- To determine if a SQL exception has occurred, check the Exception property of the e argument. If an exception has occurred, the most likely cause is a null value for a column that doesn't accept nulls. To suppress the exception, you can set the ExceptionHandled property to True. And to keep the control in edit mode, you can set the KeepInEditMode property to True.

- To determine how many rows were updated or deleted, check the AffectedRows property of the e argument. If this property is zero and an exception has *not* been thrown, the most likely cause is a concurrency error.

Figure 14-10   How to use events raised by the GridView control

How to insert a row in a GridView control

You may have noticed that although the GridView control lets you update and delete rows, it has no provision for inserting new rows. When you use the GridView control in concert with a FormView or DetailsView control, though, you can provide for insert operations with a minimum of code. You'll learn how to do that in chapter 15. Another alternative is to create a page that lets you insert data into a GridView control by using the techniques described in figure 14-11.

To provide for insertions, you must first create a set of input controls such as text boxes in which the user can enter data for the row to be inserted. Next, you must provide a button that the user can click to start the insertion. Then, in the event handler for this button, you can set the insert parameter values to the values entered by the user and call the data source's Insert method to add the new row.

This is illustrated by the code in this figure. Here, if the insertion is successful, the contents of the text boxes are cleared. But if an exception is thrown, an error message is displayed. This message indicates that an exception has occurred and uses the Message property of the Exception object to display the message that's stored in the Exception object.

Method and properties of the SqlDataSource class for inserting rows

Method	Description
`Insert()`	Executes the Insert command defined for the data source.

Property	Description
`InsertCommand`	The Insert command to be executed.
`InsertParameters("name")`	The parameter with the specified name.

Property of the Parameter class for inserting rows

Property	Description
`DefaultValue`	The default value of a parameter. This value is used if no other value is assigned to the parameter.

Code that uses a SqlDataSource control to insert a row

```
protected void btnAdd_Click(object sender, EventArgs e)
{
    SqlDataSource1.InsertParameters["CategoryID"].DefaultValue
        = txtID.Text;
    SqlDataSource1.InsertParameters["ShortName"].DefaultValue
        = txtShortName.Text;
    SqlDataSource1.InsertParameters["LongName"].DefaultValue
        = txtLongName.Text;
    try
    {
        SqlDataSource1.Insert();
        txtID.Text = "";
        txtShortName.Text = "";
        txtLongName.Text = "";
    }
    catch (Exception ex)
    {
        lblError.Text = "A database error has occurred.<br /><br />" +
            "Message: " + ex.Message;
    }
}
```

Description

- The GridView control doesn't support insert operations, but you can use the GridView's data source to insert rows into the database. When you do, the new row will automatically be shown in the GridView control.

- To provide for inserts, the page should include controls such as text boxes for the user to enter data and a button that the user can click to insert the data.

- To use a SqlDataSource control to insert a database row, first set the DefaultValue property of each insert parameter to the value you want to insert. Then, call the Insert method.

- The Insert method may throw a SqlException if a SQL error occurs. The most likely cause of the exception is a primary key constraint violation.

Figure 14-11   How to insert a row in a GridView control

A maintenance application that uses a GridView control

The Category Maintenance application

To give you a better idea of how you can use a GridView control to update, delete, and insert data, the following topics present an application that maintains the Categories table in the Halloween database.

Figure 14-12 introduces you to the Category Maintenance application. It lets the user update, delete, and insert rows in the Categories table of the Halloween database. Here, a GridView control is used to display the rows in the Categories table along with Edit and Delete buttons. In this figure, the user has clicked the Edit button for the third data row, placing that row in edit mode.

Beneath the GridView control, three text boxes let the user enter data for a new category. Then, if the user clicks the Add New Category button, the data entered in these text boxes is used to add a category row to the database. Although it isn't apparent from this figure, required field validators are used for each text box. Also, there's a label control beneath the GridView control that's used to display error messages when an update, delete, or insert operation fails.

The Category Maintenance application

Description

- The Category Maintenance application uses a GridView control to let the user update or delete rows in the Categories table.

- To edit a category, the user clicks the Edit button. This places the GridView control in edit mode. The user can then change the Short Name or Long Name and click Update. Or, the user can click Cancel to leave edit mode.

- To delete a category, the user clicks the Delete button.

- The user can add a category to the table by entering data into the text boxes beneath the GridView control and clicking the Add New Category button.

- If the user attempts to update or add a row with a column that is blank, an error message is displayed.

Figure 14-12   The Category Maintenance application

The aspx file

Figure 14-13 shows the complete aspx listing for this application. Since most of this code has already been introduced, I'll just point out a few highlights.

Part 1 of this figure shows the aspx code for the GridView control. It specifies that the data source is SqlDataSource1 and the primary key for the data is CategoryID. The five columns defined in the Columns element display the three columns from the data source, an Edit button, and a Delete button.

Part 2 of this figure shows the SqlDataSource control. Note that this data source includes the ConflictDetection and OldValuesParameterFormatString attributes. The ConflictDetection attribute indicates how update and delete operations are handled. By default, this attribute is set to CompareAllValues, which means that optimistic concurrency checking will be done. The OldValuesParameterFormatString attribute indicates the format of the parameter names that are used to hold original column values. By default, this attribute is set to original_{0}, which means that the name of each original parameter will include the name of the column prefixed with "original_".

As a result of these two attribute values, these statements are used to retrieve, delete, update, and insert category rows:

```
SELECT [CategoryID], [ShortName], [LongName]
    FROM [Categories]

DELETE FROM [Categories]
    WHERE [CategoryID] = @original_CategoryID
      AND [ShortName] = @original_ShortName
      AND [LongName] = @original_LongName

UPDATE [Categories]
   SET [ShortName] = @ShortName,
       [LongName] = @LongName
    WHERE [CategoryID] = @original_CategoryID
      AND [ShortName] = @original_ShortName
      AND [LongName] = @original_LongName

INSERT INTO [Categories]
    ([CategoryID], [ShortName], [LongName])
    VALUES (@CategoryID, @ShortName, @LongName)"
```

Here, the Where clauses implement optimistic concurrency by looking for rows that have the values originally retrieved. Then, the DeleteParameters, UpdateParameters, and InsertParameters elements in the aspx code define the parameters used by these statements.

Finally, part 3 of this figure shows the input controls used to enter the data for a new category. As you can see, each text box is validated by a required field validator that makes sure the user has entered data for the field. This validation is performed when the user clicks the Add New Category button. In addition, the MaxLength attribute is coded for each text box so the user can't enter more characters than are allowed by the associated column in the data source.

The Default.aspx file

```
<%@ Page Language="C#" AutoEventWireup="true" CodeFile="Default.aspx.cs"
Inherits="_Default" %>

<!DOCTYPE html PUBLIC "-//W3C//DTD XHTML 1.0 Transitional//EN"
"http://www.w3.org/TR/xhtml1/DTD/xhtml1-transitional.dtd">

<html xmlns="http://www.w3.org/1999/xhtml" >
<head runat="server">
    <title>Chapter 14: Category Maintenance</title>
    <style type="text/css">
        .style1 {width: 100px;}
        .style2 {width: 195px;}
    </style>
</head>
<body>
    <form id="form1" runat="server">
    <div>
        <asp:Image ID="Image1" runat="server" ImageUrl="~/Images/banner.jpg" />
        <br /><br />
        <h2>Category Maintenance</h2>
        <asp:GridView ID="GridView1" runat="server"
            AutoGenerateColumns="False" DataKeyNames="CategoryID"
            DataSourceID="SqlDataSource1" ForeColor="Black"
            OnRowDeleted="GridView1_RowDeleted"
            OnRowUpdated="GridView1_RowUpdated">
            <Columns>
                <asp:BoundField DataField="CategoryID" HeaderText="ID"
                ReadOnly="True">
                    <HeaderStyle HorizontalAlign="Left" />
                    <ItemStyle Width="100px" />
                </asp:BoundField>
                <asp:BoundField DataField="ShortName" HeaderText="Short Name">
                    <HeaderStyle HorizontalAlign="Left" />
                    <ItemStyle Width="150px" />
                </asp:BoundField>
                <asp:BoundField DataField="LongName" HeaderText="Long Name">
                    <HeaderStyle HorizontalAlign="Left" />
                    <ItemStyle Width="200px" />
                </asp:BoundField>
                <asp:CommandField ButtonType="Button" ShowEditButton="True"
                    CausesValidation="False" />
                <asp:CommandField ButtonType="Button" ShowDeleteButton="True"
                    CausesValidation="False" />
            </Columns>
            <HeaderStyle BackColor="Silver" Font-Bold="True"
                ForeColor="White" />
            <RowStyle BackColor="White" ForeColor="Black" />
            <AlternatingRowStyle BackColor="WhiteSmoke" ForeColor="Black" />
            <EditRowStyle BackColor="Blue" ForeColor="White" />
        </asp:GridView>
```

Notes

- The GridView control is bound to the data source SqlDataSource1.
- The Columns element includes child elements that define five columns. Three are for the bound fields, the other two are for the command buttons.

Figure 14-13   The aspx file of the Category Maintenance application (part 1 of 3)

The Default.aspx file

```
<asp:SqlDataSource ID="SqlDataSource1" runat="server"
    ConflictDetection="CompareAllValues"
    ConnectionString=
        "<%$ ConnectionStrings:HalloweenConnectionString %>"
    OldValuesParameterFormatString="original_{0}"
    SelectCommand="SELECT [CategoryID], [ShortName], [LongName]
        FROM [Categories]"
    DeleteCommand="DELETE FROM [Categories]
        WHERE [CategoryID] = @original_CategoryID
          AND [ShortName] = @original_ShortName
          AND [LongName] = @original_LongName"
    UpdateCommand="UPDATE [Categories]
        SET [ShortName] = @ShortName,
            [LongName] = @LongName
        WHERE [CategoryID] = @original_CategoryID
          AND [ShortName] = @original_ShortName
          AND [LongName] = @original_LongName"
    InsertCommand="INSERT INTO [Categories]
        ([CategoryID], [ShortName], [LongName])
        VALUES (@CategoryID, @ShortName, @LongName)">
    <DeleteParameters>
        <asp:Parameter Name="original_CategoryID" Type="String" />
        <asp:Parameter Name="original_ShortName" Type="String" />
        <asp:Parameter Name="original_LongName" Type="String" />
    </DeleteParameters>
    <UpdateParameters>
        <asp:Parameter Name="ShortName" Type="String" />
        <asp:Parameter Name="LongName" Type="String" />
        <asp:Parameter Name="original_CategoryID" Type="String" />
        <asp:Parameter Name="original_ShortName" Type="String" />
        <asp:Parameter Name="original_LongName" Type="String" />
    </UpdateParameters>
    <InsertParameters>
        <asp:Parameter Name="CategoryID" Type="String" />
        <asp:Parameter Name="ShortName" Type="String" />
        <asp:Parameter Name="LongName" Type="String" />
    </InsertParameters>
</asp:SqlDataSource><br />
```

Notes

- The Select statement retrieves all rows in the Categories table.
- The Where clauses in the Delete and Update statements provide for optimistic concurrency.

Figure 14-13   The aspx file of the Category Maintenance application (part 2 of 3)

The Default.aspx file   **Page 3**

```
          To create a new category, enter the category information
          and click Add New Category.<br />
          <asp:Label ID="lblError" runat="server" EnableViewState="False"
              ForeColor="Red"></asp:Label><br /><br />
          <table>
            <tr>
              <td class="style1">ID:</td>
              <td class="style1">
                <asp:TextBox ID="txtID" runat="server"
                    Width="100px" MaxLength="10">
                </asp:TextBox></td>
              <td class="style2">
                <asp:RequiredFieldValidator ID="RequiredFieldValidator1"
                    runat="server" ControlToValidate="txtID"
                    ErrorMessage="ID is a required field.">
                </asp:RequiredFieldValidator></td>
            </tr>
            <tr>
              <td class="style1">Short Name:</td>
              <td class="style1">
                <asp:TextBox ID="txtShortName" runat="server"
                    Width="200px" MaxLength="15">
                </asp:TextBox></td>
              <td class="style2">
                <asp:RequiredFieldValidator ID="RequiredFieldValidator2"
                    runat="server" ControlToValidate="txtShortName"
                    ErrorMessage="Short Name is a required field.">
                </asp:RequiredFieldValidator></td>
            </tr>
            <tr>
              <td class="style1">Long Name:</td>
              <td class="style1">
                <asp:TextBox ID="txtLongName" runat="server"
                    Width="200px" MaxLength="50">
                </asp:TextBox></td>
              <td class="style2">
                <asp:RequiredFieldValidator ID="RequiredFieldValidator3"
                    runat="server" ControlToValidate="txtLongName"
                    ErrorMessage="Long Name is a required field.">
                </asp:RequiredFieldValidator></td>
            </tr>
          </table>
          <br />
          <asp:Button ID="btnAdd" runat="server" Text="Add New Category"
              OnClick="btnAdd_Click" />
      </div>
      </form>
</body>
</html>
```

Notes

- The text boxes are used to enter data for a new row.

- The required field validators ensure that the user enters data for each column of a new row.

Figure 14-13   The aspx file of the Category Maintenance application (part 3 of 3)

The code-behind file

Although it would be nice if you could create a robust database application without writing any C# code, you must still write code to insert data into a GridView control and to catch and handle any database or concurrency errors that might occur. Figure 14-14 shows this code for the Category Maintenance application.

As you can see, this code-behind file consists of just three event handlers. The first, btnAdd_Click, sets the value of the three insert parameters to the values entered by the user. Then, it calls the Insert method of the data source control. If an exception is thrown, an appropriate error message is displayed.

The second event handler, GridView1_RowUpdated, is called after a row has been updated. This event handler checks the Exception property of the e argument to determine if an exception has been thrown. If so, an error message is displayed, the ExceptionHandled property is set to true to suppress the exception, and the KeepInEditMode property is set to true to leave the GridView control in edit mode. If an exception hasn't occurred, the e argument's AffectedRows property is checked. If it's zero, it means that a concurrency error probably occurred and an appropriate message is displayed.

The third event handler, GridView1_RowDeleted, is called after a row has been deleted. Like the event handler that's called after a row is updated, this event handler checks if an exception has been thrown or if a concurrency error has occurred. The only difference is that this event handler doesn't set the KeepInEditMode property to true, since the control isn't in edit mode when the Delete button is clicked.

The Default.aspx.cs file

```
public partial class _Default : System.Web.UI.Page
{
    protected void btnAdd_Click(object sender, EventArgs e)
    {
        SqlDataSource1.InsertParameters["CategoryID"].DefaultValue
            = txtID.Text;
        SqlDataSource1.InsertParameters["ShortName"].DefaultValue
            = txtShortName.Text;
        SqlDataSource1.InsertParameters["LongName"].DefaultValue
            = txtLongName.Text;
        try
        {
            SqlDataSource1.Insert();
            txtID.Text = "";
            txtShortName.Text = "";
            txtLongName.Text = "";
        }
        catch (Exception ex)
        {
            lblError.Text = "A database error has occurred.<br /><br />" +
                "Message: " + ex.Message;
        }
    }

    protected void GridView1_RowUpdated(object sender,
        GridViewUpdatedEventArgs e)
    {
        if (e.Exception != null)
        {
            lblError.Text = "A database error has occurred.<br /><br />" +
                "Message: " + e.Exception.Message;
            e.ExceptionHandled = true;
            e.KeepInEditMode = true;
        }
        else if (e.AffectedRows == 0)
            lblError.Text = "Another user may have updated that category." +
                "<br />Please try again.";
    }

    protected void GridView1_RowDeleted(object sender,
        GridViewDeletedEventArgs e)
    {
        if (e.Exception != null)
        {
            lblError.Text = "A database error has occurred.<br /><br />" +
                "Message: " + e.Exception.Message;
            e.ExceptionHandled = true;
        }
        else if (e.AffectedRows == 0)
            lblError.Text = "Another user may have updated that category." +
                "<br />Please try again.";
    }
}
```

Figure 14-14   The code-behind file of the Category Maintenance application

How to work with template fields

Although using bound fields is a convenient way to include bound data in a GridView control, the most flexible way is to use template fields. A *template field* is simply a field that provides one or more templates that are used to render the column. You can include anything you want in these templates, including labels or text boxes, data binding expressions, and validation controls. In fact, including validation controls for editable GridView controls is one of the main reasons for using template fields.

How to create template fields

Figure 14-15 shows how to create template fields. The easiest way to do that is to first create a regular bound field and then convert it to a template field. This changes the BoundField element to a TemplateField element and, more importantly, generates ItemTemplate and EditItemTemplate elements that include labels and text boxes with appropriate binding expressions. In particular, each EditItemTemplate element includes a text box that uses the new Bind method to implement two-way binding (please see figure 13-14 for more information about this method).

Once you've converted the bound field to a template, you can edit the template to add any additional elements you want to include, such as validation controls. In the code example in this figure, you can see that I added a RequiredFieldValidator control to the EditItem template for the ShortName column. That way, the user must enter data into the txtGridShortName text box. I also changed the names of the label and the text box that were generated for the Item and EditItem templates from their defaults (Label1 and TextBox1) to lblGridShortName and txtGridShortName.

You can also edit the templates from Design view. To do that, you use the same basic techniques that you use to work with the templates for a DataList control. The main difference is that each bound column in a GridView control has its own templates. In this figure, for example, you can see the EditItem template for the ShortName column.

Although a text box is included in the EditItem template for a column by default, you should know that you can use other types of controls too. For example, you can use a check box to work with a Boolean column, and you can use a Calendar control to work with a date column. You can also use a drop-down list that lets the user select a value from the list. To do that, you must create a separate data source that retrieves the data for the list. Then, you can bind the drop-down list to this data source by setting the DataTextField and DataValueField attributes as shown in the last chapter, and you can bind the drop-down list to a column in the GridView's data source by setting its SelectedValue attribute using the DataBindings dialog box you saw in the last chapter.

How to edit templates

GridView template elements

Element	Description
ItemTemplate	The template used for an individual field.
AlternatingItemTemplate	The template used for alternate rows.
EditItemTemplate	The template used when the row is being edited.
HeaderTemplate	The template used for the header row.
FooterTemplate	The template used for the footer row.

A template field that includes a validation control

```
<asp:TemplateField HeaderText="Short Name">
    <ItemTemplate>
        <asp:Label ID="lblGridShortName" runat="server"
            Text='<%# Bind("ShortName") %>'></asp:Label>
    </ItemTemplate>
    <EditItemTemplate>
        <asp:TextBox ID="txtGridShortName" runat="server"
            width="125px" Text='<%# Bind("ShortName") %>'></asp:TextBox>
        <asp:RequiredFieldValidator
            ID="RequiredFieldValidator5" runat="server"
            ControlToValidate="txtGridShortName"
            ErrorMessage="Short Name is a required field."
            ValidationGroup="Edit">*</asp:RequiredFieldValidator>
    </EditItemTemplate>
    <HeaderStyle HorizontalAlign="Left" />
    <ItemStyle Width="150px" />
</asp:TemplateField>
```

Description

- *Template fields* provide more control over the appearance of the columns in a GridView control. A common reason for using template fields is to add validation controls.

- To create a template field, first use the Fields dialog box to create a bound field. Then, click the Convert This Field into a TemplateField link.

- To edit a template, choose Edit Templates from the smart tag menu for the GridView control. Then, select the template you want to edit in the smart tag menu and edit the template by adding text or other controls. You may also want to change the names of the labels and text boxes that were generated when you converted to a template field. When you're finished, choose End Template Editing in the smart tag menu.

Figure 14-15   How to create template fields

The template version of the Category Maintenance application

Figure 14-16 shows a version of the Category Maintenance application that uses templates instead of bound fields in the GridView control. Then, each EditItem template includes a required field validator. In addition, the page uses a validation summary control to display any error messages that are generated by the required field validators.

The aspx code for the template version

Figure 14-17 shows the aspx code for the template version of the Category Maintenance application. Because most of this file is similar to the file shown in figure 14-13, this figure shows only the portions that are different. In particular, it shows the code for the GridView control and the ValidationSummary control. Because you've already been introduced to most of this code, I'll just point out a few highlights.

First, the GridView control uses template fields that include required field validators to validate the text box input fields. Here, each validator is assigned to a validation group named Edit. Then, in the CommandField element for the Edit button, the CausesValidation attribute is set to True and the ValidationGroup attribute is set to Edit. As a result, when a row is displayed in edit mode, just the validators that belong to the Edit group will be invoked when the Update button is clicked.

Second, the ErrorMessage attribute of each of the Edit validators provides the error message that's displayed in the ValidationSummary control. For this control, you can see that the ValidationGroup is set to Edit so the right messages will be displayed. In addition, the content of each validator specifies that an asterisk will appear to the right of each field in the GridView control. If you look closely at the screen in the last figure, you can see that these asterisks are displayed in white on the dark column dividers.

Third, the text boxes in the EditItem templates for the Short Name and Long Name fields include the MaxLength attribute. That way, the user can't enter more characters than are allowed by the data source. This is another advantage of using templates with a GridView control.

Please note that there is one other difference between this version of the application and the previous version that isn't shown in this figure. Because this version uses a validation group for the validators in the GridView control, it must also use a validation group for the validators that are outside of the GridView control. As a result, the three validators for the text boxes as well as the Add New Category button all have a ValidationGroup attribute that assigns them to the New group.

The Category Maintenance application with template fields

Description

- This version of the Category Maintenance application uses template fields in the GridView control, and the edit template for each editable field includes a required field validator.

- A ValidationSummary control is used to display the error messages generated by the required field validators.

Figure 14-16   The template version of the Category Maintenance application

The Default.aspx file

```
<asp:GridView ID="GridView1" runat="server"
    AutoGenerateColumns="False" DataKeyNames="CategoryID"
    DataSourceID="SqlDataSource1" ForeColor="Black"
    OnRowDeleted="GridView1_RowDeleted"
    OnRowUpdated="GridView1_RowUpdated">
    <Columns>
        <asp:TemplateField HeaderText="ID">
            <ItemTemplate>
                <asp:Label id="lblGridCategory" runat="server"
                    Text='<%# Bind("CategoryID") %>'></asp:Label>
            </ItemTemplate>
            <EditItemTemplate>
                <asp:Label id="lblGridCategory" runat="server"
                    Text='<%# Bind("CategoryID") %>'></asp:Label>
            </EditItemTemplate>
            <HeaderStyle HorizontalAlign="Left" />
            <ItemStyle Width="100px" />
        </asp:TemplateField>
        <asp:TemplateField HeaderText="Short Name">
            <ItemTemplate>
                <asp:Label ID="lblGridShortName" runat="server"
                    Text='<%# Bind("ShortName") %>'></asp:Label>
            </ItemTemplate>
            <EditItemTemplate>
                <asp:TextBox ID="txtGridShortName" runat="server"
                    width = "125px" MaxLength="15"
                    Text='<%# Bind("ShortName") %>'>
                </asp:TextBox>
                <asp:RequiredFieldValidator
                    ID="RequiredFieldValidator5" runat="server"
                    ControlToValidate="txtGridShortName"
                    ErrorMessage="Short Name is a required field."
                    ForeColor="White" ValidationGroup="Edit">*
                </asp:RequiredFieldValidator>
            </EditItemTemplate>
            <HeaderStyle HorizontalAlign="Left" />
            <ItemStyle Width="150px" />
        </asp:TemplateField>
```

Figure 14-17   The aspx code for the template version of the Category Maintenance application
(part 1 of 2)

The Default.aspx file   **Page 2**

```
            <asp:TemplateField HeaderText="Long Name">
                <ItemTemplate>
                    <asp:Label ID="lblGridLongName" runat="server"
                        Text='<%# Bind("LongName") %>'></asp:Label>
                </ItemTemplate>
                <EditItemTemplate>
                    <asp:TextBox ID="txtGridLongName" runat="server"
                        width = "180px" MaxLength="50"
                        Text='<%# Bind("LongName") %>'>
                    </asp:TextBox>
                    <asp:RequiredFieldValidator
                        ID="RequiredFieldValidator6" runat="server"
                        ControlToValidate="txtGridLongName"
                        ErrorMessage="Long Name is a required field."
                        ForeColor="White" ValidationGroup="Edit">*
                    </asp:RequiredFieldValidator>
                </EditItemTemplate>
                <HeaderStyle HorizontalAlign="Left" />
                <ItemStyle Width="200px" />
            </asp:TemplateField>
            <asp:CommandField ButtonType="Button" ShowEditButton="True"
                CausesValidation="True" ValidationGroup="Edit" />
            <asp:CommandField ButtonType="Button" ShowDeleteButton="True"
                CausesValidation="False" />
        </Columns>
        <HeaderStyle BackColor="Silver" Font-Bold="True"
            ForeColor="White" />
        <RowStyle BackColor="White" ForeColor="Black" />
        <AlternatingRowStyle BackColor="WhiteSmoke" ForeColor="Black" />
        <EditRowStyle BackColor="Blue" ForeColor="White" />
    </asp:GridView>
    .
    .
    .
<asp:ValidationSummary ID="ValidationSummary1" runat="server"
    HeaderText="Please correct the following errors:"
    ValidationGroup="Edit"/>
    .
    .
    .
```

Description

- The EditItem templates for the last two template fields include required field validators, which are assigned to a validation group named Edit. This group is also referenced in the code for the Edit button and the ValidationSummary control so only the validators in this group are included.

- The text boxes in the EditItem templates for the Short Name and Long Name fields include the MaxLength attribute so the user can't enter more characters than are allowed by the data source.

- The aspx code that's not shown in this figure is identical to the code in figure 14-13, except that the required field validators for the text boxes for inserting a new category and the Add New Category button specify a validation group named New.

Figure 14-17   The aspx code for the template version of the Category Maintenance application
(part 2 of 2)

Perspective

The GridView control is ideal for any application that displays a list of items retrieved from a database, and nearly all applications have that need. For instance, the Shopping Cart application of chapter 3 can easily be implemented with a GridView control if the database is enhanced so it supports shopping cart items. The GridView control is also ideal for displaying search results, such as product searches for an online catalog or document searches in an online customer support site.

In the next chapter, you'll build on your knowledge of the GridView control by learning how to use it in combination with the FormView and DetailsView controls. Both are designed to display the details for an item that's selected from a GridView control or a list control. And the combination of a GridView control and a FormView or DetailsView control can be powerful.

Terms

paging
command field
edit mode
template field

15

How to use the DetailsView and FormView controls

In this chapter, you'll learn how to use the DetailsView and FormView controls. Although both of these controls are designed to work with the GridView control to display the details of the item selected in that control, they can also be used on their own or in combination with other types of list controls such as drop-down lists or list boxes.

How to use the DetailsView control **466**
An introduction to the DetailsView control 466
Attributes and child elements for the DetailsView control 468
How to define the fields in a DetailsView control 468
How to enable paging 470
How to create a Master/Detail page 472

How to update DetailsView data **474**
An introduction to command buttons 474
How to add command buttons 476
How to use events raised by the DetailsView control 478
How to fix the optimistic concurrency bug 480
How to create template fields 482

The Product Maintenance application **484**
The operation of the application 484
The aspx file 484
The code-behind file 488

How to use the FormView control **492**
An introduction to the FormView control 492
How to work with the Item template 494
How to work with the EditItem and InsertItem templates 496

A Shopping Cart application that uses a FormView control **498**
The operation of the application 498
The aspx file for the Order page 500
The code-behind file for the Order page 500

Perspective **504**

How to use the DetailsView control

The following topics present the basics of working with the DetailsView control. However, much of what you'll learn in these topics applies to the FormView control as well.

An introduction to the DetailsView control

As figure 15-1 shows, the DetailsView control is designed to display the data for a single item of a data source. To use this control effectively, you must provide some way for the user to select which data item to display. The most common way to do that is to use the DetailsView control in combination with another control such as a GridView control or a drop-down list. At the top of this figure, you can see how the DetailsView control works with a drop-down list, and you'll see how it works with a GridView control later in this chapter.

Alternatively, you can enable paging for the DetailsView control to allow the user to select the data item to be displayed. Then, a row of paging controls appears at the bottom of the DetailsView control to allow the user to select the item. You'll learn how this works in figure 15-3.

As the code example in this figure shows, you use the DataSourceID attribute to specify the data source that a DetailsView control should be bound to. Then, the Fields element contains a set of child elements that define the individual fields to be displayed by the DetailsView control. This is similar to the way the Columns element for a GridView control works.

A DetailsView control can be displayed in one of three modes. In ReadOnly mode, the data for the current data source row is displayed but can't be modified. In Edit mode, the user can modify the data for the current row. And in Insert mode, the user can enter data that will be inserted into the data source as a new row.

A DetailsView control that displays data for a selected product

Choose a product:	Skull Fogger ▾

Product ID:	skullfog01
Name:	Skull Fogger
Short Description:	2,800 Cubic Foot Fogger
Long Description:	This fogger puts out a whopping 2,800 cubic feet of fog per minute. Comes with a 10-foot remote control.
Category ID:	fx
Image File:	skullfog01.jpg
Unit Price:	39.9500
On Hand:	50

The aspx code for the DetailsView control shown above

```
<asp:DetailsView ID="DetailsView1" runat="server" AutoGenerateRows="False"
    DataKeyNames="ProductID" DataSourceID="SqlDataSource2" Width="450px">
    <Fields>
        <asp:BoundField DataField="ProductID" HeaderText="Product ID:"
            ReadOnly="True" >
            <HeaderStyle Width="125 px" />
            <ItemStyle Width="325px" />
        </asp:BoundField>
        <asp:BoundField DataField="Name" HeaderText="Name:" />
        <asp:BoundField DataField="ShortDescription"
            HeaderText="Short Description:" />
        <asp:BoundField DataField="LongDescription"
            HeaderText="Long Description:" />
        <asp:BoundField DataField="CategoryID" HeaderText="Category ID:" />
        <asp:BoundField DataField="ImageFile" HeaderText="Image File:" />
        <asp:BoundField DataField="UnitPrice" HeaderText="Unit Price:" />
        <asp:BoundField DataField="OnHand" HeaderText="On Hand:" />
    </Fields>
</asp:DetailsView>
```

Three modes of the DetailsView control

Mode	Description
ReadOnly	Used to display an item from the data source.
Edit	Used to edit an item in the data source.
Insert	Used to insert a new item into the data source.

Description

- The DetailsView control displays data for a single row of a data source. It is usually used in combination with a drop-down list or GridView control that is used to select the item to be displayed.

- The DetailsView element includes a Fields element that contains a BoundField element for each field retrieved from the data source.

- You can edit the fields collection by choosing Edit Fields from the smart tag menu of a DetailsView control.

Figure 15-1   An introduction to the DetailsView control

Attributes and child elements for the DetailsView control

The tables in figure 15-2 list the attributes and child elements you can use to declare a DetailsView control. The first table lists the attributes you're most likely to use for this control. You can use the DataKeyNames attribute to list the names of the primary key fields for the data source. And you can set the AutoGenerateRows attribute to True if you want the DetailsView control to automatically generate data fields. Then, you'll want to delete the Fields element that was added when you created the DetailsView control.

By the way, there are many other attributes you can use on the DetailsView element to specify the control's layout and formatting. For example, you can include attributes like Height, Width, BackColor, and ForeColor. To see all of the attributes that are available, you can use the HTML Editor's IntelliSense feature.

The second table in this figure lists the child elements that you can use between the start and end tags of the DetailsView element. Most of these elements provide styles and templates that control the formatting for the different parts of the DetailsView control.

The Fields element can contain any of the child elements listed in the third table of this figure. These elements describe the individual data fields that are displayed by the DetailsView control. Although this figure doesn't show it, these child elements can themselves include child elements to specify formatting information. For example, you can include HeaderStyle and ItemStyle as child elements of a BoundField element to control the formatting for the header and item sections of a bound field. Here again, you can use the HTML Editor's IntelliSense feature to see what child elements are available and what attributes they support.

How to define the fields in a DetailsView control

Just like when you create a GridView control, one BoundField element is created for each column in the data source when you create a DetailsView control. Then, you can work with those fields or create additional fields using the Fields dialog box you saw in figure 14-2 of chapter 14. To display this dialog box, you choose the Edit Fields command from the control's smart tag menu. You can also use the HTML editor to create these fields manually. Or you can use the Add Field dialog box as described later in this chapter.

Each BoundField element that's created for a DetailsView control includes a SortExpression attribute. However, these sort expressions are only meaningful if you enable paging for the control. Because of that, you can safely delete these attributes if you're not using paging.

DetailsView control attributes

Attribute	Description
ID	The ID of this control.
Runat	Must specify "server".
DataSourceID	The ID of the data source to bind the DetailsView control to.
DataKeyNames	A list of field names that form the primary key for the data source.
AutoGenerateRows	If True, a row is automatically generated for each column in the data source. If False, you must define the rows in the Fields element.
DefaultMode	Sets the initial mode of the DetailsView control. Valid options are Edit, Insert, or ReadOnly.
AllowPaging	Set to True to allow paging.

DetailsView child elements

Element	Description
Fields	The fields that are displayed by a DetailsView control.
RowStyle	The style used for data rows in ReadOnly mode.
AlternatingRowStyle	The style used for alternate rows.
EditRowStyle	The style used for data rows in Edit mode.
InsertRowStyle	The style used for data rows in Insert mode.
CommandRowStyle	The style used for command rows.
EmptyDataRowStyle	The style used for data rows when the data source is empty.
EmptyDataTemplate	The template used when the data source is empty.
HeaderStyle	The style used for the header row.
HeaderTemplate	The template used for the header row.
FooterStyle	The style used for the footer row.
FooterTemplate	The template used for the footer row.
PagerSettings	The settings used to control the pager row.
PagerStyle	The style used for the pager row.
PagerTemplate	The template used for the pager row.

Fields child elements

Element	Description
asp:BoundField	A field bound to a data source column.
asp:ButtonField	A field that displays a button.
asp:CheckBoxField	A field that displays a check box.
asp:CommandField	A field that contains command buttons.
asp:HyperlinkField	A field that displays a hyperlink.
asp:ImageField	A field that displays an image.
asp:TemplateField	A column with custom content.

Figure 15-2   Attributes and child elements for the DetailsView control

How to enable paging

Like the GridView control, the DetailsView control supports paging. As figure 15-3 shows, a row of paging controls is displayed at the bottom of the DetailsView control when you set the AllowPaging attribute to True. Then, you can specify the paging mode by including a PagerSettings element, and you can include PagerStyle and PagerTemplate elements to specify the appearance of the pager controls.

Note that if the data source contains more than a few dozen items, paging isn't a practical way to provide for navigation. In most cases, then, a DetailsView control is associated with a list control that is used to select the item to be displayed. You'll learn how to create pages that work this way in the next figure.

A DetailsView control that allows paging

ProductID	bl01
Name	Black light (24")
Short Description:	24" black light
Long Description:	Create that creepy glow-in-the-dark effect with this powerful black light.
Category ID:	fx
Image File:	blacklight01.jpg
Unit Price:	24.9900
On Hand:	200

<< < > >>

The aspx code for the DetailsView control shown above

```
<asp:DetailsView ID="DetailsView1" runat="server" AutoGenerateRows="False"
    DataKeyNames="ProductID" DataSourceID="SqlDataSource1"
    Width="450px" AllowPaging="True" >
<PagerSettings Mode="NextPreviousFirstLast" />
<Fields>
    <asp:BoundField DataField="ProductID" HeaderText="ProductID"
        ReadOnly="True">
        <HeaderStyle Width="125px" />
        <ItemStyle Width="325px" />
    </asp:BoundField>
    <asp:BoundField DataField="Name" HeaderText="Name:" />
    <asp:BoundField DataField="ShortDescription"
        HeaderText="Short Description:" />
    <asp:BoundField DataField="LongDescription"
        HeaderText="Long Description:" />
    <asp:BoundField DataField="CategoryID"
        HeaderText="Category ID: " />
    <asp:BoundField DataField="ImageFile" HeaderText="Image File:" />
    <asp:BoundField DataField="UnitPrice" HeaderText="Unit Price:" />
    <asp:BoundField DataField="OnHand" HeaderText="On Hand:" />
</Fields>
</asp:DetailsView>
```

Description

- The DetailsView control supports paging. Then, you can move from one item to the next by using the paging controls. This works much the same as it does for a GridView control, except that data from only one row is displayed at a time.

- For more information about paging, please refer to figure 14-6 in chapter 14.

Figure 15-3   How to enable paging

How to create a Master/Detail page

As figure 15-4 shows, a *Master/Detail page* is a page that displays a list of data items from a data source along with the details for one of the items selected from the list. The list of items can be displayed by any control that allows the user to select an item, including a drop-down list or a GridView control. Then, you can use a DetailsView control to display the details for the selected item. The page shown in figure 15-1 is an example of a Master/Detail page in which the master list is displayed as a drop-down list and a DetailsView control is used to display the details for the selected item.

A Master/Detail page typically uses two data sources. The first retrieves the items to be displayed by the control that contains the list of data items. For efficiency's sake, this data source should retrieve only the data columns necessary to display the list. For example, the data source for the drop-down list in figure 15-1 only needs to retrieve the ProductName and ProductID columns from the Products table in the Halloween database.

The second data source provides the data for the selected item. It usually uses a parameter to specify which row should be retrieved from the database. In the example in this figure, the data source uses a parameter that's bound to the drop-down list. That way, this data source automatically retrieves the data for the product that's selected by the drop-down list.

A Master/Detail page typically contains:

- A control that lets the user choose an item to display, such as a drop-down list or a GridView control.

- A data source that retrieves all of the items to be displayed in the list. The control that contains the list of data items should be bound to this data source.

- A DetailsView control that displays data for the item selected by the user.

- A data source that retrieves the data for the item selected by the user. The DetailsView control should be bound to this data source. To retrieve the selected item, this data source can use a parameter that's bound to the SelectedValue property of the control that contains the list of data items.

A SqlDataSource control with a parameter that's bound to a drop-down list

```
<asp:SqlDataSource ID="SqlDataSource2" runat="server"
    ConnectionString="<%$ ConnectionStrings:HalloweenConnectionString %>"
    SelectCommand="SELECT [ProductID], [Name], [ShortDescription],
        [LongDescription], [CategoryID], [ImageFile], [UnitPrice], [OnHand]
        FROM [Products]
        WHERE ([ProductID] = @ProductID)">
    <SelectParameters>
        <asp:ControlParameter ControlID="ddlProducts" Name="ProductID"
            PropertyName="SelectedValue" Type="String" />
    </SelectParameters>
</asp:SqlDataSource>
```

Description

- A *Master/Detail page* is a page that displays a list of items from a database along with the details of one item from the list. The DetailsView control is often used to display the details portion of a Master/Detail page.

- The list portion of a Master/Detail page can be displayed by any control that contains a list of data items, including a drop-down list or a GridView control.

- A Master/Detail page usually includes two data sources, one for the master list and the other for the DetailsView control.

Figure 15-4   How to create a Master/Detail page

How to update DetailsView data

Besides displaying data for a specific item from a data source, you can also use a DetailsView control to edit, insert, and delete items. You'll learn how to do that in the following topics.

An introduction to command buttons

Much like the GridView control, the DetailsView control uses command buttons to let the user edit and delete data. Thus, the DetailsView control provides Edit, Delete, Update, and Cancel buttons. In addition, the DetailsView control lets the user insert data so it provides for two more buttons. The New button places the DetailsView control into Insert mode, and the Insert button accepts the data entered by the user and writes it to the data source. These command buttons are summarized in figure 15-5.

There are two ways to provide the command buttons for a DetailsView control. The easiest way is to use the AutoGenerate*xxx*Button attributes, which are listed in the second table and illustrated in the code example. However, when you use these attributes, you have no control over the appearance of the buttons. For that, you must use command fields as described in the next figure.

A DetailsView control with automatically generated command buttons

Product ID:	arm01
Name:	Severed Arm
Short Description:	Bloody Severed Arm
Long Description:	A severed arm, complete with protruding bones and lots of blood.
Category ID:	props
Image File:	arm01.jpg
Unit Price:	19.9500
On Hand:	200
Edit Delete New	

Command buttons

Button	Description
Edit	Places the DetailsView control in Edit mode.
Delete	Deletes the current item and leaves the DetailsView control in ReadOnly mode.
New	Places the DetailsView control in Insert mode.
Update	Displayed only in Edit mode. Updates the data source, then returns to ReadOnly mode.
Insert	Displayed only in Insert mode. Inserts the data, then returns to ReadOnly mode.
Cancel	Displayed in Edit or Insert mode. Cancels the operation and returns to ReadOnly mode.

Attributes that generate command buttons

Attribute	Description
AutoGenerateDeleteButton	Generates a Delete button.
AutoGenerateEditButton	Generates an Edit button.
AutoGenerateInsertButton	Generates a New button.

A DetailsView element that automatically generates command buttons

```
<asp:DetailsView ID="DetailsView1" runat="server"
    DataSourceID="SqlDataSource2" DataKeyNames="ProductID"
    AutoGenerateRows="False"
    AutoGenerateDeleteButton="True"
    AutoGenerateEditButton="True"
    AutoGenerateInsertButton="True">
```

Description

- The DetailsView control supports six different command buttons.
- You can use the AutoGenerateDeleteButton, AutoGenerateEditButton, and AutoGenerateInsertButton attributes to automatically generate command buttons.
- To customize command button appearance, use command fields instead of automatically generated buttons, as described in the next figure.

Figure 15-5   An introduction to command buttons

How to add command buttons

Like the GridView control, the DetailsView control lets you use CommandField elements to specify the command buttons that should be displayed by the control. One way to do that is to use the Add Field dialog box shown in figure 15-6 to add a command field to a DetailsView control. Of course, you can also use the Edit Fields dialog box to add command fields, or you can use the HTML Editor to code the CommandField elements manually.

To create a command button using the Add Field dialog box, you select CommandField as the field type. When you do, four check boxes appear that let you select which command buttons you want to show in the command field. In addition, a drop-down list lets you choose whether the command buttons should be displayed as buttons or hyperlinks.

Note that the CommandField element includes attributes that let you specify the text or image to be displayed and whether the button causes validation. For more information about using these attributes, please refer back to chapter 14.

Before I go on, you should realize that you can use the Add Field dialog box to create any of the elements shown in the third table in figure 15-2. To do that, you just select the type of field you want to create from the drop-down list at the top of the dialog box. Then, the appropriate options for that field type are displayed. If you experiment with this, you shouldn't have any trouble figuring out how it works.

The Add Field dialog box for adding a command field

Code generated by the above dialog box

```
<asp:CommandField ButtonType="Button"
    ShowDeleteButton="True"
    ShowEditButton="True"
    ShowInsertButton="True" />
```

Description

- You can add command buttons to a DetailsView control to let the user update, insert, and delete data.

- The command buttons for a DetailsView control are similar to the command buttons for a GridView control. However, the DetailsView control doesn't provide a Select button, and it does provide New and Insert buttons. For more information about command buttons, please refer to figure 14-9 in chapter 14.

- To display the Add Field dialog box, choose Add New Field from the smart tag menu of the DetailsView control.

Figure 15-6   How to add command buttons

How to use events raised by the DetailsView control

Figure 15-7 lists the events that are raised by the DetailsView control. As you can see, these events are similar to the events raised by the GridView control. Most of these events come in pairs: one that's raised before an operation occurs, and another that's raised after the operation completes. For example, the ItemDeleting event is raised before an item is deleted, and the ItemDeleted event is raised after an item has been deleted.

As with the GridView control, the most common reason to handle the before events for the DetailsView control is to provide data validation. For example, when the user clicks the Update button, you can handle the ItemUpdating event to make sure the user has entered correct data. Then, you can set the e argument's Cancel property to true if the user hasn't entered correct data. This cancels the update.

The after-action events let you check that database operations have completed successfully. To do that, you need to check for two types of errors as illustrated in the example in this figure. First, you should check for database exceptions by testing the Exception property of the e argument. If it isn't null, a database exception has occurred. Then, you should display an appropriate error message to let the user know about the problem.

If the data source uses optimistic concurrency, you should also check to make sure there hasn't been a concurrency error. You can do that by testing the AffectedRows property of the e argument. If a concurrency error has occurred, this property will be set to zero meaning that no rows have been changed. Then, you can display an appropriate error message.

If no errors occurred during the update operation, the ItemUpdated event shown in this figure ends by calling the DataBind method for the drop-down list control. This is necessary because view state is enabled for this control. As a result, this control will continue to display the old data unless you call its DataBind method to refresh its data. If view state were disabled for this control, the DataBind call wouldn't be necessary.

Unfortunately, there is a bug in the way ASP.NET data sources handle optimistic concurrency when null values are involved. For more information about this bug and how to work around it, see the next figure.

Events raised by the DetailsView control

Event	Description
ItemCommand	Raised when a button is clicked.
ItemCreated	Raised when an item is created.
DataBound	Raised when data binding completes for an item.
ItemDeleted	Raised when an item has been deleted.
ItemDeleting	Raised when an item is about to be deleted.
ItemInserted	Raised when an item has been inserted.
ItemInserting	Raised when an item is about to be inserted.
ItemUpdated	Raised when an item has been updated.
ItemUpdating	Raised when an item is about to be updated.
PageIndexChanged	Raised when the index of the displayed item has changed.
PageIndexChanging	Raised when the index of the displayed item is about to change.

An event handler for the ItemUpdated event

```
protected void DetailsView1_ItemUpdated(
    object sender, DetailsViewUpdatedEventArgs e)
{
    if (e.Exception != null)
    {
        lblError.Text = "A database error has occurred.<br /><br />" +
            "Message: " + e.Exception.Message;
        e.ExceptionHandled = true;
        e.KeepInEditMode = true;
    }
    else if (e.AffectedRows == 0)
        lblError.Text = "Another user may have updated that product."
            + "<br>Please try again.";
    else
        GridView1.DataBind();
}
```

Description

- Like the GridView control, the DetailsView control raises events that can be handled when data is updated. At the minimum, you should use these events to test for database exceptions and concurrency errors.

- To determine if a SQL exception has occurred, test the Exception property of the e parameter. If an exception has occurred, you can set the ExceptionHandled property to true to suppress the exception. You can also set the KeepInEditMode property to true to keep the DetailsView control in Edit mode. And you can set the KeepInInsertMode property to true to keep the control in Insert mode.

- If the AffectedRows property of the e argument is zero and an exception has not been thrown, a concurrency error has probably occurred.

- If the DetailsView control is used on a Master/Detail page, you should call the DataBind method of the master list control after a successful insert, update, or delete.

Figure 15-7   How to use events raised by the DetailsView control

How to fix the optimistic concurrency bug

Before you start reading this, please note that this bug has been fixed by Service Pack 1. As a result, you can skip this topic.

Optimistic concurrency works by using a Where clause that compares each column in the database row with the values saved when the row was originally retrieved. If that row can't be found, it means that another user has either updated or deleted the row. Then, the current update or delete operation isn't performed.

Unfortunately, there's a bug in the way ASP.NET generates the Where clauses for columns that allow nulls. This bug, along with a workaround for it, is described in figure 15-8. In short, the problem is that when a database column allows nulls, the comparisons generated for the Where clauses don't work. That's because SQL defines the result of an equal comparison between a null and a null as False. (Since a null represents an unknown value, no value–even another null–can be considered equal to a null.)

The Halloween database illustrates this problem because it allows nulls for the ImageFile column in the Products table. But look at the Where clause that's generated for the first Delete statement in this figure:

```
[ImageFile] = @original_ImageFile
```

In this case, if the original value of the ImageFile column is null, this comparison will never test true, so the row will never be deleted.

The workaround to this bug is to modify the generated Delete and Update statements for any database table that allows nulls in any of its columns. For the ImageFile column, you can modify the Delete statement so it looks like this:

```
( [ImageFile] = @original_ImageFile
  OR [ImageFile] IS NULL AND @original_ImageFile IS NULL )
```

Then, the comparison will test true if both the ImageFile column and the @original_ImageFile parameter are null.

A generated Delete statement that handles concurrency errors

```
DELETE FROM [Products]
      WHERE [ProductID] = @original_ProductID
        AND [Name] = @original_Name
        AND [ShortDescription] = @original_ShortDescription
        AND [LongDescription] = @original_LongDescription
        AND [CategoryID] = @original_CategoryID
        AND [ImageFile] = @original_ImageFile
        AND [UnitPrice] = @original_UnitPrice
        AND [OnHand] = @original_OnHand
```

How to modify the Delete statement for a column that allows nulls

```
DELETE FROM [Products]
      WHERE [ProductID] = @original_ProductID
        AND [Name] = @original_Name
        AND [ShortDescription] = @original_ShortDescription
        AND [LongDescription] = @original_LongDescription
        AND [CategoryID] = @original_CategoryID
        AND ( [ImageFile] = @original_ImageFile
         OR ImageFile IS NULL AND @original_ImageFile IS NULL )
        AND [UnitPrice] = @original_UnitPrice
        AND [OnHand] = @original_OnHand
```

Description

- When you select optimistic concurrency for a data source in the Data Source Configuration Wizard, the wizard adds code to the Update and Delete statements that prevents concurrency errors.

- Unfortunately, the generated code for Update and Delete statements doesn't work properly for database columns that allow nulls because two nulls aren't treated as equal.

- To fix this error, you can edit the Update and Delete statements so they include an Is Null test for each column that allows nulls.

Note: This bug has been fixed

- Although this was a known bug in the final release of the product, it was fixed by Service Pack 1.

Figure 15-8   How to fix the optimistic concurrency bug

How to create template fields

Like the GridView control, you can use template fields to control the appearance of the fields in a DetailsView control. You can do that to add validation controls or to use controls other than text boxes as described in the last chapter or to modify the text boxes that are displayed by default. Figure 15-9 illustrates how this works.

At the top of this figure, you can see two DetailsView controls displayed in Edit mode. The first control uses the default BoundField elements. Here, you can see that the text box for the long description isn't big enough to display all of the data in this column for the selected product, which makes it more difficult for the user to modify this field. In addition, to change the category, the user must enter the category ID. That makes it more likely that the user will enter a value that isn't valid.

The second DetailsView control illustrates how you can use templates to make it easier for the user to work with the data. Here, all of the text boxes have been resized so that they're appropriate for the data they will display. In particular, the text box for the long description has been changed to a multi-line text box. In addition, the text box for the category ID has been replaced by a drop-down list that displays the category name. This control is bound to a separate data source that retrieves the category IDs and category names from the Categories table.

To create template fields for a DetailsView control, you use the same techniques you use to create templates for a GridView control. That is, you convert bound fields to template fields, you switch to template-editing mode, and you select the template you want to edit. The table in this figure lists the five templates that are available for the template fields in a DetailsView control. In most cases, you'll define just the Item, EditItem, and InsertItem templates as shown in the code example in this figure.

The template field shown here is for the Name column of the Products table. Notice that in addition to setting the width of the text boxes for this column in the EditItem and InsertItem templates, I also set the MaxLength attribute. That way, the user can't enter more characters than are allowed by the Name column. As you'll see in the aspx code for the Product Maintenance application that's presented next, I used this same technique to restrict the number of characters that can be entered for the ProductID, ShortDescription, LongDescription, and ImageFile columns.

A DetailsView control in Edit mode without and with templates

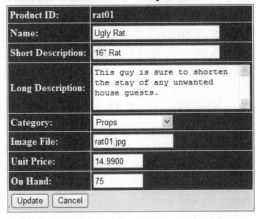

DetailsView template elements

Element	Description
ItemTemplate	The template used for an individual field.
AlternatingItemTemplate	The template used for alternating fields.
EditItemTemplate	The template used for a field in Edit mode.
InsertItemTemplate	The template used for a field in Insert mode.
HeaderTemplate	The template used for the header text for a field.

The aspx code for a custom template field

```
<asp:TemplateField HeaderText="Name:">
    <ItemTemplate>
        <asp:Label ID="Label8" runat="server" Text='<%# Bind("Name") %>'>
        </asp:Label>
    </ItemTemplate>
    <EditItemTemplate>
        <asp:TextBox ID="txtName" runat="server" Text='<%# Bind("Name") %>'
            Width="200px" MaxLength="50">
        </asp:TextBox>
    </EditItemTemplate>
    <InsertItemTemplate>
        <asp:TextBox ID="txtName" runat="server" Text='<%# Bind("Name") %>'
            Width="200px" MaxLength="50">
        </asp:TextBox>
    </InsertItemTemplate>
    <HeaderStyle HorizontalAlign="Left" Width="150px" />
    <ItemStyle Width="250px" />
</asp:TemplateField>
```

Description

- You can use template fields to control the appearance of the fields in a DetailsView control using the same techniques you use to work with template fields in a GridView control. See figure 14-15 in chapter 14 for more information.

Figure 15-9   How to create template fields

The Product Maintenance application

The following topics present an application that uses a GridView and a DetailsView control in a Master/Detail page to maintain the Products table in the Halloween database.

The operation of the application

Figure 15-10 shows the operation of the Product Maintenance application. This application uses a GridView control to list the product records on the left side of the page. This control uses paging to allow the user to scroll through the entire Products table.

When the user clicks the Select button for a product, the details for that product are displayed in the DetailsView control on the right side of the page. Then, the user can use the Edit or Delete button to edit or delete the selected product. The user can also click the New button to insert a new product.

The aspx file

Figure 15-11 shows the Default.aspx file for the Product Maintenance application. This file uses a table to control the overall layout of the page. In part 1, you can see the GridView control that displays the products as well as the data source for this control. Notice that the SelectedIndex attribute of the GridView control is set to 0. That way, the information for the first product will be displayed in the DetailsView control when the page is first displayed.

The DetailsView control is shown in parts 2 and 3 of the listing. Here, the DetailsView element includes the attributes that control the overall appearance of the control. I generated most of these attributes by applying a scheme to the DetailsView control, then editing the attributes to change the colors. You can also see that the scheme added RowStyle, EditRowStyle, and HeaderStyle elements to the control. Since an InsertRowStyle element isn't included, this style will default to the EditRowStyle.

To make it easier for the user to work with the data in the DetailsView control, all of the bound fields have been converted to template fields. Then, the EditItem and InsertItem templates for these fields were modified so the fields are displayed as shown in the second DetailsView control in figure 15-9. In addition, required field validators were added for each field except for the category ID and image file fields, and compare validators were added for the unit price and on hand fields. Finally, a command field that provides for Edit, Delete, and New buttons was added.

The Product Maintenance application

Description

- The Product Maintenance application uses a GridView control and a DetailsView control to let the user update the data in the Products table.

- To select a product, the user locates the product in the GridView control and clicks the Select button. This displays the details for the product in the DetailsView control. Then, the user can click the Edit button to change the product data or the Delete button to delete the product.

- To add a new product to the database, the user clicks the New button in the DetailsView control. Then, the user can enter the data for the new product and click the Insert button.

Figure 15-10   The Product Maintenance application

The Default.aspx file

```
<%@ Page Language="C#" AutoEventWireup="true" CodeFile="Default.aspx.cs"
Inherits="_Default" %>

<!DOCTYPE html PUBLIC "-//W3C//DTD XHTML 1.0 Transitional//EN"
"http://www.w3.org/TR/xhtml1/DTD/xhtml1-transitional.dtd">

<html xmlns="http://www.w3.org/1999/xhtml" >
<head id="Head1" runat="server">
    <title>Chapter 15: Product Maintenance</title>
    <style type="text/css">
        .style1 {width: 300px;}
        .style2 {width: 400px;}
    </style>
</head>
<body>
    <form id="form1" runat="server">
    <div>
    <asp:Image ID="Image1" runat="server" ImageUrl="~/Images/banner.jpg" />
    <br /><br />
    <table>
      <tr>
        <td class="style1" valign="top">
          <asp:GridView ID="GridView1" runat="server"
              AllowSorting="True" AllowPaging="True"
              DataKeyNames="ProductID" DataSourceID="SqlDataSource1"
              AutoGenerateColumns="False" SelectedIndex="0"
              CellPadding="4" GridLines="None" ForeColor="Black">
            <Columns>
              <asp:BoundField DataField="ProductID" HeaderText="ID"
                  ReadOnly="True">
                <HeaderStyle HorizontalAlign="Left" />
                  <ItemStyle Width="75px" />
              </asp:BoundField>
              <asp:BoundField DataField="Name" HeaderText="Name">
                <HeaderStyle HorizontalAlign="Left" />
                  <ItemStyle Width="200px" />
              </asp:BoundField>
              <asp:BoundField DataField="CategoryID" HeaderText="Category" />
              <asp:CommandField ButtonType="Button" ShowSelectButton="True" />
            </Columns>
            <HeaderStyle BackColor="Silver" Font-Bold="True"
                ForeColor="White" />
            <RowStyle BackColor="White" ForeColor="Black" />
            <AlternatingRowStyle BackColor="WhiteSmoke" ForeColor="Black" />
            <SelectedRowStyle BackColor="Blue" ForeColor="White" />
            <FooterStyle BackColor="Silver" Font-Bold="True"
                ForeColor="White" />
            <PagerStyle BackColor="Silver" ForeColor="Blue"
                HorizontalAlign="Center" />
          </asp:GridView>

          <asp:SqlDataSource ID="SqlDataSource1" runat="server"
              ConnectionString=
                  "<%$ ConnectionStrings:HalloweenConnectionString %>"
              SelectCommand="SELECT [ProductID], [Name], [CategoryID]
                  FROM [Products] ORDER BY [ProductID]">
          </asp:SqlDataSource>
        </td>
```

Figure 15-11   The aspx file for the Product Maintenance application (part 1 of 4)

The Default.aspx file   **Page 2**

```
<td class="style2" valign="top">
  <asp:DetailsView ID="DetailsView1" runat="server"
    DataSourceID="SqlDataSource2" DataKeyNames="ProductID"
    Height="50px" Width="400px" AutoGenerateRows="False"
    BackColor="White" BorderColor="White" BorderStyle="Ridge"
    BorderWidth="2px" CellPadding="3" CellSpacing="1"
    GridLines="None" OnItemDeleted="DetailsView1_ItemDeleted"
    OnItemDeleting="DetailsView1_ItemDeleting"
    OnItemInserted="DetailsView1_ItemInserted"
    OnItemUpdated="DetailsView1_ItemUpdated">
  <RowStyle BackColor="#DEDFDE" ForeColor="Black" />
  <Fields>
    <asp:TemplateField HeaderText="Product ID:">
      <ItemTemplate>
        <asp:Label ID="Label4" runat="server"
          Text='<%# Bind("ProductID") %>'></asp:Label>
      </ItemTemplate>
      <EditItemTemplate>
        <asp:Label ID="Label1" runat="server"
          Text='<%# Eval("ProductID") %>'></asp:Label>
      </EditItemTemplate>
      <InsertItemTemplate>
        <asp:TextBox ID="txtID" runat="server"
          Text='<%# Bind("ProductID") %>' Width="100px"
          MaxLength="10">
        </asp:TextBox>
        <asp:RequiredFieldValidator
          ID="RequiredFieldValidator1" runat="server"
          ControlToValidate="txtID" Display="Dynamic"
          ErrorMessage="Product ID is a required field."
          ForeColor="White">*</asp:RequiredFieldValidator>
      </InsertItemTemplate>
      <HeaderStyle HorizontalAlign="Left" Width="150px" />
      <ItemStyle Width="250px" />
    </asp:TemplateField>
      .
      .
    <asp:TemplateField HeaderText="Category:">
      <ItemTemplate>
        <asp:Label ID="Label3" runat="server"
          Text='<%# Bind("CategoryID") %>'></asp:Label>
      </ItemTemplate>
      <EditItemTemplate>
        <asp:DropDownList ID="ddlCategory" runat="server"
          DataSourceID="SqlDataSource3"
          DataTextField="LongName" DataValueField="CategoryID"
          SelectedValue='<%# Bind("CategoryID") %>' Width="130px">
        </asp:DropDownList>
      </EditItemTemplate>
      <InsertItemTemplate>
        <asp:DropDownList ID="ddlCategory" runat="server"
          DataSourceID="SqlDataSource3"
          DataTextField="LongName" DataValueField="CategoryID"
          SelectedValue='<%# Bind("CategoryID") %>' Width="130px">
        </asp:DropDownList>
      </InsertItemTemplate>
      <HeaderStyle HorizontalAlign="Left" Width="150px" />
      <ItemStyle Width="250px" />
    </asp:TemplateField>
      .
      .
```

Figure 15-11   The aspx file for the Product Maintenance application (part 2 of 4)

In part 3 of this figure, you can see the aspx code for the data source that the DetailsView control is bound to. This data source includes Delete and Update statements that use optimistic concurrency. If you look at the Where clauses for these statements, you can see the modifications that I made to correctly handle nulls for the ImageFile column.

A data source is also included for the drop-down lists that are used to display the categories in the EditItem and InsertItem templates for the CategoryID field. You can see this data source in part 4 of this figure. If you look back at the definitions of the drop-down lists, you'll see how they're bound to this data source.

The code-behind file

Figure 15-12 shows the code-behind file for the Default page of the Product Maintenance application. Even though this application provides complete maintenance for the Products table, only four event handlers are required. These event handlers respond to events raised by the DetailsView control. The first three handle database exceptions and concurrency errors for updates, deletions, and insertions.

Note that the error-handling code for the insert event handler is simpler than the error-handling code for the update and delete event handlers. That's because optimistic concurrency doesn't apply to insert operations. As a result, there's no need to check the AffectedRows property to see if a concurrency error has occurred.

The last event handler, DetailsView1_ItemDeleting, handles a problem that can occur when you apply a format to a control that's bound to the data source. In this case, the currency format is applied to the unit price field in the Item template. Because this application uses optimistic concurrency, the original values of each field are passed to the Delete statement as parameters to make sure that another user hasn't changed the product row since it was retrieved. Unfortunately, the DetailsView control sets the value of the unit price parameter to its formatted value, which includes the currency symbol. If you allow this value to be passed on to the Delete statement, an exception will be thrown because the parameter value is in the wrong format.

Before the Delete statement is executed, then, the DetailsView1_ItemDeleting event handler is called. This event handler removes the currency symbol from the parameter value so the value will be passed to the Delete statement in the correct format.

The Default.aspx file

```
            <asp:CommandField ButtonType="Button"
                ShowDeleteButton="True"
                ShowEditButton="True"
                ShowInsertButton="True" />
        </Fields>
        <HeaderStyle BackColor="Silver" Font-Bold="True" ForeColor="Black" />
        <EditRowStyle BackColor="Blue" Font-Bold="True" ForeColor="White" />
    </asp:DetailsView>
    <asp:SqlDataSource ID="SqlDataSource2" runat="server"
        ConflictDetection="CompareAllValues"
        ConnectionString=
            "<%$ ConnectionStrings:HalloweenConnectionString %>"
        OldValuesParameterFormatString="original_{0}"
        SelectCommand="SELECT [ProductID], [Name], [ShortDescription],
            [LongDescription], [CategoryID], [ImageFile],
            [UnitPrice], [OnHand]
        FROM [Products]
        WHERE ([ProductID] = @ProductID)"
        DeleteCommand="DELETE FROM [Products]
        WHERE [ProductID] = @original_ProductID
          AND [Name] = @original_Name
          AND [ShortDescription] = @original_ShortDescription
          AND [LongDescription] = @original_LongDescription
          AND [CategoryID] = @original_CategoryID
          AND ( [ImageFile] = @original_ImageFile
           OR ImageFile IS NULL AND @original_ImageFile IS NULL )
          AND [UnitPrice] = @original_UnitPrice
          AND [OnHand] = @original_OnHand"
        InsertCommand="INSERT INTO [Products] ([ProductID], [Name],
            [ShortDescription], [LongDescription], [CategoryID],
            [ImageFile], [UnitPrice], [OnHand])
        VALUES (@ProductID, @Name, @ShortDescription,
            @LongDescription, @CategoryID, @ImageFile,
            @UnitPrice, @OnHand)"
        UpdateCommand="UPDATE [Products] SET [Name] = @Name,
            [ShortDescription] = @ShortDescription,
            [LongDescription] = @LongDescription,
            [CategoryID] = @CategoryID,
            [ImageFile] = @ImageFile,
            [UnitPrice] = @UnitPrice,
            [OnHand] = @OnHand
        WHERE [ProductID] = @original_ProductID
          AND [Name] = @original_Name
          AND [ShortDescription] = @original_ShortDescription
          AND [LongDescription] = @original_LongDescription
          AND [CategoryID] = @original_CategoryID
          AND ( [ImageFile] = @original_ImageFile
           OR ImageFile IS NULL AND @original_ImageFile IS NULL )
          AND [UnitPrice] = @original_UnitPrice
          AND [OnHand] = @original_OnHand">
```

Figure 15-11   The aspx file for the Product Maintenance application (part 3 of 4)

The Default.aspx file

```
            <SelectParameters>
              <asp:ControlParameter ControlID="GridView1" Name="ProductID"
                 PropertyName="SelectedValue" Type="String" />
            </SelectParameters>
            <DeleteParameters>
              <asp:Parameter Name="original_ProductID" Type="String" />
              <asp:Parameter Name="original_Name" Type="String" />
              <asp:Parameter Name="original_ShortDescription" Type="String" />
              <asp:Parameter Name="original_LongDescription" Type="String" />
              <asp:Parameter Name="original_CategoryID" Type="String" />
              <asp:Parameter Name="original_ImageFile" Type="String" />
              <asp:Parameter Name="original_UnitPrice" Type="Decimal" />
              <asp:Parameter Name="original_OnHand" Type="Int32" />
            </DeleteParameters>
            <UpdateParameters>
              <asp:Parameter Name="Name" Type="String" />
              <asp:Parameter Name="ShortDescription" Type="String" />
              <asp:Parameter Name="LongDescription" Type="String" />
              <asp:Parameter Name="CategoryID" Type="String" />
              <asp:Parameter Name="ImageFile" Type="String" />
              <asp:Parameter Name="UnitPrice" Type="Decimal" />
              <asp:Parameter Name="OnHand" Type="Int32" />
              <asp:Parameter Name="original_ProductID" Type="String" />
              <asp:Parameter Name="original_Name" Type="String" />
              <asp:Parameter Name="original_ShortDescription" Type="String" />
              <asp:Parameter Name="original_LongDescription" Type="String" />
              <asp:Parameter Name="original_CategoryID" Type="String" />
              <asp:Parameter Name="original_ImageFile" Type="String" />
              <asp:Parameter Name="original_UnitPrice" Type="Decimal" />
              <asp:Parameter Name="original_OnHand" Type="Int32" />
            </UpdateParameters>
            <InsertParameters>
              <asp:Parameter Name="ProductID" Type="String" />
              <asp:Parameter Name="Name" Type="String" />
              <asp:Parameter Name="ShortDescription" Type="String" />
              <asp:Parameter Name="LongDescription" Type="String" />
              <asp:Parameter Name="CategoryID" Type="String" />
              <asp:Parameter Name="ImageFile" Type="String" />
              <asp:Parameter Name="UnitPrice" Type="Decimal" />
              <asp:Parameter Name="OnHand" Type="Int32" />
            </InsertParameters>
          </asp:SqlDataSource>
          <asp:SqlDataSource ID="SqlDataSource3" runat="server"
            ConnectionString=
              "<%$ ConnectionStrings:HalloweenConnectionString %>"
            SelectCommand="SELECT [CategoryID], [LongName] FROM [Categories]
              ORDER BY [LongName]">
          </asp:SqlDataSource><br />
          <asp:ValidationSummary ID="ValidationSummary1" runat="server"
            HeaderText="Please correct the following errors:" /><br />
          <asp:Label ID = "lblError" runat="server" ForeColor="Red"
            EnableViewState="False"></asp:Label>
        </td>
      </tr>
    </table>
    </div>
    </form>
</body>
</html>
```

Figure 15-11   The aspx file for the Product Maintenance application (part 4 of 4)

The Default.aspx.cs file

```
public partial class _Default : System.Web.UI.Page
{
    protected void DetailsView1_ItemUpdated(
        object sender, DetailsViewUpdatedEventArgs e)
    {
        if (e.Exception != null)
        {
            lblError.Text = "A database error has occurred.<br /><br />" +
                "Message: " + e.Exception.Message;
            e.ExceptionHandled = true;
            e.KeepInEditMode = true;
        }
        else if (e.AffectedRows == 0)
            lblError.Text = "Another user may have updated that product."
                + "<br />Please try again.";
        else
            GridView1.DataBind();
    }

    protected void DetailsView1_ItemDeleted(
        object sender, DetailsViewDeletedEventArgs e)
    {
        if (e.Exception != null)
        {
            lblError.Text = "A database error has occurred.<br /><br />" +
                "Message: " + e.Exception.Message;
            e.ExceptionHandled = true;
        }
        else if (e.AffectedRows == 0)
            lblError.Text = "Another user may have updated that product."
                + "<br />Please try again.";
        else
            GridView1.DataBind();
    }

    protected void DetailsView1_ItemInserted(
        object sender, DetailsViewInsertedEventArgs e)
    {
        if (e.Exception != null)
        {
            lblError.Text = "A database error has occurred.<br /><br />" +
                "Message: " + e.Exception.Message;
            e.ExceptionHandled = true;
            e.KeepInInsertMode = true;
        }
        else
            GridView1.DataBind();
    }

    protected void DetailsView1_ItemDeleting(
        object sender, DetailsViewDeleteEventArgs e)
    {
        e.Values["UnitPrice"]
            = e.Values["UnitPrice"].ToString().Substring(1);
    }
}
```

Figure 15-12   The code-behind file for the Product Maintenance application

How to use the FormView control

Besides the DetailsView control, ASP.NET 3.5 also provides a FormView control. Like the DetailsView control, the FormView control is designed to display data for a single item from a data source. However, as you'll see in the following topics, the FormView control uses a different approach to displaying its data.

An introduction to the FormView control

Figure 15-13 presents an introduction to the FormView control. Although the FormView control is similar to the DetailsView control, it differs in several key ways. Most importantly, the FormView control isn't restricted by the HTML table layout of the DetailsView control, in which each field is rendered as a table row. Instead, the FormView control uses templates to render all of the fields as a single row. This gives you complete control over the layout of the fields within the row.

Because you have to use template fields with a FormView control, this control can be more difficult to work with than a DetailsView control that uses bound fields. As you learned earlier in this chapter, though, you can convert the bound fields used by a DetailsView control to template fields so you have more control over them. In that case, a FormView control is just as easy to work with.

When you create a FormView control and bind it to a data source, the Web Forms Designer will automatically create default templates for you, as shown in the first image in this figure. Then, you can edit the templates to achieve the layout you want. To do that, choose Edit Templates from the smart tag menu. This places the control in template-editing mode, as shown in the second image in this figure. Here, the drop-down list shows the various templates you can use with a FormView control. For most applications, you'll use just the Item, EditItem, and InsertItem templates.

A FormView control after a data source has been assigned

A FormView control in template-editing mode

How the FormView control differs from the DetailsView control

- The DetailsView control can be easier to work with, but the FormView control provides more formatting and layout options.
- The DetailsView control can use BoundField elements or TemplateField elements with templates that use data binding expressions to define bound data fields. The FormView control can use only templates with data binding expressions to display bound data.
- The DetailsView control renders each field as a table row, but the FormView control renders all the fields in a template as a single table row.

Description

- A FormView control is similar to a DetailsView control, but its templates give you more control over how its data is displayed. To accomplish that, all the columns in the data source can be laid out within a single template.
- After you create a FormView control and assign a data source to it, you can edit the control's templates so the data is displayed the way you want.

Figure 15-13   An introduction to the FormView control

How to work with the Item template

When you use the Web Forms Designer to create a FormView control and bind it to a data source, the Web Forms Designer automatically generates basic templates for the FormView control. For instance, the code in figure 15-14 shows a typical Item template. This template is used to display the data from the data source in ReadOnly mode.

As you can see, the Item template consists of a literal header and a label control for each field in the data source. The Text attribute of each label control uses either the Bind or Eval method for data binding. The Eval method is used for columns that can't be modified. That's the case for the ProductID column in the Products table, since this is the key column.

To control the format and layout of the data that's displayed in ReadOnly mode, you can edit the Item template. In fact, it's common to include an HTML table in the Item template to control the layout of the individual fields in the template. You'll see an example of this later in this chapter.

Note that if the data source includes Update, Delete, and Insert commands, the Item template will include command buttons that let the user edit, delete, or add new rows. Although these buttons are created as link buttons, you can easily change them to regular buttons or image buttons.

The Item template generated for a FormView control

```
<asp:FormView ID="FormView1" runat="server" DataKeyNames="ProductID"
    DataSourceID="SqlDataSource2">
    <ItemTemplate>
        ProductID:
        <asp:Label ID="ProductIDLabel" runat="server"
            Text='<%# Eval("ProductID") %>' /><br />
        Name:
        <asp:Label ID="NameLabel" runat="server"
            Text='<%# Bind("Name") %>' /><br />
        ShortDescription:
        <asp:Label ID="ShortDescriptionLabel" runat="server"
            Text='<%# Bind("ShortDescription") %>' /><br />
        LongDescription:
        <asp:Label ID="LongDescriptionLabel" runat="server"
            Text='<%# Bind("LongDescription") %>' /><br />
        CategoryID:
        <asp:Label ID="CategoryIDLabel" runat="server"
            Text='<%# Bind("CategoryID") %>' /><br />
        ImageFile:
        <asp:Label ID="ImageFileLabel" runat="server"
            Text='<%# Bind("ImageFile") %>' /><br />
        UnitPrice:
        <asp:Label ID="UnitPriceLabel" runat="server"
            Text='<%# Bind("UnitPrice") %>' /><br />
        OnHand:
        <asp:Label ID="OnHandLabel" runat="server"
            Text='<%# Bind("OnHand") %>' /><br />
    </ItemTemplate>
        .
        .
        .
</asp:FormView>
```

Description

- When you bind a FormView control to a data source, the Web Forms Designer generates an Item template that includes heading text and a bound label for each column in the data source.

- The Item template is rendered whenever the FormView control is bound in ReadOnly mode.

- The Item template uses the Eval and Bind methods to create binding expressions for the columns in the data source (see figure 13-14 in chapter 13).

- If the data source includes Update, Delete, and Insert commands, the generated Item template will include Edit, Delete, and New buttons.

- The Web Forms Designer also generates an EditItem template and an InsertItem template, even if the data source doesn't include an Update or Insert command. For more information, see the next figure.

- You can add a table to a generated template to control the layout of the data that's rendered for that template.

Figure 15-14   How to work with the Item template

How to work with the EditItem and InsertItem templates

As figure 15-15 shows, the Web Forms Designer also generates an EditItem and InsertItem template when you bind a FormView control to a data source. These templates are used to display the fields in Edit and Insert mode, and they're generated even if the data source doesn't have an Update or Insert command. As a result, you can delete these templates if your application doesn't allow for edits and inserts. Although this figure only shows an EditItem template, the InsertItem template is similar.

One drawback to using the FormView control is that once you edit the Item template so the data is arranged the way you want, you'll usually want to provide similar layout code in both the EditItem template and the InsertItem template. That way, the layout in all three modes will be similar. One way to do that is to copy the code in one template and paste it into another. Then, you can make the necessary adjustments, such as replacing the labels that were generated for the Item template with the text boxes that were generated for the EditItem or InsertItem template.

Depending on the complexity of the layout, it may take considerable work to get the templates looking the way you want them. In addition, if you later decide to change that layout, you'll have to make the change to all three templates. Unfortunately, there's no escaping this duplication of effort.

A generated EditItem template as displayed in a browser window

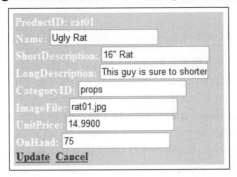

The aspx code for the edit item template shown above

```
<EditItemTemplate>
    ProductID:
    <asp:Label ID="ProductIDLabel1" runat="server"
        Text='<%# Eval("ProductID") %>'></asp:Label><br />
    Name:
    <asp:TextBox ID="NameTextBox" runat="server" Text='<%# Bind("Name") %>'>
    </asp:TextBox><br />
    ShortDescription:
    <asp:TextBox ID="ShortDescriptionTextBox" runat="server"
        Text='<%# Bind("ShortDescription") %>'>
    </asp:TextBox><br />
    .
    .          ┌─────────────────────────────────────────────────────┐
    .          │ The code generated for the LongDescription, CategoryID, │
    .          │ ImageFile, UnitPrice, and OnHand columns is similar to the │
    .          │ code generated for the ShortDescription column.        │
    .          └─────────────────────────────────────────────────────┘
    .
    <asp:LinkButton ID="UpdateButton" runat="server" CausesValidation="True"
        CommandName="Update" Text="Update">
    </asp:LinkButton> 
    <asp:LinkButton ID="UpdateCancelButton" runat="server"
        CausesValidation="False" CommandName="Cancel" Text="Cancel">
    </asp:LinkButton>
</EditItemTemplate>
```

Description

- The EditItem template determines how the FormView control is rendered in Edit mode.
  It includes a text box for each editable bound column in the data source. The Text
  attribute for each text box uses a binding expression that binds the text box to its data
  source column.

- The EditItem template also includes Update and Cancel buttons.

- The InsertItem template is similar to the EditItem template. It determines how the
  FormView control is rendered in Insert mode.

Figure 15-15   How to work with the EditItem and InsertItem templates

A Shopping Cart application that uses a FormView control

To show the versatility of the FormView control, the following topics present a version of the Order page from the Shopping Cart application that was originally presented in chapter 3. That version of the application used simple label and image controls to display the information for the product selected by the user. Because data binding didn't work for those controls, C# code was required in the Page_Load event handler to set the values of the label and image controls. In contrast, this new version of the application takes advantage of the data binding ability of the FormView control, so no Page_Load event handler is required.

Because this application doesn't allow the user to update, delete, or insert product information, it doesn't illustrate the use of the EditItem or InsertItem templates or the use of command buttons with a FormView control. If you want to see an application that does use those features, though, you can download the applications for this book from our web site, www.murach.com.

The operation of the application

To refresh your memory, figure 15-16 shows the Order page displayed by the Shopping Cart application. As you can see, this page lets the user select a product from a drop-down list. When the user selects a product, the page displays the name, description, price, and an image of the selected product. Then, the user can order the product by entering a quantity and clicking the Add to Cart button.

This time, the product information is displayed within a FormView control, and the Item template includes a simple HTML table that displays the text information on the left and the image on the right. This demonstrates the layout flexibility of the FormView control. With a DetailsView control, it wouldn't be possible to display the image to the right of the text data, because the DetailsView control displays each column of the data source in a separate table row.

The Order page as viewed in the Web Forms Designer

Description

- This is the Shopping Cart application that was originally presented in chapter 3, but this time it's implemented with a FormView control that displays the data for the selected product.
- The Item template for the FormView control includes an HTML table with cells that contain labels that are bound to the columns in the data source. It also includes an Image control whose ImageUrl property is bound to the ImageFile column in the data source.

Figure 15-16   The Shopping Cart application with a FormView control

The aspx file for the Order page

Figure 15-17 shows the aspx file for the Order page of the Shopping Cart application. Here, the FormView control includes an Item template that uses a table to format the data for the selected product. This table has four rows, each with three columns. The first column contains the labels that present the name, short description, long description, and price for the selected product. The second column (which spans all four rows) is a small spacer column to provide some space between the text and the image. And the third column (which also spans all four rows) contains the image control that displays the product's image.

Note that although the Web Forms Designer generated the EditItem and InsertItem templates, this application doesn't use them. As a result, I deleted those templates so they wouldn't clutter the listing.

There are two interesting things to notice about the format strings used in the binding expressions on this page. First, the format string used to bind the image control is this: "Images/Products/{0}". Since the ImageFile column in the Products table contains just the name of the image file for each product, not its complete path, this formatting expression prefixes the file name with the path Images/Products/ so the image file can be located.

Second, the format string used in the binding expression that displays the unit price is this: "{0:c} each". As a result, the price is displayed in currency format, followed by the word "each."

The code-behind file for the Order page

Figure 15-18 shows the code-behind file for the Order page. This code is almost identical to the code for the original version of this program that was presented back in chapter 3. In fact, there are only two substantial differences. First, this version doesn't include a Page_Load event handler because it doesn't need to do any data binding.

Second, the GetSelectedProduct method in this version is simpler than the one in the original version. Because the new application uses two data sources, a select parameter can be used to retrieve the selected product in the second data source. Then, because the second data source retrieves just a single row, a row filter isn't required. Instead, the index value 0 is used to retrieve data from the first and only row of the data source.

The Order.aspx file   **Page 1**

```
<%@ Page Language="C#" AutoEventWireup="true" CodeFile="Order.aspx.cs"
Inherits="Order" %>

<!DOCTYPE html PUBLIC "-//W3C//DTD XHTML 1.0 Transitional//EN" "http://www.w3.org/TR/
xhtml1/DTD/xhtml1-transitional.dtd">

<html xmlns="http://www.w3.org/1999/xhtml" >
<head runat="server">
    <title>Chapter 15: Shopping Cart</title>
    <style type="text/css">
        .style1 {width: 250px;}
        .style2 {width: 20px;}
    </style>
</head>
<body>
    <form id="form1" runat="server">
    <div>
        <asp:Image ID="Image1" runat="server"
            ImageUrl="~/Images/banner.jpg" /><br /><br />
        <asp:Label ID="Label1" runat="server"
            Text="Please select a product:"></asp:Label>
        <asp:DropDownList ID="ddlProducts" runat="server" Width="150px"
            AutoPostBack="True" DataSourceID="SqlDataSource1"
            DataTextField="Name" DataValueField="ProductID">
        </asp:DropDownList>
        <asp:SqlDataSource ID="SqlDataSource1" runat="server"
            ConnectionString="<%$ ConnectionStrings:HalloweenConnectionString %>"
            SelectCommand="SELECT [ProductID], [Name] FROM [Products]
                ORDER BY [Name]">
        </asp:SqlDataSource>
        <br />
        <asp:FormView ID="FormView1" runat="server"
            DataSourceID="SqlDataSource2">
            <ItemTemplate>
              <table>
                <tr>
                  <td class="style1">
                    <asp:Label ID="lblName" runat="server"
                        style="font-weight: 700; font-size: larger"
                        Text='<%# Bind("Name") %>' >
                    </asp:Label>
                  </td>
                  <td class="style2" rowspan="4" valign="top"></td>
                  <td rowspan="4" valign="top">
                    <asp:Image ID="imgProduct" runat="server" Height="200px"
                      ImageUrl='<%# Bind("ImageFile", "Images/Products/{0}") %>' />
                  </td>
                </tr>
                <tr>
                  <td class="style1">
                    <asp:Label ID="lblShortDescription" runat="server"
                        Text='<%# Bind("ShortDescription") %>'>
                    </asp:Label>
                  </td>
                </tr>
```

Figure 15-17   The aspx file for the Order page of the Shopping Cart application (part 1 of 2)

The Order.aspx file **Page 2**

```
                <tr>
                  <td class="style1">
                    <asp:Label ID="lblLongDescription" runat="server"
                        Text='<%# Bind("LongDescription") %>'>
                    </asp:Label>
                  </td>
                </tr>
                <tr>
                  <td class="style1">
                    <asp:Label ID="lblUnitPrice" runat="server"
                        style="font-weight: 700; font-size: larger"
                        Text='<%# Bind("UnitPrice", "{0:c} each") %>'>
                    </asp:Label>
                  </td>
                </tr>
              </table>
          </ItemTemplate>
      </asp:FormView>
      <asp:SqlDataSource ID="SqlDataSource2" runat="server"
          ConnectionString="<%$ ConnectionStrings:HalloweenConnectionString %>"
          SelectCommand="SELECT [ProductID], [Name], [ShortDescription],
              [LongDescription], [ImageFile], [UnitPrice]
            FROM [Products]
            WHERE ([ProductID] = @ProductID)">
          <SelectParameters>
              <asp:ControlParameter ControlID="ddlProducts" Name="ProductID"
                  PropertyName="SelectedValue" Type="String" />
          </SelectParameters>
      </asp:SqlDataSource><br />
      <asp:Label ID="Label2" runat="server" Text="Quantity:"
          Width="80px"></asp:Label>
      <asp:TextBox ID="txtQuantity" runat="server" Width="80px"></asp:TextBox>
      <asp:RequiredFieldValidator
          ID="RequiredFieldValidator1" runat="server"
          ControlToValidate="txtQuantity" Display="Dynamic"
          ErrorMessage="Quantity is a required field.">
      </asp:RequiredFieldValidator>
      <asp:CompareValidator ID="CompareValidator1" runat="server"
          ControlToValidate="txtQuantity" Display="Dynamic"
          ErrorMessage="Quantity must be greater than zero."
          Operator="GreaterThan" ValueToCompare="0">
      </asp:CompareValidator><br /><br />
      <asp:Button ID="btnAdd" runat="server" Text="Add to Cart"
          OnClick="btnAdd_Click" /> 
      <asp:Button ID="Button1" runat="server"  Text="Go to Cart"
          CausesValidation="False" PostBackUrl="~/Cart.aspx" />
    </div>
    </form>
</body>
</html>
```

Figure 15-17   The aspx file for the Order page of the Shopping Cart application (part 2 of 2)

The Order.aspx.cs file

```
public partial class Order : System.Web.UI.Page
{
    private Product selectedProduct;

    protected void btnAdd_Click(object sender, EventArgs e)
    {
        if (Page.IsValid)
        {
            selectedProduct = this.GetSelectedProduct();
            CartItem item = new CartItem();
            item.Product = selectedProduct;
            item.Quantity = Convert.ToInt32(txtQuantity.Text);
            this.AddToCart(item);
            Response.Redirect("Cart.aspx");
        }
    }

    private Product GetSelectedProduct()
    {
        DataView productsTable = (DataView)
            SqlDataSource2.Select(DataSourceSelectArguments.Empty);
        DataRowView row = (DataRowView) productsTable[0];

        Product p = new Product();
        p.ProductID = row["ProductID"].ToString();
        p.Name = row["Name"].ToString();
        p.ShortDescription = row["ShortDescription"].ToString();
        p.LongDescription = row["LongDescription"].ToString();
        p.UnitPrice = (decimal)row["UnitPrice"];
        p.ImageFile = row["ImageFile"].ToString();
        return p;
    }

    private void AddToCart(CartItem item)
    {
        SortedList cart = this.GetCart();
        string productID = selectedProduct.ProductID;
        if (cart.ContainsKey(productID))
        {
            CartItem existingItem = (CartItem)cart[productID];
            existingItem.Quantity += item.Quantity;
        }
        else
            cart.Add(productID, item);
    }

    private SortedList GetCart()
    {
        if (Session["Cart"] == null)
            Session.Add("Cart", new SortedList());
        return (SortedList) Session["Cart"];
    }
}
```

Figure 15-18   The code-behind file for the Order page of the Shopping Cart application

Perspective

The DetailsView and FormView controls are ideal for any application that displays bound data one row at a time. The choice of whether to use a DetailsView or a FormView control depends mostly on how much control you want over the layout of the data. If you want to present a simple list of fields, the DetailsView control is usually the best choice because it can automatically present data in that format. But if you need more control over the layout of the data, you'll want to use the FormView control.

In the next chapter, you'll learn about two additional controls for working with the data in a data source: the ListView control and the DataPager control. The ListView control lets you work with the data in a data source much like the GridView control. Unlike the GridView control, though, the ListView control is highly customizable. In addition, it provides for insert operations, and it provides for paging using the DataPager control. Both the ListView and DataPager controls are new to ASP.NET 3.5.

Term

Master/Detail page

16

How to use the ListView and DataPager controls

In this chapter, you'll learn how to use the ListView and DataPager controls, which are new with ASP.NET 3.5. As you'll see, the ListView control works much like the GridView control you learned about in chapter 14. However, it provides features that make it much more versatile than the GridView control. For example, you can use the ListView control to insert rows into a data source, and you can use it to display items from the data source in groups as well as other customized formats. In addition, you can use the DataPager control in conjunction with the ListView control to implement paging.

How to use the ListView control 506
An introduction to the ListView control 506
How to configure a ListView control 508
How to work with the Layout template 510
How to work with the Item template 512
How to provide for sorting 514
How to provide for paging 516
How to customize paging 518

A list application that uses a ListView control 520
The Product List application 520
The aspx file 522

How to group ListView data 526
How to define the templates for a group 526
A Product List application that uses groups 528
The aspx file for the grouped Product List application 528

How to update ListView data 532
How to use buttons to perform update operations 532
How to work with the EditItem and InsertItem templates 534
How to use events raised by the ListView control 534

A maintenance application that uses a ListView control 536
The Category Maintenance application 536
The aspx file 538
The code-behind file 538

Perspective 544

How to use the ListView control

The ListView control is a highly customizable control that was introduced with ASP.NET 3.5. In the topics that follow, you'll learn the basic skills for defining the content and appearance of this control. In addition, you'll learn how to provide sorting and paging for this control.

An introduction to the ListView control

Figure 16-1 presents a ListView control that provides for updating the data in the Categories table of the Halloween database. As you can see, this control presents the data in a row and column format just like the GridView control. In fact, if you compare this control to the GridView control shown in figure 14-1 of chapter 14, you'll see that these controls look quite similar. The main difference is that the ListView control includes an additional row for inserting a new row into the table.

The first table in this figure lists some of the basic attributes of the ListView control. In most cases, these attributes are set the way you want them by default. If you want to change the location of the row that provides for insert operations, though, you can do that by changing the value of the InsertItemPosition attribute.

To define the layout of a ListView control, you use the templates listed in the second table in this figure. At the least, a ListView control must contain a Layout template and an Item template. You use the Layout template to define the overall layout of the control, and you use the Item template to define the layout that's used for each item in the data source. You'll see how these and many of the other templates can be used as you progress through this chapter.

A ListView control that provides for updating a table

		CategoryID	ShortName	LongName
Delete	Edit	costumes	Costumes	Costumes
Update	Cancel	fx	FX	Special Effects
Delete	Edit	masks	Masks	Masks
Delete	Edit	props	Props	Props
Insert	Clear			

Basic attributes of the ListView control

Attribute	Description
ID	The ID of the control.
Runat	Must specify "server."
DataSourceID	The ID of the data source to bind to.
DataKeyNames	The names of the primary key fields separated by commas.
InsertItemPosition	The location within the ListView control where the InsertItem template is rendered. You can specify FirstItem, LastItem, or None.

Template elements used by the ListView control

Element	Description
LayoutTemplate	Defines the basic layout of the control.
ItemTemplate	The template used for each item in the data source.
ItemSeparatorTemplate	The template used to separate items in the data source.
AlternatingItemTemplate	The template used for alternating items in the data source.
EditItemTemplate	The template used when a row is being edited.
InsertItemTemplate	The template used for inserting a row.
EmptyDataTemplate	The template used when the data source is empty.
SelectedItemTemplate	The template used when a row is selected.
GroupTemplate	The template used to define a group layout.
GroupSeparatorTemplate	The template used to separate groups of items.
EmptyItemTemplate	The template used for empty items in a group.

Description

- The ListView control displays data from a data source using templates. It can be used to edit and delete data as well as insert data.

- The template elements define the formatting that's used to display data. These templates are generated automatically when you configure a ListView control. See figure 16-2 for information on configuring this control.

- The Layout template defines the overall layout of the control. This template includes an element that's used as a placeholder for the data. Then, the other templates are substituted for this placeholder as appropriate.

Figure 16-1   An introduction to the ListView control

How to configure a ListView control

The easiest way to configure a ListView control is to use the Configure ListView dialog box shown in figure 16-2. Before you do that, though, you have to add the ListView control to the page and bind it to a data source. Then, you can use the Configure ListView command in the control's smart tag menu to display this dialog box.

When you use the Configure ListView dialog box to configure a ListView control, Visual Studio generates templates based on the options you choose. If you want to generate templates that use a standard row and column format, for example, you can select the Grid layout as shown here. Then, if you want to add formatting to the templates, you can select a style. In this figure, for example, I selected the Professional style.

The other options in this dialog box let you enable editing, inserting, deleting, and paging. Note that if the data source isn't defined with Update, Insert, and Delete commands, the Enable Editing, Enable Inserting, and Enable Deleting options won't be available. Even so, EditItem and InsertItem templates are generated for the ListView control. If your application won't provide for updating and inserting data, then, you may want to delete these templates.

The Item template that's generated for a ListView control depends on the columns in the data source that the control is bound to and whether you enable editing and deleting. If you enable editing and deleting, Edit and Delete buttons are added to this template. You'll learn more about how these buttons and the other buttons used by the ListView control work later in this chapter.

If you select the Enable Paging option, a DataPager control is also added to the ListView control. The exact format of this control depends on the option you choose from the drop-down list. You'll learn more about this later in this chapter too.

As you select options in the Configure ListView dialog box, a preview of the control is displayed in the Preview window. That way, you can be sure that the ListView control is generated the way you want. And that will save you time later if you need to customize the control.

The Configure ListView dialog box

Description

- After you add a ListView control and bind it to a data source, you can configure it to generate many of the templates shown in figure 16-1. To do that, you use the Configure ListView dialog box.

- To display the Configure ListView dialog box, choose the Configure ListView command from the control's smart tag menu. Then, you can select a layout and style for the control, and you can enable editing, inserting, deleting, and paging.

- The EditItem and InsertItem templates are generated regardless of whether the data source provides for editing and inserting and whether editing and inserting are enabled for the ListView control.

- If you enable editing, an Edit button is added to the Item and AlternatingItem templates that lets the user switch to edit mode. If you enable deleting, a Delete button is added to the Item and AlternatingItem templates.

- If you enable inserting, the InsertItemPosition attribute is set to LastItem. This causes the InsertItem template to be displayed after the existing rows in the data source.

- If you enable paging, a DataPager control is added to the ListView control. See figures 16-6 and 16-7 for information on how to use this control.

Figure 16-2   How to configure a ListView control

How to work with the Layout template

Figure 16-3 shows the Layout template that was generated for the ListView control you saw in figure 16-1. This control was configured using the options shown in figure 16-2, except that no formatting was applied. That way, you can focus on the layout rather than the styles.

To start, you should notice that this template contains a table with two rows. The first row defines the layout of the data that will be displayed in the control. I'll have more to say about this row in just a minute. The second row defines the layout of the pager area. If I had enabled paging, this row would contain a DataPager control. In this case, however, paging isn't enabled, so the second row is empty.

The first row in the table within the Layout template contains a single column that contains another table. Notice that the ID attribute of this table is set to itemPlaceholderContainer. This indicates that the table will contain a placeholder where items from the data source are displayed. Although this attribute isn't required, it's included by default when you configure a ListView control using the Configure ListView dialog box.

The first row in the inner table defines the table headers (Th elements) that are displayed across the top of the ListView control. Then, the second row identifies where the data from the data source should be displayed. To do that, the ID attribute of this row is set to itemPlaceholder. To specify how the data is displayed, you use the other templates of the ListView control. In the next figure, for example, you'll see the code for a basic Item template.

Before I go on, you should notice that each element within the Layout template has a Runat attribute set to Server. This is necessary for the Table and Tr elements that specify an ID attribute since only server controls can include this attribute. Although the Runat attribute isn't required for the other elements, it's added by default when you configure the control.

You should also realize that you can't modify the templates for a ListView control from Design view. Instead, you'll need to work in Source view. The exception is the EmptyData template, which you can modify from Design view. Although that makes the ListView control more difficult to work with than the other data-bound controls, its versatility typically outweighs this shortcoming.

The Layout template for the ListView control in figure 16-1

```
<LayoutTemplate>
    <table runat="server">
        <tr runat="server">
            <td runat="server">
                <table ID="itemPlaceholderContainer" runat="server"
                        border="0" style="">
                    <tr runat="server" style="">
                        <th runat="server"></th>
                        <th runat="server">CategoryID</th>
                        <th runat="server">ShortName</th>
                        <th runat="server">LongName</th>
                    </tr>
                    <tr ID="itemPlaceholder" runat="server">
                    </tr>
                </table>
            </td>
        </tr>
        <tr runat="server">
            <td runat="server" style="">
            </td>
        </tr>
    </table>
</LayoutTemplate>
```

Description

- The Layout template that's generated for a ListView control that uses a grid layout consists of a table with two rows and one column. The first row defines the layout of the data that's displayed in the control, and the second row defines the layout of the DataPager control if paging is enabled.

- The column in the first row of the table for the Layout template contains another table with two rows. The first row defines the headers that are displayed for the columns of the data source as well as a header for any buttons that are displayed by the control. The second row defines a placeholder where the data defined by the other templates will be displayed.

- By default, the ID of the control that's used as a placeholder is set to itemPlaceholder. If you want to use a different name, you can set the ItemPlaceholderID attribute of the ListView control to the name you want to use.

- You can modify the Layout template any way you like. The only requirement is that it must contain a placeholder element that runs on the server.

- Design view doesn't support displaying the Layout template. Because of that, you must work with this template in Source view.

Figure 16-3   How to work with the Layout template

How to work with the Item template

You use the Item template to define how the items from a data source are displayed within a ListView control. To illustrate, figure 16-4 shows the Item template that was generated for the ListView control in figure 16-1. The first thing you should notice here is that this template contains a single Tr element. That's necessary because the element that defines the item placeholder in the Layout template is a Tr element. Then, at runtime, the Tr element in the Item template is substituted for the Tr element in the Layout template.

By default, the Item template contains one column for each column in the data source. As you can see, the data from each column is displayed in a label that's bound to the data source using the Eval method. In addition, if editing or deleting is enabled for the ListView control, an additional column is included in the Item template. This column contains the Edit and Delete buttons that can be used to perform edit and delete operations.

In addition to the Item template, an AlternatingItem template is generated for you when you configure a ListView control. Unless you apply a style to the control, though, this template is identical to the Item template, so each row in the control has the same appearance. If you want every other row to have a different appearance, you can modify the Item and AlternatingItem templates as appropriate. For example, you might want to set the background color for the AlternatingItem template so it's different from the background color for the Item template.

The Item template for the ListView control in figure 16-1

```
<ItemTemplate>
    <tr style="">
        <td>
            <asp:Button ID="DeleteButton" runat="server"
                CommandName="Delete" Text="Delete" />
            <asp:Button ID="EditButton" runat="server"
                CommandName="Edit" Text="Edit" />
        </td>
        <td>
            <asp:Label ID="CategoryIDLabel" runat="server"
                Text='<%# Eval("CategoryID") %>' />
        </td>
        <td>
            <asp:Label ID="ShortNameLabel" runat="server"
                Text='<%# Eval("ShortName") %>' />
        </td>
        <td>
            <asp:Label ID="LongNameLabel" runat="server"
                Text='<%# Eval("LongName") %>' />
        </td>
    </tr>
</ItemTemplate>
```

Description

- The Item template defines the layout of the data that's displayed in the ListView control. This template is substituted for the placeholder in the Layout template at runtime.

- The Item template that's generated for a ListView control with a grid layout consists of a single row with one column for each column in the data source. The data for each column is displayed in a label that's bound to the data source using the Eval method.

- If editing or deleting is enabled for the ListView control, an additional column that contains the buttons used to implement these operations is included in the Item template. See figure 16-13 for more information.

- You can modify the Item template any way you like to customize the layout that's used to display the data. To do that, you work in Source view since the Item template can't be displayed in Design view.

- The Item template is the only template that's required other than the Layout template. If editing and inserting are enabled, however, you must also include EditItem and InsertItem templates. See figure 16-14 for more information on these templates.

Figure 16-4   How to work with the Item template

How to provide for sorting

Figure 16-5 shows how you provide sorting for a ListView control. To do that, you add a button to the Layout template for each column you want to sort by. The ListView control in this figure, for example, provides for sorting by using link buttons in the column headers for the first three columns.

To indicate that a button should be used for sorting, you set the CommandName attribute of the button to Sort. Then, you set the CommandArgument attribute of the button to the name of the column in the data source that you want to sort by. If the user clicks the Product ID button in the ListView control shown here, for example, the products will be sorted by the ProductID column. Similarly, if the user clicks the Name button, the products will be sorted by the Name column.

You can also sort by two or more columns in the data source. To do that, you separate the column names with commas. You can see how this works in the link button for the Category column in this figure. If you click this button, the products will be sorted by the Name column within the CategoryID column.

By the way, the sort sequence that's used for a ListView control is the same as the sequence that's used for a GridView control. That is, the first time you click a sort button, the column is sorted in ascending sequence. The second time you click the button, the column is sorted in descending sequence. If a sort button sorts by two or more columns, only the last column toggles between ascending and descending sequence. The other columns are always sorted in ascending sequence.

Also like the GridView control, the ListView control doesn't actually do the sorting. Instead, it relies on the underlying data source to sort the data. As a result, sorting will only work if the DataSourceMode attribute for the data source is set to DataSet.

A ListView control that provides for sorting

Product ID	Name	Category	Unit Price	On Hand
pow01	Austin Powers	costumes	$79.99	25
frankc01	Frankenstein	costumes	$39.99	100
jar01	JarJar	costumes	$59.99	25
martian01	Martian	costumes	$69.99	100
super01	Superman	costumes	$39.99	100
bl01	Black light (24")	fx	$24.99	200
fogj01	Fog Juice (1qt)	fx	$9.99	500
fog01	Fog Machine	fx	$34.99	100
str01	Mini-strobe	fx	$13.99	200
skullfog01	Skull Fogger	fx	$39.95	50
vader01	Darth Vader Mask	masks	$19.99	100
fred01	Freddie	masks	$29.99	50

The Layout template for the ListView control

```
<LayoutTemplate>
  <table ID="itemPlaceholderContainer" runat="server"
         border="1" cellspacing="0" cellpadding="2">
    <tr runat="server" style="background-color: Silver">
      <th runat="server" style="width: 85px" align="left">
        <asp:LinkButton ID="lnkID" runat="server"
            CommandName="Sort" CommandArgument="ProductID">
            Product ID</asp:LinkButton></th>
      <th runat="server" style="width: 200px" align="left">
        <asp:LinkButton ID="lnkName" runat="server"
            CommandName="Sort" CommandArgument="Name">
            Name</asp:LinkButton></th>
      <th runat="server" style="width: 85px" align="left">
        <asp:LinkButton ID="lnkCategory" runat="server"
            CommandName="Sort" CommandArgument="CategoryID, Name">
            Category</asp:LinkButton></th>
      <th runat="server" style="width: 85px" align="right">
          Unit Price</th>
      <th runat="server" style="width: 85px" align="right">
          On Hand</th>
    </tr>
    <tr ID="itemPlaceholder" runat="server"></tr>
  </table>
</LayoutTemplate>
```

Description

- To sort the data in a ListView control, you add a button to the Layout template, set the button's CommandName attribute to Sort, and set its CommandArgument attribute to the name of the column you want to sort by. To sort by two or more columns, separate the column names with commas.

- For sorting to work, the DataSourceMode attribute of the data source must be set to DataSet.

Figure 16-5   How to provide for sorting

How to provide for paging

To provide paging for a ListView control, you use the new DataPager control. Figure 16-6 presents the basic skills for using this control. The easiest way to create this control is to select the Enable Paging option from the Configure ListView dialog box. When you do that, a drop-down list becomes available that lets you choose whether you want to add a *next/previous pager* or a *numeric pager*.

The ListView control at the top of this figure shows the default next/previous pager, and the first code example shows the aspx code for this pager. Notice that the DataPager control contains a Fields element. Within this element, you can code one or more NextPreviousPagerField or NumericPagerField elements. In this case, the Fields element includes a single NextPreviousPagerField element. You'll learn more about the attributes that you can code on this element in the next figure.

The second pager in this figure is a simple numeric pager. The aspx code for this pager contains a NumericPagerField element with no attributes. Because of that, the default settings for this element are used. That means that five page buttons are displayed, along with an ellipsis button (...) if additional pages are available.

A ListView control that uses a next/previous pager

Product ID	Name	Category	Unit Price	On Hand
hippie01	Hippie	masks	$79.99	40
jar01	JarJar	costumes	$59.99	25
martian01	Martian	costumes	$69.99	100
mum01	Mummy	masks	$39.99	30
pow01	Austin Powers	costumes	$79.99	25
rat01	Ugly Rat	props	$14.99	75
rat02	Uglier Rat	props	$19.99	50
skel01	Life Size Skeleton	props	$14.95	10
skullfog01	Skull Fogger	fx	$39.95	50
str01	Mini-strobe	fx	$13.99	200

First Previous Next Last

The aspx code for the next/previous pager

```
<asp:DataPager ID="DataPager1" runat="server">
    <Fields>
        <asp:NextPreviousPagerField ButtonType="Button"
            ShowFirstPageButton="True"
            ShowLastPageButton="True" />
    </Fields>
</asp:DataPager>
```

A numeric pager

1 2 3 4 5 ...

The aspx code for the numeric pager

```
<asp:DataPager ID="DataPager1" runat="server">
    <Fields>
        <asp:NumericPagerField />
    </Fields>
</asp:DataPager>
```

Description

- To provide paging for a ListView control, you use a DataPager control. To add a DataPager control to a ListView control, you can select the Enable Paging option in the Configure ListView dialog box and then select Next/Previous Pager or Numeric Pager from the drop-down list that's displayed.

- The DataPager control contains a Fields element that can contain two types of pager elements. The NextPreviousPagerField element can display first, previous, next, and last buttons. The NumericPagerField element can display page numbers as well as previous and next buttons.

- You can customize the appearance of a DataPager control by adding two or more pager elements to it. See figure 16-7 for more information.

- You can also create a DataPager control by dragging it from the Toolbox. When you do that, however, you have to add the Fields element and the pager elements manually.

Figure 16-6   How to provide for paging

How to customize paging

Figure 16-7 shows how you can customize a DataPager control. To do that, you use the attributes of the DataPager control and the NextPreviousPagerField and NumericPagerField elements shown in this figure. For example, to change the number of items that are displayed on each page, you set the PageSize attribute of the DataPager control.

Because the DataPager is a separate control, you don't have to place it inside the ListView control. Instead, you can place it anywhere you want on the page. If you do that, however, you need to set the PagedControlID attribute of the control. This attribute identifies the ListView control that it provides paging for.

By the way, the DataPager control can be used only with controls that implement the IPageableItemContainer interface. Currently, the ListView control is the only control that meets that criterion. In the future, however, I would expect other data-bound controls to implement this interface so their paging can be done from outside the controls.

The attributes of the NextPreviousPagerField element shown in this figure determine the type of buttons that are used in the pager and which buttons are displayed. The default is to display Previous and Next link buttons. Similarly, the attributes of the NumericPagerField element determine the type of buttons that are used and the number of buttons that are displayed. The default is to display five link buttons.

The code example in this figure shows a custom DataPager control that uses two next/previous pagers and one numeric pager. The resulting control is shown below this code. This should help you begin to see the flexibility that the DataPager control provides.

Attributes of the DataPager control

Attribute	Description
ID	The ID of the control.
Runat	Must specify "server."
PageSize	Specifies the number of items to be displayed on each page. The default is 10.
PagedControlID	The ID of the ListView control that the DataPager control provides paging for. Used only if the DataPager control is placed outside the ListView control.

Attributes of the NextPreviousPagerField element

Attribute	Description
ButtonType	The type of buttons to be used. You can specify Button, Image, or Link.
ShowFirstPageButton	Determines whether the first page button is displayed. The default is False.
ShowPreviousPageButton	Determines whether the previous page button is displayed. The default is True.
ShowNextPageButton	Determines whether the next page button is displayed. The default is True.
ShowLastPageButton	Determines whether the last page button is displayed. The default is False.

Attributes of the NumericPagerField element

Attribute	Description
ButtonCount	The maximum number of buttons to be displayed.
ButtonType	The type of buttons to be used. You can specify Button, Image, or Link.

Aspx code for a DataPager control that uses both types of pagers

```
<asp:DataPager ID="DataPager1" runat="server" PageSize="4">
    <Fields>
        <asp:NextPreviousPagerField ButtonType="Button"
            ShowFirstPageButton="True" ShowNextPageButton="False"
            ShowPreviousPageButton="False" />
        <asp:NumericPagerField ButtonCount="3" />
        <asp:NextPreviousPagerField ButtonType="Button"
            ShowLastPageButton="True" ShowNextPageButton="False"
            ShowPreviousPageButton="False" />
    </Fields>
</asp:DataPager>
```

The resulting DataPager control

Description

- You can use the PageSize attribute of the ListView control to specify the number of items to display on each page.

- You can place a DataPager control outside of the ListView control. Then, you must set the PagedControlID attribute of the DataPager control to the ID of the ListView control you want to use it with.

- The NextPreviousPagerField and NumericPagerField elements also have attributes that let you change the text or image for the buttons that are displayed.

Figure 16-7   How to customize paging

A list application that uses a ListView control

Now that you've learned the basic skills for working with a ListView control, the following topics present the design and code for an application that uses this control to display a list of products. If you compare this application with the list application in chapter 14 that uses a GridView control, you'll begin to see the flexibility that the ListView control provides.

The Product List application

Figure 16-8 presents the Product List application. Here, you can see that the first column in the ListView control contains the product name for each row in the Products table of the Halloween database. Then, the second column contains the headings for the other product columns that are included in the list, and the third column contains the data from each of the product columns. This type of layout wouldn't be possible with the GridView control.

You should also notice the DataPager control that's used with the ListView control. This control specifies that only four products should be displayed on each page. It's implemented using a next/previous pager with custom values for the text that's displayed on the buttons.

The Product List application

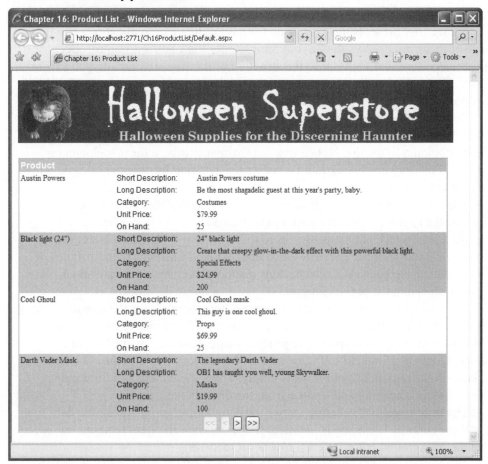

Description

- The ProductList application uses a ListView control to display a list of all the products in the Products table. The ListView control is bound to a SqlDataSource that works in DataSet mode.

- The ListView control uses Item and AlternatingItem templates to display every other row with a different background color.

- A DataPager control is used within the ListView control to display four products on each page.

Figure 16-8   The Product List application

The aspx file

Figure 16-9 presents the aspx code for the Product List application. The first page of this listing shows the Layout template for the ListView control. Because it has a structure that's similar to the structure of the Layout template you saw in figure 16-3, you shouldn't have any trouble understanding how it works. So I'll just point out a couple of differences.

First, the Th elements in the first row of the inner table have been replaced by a single Td element. This element contains the heading that's displayed for the first column in the list. Notice that the Colspan attribute for this element is set to 4. That way, the background color that's specified for the row is applied to all four columns of the row.

The second row in the outer table contains the DataPager control. As you can see, the PageSize attribute for this control has been set to 4. Then, a NextPreviousPagerField element is used to implement the control. Here, the FirstPageText, PreviousPageText, NextPageText, and LastPageText attributes of this element have been set so the buttons display less-than and greater-than signs as shown in the previous figure.

The second page of this listing shows the Item template for the control. Here, each item in the data source is represented by five rows, each with three columns. The first row displays the product name, followed by the "Short Description:" heading and the value of the ShortDescription column. The first column in the remaining four rows is empty. Then, the second and third columns contain a heading and a value from the data source.

The third page of this listing shows the AlternatingItem template for the ListView control. This code is identical to the code for the Item template except that the background color for each row is set to silver.

The SqlDataSource control is also shown on the third page of this listing. Notice here that the data source retrieves data from both the Products and Categories tables. The Categories table is included so the LongName column can be displayed instead of the CategoryID column from the Products table.

The Default.aspx file   **Page 1**

```
<%@ Page Language="C#" AutoEventWireup="true" CodeFile="Default.aspx.cs"
Inherits="_Default" %>

<!DOCTYPE html PUBLIC "-//W3C//DTD XHTML 1.0 Transitional//EN"
"http://www.w3.org/TR/xhtml1/DTD/xhtml1-transitional.dtd">

<html xmlns="http://www.w3.org/1999/xhtml">
<head runat="server">
    <title>Chapter 16: Product List</title>
</head>
<body>
  <form id="form1" runat="server">
  <div>
    <asp:Image ID="Image1" runat="server" ImageUrl="~/Images/banner.jpg" />
    <br /><br />
    <asp:ListView ID="ListView1" runat="server" DataKeyNames="ProductID"
        DataSourceID="SqlDataSource1">
      <LayoutTemplate>
        <table runat="server" border="1" cellspacing="0" cellpadding="0">
          <tr runat="server">
            <td runat="server">
              <table id="itemPlaceholderContainer" runat="server"
                    border="0" cellspacing="0" cellpadding="2">
                <tr runat="server" style="background-color: Silver">
                  <td runat="server" style="color: White;
                      font-family: Arial; font-size: 14px;
                      font-weight: bold" colspan="4">Product
                  </td>
                </tr>
                <tr ID="itemPlaceholder" runat="server"></tr>
              </table>
            </td>
          </tr>
          <tr runat="server" style="background-color: Silver" align="center">
            <td runat="server">
              <asp:DataPager ID="DataPager1" runat="server" PageSize="4">
                <Fields>
                  <asp:NextPreviousPagerField ButtonType="Button"
                      ShowFirstPageButton="True" ShowLastPageButton="True"
                      FirstPageText="&lt;&lt;" PreviousPageText="&lt;"
                      NextPageText="&gt;" LastPageText="&gt;&gt;" />
                </Fields>
              </asp:DataPager>
            </td>
          </tr>
        </table>
      </LayoutTemplate>
```

Figure 16-9   The aspx file for the Product List application (part 1 of 3)

The Default.aspx file

```
<ItemTemplate>
  <tr style="font-size: 12px">
    <td style="width: 150px">
      <asp:Label ID="NameLabel" runat="server"
          Text='<%# Eval("Name") %>' />
    <td style="width: 125px; font-family: Arial">Short Description:</td>
    <td style="width: 400px">
      <asp:Label ID="ShortDescriptionLabel" runat="server"
          Text='<%# Eval("ShortDescription") %>' /></td>
    </td>
  </tr>
  <tr style="font-size: 12px">
    <td></td>
    <td style="width: 125px; font-family: Arial">Long Description:</td>
    <td style="width: 400px">
      <asp:Label ID="LongDescriptionLabel" runat="server"
          Text='<%# Eval("LongDescription") %>' /></td>
  </tr>
  <tr style="font-size: 12px">
    <td></td>
    <td style="width: 125px; font-family: Arial">Category:</td>
    <td style="width: 400px">
      <asp:Label ID="CategoryIDLabel" runat="server"
          Text='<%# Eval("Category") %>' /></td>
  </tr>
  <tr style="font-size: 12px">
    <td></td>
    <td style="width: 125px; font-family: Arial">Unit Price:</td>
    <td style="width: 400px">
      <asp:Label ID="UnitPriceLabel" runat="server"
          Text='<%# Eval("UnitPrice", "{0:c}") %>' /></td>
  </tr>
  <tr style="font-size: 12px">
    <td></td>
    <td style="width: 125px; font-family: Arial">On Hand:</td>
    <td style="width: 400px">
      <asp:Label ID="OnHandLabel" runat="server"
          Text='<%# Eval("OnHand") %>' /></td>
  </tr>
</ItemTemplate>
```

Figure 16-9   The aspx file for the Product List application (part 2 of 3)

The Default.aspx file

```
    <AlternatingItemTemplate>
      <tr style="font-size: 12px; background-color: Silver">
        <td style="width: 150px">
          <asp:Label ID="NameLabel" runat="server"
            Text='<%# Eval("Name") %>' />
        <td style="width: 125px; font-family: Arial">Short Description:</td>
          <td style="width: 400px">
            <asp:Label ID="ShortDescriptionLabel" runat="server"
              Text='<%# Eval("ShortDescription") %>' /></td>
        </td>
      </tr>
      <tr style="font-size: 12px; background-color: Silver">
        <td></td>
        <td style="width: 125px; font-family: Arial">Long Description:</td>
        <td style="width: 400px">
          <asp:Label ID="LongDescriptionLabel" runat="server"
            Text='<%# Eval("LongDescription") %>' /></td>
      </tr>
      <tr style="font-size: 12px; background-color: Silver">
        <td></td>
        <td style="width: 125px; font-family: Arial">Category:</td>
        <td style="width: 400px">
          <asp:Label ID="CategoryIDLabel" runat="server"
            Text='<%# Eval("Category") %>' /></td>
      </tr>
      <tr style="font-size: 12px; background-color: Silver">
        <td></td>
        <td style="width: 125px; font-family: Arial">Unit Price:</td>
        <td style="width: 400px">
          <asp:Label ID="UnitPriceLabel" runat="server"
            Text='<%# Eval("UnitPrice", "{0:c}") %>' /></td>
      </tr>
      <tr style="font-size: 12px; background-color: Silver">
        <td></td>
        <td style="width: 125px; font-family: Arial">On Hand:</td>
        <td style="width: 400px">
          <asp:Label ID="OnHandLabel" runat="server"
            Text='<%# Eval("OnHand") %>' /></td>
      </tr>
    </AlternatingItemTemplate>
  </asp:ListView>
  <asp:SqlDataSource ID="SqlDataSource1" runat="server"
    ConnectionString="<%$ ConnectionStrings:HalloweenConnectionString %>"
    SelectCommand="SELECT Products.ProductID, Products.Name,
      Products.ShortDescription, Products.LongDescription,
      Categories.LongName AS Category, Products.UnitPrice,
      Products.OnHand FROM Products INNER JOIN Categories
      ON Products.CategoryID = Categories.CategoryID
      ORDER BY Products.Name">
  </asp:SqlDataSource>
  </div>
  </form>
</body>
</html>
```

Figure 16-9   The aspx file for the Product List application (part 3 of 3)

How to group ListView data

One of the most exciting features of the ListView control is its ability to group data so it's displayed in two or more columns. In the topics that follow, you'll learn the basic skills for grouping data, and you'll see a simple application that uses groups.

How to define the templates for a group

Figure 16-10 shows how to define the templates for a ListView control that uses groups. To start, you change the ID attribute for the inner table in the Layout template to groupPlaceholderContainer, and you change the ID attribute for the row within that table to groupPlaceholder. You can also use a different value for the ID attribute of the group placeholder by setting the GroupPlaceholderID attribute of the ListView control to that value.

Next, you add a Group template to the control. In most cases, this template will contain a single row with its ID set to itemPlaceholderContainer. Then, you can set the ID attribute for the single cell within that row to itemPlaceholder. When the application is run, the Item template will replace the item placeholder, and the group template will replace the group placeholder.

Finally, you set the GroupItemCount attribute of the ListView control to the number of items you want to include in each group. In this example, I set this attribute to 2. The result is shown at the top of this figure. Note that although the Item template for the ListView control isn't shown in this figure, you should be able to figure out its basic content by looking at the data for each product in the control. If you have trouble understanding how this works, however, it should become clearer when you see the complete application that's presented next.

Although you can modify a ListView control so it uses groups as I just described, you may find it easier to generate the basic code for the groups and then modify that code to customize the display. To do that, you can select the Tiled layout from the Configure ListView dialog box. Then, the ListView control is configured with Layout and Group templates like the ones shown here. In addition, the GroupItemCount attribute of the control is set to 3, and the Item template is formatted so it appears as shown in the ListView control at the top of this figure.

The beginning of a ListView control with two columns

Name: Austin Powers
ShortDescription: Austin Powers costume
LongName: Costumes
UnitPrice: $79.99
OnHand: 25

Name: Black light (24")
ShortDescription: 24" black light
LongName: Special Effects
UnitPrice: $24.99
OnHand: 200

Name: Cool Ghoul
ShortDescription: Cool Ghoul mask
LongName: Props
UnitPrice: $69.99
OnHand: 25

Name: Darth Vader Mask
ShortDescription: The legendary Darth Vader
LongName: Masks
UnitPrice: $19.99
OnHand: 100

The Layout and Group templates for the control

```
<asp:ListView ID="ListView1" runat="server" DataSourceID="SqlDataSource1"
    GroupItemCount="2">
    <LayoutTemplate>
        <table runat="server">
            <tr runat="server">
                <td runat="server">
                    <table ID="groupPlaceholderContainer" runat="server"
                        border="0" style="">
                    <tr ID="groupPlaceholder" runat="server"></tr>
                    </table>
                </td>
            </tr>
            .
            .
            .
        </table>
    </LayoutTemplate>
    <GroupTemplate>
        <tr ID="itemPlaceholderContainer" runat="server">
            <td ID="itemPlaceholder" runat="server">
            </td>
        </tr>
    </GroupTemplate>
    <ItemTemplate>
        .
        .
        .
    </ItemTemplate>
</asp:ListView>
```

Description

- You can use the Group template to display items in two or more columns. Then, the Group template replaces the element in the Layout template that has the ID "groupPlaceholder," and the Group template contains an element with the ID "itemPlaceholder" that's replaced by the Item template.

- To determine the number of columns in the group, you set the GroupItemCount attribute of the ListView control.

- The easiest way to create a Group template is to select the Tiled layout from the Configure ListView dialog box. Then, a group with three columns is created, and you can modify the aspx code to format the control any way you like.

Figure 16-10   How to define the templates for a group

A Product List application that uses groups

To illustrate how you can use groups, figure 16-11 presents a Product List application that uses groups. As you can see, this application displays the name and image for each product, and the products are displayed in three columns. Although this is a simple application, it should help you see how valuable using groups can be.

The aspx file for the grouped Product List application

Figure 16-12 presents the code for the grouped Product List application. The first thing you should notice here is that the GroupItemCount attribute of the ListView control is set to 3. This causes three items from the data source to be displayed in each row of the ListView control.

The second thing you should notice is that the Layout template includes a table row that acts as the group placeholder. This placeholder will be replaced by the Group template, which you can see at the bottom of the first page of this listing. The Group template, in turn, contains a single table row with a single cell that acts as the item placeholder.

The second page of this listing shows the Item template for the ListView control. Notice that because the item placeholder in the Group template is a table cell, the Item template must begin with a table cell. Then, a table with two rows is coded within this cell. The first row contains a column with a label that's bound to the Name column of the data source, and the second row contains a column with an image that's bound to the ImageFile column of the data source. Notice that the binding expression that's used for the image includes the path to the image file. That's necessary because the ImageFile column contains only the file name, not the path.

The SqlDataSource control that the ListView control is bound to is also shown on the second page of this listing. This data source simply retrieves the Name and ImageFile columns from the Products table and sorts the rows that are returned by the Name column.

The grouped Product List application

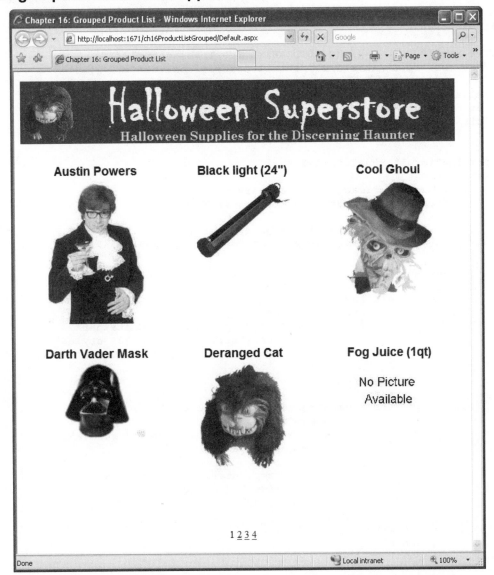

Description

- The grouped Product List application uses a ListView control to display the names and images of the products in the Products table. The products are grouped so that three products are displayed in each row.

- Although this application simply displays the product names and images, you could easily modify it to display additional information or to perform additional processing.

Figure 16-11   A Product List application that uses groups

The Default.aspx file   **Page 1**

```
<%@ Page Language="C#" AutoEventWireup="true" CodeFile="Default.aspx.cs"
Inherits="_Default" %>

<!DOCTYPE html PUBLIC "-//W3C//DTD XHTML 1.0 Transitional//EN"
"http://www.w3.org/TR/xhtml1/DTD/xhtml1-transitional.dtd">

<html xmlns="http://www.w3.org/1999/xhtml">
<head runat="server">
    <title>Chapter 16: Grouped Product List</title>
</head>
<body>
    <form id="form1" runat="server">
    <div>
        <asp:Image ID="Image2" runat="server"
            ImageUrl="~/Images/banner.jpg" /><br />

        <asp:ListView ID="ListView1" runat="server"
            DataSourceID="SqlDataSource1" GroupItemCount="3">

        <LayoutTemplate>
            <table runat="server">
                <tr runat="server">
                    <td runat="server">
                        <table ID="groupPlaceholderContainer"
                                runat="server" border="0" style="">
                            <tr ID="groupPlaceholder" runat="server"></tr>
                        </table>
                    </td>
                </tr>
                <tr runat="server" align="center">
                    <td runat="server">
                        <asp:DataPager ID="DataPager1" runat="server"
                            PageSize="6">
                            <Fields>
                                <asp:NumericPagerField />
                            </Fields>
                        </asp:DataPager>
                    </td>
                </tr>
            </table>
        </LayoutTemplate>

        <GroupTemplate>
            <tr ID="itemPlaceholderContainer" runat="server">
                <td ID="itemPlaceholder" runat="server">
                </td>
            </tr>
        </GroupTemplate>
```

Figure 16-12   The aspx file for the grouped Product List application (part 1 of 2)

The Default.aspx file   **Page 2**

```
        <ItemTemplate>
            <td>
                <table>
                    <tr>
                        <td style="font-size: 14pt;
                            font-family: Arial, Sans-Serif;
                            font-weight: bold" align="center"
                            valign="top">
                            <asp:Label ID="NameLabel" runat="server"
                                Text='<%# Eval("Name") %>' />
                        </td>
                    </tr>
                    <tr>
                        <td style="height: 250px; width: 250px"
                            align="center" valign="top">
                            <asp:Image ID="Image1" runat="server"
                                ImageUrl='<%#"~/Images/Products/" +
                                        Eval("ImageFile") %>' />
                        </td>
                    </tr>
                </table>
            </td>
        </ItemTemplate>
    </asp:ListView>

    <asp:SqlDataSource ID="SqlDataSource1" runat="server"
        ConnectionString="<%$ ConnectionStrings:HalloweenConnectionString %>"
        SelectCommand="SELECT [Name], [ImageFile] FROM [Products]
                    ORDER BY [Name]">
    </asp:SqlDataSource>

    </div>
    </form>
</body>
</html>
```

Figure 16-12   The aspx file for the grouped Product List application (part 2 of 2)

How to update ListView data

To update ListView data, you use the EditItem and InsertItem templates. I'll show you how to use these templates in just a minute. But first, I want to describe the various buttons you can use to work with data in a ListView control.

How to use buttons to perform update operations

You may recall that when you use a FormView control or a DetailsView control with templates to update data, the templates include buttons that let you insert, update, and delete data. You also use buttons to perform these operations using a ListView control. Although the buttons you need are generated automatically when you configure a ListView control, you will better understand how the ListView control works if you understand these buttons.

When the user clicks a button in a ListView control, the operation that's performed is determined by the value of the button's CommandName attribute. Figure 16-13 lists the predefined values for this attribute and describes their functions. For the most part, these values should be self-explanatory. For example, if the user clicks a button whose CommandName attribute is set to Edit, the row that contains that button is placed in edit mode. In that mode, the row is displayed using the EditItem template. As you'll see in a minute, the EditItem template contains buttons whose CommandName attributes are set to Update and Cancel. Then, if the user changes the data in that row and clicks the update button, the row in the database is updated. If the user clicks the cancel button instead, the original data is redisplayed using the Item template.

Notice that the ListView control can also contain a button whose CommandName attribute is set to Select. When this button is clicked, the selected row is displayed using the SelectedItem template. You can use a button like this to create a Master/Detail page like the one you saw in chapter 15 using a ListView control rather than a GridView control.

Buttons for working with the data in a ListView control

CommandName attribute	Description
Edit	Switches the ListView control to edit mode and displays the data using the EditItem template.
Update	In edit mode, saves the contents of the data-bound controls to the data source.
Cancel	Cancels the current operation. If a row is being edited, the original data is displayed using the Item template. If a row is being inserted, an empty InsertItem template is displayed.
Delete	Deletes the item from the data source.
Insert	Inserts the contents of the data-bound controls into the data source.
Select	Displays the contents of the data-bound controls using the SelectedItem template.

The aspx code for the Edit and Delete buttons in an Item template

```
<asp:Button ID="DeleteButton" runat="server"
    CommandName="Delete" Text="Delete" />
<asp:Button ID="EditButton" runat="server"
    CommandName="Edit" Text="Edit" />
```

Description

- To work with the data in a ListView control, you can use buttons whose CommandName attributes are set to predefined values. Then, when the user clicks these buttons, they perform the functions shown above.

- Although you must set the CommandName attribute to one of the values shown above to perform the associated function, you can set the Text attribute to anything you like.

- You can also create buttons that perform custom functions by setting the CommandName attribute to a custom value. Then, you can use the ItemCommand event of the ListView control to determine which button was clicked and perform the appropriate action.

Figure 16-13   How to use buttons to perform update operations

How to work with the EditItem and InsertItem templates

To help you understand how the EditItem and InsertItem templates work, figure 16-14 presents these templates for the ListView control you saw back in figure 16-1. This control was used to maintain the data in the Categories table of the Halloween database.

If you review the code for the EditItem template, you'll see that it includes two buttons whose CommandName attributes are set to Update and Cancel. Then, it includes a bound control for each of the three columns in the data source. The first column, CategoryID, is displayed in a label and is bound using the Eval method. That makes sense because this is the primary key for the table and shouldn't be changed. The other two columns, ShortName and LongName, are displayed in text boxes that are bound using the Bind method so they can be changed.

The InsertItem template is similar. Instead of update and cancel buttons, however, it includes insert and cancel buttons. Notice that although the CommandName attribute for the cancel button is set to Cancel just like it is for the cancel button in the EditItem template, the Text attribute is set to Clear instead of Cancel. That better describes what happens when this button is clicked. Also notice that all three columns in the data source are displayed in text boxes that are bound using the Bind method. That makes sense because all three values are required for a new category.

How to use events raised by the ListView control

The ListView control raises many of the same events as the DetailsView and FormView controls. For example, the ItemUpdating event is raised before an item is updated, and the ItemUpdated event is raised after an item has been updated. Similarly, the ItemInserting event is raised before an item is inserted, and the ItemInserted event is raised after an item has been inserted. And the ItemDeleting event is raised before an item is deleted, and the ItemDeleted event is raised after an item has been deleted. You'll typically use the before events to provide data validation, and you'll use the after events to check that the operation was successful. You'll see how some of these events are used in the maintenance application that follows.

The EditItem template for the ListView control in figure 16-1

```
<EditItemTemplate>
    <tr style="">
        <td>
            <asp:Button ID="UpdateButton" runat="server"
                CommandName="Update" Text="Update" />
            <asp:Button ID="CancelButton" runat="server"
                CommandName="Cancel" Text="Cancel" /></td>
        <td>
            <asp:Label ID="CategoryIDLabel1" runat="server"
                Text='<%# Eval("CategoryID") %>' /></td>
        <td>
            <asp:TextBox ID="ShortNameTextBox" runat="server"
                Text='<%# Bind("ShortName") %>' /></td>
        <td>
            <asp:TextBox ID="LongNameTextBox" runat="server"
                Text='<%# Bind("LongName") %>' /></td>
    </tr>
</EditItemTemplate>
```

The InsertItem template for the ListView control in figure 16-1

```
<InsertItemTemplate>
    <tr style="">
        <td>
            <asp:Button ID="InsertButton" runat="server"
                CommandName="Insert" Text="Insert" />
            <asp:Button ID="CancelButton" runat="server"
                CommandName="Cancel" Text="Clear" /></td>
        <td>
            <asp:TextBox ID="CategoryIDTextBox" runat="server"
                Text='<%# Bind("CategoryID") %>' /></td>
        <td>
            <asp:TextBox ID="ShortNameTextBox" runat="server"
                Text='<%# Bind("ShortName") %>' /></td>
        <td>
            <asp:TextBox ID="LongNameTextBox" runat="server"
                Text='<%# Bind("LongName") %>' /></td>
    </tr>
</InsertItemTemplate>
```

Description

- The EditItem template determines how an item in the ListView control is rendered in edit mode. By default, it includes a label for each column in the data source that can't be modified and a text box for each column in the data source that can be modified. These controls are bound to the columns of the data source using the Eval and Bind methods.

- The InsertItem template is similar to the EditItem template. It determines the content that's rendered for a new item that's being inserted.

- The EditItem template also includes update and cancel buttons by default, and the InsertItem template includes insert and cancel buttons.

Figure 16-14   How to work with the EditItem and InsertItem templates

A maintenance application that uses a ListView control

To give you a better idea of how you can use a ListView control to insert, update, and delete data, the topics that follow present an application that maintains the Categories table in the Halloween database. This application uses an enhanced version of the ListView control you saw in figure 16-1.

The Category Maintenance application

Figure 16-15 presents the Category Maintenance application. It uses a ListView control to display the rows in the Categories table using the Item and AlternatingItem templates, which include Edit and Delete buttons. Here, the user has clicked the button for the third category, so that row is displayed using the EditItem template. Then, the user can modify the data and click the Update button to save the changes to the database. Or, the user can click the Cancel button to cancel the changes and redisplay the original data.

The last row in the ListView control is displayed using the InsertItem template. This template lets the user enter the data for a new category into text boxes. Then, if the user clicks the Insert button, the new row is added to the database. If the user clicks the Clear button after entering data, though, the text boxes are cleared.

Note that required field validators are used for each text box in the EditItem and InsertItem templates. Then, if an error occurs, an asterisk is displayed to the right of the text box, and a message is displayed in the ValidationSummary control below the ListView control.

Before I go on, I want to point out that this application doesn't illustrate the formatting flexibility of the ListView control. In fact, except for the location of the buttons in this control, it looks almost identical to the GridView control used by the Category Maintenance application in chapter 14. However, it does illustrate the built-in capability to insert rows into a data source.

The Category Maintenance application

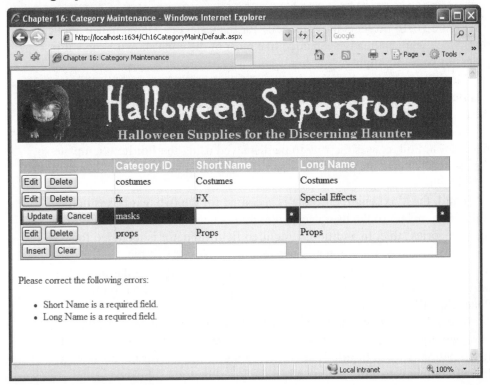

Description

- The Category Maintenance application uses a ListView control to let the user update, delete, or insert rows in the Categories table.

- To edit a category, the user clicks the Edit button for that category. This places the row for that category into edit mode. The user can then change the Short Name or Long Name and click the Update button. Or, the user can click the Cancel button to leave edit mode without performing the update.

- To delete a category, the user clicks the Delete button for that category.

- To add a category, the user enters a Category ID, Short Name, and Long Name into the last row of the ListView control and then clicks the Insert button. Or, the user can click the Clear button to clear the entries without adding the category.

- If the user attempts to update or add a row with a column that is blank, an error message is displayed in a ValidationSummary control.

Figure 16-15   The Category Maintenance application

The aspx file

Figure 16-16 presents the aspx code for the Category Maintenance application. Since you've already seen code like most of the code shown here, I'll just point out some highlights.

First, the InsertItemPosition attribute of the ListView control is set to LastItem. That causes the InsertItem template to be displayed at the bottom of the ListView control, as you saw in the previous figure.

Second, the Item and AlternatingItem templates contain two buttons. The first button, Edit, causes the row to be displayed using the EditItem template so the user can change the data for the row. The second button, Delete, lets the user delete the row.

Third, the MaxLength attribute is specified for the two text boxes in the EditItem template so the user can't enter more characters than are allowed by the Categories table. In addition, a required field validator is included for each text box so the user must enter values into them. Notice that the ValidationGroup attribute of these validators as well as the ValidationGroup attribute of the Update button is set to Edit. That way, the validation will be done when the user clicks the Update button.

The validation that's performed by the InsertItem template is similar. However, the ValidationGroup attribute for the required field validators and the Insert button is set to Insert. That way, only the validation for the controls in the InsertItem template will be done when the Insert button is clicked.

Fourth, this ListView control contains an EmptyData template. This template is displayed if no data is returned by the data source. Although it's not likely that the Categories table will be empty, this template is typically included for completeness.

Fifth, the SqlDataSource for this application doesn't use optimistic concurrency. Unfortunately, there appears to be a bug in the ListView control that doesn't let you use optimistic concurrency for delete operations. Hopefully, this bug will be corrected in an upcoming Service Pack for Visual Studio.

Finally, two ValidationSummary controls are included following the SqlDataSource control. Because the ValidationGroup attribute for the first control is set to Edit, it will be used to display errors that are detected when a row is being updated. In contrast, the ValidationGroup attribute for the second control is set to Insert, so it will be used to display errors that are detected when a row is being inserted.

The code-behind file

Figure 16-17 presents the code-behind file for the Category Maintenance application. This code is similar to the code for the maintenance applications you saw in the last two chapters, so you shouldn't have any trouble understanding how it works.

The Default.aspx file

```
<%@ Page Language="C#" AutoEventWireup="true" CodeFile="Default.aspx.cs"
Inherits="_Default" %>

<!DOCTYPE html PUBLIC "-//W3C//DTD XHTML 1.0 Transitional//EN"
"http://www.w3.org/TR/xhtml1/DTD/xhtml1-transitional.dtd">

<html xmlns="http://www.w3.org/1999/xhtml">
<head runat="server">
    <title>Chapter 16: Category Maintenance</title>
</head>
<body>
  <form id="form1" runat="server">
  <div>
    <asp:Image ID="Image1" runat="server" ImageUrl="~/Images/banner.jpg" />
    <br /><br />
    <asp:ListView ID="ListView1" runat="server" DataKeyNames="CategoryID"
        DataSourceID="SqlDataSource1" InsertItemPosition="LastItem">
      <LayoutTemplate>
        <table runat="server">
          <tr runat="server">
            <td runat="server">
              <table ID="itemPlaceholderContainer" runat="server" border="1"
                style="border-color: Silver; border-collapse: collapse">
                <tr runat="server" style="background-color: Silver;
                    color: White; font-family: Arial, Sans-Serif;
                    font-weight: bold;">
                  <td runat="server"></td>
                  <td runat="server">Category ID</td>
                  <td runat="server">Short Name</td>
                  <td runat="server">Long Name</td>
                </tr>
                <tr ID="itemPlaceholder" runat="server"></tr>
              </table>
            </td>
          </tr>
        </table>
      </LayoutTemplate>
      <ItemTemplate>
        <tr style="background-color: White; color: Black">
          <td style="width: 150px">
            <asp:Button ID="EditButton" runat="server" CommandName="Edit"
                Text="Edit" CausesValidation="false" />
            <asp:Button ID="DeleteButton" runat="server" CommandName="Delete"
                Text="Delete" CausesValidation="false" /></td>
          <td style="width: 125px">
            <asp:Label ID="CategoryIDLabel" runat="server"
                Text='<%# Eval("CategoryID") %>' /></td>
          <td style="width: 165px">
            <asp:Label ID="ShortNameLabel" runat="server"
                Text='<%# Eval("ShortName") %>' /></td>
          <td style="width: 240px">
            <asp:Label ID="LongNameLabel" runat="server"
                Text='<%# Eval("LongName") %>' /></td>
        </tr>
      </ItemTemplate>
```

Figure 16-16   The aspx file for the Category Maintenance application (part 1 of 4)

The Default.aspx file

```
<AlternatingItemTemplate>
  <tr style="background-color: #F5F5F5; color: Black">
    <td style="width: 150px">
      <asp:Button ID="EditButton" runat="server" CommandName="Edit"
        Text="Edit" CausesValidation="false" />
      <asp:Button ID="DeleteButton" runat="server" CommandName="Delete"
        Text="Delete" CausesValidation="false" /></td>
    <td style="width: 125px">
      <asp:Label ID="CategoryIDLabel" runat="server"
        Text='<%# Eval("CategoryID") %>' /></td>
    <td style="width: 165px">
      <asp:Label ID="ShortNameLabel" runat="server"
        Text='<%# Eval("ShortName") %>' /></td>
    <td style="width: 240px">
      <asp:Label ID="LongNameLabel" runat="server"
        Text='<%# Eval("LongName") %>' /></td>
  </tr>
</AlternatingItemTemplate>
<EditItemTemplate>
  <tr style="background-color: Blue; color: White">
    <td style="width: 150px">
      <asp:Button ID="UpdateButton" runat="server"
        CommandName="Update" Text="Update"
        ValidationGroup="Edit" />
      <asp:Button ID="CancelButton" runat="server"
        CommandName="Cancel" Text="Cancel" />
    </td>
    <td style="width: 125px">
      <asp:Label ID="lblCategoryID" runat="server"
        Text='<%# Eval("CategoryID") %>' /></td>
    <td style="width: 165px">
      <asp:TextBox ID="txtEditShortName" runat="server"
        Text='<%# Bind("ShortName") %>' Width="140px"
        MaxLength="15" />
      <asp:RequiredFieldValidator ID="RequiredFieldValidator1"
        runat="server" ControlToValidate="txtEditShortName"
        ErrorMessage="Short Name is a required field."
        Text="*" ForeColor="White" ValidationGroup="Edit">
      </asp:RequiredFieldValidator></td>
    <td style="width: 240px">
      <asp:TextBox ID="txtEditLongName" runat="server"
        Text='<%# Bind("LongName") %>' Width="215px"
        MaxLength="50" />
      <asp:RequiredFieldValidator ID="RequiredFieldValidator2"
        runat="server" ControlToValidate="txtEditLongName"
        ErrorMessage="Long Name is a required field."
        Text="*" ForeColor="White" ValidationGroup="Edit">
      </asp:RequiredFieldValidator></td>
  </tr>
</EditItemTemplate>
```

Figure 16-16　The aspx file for the Category Maintenance application (part 2 of 4)

The Default.aspx file   **Page 3**

```
<InsertItemTemplate>
  <tr style="background-color: Silver">
    <td style="width: 150px">
      <asp:Button ID="InsertButton" runat="server"
          CommandName="Insert" Text="Insert"
          ValidationGroup="Insert" />
      <asp:Button ID="CancelButton" runat="server"
          CommandName="Cancel" Text="Clear" />
    </td>
    <td style="width: 125px">
      <asp:TextBox ID="txtInsertCategoryID" runat="server"
          Text='<%# Bind("CategoryID") %>' Width="100px"
          MaxLength="10" />
      <asp:RequiredFieldValidator ID="RequiredFieldValidator3"
          runat="server" ControlToValidate="txtInsertCategoryID"
          ErrorMessage="Category ID is a required field."
          Text="*" ForeColor="White" ValidationGroup="Insert">
      </asp:RequiredFieldValidator>
    </td>
    <td style="width: 165px">
      <asp:TextBox ID="txtInsertShortName" runat="server"
          Text='<%# Bind("ShortName") %>' Width="140px"
          MaxLength="15" />
      <asp:RequiredFieldValidator ID="RequiredFieldValidator4"
          runat="server" ControlToValidate="txtInsertShortName"
          ErrorMessage="Short Name is a required field."
          Text="*" ForeColor="White" ValidationGroup="Insert">
      </asp:RequiredFieldValidator>
    </td>
    <td style="width: 240px">
      <asp:TextBox ID="txtInsertLongName" runat="server"
          Text='<%# Bind("LongName") %>' Width="215px"
          MaxLength="50" />
      <asp:RequiredFieldValidator ID="RequiredFieldValidator5"
          runat="server" ControlToValidate="txtInsertLongName"
          ErrorMessage="Long Name is a required field."
          Text="*" ForeColor="White" ValidationGroup="Insert">
      </asp:RequiredFieldValidator>
    </td>
  </tr>
</InsertItemTemplate>
<EmptyDataTemplate>
  <table runat="server" style="background-color: #FFFFFF;
          border-collapse: collapse; border-color: #999999;
          border-style: none; border-width: 1px">
    <tr>
      <td>
        No data was returned.
      </td>
    </tr>
  </table>
</EmptyDataTemplate>
</asp:ListView>
```

Figure 16-16   The aspx file for the Category Maintenance application (part 3 of 4)

The Default.aspx file   **Page 4**

```
<asp:SqlDataSource ID="SqlDataSource1" runat="server"
    ConnectionString="<%$ ConnectionStrings:HalloweenConnectionString %>"
    SelectCommand="SELECT [CategoryID], [ShortName], [LongName]
        FROM [Categories] ORDER BY [CategoryID]"
    DeleteCommand="DELETE FROM [Categories]
        WHERE [CategoryID] = @CategoryID"
    InsertCommand="INSERT INTO [Categories]
        ([CategoryID], [ShortName], [LongName])
        VALUES (@CategoryID, @ShortName, @LongName)"
    UpdateCommand="UPDATE [Categories]
        SET [ShortName] = @ShortName,
            [LongName] = @LongName
        WHERE [CategoryID] = @CategoryID">
    <DeleteParameters>
      <asp:Parameter Name="CategoryID" Type="String" />
    </DeleteParameters>
    <UpdateParameters>
      <asp:Parameter Name="ShortName" Type="String" />
      <asp:Parameter Name="LongName" Type="String" />
      <asp:Parameter Name="CategoryID" Type="String" />
    </UpdateParameters>
    <InsertParameters>
      <asp:Parameter Name="CategoryID" Type="String" />
      <asp:Parameter Name="ShortName" Type="String" />
      <asp:Parameter Name="LongName" Type="String" />
    </InsertParameters>
  </asp:SqlDataSource>
  <br />
  <asp:ValidationSummary ID="ValidationSummary1" runat="server"
      HeaderText="Please correct the following errors:"
      ValidationGroup="Edit" />
  <asp:ValidationSummary ID="ValidationSummary2" runat="server"
      HeaderText="Please correct the following errors:"
      ValidationGroup="Insert" />
  <asp:Label ID="lblError" runat="server" ForeColor="Red"
      EnableViewState="False"></asp:Label>
  </div>
  </form>
</body>
</html>
```

Figure 16-16   The aspx file for the Category Maintenance application (part 4 of 4)

The Default.aspx.cs file

```
public partial class _Default : System.Web.UI.Page
{
    protected void ListView1_ItemUpdated(
        object sender, ListViewUpdatedEventArgs e)
    {
        if (e.Exception != null)
        {
            lblError.Text = "A database error has occurred.<br /><br />" +
                "Message: " + e.Exception.Message;
            e.ExceptionHandled = true;
        }
        else if (e.AffectedRows == 0)
        {
            lblError.Text = "Another user may have updated that category." +
                "<br />Please try again.";
        }
    }
    protected void ListView1_ItemDeleted(
        object sender, ListViewDeletedEventArgs e)
    {
        if (e.Exception != null)
        {
            lblError.Text = "A database error has occurred.<br /><br />" +
                "Message: " + e.Exception.Message;
            e.ExceptionHandled = true;
        }
        else if (e.AffectedRows == 0)
        {
            lblError.Text = "Another user may have updated that category." +
                "<br />Please try again.";
        }
    }
    protected void ListView1_ItemInserted(
        object sender, ListViewInsertedEventArgs e)
    {
        if (e.Exception != null)
        {
            lblError.Text = "A database error has occurred.<br /><br />" +
                "Message: " + e.Exception.Message;
            e.ExceptionHandled = true;
        }
    }
}
```

Figure 16-17   The code-behind file for the Category Maintenance application

Perspective

In this chapter, you've seen three different applications that demonstrate important features of the ListView control. The Product List application demonstrates its formatting capabilities. The grouped Product List application demonstrates its grouping capabilities. And the Category Maintenance application demonstrates its insert, update, and delete capabilities. In addition, both of the Product List applications demonstrate the use of the DataPager control. With these applications to guide you, you should now be able to use these controls in your own applications.

Up to this point, all of the database applications presented in this book have relied heavily on data binding that's defined in the aspx code, using C# code only for data validation and exception handling. However, ASP.NET also has powerful features for working with data access classes written with custom code. In the next chapter, then, you'll learn how the ObjectDataSource control lets you use data-bound controls such as the GridView, DetailsView, FormView, and ListView controls with custom data access classes.

Terms

next/previous pager
numeric pager

17

How to use object data sources

This chapter is designed to introduce you to the use of object data sources as an alternative to the Access or SQL data sources that you've already learned about. The benefit of using object data sources is that they let you use a three-layer design in which the data access code is kept in data access classes. This lets you separate the presentation code from the data access code, but still lets you use the data binding features of ASP.NET.

To write the data access classes that are used with object data sources, you need to be able to use ADO.NET, which isn't presented in this book. But even if you don't understand ADO.NET, this chapter will show you how to use object data sources with existing data access classes. Then, you'll be able to decide whether you want to use object data sources in your applications and whether you want to learn how to use ADO.NET.

An introduction to object data sources **546**
How 3-layer applications work in ASP.NET 546
How to use the ObjectDataSource control 548
How to configure an ObjectDataSource control 550
How to work with bound controls 550

A Product List application **552**
The aspx file 554
The ProductDB class 556

How to create a data access class **558**
How to design a data access class 558
How to create a select method 560
How to create update, delete, and insert methods 562
How to use attributes to mark a data access class 564

A Category Maintenance application **566**
The design 566
The aspx file 566
The code-behind file 570
The CategoryDB class 572

How to use business objects with object data sources .. **576**
How to create methods that use business objects 576
The aspx file for a Category Maintenance application that uses
business objects 578
The Category business class 580
A CategoryDB class that uses business objects 580

How to use paging with object data sources **584**
How to create an ObjectDataSource control that provides for paging 584
How to create a data access class that provides for paging 586

Perspective **588**

An introduction to object data sources

The following topics introduce you to object data sources and the 3-layer architecture that they let you implement.

How 3-layer applications work in ASP.NET

As you probably know, most development experts recommend a *3-layer architecture* for web applications that separates the presentation, business rules, and data access components of the application. The *presentation layer* includes the web pages that define the user interface. The *middle layer* includes the classes that manage the data access for those objects, and it may also include classes that implement business rules such as data validation requirements or discount policies. The *database layer* consists of the database itself.

In this chapter, you'll learn how to use *object data sources* to implement the 3-layer architecture. Figure 17-1 shows how this works. Here, you can see that the ObjectDataSource control serves as an interface between the data-bound controls in the presentation layer and the *data access classes* in the middle layer.

When you use an ObjectDataSource control, you must create a data access class to handle the data access for the control. This class provides at least one method that retrieves data from the database and returns it in a form that the ObjectDataSource control can handle. It can also provide methods to insert, update, and delete data. The data access class should be placed in the application's App_Code folder.

When you code a data access class, you can use any techniques you want to access the database. In this chapter, for example, you'll see data access classes that use the ADO.NET classes that were introduced with .NET 1.0. These classes can be used to get data from a SQL Server database, from other types of databases such as Oracle or MySQL databases, or from other sources such as XML or plain text files.

If you have already developed data access classes for the database used by your application, you may be able to use those classes with an object data source. Often, though, it's better to develop the data access classes specifically for the ObjectDataSource controls that you're going to use. That way, you can design each class so it works as efficiently as possible.

Incidentally, Microsoft uses both the term *business object class* and the term *data object class* to refer to a class that provides data access for an object data source. In this chapter, though, I used the term *data access class* for this type of class because if you use static methods to provide the data access functions, an object is never instantiated from the class.

Also, you may be accustomed to using the term *3-tier architecture* for the *3-layer architecture* that's described in figure 17-1. Because some people use *3-tier* to refer to an architecture that puts the 3 layers on three different physical devices, though, I've used the term *3-layer* in this chapter. Although you could put each of the 3 layers on 3 separate devices, you don't have to.

The 3-layer architecture in ASP.NET

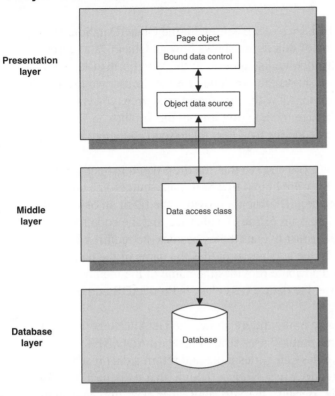

The three layers

- The **presentation layer** consists of the ASP.NET pages that manage the appearance of the application. This layer can include bound data controls and ObjectDataSource controls that bind the data controls to the data.

- The **middle layer** contains the *data access classes* that manage the data access for the application. This layer can also contain business classes that represent business entities such as customers, products, or employees and that implement business rules such as credit and discount policies.

- The **database layer** consists of the database that contains the data for the application. Ideally, the SQL statements that do the database access should be saved in stored procedures within the database, but the SQL statements are often stored in the data access classes.

Description

- An *object data source* is implemented by the ObjectDataSource control, which lets you use data binding with the *3-layer architecture* for a database application.

- An object data source is similar to a SQL data source. However, instead of directly accessing a database, the object data source gets its data through a data access class that handles the details of database access.

Figure 17-1   How 3-layer applications work in ASP.NET

How to use the ObjectDataSource control

Figure 17-2 presents the basics of working with the ObjectDataSource control. The image at the top of this figure shows how an ObjectDataSource control that's bound to a drop-down list appears in the Web Forms Designer. Then, the first code example shows the aspx code for the drop-down list and the object data source it's bound to. As with any other data source, you can add an object data source to a web page by dragging it from the Toolbox in Design view or by entering the aspx code for the ObjectDataSource element in Source view.

In the first code example, you can see that the drop-down list is bound to the object data source just as if it were bound to a SQL data source. The only difference is that the DataSourceID attribute provides the ID of an object data source rather than a SQL data source. You can also see that the code for the ObjectDataSource control has just two attributes besides the required ID and Runat attributes. The TypeName attribute provides the name of the data access class, and the SelectMethod attribute provides the name of the method used to retrieve the data. In this case, the data access class is ProductDB and the select method is GetAllCategories.

The second code example in this figure shows the GetAllCategories method of the ProductDB class. This method uses straightforward ADO.NET code to retrieve category rows from the Categories table and return a data reader that can be used to read the category rows. Notice, though, that the return type for this method is IEnumerable. Because the SqlDataReader class implements the IEnumerable interface, a data reader is a valid return object for this method. (You'll learn more about the return types that are acceptable for a select method in figure 17-8.)

A drop-down list bound to an ObjectDataSource control

The code for the drop-down list and the ObjectDataSource control

```
<asp:DropDownList ID="ddlCategories" runat="server" AutoPostBack="True"
    DataSourceID="ObjectDataSource1"
    DataTextField="ShortName"
    DataValueField="CategoryID">
</asp:DropDownList>
<asp:ObjectDataSource ID="ObjectDataSource1" runat="server"
    TypeName="ProductDB"
    SelectMethod="GetAllCategories">
</asp:ObjectDataSource>
```

The GetAllCategories method of the ProductDB class

```
[DataObjectMethod(DataObjectMethodType.Select)]
public static IEnumerable GetAllCategories()
{
    SqlConnection con = new SqlConnection(GetConnectionString());
    string sel = "SELECT CategoryID, LongName "
        + "FROM Categories ORDER BY LongName";
    SqlCommand cmd = new SqlCommand(sel, con);
    con.Open();
    SqlDataReader dr = cmd.ExecuteReader(CommandBehavior.CloseConnection);
    return dr;
}
```

Basic attributes of the ObjectDataSource control

Attribute	Description
ID	The ID of the control.
Runat	Must specify "server."
TypeName	The name of the data access class.
SelectMethod	The name of the method that retrieves the data.
UpdateMethod	The name of the method that updates the data.
DeleteMethod	The name of the method that deletes the data.
InsertMethod	The name of the method that inserts the data.
DataObjectTypeName	The name of a class that provides properties that are used to pass parameter values.
ConflictDetection	Specifies how concurrency conflicts will be detected. CompareAllValues uses optimistic concurrency checking. OverwriteValues, which is the default, does no concurrency checking.

Description

- The ObjectDataSource control specifies the name of the data access class and the methods used to select, update, delete, and insert data.

Figure 17-2   How to use the ObjectDataSource control

How to configure an ObjectDataSource control

Figure 17-3 shows how you can use the Data Source Configuration Wizard to configure an ObjectDataSource control. As you can see, the first step of the wizard lets you choose the business object that will be associated with this object data source. The selection you make here will be used in the TypeName attribute of the ObjectDataSource control. (Notice that Microsoft refers to the data access class as a *business object* in this wizard. In other contexts, though, Microsoft refers to the data access class as a *data object* or a *data component*.)

The drop-down list in the first step of the wizard lists all of the classes that are available in the App_Code folder. If you check the "Show Only Data Components" box, only those classes that identify themselves as data components will be listed. In figure 17-10, you'll learn how to mark classes this way.

When you select a data access class and click Next, the Define Data Methods step of the configuration wizard is displayed. Here, you can select the method you want to use to retrieve data for the object data source. The one you select is specified in the SelectMethod attribute of the ObjectDataSource control. (In this step, the wizard uses a .NET feature called *reflection* to determine all of the available methods, and you'll learn more about reflection in a moment.)

If you select a select method that requires parameters, the Define Parameters step lets you specify the source for each of the required parameters. Then, the wizard generates the elements that define the parameters required by the ObjectDataSource control. This works the same as it does for a SQL data source.

As you can see in this figure, the Data Source Configuration Wizard also provides tabs that let you specify the methods for update, insert, and delete operations. Later in this chapter, you'll see an application that uses these methods. But for now, I'll just focus on how you can use an ObjectDataSource control to retrieve data.

How to work with bound controls

Although you can bind a control such as a drop-down list or GridView control to an object data source, you can't use the designer to select individual fields like you can when you use a SQL data source. That's because the fields are defined in the data access class and not directly in the data source. When you bind a drop-down list, for example, you have to manually enter the names of the fields you want to display and use for the value of the control. Similarly, when you bind a GridView control, you have to manually enter the name of each field you want to bind and, if the control provides for sorting, you have to enter the name of the field for each sort expression. In addition, you have to enter the appropriate field name or names for the DataKeyNames attribute of the control. The exception is if you use business objects with object data sources, which you'll learn how to do later in this chapter. Although that makes object data sources more difficult to work with than SQL data sources, the advantages outweigh this added difficulty.

The Data Source Configuration Wizard

Description

- You can use the Data Source Configuration Wizard to configure an ObjectDataSource control by choosing Configure Data Source from its smart tag menu.

- The Choose a Business Object step of the wizard lets you select the data access class you want to use.

- The Define Data Methods step of the wizard includes tabs that let you choose the methods you want to use for select, update, insert, and delete operations.

- If you choose a method that requires parameters, a Define Parameters step will appear. This step will let you choose the source of each parameter required by the method. For example, you can specify that a drop-down list should be used as the source for a parameter.

- If you create a new data source from a bound control, the first step of the Data Source Configuration Wizard asks you to choose a data source type. To create an object data source, select the Object option. Then, when you click the Next button, the first dialog box shown above is displayed.

Figure 17-3   How to configure an ObjectDataSource control

A Product List application

To illustrate the basics of working with the ObjectDataSource control, figure 17-4 presents a Product List application. This application is identical in appearance to the Product List application that was presented in chapter 13. However, instead of using SqlDataSource controls to retrieve the data, it uses ObjectDataSource controls.

This figure also lists the methods that are provided by the data access class named ProductDB that is used by this application. The first method, GetAllCategories, returns an IEnumerable object (actually, a data reader) that contains the data for all of the categories in the Categories table. This data includes just the category ID and long name for each category.

The second method, GetProductsByCategory, returns an IEnumerable object (again, a data reader) that includes all of the products in the Products table that have the category ID that's supplied by a parameter. This parameter is bound to the SelectedValue property of the drop-down list. As a result, the ID of the category selected by the user will be passed to the GetProductsByCategory method.

This application illustrates how the use of object data sources lets you separate the presentation code from the data access code. As you will see, all of the presentation code is in the aspx file. And all of the data access code is in the data access class that's named ProductDB.

The Product List application

Methods of the ProductDB class

Method	Description
GetAllCategories()	Returns an IEnumerable object with the ID and long name of all the categories in the Categories table.
GetProductsByCategory(string CategoryID)	Returns an IEnumerable object with the ID, name, unit price, and on-hand quantity for all products in the Products table for the specified category.

Description

- The Category drop-down list is bound to an ObjectDataSource control that retrieves a list of categories from the Categories table.

- The DataList control is bound to a second ObjectDataSource control that uses a parameterized query to retrieve the products for a selected category. The CategoryID for the parameter is taken from the SelectedValue property of the drop-down list.

- Both ObjectDataSource controls use a data access class named ProductDB that contains the static methods that return a list of categories and the products for a specific category.

Figure 17-4   The Product List application

The aspx file

Figure 17-5 shows the body of the Default.aspx page for the Product List application. If you compare this listing with the listing shown in figure 13-15, you'll discover that the only difference is that the SqlDataSource elements have been replaced by ObjectDataSource elements. In other words, the code for the drop-down list and DataList controls is identical whether the application uses a SQL data source or an object data source.

In the first ObjectDataSource control, the TypeName attribute specifies ProductDB, and the SelectMethod attribute specifies GetAllCategories. As a result, the GetAllCategories method in the ProductDB data access class will be called to retrieve the category data when the drop-down list is bound.

In the second ObjectDataSource control, the SelectMethod attribute specifies GetProductsByCategory. In addition, a ControlParameter element within the SelectParameters element is used to declare the CategoryID parameter that the GetProductsByCategory method requires. This parameter is bound to the SelectedValue property of the drop-down list. As a result, the DataList control that's bound to this object data source will display only the products in the selected category.

Because the data binding for this application is defined entirely in the aspx file, there is no code-behind file for this page. As a result, the only C# code for this application is in the ProductDB class, which is presented in the next figure.

The body of the Default.aspx file

```
<body>
    <form id="form1" runat="server">
    <div>
        <asp:Image ID="Image1" runat="server"
            ImageUrl="~/Images/banner.jpg" /><br /><br />Choose a category:
        <asp:DropDownList ID="ddlCategory" runat="server" AutoPostBack="True"
            DataSourceID="ObjectDataSource1" DataTextField="LongName"
            DataValueField="CategoryID" Width="130px">
        </asp:DropDownList>
        <asp:ObjectDataSource ID="ObjectDataSource1" runat="server"
            TypeName="ProductDB" SelectMethod="GetAllCategories">
        </asp:ObjectDataSource><br /><br />
        <asp:DataList ID="DataList1" runat="server"
            DataSourceID="ObjectDataSource2" GridLines="Vertical"
            BackColor="White" BorderColor="#999999" BorderStyle="Solid"
            BorderWidth="1px" CellPadding="3" ForeColor="Black">
            <HeaderTemplate>
                <table><tr>
                    <td class="style1">ID</td>
                    <td class="style2">Product</td>
                    <td class="style3" align="right">Unit Price</td>
                    <td class="style3" align="right">On Hand</td></tr>
                </table>
            </HeaderTemplate>
            <ItemTemplate>
                <table><tr>
                    <td class="style1">
                        <asp:Label ID="lblID" runat="server"
                            Text='<%# Eval("ProductID") %>'></asp:Label></td>
                    <td class="style2">
                        <asp:Label ID="lblName" runat="server"
                            Text='<%# Eval("Name") %>'></asp:Label></td>
                    <td class="style3" align="right">
                        <asp:Label ID="lblUnitPrice" runat="server"
                            Text='<%# Eval("UnitPrice", "{0:C}") %>'>
                        </asp:Label></td>
                    <td class="style3" align="right">
                        <asp:Label ID="lblOnHand" runat="server"
                            Text='<%# Eval("OnHand") %>'></asp:Label></td></tr>
                </table>
            </ItemTemplate>
            <AlternatingItemStyle BackColor="#CCCCCC" />
            <HeaderStyle BackColor="Black" Font-Bold="True" ForeColor="White" />
        </asp:DataList>
        <asp:ObjectDataSource ID="ObjectDataSource2" runat="server"
            TypeName="ProductDB" SelectMethod="GetProductsByCategory" >
            <SelectParameters>
                <asp:ControlParameter ControlID="ddlCategory"
                    Name="CategoryID" PropertyName="SelectedValue"
                    Type="String" />
            </SelectParameters>
        </asp:ObjectDataSource>
    </div>
    </form>
</body>
```

Figure 17-5   The aspx file for the Product List application

The ProductDB class

Figure 17-6 presents the C# code for the ProductDB class. To create this class, I used the Website→Add New Item command to add a class file to the App_Code folder. Then, I added the code for the public GetAllCategories and GetProductsByCategory methods. I also created a private method named GetConnectionString. This method is used by both of the public methods to retrieve the connection string for the Halloween database.

Before I explain the details of how these methods work, I want to point out the DataObject and DataObjectMethod attributes that appear in this class. These attributes are used to identify the class and methods as data objects, and you'll learn how to use them in figure 17-10. For now, just realize that they're used by the Data Source Configuration Wizard to determine which classes and methods to display when you configure an object data source.

The GetAllCategories method starts by creating a connection to the Halloween database. To get the connection for this database, it calls the GetConnectionString method. Next, this method creates a string that contains the Select statement that will be used to retrieve data from the Halloween database:

```
SELECT CategoryID, LongName
FROM Categories
ORDER BY LongName
```

Then, a SqlCommand object is created using the string that contains the Select statement and the connection object as parameters. Finally, the connection is opened, the ExecuteReader method of the command object is called to create a data reader object that contains the requested data, and the data reader is returned to the object data source.

The GetProductsByCategory method is slightly more complicated because it uses a parameter in its Select statement:

```
SELECT ProductID, Name, UnitPrice, OnHand
FROM Products
WHERE CategoryID = @CategoryID
ORDER BY ProductID
```

Here again, a SqlCommand object is created using this Select statement and the connection object. Then, a parameter named CategoryID is added to the command's Parameters collection before the connection is opened, and the command is executed so it returns a data reader with the requested data.

The GetConnectionString method uses the ConfigurationManager class to retrieve the connection string named "HalloweenConnection" from the web.config file. As a result, the connection string for the Halloween database must be stored in this file. To refresh your memory about how to store it, please refer to figure 13-4 in chapter 13.

The ProductDB class

```
using System;
using System.Collections;
using System.Configuration;
using System.Data;
using System.Data.SqlClient;
using System.ComponentModel;

[DataObject(true)]
public static class ProductDB
{
    [DataObjectMethod(DataObjectMethodType.Select)]
    public static IEnumerable GetAllCategories()
    {
        SqlConnection con = new SqlConnection(GetConnectionString());
        string sel = "SELECT CategoryID, LongName "
            + "FROM Categories ORDER BY LongName";
        SqlCommand cmd = new SqlCommand(sel, con);
        con.Open();
        SqlDataReader dr = cmd.ExecuteReader(CommandBehavior.CloseConnection);
        return dr;
    }

    [DataObjectMethod(DataObjectMethodType.Select)]
    public static IEnumerable GetProductsByCategory(string CategoryID)
    {
        SqlConnection con = new SqlConnection(GetConnectionString());
        string sel = "SELECT ProductID, Name, "
            + "UnitPrice, OnHand "
            + "FROM Products "
            + "WHERE CategoryID = @CategoryID "
            + "ORDER BY ProductID";
        SqlCommand cmd = new SqlCommand(sel, con);
        cmd.Parameters.AddWithValue("CategoryID", CategoryID);
        con.Open();
        SqlDataReader dr = cmd.ExecuteReader(CommandBehavior.CloseConnection);
        return dr;
    }

    private static string GetConnectionString()
    {
        return ConfigurationManager.ConnectionStrings
            ["HalloweenConnectionString"].ConnectionString;
    }
}
```

Note

- The DataObject and DataObjectMethod attributes are described in figure 17-10.

Figure 17-6   The ProductDB class for the Product List application

How to create a data access class

The most challenging aspect of using object data sources is developing the data access classes that they require. So the topics that follow explain how to design and implement these classes.

How to design a data access class

As figure 17-7 shows, the data access class used by an ObjectDataSource control can have four different types of methods that are used to select, insert, update, and delete data. You can use any method names that you want for these methods, and you can design the class so that it has more than one of each of these types of methods. For example, the ProductDB class used in the previous figure has two select methods that are named GetAllCategories and GetCategoriesByProduct.

The data access methods can be static methods or instance methods. If you define them as instance methods, the ObjectDataSource control will create an instance of the data access class before it calls the method, and then destroy the object after the method has been executed. For this to work, the data access class must provide a parameterless constructor. In C#, though, a parameterless constructor is provided by default if the class has no constructors.

Because creating and destroying a data access object can be time consuming, I suggest that you use static methods for the select, insert, update, and delete methods whenever possible. That way, the ObjectDataSource control won't have to create an instance of the data access class when it calls one of the data access methods.

Although you provide the names of the methods called by the ObjectDataSource control by using the SelectMethod, InsertMethod, UpdateMethod, and DeleteMethod attributes, the ObjectDataSource control doesn't generate the parameters that will be passed to these methods until runtime. Because of that, the ObjectDataSource control must use a .NET feature called *reflection* to determine if a method it calls contains the correct parameters. It also uses reflection to determine the return type of a select method. As you'll see in the next figure, this lets you design a select method that can return the selected data in a variety of forms.

In case you haven't encountered reflection before, it's a .NET feature that provides information about compiled classes at runtime. For example, reflection can determine what methods are provided by a particular class. In addition, it can determine what parameters each method requires and the type returned by the method.

By the way, when you create an ObjectDataSource control, you'll notice that Visual Studio generates Parameter elements based on the parameters that are declared by the methods specified by the SelectMethod, InsertMethod, UpdateMethod, and DeleteMethod attributes. As you'll learn in figure 17-10, however, those aren't necessarily the parameters that the ObjectDataSource control will require.

Types of methods in a data access class

Method type	Description
Select	Retrieves data from a database and returns it as an IEnumerable object.
Insert	Inserts data for one row into the underlying database. The values for the new row are passed via parameters.
Update	Updates the data for one row in the underlying database. The values for the updated row, along with any values that are used to implement optimistic concurrency, are passed via parameters.
Delete	Deletes a row from the underlying database. The key or keys for the row to be deleted, along with any values that are used to implement optimistic concurrency, are passed via parameters.

How an object data source determines which method to call

- The name of the method used for select, insert, update, and delete operations is specified by the SelectMethod, InsertMethod, UpdateMethod, or DeleteMethod attribute.

- The ObjectDataSource control determines what parameters need to be passed to the data access class methods based on the data fields to be inserted, updated, or deleted and whether optimistic concurrency is used.

- The ObjectDataSource control uses reflection to determine the parameter signatures for the insert, update, and delete methods provided by the data access class.

- At runtime, if the class doesn't provide a method with the correct name and parameters, an exception is thrown.

Description

- A data access class can declare public methods that select, insert, update, and delete data. These methods can be instance methods or static methods.

- You can use any method names you want for the select, insert, update, and delete methods.

- If the select, insert, update, and delete methods are static methods, the methods are used without creating an instance of the data access class.

- If the select, insert, update, and delete methods are instance methods, an instance of the data access class is created and destroyed for each data access operation. In this case, the data access class must provide a parameterless constructor.

- You can use parameters to pass selection criteria or other data to the select, insert, update, and delete methods. For more information on the parameters used with insert, update, and delete methods, see figure 17-9.

- *Reflection* is a .NET feature that provides information about compiled classes and methods at runtime.

Figure 17-7   How to design a data access class

How to create a select method

Figure 17-8 shows how to design and code a select method that can be used with an ObjectDataSource control. The table at the top of this figure lists the four different types of values that a select method can return. The simplest is the IEnumerable interface, which can return a data reader or a data view since the DataReader and DataView classes implement the IEnumerable interface. Also, the IEnumerable object can be a strongly-typed collection that's created by using the generics feature of C#.

The select method can also return a DataTable or DataSet object. Because a dataset can contain more than one table, the ObjectDataSource control simply uses the first table in the dataset. As a result, you must design the select method so the first table in the dataset contains the data you want to access.

The main advantage of returning a dataset rather than a data table or data view is that the object data source can cache a dataset. Then, to enable caching, you can set the EnableCaching attribute to True for the ObjectDataSource control. In that case, the select method will be called only the first time the data is requested. For more information on caching, which works the same as it does for a SqlDataSource control, please refer back to chapter 13.

You can also pass parameters to the select method. In that case, the ObjectDataSource control must include a SelectParameters element. This element is added automatically if you use the Data Source Configuration Wizard to create the control. Then, you can create a ControlParameter element that binds a parameter to a control such as a drop-down list. You saw an example of this in figure 17-5.

Allowable return types for a select method

Return type	Description
IEnumerable	A collection such as an ArrayList or HashTable or a strongly-typed collection such as System.Collections.Generic.List. (Because the DataReader and DataView classes implement IEnumerable, the select method can also return a data reader or a data view.)
DataTable	If the select method returns a data table, the ObjectDataSource control automatically extracts a data view from the table and uses the view for data binding.
DataSet	If the select method returns a dataset, the ObjectDataSource control extracts a data view from the first data table in the dataset and uses the view for data binding.
Object	If the select method returns an object, the ObjectDataSource control wraps the object in an IEnumerable collection with just one item, then does the data binding as if the method returned an IEnumerable object.

A select method that returns a data reader

```
public static IEnumerable GetAllCategories()
{
    SqlConnection con = new SqlConnection(GetConnectionString());
    string sel = "SELECT CategoryID, LongName "
        + "FROM Categories ORDER BY LongName";
    SqlCommand cmd = new SqlCommand(sel, con);
    con.Open();
    SqlDataReader dr = cmd.ExecuteReader(CommandBehavior.CloseConnection);
    return dr;
}
```

A select method that returns a dataset

```
public static DataSet GetAllCategories()
{
    SqlConnection con = new SqlConnection(GetConnectionString());
    string sel = "SELECT CategoryID, LongName "
        + "FROM Categories ORDER BY LongName";
    SqlDataAdapter da = new SqlDataAdapter(sel, con);
    DataSet ds = new DataSet();
    da.Fill(ds, "Categories");
    return ds;
}
```

Description

- The select method returns data retrieved from the underlying database. It can return the data in several forms, including a data reader or a dataset.
- If the select method returns a dataset, the object data source can cache the data.
- The select method can also return a strongly-typed collection using C#'s generics feature. See figure 17-18 for an example.
- If the select method accepts parameters, the parameters must be declared within the SelectParameters element of the ObjectDataSource control. Within this element, you can use the ControlParameter element to declare a parameter that's bound to another control on the page.

Figure 17-8   How to create a select method

How to create update, delete, and insert methods

Besides select methods, the data access class used by an object data source can provide methods that update, delete, and insert data in the underlying database. Figure 17-9 presents some guidelines that you should follow when you create these methods.

Undoubtedly the most difficult aspect of working with object data sources is determining how the parameters for update, delete, and insert methods are passed to them from the data source. The reason for this difficulty is that these parameters aren't determined until runtime. Then, the ObjectDataSource control creates a collection of parameters that are passed to the data access class method based on several factors, including (1) the bound fields that are used by the control that the object data source is bound to, (2) the DataKeyNames attribute of the bound control, (3) whether the object data source uses optimistic concurrency checking, and (4) whether the key fields are read-only or updatable.

Once the ObjectDataSource control has determined what parameters need to be passed, it uses reflection to determine whether the data access class has a method that accepts the required parameters. If so, the method is called using these parameters. If not, an exception is thrown. This means that you must anticipate the parameters that will be passed to your method so you can code them correctly. Fortunately, though, if you code them incorrectly, you can use the message that's displayed by the exception that occurs to determine what parameters were expected and then correct your code.

If the object data source is bound to a GridView or DetailsView control that uses BoundField elements, the parameter names are determined by the DataField attributes of those elements. In contrast, if the object data source is bound to a GridView or DetailsView control that uses TemplateField elements, or if the object data source is bound to a FormView or ListView control, the parameter names are determined by the names specified in the Eval and Bind methods of the bound controls. As a result, the parameter names you use in your data access class methods must be the same as the names you use on the DataField attributes or in the Eval or Bind methods, which are the same as the names of the columns in the data source.

Note, however, that the order of the parameters doesn't matter. Instead, the ObjectDataSource control uses reflection to determine the names and order of the parameters expected by the data access methods. Then, when it calls those methods, the object data source passes the parameters in the expected order.

The most confusing aspect of how the ObjectDataSource control generates parameters has to do with cases that require two sets of values be passed to an update method. That happens if you use optimistic concurrency or if the primary key column is updatable. For optimistic concurrency, both sets of values are needed so the update statement can make sure that the data hasn't been changed before it applies the update. And if optimistic concurrency isn't used but the key column is updatable, the update statement needs the original key value so it can properly retrieve the row to be updated.

A typical Update method

```
public static void UpdateCategory(string ShortName,
    string LongName, string original_CategoryID)
{
    SqlConnection con = new SqlConnection(GetConnectionString());
    string up = "UPDATE Categories "
        + "SET ShortName = @ShortName, LongName = @LongName "
        + "WHERE CategoryID = @original_CategoryID";
    SqlCommand cmd = new SqlCommand(up, con);
    cmd.Parameters.AddWithValue("ShortName", ShortName);
    cmd.Parameters.AddWithValue("LongName", LongName);
    cmd.Parameters.AddWithValue("original_CategoryID", original_CategoryID);
    con.Open();
    cmd.ExecuteNonQuery();
}
```

How parameters are generated

- Parameters are automatically generated when an ObjectDataSource control is bound to a control that lets you update a row in a data source, including the GridView, DetailsView, FormView, and ListView controls.

- One parameter is generated for each bound column. If the column is updatable, the parameter is given the same name as the column. Otherwise, the parameter is given the name of the column prefixed with original_.

- If the ObjectDataSource control uses optimistic concurrency, an additional parameter is generated for each updatable bound column when you call the update method. These parameters hold the original values of the columns.

- If optimistic concurrency isn't used but the key column of the data source is updatable, an additional parameter is generated for the key column when you call the update method. This parameter holds the new value of the key column.

- When you call the delete method, a parameter is always generated to hold the original value of the key column.

- If you create an ObjectDataSource control that uses optimistic concurrency, Visual Studio automatically adds an OldValuesParameterFormatString attribute with a value of original_{0}. That way, the names of the parameters for the original column values will be different from the names of the parameters for the new column values.

- If you don't use optimistic concurrency but the key column is updatable, you'll need to add the OldValuesParameterFormatString attribute manually.

Description

- To properly design an update, delete, or insert method, you must be aware of how the ObjectDataSource control generates the parameters passed to these methods.

- Although the order in which the parameters appear in your update, delete, and insert methods doesn't matter, your parameter names must match the names generated by the ObjectDataSource control.

- If your methods don't use the parameters that the object data source expects, you can use the exception messages that occur at runtime to correct the parameters.

Figure 17-9   How to create update, delete, and insert methods

If you create an ObjectDataSource control that uses optimistic concurrency, Visual Studio will automatically add an OldValuesParameterFormatString attribute with a value of original_{0}. That way, the names of the parameters that are generated for an update operation to hold original column values will consist of the column names prefixed with "original_". That means that if the new value of a field named ShortName is passed via a parameter named ShortName, the original value will be passed via a parameter named original_ShortName. Without the OldValuesParameterFormatString attribute, the names of both parameters would be ShortName. That's because the default value of the OldValuesParameterFormatString attribute is {0}.

If the key column is updatable and the ObjectDataSource control doesn't use optimistic concurrency, Visual Studio doesn't generate the OldValuesParameterFormatString attribute. That means that the name of the parameter that holds the original value of the column will be the same as the name of the parameter that holds the new value of the column. To avoid that, you'll need to set the value of this attribute yourself.

The names of the parameters that are passed to a delete method also depend on whether the ObjectDataSource control is created with optimistic concurrency. If optimistic concurrency isn't used, the parameter names are simply the names of the key columns. But if optimistic concurrency is used, the delete parameters will begin with original_.

How to use attributes to mark a data access class

Figure 17-10 shows how you can use *C# attributes* to identify a data access class and its methods. In case you haven't worked with attributes before, they are simply a way to provide declarative information for classes, methods, properties, and so on. Although some of these attributes have meaning at runtime, the attributes in this figure are used at design time. In particular, the Data Source Configuration Wizard uses these attributes to determine which classes in the App_Code folder are data access classes and which methods in the data access class are select, insert, update, and delete methods.

Note, however, that you don't need to use these attributes. The only reason to use them is to help the Data Source Configuration Wizard recognize the data access classes and methods. If you haven't marked your data access classes with these attributes, you can still access them from the wizard by clearing the Show Only Data Components check box in the Choose a Business Object step of the wizard (see figure 17-3).

Attributes for marking data access classes

To mark an element as...	Use this attribute...
A data object class	`[DataObject(true)]`
A Select method	`[DataObjectMethod(DataObjectMethodType.Select)]`
An Insert method	`[DataObjectMethod(DataObjectMethodType.Insert)]`
An Update method	`[DataObjectMethod(DataObjectMethodType.Update)]`
A Delete method	`[DataObjectMethod(DataObjectMethodType.Delete)]`

A marked data access class

```
using System;
using System.Collections;
using System.Data;
using System.Data.SqlClient;
using System.Configuration;
using System.ComponentModel;

[DataObject(true)]
public static class ProductDB
{
    [DataObjectMethod(DataObjectMethodType.Select)]
    public static IEnumerable GetAllCategories()
    {
        SqlConnection con = new SqlConnection(GetConnectionString());
        string sel = "SELECT CategoryID, LongName "
            + "FROM Categories ORDER BY LongName";
        SqlCommand cmd = new SqlCommand(sel, con);
        con.Open();
        SqlDataReader dr =
            cmd.ExecuteReader(CommandBehavior.CloseConnection);
        return dr;
    }
}
```

Description

- You can use DataObject and DataObjectMethod attributes to mark data access classes and methods. Visual Studio uses these attributes to determine which classes and methods to list in the drop-down lists of the Data Source Configuration Wizard.

- The DataObject and DataObjectMethod attributes are stored in the System.ComponentModel namespace.

Figure 17-10   How to use attributes to mark a data access class

A Category Maintenance application

To give you a better idea of how you can use an object data source to update, delete, and insert data, the following topics present an application that maintains the Categories table in the Halloween database. This application is a variation of the Category Maintenance application that was presented in chapter 14.

The design

Figure 17-11 presents the design for this version of the Category Maintenance application. It uses a GridView control to let the user update and delete category rows and a DetailsView control to insert new category rows. Both the GridView and DetailsView controls are bound to a single ObjectDataSource control. But the DetailsView control is used only in Insert mode so it isn't used to display, update, or delete existing category rows.

The table in this figure shows the public methods that are provided by the CategoryDB class. These four methods provide the select, update, delete, and insert functions. Since all of these methods are defined as static, an instance of the CategoryDB class doesn't have to be created to access the database.

The aspx file

The two parts of figure 17-12 show the Default.aspx file for this application. In part 1, you can see the aspx code for the GridView control that displays the category rows. Its Columns collection includes three BoundField columns, named CategoryID, ShortName, and LongName. (I didn't use templates or validation controls for this application so it would be easier to focus on how the ObjectDataSource control is used.)

In part 2, you can see the aspx code for the ObjectDataSource control. It names CategoryDB as the data access class, then provides the names of the select, insert, update, and delete methods that will be used to access the data. Notice that the ConflictDetection attribute is set to CompareAllValues so optimistic concurrency will be used. You'll see one way to implement optimistic concurrency with an object data source when you see the C# code for this application.

You can also see the aspx code for the DetailsView control in part 2. Here, I set the DefaultMode attribute to Insert so this control is always displayed in Insert mode.

The Category Maintenance application

Methods of the CategoryDB class

Method type	Signature
Select	`public static IEnumerable GetCategories()`

Update	`public static int UpdateCategory(string ShortName,`
	`        string LongName, string original_CategoryID,`
	`        string original_ShortName, string original_LongName)`

Delete	`public static int DeleteCategory(string original_CategoryID,` `        string original_ShortName, string original_LongName)`
Insert	`public static int InsertCategory(string CategoryID,` `        string ShortName, string LongName)`

Description

- This version of the Category Maintenance application uses a GridView control to update and delete rows and a DetailsView control to insert rows. These controls are bound to an ObjectDataSource control that accesses the Categories table of the Halloween database.

- The data access class named CategoryDB provides the select, insert, update, and delete methods.

Figure 17-11   The Category Maintenance application

The Default.aspx file

```aspx
<%@ Page Language="C#" AutoEventWireup="true"  CodeFile="Default.aspx.cs"
Inherits="_Default" %>

<!DOCTYPE html PUBLIC "-//W3C//DTD XHTML 1.0 Transitional//EN"
"http://www.w3.org/TR/xhtml1/DTD/xhtml1-transitional.dtd">

<html xmlns="http://www.w3.org/1999/xhtml" >
<head runat="server">
    <title>Chapter 17: Category Maintenance</title>
</head>
<body>
    <form id="form1" runat="server">
    <div>
        <asp:Image ID="Image1" runat="server" ImageUrl="~/Images/banner.jpg" />
        <br /><br /><h2>Category Maintenance</h2>
        <asp:GridView ID="GridView1" runat="server"
            DataSourceID="ObjectDataSource1" DataKeyNames="CategoryID"
            AutoGenerateColumns="False" ForeColor="Black"
            OnRowDeleted="GridView1_RowDeleted"
            OnRowUpdated="GridView1_RowUpdated" >
            <Columns>
                <asp:BoundField DataField="CategoryID" ReadOnly="True"
                    HeaderText="Category ID" >
                    <ItemStyle Width="100px" />
                </asp:BoundField>
                <asp:BoundField DataField="ShortName" HeaderText="Short Name" >
                    <ItemStyle Width="150px" />
                </asp:BoundField>
                <asp:BoundField DataField="LongName" HeaderText="Long Name" >
                    <ItemStyle Width="200px" />
                </asp:BoundField>
                <asp:CommandField ButtonType="Button" ShowEditButton="True" />
                <asp:CommandField ButtonType="Button" ShowDeleteButton="True" />
            </Columns>
            <HeaderStyle BackColor="Silver" Font-Bold="True"
                ForeColor="White" />
            <RowStyle BackColor="White" ForeColor="Black" />
            <AlternatingRowStyle BackColor="WhiteSmoke" ForeColor="Black" />
            <EditRowStyle BackColor="Blue" ForeColor="White" />

        </asp:GridView>

        <asp:ObjectDataSource ID="ObjectDataSource1" runat="server"
            TypeName="CategoryDB"
            SelectMethod="GetCategories"
            InsertMethod="InsertCategory"
            DeleteMethod="DeleteCategory"
            UpdateMethod="UpdateCategory"
            ConflictDetection="CompareAllValues"
            OldValuesParameterFormatString="original_{0}"
            OnDeleted="ObjectDataSource1_Deleted"
            OnUpdated="ObjectDataSource1_Updated">
```

Figure 17-12   The aspx file of the Category Maintenance application (part 1 of 2)

The Default.aspx file

```
        <UpdateParameters>
            <asp:Parameter Name="ShortName" Type="String" />
            <asp:Parameter Name="LongName" Type="String" />
            <asp:Parameter Name="original_CategoryID" Type="String" />
            <asp:Parameter Name="original_ShortName" Type="String" />
            <asp:Parameter Name="original_LongName" Type="String" />
        </UpdateParameters>
        <InsertParameters>
            <asp:Parameter Name="CategoryID" Type="String" />
            <asp:Parameter Name="ShortName" Type="String" />
            <asp:Parameter Name="LongName" Type="String" />
        </InsertParameters>
        <DeleteParameters>
            <asp:Parameter Name="original_CategoryID" Type="String" />
            <asp:Parameter Name="original_ShortName" Type="String" />
            <asp:Parameter Name="original_LongName" Type="String" />
        </DeleteParameters>
    </asp:ObjectDataSource><br />

    <asp:Label ID="lblError" runat="server" EnableViewState="False"
        ForeColor="Red">
    </asp:Label><br />
    To create a new category, enter the category information
    and click Insert.<br /><br />

    <asp:DetailsView ID="DetailsView1" runat="server"
        AutoGenerateRows="False" DataSourceID="ObjectDataSource1"
        DefaultMode="Insert" Height="50px" Width="300px"
        GridLines="None" CellPadding="4" ForeColor="#333333"
        OnItemInserted="DetailsView1_ItemInserted" >
        <Fields>
            <asp:BoundField DataField="CategoryID"
                HeaderText="Category ID:" />
            <asp:BoundField DataField="ShortName"
                HeaderText="Short Name:" />
            <asp:BoundField DataField="LongName"
                HeaderText="Long Name:" />
            <asp:CommandField ButtonType="Button"
                ShowInsertButton="True" />
        </Fields>
        <FieldHeaderStyle BackColor="Silver" Font-Bold="true"
            ForeColor="White" />
        <InsertRowStyle BackColor="WhiteSmoke" ForeColor="Black" />
        <CommandRowStyle BackColor="#E1E1E1" Font-Bold="true" />
    </asp:DetailsView>
    </div>
    </form>
</body>
</html>
```

Figure 17-12   The aspx file of the Category Maintenance application (part 2 of 2)

The code-behind file

Figure 17-13 shows the code-behind file for the Default.aspx page of the Category Maintenance application. This file consists of five event handlers that handle the exceptions that might be raised and the concurrency errors that might occur when the object data source's update, delete, or insert methods are called.

The first event handler is executed after the data source is updated. This event handler retrieves the return value from the update method using the ReturnValue property of the e argument and assigns it to the AffectedRows property of the e argument. This is necessary because the AffectedRows property isn't set automatically like it is for a SQL data source. For this to work, of course, the update method must return the number of rows that were updated. You'll see the code that accomplishes that in the next figure.

The second event handler is executed after a row in the GridView control is updated, which happens after the data source is updated. This event handler checks the Exception property of the e argument to determine if an exception has been thrown. If so, an error message is displayed, the ExceptionHandled property is set to true to suppress the exception, and the KeepInEditMode property is set to true to leave the GridView control in edit mode. Notice that in addition to the Message property of the Exception object, the error message includes the Message property of the Exception object that's returned by the InnerException property of the exception if that object exists. You'll learn more about the InnerException property in chapter 23. For now, just realize that it returns the Exception object that originally caused the error.

If an exception didn't occur, this event handler continues by checking the AffectedRows property of the e argument. The value of this property is passed forward from the AffectedRows property of the object data source's Updated event. If the value of this property is zero, the row was not updated, most likely due to the concurrency checking code that was added to the SQL Update statement. As a result, an appropriate error message is displayed.

The next two event handlers are similar, except they handle the Deleted event of the ObjectDataSource control and the RowDeleted event of the GridView control. Like the Updated event handler of the ObjectDataSource control, the Deleted event handler sets the AffectedRows property of the e argument. And, like the RowUpdated event handler of the GridView control, the RowDeleted event handler checks for exceptions and concurrency errors.

The last event handler is executed after a row is inserted using the DetailsView control. It checks whether an exception has occurred and responds accordingly. Note that currency checking isn't necessary here because a concurrency error can't occur for an insert operation.

By the way, this code illustrates just one way that you can provide for concurrency errors. Another way is to write the update and delete methods so they throw an exception if a concurrency error occurs. Then, the RowUpdated and RowDeleted event handlers can test the e.Exception property to determine if this exception has been thrown. I prefer the technique illustrated here, though, because the code for the RowUpdated and RowDeleted event handlers is almost identical to the code you use with a SQL data source.

The Default.aspx.cs file

```
public partial class _Default : System.Web.UI.Page
{
    protected void ObjectDataSource1_Updated(
        object sender, ObjectDataSourceStatusEventArgs e){
        e.AffectedRows = Convert.ToInt32(e.ReturnValue);
    }

    protected void GridView1_RowUpdated(
        Object sender, GridViewUpdatedEventArgs e){
        if (e.Exception != null)
        {
            lblError.Text = "A database error has occurred.<br /><br />" +
                e.Exception.Message;
            if (e.Exception.InnerException != null)
                lblError.Text += "<br />Message: "
                    + e.Exception.InnerException.Message;
            e.ExceptionHandled = true;
            e.KeepInEditMode = true;
        }
        else if (e.AffectedRows == 0)
            lblError.Text = "Another user may have updated that category."
                + "<br />Please try again.";
    }

    protected void ObjectDataSource1_Deleted(
        object sender, ObjectDataSourceStatusEventArgs e){
        e.AffectedRows = Convert.ToInt32(e.ReturnValue);
    }

    protected void GridView1_RowDeleted(
        object sender, GridViewDeletedEventArgs e){
        if (e.Exception != null)
        {
            lblError.Text = "A database error has occurred.<br /><br />" +
                e.Exception.Message;
            if (e.Exception.InnerException != null)
                lblError.Text += "<br />Message: "
                    + e.Exception.InnerException.Message;
            e.ExceptionHandled = true;
        }
        else if (e.AffectedRows == 0)
            lblError.Text = "Another user may have updated that category. "
                + "<br />Please try again.";
    }

    protected void DetailsView1_ItemInserted(
        object sender, DetailsViewInsertedEventArgs e){
        if (e.Exception != null)
        {
            lblError.Text = "A database error has occurred.<br /><br />" +
                e.Exception.Message;
            if (e.Exception.InnerException != null)
                lblError.Text += "<br />Message: "
                    + e.Exception.InnerException.Message;
            e.ExceptionHandled = true;
            e.KeepInInsertMode = true;
        }
    }
}
```

Figure 17-13   The code-behind file for the Category Maintenance application

The CategoryDB class

The two parts of figure 17-14 present the CategoryDB class that's used as the data access class for this application. This class uses the DataObject attribute to mark the class as a data object class and the DataObjectMethod attribute to mark the methods as data object methods.

The four public methods in this class provide for the select, insert, delete, and update operations performed by this application. These methods use standard ADO.NET code to access the database. Since this code is straightforward, you shouldn't have any trouble understanding how it works. So I'll just describe it briefly here.

The GetCategories method retrieves all of the rows and columns from the Categories table in the Halloween database. This data is then returned as a data reader, and the object data source uses it to populate the GridView control.

To get a connection to the Halloween database, the GetCategories method calls the private GetConnectionString method. This method gets the connection string from the web.config file. The GetConnectionString method is also called by the other public methods.

When the user clicks the Insert button in the DetailsView control, the object data source executes the InsertCategory method. This method is declared with three parameters that correspond to the three columns in the Categories table. When the object data source executes this method, it passes the values that the user entered into the DetailsView control. Then, the method creates and executes a command that uses these parameter values to insert a new row.

The CategoryDB.cs file

```csharp
using System;
using System.Collections;
using System.Data;
using System.Data.SqlClient;
using System.Configuration;
using System.ComponentModel;

[DataObject(true)]
public static class CategoryDB
{
    [DataObjectMethod(DataObjectMethodType.Select)]
    public static IEnumerable GetCategories()
    {
        SqlConnection con = new SqlConnection(GetConnectionString());
        string sel = "SELECT CategoryID, ShortName, LongName "
            + "FROM Categories ORDER BY ShortName";
        SqlCommand cmd = new SqlCommand(sel, con);
        con.Open();
        SqlDataReader dr = cmd.ExecuteReader(CommandBehavior.CloseConnection);
        return dr;
    }

    private static string GetConnectionString()
    {
        return ConfigurationManager.ConnectionStrings
            ["HalloweenConnectionString"].ConnectionString;
    }

    [DataObjectMethod(DataObjectMethodType.Insert)]
    public static int InsertCategory(string CategoryID,
        string ShortName, string LongName)
    {
        SqlConnection con = new SqlConnection(GetConnectionString());
        string ins = "INSERT INTO Categories "
            + "(CategoryID, ShortName, LongName) "
            + "VALUES(@CategoryID, @ShortName, @LongName)";
        SqlCommand cmd = new SqlCommand(ins, con);
        cmd.Parameters.AddWithValue("CategoryID", CategoryID);
        cmd.Parameters.AddWithValue("ShortName", ShortName);
        cmd.Parameters.AddWithValue("LongName", LongName);
        con.Open();
        int i = cmd.ExecuteNonQuery();
        return i;
    }
}
```

Figure 17-14   The CategoryDB class for the Category Maintenance application (part 1 of 2)

When the user clicks the Delete button in the GridView control, the object data source executes the DeleteCategory method. This method accepts three parameters: the original category ID, short name, and long name. The values of these parameters are used within the Where clause of the Delete statement that's executed by this method to identify the row to be deleted and to perform concurrency checking.

Notice that this method is written as a function that returns an integer value. Then, when the command that contains the Delete statement is executed, the result is stored in an integer variable, which is returned to the object data source. Because this value indicates the number of rows that were deleted, it can be used as shown in the previous figure to check for a concurrency error.

The last method, UpdateCategory, is executed when the user clicks the Update button in the GridView control. It's declared with five parameters: the current short name and long name and the original category ID, short name, and long name. The values of the current short name and long name parameters are used to update the category, and the values of the original parameters are used to perform concurrency checking.

Like the DeleteCategory method, the UpdateCategory method returns an int value that indicates the number of rows that were affected by the update operation. Then, this value can be used to check for a concurrency error.

The CategoryDB.cs file   Page 2

```
[DataObjectMethod(DataObjectMethodType.Delete)]
public static int DeleteCategory(string original_CategoryID,
    string original_ShortName, string original_LongName)
{
    SqlConnection con = new SqlConnection(GetConnectionString());
    string del = "DELETE FROM Categories "
        + "WHERE CategoryID = @original_CategoryID "
        + "AND ShortName = @original_ShortName "
        + "AND LongName = @original_LongName";
    SqlCommand cmd = new SqlCommand(del, con);
    cmd.Parameters.AddWithValue("original_CategoryID",
        original_CategoryID);
    cmd.Parameters.AddWithValue("original_ShortName", original_ShortName);
    cmd.Parameters.AddWithValue("original_LongName", original_LongName);
    con.Open();
    int i = cmd.ExecuteNonQuery();
    return i;
}

[DataObjectMethod(DataObjectMethodType.Update)]
public static int UpdateCategory(string ShortName,
    string LongName, string original_CategoryID,
    string original_ShortName, string original_LongName)
{
    SqlConnection con = new SqlConnection(GetConnectionString());
    string up = "UPDATE Categories "
        + "SET ShortName = @ShortName, "
        + "LongName = @LongName "
        + "WHERE CategoryID = @original_CategoryID "
        + "AND ShortName = @original_ShortName "
        + "AND LongName = @original_LongName";
    SqlCommand cmd = new SqlCommand(up, con);
    cmd.Parameters.AddWithValue("ShortName", ShortName);
    cmd.Parameters.AddWithValue("LongName", LongName);
    cmd.Parameters.AddWithValue("original_CategoryID",
        original_CategoryID);
    cmd.Parameters.AddWithValue("original_ShortName", original_ShortName);
    cmd.Parameters.AddWithValue("original_LongName", original_LongName);
    con.Open();
    int i = cmd.ExecuteNonQuery();
    return i;
}
}
```

Figure 17-14   The CategoryDB class for the Category Maintenance application (part 2 of 2)

How to use business objects with object data sources

Although you can use a parameter for each bound field that's required by an insert, update, or delete method in a data access class, that can be cumbersome if more than just a few fields are required. In that case, you may want to use a business object that stores the data for all of the fields. In fact, because it's easier to determine what parameters are required by a method when you use business objects, and because the fields defined by a business class are available as you create a bound control with the designer, you might want to use them regardless of the number of fields you're working with.

How to create methods that use business objects

Figure 17-15 shows how to create methods that use business objects. Just as when you create methods that use individual field parameters, you need to determine what parameters are required when you use business objects. This figure summarizes how an object data source generates these parameters.

Any insert or delete method you create requires a single business object as its parameter. This business object must contain all the values required by the method, and you can give it any name you choose. If an update method doesn't provide for optimistic concurrency checking, it too requires a single business object as its parameter.

If an update method provides for optimistic concurrency checking, it requires two parameters as shown in the code at the top of this figure. The first parameter must be a business object that provides the original values for the row to be updated, and the second parameter must be a business object that provides the new values for the row. Then, the method assigns the properties of these objects to the appropriate parameters. Notice that the name of the first parameter is the same as the name of the second parameter, preceded by original_. However, the second parameter can be any name you choose.

Although two parameters are also required if the key column for a table is updatable, you should know that the object data source won't automatically generate two parameters in this case. Because of that, you will need to set the ConflictDetection property of the object data source to CompareAllValues even if the update method doesn't provide for optimistic concurrency checking, and you will need to set the OldValuesParameterFormatString accordingly. Then, the first parameter will contain an object with the original values for the row, and you can use the property that contains the value for the key column to identify the row to be updated.

This figure also lists the requirements for a business class that you can use to create the business objects. First, the class must provide a parameterless constructor. Since C# provides a parameterless constructor by default if a class isn't defined with any constructors, you may be able to omit this constructor. However, I prefer to include it for completeness.

An update method that uses business objects

```
[DataObjectMethod(DataObjectMethodType.Update)]
public static void UpdateCategory(Category original_Category,
    Category category)
{
    SqlConnection con = new SqlConnection(GetConnectionString());
    string up = "UPDATE Categories "
        + "SET ShortName = @ShortName, LongName = @LongName "
        + "WHERE CategoryID = @original_CategoryID "
        + "AND ShortName = @original_ShortName "
        + "AND LongName = @original_LongName";
    SqlCommand cmd = new SqlCommand(up, con);
    cmd.Parameters.AddWithValue("ShortName", category.ShortName);
    cmd.Parameters.AddWithValue("LongName", category.LongName);
    cmd.Parameters.AddWithValue("original_CategoryID",
        original_Category.CategoryID);
    cmd.Parameters.AddWithValue("original_ShortName",
        original_Category.ShortName);
    cmd.Parameters.AddWithValue("original_LongName",
        original_Category.LongName);
    con.Open();
    cmd.ExecuteNonQuery();
    con.Close();
}
```

How parameters are generated

- When the insert or delete method is called, one parameter of the business class type is generated and passed to the method. The parameter that's declared in the method can have any name you choose.

- One parameter of the business class type is also generated and passed to the update method when this method is called if optimistic concurrency isn't used. The parameter that's declared in the method can have any name you choose.

- If optimistic concurrency is specified, two parameters are generated and passed to the update method. The first one contains the original values, and the second one contains the new values. The name of the first object must be the name of the second object, preceded by the string that's specified by the OldValuesParameterFormatString attribute.

Requirements for the business class

- The class must provide a parameterless constructor.

- The class must have public properties with names that match the names of the bound fields that are passed to the object data source from the bound control.

- The public properties must have both get and set accessors.

Description

- Instead of using individual parameters for each bound field, you can use an object that's created from a business class that contains a property for each field.

- To use a business class with an object data source control, you set the DataObjectTypeName attribute to the name of the class.

Figure 17-15   How to create methods that use business objects

Second, the class must define a public property for each bound field that's passed from the bound control to the object data source. The names of these properties must be the same as the names specified for the DataField attribute or on the Eval or Bind method. This works just like it does when you use individual parameters for each bound field.

Third, the property for each bound field must include both a get and a set accessor. The object data source uses the set accessors to set the values of the properties based on the values passed to it from the bound control. And the insert, update, and delete methods in the data access class use the get accessors to assign the values of the properties to parameters of command objects.

Once you create the business class, you need to indicate that you want the object data source to use it with the insert, update, and delete methods. To do that, you set the DataObjectTypeName attribute of the control to the name of the class.

The aspx file for a Category Maintenance application that uses business objects

Figure 17-16 presents part of the aspx file for a version of the Category Maintenance application that uses business objects. The only difference here is in the definition of the object data source control. As you can see, the DataObjectTypeName attribute of this control is set to a class named Category. You'll see the definition of this class in the next figure.

In addition to the DataObjectTypeName attribute, you should notice that parameters are included only for the update method. These parameters are included because optimistic concurrency checking is performed by the update method, which means that this method requires two parameters: an object that contains the original values and an object that contains the new values. Because these parameters must be given appropriate names as explained in the last topic, the object data source must include parameters that specify these names. In contrast, the names of the parameters in the insert and delete methods can be anything you like, so they don't have to be defined by the object data source. Similarly, if optimistic concurrency checking isn't performed by an update method, the object data source doesn't need to define any update parameters.

Part of the Default.aspx file that uses business objects

```
...
<asp:GridView ID="GridView1" runat="server"
    DataSourceID="ObjectDataSource1" DataKeyNames="CategoryID"
    AutoGenerateColumns="False" ForeColor="Black"
    OnRowDeleted="GridView1_RowDeleted"
    OnRowUpdated="GridView1_RowUpdated" >
    <Columns>
        <asp:BoundField DataField="CategoryID" ReadOnly="True"
            HeaderText="Category ID" >
            <ItemStyle Width="100px" />
        </asp:BoundField>
        <asp:BoundField DataField="ShortName" HeaderText="Short Name" >
            <ItemStyle Width="150px" />
        </asp:BoundField>
        <asp:BoundField DataField="LongName" HeaderText="Long Name" >
            <ItemStyle Width="200px" />
        </asp:BoundField>
        <asp:CommandField ButtonType="Button" ShowEditButton="True" />
        <asp:CommandField ButtonType="Button" ShowDeleteButton="True" />
    </Columns>
    ...
</asp:GridView>
...
<asp:ObjectDataSource ID="ObjectDataSource1" runat="server"
    DataObjectTypeName="Category" TypeName="CategoryDB"
    SelectMethod="GetCategories" DeleteMethod="DeleteCategory"
    InsertMethod="InsertCategory" UpdateMethod="UpdateCategory"
    ConflictDetection="CompareAllValues "
    OldValuesParameterFormatString="original_{0}"
    OnDeleted="ObjectDataSource1_Deleted"
    OnUpdated="ObjectDataSource1_Updated" >
    <UpdateParameters>
        <asp:Parameter Name="original_Category" Type="Object" />
        <asp:Parameter Name="category" Type="Object" />
    </UpdateParameters>
</asp:ObjectDataSource>
...
<asp:DetailsView ID="DetailsView1" runat="server"
    AutoGenerateRows="False" DataSourceID="ObjectDataSource1"
    DefaultMode="Insert" Height="50px" Width="300px"
    GridLines="None" CellPadding="4" ForeColor="#333333"
    OnItemInserted="DetailsView1_ItemInserted" >

    <Fields>
        <asp:BoundField DataField="CategoryID"
            HeaderText="Category ID:" />
        <asp:BoundField DataField="ShortName"
            HeaderText="Short Name:" />
        <asp:BoundField DataField="LongName"
            HeaderText="Long Name:" />
        <asp:CommandField ButtonType="Button"
            ShowInsertButton="True" />
    </Fields>
    ...
</asp:DetailsView>
...
```

Figure 17-16   The aspx file for the Category Maintenance application that uses business objects

The Category business class

Figure 17-17 presents the Category business class that's used by the object data source shown in the previous figure. If you've used business classes like this before, you shouldn't have any trouble understanding how it works. In this case, the class includes three public properties that correspond with the three columns of the Categories table. The values of these properties are stored in the three private fields declared by this class. As required for business classes that are used by an object data source, each property is defined with both a get and a set accessor. This class also includes a parameterless constructor that's called when the object data source creates an instance of the class.

A CategoryDB class that uses business objects

Figure 17-18 presents a version of the CategoryDB class that uses business objects. Notice that although the select method in this class doesn't have to use the business object to store the results of the retrieval operation, it makes sense to do that if the insert, update, and delete methods use business objects. In this case, then, the select method returns a List<Category> object. To do that, it creates an object from the Category class for each row that's retrieved by the data reader, and it assigns the values in that row to the appropriate properties of the object. Then, it adds that object to the List<Category> object.

The insert method receives a single Category object. Then, it assigns the CategoryID, ShortName, and LongName properties of that object to the parameters that are defined in the Values clause of the Insert statement. When the Insert statement is executed, a new row with these values is inserted into the Categories table.

The delete method also receives a single Category object. This object contains the values that were originally retrieved from the Categories table. The CategoryID, ShortName, and LongName properties of this object are assigned to the parameters that are defined in the Where clause of the Delete statement. Then, if a row with these values is found, the row is deleted. Otherwise, it indicates that a concurrency error has occurred.

The update method receives two Category objects. The first one contains the values that were originally retrieved from the Categories table, and the second one contains the new values for the row. The CategoryID, ShortName, and LongName properties of the first object are assigned to the parameters that are defined in the Where clause of the Update statement, and the ShortName and LongName properties of the second object are assigned to the properties that are defined in the Set clause of the Update statement. Then, if a row with the values in the first object is found, the values of the ShortName and LongName columns of that row are updated to the values in the second object.

The Category.cs file

```
public class Category
{
    private string categoryID;
    private string shortName;
    private string longName;

    public Category()
    {
    }

    public string CategoryID
    {
        get
        {
            return categoryID;
        }
        set
        {
            categoryID = value;
        }
    }

    public string ShortName
    {
        get
        {
            return shortName;
        }
        set
        {
            shortName = value;
        }
    }

    public string LongName
    {
        get
        {
            return longName;
        }
        set
        {
            longName = value;
        }
    }
}
```

Figure 17-17   The Category business class

A CategoryDB.cs file that uses business objects   Page 1

```csharp
using System;
using System.Collections;
using System.Data;
using System.Data.SqlClient;
using System.Configuration;
using System.ComponentModel;
using System.Collections.Generic;

[DataObject(true)]
public static class CategoryDB
{
    [DataObjectMethod(DataObjectMethodType.Select)]
    public static List<Category> GetCategories()
    {
        List<Category> categoryList = new List<Category>();
        SqlConnection con = new SqlConnection(GetConnectionString());
        string sel = "SELECT CategoryID, ShortName, LongName "
            + "FROM Categories ORDER BY ShortName";
        SqlCommand cmd = new SqlCommand(sel, con);
        con.Open();
        SqlDataReader dr = cmd.ExecuteReader(CommandBehavior.CloseConnection);
        Category category;
        while (dr.Read())
        {
            category = new Category();
            category.CategoryID = dr["CategoryID"].ToString();
            category.ShortName = dr["ShortName"].ToString();
            category.LongName = dr["LongName"].ToString();
            categoryList.Add(category);
        }
        dr.Close();
        return categoryList;
    }

    private static string GetConnectionString()
    {
        return ConfigurationManager.ConnectionStrings
            ["HalloweenConnectionString"].ConnectionString;
    }

    [DataObjectMethod(DataObjectMethodType.Insert)]
    public static int InsertCategory(Category category)
    {
        SqlConnection con = new SqlConnection(GetConnectionString());
        string ins = "INSERT INTO Categories "
            + " (CategoryID, ShortName, LongName) "
            + " VALUES(@CategoryID, @ShortName, @LongName)";
        SqlCommand cmd = new SqlCommand(ins, con);
        cmd.Parameters.AddWithValue("CategoryID", category.CategoryID);
        cmd.Parameters.AddWithValue("ShortName", category.ShortName);
        cmd.Parameters.AddWithValue("LongName", category.LongName);
        con.Open();
        int i = cmd.ExecuteNonQuery();
        con.Close();
        return i;
    }
}
```

Figure 17-18   A CategoryDB class that uses business objects (part 1 of 2)

A CategoryDB.cs file that uses business objects   **Page 2**

```csharp
[DataObjectMethod(DataObjectMethodType.Delete)]
public static int DeleteCategory(Category category)
{
    SqlConnection con = new SqlConnection(GetConnectionString());
    string del = "DELETE FROM Categories "
        + "WHERE CategoryID = @CategoryID "
        + "AND ShortName = @ShortName "
        + "AND LongName = @LongName ";
    SqlCommand cmd = new SqlCommand(del, con);
    cmd.Parameters.AddWithValue("CategoryID", category.CategoryID);
    cmd.Parameters.AddWithValue("ShortName", category.ShortName);
    cmd.Parameters.AddWithValue("LongName", category.LongName);
    con.Open();
    int i = cmd.ExecuteNonQuery();
    con.Close();
    return i;
}

[DataObjectMethod(DataObjectMethodType.Update)]
public static int UpdateCategory(Category original_Category,
    Category category)
{
    SqlConnection con = new SqlConnection(GetConnectionString());
    string up = "UPDATE Categories "
        + "SET ShortName = @ShortName, "
        + "LongName = @LongName "
        + "WHERE CategoryID = @original_CategoryID "
        + "AND ShortName = @original_ShortName "
        + "AND LongName = @original_LongName";
    SqlCommand cmd = new SqlCommand(up, con);
    cmd.Parameters.AddWithValue("ShortName", category.ShortName);
    cmd.Parameters.AddWithValue("LongName", category.LongName);
    cmd.Parameters.AddWithValue("original_CategoryID",
        original_Category.CategoryID);
    cmd.Parameters.AddWithValue("original_ShortName",
        original_Category.ShortName);
    cmd.Parameters.AddWithValue("original_LongName",
        original_Category.LongName);
    con.Open();
    int i = cmd.ExecuteNonQuery();
    con.Close();
    return i;
}
}
```

Figure 17-18   A CategoryDB class that uses business objects (part 2 of 2)

How to use paging with object data sources

One complication that arises when you use an object data source is that it doesn't automatically provide for paging with controls like the GridView control. Because of that, you have to set the attributes of the object data source that provide for paging, and you have to provide for paging in the data access class. You'll learn how to do that in the two topics that follow.

How to create an ObjectDataSource control that provides for paging

To create an ObjectDataSource control that provides for paging, you set the four attributes shown in figure 17-19. The EnablePaging attribute simply indicates that the object data source supports paging. The StartRowIndexParameterName and MaximumRowsParameterName attributes specify the names of parameters that will be used by the select method in the data access class to determine which rows are returned by the method. You'll see an example of how that works in the next figure. For now, just realize that when you use a pager control to display another page of data in a bound control, the bound control passes the values that will be assigned to these two parameters to the ObjectDataSource control.

The last attribute, SelectCountMethod, names a method in the data access class that returns a count of the total number of rows that are retrieved by the select method. The control that's bound to the object data source uses this value to determine what pager controls to display. For example, if the bound control uses first, previous, next, and last pager controls, it will be able to determine when the first or last page is displayed so it can omit the first and previous or next and last pager controls. This is illustrated by the GridView control shown at the top of this figure, which is bound to the object data source shown here. In this case, the first page is displayed so the first and previous pager controls aren't included.

A GridView control that provides for paging

ID	Name	Category	Unit Price	On Hand
pow01	Austin Powers	costumes	$79.99	25
bl01	Black light (24")	fx	$24.99	200
cool01	Cool Ghoul	props	$69.99	25
vader01	Darth Vader Mask	masks	$19.99	100
cat01	Deranged Cat	props	$19.99	45
fogj01	Fog Juice (1qt)	fx	$9.99	500
fog01	Fog Machine	fx	$34.99	100
frankc01	Frankenstein	costumes	$39.99	100
		≥ ≥≥		

Attributes of the ObjectDataSource control that are used for paging

Attribute	Description
EnablePaging	True if the ObjectDataSource control supports paging.
StartRowIndexParameterName	The name of the parameter in the select method of the data access class that receives the index of the first row to be retrieved. The default is startRowIndex.
MaximumRowsParameterName	The name of the parameter in the select method of the data access class that receives the maximum number of rows to be retrieved. The default is maximumRows.
SelectCountMethod	The name of a public method in the data access class that returns the total number of rows that are retrieved by the select method.

The aspx code for an ObjectDataSource control that provides for paging

```
<asp:ObjectDataSource ID="ObjectDataSource1" runat="server"
    SelectMethod="GetProductsByPage" TypeName="ProductDB"
    EnablePaging="True" StartRowIndexParameterName="startIndex"
    SelectCountMethod="SelectCount" MaximumRowsParameterName="maxRows">
</asp:ObjectDataSource>
```

Description

- To use paging with a control like a GridView control that's bound to an object data source, you must set the four attributes of the ObjectDataSource control shown above.

- When a pager control on a bound control is clicked, the index of the starting row to be displayed and the maximum number of rows to be displayed are passed to the ObjectDataSource control. The ObjectDataSource control then passes these values to the parameters of the select method specified by the StartRowIndexParameterName and MaximumRowsParameterName attributes of the control.

- In addition to the select method that's used to retrieve the rows to be displayed, the data access class must include a method that returns the total number of rows that are retrieved. This method is named on the SelectCountMethod attribute of the ObjectDataSource control, and it's used by the bound control to determine what pager controls to display.

Figure 17-19   How to create an object data source that provides for paging

How to create a data access class that provides for paging

Figure 17-20 shows the code for a data access class that's used by the object data source you saw in the last figure. This class uses a List<Product> object named productList to store the data that's retrieved by the select method. This list is declared at the class level so both the select method and the method that returns the count of rows have access to it. As you can see, the method that returns the count of rows, which is named SelectCount as specified by the SelectCountMethod property of the ObjectDataSource control, simply returns the number of items in this list.

The most difficult aspect of creating a data access class that provides for paging is determining what rows the select method should return. To do that, the select method uses the two parameters that are passed to it from the object data source. The names of these parameters are the same as the names specified by the StartRowIndexParameterName and MaximumRowsParameterName attributes of the ObjectDataSource control.

The body of the select method starts by retrieving all the rows specified by the Select statement just as any other select method does. In this case, the select method uses the ExecuteReader method of a command object to create a data reader that contains the requested data from the Products table. Then, it retrieves each row of data from the data reader, stores it in a Product object, and adds the product object to the product list.

Next, this method gets a count of the rows in the list and stores the count in a variable named rowCount. Then, it checks to be sure that the rows specified by the values that were passed to the method aren't beyond the end of the list. That can happen if the total number of rows isn't evenly divisible by the number of rows on a page. For example, the Products table contains 23 rows, and 8 rows are displayed on each page (see figure 17-19). That means that the last page will contain only seven rows. In that case, the maximum number of rows must be adjusted so only those seven rows are returned. If you omit this code, an error will occur when you try to display the last page indicating that the index is out of range.

The last group of statements in this method retrieves the requested rows from the product list and stores them in another List<Product> object named pageList. To do that, it uses a for loop with a counter variable that varies from a value of 0 to the maximum number of rows minus 1. Then, the first statement within the loop calculates the index of the item to be retrieved from the product list by adding the value of the starting index that was passed to the method to the counter variable. Then, the item at that index is added to the page list. Finally, after all the items have been added to the page list, the list is returned to the object data source.

By the way, if you use the wizard to create an ObjectDataSource control from a data access class that provides for paging, you should know that the wizard will ask you to define the two parameters used by the select method. Because these parameters are identified by attributes of the control, however, you can just click Finish when the Define Parameters step is displayed. Then, you'll need to delete the parameters that are generated by default.

The data access class used by the object data source

```
using System;
using System.Collections;
using System.Configuration;
using System.Data;
using System.Data.SqlClient;
using System.ComponentModel;
using System.Collections.Generic;

[DataObject(true)]
public static class ProductDB
{
    private static List<Product> productList;

    [DataObjectMethod(DataObjectMethodType.Select)]
    public static List<Product> GetProductsByPage(int startIndex, int maxRows)
    {
        productList = new List<Product>();
        SqlConnection con = new SqlConnection(GetConnectionString());
        string sel = "SELECT ProductID, Name, CategoryID, UnitPrice, OnHand "
            + "FROM Products ORDER BY Name";
        SqlCommand cmd = new SqlCommand(sel, con);
        con.Open();
        SqlDataReader dr = cmd.ExecuteReader(CommandBehavior.CloseConnection);
        Product product;
        while (dr.Read())
        {
            product = new Product();
            product.ProductID = dr["ProductID"].ToString();
            product.Name = dr["Name"].ToString();
            product.CategoryID = dr["CategoryID"].ToString();
            product.UnitPrice = (decimal) dr["UnitPrice"];
            product.OnHand = (int) dr["OnHand"];
            productList.Add(product);
        }
        dr.Close();

        int rowCount = productList.Count;
        if (startIndex + maxRows > rowCount)
            maxRows = rowCount - startIndex;

        List<Product> pageList = new List<Product>();
        int rowIndex;
        for (int i = 0; i <= maxRows - 1; i++)
        {
            rowIndex = i + startIndex;
            pageList.Add(productList[rowIndex]);
        }
        return pageList;
    }

    public static int SelectCount()
    {
        return productList.Count;
    }
    .
    .
    .
}
```

Figure 17-20   A data access class that provides for paging

Perspective

In this chapter, you've learned how to work with object data sources. As you've seen, object data sources take advantage of the time-saving data binding features of ASP.NET without sacrificing the basic principle of separating presentation code from data access code. Because of that, you may want to consider using object data sources instead of SQL or Access data sources. Another option, though, is to use LINQ data sources, which you'll learn about in the next chapter.

If you decide that you do want to use object data sources in your applications, you will of course need to learn how to use ADO.NET in code. That's beyond the scope of this book, but please check our web site for the latest editions of our ADO.NET and C# books.

Terms

3-layer architecture
presentation layer
middle layer
database layer
object data source
data access class
business object class
data object class
3-tier architecture
reflection
C# attribute

18

How to use LINQ data sources

In addition to the Access, SQL, and object data sources you've already learned about, ASP.NET 3.5 provides the new LINQ data source. This data source takes advantage of the new Language-Integrated Query (LINQ) feature of C#. LINQ provides a way for you to query data using constructs that are built into C#. That way, you can use the same language to access a variety of data. In this chapter, you'll learn the basic skills for using LINQ data sources to work with SQL Server databases.

An introduction to LINQ **590**
How LINQ works 590
How to use LINQ with SQL Server databases 592

How to use the Object Relational Designer **594**
How to create an object model 594
How to create entity classes 596

How to use the LinqDataSource control **598**
An introduction to the LinqDataSource control 598
How to configure a LinqDataSource control 600
A Product List application 602
The aspx file for the Product List application 604

How to update data **606**
How to configure a LINQ data source for updates 606
How to use optimistic concurrency 606

How to group data **608**
How to configure groups 608
An Invoices By Date application that uses groups 610
The aspx file for the Invoices By Date application 610

Perspective **614**

An introduction to LINQ

LINQ, or *Language-Integrated Query*, lets you query data using the C# language. Although you won't learn how to code LINQ queries in this chapter, you should understand how LINQ works before you use LINQ data sources. In addition, since you can use LINQ data sources only with SQL Server databases, you should have a basic understanding of how that works too.

How LINQ works

To use LINQ from a C# application, you use keywords like the ones shown in figure 18-1 to define a *query expression*. If you've ever coded a query using SQL, you shouldn't have any trouble understanding what each of these keywords does. For example, you use the *from* keyword to identify the source of data for the query. You use the *where* keyword to filter the data that's returned by the query. And you use the *select* keyword to identify the fields you want to be returned by the query.

The example in this figure illustrates how this works. Here, LINQ is used to retrieve key values from a sorted list. In this case, the key for each item is an employee name, and the value is a sales amount. Then, the query expression identifies the data to be retrieved from the sorted list.

The from clause in this query expression identifies the sorted list as the source of data and declares a *range variable* that represents the elements of the list. The where clause filters the data so that only those items with values greater than 2000 are retrieved. The orderby clause sorts the data by the item values in descending sequence. And the select clause indicates that only the key for each item should be retrieved. Notice that the where, orderby, and select clauses all use the range variable that's declared in the from clause to refer to the elements that are returned by the query. Because of that, and because the from clause identifies the source of data for the query, the from clause must always be coded first.

As shown in this example, a query expression is typically stored in a *query variable*. That's necessary because this query isn't executed when it's defined. Instead, it's executed when the application accesses the elements returned by the query. In this case, it's executed by a foreach statement. This statement adds each element that's returned by the query expression to a string variable. Then, after all the elements have been processed, the string is displayed in a message box. If you compare the output with the query expression, you can see how this works.

Notice that the query variable in this example isn't declared with an explicit type. Instead, it's given a type implicitly based on the type of elements that are returned from the sorted list. In this case, because the query returns strings, the query variable is given the type IEnumerable<string>. This works because the SortedList<> class implements the IEnumerable<T> interface.

Some of the C# keywords for working with LINQ

Keyword	Description
from	Identifies the source of data for the query.
where	Provides a condition that specifies which elements are retrieved from the data source.
orderby	Indicates how the elements that are returned by the query are sorted.
select	Specifies the content of the returned elements.
group	Groups the elements by one or more data items and lets you perform aggregate functions on the groups.
join	Combines data from two data sources.

A LINQ query that retrieves key values from a sorted list

The employee sales sorted list

```
SortedList<string, decimal> employeeSales =
    new SortedList<string,decimal>();
employeeSales.Add("Anderson", 1286.45m);
employeeSales.Add("Menendez", 2433.49m);
employeeSales.Add("Thompson", 2893.85m);
employeeSales.Add("Wilkinson", 2094.53m);
```

A query expression that selects the employee names from the list

```
var employeeList = from sales in employeeSales
                   where sales.Value > 2000
                   orderby sales.Value descending
                   select sales.Key;
```

Code that executes the query

```
string employeeDisplay = "";
foreach (var employee in employeeList)
    employeeDisplay += employee + "\n";
MessageBox.Show(employeeDisplay, "Sorted Employees With Sales Over $2000");
```

The resulting dialog box

Description

- *Language-Integrated Query* (*LINQ*) provides a set of *query operators* that are available as keywords from the C# language. You use these keywords to define a *query expression* that identifies the data you want to retrieve.

- The source of data for a query must implement the IEnumerable<T> interface or another interface that implements IEnumerable<T> such as IQueryable<T>.

- LINQ can also be used with a data source such as an array or an array list that supports the non-generic IEnumerable interface.

- The implementation of LINQ shown here is called *LINQ to Objects*.

Figure 18-1   How LINQ works

How to use LINQ with SQL Server databases

In the previous figure, you saw how to use LINQ with a SortedList<> object. This implementation of LINQ is called *LINQ to Objects*. In contrast, if you want to use LINQ with a relational database, you use an implementation called *LINQ to SQL*. Unlike LINQ to Objects, LINQ to SQL lets you insert, update, and delete data as well as retrieve data. Currently, LINQ to SQL can only be used with SQL Server databases.

Figure 18-2 presents the basic concepts for using LINQ to SQL. To query a SQL Server database, you perform the three steps listed at the top of this figure. First, you create an *object model* that defines the relationships between the objects used by your application and the objects in the database. If you're working in C#, this object model is written in the C# language. You'll learn one way to create an object model in the next topic.

Once you've created an object model, you can code queries to be executed against this model. This is illustrated by the example in this figure. Here, the first statement creates an instance of a DataContext class, which is the class that provides the link between the object model and the database. In this case, the class named HalloweenDataContext provides a link between an object model for the Halloween database and the Halloween database itself.

After you create a DataContext object, you can use it as the source of data for a query. The query in this example retrieves data from the Products table of the Halloween database. Specifically, it retrieves the ProductID, Name, UnitPrice, and OnHand columns for each item that has an on-hand amount greater than zero, and it sorts the results by the ProductID column.

Notice here that the select clause uses the *new* keyword. This keyword indicates that a new type is being created that contains just ProductID, Name, UnitPrice, and OnHand properties. This is called an *anonymous type*, and it's a new feature that was added to support LINQ. An anonymous type is created whenever you select two or more, but not all, of the columns from a table. An anonymous type isn't required when a single column is selected because that column can be represented by a built-in type such as int or string. And it's not required when all the columns are selected because a type with all the columns is defined by the object model, as you'll see later in this chapter.

If you compare the query expression in this figure to the one in figure 18-1, you'll see that, except for the anonymous type that's defined in the select clause, the syntax is identical. This illustrates one of the main advantages of LINQ. That is, it lets you query different sources of data using the same language.

The example in this figure also illustrates how you can bind the results of a query to a control. To do that, you simply set the DataSource property of the control to the query variable, and then execute the Bind method of the control.

Although you can use query expressions like the one shown here to work with a SQL Server database, you can also do that by using the LinqDataSource control. You'll learn how to use the LinqDataSource control later in this chapter. But first, I'll show you how to create an object model.

The three steps for using LINQ to query a SQL Server database

1. Create an object model that maps to the data model of the database.
2. Define the query.
3. Execute the query.

Code that uses LINQ to query the Products table in the Halloween database

```
HalloweenDataContext db = new HalloweenDataContext();

var products = from product in db.Products
               where product.OnHand > 0
               orderby product.ProductID
               select new
               {
                   product.ProductID,
                   product.Name,
                   product.UnitPrice,
                   product.OnHand
               };

GridView1.DataSource = products;
GridView1.DataBind();
```

Description

- An *object model* provides a link between the objects used by your application and the objects in a relational database. The object model is written in a programming language such as C#.

- The easiest way to create an object model is to use the Object Relational Designer. See figures 18-3 and 18-4 for details.

- After you create an object model, you can define queries that work with this model. Then, when the query is executed, it's translated to a SQL statement that can be processed by the database. The results returned by this statement are then translated back to objects that can be processed by the application.

- To define a query that works with a SQL Server database, you can use the query language that's built into C# as shown above, or you can use the LinqDataSource control as shown later in this chapter.

- When you use code to define a query, the query isn't executed until the application tries to access the individual elements returned by the query. That can happen when you use the foreach statement as shown in the previous figure or when you bind the query results to a control as shown above.

- The implementation of LINQ that's used to work with relational databases is called *LINQ to SQL*. Currently, LINQ to SQL can be used only with SQL Server databases.

- When you use LINQ to SQL, you can insert, update, and delete data as well as retrieve data.

Figure 18-2   How to use LINQ with SQL Server databases

How to use the Object Relational Designer

The easiest way to create an object model is to use the Object Relational Designer. You'll learn the basic skills for working with this designer in the next two topics.

How to create an object model

Figure 18-3 presents the basic skills for creating an object model. To do that, you use the LINQ to SQL Classes template in the Add New Item dialog box. Then, a file with the name you specify and the extension *dbml* is added to the App_Code folder, and the *Object Relational Designer*, or just *O/R Designer*, is displayed as shown here.

You use the main surface of the O/R Designer to create classes that map to database tables or views. You'll learn how to do that in the next figure. You can also use the right pane of the designer to create methods that map to stored procedures or functions.

After you create an object model, you can display the generated code by double-clicking the file with the designer.cs extension that's subordinate to the dbml file. If you do, you'll see that the DataContext class that's generated by the designer is given the name you specified when you created the object model, followed by "DataContext." Since I entered the name "Halloween" for the object model in figure 18-3, for example, the DataContext class is named "HalloweenDataContext." As you saw in the previous figure, this is the class you use to work with the object model.

You can also modify the generated code to enhance the object model if you choose to do that. Keep in mind, though, that if you use the O/R Designer to modify the object model after making changes directly to this code, the changes will be lost. In most cases, then, you won't modify the generated code directly. However, you might want to enhance this code with code that's stored in separate classes. This is possible because the classes that are defined within an object model are partial classes that can be extended by other partial classes.

The Object Relational Designer for a new object model

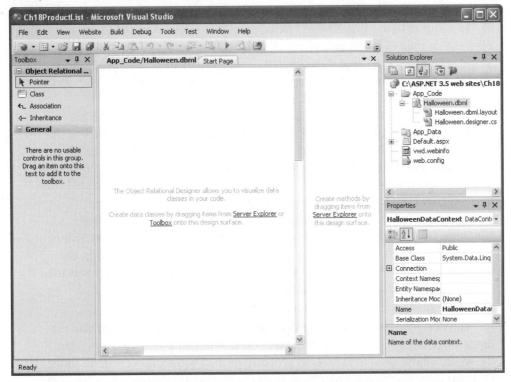

Description

- To create an object model, display the Add New Item dialog box, select the LINQ to SQL Classes template, and enter a name for the file that will define the object model.

- If the web site contains an App_Code folder, the file that defines the object model, which has the extension *dbml*, is added to that folder. Otherwise, Visual Studio will warn you that the file should be placed in the App_Code folder and ask you if you'd like to place it there. If you click the Yes button, the App_Code folder is created for you.

- After you create an object model, the *Object Relational Designer* (*O/R Designer*) is displayed. You can use this designer to create entity classes that map to database tables or views. See figure 18-4 for more information.

- If you close the O/R Designer, you can open it again by double-clicking on the dbml file in the Solution Explorer. To see the C# code that defines the object model, click the plus sign to the left of the dbml file and then double-click the designer.cs file.

- You can also use the O/R Designer to create methods that map to stored procedures or functions. If you won't be creating methods like these, you can hide the pane at the right side of the design surface by right-clicking anywhere in the designer and choosing the Hide Methods Pane command. To redisplay this pane, right-click and choose the Show Methods Pane command.

Figure 18-3   How to create an object model

How to create entity classes

In addition to the DataContext class, an object model can include *entity classes* that map to tables and views in the database. In figure 18-4, for example, you can see an object model that contains two entity classes. These classes, Category and Product, map to the Categories and Products tables in the Halloween database.

To create an entity class, you simply drag a table or view from the Server Explorer to the O/R Designer. Note that if the name of the table or view in the database is plural, the O/R Designer will give the entity class a singular name by default. That makes sense because the class will be used to create objects that represent a single item in the database. For example, an object created from the Category class represents a single category.

When you create an entity class using the O/R Designer, the designer generates C# code that defines the class. That code includes a property within the DataContext class that you can use to refer to the table in a query. In the query in figure 18-2, for example, you saw how the Products property was used to refer to the Products table in this From clause:

```
from product in db.Products
```

The designer also generates properties within the entity class that you can use to refer to each column in the table. You saw this in figure 18-2 too. Here, the where clause used the OnHand property of the Product class to refer to the OnHand column, the orderby clause used the ProductID property to refer to the ProductID column, and so on.

If you create entity classes for two tables that are related by a foreign key, the O/R Designer creates an *association* between the two classes. In this figure, for example, the arrow represents the association between the Category and Product classes. This association is defined based on the CategoryID column in the Products table, which is a foreign key to the CategoryID column in the Categories table. Because this association represents a one-to-many relationship, the Product entity class will include a property named Category that you can use in a query to refer to columns in the Categories table. In the query in figure 18-2, for example, I could have used the Category property to refer to the ShortName column like this:

```
product.Category.ShortName
```

Similarly, the Category entity class will include a property named Products that you can use to refer to the collection of products for a category.

If all this sounds a little confusing, you may want to take a look at the code that's generated for an object model as described in the previous topic. If you do, I think you'll begin to see how an object model works. I think you'll also see how much time you can save using the O/R Designer to generate code for an object model rather than entering this code yourself.

The O/R Designer for an object model that contains two entity classes

Description

- To create an *entity class*, display the Server Explorer and then drag a table or view or selected columns of a table or view from the Server Explorer to the O/R Designer.

- Each time you add an entity class, a property is added to the object model that you can use to refer to the table or view in the database. In addition, a property is added for each column in the table or view that you can use to refer to the column.

- The O/R Designer doesn't let you join data from different tables or views. However, it does recognize foreign key relationships between tables, and it creates *associations* between entity classes based on those relationships. You can use these associations to refer to one class from the other class.

- By default, if the name of a table or view in the database is plural, the O/R Designer creates a class with a singular name. If that's not what you want, display the Options dialog box (Tools→Options), expand the Database Tools node, select O/R Designer, and select False from the Enabled drop-down list in the Pluralization of Names group.

- You can display the properties of a column in an entity class by clicking on the column in the O/R Designer. However, you won't usually change these properties since they're based on the definition of the column in the database.

- You can also use the tools in the Toolbox to create entity classes manually, to add relationships (associations), and to use inheritance.

Express Edition difference

- The Server Explorer is called the Database Explorer.

Figure 18-4   How to create entity classes

How to use the LinqDataSource control

Now that you have a general idea of how LINQ works and how you create an object model, you're ready to learn how to use the LinqDataSource control. That's what you'll learn in the remaining topics of this chapter. As you'll see when you read these topics, you don't code query expressions when you use the LinqDataSource control. However, understanding how to code query expressions will help you understand what the LinqDataSource control is doing behind the scenes.

An introduction to the LinqDataSource control

Figure 18-5 introduces you to the LinqDataSource control by presenting its basic attributes. The example at the top of this figure illustrates how some of these attributes work. Here, a LinqDataSource control provides the data for a drop-down list.

The ContextTypeName attribute names the DataContext class that defines the entity classes you want to use. For this LINQ data source, the DataContext class is the one named HalloweenDataContext that was shown in figure 18-4. Then, the TableName attribute names the database table that contains the data you want to work with. Actually, this is the name of the property in the DataContext class that maps to the database table. Since the name of the property and the table are the same, however, you can think of it as the table name. This is equivalent to coding a table name on the from clause of a query expression.

The Select and OrderBy attributes are equivalent to the select and orderby clauses of a query expression. The Select attribute identifies the columns that will be included in the query results, and the OrderBy attribute indicates how the results are sorted. In this case, the CategoryID and LongName columns from the Categories table will be included in the results, and the results will be sorted by the LongName column. Notice that just like when you use C# to code a query that retrieves selected columns from a table, the new keyword is used in the Select attribute to create an anonymous type.

In addition to these attributes, you can use the Where attribute to filter the rows that are retrieved, you can use the GroupBy and OrderGroupsBy attributes to group the rows that are retrieved, and you can use the EnableInsert, EnableUpdate, and EnableDelete attributes to provide for inserting, updating, and deleting rows using the data source. You'll learn how to use these attributes later in this chapter. If you want to use paging or sorting with a control that's bound to a LINQ data source, the AutoPage or AutoSort attributes of the data source must be set to True. Since that's the default, you don't usually need to worry about these attributes.

A drop-down list that's bound to a LinqDataSource control

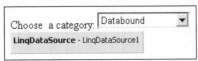

The code for the drop-down list and the LinqDataSource control

```
<asp:DropDownList ID="DropDownList1" runat="server"
    DataSourceID="LinqDataSource1" DataTextField="LongName"
    DataValueField="CategoryID" Width="130px" AutoPostBack="True">
</asp:DropDownList>
<asp:LinqDataSource ID="LinqDataSource1" runat="server"
    ContextTypeName="HalloweenDataContext"
    OrderBy="LongName"
    Select="new (CategoryID, LongName)"
    TableName="Categories">
</asp:LinqDataSource>
```

Basic attributes of the LinqDataSource control

Attribute	Description
ID	The ID of the control.
Runat	Must specify "server."
ContextTypeName	The name of the DataContext class that represents the data in the database.
TableName	The name of the table in the database whose data you want to work with.
Select	Identifies the columns to be included in the query results. If this attribute is omitted, all the columns are retrieved from the table.
Where	Specifies the conditions that must be met for a row to be retrieved from the table. If this attribute is omitted, all the rows are retrieved from the table.
OrderBy	Names the columns that are used to sort the data that's retrieved and whether each column is sorted in ascending or descending sequence.
GroupBy	Names the columns that are used to group the data that's retrieved.
OrderGroupsBy	Names the columns that are used to sort the groups of data specified by the GroupBy attribute.
EnableInsert	Indicates if the control provides for inserting rows into the table.
EnableUpdate	Indicates if the control provides for updating rows in the table.
EnableDelete	Indicates if the control provides for deleting rows from the table.
AutoPage	Indicates if the control provides for paging. The default is True.
AutoSort	Indicates if the control provides for sorting. The default is True.

Description

- The LinqDataSource control names the DataContext class and table you want to work with, identifies the data to be retrieved, and specifies how the data is sorted and grouped.
- If you want to use paging with a control that's bound to a LinqDataSource control, the AutoPage property must be set to True. If you want to using sorting with a bound control, the AutoSort property must be set to True.

Figure 18-5   An introduction to the LinqDataSource control

How to configure a LinqDataSource control

Figure 18-6 shows you the two steps of the Data Source Configuration Wizard for configuring a LinqDataSource control. The first step is displayed when you drag a LinqDataSource control from the Toolbox to a form and then select Configure Data Source from its smart tag menu. This step lets you choose the DataContext class you want to use with the control.

The second step of the wizard lets you select the table you want to retrieve data from and the columns whose data you want to retrieve. When this step is first displayed, the check box in the Select list that has an asterisk next to it is selected. This indicates that all the columns will be retrieved. If that's not what you want, you can select individual columns.

In this example, I selected the ProductID, Name, UnitPrice, and OnHand columns from the Products table. In addition, I selected the column named Category. That way, I can use this column to access the Category object for a given product. This is possible because I included both the Categories and Products tables in the object model, so an association is defined between these tables. You'll see how this works in the Product List application that's presented in the next two topics.

The second step of the wizard also lets you specify a condition that determines what rows are returned as well as a sort sequence for the rows that are returned. To do that, you use the Where and OrderBy buttons. The dialog boxes that are displayed when you click these buttons work just like the ones that are displayed for a SqlDataSource control.

The Advanced button displays a dialog box that lets you specify whether the data source provides for insert, update, and delete operations. You'll learn how this works later in this chapter.

Finally, the GroupBy drop-down list lets you select a column that the returned rows are grouped by. You'll learn how this works later in this chapter too.

By the way, you can also start the Data Source Configuration Wizard using the Choose Data Source command in the smart tag menu of a bindable control. Then, when the Choose a Data Source Type dialog box is displayed, you can select the LINQ icon and click the OK button to display the first dialog box shown here.

The Data Source Configuration Wizard

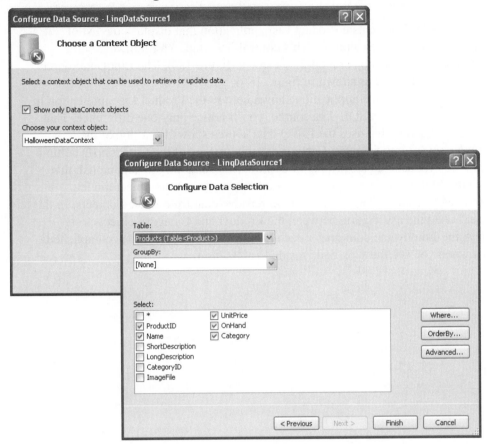

Description

- You can use the Data Source Configuration Wizard to configure a LinqDataSource control by choosing Configure Data Source from its smart tag menu.

- The Choose a Context Object step of the wizard lets you select the DataContext class you want to use.

- The Configure Data Selection step of the wizard lets you select the table and columns you want to retrieve. By default, the first check box (*) is selected, which means that all the columns will be retrieved.

- The Select list includes the properties that are defined for the entity class for the table you select. If that table is related to another table in the data context, the property that provides access to the other table is also included in the Select list.

- To specify selection criteria, click the Where button. To specify the sort order, click the OrderBy button. To insert, update, or delete rows, click the Advanced button. See figure 18-9 for more information on inserting, updating, and deleting rows.

- To group the rows that are retrieved, select a column from the GroupBy drop-down list. See figure 18-10 for more information.

Figure 18-6   How to configure a LinqDataSource control

A Product List application

Figure 18-7 presents a Product List application that displays the list of products in a GridView control. This control is bound to a LinqDataSource control that uses the object model you saw in figure 18-4. The LinqDataSource control is configured as shown in figure 18-6.

If you compare the application shown here to the Product List application in chapter 14 that uses a SQL data source, you'll notice only one difference. That is, the application that uses the LINQ data source shows the value of the LongName column from the Categories table instead of the CategoryID column from the Products table. Although I could have used a join to accomplish that with the SQL data source, you can't implement a join in an object model. However, you can use an association to retrieve data from related objects. In this case, I used the association between the Product and Category objects to retrieve the LongName column for each product. You'll see how I accomplished that when you see the aspx code for this application.

The Product List application

Description

- This version of the Product List application uses a GridView control that's bound to a LinqDataSource control. The LinqDataSource control retrieves selected columns from all the products in the Products table.

- The LinqDataSource control uses an object model that includes two entity classes named Category and Product. The Category entity is mapped to the Categories table of the Halloween database and the Product entity is mapped to the Products table.

- The Category entity is included so that the LongName column in the Categories table can be displayed for each product instead of the CategoryID column in the Products table. This is possible because of the foreign key relationship between the Products and Categories table and the association that defines this relationship in the object model.

Figure 18-7   A Product List application

The aspx file for the Product List application

Figure 18-8 presents the aspx code for this version of the Product List application. The first thing you should notice here is the definition of the LinqDataSource control. As you can see, it uses the HalloweenDataContext class, and it retrieves data from the Products table. In addition, the Select attribute creates an anonymous type that includes five properties of the Product entity class. The last property, Category, refers to the category that's related to a given product.

To see how you can use this property, take a look at the template field in the GridView control. This template uses the Category property in the SortExpression attribute to refer to the LongName column. In addition, it includes an Item template with a label that's bound to the LongName column. I used a template here because this column must be bound using the Eval method. It can't be bound using a bound field.

The body of the Default.aspx file

```
<body>
    <form id="form1" runat="server">
    <div>
        <asp:Image ID="Image1" runat="server" ImageUrl="Images/banner.jpg" />
        <br /><br />
        <asp:GridView ID="GridView1" runat="server"
            AutoGenerateColumns="False" DataSourceID="LinqDataSource1"
            AllowPaging="True" AllowSorting="True"
            CellPadding="4" ForeColor="Black" GridLines="None">
            <Columns>
                <asp:BoundField DataField="ProductID" HeaderText="ID"
                    ReadOnly="True" SortExpression="ProductID" >
                    <HeaderStyle HorizontalAlign="Left" Width="75px" />
                </asp:BoundField>
                <asp:BoundField DataField="Name" HeaderText="Name"
                    ReadOnly="True" SortExpression="Name" >
                    <HeaderStyle HorizontalAlign="Left" Width="175px" />
                </asp:BoundField>
                <asp:TemplateField HeaderText="Category"
                    SortExpression="Category.LongName, Name">
                    <ItemTemplate>
                        <asp:Label ID="Label1" runat="server"
                        Text='<%# Eval("Category.LongName") %>'></asp:Label>
                    </ItemTemplate>
                    <HeaderStyle HorizontalAlign="Left" Width="100px" />
                </asp:TemplateField>
                <asp:BoundField DataField="UnitPrice" HeaderText="Unit Price"
                    ReadOnly="True" DataFormatString="{0:c}"
                    HtmlEncode="False" >
                    <HeaderStyle HorizontalAlign="Right" Width="85px" />
                    <ItemStyle HorizontalAlign="Right" />
                </asp:BoundField>
                <asp:BoundField DataField="OnHand" HeaderText="On Hand"
                    ReadOnly="True" >
                    <HeaderStyle HorizontalAlign="Right" Width="85px" />
                    <ItemStyle HorizontalAlign="Right" />
                </asp:BoundField>
            </Columns>
            <HeaderStyle BackColor="Silver" Font-Bold="True"
                ForeColor="White" />
            <RowStyle BackColor="White" ForeColor="Black" />
            <AlternatingRowStyle BackColor="#F5F5F5" ForeColor="Black" />
            <PagerStyle BackColor="Silver" ForeColor="Blue"
                HorizontalAlign="Center" />
        </asp:GridView>
        <asp:LinqDataSource ID="LinqDataSource1" runat="server"
            ContextTypeName="HalloweenDataContext" OrderBy="ProductID"
            Select="new (ProductID, Name, UnitPrice, OnHand, Category)"
            TableName="Products">
        </asp:LinqDataSource>
    </div>
    </form>
</body>
```

Figure 18-8   The aspx file for the Product List application

How to update data

In the next two topics, you'll learn how to update data using the LinqDataSource control. As you'll see, the technique for doing that is much simpler than the technique you use with other types of data sources.

How to configure a LINQ data source for updates

To configure a LINQ data source so it provides for insert, update, and delete operations, you can use the Advanced Options dialog box shown in figure 18-9. As you can see, this dialog box simply lets you select the operations you want to perform. Then, the EnableDelete, EnableInsert, and EnableUpdate attributes of the LinqDataSource control are set depending on which options you choose.

The control shown here illustrates how this works. This control can be used to insert, update, and delete rows from the Categories table. Notice that this control doesn't include a Select attribute. This is a requirement for controls that update data because the control must return an object that contains all the properties defined by the entity class.

Once you enable updating for the LINQ data source, you can use it with any bound control that provides for updating. Then, when the LINQ data source receives a request to perform an insert, update, or delete operation, it automatically creates the command needed to perform that operation. Because of that, you don't need to provide any additional aspx or C# code. However, you may want to respond to events of the control that's bound to the LINQ data source to perform processing before or after an insert, update, or delete operation. This works just like it does with a SqlDataSource control.

Because the code for a maintenance application that uses a LINQ data source is similar to the code for an application that uses a SQL data source, I won't present a complete application here. However, a Category Maintenance application that uses the LINQ data source shown here is included in the download for this book if you want to see how it works.

How to use optimistic concurrency

The LinqDataSource control provides for optimistic concurrency by default. To do that, it stores the original values of any columns that can be changed in view state. Then, it compares those values to the current values in the database when an update or delete operation is performed.

Although this is usually what you want, you can change the way this works for individual columns using the O/R Designer. To do that, just change the value of the column's UpdateCheck property. If you don't ever want to check the column for changes, change this property to Never. If you want to check the column for changes only if its value in the program changes, change this property to When Changed.

The Advanced Options dialog box

The aspx code for a LinqDataSource control that performs insert, update, and delete operations

```
<asp:LinqDataSource ID="LinqDataSource1" runat="server"
    ContextTypeName="HalloweenDataContext"
    EnableDelete="True" EnableInsert="True" EnableUpdate="True"
    OrderBy="CategoryID" TableName="Categories">
</asp:LinqDataSource>
```

How to configure a LINQ data source for updates

- Display the Advanced Options dialog box and then select the appropriate options, or select the Enable Delete, Enable Insert, and Enable Update options from the LinqDataSource control's smart tag menu.

- To display the Advanced Options dialog box, click the Advanced button in the Configure Data Selection step of the Data Source Configuration Wizard. This button is available only if you select the first check box (*) to select all the columns in the table.

- When you enable inserting, updating, or deleting for a LinqDataSource control, the control automatically generates the commands needed to perform these operations.

- You can use the events of a control that's bound to a LINQ data source to perform processing before or after an insert, update, or delete operation. This works just like it does for a SQL data source.

How to use optimistic concurrency

- By default, the LinqDataSource control provides for optimistic concurrency by storing the original values of the data on a page in view state. Then, when an update or delete operation is performed, the original values are compared to the values in the database. If the values have changed, an exception occurs.

- You can use the O/R Designer to change which column values are used for concurrency checking. To do that, select the column and choose an option for the UpdateCheck property. The available options are Always, Never, and When Changed.

Figure 18-9   How to update data

How to group data

When you retrieve data from a table, you can group the results based on one of the columns in the table. Then, you can summarize the results for each group. In addition, you can access the individual rows in each group. You'll learn how to accomplish that in the topic that follows. Then, you'll see an application that uses groups to summarize the data in a table of invoices.

How to configure groups

If you select a column from the GroupBy drop-down list in the Configure Data Selection step of the Data Source Configuration Wizard, the dialog box changes to look like the one shown in figure 18-10. You can use this dialog box to identify the columns you want to include in the query results and to specify a sort order for the groups. By default, the results are sorted by the column that's used to group the results in ascending sequence. You can also sort by this column in descending sequence or not sort at all.

When this dialog box is first displayed, two columns are included in the Select list. The first one is for the column that's used for grouping, and it's represented by the *key* keyword. Since an *alias* is specified for this column, however, you'll refer to it in your application using this alias. By default, the alias is the name of the column, but you can change it to anything you want.

When you group data, you'll sometimes want to access the individual rows in the groups. To do that, you use the second column that's automatically included in the Select list. This column is represented by the *it* keyword, and its default alias is the name of the table.

In addition to the key and it columns, you can include one or more *aggregate columns*. An aggregate column is a column that summarizes the data in one of the columns of the table or provides a count of the number of rows returned by the query. To create an aggregate column that summarizes data, you simply select the column you want to summarize from the Column drop-down list, select the type of summary you want to perform from the Function drop-down list, and then enter an alias for the column. To create an aggregate column that provides a count of rows, you select (Count) from the Column drop-down list and then enter an alias.

The LinqDataSource control in this figure illustrates how this works. Here, the rows in the Invoices table of the Halloween database are grouped by the OrderDate column, and the groups are sorted by that column in ascending sequence. In addition to this column and the column that represents the individual invoices, the query includes an aggregate column named Sum_Total. This column will contain the sum of the Total column for the invoices in each group. You'll see how this LinqDataSource control is used in the application that follows.

The dialog box for configuring a data source that uses groups

The aspx code for a LinqDataSource control that groups data

```
<asp:LinqDataSource ID="LinqDataSource1" runat="server"
    ContextTypeName="HalloweenDataContext"
    GroupBy="OrderDate"
    OrderGroupsBy="key"
    Select="new (key as OrderDate, it as Invoices, Sum(Total) as Sum_Total)"
    TableName="Invoices">
</asp:LinqDataSource>
```

Description

- To group the rows that are returned by a LINQ data source, select a column from the GroupBy drop-down list in the Configure Data Selection step of the Data Source Configuration Wizard. Then, this step changes to the one shown above.

- The LinqDataSource control uses the *key* keyword to refer to the column that's used for grouping, and it uses the *it* keyword to refer to the individual rows in a group. Both of these columns are automatically included in the selected columns. The key column is given an *alias* that is the same as the name of the column that's used for grouping, and the it column is given an alias that is the same as the name of the table.

- A LINQ data source that groups data typically includes one or more *aggregate columns* that summarize the data in the groups. An aggregate column can return the sum of the values in the column, the average of the values, the largest value, or the smallest value. It can also return a count of the number of rows returned in each group.

- To create an aggregate column that summarizes a value, select the column you want to summarize and the summary function you want to perform from the drop-down lists in a row of the Select grid, and enter an alias for the column. To create an aggregate column that returns a count, select (Count) for the column and then enter an alias.

Figure 18-10   How to configure groups

An Invoices By Date application that uses groups

Figure 18-11 presents an application that groups the data in the Invoices table of the Halloween database by order date. For each group, it displays the order date and the invoice total in a ListView control. This ListView control includes a DataPager control that specifies that only one group should be displayed on a page at a time.

Within the first ListView control, another ListView control is used to display the invoices in each group. To accomplish that, I had to bind this control to the column that represents the individual rows in the table. You'll see how to do that when you see the aspx code for this application.

The aspx file for the Invoices By Date application

Figure 18-12 shows the aspx code for the Invoices By Date application. On the first page of this listing, you can see that the first ListView control is bound to the LinqDataSource control shown on page 2. Because this is the same LinqDataSource control you saw in figure 18-10, you shouldn't have any trouble understanding how it works.

Like any ListView control, the Layout template for this control contains a placeholder that identifies where the data from the Item template will be displayed. If you look at the Item template for this control starting at the bottom of page 1, you'll see that it includes three rows. The first row contains a label that's bound to the OrderDate column. The second row contains another ListView control. And the third row contains a label that's bound to the Sum_Total column.

Before I describe the second ListView control, you should notice that the binding expression for the Sum_Total column includes the text "Invoice Total:" that's displayed in front of the column value. This text is concatenated with the column value using the + operator. Although the expression shown here is split onto two lines, you should realize that you can't split a binding expression like this. It's split in this example only because it won't fit on a single line.

The second ListView control is bound to the Invoices column of the query results through its DataSource property. This column represents the individual invoices. Because of that, the Item template for this control can include binding expressions for any of the columns in the Invoices table. For this application, binding expressions are used to display the InvoiceNumber, Subtotal, Shipping, SalesTax, and Total columns.

By the way, I created this ListView control in Source view because there's no way to create a ListView control that's embedded in another control in Design view. When I did that, I didn't use labels to display the data from the Invoices table. Instead, I just coded the binding expression directly in each cell as shown here.

The Invoices By Date application

Description

- The Invoices By Date application uses an object model that includes just the Invoices table from the Halloween database.

- This application groups the data in the Invoices table by the order date. Then, it displays the order date and invoice total for each group in a ListView control.

- Within the first ListView control, another ListView control is used to display data for the individual invoices.

- A DataPager control is included in the outer ListView control so that only the invoices for one day are displayed on each page.

Figure 18-11   An Invoices By Date application that uses groups

The Default.aspx file   **Page 1**

```
<%@ Page Language="C#" AutoEventWireup="true" CodeFile="Default.aspx.cs"
Inherits="_Default" %>

<!DOCTYPE html PUBLIC "-//W3C//DTD XHTML 1.0 Transitional//EN"
"http://www.w3.org/TR/xhtml1/DTD/xhtml1-transitional.dtd">

<html xmlns="http://www.w3.org/1999/xhtml">
<head runat="server">
    <title>Chapter 18: Invoices By Date</title>
</head>
<body>
  <form id="form1" runat="server">
  <div>
    <asp:Image ID="Image1" runat="server" ImageUrl="~/Images/banner.jpg" />
    <br /><br />
    <asp:ListView ID="ListView1" runat="server"
        DataSourceID="LinqDataSource1">
      <LayoutTemplate>
        <table runat="server">
          <tr runat="server">
            <td runat="server">
              <table ID="itemPlaceholderContainer" runat="server"
                     cellspacing="0" cellpadding="2">
                <tr runat="server" style="background-color: Silver;
                    color: White; font-family: Arial, Sans-Serif;
                    font-weight: bold">
                 <td runat="server">Order Date</td>
                </tr>
                <tr ID="itemPlaceholder" runat="server">
                </tr>
              </table>
            </td>
          </tr>
          <tr runat="server" style="background-color: Silver" align="center">
            <td runat="server">
              <asp:DataPager ID="DataPager1" runat="server" PageSize="1">
                <Fields>
                  <asp:NextPreviousPagerField ButtonType="Button"
                      ShowFirstPageButton="True"
                      ShowLastPageButton="True" />
                </Fields>
              </asp:DataPager>
            </td>
          </tr>
        </table>
      </LayoutTemplate>
      <ItemTemplate>
        <tr style="background-color: #F5F5F5">
          <td style="width: 449px">
            <asp:Label ID="OrderDateLabel" runat="server"
                Text='<%# Eval("OrderDate", "{0:d}") %>' />
          </td>
        </tr>
```

Figure 18-12   The aspx file for the Invoices By Date application (part 1 of 2)

The Default.aspx file   **Page 2**

```
        <tr>
          <td>
            <asp:ListView ID="ListView2" runat="server"
                DataSource='<%# Eval("Invoices") %>'>
              <LayoutTemplate>
                <table id="itemPlaceholderContainer" runat="server"
                        cellspacing="0" cellpadding="2">
                  <tr runat="server">
                    <td runat="server"></td>
                    <td runat="server">Invoice No</td>
                    <td runat="server" align="right">Subtotal</td>
                    <td runat="server" align="right">Shipping</td>
                    <td runat="server" align="right">Sales Tax</td>
                    <td runat="server" align="right">Total</td>
                  </tr>
                  <tr ID="itemPlaceholder" runat="server"></tr>
                </table>
              </LayoutTemplate>
              <ItemTemplate>
                <tr>
                  <td style="width: 25px"></td>
                  <td style="width: 75px">
                    <%#Eval("InvoiceNumber")%></td>
                  <td style="width: 75px" align="right">
                    <%#Eval("Subtotal", "{0:c}")%></td>
                  <td style="width: 75px" align="right">
                    <%#Eval("Shipping", "{0:c}")%></td>
                  <td style="width: 75px" align="right">
                    <%#Eval("SalesTax", "{0:c}")%></td>
                  <td style="width: 100px" align="right">
                    <%#Eval("Total", "{0:c}")%></td>
                </tr>
              </ItemTemplate>
            </asp:ListView>
          </td>
        </tr>
        <tr style="background-color: #F5F5F5">
          <td style="width: 449px" align="right">
            <asp:Label ID="Label2" runat="server"
                Text='<%#"Invoice Total:    " +
Eval("Sum_Total", "{0:c}") %>' />
          </td>
        </tr>
      </ItemTemplate>
    </asp:ListView>
    <asp:LinqDataSource ID="LinqDataSource1" runat="server"
        ContextTypeName="HalloweenDataContext"
        GroupBy="OrderDate" OrderGroupsBy="key"
        Select="new (key as OrderDate, it as Invoices,
                  Sum(Total)as Sum_Total)"
        TableName="Invoices">
    </asp:LinqDataSource>
  </div>
  </form>
</body>
</html>
```

Figure 18-12   The aspx file for the Invoices By Date application (part 2 of 2)

Perspective

Now that you've read this chapter, you should begin to see how easy it is to create applications using LINQ data sources. Because the object model and LINQ to SQL do much of the work, it's relatively easy to configure a LinqDataSource control so it works the way you want it to. That's particularly true if you use the Data Source Configuration Wizard as shown in this chapter.

Of course, there may be times when the LinqDataSource control doesn't provide the flexibility you need. In that case, you might want to use code to work with LINQ to SQL. Although I presented a simple illustration of that in figure 18-2, there's a lot more to learn about LINQ to SQL than what's shown in this figure. So if you're interested in using LINQ to SQL without a LinqDataSource control, you'll need to get more information on how to do that from the Visual Studio documentation or from a book on LINQ.

Terms

LINQ (Language-Integrated Query)
query operator
query expression
range variable
query variable
LINQ to Objects
LINQ to SQL
object model
anonymous type
O/R (Object Relational) Designer
entity class
association
alias
aggregate column

Section 4

Professional ASP.NET skills

This section consists of eight chapters that present ASP.NET skills that are often used in professional web applications. To start, chapter 19 shows you how to use a secure connection for an application, and chapter 20 shows you how to authenticate and authorize the users of an application using the Web Site Administration Tool and the login controls. These are essential skills for e-commerce applications.

Next, chapter 21 shows you how you can use profiles to personalize an application, and chapter 22 shows you how to use two of the multi-page server controls. Then, chapter 23 shows you how to use email and custom error pages as well as how to deal with the problems that can occur when users click the Back buttons in their browsers. These are useful skills for most professional applications.

In chapter 24, you'll learn how to use web parts to develop portals that the user can customize. Although you may never need this feature, it sure comes in handy when you do need it. Then, chapter 25 introduces you to AJAX and shows you how to use the new AJAX server controls. Finally, chapter 26 shows you how to configure and deploy an application, which you'll need to do for every application that you develop. At that point, you'll be able to develop and deploy e-commerce applications at a thoroughly professional level.

Because each of the chapters in this section is written as an independent module, you can read these chapters in whatever sequence you prefer. If, for example, you want to learn how to use profiles as an alternative to session state, you can skip directly to chapter 21. Or, if you want to learn how to send email from a web application, you can skip to chapter 23. Eventually, though, you'll want to read all of the chapters because you should at least be aware of the capabilities that they offer.

19

How to secure a web site

Security is one of the most important concerns for any developer of e-commerce web sites. To secure a web site, you must make sure that private data that's sent between the client and the server can't be deciphered. To accomplish that, this chapter shows you how to use an Internet protocol called SSL.

An introduction to SSL **618**
How secure connections work 618
How digital secure certificates work 620
How to determine if a digital secure certificate is installed
on your server 620

How to get and use a digital secure certificate **622**
How to get a digital secure certificate 622
How to get a trial certificate for testing 624
How to use the IIS Certificate Wizard 626
How to work with certificates using IIS 7.0 628

How to use a secure connection **630**
How to request a secure connection 630
How to force a page to use a secure connection 632

A Halloween Store application that uses SSL **634**
The operation of the Halloween Store application 634
The code for the Halloween Store application 634

Perspective **638**

An introduction to SSL

To prevent others from reading data that's transmitted over the Internet, you can use the *Secure Sockets Layer*, or *SSL*. SSL is an Internet protocol that lets you transmit data over the Internet using data encryption. The topics that follow explain how SSL works.

How secure connections work

Figure 19-1 shows a web page that uses SSL to transfer data between the server and the client over a *secure connection*. To determine if you're transmitting data over a secure connection, you can read the URL in the browser's address bar. If it starts with HTTPS rather than HTTP, then you're transmitting data over a secure connection.

With a regular HTTP connection, all data is sent as unencrypted plain text. As a result, if a hacker intercepts this data, it is easy to read. With a secure connection, however, all data that's transferred between the client and the server is encrypted. Although a hacker can still intercept this data, he won't be able to read it without breaking the encryption code.

Note that to test an application that uses a secure connection, you must run the application under IIS. Because of that, if you created the application as a file-system web site, you'll need to use one of the techniques described in chapter 4 to run it under IIS.

A page that was requested with a secure connection

The URL starts with https:

Description

- The *Secure Sockets Layer*, or *SSL*, is the protocol used by the World Wide Web that allows clients and servers to communicate over a *secure connection*.
- With SSL, the browser encrypts all data that's sent to the server and decrypts all data that's received from the server. Conversely, the server encrypts all data that's sent to the browser and decrypts all data that's received from the browser.
- SSL is able to determine if data has been tampered with during transit.
- SSL is also able to verify that a server or a client is who it claims to be.
- The URL for a secure connection starts with HTTPS instead of HTTP.

Notes

- To test an application that uses SSL, you must run the application under the control of IIS. For information on how to do that, see chapter 4.
- With some browsers, a lock icon is displayed when a secure connection is being used.

Figure 19-1   How secure connections work

How digital secure certificates work

To use SSL to transmit data, the client and the server use *digital secure certificates* like the one shown in figure 19-2. Digital secure certificates serve two purposes. First, they establish the identity of the server or client. Second, they provide the information needed to encrypt data before it's transmitted.

By default, browsers are configured to accept certificates that come from trusted sources. If a browser doesn't recognize a certificate as coming from a trusted source, however, it informs the user and lets the user view the certificate. Then, the user can determine whether the certificate should be considered valid. If the user chooses to accept the certificate, the secure connection is established.

Sometimes, a server may want the client to authenticate itself with *SSL client authentication*. Although this isn't as common as *SSL server authentication*, it is used occasionally. For example, a bank might want to use SSL client authentication to make sure it's sending sensitive information such as account numbers and balances to the correct person. To implement this type of authentication, a digital secure certificate must be installed on the client.

How to determine if a digital secure certificate is installed on your server

Before you learn how to obtain and install digital secure certificates and trial certificates, you may want to check if a certificate is already installed on your server. If IIS is running on your local machine, chances are that a certificate hasn't been installed. But if IIS is running on a server on a network, you can use the procedure in figure 19-2 to determine if a certificate has been installed and to view the certificate.

Please note that this procedure is for Windows XP, which includes IIS 5.1, and Windows Server 2003, which includes IIS 6.0. If you're using Windows Vista or Windows Server 2008, which include IIS 7.0, the procedure for determining if a digital secure certificate is installed is somewhat different. In that case, you can refer to the topic later in this chapter on working with certificates using IIS 7.0.

The Certificate dialog box for a digital secure certificate

Types of digital secure certificates

Certificate	Description
Server certificate	Issued to trusted servers so client computers can connect to them using secure connections.
Client certificate	Issued to trusted clients so server computers can confirm their identity.

Concepts

- *Authentication* determines whether a server or client is who it claims to be.
- When a browser makes an initial attempt to communicate with a server over a secure connection that uses SSL, the server authenticates itself by sending its *digital secure certificate* to the browser.
- In some instances, the server may also request that a browser authenticate itself by presenting its own digital secure certificate. This is uncommon, however.

How to determine if a digital secure certificate is installed on your server

1. Display the IIS Management Console by double-clicking on Administrative Tools in the Control Panel and then double-clicking on Internet Information Services.

2. Expand the node for the server and the Web Sites node and then right-click on the Default Web Site node and select Properties to display the Properties dialog box.

3. Click the Directory Security tab. If a digital secure certificate is installed, the View Certificate button will be enabled. Click this button to display the dialog box shown above.

Figure 19-2   How digital secure certificates work

How to get and use a digital secure certificate

In the topics that follow, you'll first learn the general procedure for getting a digital secure certificate. Then, you'll learn how to get a trial certificate that you can use for testing web sites under IIS 5.1 or 6.0, and you'll learn how to use the IIS Certificate Wizard to manage certificates with IIS 5.1 or 6.0. Finally, you'll learn how to work with certificates using IIS 7.0.

How to get a digital secure certificate

If you want to develop an ASP.NET application that uses SSL to secure client connections, you must first obtain a digital secure certificate from a trusted source such as those listed in figure 19-3. These *certification authorities*, or *CAs*, verify that the person or company requesting the certificate is a valid person or company by checking with a *registration authority*, or *RA*. To obtain a digital secure certificate, you'll need to provide a registration authority with information about yourself or your company. Once the registration authority approves the request, the certification authority can issue the digital secure certificate.

A digital secure certificate from a trusted source isn't free, and the cost of the certificate will depend on a variety of factors including the level of security. As a result, when you purchase a digital certificate, you'll want one that fits the needs of your web site. In particular, you'll need to decide what *SSL strength* you want the connection to support. SSL strength refers to the level of encryption that the secure connection uses when it transmits data.

Most certificates sold today provide for up to 128-bit SSL strength. It's nearly impossible to break the encryption code provided by this SSL strength, and the most popular browsers support it. If a browser doesn't support it, however, the browser will use the maximum strength it does support, which is either 40-bit or 56-bit. Some CAs also sell certificates that provide for 256-bit SSL strength, but this strength isn't currently supported by IIS.

In addition to SSL strength, you should consider whether a certificate is a single root certificate or a chained root certificate. A *single root certificate* is a certificate from a trusted source that has already been added to the most popular browsers. These certificates are stable and easy to install. In contrast, a *chained root certificate* is a certificate that inherits a certificate that browsers recognize. Although chained root certificates can be less expensive than single root certificates, they are less stable and more difficult to install.

Common certification authorities that issue digital secure certificates

```
www.verisign.com
www.geotrust.com
www.entrust.com
www.thawte.com
```

SSL strengths

Strength	Pros and Cons
40-bit	Most browsers support it, but it's relatively easy to break the encryption code.
56-bit	It's thousands of times stronger than 40-bit strength and most browsers support it, but it's still possible to break the encryption code.
128-bit	It's over a trillion times a trillion times stronger than 40-bit strength, which makes it extremely difficult to break the encryption code, but it's more expensive and not all browsers support it.
256-bit	It's much stronger than 128-bit encryption, but it's not supported by many web servers and browsers.

Description

- To use SSL in your web applications, you must first purchase a digital secure certificate from a trusted *certification authority*, or *CA*. Once you obtain the certificate, you send it to the people who host your web site so they can install it on the server.

- A certification authority is a company that issues and manages security credentials. To verify information provided by the requestor of the secure certificate, a CA must check with a *registration authority*, or *RA*. Once the registration authority verifies the requestor's information, the certification authority can issue a digital secure certificate.

- Since SSL is built into all major browsers and web servers, installing a digital secure certificate enables SSL.

- *SSL strength* refers to the length of the generated key that is created during the encryption process. The longer the key, the more difficult it is to break the encryption code.

- The SSL strength that's used depends on the strength provided by the certificate, the strength supported by the web server, and the strength supported by the browser. If a web server or browser isn't able to support the strength provided by the certificate, a lesser strength is used.

- Most certificates are issued by trusted certification authorities who own and use their own certificates. These CAs are known to browser vendors, and their certificates have been added to many of the most popular browsers. This type of certificate is called a *single root certificate*.

- A *chained root certificate* is one that inherits the recognition of a trusted certification authority. This type of certificate is more difficult to install and some web servers and web applications can't use them.

Figure 19-3   How to get a digital secure certificate

How to get a trial certificate for testing

Most certification authorities will provide you with a free trial certificate that you can use for testing purposes. The trial certificate typically expires after a relatively short period of time, such as two weeks or a month. Although you can continue to use the trial certificate after the testing period expires, the page shown at the top of figure 19-4 will appear each time you enter a secure connection. This page simply informs you that there's a problem with the certificate.

Of course, you shouldn't run an ASP.NET application in a production environment using an expired certificate. When you're ready to deploy your application, then, you should contact the certification authority to obtain a valid certificate.

Another way to obtain certificates for testing purposes is to set up your own certification authority using Microsoft Certificate Services, which comes with Windows Server 2003. You can then use the certificate server to issue certificates for testing purposes. To learn more about Microsoft Certificate Services, you can review the online help for Windows Server 2003 or you can visit Microsoft's web site.

The page that's displayed when your trial certificate has expired

Description

- To test SSL connections in a local environment, you can request a free trial certificate from an established certification authority. The certificate typically expires in 14 to 30 days.

- After the certificate expires, you can still use it for testing purposes. When you switch to a secure connection and the certificate has expired, the page shown above will be displayed. Then, you can click the "Continue to this website" link to proceed with the secure connection even though the certificate has expired.

- The certification authority's web site will have detailed instructions you can follow to request, download, and install a trial certificate.

- An alternative to requesting a trial certificate from a certification authority is to become your own certification authority. To do that, you need to install Microsoft Certificate Services on a separate server computer on your network. Then, you can use the certificate server to create certificates you can use for testing.

- Certificates issued by a certification authority on a local network won't be trusted outside of your network, but they will be adequate for testing ASP.NET applications that use SSL.

Figure 19-4   How to get a trial certificate for testing

How to use the IIS Certificate Wizard

Microsoft's web server, Internet Information Services (IIS), includes a Certificate Wizard you can use to manage digital certificates. Figure 19-5 describes how you use this wizard.

If your IIS server doesn't have a certificate installed, the wizard walks you through the steps needed to create a file that contains the information a certification authority needs to issue a certificate. Once you create this file, you'll need to go to the certification authority's web site for instructions on how to request a certificate. Then, when you receive the certificate, you can return to the Certificate Wizard to install it.

You can also use the Certificate Wizard to manage existing certificates for your IIS server. For example, you can use it to remove certificates or renew expired certificates. You can also use it to assign a certificate that was previously installed but has been removed or to import a certificate used by another server.

The Certificate Wizard options for an IIS server that doesn't have a certificate installed

How to start the IIS Certificate Wizard

1. Display the Properties dialog box for the Default Web Site node of the server as described in figure 19-2 and display the Directory Security tab.

2. Click the Server Certificate button to display the first Certificate Wizard dialog box. This dialog box indicates whether a certificate is installed or a request is pending and summarizes the functions the wizard can help you perform.

Description

- The IIS Certificate Wizard manages the process of requesting certificates from certification authorities and installing certificates in IIS.

- If a certificate is already installed on your IIS server, the wizard lets you renew the certificate if it's expired, remove the certificate, or replace it with another certificate.

- If no certificate is installed, the wizard lets you create a certificate file that you can use to request a certificate from a certification authority, assign a certificate that was previously installed, or import a certificate from a copy exported from another server.

- If you have requested a certificate from a certification authority but haven't installed the resulting certificate, the wizard lets you complete the request and install the certificate or cancel the request.

Note

- When you request a certificate from a certification authority, it's usually sent to you as an email attachment. Then, you can save the attachment on your hard drive and use the Wizard to install it. If the certificate is sent as text within the email instead, you'll need to copy and paste it into a file using a program such as WordPad and then save it with the extension *cer*.

Figure 19-5 How to use the IIS Certificate Wizard

How to work with certificates using IIS 7.0

So far in this chapter, you've learned how to work with certificates using the versions of IIS that come with Windows XP and Windows Server 2003. If you have Windows Vista or Windows Server 2008, however, you'll need to know how to use IIS 7.0, which is the version that comes with these operating systems. Figure 19-6 summarizes the techniques you use to work with certificates using IIS 7.0.

To start, you can determine if a digital secure certificate is already installed by selecting the server in the Connections pane of the IIS Manager and then double-clicking the Server Certificates icon in the main part of the window. Then, a list of the certificates that are installed is displayed. In this figure, for example, you can see that one test certificate is installed.

Although you can request and install a trial certificate from a certification authority just as you can with IIS 5.1 or 6.0, IIS 7.0 also lets you create a *self-signed certificate*. This is simply a certificate that IIS creates for its own use, and you can use it to test security as you develop a web site. Then, if you deploy the web site to a server that doesn't already have a digital secure certificate installed, you can request a certificate from a certification authority and install it as described in this figure.

Unlike IIS 5.1 or 6.0, IIS 7.0 requires that you create a *binding* to use the HTTPS protocol. A binding defines how a web site can be accessed, and each web site is defined with a binding that uses the HTTP protocol by default. To use SSL with a web site, you must define a binding that uses the HTTPS protocol. When you define that binding, you must also select the certificate you want to use as described in this figure.

The IIS Management Console with a certificate installed

How to start IIS

- Open the Control Panel, double-click on Administrative Tools, and then double-click on Internet Information Services (IIS) Manager.

How to determine if a digital secure certificate is installed

- Select the server in the Connections pane, and then double-click Server Certificates in the main window. If a certificate is installed, it will be listed in the Server Certificates window as shown above. Then, you can select it and click View in the Actions pane to display the certificate.

How to create and install certificates

- IIS 7.0 lets you create a *self-signed certificate* that can be used for testing purposes. To do that, click Create Self-Signed Certificate in the Actions pane and then complete the dialog box that's displayed.
- To create a certificate file that you can use to request a certificate from a certification authority, click Create Certificate Request in the Actions pane and then complete the dialog boxes that are displayed.
- To install a certificate from a certification authority, click Complete Certificate Request in the Actions pane and then complete the dialog box that's displayed.

How to create a binding for the HTTPS protocol

- Before you can use the HTTPS protocol, you must create a *binding* for that protocol. To do that, select the Default Web Site node in the Connections pane, click Bindings in the Actions pane, and click the Add button in the dialog box that's displayed. Then, select https from the Type drop-down list, select a certificate from the SSL Certificate drop-down list, and click the OK button.

Figure 19-6   How to work with certificates using IIS 7.0

How to use a secure connection

In the topics that follow, you'll first learn how to request secure connections for the pages of your applications. Then, you'll learn how to force a page to use a secure connection when a user bypasses your navigation features.

How to request a secure connection

Figure 19-7 shows how to request a secure connection in an ASP.NET application. To do that, you simply execute a Response.Redirect method with a URL that specifies HTTPS as the protocol rather than HTTP. Then, depending on how the user's browser is configured, the user may see a dialog box similar to the one shown in this figure before the application enters the secure connection. In addition, if a trial or self-signed certificate is being used, a Certificate Error page like the one you saw on figure 19-4 will be displayed. Then, you can click the "Continue to this website" link on this page to display the requested page with a secure connection.

To request a secure connection using HTTPS, you must use an absolute URL. That means that the URL must include the complete application path, including the web server's domain name and the directory path that leads to the application. For example, the first URL in this figure specifies //localhost as the web server's domain name and /ASPNET2008/Ch19HalloweenStore as the directory path.

Rather than coding this information into each URL, you may want to store the application path in the web.config file as shown in the second coding example in this figure. As you can see, you store this information as an element within the appSettings section of this file. Then, you can use the AppSettings property of the ConfigurationManager class to retrieve the value of the element that contains the path. This is illustrated in the third coding example. If you use this technique, you'll only need to change the application path in the web.config file if you deploy the application to a different location.

Once your application has established a secure connection, it can navigate to other pages using relative URLs while maintaining the secure connection. To close the secure connection, the application must navigate to another page by specifying an absolute URL with HTTP rather than HTTPS as the protocol. This is illustrated in the last coding example in this figure.

A dialog box that may be displayed for secure connections

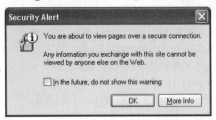

A URL that requests a secure connection

```
https://localhost/ASPNET2008/Ch19HalloweenStore/CheckOut1.aspx
```

A web.config file that defines the AppPath setting

```xml
<?xml version="1.0"?>
<configuration xmlns="http://schemas.microsoft.com/.NetConfiguration/v2.0">
    <appSettings>
        <add key="AppPath"
             value="//localhost/ASPNET2008/Ch19HalloweenStore/" />
    </appSettings>
    <system.web>
    .
    .
```

Code that retrieves the application path from the web.config file

```csharp
string url = "https:"
    + ConfigurationManager.AppSettings["AppPath"]
    + "CheckOut1.aspx";
Response.Redirect(url);
```

Code that returns to an unsecured connection

```csharp
string url = "http:"
    + ConfigurationManager.AppSettings["AppPath"]
    + "Order.aspx";
Response.Redirect(url);
```

Description

- To request a secure connection, you must use an absolute URL that specifies HTTPS as the protocol. Once you establish a secure connection, you can use relative URLs to continue using the secure connection.

- To return to an unsecured connection after using a secure connection, you must code an absolute URL that specifies the HTTP protocol.

- Instead of coding the application's path into each URL, you can store it in the appSettings section of the web.config file. That way, if the path changes, you can change it in just one location.

- You can use the AppSettings property of the ConfigurationManager class within the application to access the elements in the appSettings section of the web.config file.

- Depending on the security settings in your browser, a dialog box may be displayed before a secure connection is established or before a secure connection is closed.

Figure 19-7   How to request a secure connection

How to force a page to use a secure connection

When you build a complete web application, you usually include navigation features such as menus or hyperlinks that guide the user from page to page. Unfortunately, users sometimes bypass your navigation features and access pages in your application directly. For example, a user might bookmark a page in your application and return to it later. Other users might simply type the URL of individual pages in your application into their browser's address bar. Some users do this innocently; others do it in an attempt to bypass your application's security features.

Because of that, a page that should use SSL to send or receive sensitive information shouldn't assume that a secure connection has been established. Instead, it should check for a secure connection and establish one if necessary. To do that, you can use the properties of the HttpRequest class shown in figure 19-8.

To check for a secure connection, you use the IsSecureConnection property. Then, if the connection isn't secure, you can use the Url property to retrieve the URL for the page and modify that URL so it uses the HTTPS protocol. After you do that, you can use the Redirect method to redirect the browser using the new URL. Notice that you typically include this code at the beginning of the Load event handler for the page. That way, you can be sure that no other code is executed until a secure connection is established.

Another way to force a page to use a secure connection is by setting a property of the page from IIS. You can also use this technique to change the minimum SSL strength that's required from 40-bit to 128-bit. When you use this technique, a user won't be able to access the page without using a secure connection. In other words, he won't be able to bypass the navigation features provided by your application. For more information on how to use this technique, please see appendix B (Windows XP) or Appendix C (Windows Vista).

Properties of the HttpRequest class for working with secure connections

Property	Description
IsSecureConnection	Returns True if the current connection is secure. Otherwise, returns False.
Url	The URL of the current request.

A Page_Load event handler that forces the page to use a secure connection

```
protected void Page_Load(object sender, EventArgs e)
{
    if (!Request.IsSecureConnection)
    {
        string url = Request.Url.ToString().Replace("http:", "https:");
        Response.Redirect(url);
    }
}
```

Description

- If a page requires the user to enter sensitive information, such as passwords or credit card data, it should make sure that it's operating on a secure connection. To do that, the page should check the IsSecureConnection property of the HttpRequest object in its Load event handler.

- If the page isn't using a secure connection, it should switch to a secure connection to protect the privacy of the user's data. To do that, it can replace the HTTP protocol in the URL to HTTPS and then redirect the browser to the new URL.

- You can also prevent a user from accessing a page without a secure connection by setting a property of the page from the Internet Information Services program. When you use this technique, you can also set the default SSL strength to 128-bit. For more information, see appendix B (Windows XP) or Appendix C (Windows Vista).

Figure 19-8   How to force a page to use a secure connection

A Halloween Store application that uses SSL

To show how secure connections are used in a typical application, the next two topics present a version of the Halloween Store application that uses SSL.

The operation of the Halloween Store application

Figure 19-9 shows the five pages of the Halloween Store application. As you can see, this application lets the user select products and display the shopping cart without establishing a secure connection. When the user clicks the Check Out button from the Cart page, however, a secure connection is established. The secure connection is then maintained while the two Check Out pages and the Confirmation page are displayed. When the user clicks the Return to Order Page button, however, the Order page is redisplayed with an unsecured connection.

The code for the Halloween Store application

Figure 19-10 presents the code for using SSL in the Halloween Store application. At the top of the first page of this figure, you can see the code for the Click event of the Check Out button on the Cart page. (The code for the Click event of the Check Out button on the Order page is identical.) This code creates a URL that uses the HTTPS protocol and the path that's specified in the appSettings section of the web.config file. Then, it redirects the browser to the first Check Out page using a secure connection.

In the code for the first Check Out page, you can see that the Load event handler checks if a secure connection has been established. If not, the URL is retrieved from the request and the HTTP protocol is replaced with HTTPS. Then, the browser is redirected to that URL, which uses a secure connection.

If the user clicks the Continue Checkout button, a relative URL is used to display the second Check Out page, which means that the secure connection is maintained. If the user clicks the Cancel or Continue Shopping button, however, the browser is redirected to the Order page with an unsecured connection.

The code for the second Check Out page is shown in part 2 of this figure. Like the first Check Out page, its Load event handler makes sure that a secure connection is established before proceeding. In addition, if the user clicks the Cancel or Continue Shopping button, the Order page is redisplayed with an unsecured connection. If the user clicks the Accept Order button, however, the secure connection is maintained and the Confirmation page is displayed.

The code for the Confirmation page is also shown in this figure. As you can see, if the user clicks the Return to Order Page button on this page, the Order page is redisplayed with an unsecured connection.

How security is used by the Halloween Store application

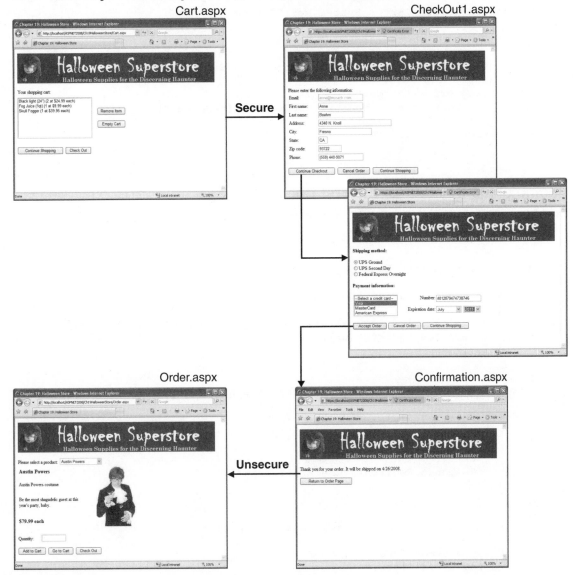

Description

- When the user clicks the Check Out button from the Cart page (or the Order page), the browser is redirected to the first Check Out page using a secure connection.

- When the user clicks the Continue Checkout button from the first Check Out page, the browser is redirected to the second Check Out page and remains in the secure connection.

- When the user clicks the Accept Order button from the second Check Out page, the browser is redirected to the Confirmation page and remains in the secure connection.

- When the user clicks the Return to Order Page button from the Confirmation page, the browser is redirected to the Order page in an unsecured connection.

Figure 19-9   The operation of the Halloween Store application with SSL

Some of the C# code for the Cart page

```
public partial class Cart : System.Web.UI.Page
{
    .
    .
    protected void btnCheckOut_Click(object sender, EventArgs e)
    {
        string url = "https:"
            + ConfigurationManager.AppSettings["AppPath"]
            + "CheckOut1.aspx";
        Response.Redirect(url);
    }
}
```

Some of the C# code for the first Check Out page

```
public partial class CheckOut1 : System.Web.UI.Page
{
    .
    .
    protected void Page_Load(object sender, EventArgs e)
    {
        if (!Request.IsSecureConnection)
        {
            string url = Request.Url.ToString().Replace("http:", "https:");
            Response.Redirect(url);
        }
    }

    protected void btnCheckOut_Click(object sender, EventArgs e)
    {
        if (Page.IsValid)
        {
            .
            .
            Response.Redirect("CheckOut2.aspx");
        }
    }

    protected void btnCancel_Click(object sender, EventArgs e)
    {
        Session.Remove("Cart");
        string url = "http:"
            + ConfigurationManager.AppSettings["AppPath"]
            + "Order.aspx";
        Response.Redirect(url);
    }

    protected void btnContinue_Click(object sender, EventArgs e)
    {
        string url = "http:"
            + ConfigurationManager.AppSettings["AppPath"]
            + "Order.aspx";
        Response.Redirect(url);
    }
}
```

Figure 19-10   The code for the Halloween Store application (part 1 of 2)

Some of the C# code for the second Check Out page

```csharp
public partial class CheckOut2 : System.Web.UI.Page
{
    .
    .
    protected void Page_Load(object sender, EventArgs e)
    {
        if (!Request.IsSecureConnection)
        {
            string url = Request.Url.ToString().Replace("http:", "https:");
            Response.Redirect(url);
        }
    }

    protected void btnAccept_Click(object sender, EventArgs e)
    {
        if (Page.IsValid)
        {
            .
            .
            Response.Redirect("Confirmation.aspx");
        }
    }

    protected void btnCancel_Click(object sender, EventArgs e)
    {
        Session.Remove("Cart");
        string url = "http:"
            + ConfigurationManager.AppSettings["AppPath"]
            + "Order.aspx";
        Response.Redirect(url);
    }

    protected void btnContinue_Click(object sender, EventArgs e)
    {
        string url = "http:"
            + ConfigurationManager.AppSettings["AppPath"]
            + "Order.aspx";
        Response.Redirect(url);
    }
```

Some of the C# code for the Confirmation page

```csharp
public partial class Confirmation : System.Web.UI.Page
{
    .
    .
    protected void btnReturn_Click(object sender, EventArgs e)
    {
        string url = "http:"
            + ConfigurationManager.AppSettings["AppPath"]
            + "Order.aspx";
        Response.Redirect(url);
    }
}
```

Figure 19-10   The code for the Halloween Store application (part 2 of 2)

Perspective

Now that you've completed this chapter, you should be able to use SSL encryption to secure the data transmissions between client and server. That's one part of securing an application. The other part is making sure that only authorized users are able to use your application, and you'll learn how to provide for that in the next chapter.

By the way, if you're interested in seeing the rest of the code for the Halloween Store application in this chapter, you should know that you can download all of the applications in this book from our web site (www.murach.com).

Terms

Secure Sockets Layer (SSL)
secure connection
authentication
server authentication
client authentication
digital secure certificate
certification authority (CA)
registration authority (RA)
SSL strength
single root certificate
chained root certificate
self-signed certificate
binding

20

How to authenticate and authorize users

In the last chapter, you learned how to secure the transmission of data between client and server. Now, you'll learn how to restrict access to some of the pages of an application, but let authorized users access those pages. To provide this functionality without writing a single line of code, you can use the Web Site Administration Tool and the login controls.

An introduction to authentication **640**
Three types of authentication 640
How forms-based authentication works 642

How to set up authentication and authorization **644**
How to start the Web Site Administration Tool 644
How to enable forms-based authentication 646
How to create and manage roles 648
How to create and manage users 650
How to create and manage access rules 652
How to modify the membership and role provider 654

How to use the login controls **656**
How to use the Login control 656
How to use the LoginStatus and LoginName controls 658
How to use the CreateUserWizard control 660
How to use the PasswordRecovery control 662
How to use the ChangePassword control 664
How to use the LoginView control 666

The Authentication application **668**
The pages 668
The directory structure 672
The access rules 672
The web.config files 674

How to use code to work with authentication **676**
How to use the Membership class 676
How to use the MembershipUser class 678
How to use the FormsAuthentication class 680
How to use the Roles class 682

Perspective **684**

An introduction to authentication

If you want to limit access to all or part of your ASP.NET application to certain users, you can use *authentication* to verify each user's identity. Then, once you have authenticated the user, you can use *authorization* to check if the user has the appropriate privileges for accessing a page. That way, you can prevent unauthorized users from accessing pages that they shouldn't be able to access.

Three types of authentication

Figure 20-1 describes the three types of authentication you can use in ASP.NET applications. The first, called *Windows-based authentication*, requires that you set up a Windows user account for each user. Then, you use standard Windows security features to restrict access to all or part of the application. When a user attempts to access the application, Windows displays a login dialog box that asks the user to supply the user name and password of the Windows account.

To use *forms-based authentication*, you add a login page to your application that typically requires the user to enter a user name and password. Then, ASP.NET displays this page automatically when it needs to authenticate a user who's trying to access the application. ASP.NET automatically creates a database to store user data such as user names and passwords, and it includes login controls that automatically generate code that reads data from and writes data to this database. As a result, you can implement forms-based authentication without having to write a single line of code. That makes this type of authentication easy to use, and you'll see how this works as you progress through this chapter.

Windows Live ID authentication, previously called *Passport authentication*, relies on the *Windows Live ID* service to authenticate users. Windows Live ID is a centralized account management service that lets users access multiple web applications with a single user account. Before you can use Windows Live ID with a web site, you must register the web site with Microsoft. Then, you can download the Windows Live ID Web Authentication software development kit (SDK) and use it in your web site to authenticate users of the site. For more information, go to www.msdn.microsoft.com and search for Windows Live ID.

Windows-based authentication

- Causes the browser to display a login dialog box when the user attempts to access a restricted page.
- Is supported by most browsers.
- Is configured through the IIS management console.
- Uses Windows user accounts and directory rights to grant access to restricted pages.

Forms-based authentication

- Lets developers code a login form that gets the user name and password.
- The user name and password entered by the user are encrypted if the login page uses a secure connection.
- Doesn't rely on Windows user accounts. Instead, the application determines how to authenticate users.

Windows Live ID authentication

- *Windows Live ID* is a centralized authentication service offered by Microsoft.
- Windows Live ID lets users maintain a single user account that lets them access any web site that participates in Windows Live ID. The advantage is that the user only has to maintain one user name and password.
- To use Windows Live ID, you must register your web site with Microsoft to obtain an application ID and then download the Windows Live ID Web Authentication SDK.

Description

- *Authentication* refers to the process of validating the identity of a user so the user can be granted access to an application. A user must typically supply a user name and password to be authenticated.
- After a user is authenticated, the user must still be authorized to use the requested application. The process of granting user access to an application is called *authorization*.

Figure 20-1   Three types of authentication

How forms-based authentication works

To help you understand how forms-based authentication works, figure 20-2 shows a typical series of exchanges that occur between a web browser and a server when a user attempts to access a page that's protected by forms-based authentication. The authentication process begins when a user requests a page that is part of a protected application. When the server receives the request, it checks to see if the user has already been authenticated. To do that, it looks for a cookie that contains an *authentication ticket* in the request for the page. If it doesn't find the ticket, it redirects the browser to the login page.

Next, the user enters a user name and password and posts the login page back to the server. Then, if the user name and password are found in the database, which means they are valid, the server creates an authentication ticket and redirects the browser back to the original page. Note that the redirect from the server sends the authentication ticket to the browser as a cookie. As a result, when the browser requests the original page, it sends the cookie back to the server. This time, the server sees that the user has been authenticated and the requested page is sent back to the browser.

By default, the authentication ticket is sent as a session cookie. In that case, the user is authenticated only for that session. However, you also can specify that the ticket be sent as a persistent cookie. Then, the user will be authenticated automatically for future sessions, until the cookie expires.

HTTP requests and responses with forms-based authentication

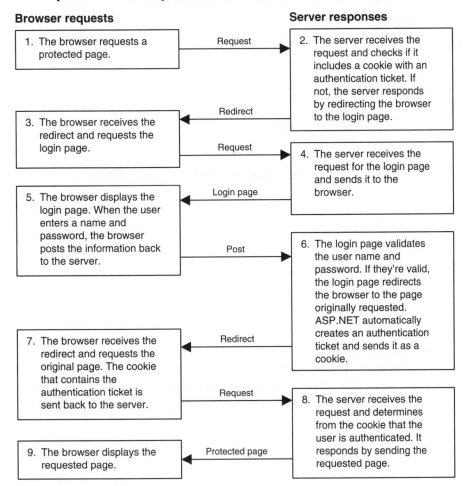

Browser requests

Server responses

1. The browser requests a protected page.

→ Request →

2. The server receives the request and checks if it includes a cookie with an authentication ticket. If not, the server responds by redirecting the browser to the login page.

← Redirect ←

3. The browser receives the redirect and requests the login page.

→ Request →

4. The server receives the request for the login page and sends it to the browser.

← Login page ←

5. The browser displays the login page. When the user enters a name and password, the browser posts the information back to the server.

→ Post →

6. The login page validates the user name and password. If they're valid, the login page redirects the browser to the page originally requested. ASP.NET automatically creates an authentication ticket and sends it as a cookie.

← Redirect ←

7. The browser receives the redirect and requests the original page. The cookie that contains the authentication ticket is sent back to the server.

→ Request →

8. The server receives the request and determines from the cookie that the user is authenticated. It responds by sending the requested page.

← Protected page ←

9. The browser displays the requested page.

Description

- When ASP.NET receives a request for a page that's protected from a user who has not been authenticated, the server redirects the user to the login page.

- To be authenticated, the user's computer must contain an *authentication ticket*. By default, this ticket is stored as a session cookie.

- ASP.NET automatically creates an authentication ticket when the application indicates that the user should be authenticated. ASP.NET checks for the presence of an authentication ticket any time it receives a request for a restricted page.

- The authentication ticket cookie can be made persistent. Then, the user will be authenticated automatically in future sessions, until the cookie expires.

Figure 20-2   How forms-based authentication works

How to set up authentication and authorization

By default, all pages of a web site can be accessed by all users whether or not they are authenticated. As a result, if you want to restrict access to all or some of the pages of the web site, you need to set up authentication and authorization. The easiest way to do that is to use the ASP.NET Web Site Administration Tool as shown in the topics that follow.

How to start the Web Site Administration Tool

To start the ASP.NET Web Site Administration Tool, you use the Website→ASP.NET Configuration command. This starts a web browser that displays the home page for this tool. Then, you can click on the Security tab to access a web page like the one shown in figure 20-3. This page lets you set up users, create groups of users known as *roles*, and create *access rules* that control access to parts of your application.

To set up authentication for the first time, you can click on the link that starts the Security Setup Wizard. This wizard walks you through several steps that allow you to set up the security for your application. Alternatively, you can use the links at the bottom of the page to select the authentication type and manage the users, roles, and access rules for your application.

The Security tab of the Web Site Administration Tool

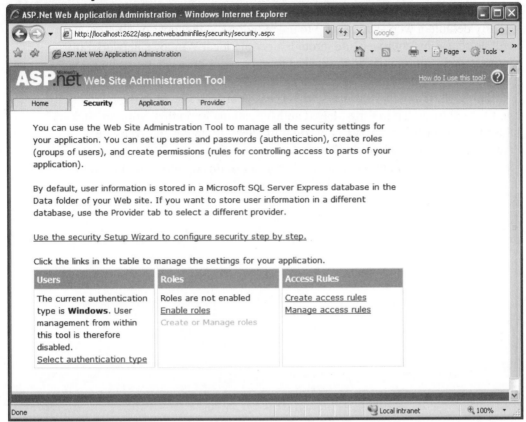

Description

- To start the ASP.NET Web Site Administration Tool, use the Website→ASP.NET Configuration command.

- You can use the ASP.NET Web Site Administration Tool to set up users, roles, and access rules.

Figure 20-3   How to start the Web Site Administration Tool

How to enable forms-based authentication

By default, a web site is set up to use Windows authentication. If all users will be accessing your web site through a private local Windows network (an intranet), this option may be the easiest to implement because it uses built-in Windows dialog boxes to allow users to log in.

However, if any of your users will access your web site from the Internet, you'll need to switch to forms-based authentication. To do that, you can click on the Select Authentication Type link from the Security tab of the Web Site Administration Tool to display the page shown in figure 20-4. Then, you can select the From the Internet option. When you use this option, you'll need to create a web form that allows users to log in as shown later in this chapter.

How to enable forms-based authentication

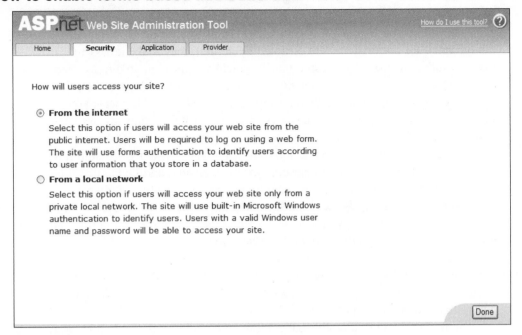

Description

- By default, a web site is set up to use Windows authentication. However, this option is only appropriate for accessing a web site through a local intranet.
- To switch to forms-based authentication, select the From the Internet option. This is the option that you'll need to use if you intend to deploy the application so it's available from the Internet.
- When you switch to forms-based authentication, Create User and Manage Users links become available from the main security page.

Figure 20-4   How to enable forms-based authentication

How to create and manage roles

Roles allow you to apply the same access rules to a group of users. Although roles are optional and are disabled by default, they make it easy to manage authentication. As a result, you'll typically want to enable roles. And since you use roles when you create users and access rules, it's often helpful to set up the roles before you create the users and access rules. That way, you don't have to go back later and edit your users and access rules so they are associated with the correct roles.

To understand how roles work, let's say you create a role named admin for all employees that will be administrators for the web site, and you assign this role to multiple users. Later, if you want to give all users in the admin role additional permissions, you don't have to give the permissions to each user. Instead, you just need to give the additional permissions to the admin role and all users with that role will get the new permissions.

Before you can work with roles using the Web Site Administration Tool, you must enable them. To do that, you click on the Enable Roles link in the Security tab. Then, you can click on the Create or Manage Roles link to display a page like the one in figure 20-5.

The first two controls on this page allow you to add roles. To do that, you just enter a name for the role and click on the Add Role button, and the role will appear in the table at the bottom of the page. Then, you can click on the Manage link for the role to add users to the role or to remove users from the role. Or, you can click the Delete link for the role to delete the role entirely.

User names and roles

```
User name     Roles
anne          admin
joel          admin, custserv
kelly         custserv
```

How to create and manage roles

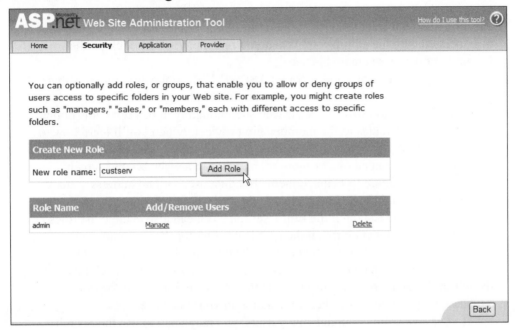

Description

- A *role* allows you to apply the same access rules to a group of users.
- Each user may be associated with one or more roles.
- By default, roles are disabled. To enable them, you need to click on the Enable Roles link in the Security tab.
- Once you enable roles, you can click on the Create or Manage Roles link in the Security tab to display the page shown above. This page lets you add roles, manage all users associated with the role, and delete roles.

Figure 20-5   How to create and manage roles

How to create and manage users

The first page displayed in figure 20-6 shows how to use the Web Site Administration Tool to create users. To do that, you start by entering all of the required information for a user. This information includes a user name, a password, an email address, and a security question and answer. If you want to associate the user with one or more roles, you can select the check box next to each role that you want to apply to the user. In this figure, for example, the user is associated with the admin role. When you're done, you can click on the Create User button to create the user.

The default password policy for an ASP.NET 3.5 application requires that you enter at least seven characters with one of them being a non-alphanumeric character. If that's too strict for your web site, though, you can relax this policy by adding two attributes to the membership provider, which you'll learn how to do in figure 20-8.

Once you've created one or more users, you can use the second screen displayed in this figure to manage them. To edit a user's email address, enter or change the description for a user, change the roles assigned to a user, or change a user's status, you can click the Edit User link. You can also change the roles assigned to a user by clicking on the Edit Roles link for the user and then working with the check boxes that are displayed in the Roles column of the table. And you can change a user's status by clearing the Active check box to the left of the user's name. This prevents the user from logging into your application but retains his or her information in your database.

If your application contains many users, you may need to use the Search For Users controls to search for users. When you use these controls, you can search by user name or email address. For example, to search by email address, you can select the E-mail option from the Search By drop-down list, enter the email address in the For text box, and click on the Find User button. If necessary, you can use the asterisk (*) wildcard for multiple characters, and you can use the question mark (?) wildcard for a single character. Alternatively, you can click on the letters displayed on this page to display all users whose user name or email address begins with the specified letter. Either way, you should be able to quickly find the user that you're looking for.

How to create a user

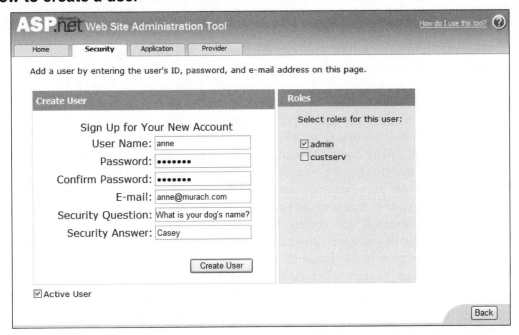

How to manage users

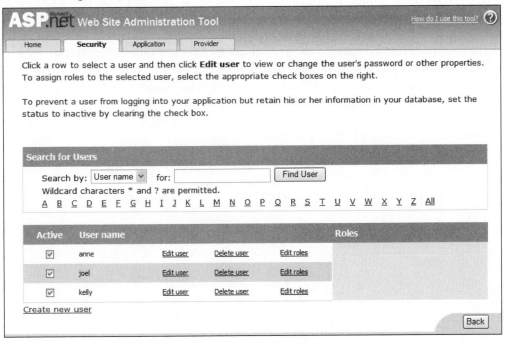

Figure 20-6   How to create and manage users

How to create and manage access rules

The first page in figure 20-7 shows how to create an *access rule* that restricts access to all or part of a web application. If you want to apply an access rule to the entire web application, you can select the root directory for the web application and apply the rule. Then, this rule will apply to all subfolders. For example, if you want to allow only authenticated users to access your web site, you can select the root directory (Ch20Authentication in this example), and create a rule that denies access to anonymous users.

However, it's more common to allow all users including anonymous users to access the pages in the root directory. That way, all users can view your home page and any other pages that you want to make available to the general public. Then, you can restrict access to the pages in your application that are stored in subfolders. For example, this screen shows how to create a rule for the Maintenance folder that denies access to all users.

The second page in this figure shows how to manage the access rules for a folder. To do that, you can select the folder to display all of the access rules for that folder. Then, you can move rules up or down, which is important since they're applied in the order in which they're displayed. Or, you can delete any rules that you no longer want to apply.

In this example, you can see the rules that restrict access to the Maintenance folder. Here, the bottom rule (which is dimmed) is the rule that's automatically applied to all pages of a web site if you don't create new rules. This rule allows access to all users including anonymous users. Then, the middle rule overrides the bottom rule and denies access to all users including authenticated users. However, the top rule overrides the middle rule and allows access to users in the admin role. As a result, only authenticated users in the admin role are able to access the pages in the Maintenance folder.

How to create an access rule

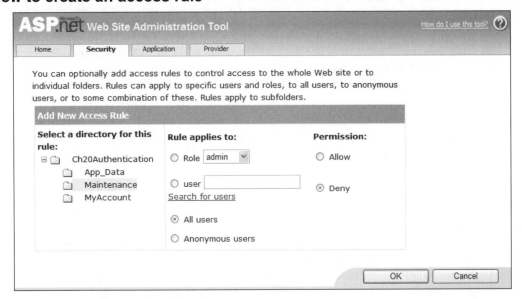

How to manage access rules

Description

- An *access rule* determines which users have access to portions of a web site.

- Each rule overrides the rules below it. As a result, for the Maintenance directory shown above, users in the admin role are allowed and all other users are denied.

Figure 20-7   How to create and manage access rules

How to modify the membership and role provider

When you add roles and users, a class known as a *data provider* contains the code that reads and writes the data for the users and roles. A data provider that works with membership data is often called a *membership provider*, and a data provider that works with roles data is often called a *role provider*. By default, a data provider named AspNetSqlProvider is used to store both membership and role data in a SQL Server Express database named AspNetDb.mdf that's stored in the App_Data folder of your web site. This database is created for you automatically, and it usually works the way you want, at least for prototyping.

However, the data provider architecture lets you use different data providers if you want to. If, for example, you want to use one data provider for the membership data and another for role data, you can use the Provider tab shown in figure 20-8 to select separate providers. The only provider for membership data is AspNetSqlMembershipProvider. Two providers are available for role data: AspNetSqlRoleProvider and AspNetWindowsTokenRoleProvider. If you use the Windows token provider, the role information will be based on Windows accounts. Because of that, you won't create roles and users as described in the previous topics. In addition, you won't use forms-based authentication. Instead, you'll need to use Windows-based authentication.

If the data providers that ship with ASP.NET 3.5 aren't adequate for your application, you may need to write a custom data provider. If, for example, you need to store membership data in an Oracle database, a MySQL database, or even on a midrange or mainframe computer, you can write a custom membership provider to do that. Or, if you need to work with existing membership data that's stored in a SQL Server database, you can write a custom provider to work with that data.

To write a membership provider, you need to code a class that implements the abstract MembershipProvider class. To write a role provider, you need to code a class that implements the abstract RoleProvider class. After you implement all of the necessary properties and methods of these classes, you can edit the machine.config or web.config file to add the providers to the list for all applications or the list for one application. Then, you can use the Provider tab to select the data providers for memberships and roles. Once you do that, the rest of the authentication features should work as described in this chapter.

This figure also shows how you can modify the attributes of a data provider to change the way that the data provider behaves. In particular, it shows how you can relax the strict password requirements for an application. To do that, you can copy the Membership element from the machine.config file (which applies to all web applications) to the web.config file (which applies to your application). Then, you can edit the Name attribute of the Add element to create a unique name for the modified provider, and you can add and set the minRequiredPasswordLength and minRequiredNonAlphanumericCharacters attributes. In this case, these attributes are set so each password requires 6 characters and zero special characters. Last, you can add the defaultProvider attribute to the Membership element so your application uses this provider.

The Provider tab of the Web Site Administration Tool

Elements in the web.config file that relax the default password policy

```
<membership defaultProvider="AspNetSqlMembershipProviderRelaxed">
  <providers>
    <add name="AspNetSqlMembershipProviderRelaxed"
         type="System.Web.Security.SqlMembershipProvider,
               System.Web, Version=2.0.0.0, Culture=neutral,
               PublicKeyToken=b03f5f7f11d50a3a"
         connectionStringName="LocalSqlServer"
         enablePasswordRetrieval="false"
         enablePasswordReset="true"
         requiresQuestionAndAnswer="true"
         applicationName="/"
         requiresUniqueEmail="false"
         passwordFormat="Hashed"
         maxInvalidPasswordAttempts="5"
         passwordAttemptWindow="10"
         passwordStrengthRegularExpression=""
         minRequiredPasswordLength="6"
         minRequiredNonalphanumericCharacters="0" />
  </providers>
</membership>
```

Description

- By default, a *data provider* named AspNetSqlProvider is used to store both membership and role data in a SQL Server Express database named AspNetDb.mdf. However, you can use separate membership and role providers, and you can write your own custom providers.

- The definitions for the default membership and role providers can be found in the machine.config file. This file is stored in the Config folder subordinate to the .NET Framework 2.0 installation folder.

- To relax the password restrictions for a provider, you can change the attributes for password length and non-alphanumeric characters in the web.config file for an application.

Figure 20-8   How to modify the membership and role provider

How to use the login controls

Once you've restricted access to some or all of the pages of your web application, you need to allow users with the proper permissions to log in and access the restricted pages. In addition, you may want to provide other features such as allowing users to log out, to create an account by themselves, to recover a forgotten password, or to change a password. You can use the controls in the Login group of the Toolbox to automatically handle these tasks.

How to use the Login control

Figure 20-9 shows how to create a login page that contains a Login control. When you create a login page, you should name it Login.aspx. That's because ASP.NET looks for a page with this name when it attempts to authenticate a user. Also, since this page is used for the entire application, you usually want to use a simple format so it works equally well for all parts of the application.

Once you've created a page named Login.aspx, you can add all of the login functionality just by adding a Login control to the page. To do that, drag the Login control that's in the Login group of the Toolbox onto the page.

Like most login pages, the Login control includes two text boxes that let the user enter a user name and a password. In addition, it includes a check box that lets the users indicate whether or not they want to be logged in automatically the next time the application is accessed. If the user selects this check box, the application can create a persistent cookie that contains the authentication ticket.

When the user clicks the Log In button within the Login control, the code for the control tries to authenticate the user. It does that by checking to see whether the user name and password are in the membership data store. Then, if the user is authenticated, the code checks the role provider to see whether the user has the proper authorization for the requested page. If so, this code continues by redirecting the browser to that page.

If you want to automatically apply formatting to the Login control, you can select the Auto Format command from the control's smart tag menu. Then, you can use the resulting Auto Format dialog box to select a scheme that you like. When you do, Visual Studio will change many of the control's formatting properties. This feature works similarly for the CreateUserWizard, PasswordRecovery, and ChangePassword controls described in the pages that follow.

Although it's not shown in this figure, a login page should always force the page to use a secure connection. Then, if a hacker manages to intercept a user's user name and password, your application won't be compromised.

A Login control in the Web Forms Designer

The aspx code for the Login control

```
<asp:Login ID="Login1" runat="server">
</asp:Login>
```

Common attributes of the Login control

Attribute	Description
DisplayRememberMe	Determines whether the RememberMe check box is displayed. By default, this is set to True.
RememberMeText	The text for the label of the RememberMe text box.
RememberMeSet	Determines whether a persistent cookie is sent to the user's computer, which is based on whether the RememberMe check box is selected.
FailureText	The text that's displayed when a login attempt fails.

Description

- When a user attempts to access a page that requires authentication, ASP.NET automatically redirects the user to the application's login page. This page must be named Login.aspx.

- To automatically apply formatting to the Login control, select the AutoFormat command from the control's smart tag menu. Then, select a scheme from the dialog box that's displayed.

Figure 20-9   How to use the Login control

How to use the LoginStatus and LoginName controls

Figure 20-10 shows how you can use the LoginStatus and LoginName controls. In the page at the top of this figure, you can see that the LoginName control provides the name of a logged in user. In contrast, the LoginStatus control provides a Login link if a user hasn't logged in yet, and a Logout link if the user has logged in. Notice that this page also includes a hyperlink that the user can click if the user name that's displayed is incorrect. This hyperlink is not part of the LoginName or LoginStatus control.

To use these controls, you just drag them onto the form from the Login group of the Toolbox. Then, you can change the properties as needed. For instance, you can use the LoginText and LogoutText attributes of the LoginStatus control to change the text that's displayed by the links. And you can use the FormatString attribute of the LoginName control to add text before or after the placeholder for the user name.

When the user clicks on the Login link of a LoginStatus control, the user will be redirected to the login page and required to enter a user name and password. Then, after the user has been authenticated, the user will be redirected to the original page. Conversely, when the user clicks the Logout link, the user will be redirected to the login page (Login.aspx).

When a user has been authenticated, the LoginName control will display the user name. Otherwise, the control won't display the user name. However, it will display any other text that has been specified in the FormatString attribute.

The LoginName and LoginStatus controls displayed in a browser

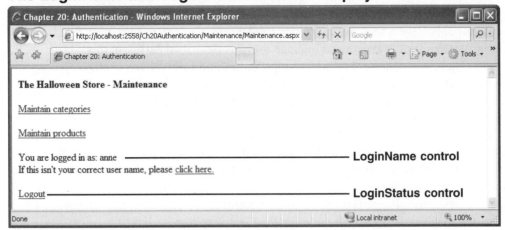

LoginName control

LoginStatus control

The LoginName and LoginStatus controls in the Web Forms Designer

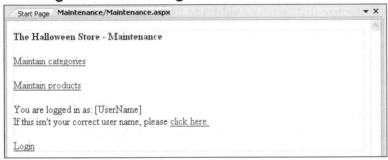

The aspx code for the LoginName and LoginStatus controls

```
<asp:LoginName ID="LoginName1" runat="server"
    FormatString="You are logged in as: {0}" />

<asp:LoginStatus ID="LoginStatus1" runat="server" />
```

Common attribute of the LoginName control

Attribute	Description
FormatString	The text that's displayed with the user name. This string uses "{0}" to identify the UserName parameter, and you can add text before or after this parameter.

Common attributes of the LoginStatus control

Attribute	Description
LoginText	The text that's displayed for the login link.
LogoutText	The text that's displayed for the logout link.

Figure 20-10   How to use the LoginStatus and LoginName controls

How to use the CreateUserWizard control

If you only have a few users for your application, you can use the Web Site Administration Tool to create and manage users as described earlier in this chapter. Then, you can use the Login, LoginStatus, and LoginName controls to allow users to log in and out. Often, though, you'll want to allow users to create user accounts for themselves. To do that, you can use the CreateUserWizard control as shown in figure 20-11.

By default, the CreateUserWizard control uses two steps to create a new user: the Create User step and the Complete step. To display these steps, you can use the drop-down list in the smart tag menu as shown in this figure. Usually, these steps work like you want them to. In that case, you can simply set the ContinueDestinationPageUrl property of the control to indicate what page the user is directed to when the Continue button in the Complete step is clicked.

If you need to modify the behavior of either of the steps, you can do that by selecting the Customize command for that step from the smart tag menu for the control. Then, you can customize that step by modifying the controls and properties of the step. If you modify the Complete step, note that you can specify the page that's displayed when the user clicks the Continue button by setting the PostBackUrl property of that button rather than by setting the ContinueDestinationPageUrl property of the CreateUserWizard control.

When you use the pages that result from the CreateUserWizard control, you should realize that the membership provider is being used to write the data to the appropriate data source. This works the same as it does for the Web Site Administration Tool.

A CreateUserWizard control with the smart tag menu shown

The two steps of a customized CreateUserWizard control in a browser

Description

- If you select the CreateUserWizard control in the Web Forms Designer, you can use the smart tag menu to switch between its two steps and customize or reset either step.

- To identify the page that the user is directed to when the Continue button in the Complete step is clicked, you can set the ContinueDestinationPageUrl property of the control. Or, if you've customized the Complete step, you can set the PostBackUrl property of the Continue button.

Figure 20-11   How to use the CreateUserWizard control

How to use the PasswordRecovery control

It's inevitable that some users will forget their passwords. Fortunately, the PasswordRecovery control makes it easy to automate the process of recovering forgotten passwords. This process is described in figure 20-12, and it's especially useful if you are managing a site with a large number of users.

When you use the PasswordRecovery control, the password is sent to the user via email. As a result, you need to make sure that your system is set up so it can send email before you test this control. By default, an application will try to send email to an SMTP server set to localhost on port 25.

The most important element of the PasswordRecovery control is the MailDefinition element. In particular, you must set the From attribute of the MailDefinition element to the email address that's sending the email message or an error will occur when your system attempts to send the email. Typically, the From email address is set to the email address that's used by the web site administrator. If you set this attribute correctly, a standard message will be sent to the user. To customize the subject line and message body, you can edit the other attributes of the MailDefinition element.

The PasswordRecovery control uses three views. In the Web Forms Designer, you can switch between these three views by using the smart tag menu, and you can edit the properties for any of these views as necessary.

When you display this control in a browser, the first view asks the user to enter a user name. Then, the second view requires the user to answer the security question. If the answer to this question is correct, the password is emailed to the address that's associated with the user name, and the third view is displayed. This view displays a message that indicates that the password recovery was successful and that the password has been sent to the user via email.

The PasswordRecovery control in the Web Forms Designer

The first two views of the PasswordRecovery control

The aspx code for the PasswordRecovery control

```
<asp:PasswordRecovery ID="PasswordRecovery1" runat="server">
    <MailDefinition From="anne@murach.com">
    </MailDefinition>
</asp:PasswordRecovery>
```

Description

- After the second view is completed, the password is emailed to the user. For this to work, you need to edit the From attribute of the MailDefinition element to supply the from address for this email. In addition, the web server that you're using must be configured to work with an SMTP server.

- By default, an application will try to send email to an SMTP server set to localhost on port 25. For information on how to change these settings, see chapter 23.

Figure 20-12   How to use the PasswordRecovery control

How to use the ChangePassword control

Another common task associated with the authentication process is allowing users to change their passwords. To make that easy for you, ASP.NET provides the ChangePassword control, and figure 20-13 shows how to use it.

The ChangePassword control uses two views. The first view lets the user enter the current password and the new password twice. Then, if the old password is correct and the two new passwords match, the second view is displayed. This view tells the user that the password has been successfully changed.

Once you've placed the PasswordControl on the form, it usually works the way you want it to. However, you may need to edit the Url attributes so they point to the pages that you want to navigate to when the user clicks on the Cancel and Continue buttons.

The first view of the ChangePassword control in the Web Forms Designer

The second view of the ChangePassword control

The aspx code for the ChangePassword control

```
<asp:ChangePassword ID="ChangePassword1" runat="server"
    CancelDestinationPageUrl="MyAccount.aspx"
    ContinueDestinationPageUrl="MyAccount.aspx">
</asp:ChangePassword>
```

Description

- The ChangePassword control uses two views to allow users to change their passwords. The first view lets the user change the password. The second view is displayed when the change has been successful.

- The CancelDestinationPageUrl and ContinueDestinationPageUrl attributes provide the URLs that are navigated to when the Cancel or Continue buttons are clicked.

Figure 20-13   How to use the ChangePassword control

How to use the LoginView control

If your web site uses authentication, you often need to display one message to users who are logged in and another message to users who aren't logged in. For example, when a user isn't logged in, you may want to display a message that asks the user to log in. Conversely, if a user is logged in, you may want to display a message that welcomes the user back and allows the user to log out. Figure 20-14 shows how to use the LoginView control to accomplish these tasks.

The LoginView control uses two views. The first view contains the controls that are displayed to users who aren't logged in (*anonymous users*). The second view contains the controls that are displayed to users who are logged in (*authenticated users*). In this figure, each view of the LoginView control contains a Label control followed by a LoginStatus control. This is a fairly typical use of the LoginView control. However, the LoginView control can store entire tables if that's necessary. Then, the height and width of the LoginView control will be adjusted automatically to accommodate the controls that you place inside of it.

The LoginView control in the Web Forms Designer

The aspx code for the LoginView control

```
<asp:LoginView ID="LoginView1" runat="server">
    <LoggedInTemplate>
        <asp:Label ID="Label2" runat="server"
            Text="You are logged in." Width="155px"></asp:Label><br />
        <asp:LoginStatus ID="LoginStatus2" runat="server" />
    </LoggedInTemplate>
    <AnonymousTemplate>
        <asp:Label ID="Label1" runat="server"
            Text="You are not logged in." Width="175px"></asp:Label><br />
        <asp:LoginStatus ID="LoginStatus1" runat="server" />
    </AnonymousTemplate>
</asp:LoginView>
```

The LoginView control displayed in a browser

Description

- The LoginView control lets you change what's on the web page depending on whether the user isn't logged in (an *anonymous user*) or is logged in (an *authenticated user*).

Figure 20-14   How to use the LoginView control

The Authentication application

To show how to use forms-based authentication to restrict access to a web application, this topic presents part of a Halloween Store application that we'll refer to as the Authentication application. This application restricts access to all pages in the Maintenance folder to users with admin privileges. In addition, it restricts access to all pages in the MyAccount folder to users who have created an account and logged in.

As you review this application, please keep in mind that the authentication and authorization features don't require any code. That's why the figures that follow show only the pages, the directory structure, the access rules, and the web.config files.

The pages

Figure 20-15 shows just four pages of the Authentication application, but you can also think of the pages in figures 20-11 through 20-13 as part of this application. For instance, the Forgot Your Password link on the Login page goes to the page in figure 20-12, and the Need to Create a New Account link goes to the page in figure 20-11. Also, the Change Password link on the MyAccount page goes to a ChangePassword page like the one in figure 20-13.

To start this application, the Menu page in figure 20-15 contains three links that allow you to perform some tests to make sure that the authentication and authorization features are working correctly. The first link on this page lets the user access an Order page to begin placing an order. When the user clicks on this link, the system tries to authenticate the user by checking whether the user has a cookie with a valid authentication ticket. If so, the user will be authenticated automatically. If not, the user can view the Order page as an anonymous user. Either way, the Order page will be displayed. In other words, this page is available to both anonymous and authenticated users.

The second link on the Menu page lets the user access the MyAccount page where the user can edit settings for his or her personal account. To be able to access this page, the user must be authenticated. When the user clicks on this link, the system attempts to authenticate the user by checking if the browser has a cookie with a valid authentication ticket. If so, the user will be authenticated automatically and allowed to access the MyAccount page. If not, the user will be redirected to the Login page so he or she can log in. Once the user supplies a valid user name and password on the Login page, the browser will be redirected to the MyAccount page.

The Menu page

The Login page

Description

- The Menu page contains three links. The first lets anonymous users or authenticated users access the Order page. The second lets authenticated users access the MyAccount page. The third lets authenticated users who are associated with the admin role access the Maintenance page.

- The Login page is only displayed if the user clicks on the second or third link and the browser doesn't contain a cookie that authenticates the user.

- If the user clicks on the Forgot your Password link on the Login page, the PasswordRecovery page in figure 20-12 is displayed. If the user clicks on the Need to Create a New Account link, the CreateUser page in figure 20-11 is displayed.

Figure 20-15   The pages of the Authentication application (part 1 of 2)

The third link on the Menu page lets users access the Maintenance page that can be used to manage data that's stored in the Categories and Products tables of the database for the web site. To be able to access this page, the user must be authenticated and the user must be associated with the admin role. When the user clicks on this link, the system attempts to authenticate the user by checking if the browser has a cookie with a valid authentication ticket. If so, the user will be authenticated automatically. If not, the user will be redirected to the Login page so he or she can log in. Once the user is authenticated, the browser will be redirected to the Maintenance page if the user has admin privileges.

When you're using the MyAccount and Maintenance pages, the LoginStatus control on these pages allows the users to log out when they're done. This removes the authentication ticket from the browser. As a result, the application won't remember the user the next time the user attempts to access the application, even if the user has selected the Remember Me check box to store the authentication ticket in a persistent cookie.

The MyAccount page

The Maintenance page

Description

- The MyAccount page lets a user edit account data. The user must be authenticated, but need not be associated with any role. When the user clicks on the Change Password link, a page like the one in figure 20-13 is displayed.

- The Maintenance page lets a user maintain data in the Categories and Products tables. The user must be authenticated and must be associated with the admin role.

- The LoginStatus controls on these pages let the user log out when done. This removes the authentication ticket from the browser. As a result, the application won't be able to remember the user the next time the user attempts to access the application.

Figure 20-15   The pages of the Authentication application (part 2 of 2)

The directory structure

Figure 20-16 shows the directory structure for the Authentication application. This shows the App_Data folder with the SQL Server Express database that's used to store the data about the web site's registered users and their roles. In addition, it shows two directories that store web pages that have restricted access. First, it shows the Maintenance directory, which contains the Maintenance page shown in the previous figure. Second, it shows the MyAccount directory, which contains the MyAccount page shown in the previous figure.

In addition, there are three web.config files for this application: one for the root directory, one for the Maintenance directory, and one for the MyAccount directory. The complete listings for these files are shown in figure 20-17.

The access rules

Figure 20-16 also shows the one access rule for the MyAccount directory. This rule denies access to anonymous users. As a result, only users who are authenticated can access the MyAccount directory.

The Maintenance directory, on the other hand, contains two access rules. The first rule denies access to all users. Then, the second rule allows access to authenticated users who are associated with the admin role. To refresh your memory about how this works, please refer back to figure 20-7.

The directory structure for the Authentication application

The access rules for the My Account directory

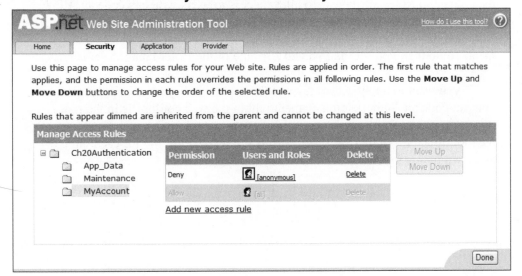

Description

- The MyAccount page lets a user edit personal account data. The user must be authenticated, but doesn't need to be associated with any role.

Figure 20-16   The directory structure and access rules for the Authentication application

The web.config files

Figure 20-17 shows the three web.config files for the Authentication application. When you use the Web Site Administration Tool to create access rules, it automatically creates and modifies these web.config files. As a result, you don't have to edit them manually. However, it's good to have an idea of what's going on under the hood as you use the Web Site Administration Tool.

In addition, once you become familiar with these files, you may find that you prefer to edit or review them manually. But first, you need to understand the XML code that's used by these files to store configuration settings.

To enable forms-based authentication, you can use the Mode attribute of the Authentication element. This attribute is set to Windows by default to use Windows authentication, but you can set it to Forms to enable forms-based authentication.

Once you've enabled forms-based authentication, you can use the Authorization element to deny or allow access to specified users. To deny access to users, you can code a Deny element within the Authorization element and set the Users and Roles attributes. To allow access to users, you can code an Allow element within the Authorization element and set the Users and Roles attributes. Note that before you can use the Roles attribute, you must enable role management. To do that, you set the Enabled attribute of the RoleManager element to True.

If you want to apply access rules to the root directory for the application, you can code an Authorization element within the web.config file in the root directory. However, it's more common to apply access rules to subdirectories of the root directory. In that case, you can code a web.config file for each directory as shown in this figure.

The web.config files for the Authentication application

For the root directory

```xml
<?xml version="1.0"?>
<configuration>
    <system.web>
        <authentication mode="Forms"/>
        <roleManager enabled="True"/>
        ...
    </system.web>
</configuration>
```

For the MyAccount directory

```xml
<?xml version="1.0" encoding="utf-8"?>
<configuration>
    <system.web>
        <authorization>
            <deny users="?" />
        </authorization>
    </system.web>
</configuration>
```

For the Maintenance directory

```xml
<?xml version="1.0" encoding="utf-8"?>
<configuration>
    <system.web>
        <authorization>
            <allow roles="admin" />
            <deny users="*" />
        </authorization>
    </system.web>
</configuration>
```

Wildcard specifications in the users attribute

Wildcard	Description
*	All users, whether or not they have been authenticated.
?	All unauthenticated users.

Discussion

- When you use the Web Site Administration Tool, it automatically creates and modifies the web.config files for an application. If you prefer, you can manually edit these files and you can read them to quickly review the settings for an application.

- To enable forms-based authentication, set the Mode attribute of the Authentication element to Forms. This attribute is set to Windows by default.

- To enable role management, set the Enabled attribute of the roleManager element to True.

- To deny access to users, you can code a Deny element within the Authorization element. To allow access to users, you can code an Allow element within the Authorization element. Then, you can set the Users and Roles attributes of these elements.

Figure 20-17   The web.config files for the Authentication application

How to use code to work with authentication

For most web applications, you can use the Web Site Administration Tool to create users, roles, and access rules. Then, you can use the login controls to allow authorized users to access the restricted pages. And you can do all of this without having to write any code. However, if you do need to write code to work with authentication, ASP.NET provides four classes that make it easy to do that: the Membership, MembershipUser, FormsAuthentication, and Roles classes. All of these classes are stored in the System.Web.Security namespace.

How to use the Membership class

If you need to work with user data, you can use the Membership class as shown in figure 20-18. This class uses the membership provider that's specified for the application to read and write data from the data store. For more information about how this works, see figure 20-8.

All methods of the Membership class are static. As a result, you never need to create an instance of this class to use its methods. To give you an idea of the types of methods that are available from the Membership class, some of the most commonly used methods are summarized in this figure. However, for a full list of methods, you should consult the documentation for the Membership class.

You can use these methods to create or delete a user. When you use some of these methods, you may need to catch the exceptions that they can throw. For example, when you create a user, you need to catch the MembershipCreateUserException that's thrown when the user can't be created. Note that the two CreateUser methods shown here don't require a security question and answer. For this to work, you must set the RequiresQuestionAndAnswer attribute in the membership provider to false since the default is true.

You can also use these methods to retrieve and update the data that's stored for a user. To do that, you must work with an object created from the MembershipUser class. For example, the GetUser method returns a MembershipUser object that contains the data for the user such as the user name, password, email address, security question, and security answer. For more information about working with this class, see the next figure.

If you create a custom login page that doesn't use the Login control shown earlier in this chapter, you can use the ValidateUser method of the Membership class to authenticate the user. Then, if the specified user name and password exist in the database and the user has the proper authorization, this method will return a True value. In that case, you can safely redirect the request to the original page that caused the custom login page to be displayed. You can see an example of how this works in figure 20-20.

Common methods of the Membership class

Method	Description
ValidateUser(userName, password)	Returns a Boolean value that indicates whether the user is authenticated and authorized.
CreateUser(userName, password)	Creates a user with the specified user name and password.
CreateUser(userName, password, email)	Creates a user with the specified user name, password, and email address.
GetUser()	Returns a MembershipUser object that contains data about the currently logged-on user. Updates the last activity date-time stamp.
GetUser(userName)	Returns a MembershipUser object that contains data about the user with the specified user name. Updates the last activity date-time stamp.
GetUserNameByEmail(email)	Returns a string that contains the user name that corresponds with the specified email address.
GetAllUsers()	Returns a MembershipUserCollection object that contains MembershipUser objects.
DeleteUser(userName)	Deletes the user with the specified user name.
UpdateUser(membershipUser)	Updates the user with the data that's stored in the specified MembershipUser object.

A statement that checks if a user is valid

```
bool validUser;
validUser = Membership.ValidateUser(txtUserName.Text, txtPassword.Text);
```

A statement that creates a user

```
try
{
    Membership.CreateUser(txtUserName.Text, txtPassword.Text);
}
catch(MembershipCreateUserException ex)
{
    lblStatus.Text = ex.Message;
}
```

A statement that gets the current user and updates the last activity timestamp

```
MembershipUser user = Membership.GetUser();
```

A statement that deletes a user

```
Membership.DeleteUser(txtUserName.Text);
```

Description

- All methods of the Membership class are static.
- For more information about the MembershipUser class, see the next figure.
- The Membership class is in the System.Web.Security namespace.

Figure 20-18   How to use the Membership class

How to use the MembershipUser class

Figure 20-19 shows how to use the MembershipUser class. To start, you typically use a method of the Membership class to retrieve a MembershipUser object from the data store that's used for authentication. Then, you can use the properties and methods of the MembershipUser object to get or modify the data that's stored in this object.

For example, you might want to use the Email property to get the email address from the MembershipUser object. Or, you might want to set the IsApproved property to False if the user is unsuccessful at logging in a given number of times. Then, the user would not be allowed to log in until the password question was answered correctly, at which time the IsApproved property could be reset to True.

You might also want to use the ChangePassword method to change the password for the object. When you use this and other methods from the MembershipUser object, it updates the data in the MembershipUser object and it updates the data in the membership data store. As a result, you don't need to use the UpdateUser method of the Membership class to update the data in the data store.

Common properties of the MembershipUser class

Property	Description
Username	The user name for the membership user.
Email	The email address for the membership user.
PasswordQuestion	The password question for the membership user.
CreationDate	The date and time when the user was added to the membership data store.
LastLoginDate	The date and time when the membership user was last authenticated.
LastActivityDate	The date and time when the membership user was last authenticated or accessed the application.
IsApproved	A Boolean value that indicates whether the membership user can be authenticated.

Common methods of the MembershipUser class

Method	Description
GetPassword()	Gets the password for the membership user from the membership data store.
ChangePassword(oldPassword, newPassword)	Updates the password for the membership user in the membership data store.
ResetPassword()	Resets a user's password to a new, automatically generated password.
ChangePasswordQuestionAndAnswer(password, question, answer)	Updates the password question and answer for the membership user in the membership data store.

Code that changes a user's password

```
MembershipUser user = Membership.GetUser();
try
{
    user.ChangePassword(txtOldPassword.Text, txtNewPassword.Text);
}
catch(Exception ex)
{
    lblStatus.Text = "Error changing password: " + ex.Message;
}
```

Description

- The MembershipUser class is in the System.Web.Security namespace.
- The methods shown here update the MembershipUser object and the data that's stored in the membership data store.

Figure 20-19   How to use the MembershipUser class

How to use the FormsAuthentication class

If you don't want to use the Login control described earlier in this chapter, you can create a login form that includes text boxes that allow the user to enter a user name and password. Then, you can write code that authenticates the user and redirects the user from the login page to the page that was originally requested. To do that, you can use the ValidateUser method of the Membership class with the RedirectFromLoginPage method of the FormsAuthentication class as shown in figure 20-20.

When a login page has established that a user has entered a correct user name and password, it can use the RedirectFromLoginPage method to create an authentication ticket for the user and redirect the browser to the page that the user originally tried to access. The two arguments for this method specify the user name and whether or not the authentication ticket should be saved in a persistent cookie. Because the example in this figure specifies False for the second argument, the authentication ticket will be saved in a session cookie.

Whether the authentication ticket is saved in a session cookie or a persistent cookie, you can use a SignOut method like the one shown in the second code example to log a user off your application. This method removes the authentication ticket from the user's computer. Then, the user will have to be authenticated again the next time the application is accessed.

Common methods of the FormsAuthentication class

Method	Description
RedirectFromLoginPage(userName, createPersistentCookie)	Issues an authentication ticket for the user and redirects the browser to the page it was attempting to access when the login page was displayed. If the createPersistentCookie argument is true, the cookie that contains the authentication ticket is persisted across browser restarts. Otherwise, the cookie is only available for the current session.
SignOut()	Logs the user off by removing the cookie that contains the authentication ticket.

Code that redirects the browser to the originally requested page

```
if (Membership.ValidateUser(txtUserName.Text, txtPassword.Text))
    FormsAuthentication.RedirectFromLoginPage(txtUserName.Text, false);
else
    lblStatus.Text = "Invalid user! Try again.";
```

A statement that logs a user off

```
FormsAuthentication.SignOut();
```

Discussion

- After you authenticate a user, you can use the RedirectFromLoginPage method of the FormsAuthentication class to redirect the browser to the page that was originally requested. This method creates an authentication ticket that's passed as a cookie to the browser.

- The FormsAuthentication class is in the System.Web.Security namespace.

Figure 20-20   How to use the FormsAuthentication class

How to use the Roles class

The Roles class in figure 20-21 works similarly to the Membership class. First, all methods of the Roles class are static methods. Second, you can use the Roles class to read data from and write data to the data store that's specified by the role provider for the application.

Although you can use the Roles class to add and delete roles from the roles data store, you probably won't need to do that. However, you might need to provide some custom code that works with roles in another way. To illustrate, let's say you've used the Web Site Administration Tool to define a role named premium. Then, when users pay a small fee, they can access the premium pages of the web site. In that case, you might need to write code that adds the current user to the premium role after the user has paid for the premium subscription. To do that, you can use the AddUserToRole method of the Roles class as shown in the third example in this figure.

Common methods of the Roles class

Method	Description
`CreateRole(roleName)`	Adds a new role to the data store.
`GetAllRoles()`	Gets a string array containing all the roles for the application.
`AddUserToRole(userName, roleName)`	Adds the specified user to the specified role.
`GetRolesForUser(userName)`	Gets a string array containing the roles that a user is in.
`GetUsersInRole(roleName)`	Gets a string array containing users in the specified role.
`IsUserInRole(userName, roleName)`	Gets a Boolean value indicating whether a user is in the specified role.
`RemoveUserFromRole(userName, roleName)`	Removes the specified user from the specified role.
`DeleteRole(roleName)`	Removes a role from the data store.

Code that creates a role

```
try
{
    Roles.CreateRole(txtRoleName.Text);
}
catch(Exception ex)
{
    errorMessage = "Error creating role: " + ex.Message;
}
```

A statement that gets all roles in the system

```
string[] roles = Roles.GetAllRoles();
```

A statement that adds a user to a role

```
Roles.AddUserToRole(currentUserName, "premium");
```

A statement that removes a user from a role

```
Roles.RemoveUserFromRole(txtUserName.Text, cboRoles.SelectedValue);
```

Description

- The Roles class is in the System.Web.Security namespace.
- All methods of the Roles class are static.

Figure 20-21   How to use the Roles class

Perspective

This chapter has presented the skills that you need for using forms-based authentication to restrict access to a web application. When you combine these skills with those of the previous chapter, you should have all of the skills you need for providing the security that an e-commerce application requires.

Terms

authentication
authorization
Windows-based authentication
forms-based authentication
Windows Live ID authentication
Passport authentication
Windows Live ID
authentication ticket
role
access rule
data provider
membership provider
role provider
anonymous user
authenticated user

21

How to use profiles to personalize a web site

In the last chapter, you learned how to work with authentication. In particular, you learned how to create user accounts that include information about a user such as user name, password, and email address. Once you understand how authentication works, you're ready to learn how to use profiles.

You can use the profile feature to store additional information about a user such as the user's mailing address or the preferences that a user has for working with your web application. You can also use it as an easier way to store and retrieve session data like a shopping cart. By default, the profile feature is designed to work with authenticated users, but you can also use it to work with anonymous users.

An introduction to profiles **686**
Profiles compared with session state 686
An overview of how profiles work 688
How the default profile provider works 690

How to use profiles with authenticated users **692**
How to define profile properties 692
How to specify data types 694
How to group profile properties 696
How to specify default values 698
How to specify read-only properties 698
How to use custom types 700

How to use profiles with anonymous users **702**
How to enable anonymous identification 702
How to allow anonymous users to access profile properties 702
How to migrate data from anonymous to authenticated users 704

The Cart Profile application **706**
The pages 706
The code 710

Perspective **716**

An introduction to profiles

The *profile feature* is part of the *personalization feature* that includes the forms-based authentication you learned about in the last chapter and the web parts feature you'll learn about in chapter 24. As you will see, the use of profiles has several advantages, along with a few potential pitfalls.

Profiles compared with session state

The profile feature lets you use the ProfileCommon class to store and retrieve data that's associated with a user, which can be referred to as a *profile*. This works similarly to storing user data in session state, but the profile feature has several advantages over the HttpSessionState class. Figure 21-1 describes three of these advantages.

First, the profile feature is designed to store data in a persistent data store that's available for future sessions. In contrast, session state is designed to work with temporary data that's available for only the current session.

Second, the ProfileCommon class uses strongly typed data. As a result, you can use IntelliSense to discover the properties that are stored in a profile, and you typically don't need to use casting when retrieving profile data. In contrast, session state uses keys to retrieve objects of the Object type. As a result, you must know the name of the key to be able to access an object, and then you must cast the object to its appropriate type when you retrieve it.

Third, the profile feature works more efficiently than session state because it only retrieves data when the data is requested. In contrast, the session state object is retrieved on each request, whether or not its values are used.

This figure also describes some of the difficulties of working with the profile feature. These difficulties are mainly due to the complexities that are brought on by the challenges of storing persistent data.

First, if you have an existing data store that you want to use, you have to write a significant amount of code to get the profile feature to work with this data. That's because, by default, the profile feature uses a data provider to store profile data in a SQL Server Express database named AspNetDb.mdf. This type of provider is called a *profile provider*. To change the way this works, you need to write a custom profile provider that will use your existing data store, but this is a significant undertaking.

Second, if you decide to use the profile feature to store data about anonymous users, the amount of data in your database can quickly grow so that it contains stale and redundant data that isn't useful and will eventually slow the performance of your site. That's especially true if you have a high volume site with a large number of anonymous users. As a result, you'll need to implement a strategy for managing this data. For example, you'll need to find a way to delete data when it becomes stale or redundant.

Advantages of using the profile feature

Persistent data storage

Unlike session state, which only stores data for the current session, the profile feature stores data in a persistent data store. As a result, you can retrieve the data in later sessions.

Strongly typed data access

Unlike session state, which requires that you use keys and casting to retrieve data, the profile feature uses properties that have data types. This lets you use the IntelliSense feature to display the properties that are stored in the profile, and it lets you retrieve data without casting.

Efficient data retrieval

Unlike session state, which retrieves data each time a page is posted, the profile feature only retrieves data when necessary.

Disadvantages of using the profile feature

Difficulty accessing legacy data

By default, the profile feature creates and lets you work with the data in a SQL Server Express database. However, if you have data that's stored in an existing database and want to use the profile feature to work with that data, you need to write a custom profile provider and configure your web application to use that profile provider.

Data that's stale and redundant

Since the profile feature stores data persistently about each user, it's easy for your database to become full of stale and redundant data. This is especially true if you store data about anonymous users. If this begins to slow the performance of your site, you'll need to develop a strategy for managing this data.

Description

* The *profile feature* is used to persistently store data associated with a user such as first name, birth date, display preferences, shopping cart, and so on. This data can be referred to as a *profile*.
* To implement the profile feature, ASP.NET uses a data provider called a *profile provider*.

Figure 21-1   Profiles compared with session state

An overview of how profiles work

Figure 21-2 gives an overview of how the profile feature works. To start, you define the properties of the ProfileCommon class in the web.config file for the application. Then, when you run the application, ASP.NET generates the ProfileCommon class based on the properties you defined. It also creates an instance of that class that you can refer to using the Profile property of the HttpContext object.

If you take a closer look at the web.config file in this figure, you can see that it uses the Profile, Properties, and Add elements to define the profile properties. Within each Add element, you must use the Name attribute to specify the name for the property. Then, if you want to specify a data type other than the String type, you can use the Type attribute to specify the data type. In addition, you can use other attributes to specify other behaviors for the profile property. As you progress through this chapter, you'll learn the details for working with the attributes that are available for the Add element.

By default, the data that's stored by the profile feature can only be read by authenticated users. As a result, the user must log in or submit a cookie with a valid authentication ticket before retrieving or storing profile data. However, it's possible to use the profile feature with another ASP.NET feature known as *anonymous identification* that allows anonymous users to use the profile feature. Anonymous identification lets ASP.NET identify users by storing a unique identifier for each user, usually as a cookie within the user's browser.

In this figure, the web.config file allows anonymous identification by setting the Enabled attribute of the anonymousIdentification element to true. Then, to allow the Cart property to use anonymous identification, the AllowAnonymous attribute of the Cart property is set to true. As a result, users can persistently store items in their cart even if they don't log in.

Once you've defined the profile properties in the web.config file, you can use the Profile property of the HttpContext object to get and set these properties. Since the properties are strongly typed, you don't need to use casting when you retrieve data from the profile. However, if you want to display non-string data in a text box, you need to use a ToString method to convert the data type to a string. For example, since the LastActivityDate property is of the DateTime type, the ToShortDateString method is used to convert the property to a string that can be displayed in a text box. Conversely, you may sometimes need to convert a value that's entered as a string to another data type before you can store it in a profile property.

A web.config file that configures a profile

```
<system.web>

  <anonymousIdentification enabled="true" />

  <profile>
    <properties>

      <add name="FirstName" />

      <add name="LastActivityDate"
           type="System.DateTime" />

      <add name="Cart"
           type="Cart"
           serializeAs="Binary"
           allowAnonymous="true" />

    </properties>
  </profile>
</system.web>
```

C# code that stores profile data

```csharp
protected void btnAdd_Click(object sender, EventArgs e)
{
    Profile.FirstName = txtFirstName.Text;
    Profile.LastActivityDate = DateTime.Now;
    Profile.Cart = cart;
}
```

C# code that retrieves profile data

```csharp
ShoppingCart cart;

protected void Page_Load(object sender, EventArgs e)
{
    if (!IsPostBack)
    {
        txtFirstName.Text = Profile.FirstName;
        txtLastActivityDate.Text =
            Profile.LastActivityDate.ToShortDateString();
        cart = Profile.Cart;
    }
}
```

Description

- After you define the properties of a profile in the web.config file, you can use the Profile property of the HttpContext object to store and retrieve the data.

- By default, the profile feature only allows you to access data for users who have been authenticated. However, it's also possible to store data about anonymous users.

Figure 21-2   An overview of how profiles work

How the default profile provider works

The machine.config file sets the defaults for all web applications on the current machine. In figure 21-3, you can see the elements that set the default profile provider.

To start, this figure shows the default connection string. This connection string is named LocalSqlServer, and it connects to a SQL Server Express database named AspNetDb.mdf that's stored in the App_Data directory of the application. This is the same connection string and database that's used for the membership and role providers that are described in chapter 20.

Then, this figure shows the code that configures the profile feature so it uses a profile provider named AspNetSqlProfileProvider. This provider uses the LocalSqlServer connection string to connect to the AspNetDb.mdf database using the SqlProfileProvider class that's stored in the System.Web.Profile namespace.

If you're developing a web application from scratch, you may want to use this default provider as is. It works well for prototyping and may be acceptable for some small to medium-sized web applications. Then, since the database is automatically created and configured, you can use the ProfileCommon class to store and retrieve data without having to write any data access code.

However, if you need to work with an existing data store, or if you need to gain control over low-level data access details, the default profile provider won't work for your application. If, for example, you need to access data that's stored in an existing SQL Server database that uses a different database schema, the default provider won't work. Or, if you need to access data that's stored in an Oracle database, the default provider won't work.

In that case, one option is to avoid the profile feature altogether. After all, if you have an existing database, you may already have existing classes that read and write profile data to and from the database. If not, you can write this data access code yourself. Typically, that means storing temporary profile data in the session state object. Although this alternative may not be as slick as using the profile feature, it will give you more control over when and how profile data is stored.

Another option is to implement a custom profile provider. To do that, you need to write a class that implements all of the abstract methods of the abstract ProfileProvider class. Then, you need to modify the web.config file for your application so it uses this custom profile provider.

The elements of the machine.config file that are used by the profile feature

The default connection string for SQL Server Express

```
<connectionStrings>
  <add name="LocalSqlServer"
       connectionString="data source=.\SQLEXPRESS;Integrated
          Security=SSPI;AttachDBFilename=|DataDirectory|aspnetdb.mdf;User
          Instance=true"
       providerName="System.Data.SqlClient" />
</connectionStrings>
```

The default profile provider

```
<system.web>

  <profile>
    <providers>
      <add name="AspNetSqlProfileProvider"
           connectionStringName="LocalSqlServer"
           applicationName="/"
           type="System.Web.Profile.SqlProfileProvider,
              System.Web, Version=2.0.0.0, Culture=neutral,
              PublicKeyToken=b03f5f7f11d50a3a" />
    </providers>
  </profile>

</system.web>
```

Description

- To store data, the profile feature uses a *profile provider*.
- By default, the profile feature uses a profile provider named AspNetSqlProfileProvider to store and retrieve data from a SQL Server Express database named AspNetDb.mdf.
- To use the ProfileCommon class with data that's stored in an existing database, you must write and configure a custom profile provider.

Figure 21-3   How the default profile provider works

How to use profiles with authenticated users

By default, the profile feature only works for authenticated users. Most of the time, this makes sense. For example, you typically want a user to create an account and log in before you allow the user to read or write personalized data such as first name, last name, or preferences for the web application. The topics that follow show you how to use profiles, but they assume that the user has been authenticated before accessing the specified web pages.

How to define profile properties

Figure 21-4 shows the details of how to define and use a profile property for a String data type. To start, you must code a Profile element and a Properties element within the System.web element of the web.config file. Within the Properties element, you can code one or more Add elements to add profile properties. Then, you can use the Name attribute of the Add element to specify the name of the property. In this figure, the web.config file contains two properties named FirstName and LastName. Since the Add elements don't specify a data type, the String data type is used by default.

Once you have defined profile properties in the web.config file, you can write code that uses the Profile property of the HttpContext object to store and retrieve the profile properties. Remember, though, that these properties can only be accessed for a user after the user has been authenticated. In this figure, for example, let's assume that the code that stores profile data is in the code-behind file for a page named MyAccount.aspx that can only be accessed by an authenticated user. As a result, the user must log in or submit a cookie with a valid authentication ticket before being allowed to access the MyAccount page.

When the user accesses this page, the code that's in the Load event handler for the page uses the Profile property to read the user's first and last name from the data store. Since this data is stored as the String type, it can be loaded directly into a text box without any casting or conversions. Then, the MyAccount page will be displayed with the FirstName and LastName properties for the current authenticated user displayed in the text boxes. If no data exists for the current user, though, the FirstName and LastName properties will return empty strings. In that case, you should leave the text boxes at their default values of empty strings.

At this point, the user can enter or edit his or her first or last name in these text boxes. Then, the user can click on the Save button to execute the event handler for the Click event of the button. This event handler saves the data that's in the text boxes for the first and last names to the FirstName and LastName properties of the profile. Again, since these properties are of the String type, no casting or conversion is needed.

How to define profile properties in the web.config file

```
<system.web>

  <profile>
    <properties>

      <add name="FirstName" />
      <add name="LastName" />

    </properties>
  </profile>

</system.web>
```

C# code that retrieves profile data

```csharp
protected void Page_Load(object sender, EventArgs e)
{
    if (!IsPostBack)
    {
        txtFirstName.Text = Profile.FirstName;
        txtLastName.Text = Profile.LastName;
    }
}
```

C# code that stores profile data

```csharp
protected void btnSave_Click(object sender, EventArgs e)
{
    Profile.FirstName = txtFirstName.Text;
    Profile.LastName = txtLastName.Text;
}
```

Description

- To define the properties that can be used by a profile in the web.config file, you code an Add element within the Properties element of the Profile element. The only attribute that's required within an Add element is the Name attribute, which specifies the name that's used to access the property.

- By default, all profile properties are stored with the String data type.

- By default, the user must be authenticated before the profile properties can be accessed. If the user isn't authenticated, the property will return an empty string.

Note

- If a web.config file hasn't already been added to your application, you can add it by right-clicking the project, selecting the Add New Item command, and then selecting the Web Configuration File template from the dialog box that's displayed.

Figure 21-4   How to define profile properties

How to specify data types

Figure 21-5 shows how to use the Type attribute of a profile property to specify a data type other than the String type. To start, this figure shows the XML code for the FirstName property displayed in the last figure. Then, it shows the XML code for a property named BirthDate that uses the DateTime data type. Last, it shows the XML code for a property named AccessCount that uses an integer data type.

When you specify a .NET data type, you must qualify it by including the name of the namespace that contains the type. For example, you must use System.DateTime for the DateTime data type, and you must use System.Int32 for the int type. In contrast, you can use C# data types like int and decimal without any qualification.

In addition, if you use a custom data type and that data type is stored within the application's App_Code folder, you only need to include the namespace name if the custom data type is stored in a namespace. For example, let's assume that you store a class named Customer within the App_Code folder. Let's also assume that this class isn't coded within a namespace. In that case, you can specify the Customer type like this:

```
<add name="Customer" type="Customer" />
```

However, if this class is coded within the Business namespace, you must specify the Customer type like this:

```
<add name="Customer" type="Business.Customer" />
```

You'll learn more about working with custom data types later in this chapter.

When you work with profile properties that use data types, you need to convert these properties to a different data type so they can be displayed in a control. For example, the BirthDate property in this figure (which is of the DateTime type) is stored in a text box (which takes a String type). That's why the code in this figure uses the ToShortDateString method to convert the BirthDate property to a string, and that's why the ToDateTime method of the Convert class is used to convert the string that's stored in the text box to a valid DateTime object before it's stored in the BirthDate property.

However, if you don't need to convert a profile property to get it to work with a control, you can often work with it directly. For example, the last statement in this figure shows how you can update the AccessCount property (which is an integer type). To do this, you just use the increment operator after the property. This updates AccessCount and causes the updated count to be stored in the data source.

How to specify data types for profile properties in the web.config file

```
<!-- System.String is the default type -->
<add name="FirstName" />

<add name="BirthDate"
     type="System.DateTime" />

<add name="AccessCount"
     type="System.Int32" />
```

C# code that retrieves typed profile data

```
txtFirstName.Text = Profile.FirstName;

txtBirthDate.Text =
    Profile.BirthDate.ToShortDateString();

lblCount.Text =
    Profile.AccessCount.ToString();
```

C# code that stores typed profile data

```
Profile.FirstName = txtFirstName.Text;

Profile.BirthDate =
    Convert.ToDateTime(txtBirthDate.Text);

Profile.AccessCount++;        // updates and stores the access count
```

Description

- You can use the Type attribute of the Add element to specify the data type for a profile property in the web.config file.
- By default, all profile properties are stored with the String data type.
- To specify the Type attribute for a .NET data type, you must include the namespace name.
- To specify the Type attribute for a custom data type that's in the App_Code folder, you only need to include the namespace name if the data type is stored in a namespace (see figure 21-8).

Figure 21-5   How to use data types with profile properties

How to group profile properties

Figure 21-6 shows how to group profile properties. To do that, you code a Group element within the Profile and Properties elements. Within this Group element, you must code a Name attribute that specifies the name of the group. In this figure, for example, the Name attribute creates a group named Preferences.

Within the Group element, you can code one or more Add elements to specify the properties for the group. In this figure, for example, the Preferences group contains two properties of the Boolean type named SendPromotions and SendNewProducts. These properties can be used to determine whether to send a user emails about special product promotions or announcements for new products. Please note, however, that you can't nest one group within another.

Once you've defined a group and its properties within the web.config file, you can access them just as you would any other property. The only difference is that you need to specify the name of the group before the name of the property. To illustrate, the examples in this figure show how to use the SendPromotions and SendNewProducts properties with the Checked property of a check box. Since the Checked property expects a Boolean value, no casting or conversion is required to synchronize the check box with the profile property.

This figure also shows that the IntelliSense feature works with groups just as it does for regular properties. To access it, you just type "Profile" followed by a period to display a list that includes all of the groups that are available from the ProfileCommon class. Then, you can select a group by typing the first few letters of the group's name and pressing the Tab key. Finally, you can enter a period and then select a property within the group.

How to group profile properties

```
<group name="Preferences">

    <add name="SendPromotions"
        type="System.Boolean" />

    <add name="SendNewProducts"
        type="System.Boolean" />

</group>
```

C# code that retrieves grouped profile properties

```
chkPromotions.Checked = Profile.Preferences.SendPromotions;
chkNewProducts.Checked = Profile.Preferences.SendNewProducts;
```

C# code that stores grouped profile properties

```
Profile.Preferences.SendPromotions = chkPromotions.Checked;
Profile.Preferences.SendNewProducts = chkNewProducts.Checked;
```

How IntelliSense makes it easy to work with profile properties

Description

- To group properties, you can code a Group element around any Add elements within the Profile and Properties elements in the web.config file. The only attribute that's required within a Group element is the Name attribute, which specifies the name for the group.

- You can't nest a second Group element within the first Group element.

Figure 21-6   How to group profile properties

How to specify default values

The first example in figure 21-7 shows how to use the DefaultValue attribute of the Add element to specify a default value for a profile property. Here, the default value for the Boolean SendPromotions property is set to true. As a result, the first time you use the ProfileCommon class to retrieve this property it will be a true value. If you don't code a default value, a false value will be returned for this property.

How to specify read-only properties

By default, you can read and write all profile properties. However, if you want to make a profile property read-only, you can set the ReadOnly attribute of the Add element to true. This is shown in the second example in figure 21-7.

How to specify default values for profile properties

```
<add name="SendPromotions"
     type="System.Boolean"
     defaultValue="true" />
```

How to specify read-only profile properties

```
<add name="DisplayName"
     readOnly="true" />
```

Description

- You can use the DefaultValue attribute of the Add element to initialize the value of a property.
- You can set the ReadOnly attribute of the Add element to true to prevent the application from writing to that property.

Figure 21-7   How to specify two more profile property attributes

How to use custom types

Figure 21-8 shows how to use a custom type named Customer. To start, this figure shows the Customer class, which specifies the types of data that are stored within a Customer object. The Serializable attribute at the start of the class lets the .NET Framework know that it's OK to convert this class to the specified format. You'll see how to specify the format that's used in just a moment.

In this example, each of the eight public fields of the Customer class store string data. However, you can use any of the data types for a class like this. If, for example, you want to store a DateTime data type, you can do that. Or, if you want to store a custom data type named Address to store street address information, you can do that as long as you mark that data type as serializable too.

To specify the format you want to use to store a custom type, you use the SerializeAs attribute of the Add element for a profile property. The default value of this attribute is String, which stores all the public fields and properties of a custom type as plain text. For many custom types, this setting is adequate. Note that you don't need to mark a custom type as serializable to use this setting. However, we recommend that you mark all your custom types as serializable in case you decide to save the data in a different format later on.

If a custom type contains a reference to another object, or if you need to save the private fields of the custom type, you'll need to set the SerializeAs attribute to binary. Although neither of these conditions apply to the Customer type, I used binary serialization here for illustrative purposes. Because of that, a Customer object will be converted to binary data before it's saved to a column in the database. Conversely, the binary data will be converted to a Customer object when the column is retrieved from the database.

The C# code in the examples shows how to work with the Customer type. To start, you can retrieve the Customer object for a user just as you would retrieve any other type of profile property. But note that if you try to retrieve a Customer object and no object exists, one is created using the default constructor. Conversely, you can save the Customer object for a user just as you would save any other type of profile property.

Since the profile property named Customer is of the Customer type, you can use it to directly access any of the properties stored within the Customer object. For example, to retrieve the Email property of the Customer object for the user, you can use this statement:

```
txtEmail.Text = Profile.Customer.Email;
```

This retrieves the Customer object for the user, accesses the Email property, and stores it in the email text box. Conversely, to store a change that's made in the email text box, you can use this statement:

```
Profile.Customer.Email = txtEmail.Text;
```

Although you can also set the SerializeAs attribute to XML or ProviderSpecific, you probably won't need to use these settings unless you create a custom profile provider. In that case, you may want to set the SerializeAs attribute to ProviderSpecific so the profile provider can determine how to store and retrieve each object.

The Customer class in the App_Code folder

```
[Serializable]
public class Customer
{
    public string Email;
    public string LastName;
    public string FirstName;
    public string Address;
    public string City;
    public string State;
    public string ZipCode;
    public string Phone;
}
```

How to specify a custom type for a profile property

```
<add name="Customer"
    type="Customer"
    serializeAs="Binary" />
```

Possible values for the SerializeAs attribute

Value	Description
String	Converts the object to plain text and stores it within the specified data store for the application. This is the default setting.
Binary	Converts the object to binary data and stores it within the specified data store for the application. For this to work, the .NET Framework must be able to serialize the object.
XML	Converts the object to XML and stores it in the specified data store for the application.
ProviderSpecific	Allows a custom profile provider to decide how to store the object.

C# code that retrieves custom typed data

```
Customer c = Profile.Customer;
```

C# code that stores custom typed data

```
Customer c = new Customer();
c.Email = txtEmail.Text;
c.LastName = txtLastName.Text;
c.FirstName = txtFirstName.Text;
Profile.Customer = c;
```

Description

- To specify the Type attribute of the Add element for a custom type that's in the App_Code folder, you can code just the name of the class. However, if the class is coded within a namespace, you must include the name of the namespace.

- To store a custom type as binary data, you need to mark it as serializable by coding the Serializable attribute just before the declaration of the class. Then, you can set the SerializeAs attribute of the Add element to Binary to specify that the data should be stored as binary data.

Figure 21-8   How to use custom types

How to use profiles with anonymous users

By default, the profile feature only works with authenticated users. However, there are times when you may want to use profiles with anonymous users. For example, you probably don't want to force a user to log in before he or she can add items to a shopping cart. Fortunately, the ASP.NET *anonymous identification* feature lets you use profiles with anonymous users.

How to enable anonymous identification

Before you can identify anonymous users, you need to enable the anonymous identification feature as shown in figure 21-9. To do that, you just code an anonymousIdentification element with an Enabled attribute set to true. Once you do that, a cookie will be stored for each user that visits your web site. This cookie will be named .ASPXANONYMOUS, and it will be stored on the user's machine for 100,000 minutes, which is almost 70 days. That way, each time an anonymous user visits your site, the user's browser passes a cookie to the site that contains an identifier that uniquely identifies the user.

Most of the time, that's all you need to do to enable anonymous identification. However, if you want to change the name of the cookie, you can use the CookieName attribute. Or, if you want to shorten or lengthen the amount of time that the cookie is stored on the user's system, you can use the CookieTimeout attribute. Or, if you need to make sure that this works even if the user's browser doesn't support cookies (which is rare), you can use the Cookieless attribute. In that case, you typically set this attribute to AutoDetect so cookies can be used if they're available.

How to allow anonymous users to access profile properties

Once you've enabled anonymous identification, you must specify which profile properties can be accessed by an anonymous user. To do that, you can set the AllowAnonymous attribute of the Add element to true. In this figure, for example, the Cart property can be accessed by anonymous users, but the Customer property can't. Note that the Cart property uses a ShoppingCart data type that's defined by the ShoppingCart class shown in figure 21-12.

How to use profile properties with anonymous users

```
<system.web>

    <anonymousIdentification enabled="true" />

    <profile>
      <properties>

        <add name="Customer"
             type="Customer"
             serializeAs="Binary" />

        <add name="Cart"
             type="ShoppingCart"
             serializeAs="Binary"
             allowAnonymous="true" />

      </properties>
    </profile>

</system.web>
```

Attributes of the anonymousIdentification element

Attribute	Description
Enabled	Enables or disables anonymous identification. The default setting is False.
CookieName	Sets the name of the cookie that's stored for each anonymous user. The default setting is .ASPXANONYMOUS.
CookieTimeout	Sets the length of time that the cookie will be stored on the user's machine in minutes. The default setting is 100,000 minutes, which is almost 70 days.
Cookieless	Specifies how to identify anonymous users. You can use one of the four values shown below.

Possible values for the Cookieless attribute

Value	Description
UseCookies	Uses cookies to store the anonymous identifier. This is the default setting.
UseUri	Stores the anonymous identifier in a query string.
AutoDetect	Allows ASP.NET to detect whether the browser can support cookies. If so, it uses cookies to store the anonymous identifier. If not, it uses a query string.
UseDeviceProfile	Configures the anonymous identifier for the device or browser.

Description

* Once you've enabled *anonymous identification*, you can set the AllowAnonymous attribute of any Add element to true to allow anonymous users to access the specified profile property.

Figure 21-9   How to enable anonymous identification

How to migrate data from anonymous to authenticated users

Once you begin storing personalized data for anonymous users, you need to develop a strategy for what to do if the anonymous user creates an account and authenticates. To illustrate, let's assume an anonymous user has added items to his or her cart and that this cart has been saved to the data store. Then, the anonymous user decides to purchase the items in the cart. At this point, the user must get authenticated by creating an account or by logging in, and you must decide what to do with the data that's stored in the anonymous user's cart.

Figure 21-10 shows how you can use the Profile_MigrateAnonymous event handler to handle this situation. To start, you can create a global.asax file for your application if one doesn't already exist. Then, you can code the Profile_MigrateAnonymous event handler in this file. Because Profile_MigrateAnonymous is an application-wide event, it will be called whenever a user authenticates. In fact, unless you remove the cookie that contains the anonymous identifier as shown in the second example in this figure, this method may be called twice each time the user authenticates.

One way to migrate data is to copy the data that's stored in the Cart property for the anonymous user to the Cart property for the authenticated user as shown in the first example in this figure. Here, the first statement retrieves the profile for the anonymous user and stores it in a ProfileCommon object named p. To accomplish this, this statement uses the AnonymousId property of the ProfileMigrateEventsArg object to retrieve the unique identifier for the user, and it uses the static GetProfile method of the ProfileCommon class. Then, the second statement copies the Cart property from the anonymous user's profile to the Cart property for the newly authenticated user's profile. This will replace any items in the authenticated user's cart with the items in the anonymous cart.

At this point, the data for the ShoppingCart object is stored for both the anonymous user and the authenticated user. As a result, if the user logs out and becomes anonymous again, the user's cart will still contain all of the same items. On the other hand, if the user logs in and becomes authenticated, the user's cart will be replaced by whatever items are stored in the anonymous cart.

Although this solution works, it doesn't provide for an anonymous user that already has stored items in the cart for his authenticated account. In that case, you may not want to replace the authenticated Cart property with the anonymous Cart property. Instead, you may want to merge the items in the two carts as shown in the second example. In this case, if the same item is in both carts, the AddItem method of the ShoppingCart class increases the quantity for the item appropriately.

After the items in the two carts have been merged, this code uses a method of the ProfileManager class to delete the anonymous profile from the data store. Then, it uses a method of the AnonymousIdentificationModule class to clear the cookie that stores the anonymous identifier from the client's browser. This reduces the size of the data store, it deletes all items from the anonymous cart, and it prevents the Profile_MigrateAnonymous event handler from being run twice each time a user authenticates.

Code that copies the data for an anonymous user to an authenticated user

```
void Profile_MigrateAnonymous(object sender,
    ProfileMigrateEventArgs e)
{
    ProfileCommon p = Profile.GetProfile(e.AnonymousID);
    Profile.Cart = p.Cart;
}
```

Code that merges data for an anonymous user with data for an authenticated user

```
void Profile_MigrateAnonymous(object sender,
    ProfileMigrateEventArgs e)
{
    // get the anonymous profile
    ProfileCommon p = Profile.GetProfile(e.AnonymousID);

    if (p.Cart.Count > 0 && Profile.Cart.Count == 0)
    {
        // copy the anonymous cart to the authenticated cart
        Profile.Cart = p.Cart;
    }
    else if (Profile.Cart.Count > 0 && p.Cart.Count > 0)
    {
        // put all anonymous items in the authenticated cart
        CartItem[] items = p.Cart.GetItems();
        foreach (CartItem item in items)
        {
            If (item != null)
                Profile.Cart.AddItem(item);
        }
    }

    // delete the anonymous profile data from the data store
    ProfileManager.DeleteProfile(e.AnonymousID);

    // clear the cookie that identifies the anonymous user
    AnonymousIdentificationModule.ClearAnonymousIdentifier();
}
```

Description

- Since the Profile_MigrateAnonymous event handler may be called from multiple web pages, it is often stored in the global.asax file. This event handler is executed whenever a user is authenticated.

- If you don't delete the profile data for the anonymous user and remove the anonymous identifier after the data for an anonymous user has been migrated to the authenticated user, the Profile_MigrateAnonymous event handler will be executed twice each time a user is authenticated.

- The code for the GetItems and AddItem methods of the ShoppingCart class is shown in figure 21-12.

Figure 21-10   How to migrate data from anonymous to authenticated users

The Cart Profile application

Now that you've seen the details for how to use profiles to work with authenticated users and anonymous users, you're ready to see how these details fit together within an application. In particular, you're ready to see how the Halloween Store application can use profiles to provide for a shopping cart that persists across sessions for both anonymous and authenticated users, and you're ready to see how this application can use profiles to store other user data for authenticated users. We'll call this the Cart Profile application.

The pages

Part 1 of figure 21-11 shows how the Cart page of this application can be displayed for an anonymous user or an authenticated user. The first Cart page contains a single item, and you can tell that the user is an anonymous user because the Login control at the bottom of the page says, "Login."

The second Cart page shows that the user is an authenticated user because the Login control at the bottom of the page says, "Logout." In addition, you can tell that this authenticated user has previously saved first name data because the page displays "Anne's shopping cart" instead of "Your shopping cart" above the list box that's used for the shopping cart. Last, the cart for the authenticated user contains two items instead of one because the application has merged the anonymous cart with the authenticated cart.

The Cart page before the user logs in

The Cart page after the user logs in

Figure 21-11   The pages of the Cart Profile application (part 1 of 2)

Part 2 of figure 21-11 shows the CheckOut1 page that's displayed when the user clicks on the Check Out button on the Cart page. This page can only be accessed by an authenticated user, which is appropriate since this page allows the user to enter and edit personalized customer data. If an anonymous user tries to access this page, the user is transferred to the Login page using the techniques of the last chapter.

In this application, you can only display the CheckOut1 page by clicking on the Check Out button from the Cart page. However, in a more full-featured application, you might want to add a "My Account" link that allows a user to edit this type of information at his or her convenience. That way, a user can create an account, authenticate, and begin storing personalized data like the data shown in this figure without having to begin the check out process.

The CheckOut1 page

Description

- The Cart page can display the cart for an anonymous user or an authenticated user. When an anonymous user logs in, all items in the anonymous user's cart are copied into the authenticated user's cart, adding to the quantity as necessary for duplicate items.

- The CheckOut1 page can only be accessed by an authenticated user. This page allows the user to enter or edit personalized user data.

- If an anonymous user clicks on the Check Out button on the Cart page, the Login page is automatically displayed by using the techniques presented in chapter 20.

Figure 21-11   The pages of the Cart Profile application (part 2 of 2)

The code

Part 1 of figure 21-12 shows the code for the ShoppingCart class. Since this is a typical business class, you shouldn't have any trouble understanding it. However, there are three things you should notice.

First, the Serializable attribute is coded at the beginning of this class to mark it as serializable. This allows the profile feature to store and retrieve ShoppingCart objects from the data store. Note that because the ShoppingCart class uses the CartItem and Product classes, these classes must also be marked as serializable for the ShoppingCart class to be serialized successfully.

Second, the AddItem method contains all of the logic that's used to add an item to the cart. In particular, if the item already exists in the cart, the quantity of that item is increased appropriately. Note that you can access this code from any point in the application. For example, the Order page calls this method to add an item to the cart, and the global.asax file calls this method to migrate items from the anonymous cart to the authenticated cart.

Third, the ShoppingCart class works with strongly typed data. For example, the AddItem method only accepts objects of the CartItem type. As a result, it's impossible for a programmer to accidentally add another type of object to the cart (which could cause a nasty debugging problem). Conversely, the GetItems method returns an array of CartItem objects. As a result, you don't need to use casting to retrieve the CartItem objects.

The code for the ShoppingCart class

```
using System;
using System.Collections;

[Serializable]
public class ShoppingCart
{
    SortedList cart = new SortedList();

    public int Count
    {
        get
        {
            return cart.Count;
        }
    }

    public void AddItem(CartItem item)
    {
        string productID = item.Product.ProductID;
        if (cart.ContainsKey(productID))
        {
            CartItem existingItem = (CartItem) cart[productID];
            existingItem.Quantity += item.Quantity;
        }
        else
            cart.Add(productID, item);
    }

    public CartItem[] GetItems()
    {
        CartItem[] items = new CartItem[cart.Count];
        for (int i = 0; i < cart.Count; i++)
            items[i] = (CartItem) cart.GetByIndex(i);
        return items;
    }

    public void Clear()
    {
        cart.Clear();
    }

    public void RemoveAt(int i)
    {
        cart.RemoveAt(i);
    }
}
```

Description

- The ShoppingCart class uses the CartItem and Product classes that were presented in chapter 3. The only difference is that the Serializable attribute has been added to these classes to mark them as serializable.

Figure 21-12   The code for the Cart Profile application (part 1 of 3)

Part 2 of figure 21-12 presents the code for the Cart page. To start, when the page is loaded, the Page_Load event handler sets the title for the cart. First, this event handler declares the default title that's displayed for anonymous users and for authenticated users who have not saved their first names in the data store. Then, this event handler uses the Profile property of the application to check if the FirstName property of the Customer object contains a null value or an empty string. If not, the first name is used to personalize the title for the cart. Finally, the DisplayCart method is called to load all items in the cart into the list box for the cart.

The DisplayCart method begins by clearing any existing items from the list box. Then, it uses a foreach loop to add each item in the cart to the list box. To do that, it uses the GetItems method of the Cart property of the profile to get an array of CartItem objects.

The btnRemove_Click and the btnEmpty_Click event handlers both use the Cart property of the profile to update the items that are stored in the cart. These updates are automatically made to the data store as soon as the statements are executed. If, for example, you click the Empty Cart button, the code that's in the btnEmpty_Click event handler will clear all items from the Cart property of the profile, which will delete all cart items from the data store.

The code for the Cart page

```
public partial class Cart : System.Web.UI.Page
{
    protected void Page_Load(object sender, EventArgs e){
        if (!IsPostBack)
        {
            string title = "Your shopping cart:";
            string fn = Profile.Customer.FirstName;
            if (fn != null && !fn.Equals(""))
                title = fn + "'s shopping cart:";
            lblCartTitle.Text = title;
            this.DisplayCart();
        }
    }

    private void DisplayCart(){
        lstCart.Items.Clear();
        CartItem[] items = Profile.Cart.GetItems();
        foreach (CartItem i in items)
            lstCart.Items.Add(i.display);
    }

    protected void btnRemove_Click(object sender, EventArgs e){
        if (Profile.Cart.Count > 0)
        {
            if (lstCart.SelectedIndex > -1)
            {
                Profile.Cart.RemoveAt(lstCart.SelectedIndex);
                this.DisplayCart();
            }
            else
            {
                lblMessage.Text = "Please select the item you want to remove.";
            }
        }
    }

    protected void btnEmpty_Click(object sender, EventArgs e){
        Profile.Cart.Clear();
        lstCart.Items.Clear();
    }

    protected void btnCheckOut_Click(object sender, EventArgs e){
        Response.Redirect("~/CheckOut/CheckOut1.aspx");
    }
}
```

Description

- Within the Page_Load event handler, the Profile.Customer property is used to display a different title for the cart if the user is authenticated and has stored a first name in the database.

- Within the other methods, the Profile.Cart property is used to work with the items that are stored in the cart for the current user. Since this property is of the ShoppingCart type, you can use the methods defined in the ShoppingCart class to work with it.

Figure 21-12   The code for the Cart Profile application (part 2 of 3)

Part 3 of figure 21-12 presents the code for the CheckOut1 page. To start, when this page loads, it binds the states data in a class named US_States to the State drop-down list. Then, it uses the Profile property to return a Customer object and display the properties of the Customer object within the text boxes and drop-down list on the page. Remember that the first statement shown here will create a Customer object if one doesn't already exist. Because of that, you need to check this object to be sure it isn't null before you assign its properties to the text boxes. If you don't, an error will occur because the properties of the object will be null.

If the user clicks the Continue Checkout or Continue Shopping button, the UpdateCustomer method is called. This method begins by creating a new Customer object. Then, it sets the properties of this Customer object to the string values that are stored in the text boxes and drop-down list on the page. Last, it saves the updated Customer object in the profile.

If, on the other hand, the user clicks on the Cancel button, the UpdateCustomer method isn't called. As a result, the customer data on the CheckOut1 page isn't saved. Instead, the Cart property of the user's authenticated profile is cleared, and the user is redirected to the Order page.

The code for the CheckOut1 page

```
public partial class CheckOut_CheckOut1 : System.Web.UI.Page
{
    protected void Page_Load(object sender, EventArgs e){
        if (!IsPostBack){
            US_States states = new US_States();
            ddlState.DataSource = states;
            ddlState.DataMember = "US_States.State";
            ddlState.DataValueField = "Abbreviation";
            ddlState.DataTextField = "Name";
            ddlState.DataBind();

            Customer c = Profile.Customer;
            if (c != null){
                txtLastName.Text = c.LastName;
                txtFirstName.Text = c.FirstName;
                txtAddress.Text = c.Address;
                txtCity.Text = c.City;
                ddlState.SelectedValue = c.State;
                txtZipCode.Text = c.ZipCode;
                txtPhone.Text = c.Phone;
                txtEmail.Text = c.Email;
            }
        }
    }

    protected void UpdateCustomer(){
        Customer c = new Customer();
        c.LastName = txtLastName.Text;
        c.FirstName = txtFirstName.Text;
        c.Address = txtAddress.Text;
        c.City = txtCity.Text;
        c.State = ddlState.SelectedValue;
        c.ZipCode = txtZipCode.Text;
        c.Phone = txtPhone.Text;
        c.Email = txtEmail.Text;
        Profile.Customer = c;
    }

    protected void btnContinue_Click(object sender, EventArgs e){
        UpdateCustomer();
        Response.Redirect("~/Order.aspx");
    }

    protected void btnCheckout_Click(object sender, EventArgs e){
        UpdateCustomer();
        lblMessage.Text = "Sorry, that function hasn't been implemented yet.";
    }

    protected void btnCancel_Click(object sender, EventArgs e){
        Profile.Cart.Clear();
        Response.Redirect("~/Order.aspx");
    }
}
```

Description

- This page uses the Profile.Customer property to store and retrieve Customer objects.

Figure 21-12   The code for the Cart Profile application (part 3 of 3)

Perspective

This chapter has presented the skills you need for using the profiles feature to store data for authenticated and anonymous users. Now, you should be able to use profiles to quickly prototype a new application without writing any of the data access code. That is one of the strengths of this feature. Then, once you get the prototype working, you can decide whether you need to write a custom profile provider to gain control of how this feature stores your data.

Terms

profile feature
personalization feature
profile
profile provider
anonymous identification

22

How to use the MultiView and Wizard controls

The MultiView and Wizard controls provide two ways to divide a page into multiple views or steps. Both of these controls let you navigate between views or steps without writing any C# code, and they make it easy to work with the data that's stored within these views or steps.

How to use the MultiView control **718**
How the MultiView control works 718
How to add views 720
How to add controls to a view 722
How to navigate between views with commands 724
How to access the data stored in a MultiView control 726
Properties and events of the MultiView and View controls 728

How to use the Wizard control **730**
How the Wizard control works 730
How to add or remove steps 732
How to add a Cancel button 734
How to add a completion step 736
Properties and events of the Wizard and WizardStep controls ... 738
How to use templates and styles with a Wizard control 740

Perspective **742**

How to use the MultiView control

In the topics that follow, you'll see how a MultiView control can be used as part of a Checkout application. Of course, the MultiView control can also be used for any application that lets the user navigate between related pages.

How the MultiView control works

Figure 22-1 shows a Checkout application that uses three *views* of a MultiView control. Although each of these views appears to be a separate page, each view is actually on the same page (the Checkout.aspx page). When the user clicks on any of the buttons within a MultiView control, the page requires a postback. As a result, all of the data on the page is posted each time the user clicks on a navigation button to switch views. For example, when the user clicks on the Next button in the first view, the data that's stored in all three views is posted. Although this isn't as efficient as coding three separate pages, the views are easier to develop and maintain.

The first view of a MultiView control

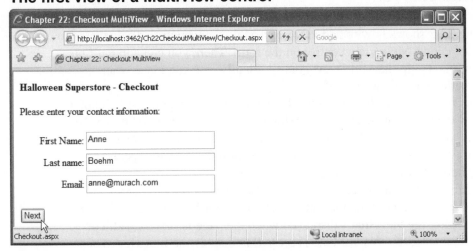

The second view of a MultiView control

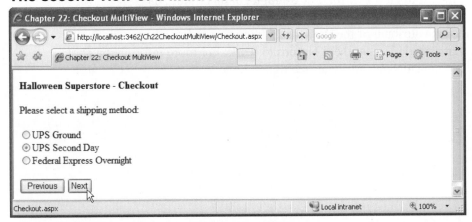

The third view of a MultiView control

Figure 22-1   How the MultiView control works

How to add views

Figure 22-2 shows how to add views to a MultiView control. To do that, you begin by placing a MultiView control on the form. Then, you can add multiple View controls within the MultiView control. Finally, you can place other controls within each View control.

In this figure, the MultiView control is named mvCheckout, and it contains three View controls named vContact, vShippingMethod, and vCreditCard. To keep this figure simple, each view only contains some plain text and a Button control or two. This allows you to get the navigation for the views set up correctly before adding other controls to each view.

The MultiView control lets you navigate between views without writing any C# code. To start, you can set the ActiveViewIndex attribute of the MultiView control to select the view that's displayed when the page is first loaded. For example, in this figure, this attribute is set to 0 to display the first view. Then, you can set a button's CommandName attribute to one of the commands that work with the MultiView control. For example, in this figure, the CommandName attribute of the Next button is set to NextView, and the CommandName attribute of the Previous button is set to PrevView. This is all the code that's needed to get these buttons to work! For more information about using the CommandName attribute, see figure 22-4.

A MultiView control with three View controls

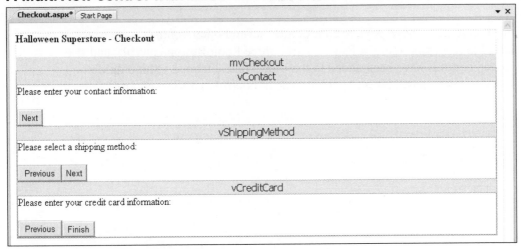

The aspx code for these controls

```
<asp:MultiView ID="mvCheckout" runat="server" ActiveViewIndex="0">
    <asp:View ID="vContact" runat="server">
        Please enter your contact information:<br /><br />
        <asp:Button ID="Button1" runat="server"
            CommandName="NextView" Text="Next" />
    </asp:View>
    <asp:View ID="vShippingMethod" runat="server">
        Please select a shipping method:<br /><br />
        <asp:Button ID="Button2" runat="server"
            CommandName="PrevView" Text="Previous" /> 
        <asp:Button ID="Button3" runat="server"
            CommandName="NextView" Text="Next" />
    </asp:View>
    <asp:View ID="vCreditCard" runat="server">
        Please enter your credit card information:<br /><br />
        <asp:Button ID="Button4" runat="server"
            CommandName="PrevView" Text="Previous" />
        <asp:Button ID="btnFinish" runat="server"
            Text="Finish" PostBackUrl="~/Completion.aspx" />
    </asp:View>
</asp:MultiView>
```

Description

- Once you add a MultiView control to a page, you can add one or more View controls within the MultiView control, and you can add other controls such as labels, text boxes, and buttons within the View control.

- To display the first view when the page is loaded, set the ActiveViewIndex attribute of the MultiView control to 0.

- To use commands to navigate to the next or previous view, you can add any control that has a CommandName attribute such as a Button control. Then, you can set the CommandName attribute to NextView or PrevView.

Figure 22-2   How to add views

How to add controls to a view

Figure 22-3 shows a View control after several other controls have been added to it. In this figure, a Panel control, three RadioButton controls, and two Button controls have been added to the View control named vShippingMethod. However, you can add just about any type of control to a View control.

The second view of figure 22-1

The aspx code for the second View control

```
<asp:MultiView ID="mvCheckout" runat="server" ActiveViewIndex="0">

    <asp:View ID="vContact" runat="server">
        <!-- code for the first view goes here -->
    </asp:View>

    <asp:View ID="vShippingMethod" runat="server">
        <asp:Panel ID="Panel1" runat="server" Width="492">
            Please select a shipping method:<br /><br />
            <asp:RadioButton ID="rdoUPSGround" runat="server"
                Text="UPS Ground" GroupName="ShipVia"
                Checked="True" /><br />
            <asp:RadioButton ID="rdoUPS2Day" runat="server"
                Text="UPS Second Day" GroupName="ShipVia" /><br />
            <asp:RadioButton ID="rdoFedEx" runat="server"
                Text="Federal Express Overnight" GroupName="ShipVia" /><br />
        </asp:Panel><br />
        <asp:Button ID="Button2" runat="server"
            CommandName="PrevView" Text="Previous" />
        <asp:Button ID="Button3" runat="server"
            CommandName="NextView" Text="Next" />
    </asp:View>

    <asp:View ID="vCreditCard" runat="server">
        <!-- code for the third view goes here -->
    </asp:View>

</asp:MultiView>
```

Description

- Within a View control, you can add any other controls including controls such as panels and tables that contain other controls such as labels, text boxes, radio buttons, check boxes, combo boxes, buttons, and so on.

Figure 22-3   How to add controls to a view

How to navigate between views with commands

For most MultiView controls, you can navigate between the views by adding one or more buttons to each view and then setting the CommandName attribute of each button to NextView or PrevView as shown in figure 22-2. However, in some cases, you'll need to be able to navigate to a view other than the previous or next view. To do that, you can use the CommandName and CommandArgument attributes of a button as shown in figure 22-4.

If you need to navigate to a view with a specified index, you can set the CommandName attribute to SwitchViewByIndex. Then, you can set the CommandArgument attribute to the appropriate index (where 0 is the first view, 1 is the second view, and so on).

If you prefer to navigate to a view with a specified ID, you can set the CommandName attribute to SwitchViewByID. Then, you can set the CommandArgument attribute to the ID.

Within a MultiView control, you can use any control that has CommandName and CommandArgument attributes to navigate between the views. All button controls (Button, ImageButton, and LinkButton) have both of these attributes. That's why this figure can use LinkButton controls instead of the Button controls that were used in figure 22-2.

A view that allows you to navigate to other views

How to navigate by index

```
<asp:View ID="vNavigate" runat="server">
    <asp:LinkButton ID="LinkButton1" runat="server"
        CommandName="SwitchViewByIndex" CommandArgument="0">
        View 1: Contact Info</asp:LinkButton><br />
    <asp:LinkButton ID="LinkButton2" runat="server"
        CommandName="SwitchViewByIndex" CommandArgument="1">
        View 2: Shipping Method</asp:LinkButton><br />
    <asp:LinkButton ID="LinkButton3" runat="server"
        CommandName="SwitchViewByIndex" CommandArgument="2">
        View 3: Credit Card Info</asp:LinkButton>
</asp:View>
```

How to navigate by ID

```
<asp:View ID="vNavigate" runat="server">
    <asp:LinkButton ID="LinkButton1" runat="server"
        CommandName="SwitchViewByID" CommandArgument="vContact">
        View 1: Contact Info</asp:LinkButton><br />
    <asp:LinkButton ID="LinkButton2" runat="server"
        CommandName="SwitchViewByID" CommandArgument="vShippingMethod">
        View 2: Shipping Method</asp:LinkButton><br />
    <asp:LinkButton ID="LinkButton3" runat="server"
        CommandName="SwitchViewByID" CommandArgument="vCreditCard">
        View 3: Credit Card Info</asp:LinkButton>
</asp:View>
```

Description

- If a control within a MultiView control has CommandName and CommandArgument attributes, you can use those attributes to navigate between the available views. For example, both the Button and LinkButton controls have CommandName and CommandArgument attributes.

- To navigate to the next or previous view, you can set the CommandName attribute to NextView or PrevView as shown in figure 22-2.

- To navigate to the view with the specified index, you can set the CommandName attribute to SwitchViewByIndex, and you can set the CommandArgument attribute to the appropriate index where 0 is the first view, 1 is the second view, and so on.

- To navigate to the view with the specified ID, you can set the CommandName attribute to SwitchViewByID, and you can set the CommandArgument attribute to the ID.

Figure 22-4   How to navigate between views with commands

How to access the data stored in a MultiView control

To show how to access the data that's stored within a MultiView control, figure 22-5 presents a fourth and final view that displays all of the data that's entered in the three views shown in figure 22-1. This final view is displayed when the user clicks on the Finish button that's available from the third view. Since the data for each of the previous views is automatically stored in the view state of the page, the code for this final view can access that data. In other words, the state of these controls is automatically maintained. And since all of the controls are on the same page, you can directly access them just as you would any control.

For example, the code in the DisplayMessage method begins by getting the shipping type from the radio buttons that are in the second view. Then, this code builds a string that contains the data that's stored in the first three views. To do that, it directly accesses the text box, list box, and drop-down list controls from the first and third views. Finally, it displays this message in the multi-line text box of the fourth and final view.

In this figure, the code only converts the text to a string and displays it in a text box. However, this code could store this data in the session state object so it's available to other pages within the current session. Or, this code could store this data in a database so it's available for future sessions. Regardless, this figure shows how the MultiView control makes it easy to access the data that's stored within any of its views.

A view that displays the data of the MultiView control

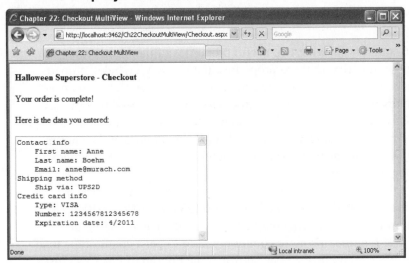

Code that accesses the data that's stored in the MultiView control

```
protected void btnFinish_Click(object sender, EventArgs e)
{
    this.DisplayMessage();
}

private void DisplayMessage()
{
    string shipVia = "";
    if (rdoUPSGround.Checked)
        shipVia = "UPSG";
    else if (rdoUPS2Day.Checked)
        shipVia = "UPS2D";
    else if (rdoFedEx.Checked)
        shipVia = "FEDEX";

    string message =
        "Contact info\n" +
        "    First name: " + txtFirstName.Text + "\n" +
        "    Last name: " + txtLastName.Text + "\n" +
        "    Email: " + txtEmail.Text + "\n" +
        "Shipping method\n" +
        "    Ship via: " + shipVia + "\n" +
        "Credit card info\n" +
        "    Type: " + lstCardType.SelectedValue + "\n" +
        "    Number: " + txtCardNumber.Text + "\n" +
        "    Expiration date: " + ddlExpirationMonth.SelectedValue + "/"
                                + ddlExpirationYear.SelectedValue;
    txtMessage.Text = message;
}
```

Description

- Because the state of each control in the MultiView and View controls is stored in view state, it's easy to access the data for the controls from the code-behind file.

Figure 22-5   How to access the data stored in a MultiView control

Properties and events of the MultiView and View controls

Figure 22-6 starts by showing two useful properties of the MultiView control. You can use the first of these properties, the ActiveViewIndex property, to get or set the zero-based index for the active view. This is useful if you need to write code to display the index of the active view or if you need to write code to change the active view. For example, the code shown at the bottom of this figure uses the ActiveViewIndex property to display the number of the current view. However, you could also set the ActiveViewIndex property to the index of the view you want to display.

You can use the second of these properties, the Views property, to access the collection of View objects that are stored in the MultiView control. Although this property allows you to perform complex operations such as adding or removing a view at runtime, it's more commonly used to get a count of the total number of views. For example, the code shown at the bottom of this figure uses the Count property of the Views collection to display the total number views.

For a MultiView control like the one presented in figure 22-1, you don't usually need to use the events of the MultiView or View controls. However, if you add controls outside of the MultiView control that need to be synchronized with the MultiView control, you may need to code event handlers for the events shown in this figure. For example, the code shown at the bottom of this figure is an event handler for the ActiveViewChanged event of the MultiView control. The code within this event handler changes the text that's displayed in a label that's placed outside of the MultiView control. This causes the label to display a message for each view like this:

    View 1 of 4

Since this event handler is executed every time the active view changes, the text within this label will always be synchronized with the view that's displayed.

Properties of the MultiView control

Property	Description
ActiveViewIndex	Gets or sets the index for the active view, where 0 is the first view, 1 is the second view, and so on. By default, this is set to -1 so no view is selected as the active view.
Views	Gets the collection of View objects contained within the MultiView control. The Count property of this collection can be used to determine the total number of View controls in the MultiView control.

Button properties that work with the MultiView control

Property	Description
CommandName	Sets the navigation command for the button. This property can be set to NextView, PrevView, SwitchViewByIndex, or SwitchViewByID. For more information, see figure 22-2 and figure 22-4.
CommandArgument	Sets the arguments required by the SwitchViewByIndex and SwitchViewByID commands. For more information, see figure 22-4.

An event of the MultiView control

Event	Description
ActiveViewChanged	Fires every time the active view changes.

Events of the View control

Event	Description
Activate	Fires every time the view is activated.
Deactivate	Fires every time the view is deactivated.

Code that uses the ActiveViewChanged event of the MultiView control

```
protected void mvCheckout_ActiveViewChanged(object sender, EventArgs e)
{
    int viewNumber = mvCheckout.ActiveViewIndex + 1;
    lblStatus.Text = "View " + viewNumber + " of " + mvCheckout.Views.Count;
}
```

Figure 22-6   Properties and events of the MultiView and View controls

How to use the Wizard control

In the topics that follow, you'll see how a Wizard control can be used to code a Checkout application that's similar to the one presented earlier in this chapter. This will help you compare the MultiView control to the Wizard control.

How the Wizard control works

Figure 22-7 shows a Checkout application that uses three *steps* of a Wizard control. Although each of these steps appears to be a separate page, each step is actually part of the same page (Checkout.aspx). This works like the views within a MultiView control. The main difference is that, by default, the Wizard control includes a *side bar* on the left side of the control, which provides links to each step in the control. As a result, you can easily navigate to any step in the wizard.

In addition, by default, the Wizard control automatically includes the Next, Previous, and Finish buttons shown on these steps. As a result, if you want to include these features, you may prefer using a Wizard control over a MultiView control.

Step 1 of a Wizard control

Step 2 of a Wizard control

Step 3 of a Wizard control

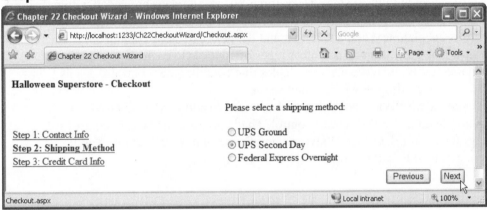

Figure 22-7   How the Wizard control works

How to add or remove steps

Figure 22-8 shows how to add or remove steps from a Wizard control. To start, you place a Wizard control on a page. Next, you select the Add/Remove WizardSteps command from the smart tag menu to display the WizardStep Collection Editor. Then, you can use the Add and Remove buttons on this editor to add or remove steps. In addition, you can use this dialog box to edit the properties for each step. In particular, you'll want to set the Title property, which determines the text that's displayed for the step in the side bar.

Once you get the correct number of steps for your wizard, you can add controls to each step. To do that, you can use the smart tag menu to select and display the step. Then, you can use any standard technique to add controls to the step. In this figure, for example, a TextBox control has been placed on the first step immediately after some plain text.

Whenever you prefer, you can work with the steps of a wizard directly in the aspx code. For example, this figure shows the aspx code for the beginning of a Wizard control with three steps. Here, three WizardStep tags are coded within the WizardSteps tag, which is coded within the Wizard tag. The first step contains some plain text and a text box, and the next two steps contain only plain text. However, you can add other types of controls to each step, including container controls such as panels and tables that contain other controls such as labels, text boxes, drop-down lists, and so on.

Unlike the MultiView control, you don't need to add buttons to provide for navigation features for the Wizard control. That's because the Wizard control displays the appropriate Next, Previous, and Finish buttons by default. You'll learn more about how this works in the next two figures.

A wizard with three steps

The WizardStep Collection Editor

The aspx code for a Wizard control

```
<asp:Wizard ID="Wizard1" runat="server" ActiveStepIndex="0" Width="344px">
    <WizardSteps>
        <asp:WizardStep runat="server" Title="Step 1">
            Please enter your contact information:<br /><br />
            First Name:<asp:TextBox ID="txtFirstName" runat="server">
                </asp:TextBox><br /><br />
        </asp:WizardStep>
        <asp:WizardStep runat="server" Title="Step 2">
            Please select a shipping method:</asp:WizardStep>
        <asp:WizardStep runat="server" Title="Step 3">
            Please enter your credit card information:</asp:WizardStep>
    </WizardSteps>
</asp:Wizard>
```

Description

- To add or remove steps or to edit the properties for a step, you can use the WizardStep Collection Editor, or you can edit the aspx code.

- To access the WizardStep Collection Editor, select the Add/Remove WizardSteps command from the smart tag menu for the Wizard control.

Figure 22-8   How to add or remove steps

How to add a Cancel button

Figure 22-9 shows how to add a Cancel button to each step in a Wizard control. To do that, you set the DisplayCancelButton property of the wizard to True. Once you display the Cancel button, you can code an event handler to handle the CancelButtonClick event that occurs when the user clicks this button. You can see an example of this in the event handler in this figure.

The code within this event handler displays the first step and clears all of the text from the text box controls on this page. To display the first step, this code sets the ActiveStepIndex property of the wizard to 0. Then, it sets the Text property of the three text box controls on this step to an empty string. This shows that you can directly access all of the controls within the wizard from the code-behind file for the page.

A wizard with a Cancel button

A Wizard tag that displays a Cancel button

```
<asp:Wizard ID="wizCheckout" runat="server" Width="739px"
    DisplayCancelButton="True"
    OnCancelButtonClick="wizCheckout_CancelButtonClick">
```

C# code that works with the Cancel button

```
protected void wizCheckout_CancelButtonClick(object sender, EventArgs e)
{
    wizCheckout.ActiveStepIndex = 0;
    txtFirstName.Text = "";
    txtLastName.Text = "";
    txtEmail.Text = "";
}
```

Description

- You can display a Cancel button for each step of a wizard by setting the DisplayCancelButton property of the Wizard control to True. By default, this property is set to False.

- You can use the CancelButtonClick event of the Wizard control to respond to the user clicking on the Cancel button.

- You can use the ActiveStepIndex property of the Wizard control to get or set the active step where 0 is the first step, 1 is the second step, and so on.

Figure 22-9   How to add a Cancel button

How to add a completion step

Figure 22-10 shows how to add a fourth and final step to the wizard that's displayed in figure 22-7. This step is displayed when the user clicks on the Finish button in the third step. But first, the event handler that handles the FinishButtonClick event of the wizard is executed. In this figure, this event handler calls the DisplayMessage method, which displays all of the data that's been entered in the first three steps in the multiline text box of the fourth step.

The DisplayMessage method called by this event handler contains the same code as the DisplayMessage method that was presented in figure 22-5. This shows that the technique for accessing the data that's stored in a Wizard control is the same as the technique for accessing the data that's stored in a MultiView control. That's because, like the MultiView control, the Wizard control stores its data in the view state for the page.

The primary difference between the fourth step and the first three steps is that it doesn't have a side bar or navigation buttons. That's because the StepType attribute for this step has been set to Complete. This attribute is left at the default setting of Auto for the first three steps. As a result, the first step only contains a Next button, the second step contains Previous and Next buttons, and the third step contains Previous and Finish buttons. That's usually what you want, but if it isn't, you can use the StepType attribute to change it.

A wizard with a completion step

A WizardStep tag that defines a completion step

```
<asp:WizardStep ID="WizardStep4" runat="server"
    StepType="Complete" Title="Step 4: Complete">
        Congratulations. You have completed the Checkout wizard.<br /><br />
        Here is the data you entered:<br /><br />
    <asp:TextBox ID="txtMessage" runat="server" Height="166px"
        TextMode="MultiLine" Width="489px"></asp:TextBox>
</asp:WizardStep>
```

C# code that displays a message on the completion page

```
protected void wizCheckout_FinishButtonClick(object sender,
    WizardNavigationEventArgs e)
{
    this.DisplayMessage();
}
```

Possible values for the StepType attribute

Value	Description
Auto	Automatically sets the first step to Start, the last step to Finish, and any intermediate steps to Step. This is the default.
Start	Defines a step that doesn't have a Previous button.
Step	Defines a step that has Previous and Next buttons.
Finish	Defines a step that has Previous and Finish buttons.
Complete	Defines a step that doesn't have a side bar or any buttons. This step is typically used to display a completion message.

Description

- To add a completion step, you can add a final WizardStep tag and set its StepType attribute to Complete.

Figure 22-10 How to add a completion step

Properties and events of the Wizard and WizardStep controls

Figure 22-11 starts by summarizing three useful properties of the Wizard control. First, you can use the ActiveStepIndex property to get or set the active step. For example, the event handler for the Cancel button shown in figure 22-9 sets this property to 0 to display the first step. Second, you can set the DisplayCancelButton property to True to display a Cancel button for each step of the wizard as described in figure 22-9. Third, if you don't want to display the side bar, you can set the DisplaySideBar property to False.

Besides these properties, there are many other properties of the Wizard control that you can use to control the appearance and function of the wizard. For example, you can change the text that's displayed on the navigation buttons. Or, you can change the type of button that's used for the navigation buttons. By default, the wizard uses regular Button controls, but it's also possible to use ImageButton or LinkButton controls. If you use the Auto Format command that's available from the smart tag menu for a wizard, you can automatically change many of these properties.

In a typical wizard, you only need to handle the FinishButtonClick event that's fired when the user clicks on the Finish button. You saw an example of this in figure 22-10. Within this event handler, you can store the data that has been gathered by the wizard and redirect the application to the next page. However, if you add a Cancel button, you'll probably want to add an event handler for the CancelButtonClick event of the wizard like the one you saw in figure 22-9 that's executed when the Cancel button is clicked. And, if necessary, you can write event handlers for any of the other events shown in this figure. For example, you may want to write an event handler for the ActiveStepChanged event to synchronize any controls that are placed outside of the Wizard control with the wizard's current step.

This figure finishes by presenting two properties of the WizardStep control that can be used to control the types of buttons that are displayed on the step. First, you can set the StepType property to any of the values shown in figure 22-10. Second, you can set the AllowReturn property to False to remove the Previous button from the step. However, the user can still return to the previous step by clicking the browser's Back button or by clicking on the links in the side bar if it's displayed. As a result, if it's critical to your application to prevent the user from returning to the previous step, you'll need to remove the side bar and disable the browser's Back button.

Properties of the Wizard control

Property	Description
ActiveStepIndex	Gets or sets the index for the active page where 0 is the first page, 1 is the second page, and so on. By default, this property is set to the page that's selected in Design view.
DisplayCancelButton	To show a Cancel button on every step, you can set this property to True. The default is False.
DisplaySideBar	To hide the side bar, you can set this property to False. The default is True.

Events of the Wizard control

Event	Description
ActiveStepChanged	Fires every time the active step changes.
NextButtonClick	Fires every time a Next button is clicked.
PreviousButtonClick	Fires every time a Previous button is clicked.
CancelButtonClick	Fires every time a Cancel button is clicked.
FinishButtonClick	Fires every time the Finish button is clicked.
SideBarButtonClick	Fires every time one of the side bar links is clicked.

Properties of the WizardStep control

Property	Description
StepType	Changes the types of buttons (Previous, Next, Finish) that are available for the step (see figure 22-10).
AllowReturn	To remove the Previous button from the step, you can set this property to False. The default is True.

Description

- You can use other properties of the Wizard control to control the formatting options for a wizard.

- You can use the Auto Format command that's available from the smart tag menu for a Wizard control to automatically apply many formatting options.

Figure 22-11   Properties and events of the Wizard and WizardStep controls

How to use templates and styles with a Wizard control

Figure 22-12 shows how you can use templates and styles to customize the default controls and formatting for your wizard. For example, you can use templates to override the default controls for the parts of a wizard. Or, you can use styles to change the formatting for the parts of a wizard.

To begin working with templates, you can select the Edit Templates command from the wizard's smart tag menu to enter template-editing mode. In template-editing mode, you can select the template that you want to edit from the smart tag menu. In this figure, for example, you can see the StartNavigation template that contains the navigation buttons for the start step.

Once you've displayed a template, you can use standard techniques to add controls to the template. In this figure, for example, a LinkButton control has been added to the StartNavigation template. This causes the LinkButton control on this template to override the Button control that's used by default.

When you're done modifying the templates, you can select the End Template Editing command from the smart tag menu. Then, you can run the application and see how the new templates work.

Once you understand how to modify one template, you shouldn't have much trouble modifying the other ones. You can use the three navigation templates to modify the navigation buttons for the start, step, and finish steps. You can use the side bar template to modify the links displayed in the side bar. And you can use the header template to add a header to the wizard control. By default, the header template doesn't contain any controls, so adding controls to this template activates a new part of the wizard.

To work with styles, you can use the Properties window or you can work directly in Source view. The example in this figure shows two styles. The Navigation style sets the horizontal alignment for all navigation buttons to left. Then, the SideBar style makes the font size smaller for the links in the side bar. As a result, the side bar won't take up as much horizontal space.

Although it might seem like a lot of extra work to set up templates and styles for a wizard, the extra work will pay off in certain situations. For example, you might want to use templates and styles if you have an application that will include multiple wizards with custom formatting. In that case, you can create the templates and styles for one wizard and then copy them to the other wizards.

A Wizard control in template-editing mode

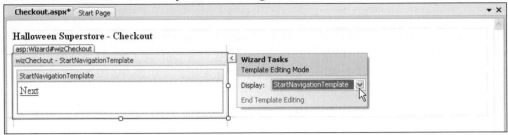

Aspx code for wizard templates and styles

```
<asp:Wizard ID="wizCheckout" runat="server">

    <StartNavigationTemplate>
        <asp:LinkButton ID="LinkButton1" runat="server">Next
        </asp:LinkButton>
    </StartNavigationTemplate>

    <NavigationStyle HorizontalAlign="Left" />
    <SideBarStyle Font-Size="Small" />

    <WizardSteps>
        <!-- wizard steps go here -->
    </WizardSteps>
</asp:Wizard>
```

Wizard templates and styles

Template	Style
HeaderTemplate	HeaderStyle
StartNavigationTemplate	StepNextButtonStyle
StepNavigationTemplate	StepPreviousButtonStyle
	StepStyle
FinishNavigationTemplate	FinishCompleteButtonStyle
	FinishPreviousButtonStyle
SideBarTemplate	SideBarButtonStyle
	SideBarStyle
	CancelButtonStyle
	NavigationButtonStyle
	NavigationStyle

Description

- You can use templates and styles to customize the default controls and formatting for a Wizard control.

Figure 22-12   How to use templates and styles with a Wizard control

Perspective

The MultiView and Wizard controls make it easy to develop a set of related views or steps that gather or display information. They also make it easy to access the data that's gathered by these views or steps. That's why you're going to want to use these controls whenever you find the need for them.

Terms

view
step
side bar

23

How to use email, custom error pages, and back-button control

Once you've got an application working the way it's supposed to, you can add enhancements that make it work even better. In this chapter, you'll learn how to add three of the most useful enhancements. First, you'll learn how to send email from an ASP.NET application. Then, you'll learn how to create and use custom error pages. And last, you'll learn how to handle the problems that can occur when the user uses the Back button to access a page that has already been posted.

How to send email **744**
An introduction to email 744
How to configure the SMTP service in IIS 746
How to create an email message 748
How to send an email message 750
How to add an attachment to an email message 752
How to create an HTML message 754

How to use custom error handling **756**
An introduction to custom error handling 756
How to get and use the Exception object for an error 758
How to code methods that redirect to a custom error page 760
The code for a custom error page 762
How to handle HTTP errors with the web.config file 764

How to handle the back-button problem **766**
An introduction to the back-button problem 766
How to disable browser page caching 768
How to use timestamps to avoid the back-button problem 770

Perspective **772**

How to send email

When you create a web application, you often need to send email messages from the application. For instance, when a user makes a purchase from an e-commerce site, a web application usually sends an email to the customer that confirms the order. Or, if a serious error occurs, the web application often sends an email message to the support staff that documents the error. In the topics that follow, you'll learn how to send email from your ASP.NET applications.

An introduction to email

You're probably familiar with *mail client* software such as Microsoft Outlook or Outlook Express that allows you to send and retrieve email messages. This type of software communicates with a *mail server* that actually sends and retrieves your email messages. Most likely, your mail server software is provided by your Internet Service Provider (ISP) or through your company.

The diagram in figure 23-1 shows how this works. The two protocols that are commonly used to send email messages are *SMTP* and *POP*. When you send an email message, the message is first sent from the mail client software on your computer to your mail server using the SMTP protocol. Then, your mail server uses SMTP to send the mail to the recipient's mail server. Finally, the recipient's mail client uses the POP protocol to retrieve the mail from the recipient's mail server.

A third protocol you should know about is *MIME*, which stands for *Multipurpose Internet Mail Extension*. Unlike SMTP or POP, MIME isn't used to transfer email messages. Instead, it defines how the content of an email message and its attachments are formatted. In this chapter, you'll learn how to send messages that consist of simple text as well as messages that use HTML format.

How email works

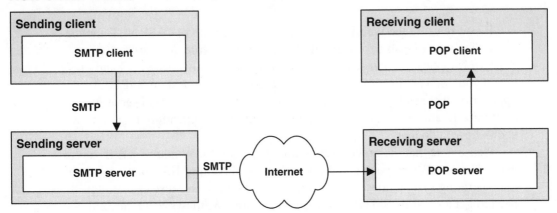

Three email protocols

Protocol	Description
SMTP	*Simple Mail Transfer Protocol* is used to send a message from one mail server to another.
POP	*Post Office Protocol* is used by mail clients to retrieve messages from mail servers. POP version 3, known as POP3, is the most widely used version, but a specification for POP version 4 has been developed.
MIME	The *Multipurpose Internet Mail Extension* specifies the type of content that can be sent as a message or attachment.

Three common reasons for sending email from an ASP.NET application

- **To confirm receipt of an order.** When the user completes an order, the application can email a confirmation of the order to the user.

- **To remind a registered user of a forgotten password.** If the user forgets his or her password, the application can email the password to the email address that's on file for the user. You can also accomplish this using the PasswordRecovery control presented in chapter 20.

- **To notify support personnel of a problem.** If a problem like an unhandled exception occurs, the application can email a message that summarizes the problem to the appropriate support person.

Description

- When an email message is sent, it goes from the sender's *mail client* to the sender's *mail server* to the receiver's mail server to the receiver's mail client.

- *SMTP* and *POP* are the protocols that are commonly used for sending and retrieving email messages. *MIME* is the protocol for defining the format of an email message.

Figure 23-1   An introduction to email

How to configure the SMTP service in IIS

If you're using the Web Development Server to test your ASP.NET applications, they won't be able to send email. As a result, before you can test an ASP.NET application that sends email messages, you must install IIS and use it to run your web applications. In addition, before you can test an ASP.NET application that sends email messages, you must enable the email server that's built into IIS and configure it to send mail from your application. Figure 23-2 shows how to do that.

Please note that the procedures in this figure are for Windows XP. If you're using Windows Vista, you should know that the version of IIS that comes with that operating system doesn't include an SMTP server. Because of that, you'll need to get a separate SMTP server if you're using Windows Vista. Several servers can be downloaded for free from the Internet.

The first step is to start the SMTP service. You do that from the IIS Management Console, which you can reach by opening the Control Panel and then opening Administrative Tools and double-clicking the Internet Information Services icon. Once you've opened the IIS Management Console, you can expand the tree to display the Default SMTP Virtual Server node. Then, you can start the SMTP service by selecting it in the tree and clicking the Start button in the toolbar.

Once you've started the SMTP service, you must configure it so that it allows your ASP.NET applications to send mail. To do that, you enable relaying for the local computer. This allows the mail server to accept mail from a specified computer and deliver it to the intended recipient. To configure the SMTP service to relay mail from the local computer, open the Relay Restrictions dialog box as described in this figure and add the localhost address (127.0.0.1) to the list of computers that the SMTP server will relay mail for.

How to make sure SMTP is running on your local server

Start/Stop/Pause buttons

1. Open the Control Panel, double-click on Administrative Tools, and then double-click on Internet Information Services to open the IIS Management Console shown above.
2. Expand the tree to display your local computer's IIS server and the services running under it.
3. Select the Default SMTP Virtual Server service.
4. If the SMTP service is *not* running, the Stop button (■) will be disabled. In that case, click the Start button (▶) to start the SMTP service.

How to allow relaying for the local host

1. In the IIS Management Console, right-click the Default SMTP Virtual Server node and choose the Properties command.
2. Click the Access tab, then click the Relay button. This displays the Relay Restrictions dialog box shown above.
3. Click the Add button to display the Computer dialog box shown above. Then, select Single Computer, type 127.0.0.1 into the IP address field, click OK to close the Computer dialog box, and click OK again to close the Relay Restrictions dialog box.

Note

- These procedures are for Windows XP. The version of IIS that comes with Windows Vista doesn't include an SMTP server.

Figure 23-2   How to configure the SMTP service in IIS

How to create an email message

Figure 23-3 shows the constructors and properties of the MailMessage class that you use to create email messages. It also shows the constructors of the MailAddress class. This class is used to create the addresses that are stored in the From, To, CC, and Bcc properties of a mail message.

The first example in this figure illustrates how you can use these classes to create a mail message that includes a carbon copy (cc). Here, all of the values needed to create the email message are passed to the method as arguments. Then, the first three statements of the method create MailAddress objects for the from, to, and cc addresses. Notice that the MailAddress object for the from address includes both an email address and a display name. When a display name is included, it's displayed in the mail client's email list instead of the email address.

The fourth statement in this method creates a MailMessage object using the to and from MailAddress objects. Then, the next two statements set the Subject and Body properties of the message. Finally, the last statement adds the cc MailAddress object to the collection of objects in the CC property.

The second example in this figure shows how to create the same email as in the first example without setting the display name for the sender. To do that, you simply create the MailMessage object using the from and to addresses and the subject and body. This example also illustrates how you can create a MailAddress object for the carbon copy and add it to the collection of objects using a single statement.

Although the examples in this figure create messages that will be sent to a single recipient, you should realize that you can send a message to any number of recipients. To do that, you need to use the first constructor for the MailMessage class shown here to create an empty mail message. Then, you can create a MailAddress object for the sender and assign it to the From property of the message. And you can create a MailAddress object for each recipient and add it to the collection of MailAddress objects returned by the To property of the mail message. For example, to create a message that will be sent to two people, your code will look something like this:

```
MailMessage msg = new MailMessage();
msg.From = new MailAddress("anne@murach.com");
msg.To.Add(new MailAddress("joel@murach.com"));
msg.To.Add(new MailAddress("kelly@murach.com"));
```

Constructors and properties of the MailMessage class

Constructor	Description
`MailMessage()`	Creates an empty mail message.
`MailMessage(from, to)`	Creates a mail message with the to and from addresses specified as strings or MailAddress objects.
`MailMessage(from, to, subject, body)`	Creates a mail message with the to address, from address, subject, and body specified as strings.

Property	Description
`From`	A MailAddress object for the message sender.
`To`	A collection of MailAddress objects for the message recipients.
`CC`	A collection of MailAddress objects for the copy recipients.
`Bcc`	A collection of MailAddress objects for the blind copy recipients.
`Subject`	The subject line for the message.
`Body`	The body of the message.
`IsBodyHtml`	A Boolean value that indicates if the body of the message contains HTML. The default is False.
`Attachments`	A collection of Attachment objects.

Constructors of the MailAddress class

Constructor	Description
`MailAddress(address)`	Creates an email address with the specified address string.
`MailAddress(address, displayName)`	Creates an email address with the specified address and display strings.

Code that creates an email message with a carbon copy

```
private void SendTextMessageCC(string fromAddress, string fromName,
    string toAddress, string subject, string body, string ccAddress)
{
    MailAddress fromAdd = new MailAddress(fromAddress, fromName);
    MailAddress toAdd = new MailAddress(toAddress);
    MailAddress ccAdd = new MailAddress(ccAddress);
    MailMessage msg = new MailMessage(fromAdd, toAdd);
    msg.Subject = subject;
    msg.Body = body;
    msg.CC.Add(ccAdd);
}
```

Another way to create a message

```
MailMessage msg = new MailMessage(fromAddress, toAddress, subject, body);
msg.CC.Add(new MailAddress(CCAddress));
```

Description

- To create an email message, you use the MailMessage and MailAddress classes that are in the System.Net.Mail namespace.

- To add an address to a collection of MailAddress objects, you use the Add method of the collection.

Figure 23-3   How to create an email message

How to send an email message

After you create an email message, you use the SmtpClient class shown in figure 23-4 to send the message. The technique you use to do that depends on the message you're sending and on whether you have set the SMTP configuration settings for the application. To set the SMTP configuration settings, you use the Web Site Administration Tool as shown in this figure. Then, these settings are saved in the web.config file.

To illustrate, the first example in this figure shows you how to send a message using settings in the web.config file. When you use this technique, you don't have to specify the name or port for the SMTP server when you create the SmtpClient object. Instead, these settings are taken from the Smtp section of the web.config file.

The first example also illustrates how to send a message that's been stored in a MailMessage object. To do that, you simply name the MailMessage object on the Send method.

If you haven't set the SMTP configuration options, or if you want to override these options, you can specify the domain name of the server when you create the SmtpClient object. This is illustrated in the second example in this figure. Here, the name "localhost" is specified so that the SMTP server that's built into the local IIS server will be used. Notice that when you use the local IIS server, you don't have to specify a port number. That's because the default port number is 25, which is also the default port for the IIS server. If you use a server at a different port, though, you'll have to specify the port number.

The second example also illustrates how you can send a mail message without creating a MailMessage object. To do that, you just pass the from and to addresses and the subject and body text to the Send method. Then, the Send method creates the MailMessage object for you and sends it. You can use this format of the Send method if the message is in simple text format, you don't need to send the message to more than one person, you don't need to send copies of the message to anyone, and you don't need to send attachments with the message.

If you've read chapter 20, you know that another way to send an email is to use the PasswordRecovery control. This control sends an email to a user that includes the user's password. Because you don't specify the server that's used to send the message when you use this control, you must set the server name (and port if necessary) in the web.config file for it to work. In addition, you should set a from address to appear in the email that's sent by this control.

How to set the SMTP configuration settings

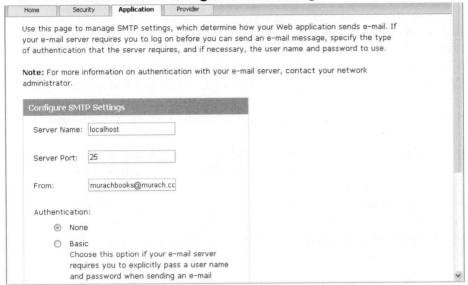

| Home | Security | **Application** | Provider |

Use this page to manage SMTP settings, which determine how your Web application sends e-mail. If your e-mail server requires you to log on before you can send an e-mail message, specify the type of authentication that the server requires, and if necessary, the user name and password to use.

Note: For more information on authentication with your e-mail server, contact your network administrator.

Configure SMTP Settings

Server Name: `localhost`

Server Port: `25`

From: `murachbooks@murach.cc`

Authentication:

⦿ None

○ Basic
Choose this option if your e-mail server requires you to explicitly pass a user name and password when sending an e-mail

Constructors and methods of the SmtpClient class

Constructor	Description
`SmtpClient()`	Creates a client using the settings specified in the web.config file.
`SmtpClient(name)`	Creates a client that can send email to the specified SMTP server.
`SmtpClient(name, port)`	Creates a client that can send email to the specified SMTP server and port.

Method	Description
`Send(message)`	Sends the specified MailMessage object.
`Send(from, to, subject, body)`	Creates and sends an email message using the specified from, to, subject, and body strings.

Code that sends a message using settings in the web.config file

```
SmtpClient client = new SmtpClient();
client.Send(msg);
```

Code that creates and sends a message to a named server

```
SmtpClient client = new SmtpClient("localhost");
client.Send(fromAddress, toAddress, subject, body);
```

Description

- To send an email message, you use the SmtpClient class in the System.Net.Mail namespace.

- You can use the Web Site Administration Tool to specify the settings that will be used to send email messages. To do that, select the Website→ASP.NET Configuration command, display the Application tab, click the Configure SMTP E-mail Settings link, and enter the values on the page that's displayed.

Figure 23-4   How to send an email message

How to add an attachment to an email message

An *attachment* is a file that's sent along with an email message. The most common types of attachments are text files, word processing documents, spreadsheets, pictures, and other media files such as sound and video files.

Figure 23-5 shows how you can create an attachment and add it to an email message. After you create an attachment object using the Attachment class, you add the object to the mail message's Attachments collection. Then, you can send the message.

Since the SMTP protocol is designed to send text messages, not binary files, any email attachment for a binary file must be converted to text format before it can be sent. Then, the text attachment must be converted back to a binary file when it's received. The most common format for converting attached binary files to text and back to binary is called *UUEncode*, and it's used by default. The other available format for converting binary files is called *Base64*. Since you shouldn't need to use this format, I haven't shown you how to create an attachment that uses it here.

The syntax for creating an attachment

```
new Attachment(fileName)
```

One way to create a new attachment and add it to a message

```
string fileName = "C:\\HalloweenStore\\Attachments\\ReturnPolicy.doc";
Attachment attach = new Attachment(fileName);
MailMessage msg = new MailMessage(fromAddress, toAddress, subject, body);
msg.Attachments.Add(attach);
```

Another way to create a new attachment and add it to a message

```
string fileName = "C:\\HalloweenStore\\Attachments\\ReturnPolicy.doc";
MailMessage msg = new MailMessage(fromAddress, toAddress, subject, body);
msg.Attachments.Add(new Attachment(fileName);
```

Description

- An *attachment* is a file that is sent along with an email message. When the recipient receives the email message, he or she can open or save the attachment.

- To add an attachment to an email message, you create the attachment using the Attachment class. Then, you add the attachment to the message using the Add method of the Attachments collection of the MailMessage class.

- If an email attachment contains a binary file, it must be converted to text before it can be sent, and it must be converted back to binary when it's received. By default, binary files are converted to a format called *UUEncode*. However, you can also use a format called *Base64*.

Figure 23-5   How to add an attachment to an email message

How to create an HTML message

By default, email messages consist of plain text with no formatting. However, you can create a formatted message by using HTML as the MIME type as described in figure 23-6. When you set the IsBodyHtml property of the MailMessage object to true, you can use HTML formatting tags in the body of the message.

The example in this figure calls a private method named GetConfirmationMessage that formats the HTML for the body of an order confirmation message. This method uses basic HTML formatting tags to create a message that includes an image and some text. Note that if you refer to an image in the body by including an <img> tag, you must include the image file as an attachment as shown here. Otherwise, the recipient won't be able to see the image.

How an HTML message appears in an email client

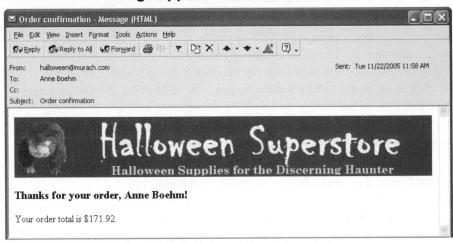

A method that creates and sends a simple HTML message

```
private void SendConfirmation()
{
    MailMessage msg = new MailMessage("halloween@murach.com", toAddress);
    msg.Subject = "Order Confirmation";
    msg.Body = this.GetConfirmationMessage();
    msg.IsBodyHtml = true;
    string file =
        "C:\\ASP.NET 3.5 Web sites\\Ch23HalloweenStore\\Images\\banner.jpg";
    msg.Attachments.Add(new Attachment(file));
    SmtpClient client = new SmtpClient("localhost");
    client.Send(msg);
}

private string GetConfirmationMessage()
{
    string message = "<HTML><head><title>Order confimation</title></head>"
                   + "<body><img src='banner.jpg' alt='Halloween Store' />"
                   + "<br /><br /><h3>Thanks for your order, "
                   + dvCustomer[0]["FirstName"].ToString() + " "
                   + dvCustomer[0]["LastName"].ToString() + "!</h3>"
                   + "<p>Your order total is " + total.ToString("c")
                   + ".</p></body></HTML>";
    return message;
}
```

Description

- To create an email message in HTML format, set the IsBodyHtml property to True. Then, you can use HTML in the message that you assign to the Body property.

- An HTML email message can include links to your web site. However, you should avoid sending HTML that includes scripts or web form controls. Many mail servers will reject them because they might be malicious.

- If the HTML includes <img> tags, you should include the image files as attachments. Otherwise, recipients won't be able to see the images in your email.

Figure 23-6   How to create an HTML message

How to use custom error handling

When an error occurs in an ASP.NET application, an exception is thrown. Then, if the exception isn't handled by the application, an ASP.NET Server Error page is displayed. This page includes an error message, a portion of the source code that threw the unhandled exception, and other debugging information. Since this type of error page usually isn't appropriate for the users of an application, you typically replace the generic error pages with your own custom error pages after you're done testing the web site but before you go live with it.

An introduction to custom error handling

Figure 23-7 describes four techniques you can use to display your own custom error pages. Depending on the needs of your application, you may use one or more of these techniques.

The first technique is to enclose code that might generate exceptions in a try block of a try-catch statement. Then, you can redirect to a custom error page in the catch block if an exception does occur.

The second technique is to code a Page_Error event handler in the code-behind file for a page. This event handler is called whenever an unhandled exception occurs on the page. Then, within this event handler, you redirect the user to a custom error page.

The third technique is to code an Application_Error event handler in the global.asax file. This event handler is called whenever an unhandled exception occurs on a page that doesn't have a Page_Error event handler. Then, the Application_Error event handler can redirect the user to a custom error page.

The fourth technique is to use the customErrors element in the web.config file to designate custom error pages. This technique is used to display custom error pages when common HTTP errors such as a 404 – Not Found error occur.

A custom error page in a browser

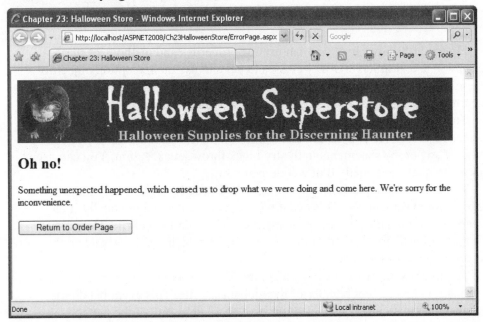

Four ways to display a custom error page when an exception occurs

- Use try-catch statements to catch exceptions as they occur, then redirect or transfer to a custom error page.
- Use the Page_Error event handler in a code-behind file to catch unhandled exceptions at the page level, then redirect or transfer to a custom error page.
- Use the Application_Error event handler in the global.asax file to catch unhandled exceptions at the application level, then redirect or transfer to a custom error page.
- Use the customErrors element of the web.config file to specify custom error pages that are displayed for specific types of HTTP errors.

Description

- If an unrecoverable error occurs, most applications display a custom error page to inform the user that a problem has occurred.
- Behind the scenes, the custom error page may also record the error in a log or send an email message to the application's support staff to notify them of the error.
- Custom error pages often use an Exception object to display a detailed message that describes the error.

Figure 23-7   An introduction to custom error handling

How to get and use the Exception object for an error

Figure 23-8 shows how you can use the properties and methods of the Exception and HttpServerUtility classes to get and use the Exception object for an error. This is the object that contains information about the exception that has occurred. The examples in this figure show how this works.

The first example shows how you can use a try-catch statement to get the Exception object. As you should know, the catch block catches the Exception object if any of the statements in the try block throw an exception. You can use this technique in any method of a code-behind file.

The second example shows how to get the Exception object within the Page_Error event handler. This event handler is executed automatically if an exception isn't handled by the other methods of a code-behind file. Here, you use the GetLastError method of the Server object, which you access using the Server property of the page.

The third example shows how to get the Exception object within the Application_Error event handler of the global.asax file. This event handler is executed automatically if an exception isn't handled by any of the methods in the code-behind file including the Page_Error event handler. In the Application_Error event handler, however, the GetLastError method doesn't return the correct Exception object. That's because a second exception called HttpUnhandledException is thrown if an exception occurs and the exception isn't handled by a try-catch statement or a Page_Error event handler. As a result, the GetLastError method returns the HttpUnhandledException exception, not the exception that originally caused the error. To access the original exception, you must use the InnerException property of the Exception object that's returned by the GetLastError method.

Although you might think that you could use the ClearError method to clear the HttpUnhandledException exception and then use GetLastError to get the original exception, that won't work. That's because you can only use GetLastError to get the Exception object for the last exception that occurred. In this case, that's the HttpUnhandledException exception.

The fourth example shows how you might use the properties of an Exception object as you test an application. Here, the Write method of the HttpResponse object is used to display the Message and Source properties on the page. Notice that before this method is executed, the ClearError method of the Server object is used to clear the error. That way, the ASP.NET Server Error page won't be displayed.

Common properties of the Exception class

Property	Description
Message	A message that describes the error.
Source	The name of the application or object that caused the error.
InnerException	The Exception object that caused the exception at the application level.

Methods of the HttpServerUtility class for working with exceptions

Method	Description
GetLastError()	Gets the most recent exception.
ClearError()	Clears the most recent exception.

Code that gets the Exception object at the method level

```
try
{
    statements that could throw an exception
}
catch (Exception ex)
{
    statements that use the Exception object named ex
}
```

A statement that gets the Exception object at the page level

```
Exception ex = Server.GetLastError();
```

A statement that gets the Exception object at the application level

```
Exception ex = Server.GetLastError().InnerException;
```

Code that displays the error message and source of the Exception object

```
Server.ClearError();
Response.Write(ex.Message + "<br />" + ex.Source);
```

Description

- You can use a try-catch statement in any method of a code-behind file to get the Exception object for an error.

- The Page_Error event handler is executed when an unhandled exception occurs. Within this event handler, you use the GetLastError method of the Server object to get the Exception object for the error.

- If you don't handle an exception with a try-catch statement or a Page_Error event handler, an HttpUnhandledException is thrown. Then, you can use the Application_Error event handler in the global.asax file to handle the exception. To do that, you use the GetLastError method of the Server object to get the Exception object for the HttpUnhandledException, and you use the InnerException property of that exception to get the Exception object that caused the error.

- During testing, you may want to use the Write method of the HttpResponse object to write information about the exception to the page. Before you do that, you need to clear the error from the Server object so that the ASP.NET Server Error page isn't displayed.

Figure 23-8   How to get and use the Exception object for an error

How to code methods that redirect to a custom error page

Figure 23-9 shows three ways to redirect to a custom error page when an exception occurs in an ASP.NET application. The first example shows how you can redirect to a custom error page from a try-catch statement. Here, a call to the Insert method of a SQL data source is placed in a try block so any database exceptions can be handled in the catch block. If an exception occurs, the catch block adds the Exception object to session state and redirects to the error page. Then, the error page can use the Exception object to get information about the exception.

The second example shows how you can use a Page_Error event handler to catch all unhandled exceptions for a page and redirect to a custom error page. Here, the GetLastError method is used to get the Exception object. Then, the event handler adds the Exception object to session state and redirects to the custom error page.

The third example shows how you can use an Application_Error event handler in the global.asax file to catch all unhandled exceptions for an entire application. Here, the GetLastError method is used to get the Exception object, and the InnerException property of the Exception object is used to get the exception that caused the error. Then, the event handler adds the Exception object to session state and redirects to the custom error page.

A try-catch statement that redirects to a custom error page if an exception occurs during a database operation

```
try
{
    SqlDataSource1.Insert();
}
catch (Exception ex)
{
    Session["Exception"] = ex;
    Response.Redirect("ErrorPage.aspx");
}
```

A Page_Error event handler that redirects to a custom error page

```
private void Page_Error(object sender, EventArgs e)
{
    Exception ex = Server.GetLastError();
    Session["Exception"] = ex;
    Response.Redirect("ErrorPage.aspx");
}
```

An Application_Error event handler in the global.asax file that redirects to a custom error page

```
void Application_Error(object sender, EventArgs e)
{
    Exception ex = Server.GetLastError().InnerException;
    Session["Exception"] = ex;
    Response.Redirect("ErrorPage.aspx");
}
```

Description

- You can redirect to a custom error page from a try-catch statement, a Page_Error event handler, or an Application_Error event handler in the global.asax file.
- Before redirecting to a custom error page, the Exception object should be added to session state so it can be used by the error page.

Figure 23-9   How to code methods that redirect to a custom error page

The code for a custom error page

Figure 23-10 shows the aspx code and the code-behind file for the custom error page that's shown in figure 23-7. Here, the aspx code should be self-explanatory because it simply displays a message and provides a button for returning to the Order page.

The code-behind file for the error page is more interesting, though, because it sends an email message to the support personnel that describes the error that has occurred. This assumes that the try-catch statement, Page_Error event handler, or Application_Error event handler that redirects to the error page has added the Exception object to session state. Then, the Load event handler for the error page gets the Exception object from session state and passes it to the SendEmail method, which sends the email message. After that, the Load event handler removes the Exception object from session state.

The aspx code for the body of the Error page

```
<body>
    <form id="form1" runat="server">
    <div>
        <asp:Image ID="Image1" runat="server"
            ImageUrl="~/Images/banner.jpg" /><br />
        <h2>Oh no!</h2>
        Something unexpected happened, which caused us to drop what we were
        doing and come here. We're sorry for the inconvenience.<br /><br />
        <asp:Button ID="btnReturn" runat="server"
            Text="Return to Order Page" PostBackUrl="~/Order.aspx" />
    </div>
    </form>
</body>
```

The C# code for the Error page

```csharp
using System.Net.Mail;

public partial class ErrorPage : System.Web.UI.Page
{
    protected void Page_Load(object sender, EventArgs e)
    {
        if (!IsPostBack)
        {
            Exception ex = (Exception)Session["Exception"];
            this.SendEmail(ex);
            Session.Remove("Exception");
        }
    }

    private void SendEmail(Exception ex)
    {
        string body = "An exception occurred at "
                    + DateTime.Now.ToLongTimeString()
                    + " on " + DateTime.Now.ToLongDateString()
                    + "<br />" + ex.Message;
        MailMessage msg = new MailMessage("halloween@murach.com",
            "support@murach.com");
        msg.Subject = "Exception in Halloween application";
        msg.Body = body;
        msg.IsBodyHtml = true;
        SmtpClient client = new SmtpClient("localhost");
        client.Send(msg);
    }
}
```

Note

- This code assumes that the Exception object has been placed in session state.

Figure 23-10   The code for a custom error page

How to handle HTTP errors with the web.config file

Not all unrecoverable errors cause ASP.NET to throw an exception. As figure 23-11 shows, some error conditions result in HTTP errors that are handled by the web server itself. For these errors, you can use the customErrors element in the web.config file to specify custom error pages.

Although there are many different types of HTTP errors that can occur, the common types are listed in this figure. Of these, the most common is the 404 error. This error occurs when a user attempts to retrieve a page that doesn't exist. In some cases, a 404 error is caused by a missing page or a page that has been renamed. In other cases, a 404 error is caused by an error in your application's navigation controls, such as a hyperlink that uses an incorrect URL.

As this figure shows, you include an Error element in the web.config file for each HTTP error that you want to redirect to a custom error page. In the example, this is done for two types of errors. The first Error element specifies that the page named E404.aspx should be displayed if a 404 error occurs. The second element specifies that the page named E500.aspx should be displayed if a 500 error occurs.

You can also specify a default error page that's displayed if an HTTP error that isn't specifically listed in an Error element occurs. In the example in this figure, the defaultRedirect attribute specifies that a page named DefaultError.aspx should be displayed if an HTTP error other than 404 or 500 occurs.

A customErrors element in the web.config file that designates custom error pages

```
<customErrors mode="On" defaultRedirect="DefaultError.aspx">
    <error statusCode="404" redirect="E404.aspx" />
    <error statusCode="500" redirect="E500.aspx" />
</customErrors>
```

Common HTTP error codes

Code	Description
401	Unauthorized request. The client must be authorized to access the resource.
403	Forbidden request. The client is not allowed to access the resource.
404	File Not Found. The resource could not be located.
500	Internal Server Error. This is usually the result of an unhandled exception.

Description

- The customErrors element in the web.config file lets you designate custom error pages that are automatically displayed when unrecoverable HTTP errors occur. You don't have to write any code to redirect or transfer to these pages.

- To enable custom error pages, add a customErrors element to the web.config file. Then, set the Mode attribute to On, and set the defaultRedirect attribute to the name of the generic error page.

- To associate a custom error page with an HTTP error, add an Error element that specifies the HTTP error code in the statusCode attribute and the name of the custom error page in the Redirect attribute.

- You can also add a customErrors element to the web.config file using the Web Site Administration Tool. To do that, select the Website→ASP.NET Configuration command, display the Application tab, click the Define Default Error Page link, and then select the appropriate settings.

Note

- You shouldn't use a customErrors element if you use the Application_Error event handler to handle errors. If you do, the customErrors element will be ignored.

Figure 23-11   How to handle HTTP errors with the web.config file

How to handle the back-button problem

If the user clicks the Back button in the browser window to return to a previous ASP.NET form and then posts the form, the application's session state may not correspond to that form. In some cases, this can result in a problem that we refer to as the *back-button problem*. The topics that follow show you how to deal with this problem.

An introduction to the back-button problem

Figure 23-12 illustrates the back-button problem in a shopping cart application. Here, the contents of the user's shopping cart are stored in session state and displayed on the page. The user then deletes one of the two items, which changes the data in session state. At that point, the user changes his mind and clicks the Back button, which displays both items again, even though session state only includes one item.

If the user now proceeds to check out, the order is likely to show one item when the user thinks he has ordered two items. But that depends upon how the application is coded. In the worst cases, the back-button problem may cause an application to crash. In the best cases, clicking on the Back button won't cause a problem at all.

In general, there are two ways to handle the back-button problem. The first is to try to prevent pages from being saved in the browser's cache. Then, when the user clicks the Back button, the old page can't be retrieved and a new request for the page is sent to the server. As you will see in the next figure, ASP.NET provides four methods for doing that, but they don't work if the user's browser ignores the page cache settings that are sent with a response.

The second way is to code critical web forms so they detect when the user attempts to post a page that isn't current. To do that, a form can use timestamps or random numbers to track the use of pages. Because there's no reliable way to prevent a page from being cached and retrieved via the Back button, you should use this second technique whenever possible.

An example of a back-button problem in the Cart page of the Halloween Store application

1. The user adds two products to the shopping cart. The shopping cart data is stored in session state and currently contains two items: one Cool Ghoul at $69.99 and one Deranged Cat at $19.99. The shopping cart displayed in the browser window looks like this:

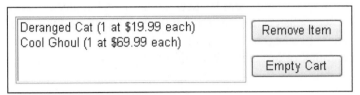

2. The user selects the first product and clicks the Remove Item button to delete it. The first line item is deleted from the shopping cart in session state and the updated page is sent to the browser:

3. The user decides that he or she wants to purchase the Deranged Cat after all and clicks the browser's Back button, thinking this will undo the Delete action. The browser retrieves the previous page from its local cache:

    Because the browser redisplayed this page directly from its cache, the first line item was not added back to the shopping cart in session state. As a result, session state contains only one item even though the web page displays two items.

Two ways to handle the back-button problem

*   Disable browser page caching for user input forms.
*   Use timestamps or random numbers to track pages so you can detect when a page isn't current.

Description

*   When a user clicks the browser's Back button, the browser retrieves a locally cached copy of the previous page without notifying the server. As a result, the information stored in session state can become out of sync with the data displayed in the browser window.

Figure 23-12   An introduction to the back-button problem

How to disable browser page caching

Figure 23-13 shows how you can use four ASP.NET methods to prevent a user's browser from caching pages. All of these methods work by adding information to the HTTP headers that are sent to the browser along with the page.

Unfortunately, some browsers ignore these headers, so these techniques don't guarantee that a page won't be cached. Still, it's not a bad idea to add the code in this figure to the Page_Load event handler of any ASP.NET page that gets important data like customer or product information.

The warning message that's displayed if the user returns to a page and caching is disabled

Methods that set page caching options

Method	Description
`Response.Cache.SetCacheability()`	Indicates how the page should be cached. Specify HttpCacheability.NoCache to suppress caching.
`Response.Cache.SetExpires()`	Specifies when the cached page should expire. Specify Now().AddSeconds(-1) to mark the page as already expired.
`Response.Cache.SetNoStore()`	Specifies that the browser should not cache the page.
`Response.AppendHeader()`	Adds a header to the HTTP response object. Specifying "Pragma" for the key and "no-cache" for the value disables caching.

Code that disables caching for a page

```
Response.Cache.SetCacheability(HttpCacheability.NoCache);
Response.Cache.SetExpires(DateTime.Now.AddSeconds(-1));
Response.Cache.SetNoStore();
Response.AppendHeader("Pragma", "no-cache");
```

Description

- You can limit the effect of the Back button by directing the browser to not cache pages that contain state-sensitive data. Then, when the user attempts to return to a page using the Back button, the warning message at the top of this figure is displayed.

- You can place the code to disable browser page caching in the event handler for the Load event of the page. This code should be executed each time the page is loaded.

- Unfortunately, the technique described in this figure doesn't ensure that the user's browser won't cache the page because the user's browser may ignore the page cache settings. As a result, you should use the technique in the next figure to prevent back-button problems.

Figure 23-13   How to disable browser page caching

How to use timestamps to avoid the back-button problem

Figure 23-14 illustrates the most reliable way to avoid the back-button problem. Here, you see the code for a web page that uses timestamps to determine whether the posted page is current. The basic technique is to record a timestamp in two places when a page is posted: view state and session state. Then, the view state stamp is sent back to the browser and cached along with the rest of the information on the page, while the session state stamp is saved on the server.

Later, when the user posts a form for the second time, the Page_Load event handler calls a private method named IsExpired. This method retrieves the timestamps from view state and session state and compares them. If they are identical, the page is current and IsExpired returns false. But if they are different, it indicates that the user has posted a page that was retrieved from the browser's cache via the Back button. In that case, the IsExpired method returns true. Then, the Page_Load event handler redirects to a page named Expired.aspx, which in turn displays a message indicating that the page is out of date and can't be posted.

Notice that before comparing the timestamp items in session state and view state, the IsExpired method checks that both of these items exist. If not, the method returns false so that current timestamps can be saved in both session state and view state.

Incidentally, this technique can also be used to deal with problems that occur when the user clicks the Refresh button. This posts the page to the server and gets a new response, which refreshes the page, so it has nothing to do with the browser's cache. However, this can cause problems like a user ordering a product twice without realizing it. Because most users tend to click the Back button far more than the Refresh button, though, the Refresh button causes far fewer errors. That's why most web developers ignore this problem.

A page that checks timestamps to avoid the back-button problem

```
public partial class Cart : System.Web.UI.Page
{
    private SortedList cart;

    protected void Page_Load(object sender, EventArgs e)
    {
        if (IsExpired())
            Response.Redirect("Expired.aspx");
        else
            this.SaveTimeStamps();
        this.GetCart();
        if (!IsPostBack)
            this.DisplayCart();
    }

    private bool IsExpired()
    {
        if (Session["Cart_TimeStamp"] == null)
            return false;
        else if (ViewState["TimeStamp"] == null)
            return false;
        else if (ViewState["TimeStamp"].ToString()
            == Session["Cart_TimeStamp"].ToString())
            return false;
        else
            return true;
    }

    private void SaveTimeStamps()
    {
        DateTime dtm = DateTime.Now;
        ViewState.Add("TimeStamp", dtm);
        Session.Add("Cart_TimeStamp", dtm);
    }
    .
    .
    .
}
```

Description

- One way to avoid back-button problems is to use timestamps. The page saves two copies of a timestamp obtained via the Now method: one in view state, the other in session state.
- The IsExpired method tests the view state and session state timestamps to make sure they are the same. If they aren't, the user has posted a page that has been retrieved from the browser's cache.

Note

- Some developers prefer to use random numbers rather than timestamps. Either technique will work.

Figure 23-14 How to use timestamps to avoid the back-button problem

Perspective

This chapter has presented three types of enhancements that you can add to an application once you've got the basic functions working right. In practice, most serious applications use both email and custom error pages to make an application more user friendly and less error prone.

In contrast, many serious applications ignore the back-button problem on the theory that the users should be smart enough to avoid that problem themselves. As a result, clicking on the Back button and re-posting a page will cause a problem on many e-commerce sites. That's why you may want to use the techniques in this chapter to handle that problem on your own web site.

Terms

Simple Mail Transfer Protocol (SMTP)
Post Office Protocol (POP)
Multipurpose Internet Mail Extension (MIME)
mail client
mail server
attachment
UUEncode
Base64 encoding
back-button problem

24

How to use web parts to build portals

Portals are web pages that display modular content that can be customized by the user. With ASP.NET, you can develop a portal by writing just a few lines of code. To make this possible, ASP.NET provides a built-in portal framework that's conceptually similar to the framework that's used by Microsoft SharePoint. In addition, Visual Studio 2008 provides full support for building portals, and the .NET Framework exposes an API that can be used to work with portals.

An introduction to the portal framework **774**
A portal that uses web parts 774
How user configurations are stored 778
SharePoint and ASP.NET 778
Types of controls that can be used as web parts 780

How to use web parts **782**
How to create a page that uses web parts 782
How to add a user control to a web part zone 786
How to let the user move web parts between zones 790
How to let the user add web parts to a zone 792
How to let the user edit the properties of a web part 794
How to apply formatting to web parts 798

How to write code that works with web parts **800**
Classes for working with web parts 800
How to develop and use a custom WebPart control 802

Perspective **804**

An introduction to the portal framework

The topics that follow introduce you to the ASP.NET portal framework that allows you to easily develop *portals*, which are web pages that provide modular content that can be customized by each user of the page. To start, you'll see five screens that illustrate some of the features for a portal that might be used by a salesperson employed by the company that runs the Halloween Store web site. Then, you'll learn how portal configurations are stored, and you'll learn how the ASP.NET portal framework compares with the Microsoft SharePoint portal framework. Finally, you'll learn about the types of controls that can be used as *web parts*, which are the controls that provide modular content that can be used by a portal.

A portal that uses web parts

Each portal page contains one or more web parts. In part 1 of figure 24-1, for example, the Sales Portal page contains three web parts: Order Calculator, Days to Halloween, and Product List. In the first screen, the user has pulled down the control menu for the Product List part and is about to minimize it. In the second screen, the Product List has been minimized. As a result, only its title bar is displayed. In addition, the user is about to click on a radio button to switch to another display mode that allows the user to move web parts.

A portal page that displays three web parts

The same page after one web part has been minimized

Figure 24-1   A page that uses web parts (part 1 of 3)

In part 2 of figure 24-1, the user has switched to the mode that allows the web parts to be moved between different areas of the page. This causes the header text and borders for these areas, which are known as *web part zones*, to be displayed. For example, the header text for the first web part zone is "Zone 1 – Horizontal Layout." That's because this zone lays out web parts horizontally from left to right. In contrast, the header text for the second web part zone is "Zone 2 – Vertical Layout." That's because this zone lays out the web parts vertically from top to bottom.

Once the user has switched to the mode that allows the web parts to be moved, the user can drag a web part from one zone to another. For instance, in part 2 of this figure, the user drags the Days to Halloween part from the first web part zone to the second one. In part 3, you can see how the Sales Portal page appears after the Product List web part has been restored.

Although this figure doesn't illustrate it, this portal also lets a user add web parts to a web part zone, and it lets a user edit the appearance and behavior of web parts. If, for example, the user clicks on the Add Parts radio button, the page displays a zone that lets the user add a part by selecting it from a catalog that contains all available parts for the page. Or, if the user clicks on the Edit Parts radio button, an Edit command is added to the control list menu for each web part. Then, the user can select this command to edit the appearance and behavior of this web part. Later in this chapter, you'll see examples that show how both of these features work.

The same page as a web part is being moved

The same page after the move has been completed

Figure 24-1   A page that uses web parts (part 2 of 3)

How user configurations are stored

The web parts feature uses a *personalization provider* to store the portal configuration for each user in the AspNetDb.mdf database file. That means that whenever a user moves a web part to a new zone, minimizes a web part, or modifies the portal configuration in some other way, the new configuration is saved in this database. That way, the customized page can be displayed the next time the user visits the site.

Note that to use the web parts feature, a user must be authenticated. The best way to authenticate a user is to use forms-based authentication as described in chapter 20. If you want to use Windows authentication, however, you should know that you'll run into a problem if you try to run the application under IIS. That's because, by default, IIS allows anonymous access to an application. Although you can change a property of the virtual directory for the application to correct this problem, it's easiest to avoid the problem by creating a file-system web site.

SharePoint and ASP.NET

Microsoft SharePoint is an older technology that provides a robust portal framework that can, among other things, be used to develop web parts. The ASP.NET portal framework and SharePoint are similar from a conceptual point of view. In fact, SharePoint 3.0 fully supports ASP.NET web parts. That means that you can use custom web parts you develop with ASP.NET in a SharePoint portal. You'll learn how to develop custom web parts later in this chapter.

If you already know how to build portals with SharePoint, you'll be able to use many of the same skills for building portals with ASP.NET. Conversely, many of the skills that you learn for building portals with ASP.NET also apply to building portals with SharePoint.

The same page after the minimized part has been restored

Description

- ASP.NET comes with a built-in portal framework that allows you to easily develop *portals*, which are web pages that can be customized by users. To customize a portal, a user must be authenticated.

- A *web part* is a special type of control that can be displayed within a *web part zone*. Most portals let the user customize the appearance of the page by minimizing, restoring, closing, and moving the web parts. In addition, most portals let the user add web parts to the page, and some portals let the user edit the properties of the web parts.

- The portal configuration for each user is stored in the AspNetDb.mdf database. To accomplish that, the web parts feature uses a *personalization provider*.

Figure 24-1   A page that uses web parts (part 3 of 3)

Types of controls that can be used as web parts

Figure 24-2 shows the types of controls that can be placed within a web part zone. To start, you can place any ASP.NET control within a web part zone. This includes standard ASP.NET controls such as Label and Calendar controls, it includes user controls, and it includes custom server controls. When you add one of these controls to a web part zone, the control will automatically be wrapped by the GenericWebPart class at runtime. This class allows the control to behave like a web part.

The advantage of this approach is that you can use the ASP.NET skills that you're already familiar with to quickly develop controls that can be used as web parts. The disadvantage is that the GenericWebPart class doesn't let you take advantage of several advanced features of web parts. For example, when you use the GenericWebPart class, you can't create a connection between two web parts and share data between them.

If you need to use any of the advanced features, you can develop custom WebPart controls that inherit the WebPart class. Keep in mind, though, that custom WebPart controls are significantly more difficult to develop than the user controls that are used in this chapter.

The WebPart hierarchy in this figure shows that all web parts begin by inheriting the Panel class. Then, the Part and WebPart classes provide additional members that can be used to work with web parts. Finally, the GenericWebPart class provides the functionality that's necessary to wrap ASP.NET controls so they can appear and behave as WebPart controls at runtime.

Types of controls that can be used as web parts

ASP.NET controls that can be placed in a web part zone

- Standard controls (such as the Label control in figure 24-3)
- User controls (such as the ProductList control in figure 24-4)
- Custom server controls

Custom WebPart controls

- Custom WebPart controls (such as the HalloweenCounter control in figure 24-10)

The WebPart hierarchy

```
Panel
    Part
        WebPart
            GenericWebPart
```

Description

- When you add an ASP.NET control such as a user control to a web part zone, the control is automatically wrapped by the GenericWebPart class. This class allows ASP.NET controls to behave like web parts.

- A custom WebPart control inherits the WebPart class. As a result, custom WebPart controls let you take advantage of several advanced web part features that aren't available for other ASP.NET controls. However, custom WebPart controls can be difficult to develop.

- You can learn how to develop user controls and custom server controls in chapters 27 and 28. In this chapter, then, you can just focus on how you use these controls as web parts.

Figure 24-2   Types of controls that can be used as web parts

How to use web parts

Now that you have a general idea of what web parts are and how they work, you're ready to learn how to use Visual Studio to create portals that use web parts. As you'll see in a moment, you only need to write a few lines of code to create a fully functional portal.

How to create a page that uses web parts

Figure 24-3 shows how to create a page that uses two web part zones and three web part controls. To start, you open the page in Design view, go to the WebParts group of the Toolbox, and drag a WebPartManager control onto the page. This control manages the web parts and zones, and each portal page must include one of these controls.

Once you've added a WebPartManager control to a page, you can add WebPartZone controls by dragging them from the Toolbox onto the page. To keep things simple, the page in this figure contains only two zones, but it's common to place several web part zones on a page. Often, these web part zones are added within a table. Then, you can add a web part zone to each cell of the table to give the user more flexibility for how the page can be organized.

Once you've added the WebPartZone controls to the page, you can add web parts to the web part zones. In this figure, for example, two Label controls have been added to the first web part zone, and one Label control has been added to the second web part zone. These controls are coded within the ZoneTemplate element of the WebPartZone controls. This template specifies the web parts that are displayed the first time a user accesses the portal. However, if the user closes or moves these web parts, the user's changes will be stored in the AspNetDb.mdf database, and the changes will be displayed the next time the user accesses the portal.

Any control that's placed within a WebPartZone control is automatically wrapped by the GenericWebPart class so it can behave like a web part. As a result, for the Label controls in this figure, you can set any attributes that are available to the GenericWebPart class. Of these attributes, the Title attribute is commonly used to set the title of a web part. This attribute is stored in the Part class, which is ultimately inherited by the GenericWebPart class.

A page that contains two web part zones and three web parts

The tags for the page

```
<h1>Halloween Store - Sales Portal</h1>

<asp:WebPartManager ID="WebPartManager1" runat="server">
</asp:WebPartManager>

<asp:WebPartZone ID="WebPartZone1" runat="server"
    LayoutOrientation="Horizontal"
    HeaderText="Web Part Zone 1 - Horizontal Layout">
    <ZoneTemplate>
        <asp:Label ID="Label1" runat="server" Title="Part 1 Title"
            Text="Part 1 Content"></asp:Label>
        <asp:Label ID="Label2" runat="server" Title="Part 2 Title"
            Text="Part 2 Content"></asp:Label>
    </ZoneTemplate>
</asp:WebPartZone><br />

<asp:WebPartZone ID="WebPartZone2" runat="server"
    HeaderText="Web Part Zone 2 - Vertical Layout">
    <ZoneTemplate>
        <asp:Label ID="Label3" runat="server" Title="Part 3 Title"
            Text="Part 3 Content"></asp:Label>
    </ZoneTemplate>
</asp:WebPartZone>
```

Figure 24-3   How to create a page that uses web parts (part 1 of 2)

If necessary, you can use the HeaderText attribute of a WebPartZone control to specify the header text for the web part zone. Then, this text will be displayed above the control in Design view, and it will be displayed above the control at runtime whenever the portal enters certain modes such as the mode that allows the user to move web parts between zones.

You may also want to set the LayoutOrientation attribute of a WebPartZone control to specify the layout orientation. In this figure, for example, the first web part zone specifies a horizontal orientation, so the web parts are displayed from left to right. In contrast, the second web part zone doesn't specify a layout orientation, so the default orientation is used to display the web parts vertically.

When you run a page like the one in this figure, the default features provide a lot of built-in functionality. For example, the control menu for each web part will contain Minimize and Close commands for any parts that haven't been minimized and Restore and Close commands for any parts that have been minimized. So, if you use the Minimize command to minimize a web part, you can use the Restore command to restore that web part. However, if you select the Close command, the web part will be removed from the page. In that case, there's no way for the user to add that part back to the page unless the page provides for it as described in figure 24-6.

The page when it's displayed in a browser

Description

- In the Toolbox, all of the controls for working with web parts are stored in the WebParts group.

- Each portal must have one (and only one) WebPartManager control. This control manages the web parts and zones on the page.

- Most portals have two or more WebPartZone controls that define the web part zones that are available on the page. These controls are often coded within a table that specifies the number of rows and columns to be used for the page.

- The ZoneTemplate element of a WebPartZone control specifies the web parts that are displayed the first time a user accesses the portal. When you add a control to a web part zone from Design view, the control is added within a ZoneTemplate element.

- The HeaderText attribute of a WebPartZone control specifies the header text that's used for the zone when it's displayed in Design view. This text is also displayed at runtime when the portal enters certain modes such as the mode that allows the user to move web parts between zones.

- The Title attribute can be added to any control in a web part zone. That's because each control added to a web part zone is automatically wrapped by the GenericWebPart class, which provides access to the Title attribute of the Part class. Because the controls aren't wrapped until runtime, however, the Title attribute isn't available from the Properties window or from the IntelliSense completion list.

Figure 24-3   How to create a page that uses web parts (part 2 of 2)

How to add a user control to a web part zone

Although figure 24-3 shows how to add a standard Label control to a web part zone, it's more common to add a user control to a web part zone as shown in figure 24-4. Then, this user control will automatically be wrapped by the GenericWebPart class so it behaves like a web part.

In chapter 27, you can learn how to develop user controls. To do that, you (1) add a user control (ascx file) to the project, (2) use the User Control Designer to design the control, and (3) use the Code Editor to write any code that's necessary to get the control to work.

In this figure, for example, a user control file named ProductList.ascx has been added to the project. This user control contains a SqlDataSource control that specifies the connection string and the Select statement needed to retrieve the data for the user control. In addition, it contains a GridView control that displays a list of the products that are retrieved by the SqlDataSource control.

The ProductList user control in Design view

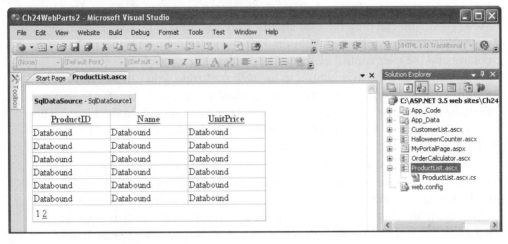

The aspx code for the ProductList control

```
<%@ Control Language="C#" AutoEventWireup="true" CodeFile="ProductList.ascx.cs"
        Inherits="ProductList" %>

<asp:SqlDataSource ID="SqlDataSource1" runat="server"
    ConnectionString="Data Source=localhost\SQLExpress;
        Initial Catalog=Halloween;Integrated Security=True"
    SelectCommand="SELECT ProductID, Name, UnitPrice
        FROM Products ORDER BY Name">
</asp:SqlDataSource>

<asp:GridView ID="GridView1" runat="server" DataSourceID="SqlDataSource1"
    AllowPaging="True" AllowSorting="True" AutoGenerateColumns="False"
    PageSize="6" Width="400px">
    <Columns>
        <asp:BoundField DataField="ProductID" HeaderText="ProductID"
            ReadOnly="True" SortExpression="ProductID" />
        <asp:BoundField DataField="Name" HeaderText="Name"
            SortExpression="Name" />
        <asp:BoundField DataField="UnitPrice" HeaderText="UnitPrice"
            DataFormatString="{0:c}" HtmlEncode="false"
            SortExpression="UnitPrice" />
    </Columns>
</asp:GridView>
```

Description

- In chapter 27, you can learn how to create a user control. In brief, you add a user control (ascx file) to the project, use the User Control Designer to design the control, and use the Code Editor to write any code that's necessary to get the control to work.

Figure 24-4   How to add a user control to a web part zone (part 1 of 2)

Once you've created a user control and added it to your project, you can add it to your portal page. The easiest way to do that is to view the page in Design view. Then, you can drag the user control from the Solution Explorer onto the page. This automatically generates the Register directive that registers the control and the user control element that displays the control.

Once you add the user control to the web part zone, you can switch to Source view and add a Title attribute to the control. In this figure, for example, the Title attribute for the ProductList control has been set to "Product List." This works the same for user controls as for the Label controls described in figure 24-3.

Although this figure only shows the code for the ProductList user control, you can use the same coding techniques to create other user controls such as the Order Calculator and Days to Halloween controls. In many ways, these controls are easier to develop than the ProductList user control since they don't access a database. Instead, the Order Calculator control allows the user to calculate a total based on quantity and price, and the Days to Halloween control calculates the number of days to Halloween and displays the result within a label.

A page that includes three user controls

The code that registers a user control for a page

```
<%@ Register Src="ProductList.ascx" TagName="ProductList" TagPrefix="uc1" %>
```

The code that adds a user control to a web zone

```
<asp:WebPartZone ID="WebPartZone2" runat="server"
    HeaderText="Web Part Zone 2 - Vertical Layout">
    <ZoneTemplate>
        <uc1:ProductList ID="ProductList1" runat="server" Title="Product List">
        </uc1:ProductList>
    </ZoneTemplate>
</asp:WebPartZone>
```

Description

- In Design view, you can register a user control and add it to the page by dragging it from the Solution Explorer onto the page.

- In Source view, you can register a user control and add it to the page by coding the Register directive and by coding the element for the user control.

Figure 24-4   How to add a user control to a web part zone (part 2 of 2)

How to let the user move web parts between zones

By default, a page that contains web parts runs in *browse display mode*. In this mode, you can only minimize, restore, and close web parts. Then, if you want to let the user move web parts between zones, you must switch into *design display mode*. In this mode, which is shown in figure 24-5, the header text and borders appear for each web part zone, and the user can move web parts between zones by dragging them from one zone to another. In this figure, the user is moving the Days to Halloween web part from the first web part zone to the second web part zone.

To switch between display modes in the code-behind file for a page, you set the DisplayMode property of the WebPartManager control equal to one of the DisplayMode constants that are available from the WebPartManager class. In this figure, for example, the page includes a RadioButtonList control that lets the user choose between browse display mode and design display mode. If the user chooses the second option, the page enters design display mode so the user can move web parts between zones. Then, when the user is done moving web parts, the user can select the first option. This will cause the page to enter browse display mode, which is the optimal mode for browsing the data that's displayed on a page.

A page that lets the user move web parts between zones

A radio button list that switches between display modes

```
<asp:RadioButtonList ID="rdoDisplayMode" runat="server" AutoPostBack="True"
    RepeatDirection="Horizontal"
    OnSelectedIndexChanged="rdoDisplayMode_SelectedIndexChanged">
    <asp:ListItem Value="Browse Page" Selected="True">
        Browse Page</asp:ListItem>
    <asp:ListItem Value="Move Parts">Move Parts</asp:ListItem>
</asp:RadioButtonList>
```

The event handler for the radio button list

```
protected void rdoDisplayMode_SelectedIndexChanged(object sender, EventArgs e)
{
    if (rdoDisplayMode.SelectedIndex == 0)
        WebPartManager1.DisplayMode = WebPartManager.BrowseDisplayMode;
    else if (rdoDisplayMode.SelectedIndex == 1)
        WebPartManager1.DisplayMode = WebPartManager.DesignDisplayMode;
}
```

Description

* You can use the DisplayMode property of the WebPartManager class to switch between display modes. To do that, you can set this property equal to any of the constant values stored in the WebPartManager class such as BrowseDisplayMode and DesignDisplayMode.

Figure 24-5   How to let the user move web parts between zones

How to let the user add web parts to a zone

If a user closes a web part when working in browse or design display mode, the part is removed from the page and there's no way for the user to add the web part back to the page. However, you can add functionality to the page that lets the user add web parts that have been closed back to the page and add web parts that aren't on the page by default. To do this, you must perform three tasks.

First, you must provide a way for the user to switch to the *catalog display mode* that's shown in figure 24-6. To do that, you can extend the RadioButtonList control shown in figure 24-5 so it includes a third option that lets the user switch into catalog display mode.

Second, you must add a CatalogZone control to the page. To do that, you can drag the CatalogZone control from the Toolbox onto the page.

Third, you must add one or more of the CatalogPart controls within the CatalogZone control. In this figure, for example, the CatalogZone control contains a PageCatalogPart control followed by a DeclarativeCatalogPart control. The DeclarativeCatalogPart control includes a WebPartsTemplate element that declares any web parts that aren't on the default page but should also be available. In this example, the CustomerList part is the only part in this catalog, but you can include as many parts as you need.

When the page is running in browse display mode, the catalogs of available web parts that are defined by the CatalogZone and CatalogPart controls aren't displayed. However, if the user switches to catalog display mode, the catalog is displayed. In this figure, for example, the CatalogZone control is displayed in the bottom half of the page, starting with the heading (Catalog of Web Parts) that's provided by the HeaderText attribute.

After the heading, the CatalogZone control displays "Select the catalog you would like to browse" and a menu that lets you switch between the CatalogPart controls within the zone. In this figure, the choices are Page Catalog and Declarative Catalog, and the user has selected Page Catalog. This displays a list of all the web parts that were on the page by default, but were closed by the user (this list includes just the Product List part). In contrast, if the user selects Declarative Catalog, the list displays all of the web parts in that catalog. The number in parentheses after each menu item for the catalog zone indicates the number of items in each list (one each).

Under the catalog list, the CatalogZone control generates controls for adding a selected web part. Here, the user is using the drop-down list to specify the zone that the selected web part should be added to. Then, when the user clicks the Add button, the selected part is added to that zone.

By default, the CatalogZone control also displays a Close link in its header and a Close button next to the Add button. This provides the user with a way to close the CatalogZone control and exit catalog display mode. However, this also causes the display mode to get out of synch with the RadioButtonList control. As a result, the Visible attribute of the HeaderCloseVerb and CloseVerb elements has been used to hide these elements. (When working with web parts, the term *verb* is used to refer to the actions that are executed by the buttons, links, and menu items that are available from a web part.)

A page that lets the user add web parts to a zone

The asp tags for the catalog

```
<asp:CatalogZone ID="CatalogZone1" runat="server"
    HeaderText="Catalog of Web Parts">
    <ZoneTemplate>
        <asp:PageCatalogPart ID="PageCatalogPart1" runat="server" />
        <asp:DeclarativeCatalogPart ID="DeclarativeCatalogPart1" runat="server">
            <WebPartsTemplate>
                <uc1:CustomerList ID="CustomerList1" runat="server"
                    Title="Customer List"/>
            </WebPartsTemplate>
        </asp:DeclarativeCatalogPart>
    </ZoneTemplate>
    <HeaderCloseVerb Visible="False" />
    <CloseVerb Visible="False" />
</asp:CatalogZone>
```

The code that switches to catalog display mode

```
WebPartManager1.DisplayMode = WebPartManager.CatalogDisplayMode;
```

Description

- To let the user add web parts to a page, you must (1) provide a way to switch to *catalog display mode*, (2) add a CatalogZone control to the page, and (3) place one or more of the CatalogPart controls within the CatalogZone control. (The CatalogPart controls are the PageCatalogPart, DeclarativeCatalogPart, and ImportCatalogPart controls.)

Figure 24-6   How to let the user add web parts to a zone

How to let the user edit the properties of a web part

Most of the time, you can provide all of the customization that's necessary for a portal by letting the user minimize, restore, close, move, and add web parts as described in the last three figures. However, there are times when you may also want to let the user edit the properties that control the appearance and behavior of a web part. To do this, you must perform three tasks that are similar to the three tasks for letting the user add a web part to a page.

First, you must provide a way for the user to switch to the *edit display mode* that's shown in figure 24-7. To do that, you can extend the RadioButtonList control shown in figure 24-6 so it includes a fourth option that lets the user switch to this mode. Once the switch has been made, an Edit command is included in the drop-down control menu for each web part as shown in the first screen in this figure. Then, the user can select this command to display the properties that can be edited, as shown in the second screen.

Second, you must add an EditorZone control to the page. To do that, you can drag the EditorZone control from the Toolbox onto the page. This control is a container control that works similarly to the WebPartZone and CatalogZone controls.

Third, you must add one or more of the EditorPart controls within the EditorZone control. In this figure, for example, the EditorZone control contains just one EditorPart control, the AppearanceEditorPart control. But you could add other EditorPart controls such as the BehaviorEditorPart, LayoutEditorPart, or PropertyGridEditorPart control.

By default, the EditorZone control displays a Close link in its header. This lets the user close the EditorZone control, which hides this control and any subordinate EditorPart controls, but doesn't exit edit display mode. As a result, the Edit command is still available from each of the web parts on the page.

A page that lets the user edit web parts

An editor zone for the Product List part

Figure 24-7   How to let the user edit the properties of a web part (part 1 of 2)

Although the EditorPart controls let the user modify the properties of a web part, most of these properties only provide for minor cosmetic changes. In this figure, for example, the user has modified the Product List web part by changing the title from "Product List" to "Halloween Product List" and by turning off the border. Since this type of change is so trivial, you may not want to bother with this type of editing support.

When working with web parts, the term *chrome* is used to refer to the non-content area of a web part such as the border, title bar, minimize/close buttons, and so on. In this figure, for example, the user can use the Chrome Type combo box to change the type of chrome that's used for the Product List web part. In the next figure, you'll see how you can use the PartChromeStyle element of the WebPartZone control to change the style of the chrome for each web part within a web part zone.

A page after the appearance of the Product List part has been edited

The asp tags for the editor zone

```
<asp:EditorZone ID="EditorZone1" runat="server">
    <ZoneTemplate>
        <asp:AppearanceEditorPart ID="AppearanceEditorPart1" runat="server" />
    </ZoneTemplate>
</asp:EditorZone>
```

The code that switches to EditDisplayMode

```
WebPartManager1.DisplayMode = WebPartManager.EditDisplayMode;
```

The EditorPart controls

```
AppearanceEditorPart
BehaviorEditorPart
LayoutEditorPart
PropertyGridEditorPart
```

Description

- To let the user edit the web parts on a page, you must (1) provide a way to switch to *edit display mode*, (2) add an EditorZone control to the page, and (3) place one or more of the EditorPart controls within the EditorZone control.

- When a page enters edit display mode, an Edit command becomes available from the drop-down control menu for each web part. When a user selects this command, the properties of the web part are displayed so the user can edit them.

- When working with web parts, the term *chrome* is used to refer to the non-content area of a web part such as the border, title bar, minimize/close buttons, and so on.

Figure 24-7   How to let the user edit the properties of a web part (part 2 of 2)

How to apply formatting to web parts

So far, the examples in this topic haven't included any formatting. That's why they appear as white controls with black borders. However, for a typical portal, each web part should be formatted in a way that's appropriate for that portal. Most of the time, that means applying formatting that gives the portal a professional and pleasing appearance as shown in figure 24-8.

The easiest way to apply formatting to all of the web parts in a web part zone is to use the Auto Format feature. To do that, select the Auto Format command from the web part zone's smart tag menu and then choose a scheme from the dialog box that's displayed. When you do, the appropriate attributes and elements will be added to the WebPartZone tag. Then, if necessary, you can edit these tags. In this figure, for example, I applied the Professional scheme to the first web part zone. Then I modified the attributes and elements slightly to make them more appropriate for the application.

If you want to apply the same formatting to multiple web part zones, you can store the formatting for the WebPartZone control in a skin file within a theme as described in chapter 11. To get the formatting for a web part zone into a skin file, you can copy the tag for the WebPartZone control from the aspx file into the skin file. Then, you can delete any attributes or elements that aren't used to control the formatting of web parts such as the ID attribute, the LayoutOrientation attribute, the HeaderText attribute, and the ZoneTemplate element. When that's done, you end up with a WebPartZone element like the one in this figure that only contains the attributes and elements that apply formatting. Then, this formatting can automatically be applied to all web part zones on the page or to all web part zones in the entire application.

As you might expect, you can use similar techniques to apply formatting to the CatalogZone and EditorZone controls, which will change the appearance of the CatalogPart and EditorPart controls within these zones. Although the tags that apply this type of formatting aren't shown in this figure, you can see them in the application for this chapter that you can download from our web site.

A page after formatting has been applied to the web parts

The asp tags that apply formatting to a web part zone

```
<asp:WebPartZone runat="server"
    BorderColor="#CCCCCC"
    Font-Names="Verdana"
    Padding="6">
    <PartChromeStyle
        BackColor="#F7F6F3"              BorderColor="#E2DED6"
        Font-Names="Verdana"             ForeColor="White" />
    <MenuLabelHoverStyle                 ForeColor="#E2DED6" />
    <MenuLabelStyle                      ForeColor="White" />
    <MenuVerbHoverStyle
        BackColor="#F7F6F3"              BorderColor="#CCCCCC"
        BorderStyle="Solid"              BorderWidth="1px"
        ForeColor="#333333" />
    <HeaderStyle
        ForeColor="#CCCCCC"              HorizontalAlign="Center" />
    <MenuVerbStyle
        BorderColor="#5D7B9D"            BorderStyle="Solid"
        BorderWidth="1px"                ForeColor="White" />
    <PartStyle
        ForeColor="#333333" />
    <TitleBarVerbStyle
        Font-Underline="False"           ForeColor="White" />
    <MenuPopupStyle
        BackColor="#5D7B9D"              BorderColor="#CCCCCC"
        BorderWidth="1px" />
    <PartTitleStyle
        BackColor="#5D7B9D"              Font-Bold="True"
        ForeColor="White" />
</asp:WebPartZone>
```

Description

- You can use the Auto Format feature to automatically format all of the parts in a web part zone, catalog zone, or editor zone. To do that, select the Auto Format command from the zone's smart tag menu and then choose a scheme from the dialog box that's displayed.

- You can use a theme to apply formatting to all of the zones on a page (or to the entire web site). For more information about themes, see chapter 11.

Figure 24-8   How to apply formatting to web parts

How to write code that works with web parts

You can develop most portals using just the skills that have already been presented in this chapter. However, if you need to customize a portal beyond what has been shown, the portal framework exposes an API that lets you write code that works with web parts. This API also lets you develop custom WebPart controls that can take advantage of some of the advanced features of the portal framework. What follows is just an introduction to this subject, but it should get you started.

Classes for working with web parts

Figure 24-9 shows some of the classes that are commonly used to work with web parts. Of these classes, the WebPartManager class is the one that's most commonly used to work with portals. As you learned earlier in this chapter, you can use this class to switch between display modes. In addition, you can use this class to access a collection of WebPart and WebPartZone objects that correspond to the web parts and zones available from the page. And you can use this class to respond to the events that occur on a web portal such as switching display modes or adding or removing a web part or zone.

In general, the classes described in this figure correspond with the controls that are available from the WebParts group in Visual Studio's Toolbox. Most of the time, you can use Visual Studio to set the properties for these controls at design time. Whenever necessary, though, you can write code that uses these classes to work with these controls at runtime. To do that, you often need to get a more complete description of the class for the control by looking it up in the documentation for the .NET Framework class library.

Classes for working with web parts

Class	Description
WebPartManager	Can be used to work with all of the zones and web parts on the page, to change display modes for the page, and to respond to events that are raised by the zones and web parts on the page.
WebPartZone	Can be used to modify the properties of a web part zone. Many of these properties control the appearance of the web parts within this zone.
CatalogZone	Can be used to modify the properties of a catalog zone. Many of these properties control the appearance of the catalog parts within this zone.
EditorZone	Can be used to modify the properties of an editor zone. Many of these properties control the appearance of the editor parts within this zone.
ConnectionsZone	Can be used to work with connections between custom WebPart controls.
WebPartVerb	Can be used to work with a *verb*, which is a button, link, or menu item in the title bar of a web part.
WebPart	Can be used to work with web parts at runtime, or it can be overridden to create a custom WebPart that takes advantage of the advanced features of the portal framework (see figure 24-10).
GenericWebPart	Can be used to work with user controls and custom server controls within a web part zone. Many of its properties are inherited from the Panel and Part classes. The ASP.NET portal framework automatically uses this class whenever it needs to wrap ASP.NET controls such as standard controls, user controls, and custom server controls so they behave like web parts.
PageCatalogPart	Can be used to work with the web parts in the page catalog, including parts that a user has closed.
DeclarativeCatalogPart	Can be used to work with the web parts in the declarative catalog.
ImportCatalogPart	Can be used to import a catalog of web parts.
BehaviorEditorPart	Can be used to apply behavior changes to an associated web part.
AppearanceEditorPart	Can be used to apply appearance changes to an associated web part.
LayoutEditorPart	Can be used to apply layout changes to a web part.
PropertyGridEditorPart	Can be used to change the property grid of a web part.

Description

- For a complete description of each class, including its constructors, properties, methods, and events, look up the class in the documentation for the .NET Framework class library.

Figure 24-9   Classes for working with web parts

How to develop and use a custom WebPart control

To show you how to develop a custom WebPart control, figure 24-10 presents the HalloweenCounter class. This class defines a custom WebPart control that displays a message that indicates the number of shopping days until Halloween. To start, this class inherits the WebPart class. Since this WebPart class inherits the Panel class and the Part class, the HalloweenCounter class inherits these classes too.

Next, the constructor for the HalloweenCounter class sets the Title property to "Days to Halloween." This is possible because the Title property is available from the Part class, which is inherited by the WebPart class and the HalloweenCounter class.

Then, the HalloweenCounter class overrides the RenderContents method of the WebControl class. Like all web server controls, the Panel class inherits the WebControl class. Because the Part class inherits the Panel class, the RenderContents method is available from the HalloweenCounter class. This method is called by the web page whenever the page needs to display the control. The code within this method calculates the number of shopping days to Halloween, creates a message that includes the results of this calculation, and uses the HtmlTextWriter object to write that message to the page.

Since the message doesn't include any HTML tags, this HalloweenCounter class causes plain text to be displayed as the content of the web part. However, you can include HTML tags in the message if you want to format it. Also, if you know how to render controls as HTML, you can create complex controls using this method. In this regard, the skills for developing a custom WebPart control are similar to the skills for developing a custom server control, as you will see in chapter 28.

The last two statements in this figure show how to register a custom WebPart control and place it on the page. First, you code a Register directive that specifies the namespace for the control and a prefix for the control's tag. Then, you code the tag for the control, using the prefix followed by the name of the class that defines the control. Once you do that, the page will display the custom WebPart control just as it would display a user control that was wrapped in the GenericWebPart class.

The code that defines the custom WebPart control

```
using System;
using System.Web.UI;
using System.Web.UI.WebControls.WebParts;

namespace murach
{
    public class HalloweenCounter : WebPart
    {
        public HalloweenCounter()
        {
            this.Title = "Days to Halloween";
        }

        protected override void RenderContents(HtmlTextWriter writer)
        {
            DateTime today = DateTime.Today;
            DateTime halloween = new DateTime(DateTime.Today.Year, 10, 31);
            if (today > halloween)
                halloween = halloween.AddYears(1);
            TimeSpan span = halloween - today;
            string content = "There are " + span.Days
                + " shopping days until Halloween.";

            writer.Write(content);
        }
    }
}
```

Code that registers a custom WebPart control for a page

```
<%@ Register TagPrefix="mma" Namespace="murach" %>
```

Code that places a custom WebPart control on a page

```
<mma:HalloweenCounter ID="HalloweenCounter1" runat="server" />
```

Description

- To develop a custom WebPart control, code a class that inherits the WebPart class. Then, override the RenderContents method of the WebControl class to render the contents of the web part.

- To use a custom WebPart control, code a Register directive that specifies the namespace for the control and a prefix for the control's tag. Then, code the tag for the control using the prefix followed by the name of the class that defines the control.

Figure 24-10   How to develop and use a custom WebPart control

Perspective

Now that you've finished this chapter, you should have the skills you need to develop portals with web parts. In particular, you should be able to develop a portal that lets the user move web parts between zones, add web parts to a page, and even edit the properties of a web part. You should also be able to develop some custom WebPart controls.

Of course, there's more to developing portals than has been presented in this chapter. In chapters 27 and 28, for example, you can learn how to develop the user controls and custom server controls that you need for your portals. Also, if you want to do something like share data between web parts, you're going to have to dig into the documentation for the classes that let you work with web parts. For many portals, though, this chapter should provide all of the skills that you're going to need.

Terms

portal
web part
web part zone
personalization provider
browse display mode
design display mode
catalog display mode
verb
edit display mode
chrome

25

How to use AJAX

This chapter introduces you to the new ASP.NET server controls that provide
for building AJAX-enabled web pages. These controls let you develop web
applications that are more responsive to users and that help reduce the load on
the web server. As you'll see, these controls are completely integrated with
ASP.NET 3.5 and Visual Studio 2008.

An introduction to AJAX **806**
AJAX concepts 806
How AJAX works 808

An introduction to ASP.NET AJAX **810**
How ASP.NET AJAX works 810
The Microsoft AJAX Library 812
The ASP.NET AJAX server controls 814
The ASP.NET AJAX Control Toolkit 816

How to use the ASP.NET AJAX server controls **818**
How to use the ScriptManager control 818
How to use the ScriptManagerProxy control 820
How to use the UpdatePanel control 822
How to use the Timer control 824
How to use the UpdateProgress control 826

An application that uses AJAX **828**
The Shout Box application 828
The ShoutItem class 830
The ShoutItemList class 830
The aspx file 832
The css file 832
The code-behind file 836

Perspective **838**

An introduction to AJAX

Over the years, web sites have changed from collections of static web pages to complex, dynamic, data-driven web applications. As web applications started performing many of the same functions as traditional desktop applications, users wanted their web applications to perform in the same way. A *rich Internet application (RIA)* is a web application that provides users with an enhanced user interface, advanced functionality, and a quick response time like desktop applications.

There are many frameworks you can use to build a RIA, including Java applets, Adobe Flash player, and Microsoft Silverlight. For most frameworks to work, however, the user must install a plug-in into the web browser. Only one framework uses just the features that are built into all modern web browsers. That framework is known as *Asynchronous JavaScript and XML*, or *AJAX*.

AJAX concepts

AJAX is not a single technology. It is a collection of technologies that, when used together, enable developers to build a RIA. These technologies allow a web page to communicate with a web server and update the page after it's loaded without having to reload the entire page.

As you saw in chapter one, when a web browser sends an HTTP request to a web server, the server returns an HTTP response that contains the content to be displayed for the page. Whether the page is static or dynamic, once the page is returned, the connection to the server is closed. Even if state is maintained with application variables, session variables, or cookies, a full HTTP request and response cycle must take place to update the web page. This is illustrated in the first diagram in figure 25-1.

In contrast, if portions of a web page are AJAX-enabled, AJAX can update the web page after it's loaded without having to perform a full HTTP request and response cycle. This is illustrated in the second diagram in this figure. Here, AJAX initiates a request that sends just the data that will be needed by the server to respond to the request. That can include information about what event triggered the request, as well as the contents of the relevant controls on the page. Then, when the server sends its response back to the browser, the browser can use the data in the response to update the contents of the web page without having to reload the entire page.

AJAX-initiated requests can be repeated as many times as necessary to update a page. For example, one common use for AJAX is to update information on a page at a given time interval. In that case, a full HTTP request and response cycle would only be performed when part of the page that is not AJAX-enabled needs to be updated or when a different page needs to be loaded.

Standard request and response cycle

AJAX-enabled request and response cycle

Description

- A *rich Internet application* (*RIA*) is an application that is displayed in a web browser, but has some of the features of a desktop application such as an enhanced user interface and quick response time.

- *Asynchronous JavaScript and XML* (*AJAX*) is one way to build a RIA. It lets you update part of a web page without having to reload the entire page. This can also reduce the load on the web server.

- Each time a standard HTTP request and response cycle is performed, the entire page is returned from the server and the page is loaded into the browser. This type of request and response is required the first time a page is requested even if the page is AJAX-enabled.

- With an AJAX HTTP request and response cycle, the browser can request just the information it needs to update the page. Then, the updated information that's returned from the server can be used to update the page without having to reload it.

- A number of JavaScript libraries that support AJAX application development are available. The one you'll use with ASP.NET AJAX application development is the Microsoft AJAX Library.

Figure 25-1   AJAX concepts

How AJAX works

HTML by itself can only describe a static web page. Other technologies are needed to provide an enhanced user interface and to communicate with a server from within a web page. Figure 25-2 illustrates how these technologies work in an AJAX-enabled web page.

The technologies that enable AJAX web applications are *JavaScript*, the *Document Object Model* (*DOM*), Cascading Style Sheets (CSS), the XMLHttpRequest object, a server-side scripting language, Extensible Markup Language (XML), and *JavaScript Object Notation* (*JSON*). JavaScript, DOM, and CSS, together with HTML, are used to implement *Dynamic HTML* (*DHTML*), which provides for interactive and animated web pages.

JavaScript is a programming language that's built into the web browser that can read and write the properties of HTML tags on a web page. The JavaScript language has no built-in mechanisms for gathering input or displaying output. It only provides mathematical capabilities, structured programming statements, and a few data types and objects. It has to rely on its host environment to provide other facilities.

The DOM provides most of JavaScript's input and output facilities in a web browser. It consists of a hierarchy of objects that represents the content on the web page. It is built by the web browser from the HTML and CSS in the web page, and it is made available to the JavaScript environment. The browser object model provides the rest of JavaScript's input and output capabilities, but these capabilities aren't typically used in an AJAX-based web application.

JavaScript can read the properties of objects in the DOM to find out what's on the web page. These properties include the style of text elements, the contents of form fields, and the state of form controls. When JavaScript code updates an object in the DOM, the web browser updates the web page that's displayed to reflect the changes.

When an event occurs on an object in the DOM, JavaScript code can run to handle the event. These events include user actions such as when the user clicks the mouse, types on the keyboard, or changes elements on a form. They can also include events initiated by the web page, such as a timer expiring.

The XMLHttpRequest object is also provided by the web browser. It has methods that can initiate an HTTP request to the web server. The scripting language on the web server then processes the data in the request and generates a response that's sent back to the browser. When the browser receives the response, it stores it in the XMLHttpRequest object for JavaScript to use as a basis for updating the web page by manipulating the DOM.

Although the XMLHttpRequest object was designed to send and receive XML documents, any text-based format can be used. Because XML documents are hard to create and process in JavaScript, they're typically used only to send data to the server. Then, JSON, which provides a plain text representation of a JavaScript object, is used to send data back to the browser.

The architecture of AJAX

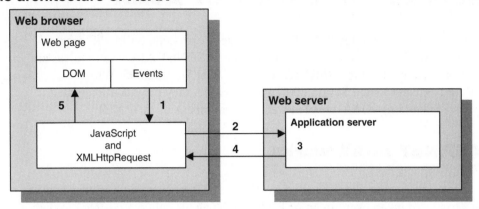

How AJAX updates the contents of a web page

1. An event happens on the web page. This can be the user moving the mouse, clicking a button, or changing a field or a timer going off. This event triggers JavaScript code to execute.

2. JavaScript prepares a request and sends it to the web server. The request contains information about the event and the current state of the controls on the web page.

3. The server receives the data and processes it. Although processing can take place on the client, some actions, such as database access, must happen on the server.

4. The server prepares a response and sends it back to the browser. The response contains the updated state of the controls on the web page.

5. JavaScript parses the response and uses the data it contains to update the contents of the web page by modifying objects in the DOM. The browser then updates the user's screen.

Description

- The web page that is downloaded from the web server contains HTML, CSS, and *JavaScript*. JavaScript is a programming language that's built into the web browser.

- The web browser uses the HTML and CSS to build the *Document Object Model* (*DOM*), which is an object-oriented representation of the content in the page. This content is displayed on the screen for the user. Whenever the objects in the DOM are modified, the web browser updates the content on the screen to display those changes.

- JavaScript is used to run code when events occur in the web page. JavaScript also has access to the DOM to determine the state of controls on the page and to make changes to the DOM that will be shown to the user.

- The XMLHttpRequest object that's built into the web browser is used to communicate with the web server. JavaScript is used to access the functionality of the XMLHttpRequest object.

- When AJAX was first developed, it used XML to format the data that's sent between the web browser and web server. For most requests, *JavaScript Object Notation* (*JSON*) is now used to send data back to the web browser.

Figure 25-2   How AJAX works

An introduction to ASP.NET AJAX

Microsoft developed ASP.NET AJAX so developers can build a RIA out of standard ASP.NET controls. The components of ASP.NET AJAX were released as a separate download for ASP.NET 2.0 and Visual Studio 2005. When ASP.NET 3.5 and Visual Studio 2008 were released, they provided integrated support for building AJAX-enabled web applications using ASP.NET.

How ASP.NET AJAX works

As you learned in chapter one, a standard HTTP request and response cycle that's triggered by an event in an ASP.NET web page is called a postback. When a postback occurs, the view state of the controls on the page is sent to the server as part of the request. Then, the server processes the request, updates the view state as necessary, and sends a response back to the browser that contains a new page with the new view state.

In contrast, ASP.NET AJAX enables a process known as an *asynchronous postback*. This is similar to a standard postback in that the view state of controls on the page is sent to the server in response to an event on the page. In an asynchronous postback, however, the XMLHttpRequest object is used to send the view state to the server. Then, the response that's returned by the server is used to update the controls on the page without having to reload the entire web page in the browser.

Figure 25-3 shows the three components of ASP.NET AJAX and illustrates how they work. The *Microsoft AJAX Library* is a JavaScript library that is loaded by the web browser when an AJAX-enabled ASP.NET page is displayed. It provides functionality that's not available in JavaScript. For example, it makes it easier to write JavaScript code that interacts with the web page through the DOM. It also allows JavaScript code to interact with the ASP.NET application server through the XMLHttpRequest object it encapsulates.

ASP.NET AJAX also provides five server controls. They are used to AJAX-enable the ASP.NET web page so that other ASP.NET server controls can be updated in the web browser without having to reload the page. These controls render JavaScript code as part of the web page just as other controls render HTML and CSS. The code they render uses the Microsoft AJAX Library to process events in the web page, manage and update controls in the web page, and trigger an asynchronous postback to interact with the server.

The Microsoft AJAX Library and the ASP.NET AJAX server controls are built into ASP.NET 3.5 and Visual Studio 2008. In contrast, the *ASP.NET AJAX Control Toolkit* is not. Instead, it's available as a separate download for Visual Studio 2008. This toolkit consists of components and server control extensions that provide a variety of effects, animations, and interactive features.

The architecture of ASP.NET AJAX

Components of ASP.NET AJAX

Component	Description
Microsoft AJAX Library	A JavaScript library that provides enhancements to the JavaScript language to better support AJAX development in an ASP.NET environment.
ASP.NET AJAX server controls	Five server controls that encapsulate other ASP.NET controls on the web page to indicate that they will be controlled on the client by the Microsoft AJAX Library.
ASP.NET AJAX Control Toolkit	An open source, community supported project that provides AJAX-related enhancements to existing ASP.NET server controls.

Description

- Microsoft developed a set of extensions to ASP.NET code-named Atlas that provided AJAX support. These extensions were released as a fully supported extension of ASP.NET 2.0 in January of 2007. They were incorporated as built-in features of ASP.NET 3.5 and Visual Studio 2008.

- An *asynchronous postback* is the process used by ASP.NET to perform a partial-page update. During an asynchronous postback, the view state of the web page is sent to the server, which processes the request and sends back the new view state of the controls being updated.

- The ASP.NET AJAX server controls enclose other ASP.NET server controls to make them AJAX-enabled. These controls can then be updated using an asynchronous postback.

- A single page can have one or more groups of AJAX-enabled controls that can be updated independently or simultaneously. Server controls that are not AJAX-enabled will still trigger a full postback that causes the entire page to be reloaded.

- The ASP.NET AJAX Control Toolkit adds animation and effects to standard server controls. It is not officially supported by Microsoft.

Figure 25-3   How ASP.NET AJAX works

The Microsoft AJAX Library

The Microsoft AJAX Library provides numerous enhancements to the JavaScript language. These enhancements provide a rich client-side environment in which the ASP.NET AJAX server controls can more easily implement AJAX-enabled web pages. Although you won't typically use this library directly, you should be familiar with the features it provides. Figure 25-4 summarizes those features.

To start, the Microsoft AJAX Library is written to work with three popular browsers: Microsoft Internet Explorer, Mozilla Firefox, and Apple Safari. Although all three of these web browsers use HTML, CSS, DOM, JavaScript and the XMLHttpRequest object, they implement them differently. Because of that, the Microsoft AJAX Library abstracts common functionality into methods that will work properly no matter which web browser is used.

The library also extends the core JavaScript types and classes to better match those provided by C#. This makes it easier for ASP.NET to render C# code in JavaScript so that it can execute in the web browser.

The library also adds the concept of namespaces to JavaScript. This allows a large number of functions to be organized in a hierarchy, which reduces the probability of conflicts between function names. The Sys namespace is created and used by the Microsoft AJAX Library to organize the functions in the library.

In addition, the library adds better object-oriented programming support within JavaScript. Although JavaScript is object-based, it isn't truly object-oriented. By adding object-oriented support, the developer can use object-oriented practices such as classes, interfaces, polymorphism, and type reflection.

Next, the library enhances the event management, exception handling, and debugging capabilities of JavaScript. This allows code that uses the library to better deal with error conditions and to return more meaningful error messages for unhandled exceptions.

The library also provides enhanced support for many network related features. That includes a single interface to the XMLHttpRequest object. It includes web service proxy classes that can represent an ASP.NET web service, which make it easy to use the web service from within JavaScript code. It includes methods to convert JavaScript objects to and from JSON text strings. And it includes classes that provide access to ASP.NET authentication, profile, and membership services across the network from within JavaScript.

Finally, the library adds globalization methods so that data can be formatted based on regional settings. It also adds localization methods so that multiple translations of text strings can be provided and used based on language settings in the browser. And it adds classes to represent the ASP.NET server controls in JavaScript. These classes are used to trigger an asynchronous postback and to update the controls on the page based on the result of the postback.

The Microsoft AJAX Library

Feature	Description
Cross-browser compatibility	Ensures that the library works correctly in three major web browsers. Also adds methods to manage the DOM in all three browsers.
JavaScript type extensions	Adds methods to the Array, Boolean, Date, Number, and String types to match methods available in the corresponding .NET types.
Event handling	Adds event functionality to all JavaScript objects and the ability to register functions as event listeners.
Classes and namespaces	Provides a mechanism for creating classes in JavaScript and to organize them into a hierarchical structure.
Inheritance and interfaces	Enables object-oriented development in JavaScript by supporting polymorphism and method overriding.
Reflection	Provides methods for inspecting objects to determine the object type and to enumerate its properties and methods.
Exception handling	Adds typed exception handling to the JavaScript Error object.
Debugging	Supports debugging by adding code tracing and trace dumping.
Globalization and localization	Add methods to format data and allow for multiple translations of text strings based on language settings.
Networking	Encapsulates the XMLHttpRequest object and provides access to ASP.NET web services.
JSON serialization	Provides methods for encoding JavaScript objects into JSON strings and decoding JSON strings back into objects.
Components	Provides classes for managing ASP.NET user interface elements on the page.
Partial-page updates	Provides classes for managing the asynchronous postback process on the client.
Application services	Adds methods that provide ASP.NET authentication, profiles, and membership services in JavaScript.

Description

- The *Microsoft AJAX Library* supports the Internet Explorer, Mozilla Firefox, and Apple Safari browsers.

- Extensions to the built-in JavaScript objects are in the global namespace, which is the root namespace for all other namespaces. All other enhancements are in the Sys namespace that the Microsoft AJAX Library creates within the global namespace.

- Although this library is needed for ASP.NET AJAX to work, most developers won't use the library directly. Instead, it will be included and used automatically by the ASP.NET AJAX server controls that the developer includes on the web page.

- The Microsoft AJAX Library can be used with server-side languages other than ASP.NET, such as PHP.

Figure 25-4   The Microsoft AJAX Library

The ASP.NET AJAX server controls

Figure 25-5 describes the five ASP.NET AJAX server controls that you can use to enable and manage asynchronous postbacks on a web page. These controls allow the other controls on the page to participate in an asynchronous postback. You'll find these controls in the AJAX Extensions group of the Toolbox in Visual Studio 2008.

The ScriptManager control is the primary control that enables asynchronous postbacks, and it must be on a page for ASP.NET AJAX to work. It is often placed on a Master page so all the pages that use the Master page will be AJAX-enabled. The other AJAX controls can then be placed on either the Master page or content pages.

In addition to enabling asynchronous postbacks, the ScriptManager control provides for loading and managing additional JavaScript files. It also provides for registering web services so they can be accessed by JavaScript code on the client through a web service proxy. You'll learn more about how this works in figure 25-7.

Note that you can have only one ScriptManager control on a page. In addition, if you add a ScriptManager control to a Master page, you can't also add one to a content page that uses the master page. However, you can add a ScriptManagerProxy control to the content page. This control lets you load additional JavaScript files or register additional web services needed by the content page but not by all the pages that use the Master page.

After you add a ScriptManager control to a page, you can use the UpdatePanel control to enclose standard ASP.NET server controls. Then, the controls inside the UpdatePanel control will be updated in place when an asynchronous postback occurs. Note that you can have multiple UpdatePanel controls on a page. You can also have controls outside the UpdatePanel controls. If an event occurs on one of those controls, a full postback will occur on the web page.

If you want to provide a visual indication that an asynchronous postback is in progress, you can use the UpdateProgress control. This lets users know that their actions were detected and their request is being processed. That's useful if an operation takes more than a few seconds to perform.

If you want to trigger an asynchronous postback at a set time interval, you can use the Timer control. This can be useful if you want to poll the server for any updates that need to be displayed. Keep in mind, however, that if an asynchronous postback is triggered too often, the load on the server can increase dramatically.

ASP.NET AJAX server controls

Control	Description
ScriptManager	Enables the use of the other ASP.NET AJAX controls, loads the Microsoft AJAX Library, and manages client-side JavaScript code.
ScriptManagerProxy	Extends the scripting services provided by a ScriptManager control.
UpdatePanel	Identifies a set of server controls to be updated using an asynchronous postback.
UpdateProgress	Provides visual feedback that an asynchronous postback is in progress.
Timer	Periodically triggers an asynchronous postback on an UpdatePanel control.

The ScriptManager control

* You can only have one ScriptManager control on a page. This includes master and content pages. If you put a ScriptManager control on a master page, you can't use one on a content page. If there is more than one ScriptManager control on a page, an Invalid Operation exception will be generated.

* The ScriptManager control can also be used to load and manage additional JavaScript files and to register web services so they can be accessed by JavaScript code on the client through a web service proxy. See figure 25-7 for details.

The ScriptManagerProxy control

* The ScriptManagerProxy control lets you load JavaScript files and register web services. It can be used in a content page if the master page contains a ScriptManager control or in a user control that will be used on pages that contain a ScriptManager control. See chapter 27 for more information on user controls.

The UpdatePanel control

* The UpdatePanel control is a container control that holds other server controls that will be updated during an asynchronous postback. All controls inside an UpdatePanel control will be updated at the same time. A page can contain multiple UpdatePanel controls, each with a different set of controls.

The UpdateProgress control

* Although an asynchronous postback is faster than a full postback, there are times when an asynchronous postback will take a few seconds or more to complete. In that case, you can use the UpdateProgress control to visually indicate that an asynchronous postback is in progress and that the user should wait until it's completed before doing anything else on the page.

The Timer control

* When one or more UpdatePanel controls need to be updated automatically, you can use the Timer control to trigger partial-page updates at a set time interval.

Figure 25-5   The ASP.NET AJAX server controls

The ASP.NET AJAX Control Toolkit

The ASP.NET AJAX Control Toolkit provides more dynamic, visually appealing user interface controls. It is not a required component of ASP.NET AJAX and it is not built into Visual Studio 2008. Instead, it's an open source project hosted at Microsoft's Codeplex web site that you can download and use for free.

Figure 25-6 lists some of the most common controls in the toolkit. These controls extend the functions of existing ASP.NET controls. For example, the Calendar control extends the function of a TextBox control.

The toolkit currently contains over thirty control extensions, and more are being added with every release. To view descriptions of these controls along with live examples, you can go to the first web site listed in this figure. To download the toolkit, you can go to the second web site.

The ASP.NET AJAX Control Toolkit is developed by volunteers and is not supported by Microsoft. Because of that, developers are responsible for checking for security updates related to the toolkit. If you publish a web page that uses an extension from the toolkit that is later found to have a security weakness, you must download the updated toolkit and republish the web page. You may also want to check the toolkit periodically for new features and bug fixes.

Common ASP.NET AJAX Control Toolkit controls

Control	Description
Accordion	Contains multiple panes of content, but only displays one at a time.
Animation	Adds methods to change the position, size, opacity, and color of a control. They can be combined to create many dynamic effects.
Calendar	Shows a calendar in a pop-up window for easy date entry.
CollapsiblePanel	Provides a one-click, hide/show effect for a control.
DragPanel	Lets the user move a panel of content around on the page.
DropShadow	Adds a drop shadow to a control.
HoverMenu	Displays a menu when the user hovers over a control.
ModalPopup	A pop-up control that hides the page until the user selects an option.
NumericUpDown	Adds up and down arrows to a text box for changing the value.
PagingBulletedList	Displays a long list of items across multiple pages.
PopupControl	Hides a set of controls until they are displayed in a pop-up window.
RoundedCorners	Adds rounded corners to a control.
Slider	Lets the user enter a value by dragging a slider.
SlideShow	Shows multiple images in one image tag. The images can change automatically or the user can manually scroll back and forth.
TabContainer	Shows multiple panes of content in a tabbed format.
TextBoxWatermark	Displays a message in an "empty" text box with a custom style. The text goes away when the user clicks in the text box.
ToggleButton	Replaces a check box with two images that indicate whether the check box is checked or not.

Web sites related to the ASP.NET AJAX Control Toolkit

URL	Description
http://www.asp.net/ajax/ ajaxcontroltoolkit/samples/	You can view live examples of the toolkit at this address.
http://www.codeplex.com/ AtlasControlToolkit/Release/ ProjectReleases.aspx	You can download the latest toolkit at this address.

Description

- The ASP.NET AJAX Control Toolkit provides extensions to ASP.NET controls that enable animations, special effects, and dynamic data bindings through asynchronous postbacks.

- The toolkit is not an official part of ASP.NET. It is an open source project developed by the community at Microsoft's Codeplex web site.

- The toolkit is constantly being updated. You should check the toolkit site often for new features, bug fixes, and security vulnerabilities.

Figure 25-6   The ASP.NET AJAX Control Toolkit

How to use the ASP.NET AJAX server controls

The ASP.NET AJAX server controls can be added to almost any page to manage asynchronous postbacks. In the topics that follow, you'll learn the details of using each of the five controls.

How to use the ScriptManager control

As you know, you must add a ScriptManager control to a web page to enable asynchronous postbacks. Figure 25-7 presents some common attributes of this control along with some code examples. Note that this code must be added inside a Form element before any other ASP.NET AJAX controls.

By default, all the JavaScript code for a page is loaded before the user interface is displayed. This ensures that the user interface is fully functional when it's displayed, which is usually what you want. In some case, though, the user interface will take too long to display. Then, you should consider setting the LoadScriptsBeforeUI attribute to False so the user interface is displayed before the JavaScript is loaded. If you do that, keep in mind that the user interface may not be fully functional when it's first displayed.

The AsyncPostBackTimeout attribute determines how long the Microsoft AJAX Library will wait for a response after triggering an asynchronous postback. If a response isn't received within the specified time period, an exception is raised and the postback is cancelled. If the value of this attribute is set to a time interval that's too short, users will see a larger number of errors. If it's set to a time interval that's too long, users will wait too long to find out that there's a problem with the request.

The IsInAsyncPostBack attribute is a read-only Boolean value that is set to True while an asynchronous postback is in progress. This attribute can be examined by either client-side or server-side code. In most cases, you'll use it in the Load event handler for a web page. Because this event handler is executed for full postbacks as well as asynchronous postbacks, you can use the IsInAsyncPostBack attribute to execute code depending on which type of postback is being performed. For example, code that initializes a control would not run during an asynchronous postback.

In addition to setting attributes of the ScriptManager control, you can add Scripts and Services child elements. You use the Scripts element to load additional JavaScript code. Within this element, you code asp:ScriptReference elements that identify the files that contain the code.

You use the Services element to create *web service proxies* that allow the use of web services in JavaScript code. Within this element, you code asp:ServiceReference elements that specify the location of the asmx file for each web service.

Common attributes of the ScriptManager control

Attribute	Description
AsyncPostBackTimeout	Sets the time in seconds before an asynchronous postback times out if there is no response. The default is 90.
EnablePageMethods	Determines if static methods on an ASP.NET page that are marked as web methods can be called from client scripts as if they're part of a web service. The default is False.
EnableScriptGlobalization	Determines if globalized functions in the Microsoft AJAX Library can display culture-specific information. The default is False.
EnableScriptLocalization	Determines if the server will look for localized versions of script files and use them if they exist. The default is True.
IsInAsyncPostBack	A read-only Boolean value that is True if the page is currently processing an asynchronous postback.
LoadScriptsBeforeUI	Determines if scripts are loaded before or after user interface elements. If False, the user interface may load more quickly but not be functional at first. The default is True.

The aspx code for a ScriptManager control

```
<asp:ScriptManager ID="ScriptManager1" runat="server">
</asp:ScriptManager>
```

The aspx code for a ScriptManager control that registers scripts

```
<asp:ScriptManager ID="ScriptManager1" runat="server">
    <Scripts>
        <asp:ScriptReference Path="~/Scripts/SampleScript.js" />
        <asp:ScriptReference Assembly="SampleAssembly"
            Name="SampleAssembly.SampleScript.js" />
    </Scripts>
</asp:ScriptManager>
```

The aspx code for a ScriptManager control that registers a web service

```
<asp:ScriptManager ID="ScriptManager1" runat="server">
    <Services>
        <asp:ServiceReference Path="~/Services/SampleService.asmx" />
    </Services>
</asp:ScriptManager>
```

Description

- The Scripts element of a ScriptManager control can contain asp:ScriptReference elements that cause the ScriptManager control to load and manage additional scripts. The asp:ScriptReference elements can load JavaScript code from a file using the Path attribute or from an assembly using the Assembly and Name attributes.

- The Services element of a ScriptManager control can contain asp:ServiceReference elements that cause the ScriptManager to create *web service proxies*. This allows client-side scripts to access these services. The asmx file for a web service is given in the Path attribute.

Figure 25-7   How to use the ScriptManager control

How to use the ScriptManagerProxy control

The ScriptManagerProxy control is used to extend the capabilities of a ScriptManager control. The most common scenario for using a ScriptManagerProxy control is when you use a ScriptManager control on a Master page and you want to add either JavaScript code or a web service proxy to a content page that uses that master page. This is illustrated in figure 25-8. Here, you can see a content page that uses a master page that contains an image and a ScriptManager control.

Unlike the ScriptManager control, you can have more than one ScriptManagerProxy controls on a page. However, these controls can't be used to modify the properties of the ScriptManager control. They can only add additional asp:ScriptReference and asp:ServiceReference elements to a page. As you can see in the second and third examples in this figure, you code these elements just like you do for a ScriptManager control.

A content page with a ScriptManagerProxy control

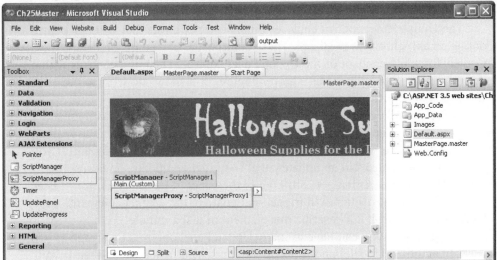

The aspx code for the ScriptManagerProxy control

```
<asp:ScriptManagerProxy ID="ScriptManagerProxy1" runat="server">
</asp:ScriptManagerProxy>
```

The aspx code for a ScriptManagerProxy control that registers scripts

```
<asp:ScriptManagerProxy ID="ScriptManager1" runat="server">
    <Scripts>
        <asp:ScriptReference Path="~/Scripts/SampleScript.js" />
        <asp:ScriptReference Assembly="SampleAssembly"
            Name="SampleAssembly.SampleScript.js" />
    </Scripts>
</asp:ScriptManagerProxy>
```

The aspx code for a ScriptManagerProxy control that registers a web service

```
<asp:ScriptManagerProxy ID="ScriptManager1" runat="server">
    <Services>
        <asp:ServiceReference Path="~/Services/SampleService.asmx" />
    </Services>
</asp:ScriptManagerProxy>
```

Description

- The ScriptManagerProxy control lets you extend the scripting services that are provided by a ScriptManager control. It's used most often on a content page whose master page contains a ScriptManager control.

- You can have multiple ScriptManagerProxy controls on a page. However, the ScriptManagerProxy controls can't override the properties of the ScriptManager control.

- The Scripts and Services elements of the ScriptManagerProxy control work the same as they do in the ScriptManager control.

Figure 25-8   How to use the ScriptManagerProxy control

How to use the UpdatePanel control

The UpdatePanel control encloses other server controls that will be updated during an asynchronous postback. These controls are placed inside the ContentTemplate element of the UpdatePanel control. Then, the controls within this element will be updated as a group. Figure 25-9 shows how to use the UpdatePanel control.

When controls are added to an update panel, they are automatically made triggers for the panel. That means that if any of the controls cause an asynchronous postback, the panel is updated. In most cases, that's what you want. If you don't want the controls in an update panel to trigger an update, however, you can set the ChildrenAsTriggers attribute of the panel to False. Then, you'll need to identify the controls that will trigger an update in the Triggers element of the UpdatePanel control. I'll describe this element in just a minute.

As you know, you can have as many UpdatePanel controls on a page as you need. In addition, UpdatePanel controls can be nested inside each other. If you nest UpdatePanel controls, you should know that server controls in a child update panel won't trigger the update of the parent panel. That's true even if the ChildrenAsTriggers attribute of the panels is set to True.

By default, a panel will be updated any time an asynchronous postback occurs on the page. This behavior is controlled by the UpdateMode attribute of the UpdatePanel control, which is set to Always by default. If you want a panel to be updated only when an asynchronous postback is caused by one of the panel's triggers, you can set the UpdateMode attribute to Conditional. Note that if an UpdatePanel control is nested inside another UpdatePanel control, it will always be updated when its parent UpdatePanel control is updated. Also note that if you set the ChildrenAsTriggers attribute to False, you must set the UpdateMode attribute to Conditional or an exception will occur.

You can specify the controls that cause a panel to be updated in the Triggers element of the control, as illustrated in the second example in this figure. Here, the Triggers element includes two asp elements. The first one, asp:AsyncPostBackTrigger, identifies a control that will cause an asynchronous postback to occur. In this case, the control is defined outside the update panel. However, you can also use this element for a control that's defined within an update panel. Notice that, in addition to naming the control that will cause the postback to occur, the EventName attribute names the event that will cause the postback. This isn't required, however. If this attribute is omitted, the postback will occur for the default event of the control.

The second element, asp:PostBackTrigger, names a control inside the update panel that causes a full postback to occur rather than an asynchronous postback. In other words, instead of causing just the panel to be updated, it causes the entire page to be reloaded.

This figure also lists some compatibility issues you may encounter when you use certain controls within an UpdatePanel control. You'll want to review this list before you use the UpdatePanel control so you're aware of any potential problems when you use these controls.

Two attributes of the UpdatePanel control

Attribute	Description
ChildrenAsTriggers	Determines if the controls in a panel are treated as triggers that cause the content of the panel to be updated when a control causes a postback. The default is True.
UpdateMode	Determines when the content of a panel is updated. If set to Always, the panel will be updated whenever a postback occurs. If set to Conditional, the panel will be updated only when one if its own triggers causes a postback. A nested UpdatePanel control will always be updated when its parent UpdatePanel control is updated. The default is Always.

The starting aspx code for an UpdatePanel control

```
<asp:UpdatePanel ID="UpdatePanel1" runat="server">
    <ContentTemplate>
    </ContentTemplate>
</asp:UpdatePanel>
```

The aspx code for an UpdatePanel control that specifies triggers

```
<asp:UpdatePanel ID="UpdatePanel1" runat="server">
    <ContentTemplate>
        <asp:Button ID="Button2" runat="server" Text="Add" />
    </ContentTemplate>
    <Triggers>
        <asp:AsyncPostBackTrigger ControlID="Button1" EventName="Click" />
        <asp:PostBackTrigger ControlID="Button2" />
    </Triggers>
</asp:UpdatePanel>
```

Description

- The ContentTemplate element of an UpdatePanel control contains the controls that will be updated during an asynchronous postback. UpdatePanel controls can be nested.

- You can use the Triggers element to specify controls that will cause the panel to be updated. The asp:AsyncPostBackTrigger element identifies a control inside or outside of the UpdatePanel control that will trigger an asynchronous postback. The asp:PostBackTrigger element identifies a control inside the UpdatePanel control that will trigger a full postback.

Compatibility issues with other controls

- The GridView and DetailsView controls can't be used in an update panel if you set their EnableSortingAndPagingCallbacks attributes to True.

- The TreeView control can't be used in an update panel if you enable callbacks that are not part of an asynchronous postback, set its styles directly as control attributes, or set the EnableClientScript attribute to False.

- The Menu control can't be used if you set its styles directly as control attributes.

- A FileUpload control can only be used as a postback trigger for an update panel.

- The Login, PasswordRecovery, ChangePassword, and CreateUserWizard controls can only be used if you convert their contents to editable templates.

Figure 25-9   How to use the UpdatePanel control

How to use the Timer control

The Timer control triggers a periodic asynchronous postback. This control is typically placed inside the ContentTemplate element of the UpdatePanel control that will be updated when the postback occurs. If it isn't placed inside an UpdatePanel control, it will trigger a full postback of the entire page.

Figure 25-10 illustrates how the Timer control works. To start, you can determine how often an asynchronous postback occurs by setting the Interval attribute of the control. This attribute is measured in milliseconds (1/1000th of a second). In the example in this figure, the Interval attribute is set to 10,000, or 10 seconds.

When you set the Interval attribute, you should be careful not to specify a value that's too small. If you do, it can cause a severe load on the server, particularly when many people have the page displayed. A value of 5,000 to 10,000 milliseconds is probably the smallest value you would want to use under most circumstances.

Also, you shouldn't expect the timer to be very accurate. That's because it's controlled by the timing mechanisms available to JavaScript in the web browser, and these mechanisms can be off by several hundred milliseconds.

If you need to, you can have two or more Timer controls on the same page. In most cases, you'll place these controls in different update panels. Then, you'll typically set the UpdateMode attribute of the UpdatePanel controls to Conditional so that the Timer in one panel won't trigger the update of another panel.

Although you can use two or more Timer controls in the same update panel, there's usually no need to do that. Instead, if you need an update panel to refresh at different rates depending on what's happening in the web page, you can use a single Timer control and change its Interval attribute. If you want to use two or more Timer controls with preset intervals, however, you can use the Enabled attribute of the controls to determine which control will be used at any given time.

A Timer control in Design view

Two attributes of the Timer control

Attribute	Description
Interval	Determines how often in milliseconds the control will trigger an asynchronous postback. The default value is 60,000 milliseconds (60 seconds).
Enabled	Determines whether a postback occurs when the time specified by the Interval attribute elapses. The default is True. You might set this attribute to False if you include more than one Timer control in the same panel, but you want only one to initiate a postback at any given time.

The aspx code for an UpdatePanel control with a Timer control

```
<asp:UpdatePanel ID="UpdatePanel1" runat="server">
    <ContentTemplate>
        <asp:Timer ID="Timer1" runat="server" Interval="10000">
        </asp:Timer>
    </ContentTemplate>
</asp:UpdatePanel>
```

Description

- The Timer control should be placed inside the ContentTemplate element of the UpdatePanel control that will be updated when the timer triggers an asynchronous postback.
- Setting the value of the Interval attribute too small can cause an increase in the load on the web server and an increase in the amount of traffic to the web server.
- The accuracy of the Timer control is determined by the accuracy of the JavaScript implementation in the user's web browser.

Figure 25-10   How to use the Timer control

How to use the UpdateProgress control

The UpdateProgress control displays information to the user when an asynchronous postback is in progress. You code this information within the ProgressTemplate element of the control as shown in figure 25-11. Here, the information consists of simple text, but you can include controls as well. Note that this text is displayed only when an asynchronous postback is taking place. Otherwise, it's hidden.

The DynamicLayout attribute of the UpdateProgress control determines how space is allocated for the content of the control. By default, space is allocated only when the content is being displayed. That means that any elements on the page that appear after the UpdateProgress control will be shifted down when the content is being displayed and will shift back up when the content is hidden again. If that's not what you want, you can allocate space for the content even when it isn't being displayed by setting the DynamicLayout attribute to False. It's up to the developer to determine which layout works best for the page.

In some cases, an asynchronous postback will happen so quickly that the content of the UpdateProgress control will simply flicker on the screen. To prevent that from happening, you can set the DisplayAfter attribute to determine how long the control should wait after the asynchronous postback starts to display its content. By default, this attribute is set to 0.5 seconds. Then, if the postback takes longer than that to complete, the content of the UpdateProgress control will be displayed on the page.

In most cases, you'll code the UpdateProgress control within an UpdatePanel control as shown in this figure. Then, its content will be displayed only when an asynchronous postback occurs on that panel. However, you can also code an UpdateProgress control outside an UpdatePanel control. Then, you can set its AssociatedUpdatePanelID attribute to the ID of the panel you want to use it with. Or, you can omit this attribute, in which case its content will be displayed anytime an asynchronous postback occurs.

An UpdateProgress control in Design view

Three attributes of the UpdateProgress control

Attribute	Description
DynamicLayout	Determines whether space is allocated on the page for the content of the control when it isn't displayed. The default is True, which means that space will be dynamically allocated. If set to False, space will be allocated for the content even though it won't be seen until an asynchronous postback occurs.
DisplayAfter	Determines how long in milliseconds after the asynchronous postback has started to display the content. The default is 500 milliseconds (0.5 seconds). This value can prevent the content from flickering when the postback happens quickly.
AssociatedUpdatePanelID	The ID of the UpdatePanel control that the control is associated with.

The aspx code for an UpdatePanel control with an UpdateProgress control

```
<asp:UpdatePanel ID="UpdatePanel1" runat="server">
    <ContentTemplate>
        <asp:UpdateProgress ID="UpdateProgress1" runat="server">
            <ProgressTemplate>
                Please wait. The update is in progress.
            </ProgressTemplate>
        </asp:UpdateProgress>
    </ContentTemplate>
</asp:UpdatePanel>
```

Description

- An UpdateProgress control must contain a ProgressTemplate element that defines the content of the control. This content is displayed only while an asynchronous postback is in progress. It is hidden after the asynchronous postback is complete.

- The content of an UpdateProgress control is displayed for the UpdatePanel control that contains it. If it's coded outside an UpdatePanel control, its content is displayed for any asynchronous postback unless the AssociatedUpdatePanelID attribute is specified.

Figure 25-11   How to use the UpdateProgress control

An application that uses AJAX

To illustrate how an application that uses AJAX works, the topics that follow present an application that uses a shout box. A shout box can be used to implement an informal comment system on a web site. Unlike traditional comment systems, users aren't required to register to enter shouts and shouts are typically displayed only for a short period of time. By AJAX-enabling this shout box, it can be updated without interfering with what the user is doing.

The Shout Box application

Figure 25-12 presents the Shout Box application. To start, this application lets the user display the products in a selected category in a DataList control. This part of the web page is not AJAX-enabled and works just like the Product List application you saw in chapter 13.

To the right of the DataList control are the controls that are used to implement the shout box. These controls are placed inside two UpdatePanel controls. The first update panel includes a label that displays the shout box, along with a Timer control that causes the shout box to be updated every five seconds. The second update panel includes two text boxes that let the user enter the information for a shout, labels that identify the text boxes, required field validators for the text boxes, a button that submits the shout, and an UpdateProgress control.

Notice that the shouts in the shout box are displayed in reverse chronological order. In other words, they're displayed from the newest shout to the oldest shout. That way, if there are many shouts being displayed, the user won't have to scroll down to see the newest ones.

The shouts for this application will be displayed in the shout box for three minutes. The shouts that are currently displayed are stored in a list in application state. That makes sense since the shouts are temporary. If you wanted to have a permanent record of the shouts, however, you could store them in a database and then display just the most recent shouts in the shout box.

To keep this application simple, it doesn't provide for filtering user entries. In most cases, though, you'd want to be sure that an application like this checks for objectionable material. The easiest way to do that would be to use a custom validator that scans the text of each shout for objectionable words and phrases. You could also store the list of objectionable material that's scanned for in a database so that administrators could update the list.

The Shout Box application

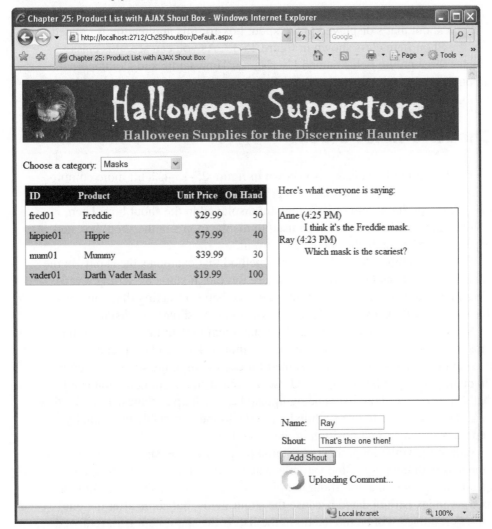

Description

- The Shout Box application is a variation of the Product List application you saw in chapter 13. It lets users post short messages, called shouts, which are then displayed in a shout box for other users to see.

- A list of the shout items that are currently displayed is stored in an application state variable. Shout items that are over three minutes old are deleted from this list whenever the shout box is updated or displayed.

- To implement the shout box, this page uses two UpdatePanel controls. The first one contains a label that's used to display the shout items and a Timer control that updates the panel every five seconds. The second one contains the controls that are used to submit a shout and display a progress indicator. It also contains required field validators for the two text boxes.

Figure 25-12   The Shout Box application

The ShoutItem class

Each shout that's displayed in the shout box for this application is created from the ShoutItem class shown in figure 25-13. As you can see, this class includes three public fields named UserName, Timestamp, and Comment. Although you'd typically define these fields as private and then code public methods for accessing them, that wasn't necessary for this application.

The ShoutItemList class

The ShoutItemList class, also shown in figure 25-13, is a bit more complicated. This class starts by declaring a private field named shoutList that will store the list of ShoutItem objects that are displayed in the shout box. Then, it includes three methods that will be used to display items in the shout box and keep the list of items in the shout box current.

The first method, Purge, is a private method that examines the shouts in the shoutList variable and removes any that are too old. It starts by setting a variable named purgeTime to the current time and then subtracting three minutes. This variable will be used to determine how long the shouts are displayed.

Next, the Purge method uses a while statement to determine if any of the items in the shout list are older than three minutes. The condition on this statement causes the loop to be executed for each item in the shoutList variable. Although you might think you could use a foreach statement here, you can't. That's because the shout list is being updated as the loop executes. To make this work, then, you have to use a while loop with an index variable to manually keep track of the current position in the shout list.

Within the while loop, the TimeStamp property of the current shout item is compared with the purgeTime variable. Then, if the timestamp is less than or equal to the purge time, the shout item is removed from the shout list. In that case, the index isn't updated because the shout items that come after the one that was removed will be moved up in the list. If the shout item isn't removed from the list, however, the index variable is increased by one so the next item can be checked.

The public Add method adds the shout item that's passed to it to the beginning of the shout list. But first, it calls the Purge method to remove any old shout items. In addition, it executes the Sleep method of the current thread to delay the Add method by two seconds. I included this method to ensure that the UpdateProgress control is displayed. Of course, you wouldn't want to include code like this in a production application.

The public Display method returns a text string that contains the contents of the shout box. Like the Add method, it starts by calling the Purge method. Then, it creates a StringBuilder object that will store the shout box text.

If the shout list contains at least one item, the Display method continues by adding a <dl> tag to the StringBuilder object. This tag defines a definition list, which can contain a formatted list of text items. Then, it uses a foreach loop to add the information for each shout item to this list. In this case, the user name and timestamp are coded within a <dt> tag, which defines a definition term, and

The ShoutItem.cs file

```
using System;

public class ShoutItem
{
    public string UserName;
    public DateTime Timestamp;
    public string Comment;
}
```

The ShoutItemList.cs file

```
using System;
using System.Collections.Generic;
using System.Text;

public class ShoutItemList
{
    private List<ShoutItem> shoutList = new List<ShoutItem>();

    private void Purge(){
        DateTime purgeTime = DateTime.Now;
        purgeTime = purgeTime.AddMinutes(-3);

        int i = 0;
        while (i < shoutList.Count){
            if (shoutList[i].Timestamp <= purgeTime)
                shoutList.RemoveAt(i);
            else
                i += 1;
        }
    }

    public void Add(ShoutItem shout){
        Purge();
        System.Threading.Thread.Sleep(2000);
        shoutList.Insert(0, shout);
    }

    public string Display(){
        Purge();
        StringBuilder shoutBoxText = new StringBuilder();
        if (shoutList.Count > 0){
            shoutBoxText.AppendLine("<dl>");
            foreach (ShoutItem shout in shoutList){
                shoutBoxText.Append("<dt>" + shout.UserName);
                shoutBoxText.Append(" (");
                shoutBoxText.Append(shout.Timestamp.ToShortDateString());
                shoutBoxText.AppendLine(")</dt>");
                shoutBoxText.AppendLine("<dd>" + shout.Comment + "</dd>");
            }
            shoutBoxText.AppendLine("</dl>");
        }
        return shoutBoxText.ToString();
    }
}
```

Figure 25-13   The ShoutItem and ShoutItemList classes

the comment is coded within a <dd> tag, which defines a definition. The <dt> tag causes the text to be left-aligned with no space above or below it. The <dd> tag causes the text to be indented. If you look back at the shout box in figure 25-12, you'll see how this works.

The aspx file

Figure 25-14 presents the aspx file for this application. Since you've already seen code like much of what's presented here, I'll just focus on the code that implements the AJAX controls. This code starts near the middle of page 2 of this listing.

To start, a ScriptManager control is used to AJAX-enable the page. This control is followed by an UpdatePanel control that contains the label that displays the text of the shout box and the Timer control that's used to refresh the shout box. Because the Interval attribute of this control is set to 5000, it will cause an asynchronous postback of the panel to occur every five seconds.

This panel also needs to be refreshed when the user adds a new shout. Because the UpdateMode attribute of the update panel has been left at its default of Always, this will happen automatically. In case this attribute is ever changed, though, I included a Triggers element in the UpdatePanel control. This element contains a trigger that will cause an asynchronous postback to occur when the user clicks the Add Shout button.

The second UpdatePanel control contains the controls for submitting a shout. Notice that the UpdateMode attribute of this control is set to Conditional. That way, the panel will be updated only when one of its own controls causes a postback.

On page 3 of this listing, you can see that this update panel also contains an UpdateProgress control. Because the DynamicLayout attribute of this control has been set to False, space will be reserved for it on the page even when it's not displayed. The content of this control includes a simple animated gif and a text comment.

The css file

The ShoutBox.css file, also shown in figure 25-14, is used to apply styles to the shout box. If you look back to page 1 of this listing, you'll see that this file is identified in a Link element within the Head element of the document.

The first style specifies the height of the shout box in pixels, and it applies a solid black border to the shout box. It also specifies Auto for the Overflow style property, which causes scroll bars to be displayed if the content of the shout box exceeds its height or width. (In this case, the width is defined by the table column that contains it.) The second style sets the margin of the definition list (dl) that's displayed in the shout box to zero pixels so that the list is displayed at the top of the shout box in all web browsers.

Notice that the names of both of these styles starts with a number sign (#). This indicates that the element it applies to is identified by its ID.

The Default.aspx file

```
<%@ Page Language="C#" AutoEventWireup="true" CodeFile="Default.aspx.cs"
Inherits="_Default" %>

<!DOCTYPE html PUBLIC "-//W3C//DTD XHTML 1.0 Transitional//EN"
"http://www.w3.org/TR/xhtml1/DTD/xhtml1-transitional.dtd">

<html xmlns="http://www.w3.org/1999/xhtml">
<head runat="server">
  <title>Chapter 25: Product List with AJAX Shout Box</title>
    <style type="text/css">
        .style1 {width: 100px;}
        .style2 {width: 200px;}
        .style3 {width: 80px;}
        .style4 {width: 390px;}
        .style5 {width: 10px;}
        .style6 {width: 290px;}
        .style7 {width: 75px;}
        .style8 {width: 225px;}
    </style>
    <link href="ShoutBox.css" rel="stylesheet" type="text/css" />
</head>
<body>
  <form id="form1" runat="server">
  <div>
    <asp:Image ID="Image1" runat="server" ImageUrl="~/Images/banner.jpg" />
    <br /><br />
    Choose a category: 
    <asp:DropDownList ID="Category" runat="server" AutoPostBack="True"
        Width="130px" DataSourceID="SqlDataSource1" DataTextField="LongName"
        DataValueField="CategoryID">
    </asp:DropDownList>
    <asp:SqlDataSource ID="SqlDataSource1" runat="server"
        ConnectionString="<%$ ConnectionStrings:HalloweenConnectionString %>"
        SelectCommand="SELECT [CategoryID], [LongName]
                       FROM [Categories]
                       ORDER BY [LongName]">
    </asp:SqlDataSource>
    <br /><br />
    <table>
      <tr>
        <td class="style4" valign="top">
          <asp:DataList ID="DataList1" runat="server"
              DataSourceID="SqlDataSource2" BackColor="White"
              BorderColor="#999999" BorderStyle="Solid" BorderWidth="1px"
              CellPadding="3" ForeColor="Black" GridLines="Vertical">
            <HeaderTemplate>
              <table>
                <tr>
                  <td class="style1">ID</td>
                  <td class="style2">Product</td>
                  <td class="style3" align="right">Unit Price</td>
                  <td class="style3" align="right">On Hand</td>
                </tr>
              </table>
            </HeaderTemplate>
```

Figure 25-14   The aspx and css files for the Shout Box application (part 1 of 3)

The Default.aspx file   **Page 2**

```
      <ItemTemplate>
        <table>
          <tr>
            <td class="style1">
              <asp:Label ID="ProductID" runat="server"
                  Text='<%# Eval("ProductID") %>'></asp:Label></td>
            <td class="style2">
              <asp:Label ID="ProductName" runat="server"
                  Text='<%# Eval("Name") %>'></asp:Label></td>
            <td class="style3" align="right">
              <asp:Label ID="UnitPrice" runat="server"
                  Text='<%# Eval("UnitPrice", "{0:c}") %>'>
              </asp:Label></td>
            <td class="style3" align="right">
              <asp:Label ID="OnHand" runat="server"
                  Text='<%# Eval("OnHand") %>'></asp:Label></td>
          </tr>
        </table>
      </ItemTemplate>
      <AlternatingItemStyle BackColor="#CCCCCC" />
      <HeaderStyle BackColor="Black" Font-Bold="True"
          ForeColor="White" />
  </asp:DataList></td>
<td class="style5"></td>
<td class="style6" valign="top">
  <asp:ScriptManager ID="ScriptManager1" runat="server">
  </asp:ScriptManager>
  Here's what everyone is saying:<br /><br />
  <asp:UpdatePanel ID="ShoutBoxPanel1" runat="server">
    <ContentTemplate>
      <asp:Label ID="lblShoutBox" runat="server"></asp:Label>
      <asp:Timer ID="Timer1" runat="server" Interval="5000">
      </asp:Timer>
    </ContentTemplate>
    <Triggers>
      <asp:AsyncPostBackTrigger ControlID="btnAddShout"
          EventName="Click" />
    </Triggers>
  </asp:UpdatePanel><br />
  <asp:UpdatePanel ID="ShoutBoxPanel2" runat="server"
      UpdateMode="Conditional">
    <ContentTemplate>
      <table>
        <tr>
          <td class="style7">Name:</td>
          <td class="style8">
            <asp:TextBox ID="txtUserName" runat="server"
                MaxLength="15" Width="100px"></asp:TextBox></td>
        </tr>
        <tr>
          <td class="style7">Shout:</td>
          <td class="style8">
            <asp:TextBox ID="txtShout" runat="server"
                MaxLength="255" Width="220px"></asp:TextBox></td>
        </tr>
      </table>
```

Figure 25-14   The aspx and css files for the Shout Box application (part 2 of 3)

The Default.aspx file   Page 3

```
            <asp:RequiredFieldValidator ID="RequiredFieldValidator1"
                runat="server" ErrorMessage="Name is required."
                ControlToValidate="txtUserName" Display="Dynamic">
            </asp:RequiredFieldValidator>
            <asp:RequiredFieldValidator ID="RequiredFieldValidator2"
                runat="server" ErrorMessage="Shout is required."
                ControlToValidate="txtShout" Display="Dynamic">
            </asp:RequiredFieldValidator>
            <asp:Button ID="btnAddShout" runat="server" Text="Add Shout" />
            <asp:UpdateProgress ID="UpdateProgress1" runat="server"
                DynamicLayout="False">
              <ProgressTemplate>
                <img src="Images/spinner.gif" alt="Please Wait"
                    style="vertical-align: middle" />
                Uploading Comment...
              </ProgressTemplate>
            </asp:UpdateProgress>
          </ContentTemplate>
        </asp:UpdatePanel>
      </td>
    </tr>
  </table>
  <asp:SqlDataSource ID="SqlDataSource2" runat="server"
      ConnectionString="<%$ ConnectionStrings:HalloweenConnectionString %>"
      SelectCommand="SELECT [ProductID], [Name], [UnitPrice], [OnHand]
                    FROM [Products]
                    WHERE ([CategoryID] = @CategoryID)
                    ORDER BY [ProductID]">
    <SelectParameters>
      <asp:ControlParameter Name="CategoryID" Type="String"
          ControlID="Category" PropertyName="SelectedValue" />
    </SelectParameters>
  </asp:SqlDataSource>
  </div>
  </form>
</body>
</html>
```

The ShoutBox.css file

```
#ShoutBoxPanel1
{
  height: 300px;
  border: solid 1px black;
  overflow: auto;
}

#ShoutBoxPanel1 dl
{
  margin-top: 0px;
}
```

Figure 25-14   The aspx and css files for the Shout Box application (part 3 of 3)

The code-behind file

Figure 25-15 presents the code-behind file for the Shout Box application. This file consists of two event handlers. The first one is executed each time the page is posted back to the server, and the second one occurs when the user clicks the Add Shout button.

The Page_Load event handler starts by declaring a shout box object from the ShoutItemList class. Then, it checks if the application state object contains an item named ShoutBox. If it doesn't, a new shout box object is created from the ShoutItemList class, and this object is added to application state. Otherwise, the ShoutBox item in application state is assigned to the shout box object, the Display method of that object is used to get the text for the shout box, and that text is assigned to the Text property of the label that displays the shout box.

Finally, the Load event handler checks if the page is being processed as the result of an asynchronous postback. If it isn't, the focus is moved to the User Name text box to make it easy for the user to enter a shout.

If the user enters data into the Name and Shout text boxes and then clicks the Add Shout button, the Click event handler for that button is executed. This event handler starts by creating a new shout from the ShoutItem class. Then, it assigns the text in the Name and Shout text boxes to the UserName and Comment properties of the shout item, and it assigns the current time to the Timestamp property.

Next, this event handler locks application state so that another user can't modify it at the same time. Then, it gets a reference to the ShoutBox item in application state, stores it in a ShoutItemList variable named shoutBox, adds the shout to the shout box, and unlocks application state.

Finally, the Display method of the shout box is called to get the updated text for the shout box, and this text is assigned to the Text property of the label for the shout box. In addition, the Text property of the Shout text box is cleared and the focus is moved to that text box to prepare for the user's next entry.

The Default.aspx.cs file

```
using System;
using System.Configuration;
using System.Data;
using System.Linq;
using System.Web;
using System.Web.Security;
using System.Web.UI;
using System.Web.UI.HtmlControls;
using System.Web.UI.WebControls;
using System.Web.UI.WebControls.WebParts;
using System.Xml.Linq;

public partial class _Default : System.Web.UI.Page
{
    protected void Page_Load(object sender, EventArgs e)
    {
        ShoutItemList shoutBox;
        if (Application["ShoutBox"] == null)
        {
            shoutBox = new ShoutItemList();
            Application.Add("ShoutBox", shoutBox);
        }
        else
        {
            shoutBox = (ShoutItemList) Application["ShoutBox"];
            lblShoutBox.Text = shoutBox.Display();
        }
        if (ScriptManager1.IsInAsyncPostBack != true)
            txtUserName.Focus();
    }

    protected void btnAddShout_Click(object sender, EventArgs e)
    {
        ShoutItem shout = new ShoutItem();
        shout.UserName = txtUserName.Text;
        shout.Comment = txtShout.Text;
        shout.Timestamp = DateTime.Now;

        Application.Lock();
        ShoutItemList shoutBox = (ShoutItemList) Application["ShoutBox"];
        shoutBox.Add(shout);
        Application.UnLock();

        lblShoutBox.Text = shoutBox.Display();
        txtShout.Text = "";
        txtShout.Focus();
    }
}
```

Figure 25-15   The code-behind file for the Shout Box application

Perspective

In this chapter, you've learned how AJAX works and how it's implemented in ASP.NET. At this point, you should have a basic understanding of the features that the Microsoft AJAX Library provides. In addition, you should be able to use the ASP.NET AJAX server controls to develop AJAX-enabled web applications of your own.

Of course, there's a lot more to learn about AJAX than what's presented here. In particular, you'll want to learn more about the controls that are available in the ASP.NET AJAX Control Toolkit. The best way to do that is to go to the web site listed in figure 25-6 and review the controls it contains. Then, you can download this toolkit and use any of these controls in your own applications.

Terms

rich Internet application (RIA)
Asynchronous JavaScript and XML (AJAX)
JavaScript
Document Object Model (DOM)
JavaScript Object Notation (JSON)
Dynamic HTML (DHTML)
asynchronous postback
Microsoft AJAX Library
ASP.NET AJAX Control Toolkit
web service proxy

26

How to configure and deploy ASP.NET applications

This chapter presents the ways that ASP.NET applications can be configured and deployed. After this chapter presents two tools for configuring an application, it presents three general ways to deploy an application. Then, it presents four specific deployment techniques.

How to configure an ASP.NET application 840
How to use the Web Site Administration Tool 840
How to use the IIS Management Console with Windows XP 842
How to use the IIS Management Console with Windows Vista 844
How to deploy an ASP.NET application 846
Three ways to deploy a ASP.NET application 846
How to use the Copy Web Site command for XCopy deployment 848
How to use the Publish Web Site command for precompiled deployment 850
How to use the aspnet_compiler command for precompiled deployment 852
How to create a Web Setup project 854
How to create and use a Setup program 856
Perspective 858

How to configure an ASP.NET application

As with previous versions of ASP.NET, the web.config file controls the configuration of an ASP.NET 3.5 application. As a result, you usually need to change this file not only during the development of an application but also when it is deployed. For example, you need to create a connection string to access the application's database when you develop the application. But if you move the database to another server when the application is deployed, you need to adjust the connection string to point to the correct database.

Although you can edit the web.config file for an application manually, this technique is error prone. Because of that, you'll want to use one of the GUI tools for working with an application's configuration. These tools are presented in the topics that follow.

How to use the Web Site Administration Tool

As figure 26-1 shows, the Web Site Administration Tool is a web-based editor that lets you specify certain configuration options. This tool uses a tabbed interface that lets you switch between the home page and the pages that configure security, application, and provider settings.

The Security and Provider tabs let you configure the ASP.NET authentication and provider features. You can refer to chapter 20 for more information on using the Security tab. And if you ever create your own custom providers, you shouldn't have any trouble using the Provider tab.

The Application tab lets you create custom application settings that appear in the appSettings element of the web.config file and can be accessed in code by using the System.Configuration.ConfigurationManager class. In chapter 19, for example, you saw how to add a setting that specifies the path for an application. To enter this infomation using the Web Site Administration Tool, you can click the Create Application Settings link on the Application tab. Then, you can use the page that's displayed to enter the key and value for the setting.

The Application tab also lets you configure a web site to work with an SMTP server so it can send and receive email. You saw how this works in chapter 23. It also lets you configure debugging options for the site. And it lets you start and stop the site.

When you use the Web Site Administration Tool, you need to remember that it has two limitations. First, it doesn't let you set all of the configuration options that are available via the web.config file. For example, you can't use it to change the connection strings stored in the file or specify custom error pages. To edit these configuration settings, you must manually edit the web.config file or use the IIS Management Console that's described in the next two figures.

The second limitation is that you can only use the Web Site Administration Tool from within Visual Studio. As a result, you can't use this tool for a web site that's been deployed to a production server unless you can open the web site in Visual Studio.

The home page of the Web Site Administration Tool

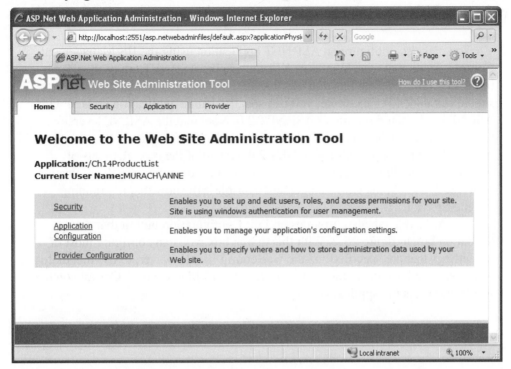

The four tabs of the Web Site Administration Tool

- **Home:** Displays the home page.
- **Security:** Lets you configure security features. For more information, see chapter 20.
- **Application:** Lets you create custom application settings, configure SMTP email support (see chapter 23), control debugging and tracing settings, and start or stop the application.
- **Provider:** Lets you configure providers for features such as membership and profiles.

Description

- The Web Site Administration Tool lets you configure certain web.config settings using a browser-based interface.
- To start the Web Site Administration Tool, open the project in Visual Studio 2008 and choose Website→ASP.NET Configuration.

Figure 26-1   How to use the Web Site Administration Tool to configure an ASP.NET 3.5 application

How to use the IIS Management Console with Windows XP

You can also configure an ASP.NET application using the IIS Management Console. To do that from Windows XP, you use the ASP.NET tab of the Properties dialog box. This tab lets you set the ASP.NET version that an application should run under. For example, you can specify that an application created with ASP.NET 1.1 should run under ASP.NET 2.0. Note that the ASP.NET versions that are available from this tab don't include ASP.NET 3.5. That's because ASP.NET 3.5 is a superset of ASP.NET 2.0, and all of the core elements of ASP.NET are included in ASP.NET 2.0. So even if you create a web application with ASP.NET 3.5, the IIS Management Console will show that it's running under ASP.NET 2.0.

The ASP.NET tab also provides an Edit Configuration button that displays the dialog box in figure 26-2. With this dialog box, you can configure most of the settings that are specified via the web.config file. However, to use this dialog box, you must have the authorization to run the IIS Management Console on the server that hosts the application.

The ASP.NET Configuration Settings dialog box

The seven tabs of the ASP.NET Configuration Settings dialog box

- **General:** Creates connection strings and application settings.
- **Custom Errors:** Configures custom error pages.
- **Authorization:** Creates authorization rules.
- **Authentication:** Specifies the authentication mode and configures membership and role providers.
- **Application:** Configures application settings such as the default master page and theme.
- **State Management:** Configures session state settings.
- **Locations:** Adds Location elements to the web.config file that let you apply configuration settings to specific parts of the application.

Description

- The IIS Management Console includes an ASP.NET Configuration Settings dialog box that lets you configure the web.config file for an ASP.NET application.
- The ASP.NET Configuration Settings dialog box lets you configure more web.config settings than the Web Site Administration Tool, but it only works for IIS-based applications.
- To open the ASP.NET Configuration Settings dialog box, open the IIS Management Console, right-click the web site, and choose Properties. Then, click the ASP.NET tab and click the Edit Configuration button.

Figure 26-2   How to use the IIS Management Console to configure an ASP.NET application with Windows XP

How to use the IIS Management Console with Windows Vista

You can also use the IIS Management Console to configure an ASP.NET application under Windows Vista. However, the user interface for this program under Windows Vista is quite different from the interface under Windows XP. In figure 26-3, for example, you can see the home page that's displayed for a web site.

To configure an ASP.NET application, you use the features that are listed in the ASP.NET area of the home page. To define the roles for an application, for example, you can double-click on the .NET Roles icon. Then, you can use the page that's displayed along with the commands in the Actions menu to create new roles and work with existing roles.

The IIS Management Console for an ASP.NET application

Description

- You can configure the web.config file for an ASP.NET application from the Home page for the application in the IIS Management Console. To do that, you work with the features that are available from the ASP.NET area of this page.

- The IIS Management Console for Windows Vista provides many of the same features for configuring ASP.NET applications as Windows XP. These features are organized and presented differently, however.

- To configure an ASP.NET application, highlight it in the Connections pane, and then double-click on a feature in the Home page to display a page for working with that feature.

Figure 26-3   How to use the IIS Management Console to configure an ASP.NET application with Windows Vista

How to deploy an ASP.NET application

Deployment refers to the process of copying an ASP.NET web application from the development system to the production server on which the application will be run. As the following topics explain, ASP.NET provides several alternatives for deploying web applications.

Three ways to deploy a ASP.NET application

Figure 26-4 lists the three basic approaches to deploying an ASP.NET application. The first is commonly called *XCopy deployment* because it simply copies the files required by the application to the production server. To do that, you can use the DOS XCopy command, or you can use the Copy Web Site command from within Visual Studio as described in figure 26-5.

The second way to deploy a web site is called *precompiled deployment*. This type of deployment that lets you compile the pages of an application before deploying the application to the production server. Then, the precompiled assemblies are copied to the server. To use this method of deployment, you can use the Publish Web Site command from within Visual Studio as shown in figure 26-6. Or, you can use the aspnet_compiler command from a command prompt as shown in figure 26-7.

The third way to deploy a web application is to develop a Web Setup project that creates a Windows *Setup program* for the application. Then, you can run this Setup program on the production server to install the application. This approach is described in figures 26-8 and 26-9.

Which of these deployment alternatives is the best choice depends on the particular needs of each application. XCopy deployment is the easiest, and it's often used during development to create copies of an application on different servers for testing purposes. For small applications, XCopy deployment may also be the best choice for production deployment.

Precompiled deployment has several advantages over XCopy deployment. For example, precompiled deployment provides better performance for the first users that access the site. In addition, it provides increased security because you don't have to copy the application's source files to the server.

For applications that are deployed to one or just a few servers, precompiled deployment is usually the best choice. However, if you're distributing an application to many different servers, you should consider creating a Setup program for the application. Although creating this program can involve considerable work, the effort will be repaid each time you use the program to install the application.

XCopy deployment

- To manually copy the files of an ASP.NET web site to a server, you can use the XCopy command from a command prompt. Then, you can use the IIS Management Console to create a virtual directory that's mapped to the directory that you copied the web site to.
- To automate the deployment, you can create a batch file for the XCopy command. Then, you can run the batch file any time you make changes to the application and want to deploy the updated code.
- You can also do XCopy deployment from Visual Studio by using the Copy Web Site command (see figure 26-5).

Precompiled deployment

- Deploys precompiled assemblies to the specified server.
- Lets you deploy the web site with or without the source files.
- Can be done from within Visual Studio using the Publish Web Site command (see figure 26-6) or from a command prompt using the aspnet_compiler command (see figure 26-7).

Setup program deployment

- Uses a Web Setup project to build a Windows Setup program that can be run to deploy a web application to a server (see figures 26-8 and 26-9).
- Useful if you want to distribute a web application to multiple servers.
- Can be used to deploy precompiled assemblies and can be configured to include or omit the source files.
- An application that's installed by a Setup program can be removed by using the Add or Remove Programs dialog box that can be accessed from the Control Panel.

Description

- There are three general methods for deploying ASP.NET applications: *XCopy deployment*, *precompiled deployment*, and *Setup program* deployment.
- The method you should use for deployment depends on how often the application will need to be deployed and whether you want to include the source code with the deployed application.

Figure 26-4   Three ways to deploy an ASP.NET application

How to use the Copy Web Site command for XCopy deployment

To implement XCopy deployment from within Visual Studio, you use the Copy Web Site command shown in figure 26-5. This command lets you copy a web site to a file system, local IIS, FTP, or remote IIS web site. In addition, it lets you copy all of the files in the web site or just selected files, and you can use it to synchronize web sites so that both sites have the most recently updated versions of each file.

To use this command, open the web site you want to copy and start the command to display the dialog box shown in this figure. Here, the Source Web Site section lists the files in the current web site. Next, click the Connect button to display an Open Web Site dialog box that lets you pick the location you want to copy the web site to. If you're copying to a local or remote IIS system, you can also use this dialog box to create a new IIS or virtual directory on the server if the directory doesn't already exist.

Once you select the remote web site, its files will appear in the Remote Web Site section of the dialog box. You can then select the files you want to copy in the Source Web Site list and click the right-arrow button that appears between the lists to copy the files from the source web site to the remote web site. You can use the other buttons to copy files from the remote web site to the source web site, to synchronize files in the web sites, or to stop a lengthy copy operation.

The Copy Web Site dialog box

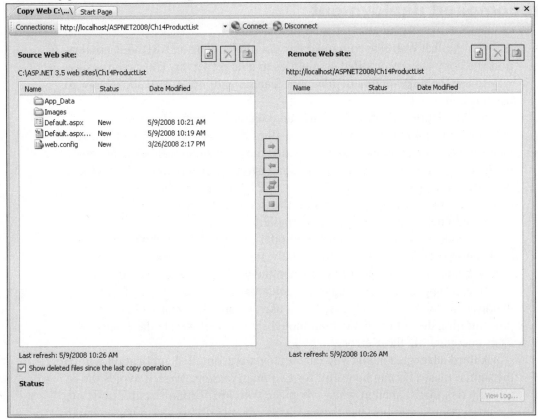

How to use the Copy Web Site command

1. In Visual Studio, open the web site you want to deploy and choose the Website→Copy Web Site command.
2. Click the Connect button to display an Open Web Site dialog box that lets you choose the destination you want to copy the web site to.
3. Select the files you want to copy. (Press Ctrl+A to select all of the site's files.)
4. Click the → button to copy the files from the source web site to the remote web site.

Description

*   You can use the Copy Web Site command to deploy a web application with XCopy deployment.

Figure 26-5   How to use the Copy Web Site command for XCopy deployment

How to use the Publish Web Site command for precompiled deployment

The Publish Web Site command lets you precompile an ASP.NET application and copy the precompiled assemblies to a target server. This is the easiest way to use the precompiled deployment feature, and figure 26-6 shows how to use this command.

As this figure indicates, there are three main advantages to using precompiled deployment. First, because all of the pages are compiled before the web site is deployed to the server, it avoids the delays that can be encountered by the first visitors to the web site. In contrast, when precompiled deployment isn't used, each page is compiled by the ASP.NET runtime the first time the page is accessed by a user. As a result, the first user to retrieve each page will encounter a delay while the page is compiled.

A second advantage is that any compiler errors will be found before the application is deployed. Although unlikely, it's possible for pages in a production web site to become out of sync when the application is deployed. For example, a supporting class might be accidentally omitted. Then, when a page that uses that class is first accessed by a user, a compiler error will occur. By precompiling the entire application, though, you can eliminate the chance of users encountering these errors.

A third advantage is that you can deploy a precompiled application without the source files. This can be useful for two main reasons. First, it avoids the security risk that's inherent when you place your application's source code on the production server because there's always the possibility that a hacker might exploit a vulnerability in IIS and access your code. Second, if you develop a commercial application and don't want your customers to be able to access your source code, this makes that possible.

To omit the source code from a precompiled application, you uncheck the Allow This Precompiled Site To Be Updatable box. Then, the source files won't be copied to the production server. Instead, dummy files with the same names as the source files will be copied to the server. If you open one of these files, you'll find that it contains a single line with the following text:

```
This is a marker file generated by the precompilation tool,
and should not be deleted!
```

Although these dummy files are required for the application to work, their contents are ignored by the ASP.NET runtime.

The Publish Web Site dialog box

Advantages of precompiling a web site

- Avoids delays caused by compiling web pages when they are first accessed by a user.
- Finds compile errors before the site is deployed.
- Can copy just the executable files and not the source files to the server.

Description

- The Build→Publish Web Site command compiles all of the files that make up an ASP.NET application, and then deploys the compiled assemblies to the location you specify.
- If you check the Allow This Precompiled Site To Be Updatable box, the source files are deployed along with the executable files. If you leave this box unchecked, the source files aren't deployed.

Note

- The Publish Web Site command isn't available in the Visual Web Developer Express Edition.

Figure 26-6   How to use the Publish Web Site command for precompiled deployment

How to use the aspnet_compiler command for precompiled deployment

Figure 26-7 shows how to use the aspnet_compiler command from a command prompt to precompile a web site. This is simply a command-line version of the Publish Web Site command.

When you use the aspnet_compiler command, the precompiled assemblies are copied to the target directory. If you specify the –u switch, the source files are copied along with the precompiled assemblies and the site will be updateable. If you omit this switch, the source files won't be copied and the site will not be updateable.

Note that the aspnet_compiler command is located in the .NET Framework directory, and the exact name of this directory may be slightly different on your system. On my system, for example, this directory is C:\Windows\Microsoft.NET\Framework\v2.0.50727.

The syntax of the aspnet_compiler command

```
aspnet_compiler -v virtual-directory [-u] [-d] [-f] [target-directory]
```

Switches

Switch	Description
-v	Precedes the name of the virtual directory of the existing web site to be precompiled.
-u	The precompiled web site will be updateable.
-d	Debug information will be included in the compiled assemblies.
-f	Overwrites the target directory if it already exists.

Examples

Precompiles an existing web site

```
aspnet_compiler -v Ch05ProductList c:\Deploy\Ch05ProductList
```

Precompiles a web site in place

```
aspnet_compiler -v Ch05ProductList
```

Creates an updateable precompiled web site with debugging information

```
aspnet_compiler -v Ch05ProductList -u -d c:\Deploy\Ch05ProductList
```

Description

- You can use the aspnet_compiler command to precompile a web site from a command prompt.
- If you specify a target directory, the precompiled web site is stored in the directory you specify. If you don't specify a target directory, the web site is precompiled in place.
- If the target directory isn't the final destination for an application, you can use XCopy deployment to move the precompiled web site to that destination.

Note

- The aspnet_compiler command is located in the .NET Framework 2.0 directory, which is %systemroot%\Microsoft.NET\Framework\v2.0.xxxxx, where *%systemroot%* is the root directory for Windows and *xxxxx* is the five-digit build number.

Figure 26-7   How to use the aspnet_compiler command for precompiled deployment

How to create a Web Setup project

Another way to deploy a web application is to develop a *Web Setup project* that creates a standard Windows *Setup program* that you can use to install the web application on an IIS server. As figure 26-8 shows, you start by adding a Web Setup project to an existing web site. Then, you configure the Web Setup project so it installs the files required by the web application. You can also use the setup editors to configure many custom options that control how the application will be installed.

You can use the File System Editor shown in this figure to add files and folders to the setup project. To add a Readme file, for example, you can right-click the Web Application Folder in the left pane of the File System Editor and then select Add→File. Note that the Web Application Folder represents the virtual directory where the web application will be installed, and it has properties that define that virtual directory. The two properties you're most likely to change are VirtualDirectory, which specifies the name of the virtual directory, and DefaultDocument, which specifies the page that's displayed by default.

You can use the Registry Editor to specify the keys and values that should be added to the registry on the target computer. And you can use the File Types Editor to establish a file association between a file extension and an application on the target computer. Since most web applications don't need to adjust registry settings or create file type associations, you shouldn't need either of these editors. However, the other three editors can be useful.

The User Interface Editor lets you customize the dialog boxes that are displayed when you run the Setup program to install a web application. For example, you can change the BannerBitMap property of any dialog box to display your company's logo in that dialog box. This editor also lets you add your own dialog boxes to those that are displayed by the Setup program.

The Custom Actions Editor lets you add actions to those that are performed by the Setup program. For example, you can use a custom action to create a SQL Server database when the application is installed. Before you can add a custom action to a Setup project, though, you must first develop a batch file, a script, or an executable program that implements the action.

Finally, the Launch Conditions Editor lets you set conditions that must be met before the application can be installed. For example, you can use a launch condition to check the operating system version or to see if a particular file exists on the target system. If the condition isn't met, the Setup program aborts the installation.

In addition to using the setup editors, you can set properties of the Setup project. Some of those properties provide support information and are displayed in the Support Info dialog box. The user can display this information by opening Add or Remove Programs in the Control Panel, selecting the application, and clicking the Click Here for Support Information link for the application. Other properties provide additional information about the application, such as the icon that's displayed for the application in the Add or Remove Programs dialog box and the product name that's displayed by the Setup program and in the Add or Remove Programs dialog box.

A Web Setup project with the File System Editor displayed

How to create a Setup project

- Choose the File→Add→New Project command to display the Add New Project dialog box. Then, choose Setup and Deployment in the Other Project Types list, select Web Setup Project as the template, enter a name for the Web Setup project, and click OK.

- In the Solution Explorer, right-click the Web Setup project and choose the Add→Project Output command to display the Add Project Output Group dialog box. Then, click OK to add the content files from your web site to the Web Setup project.

- Use the buttons that are displayed at the top of the Solution Explorer when the Web Setup project is selected to access setup editors that let you customize various aspects of the Web Setup project.

Description

- A *Web Setup project* creates a standard Windows *Setup program* that installs the web application on an IIS server. To create a Web Setup project, add a Web Setup project to the web site you want to deploy and then configure it using the setup editors.

- You can set project properties that provide support and other information for the application. You can also set properties that provide information about the virtual directory where the application will be installed, which is represented by the Web Application Folder in the File System Editor shown above.

Figure 26-8   How to create a Web Setup project

How to create and use a Setup program

Once you've configured the Web Setup project, you can create the Setup program and install the application as described in figure 26-9. To start, you should choose whether you want to create a debug or release version of the application. Because the debug version contains symbolic debugging information that you don't typically need in a production application, and because this version isn't optimized, you'll usually create a release version. On the other hand, you may want to create a debug version during testing. To determine which version is created, you can use the Configuration Manager as described in this figure.

Next, you build the Setup project. This creates the setup files (Setup.exe and Setup.msi) in the Debug or Release folder of the project, depending on whether a debug or release version is created. Then, in most cases, you'll copy these files to a network server or burn them to a CD or DVD. Finally, you can install the application by running the Setup.exe program from the server that will host the application.

Note that the Setup program itself is a standard Windows application, not a web application. As a result, the Setup.exe and Setup.msi files aren't found in the same directory as the web application. Instead, you'll find these files in the project directory for the Web Setup project, which you can find under My Documents\Visual Studio 2008\Projects by default.

When you run a Setup program to install the web application on the host server, it steps you through the installation process. In this figure, for example, you can see the screen for one of the steps of a typical Setup program. Here, the application will be deployed to the default web site in a virtual directory named HalloweenProductList.

The Select Installation Address step of a typical Setup program

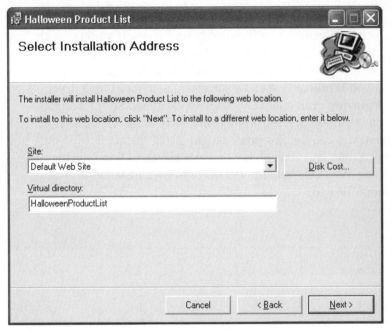

Description

- To create a Setup program, right-click the Setup project in the Solution Explorer and then use the Build command. When you do, Visual Studio creates files named Setup.exe and Setup.msi. Setup.exe is the file you will run to install the application, and Setup.msi contains all of the files to be installed.

- The Setup.exe and Setup.msi files are stored in the Web Setup project's Debug or Release folder, depending on whether Visual Studio is configured to create a debug or release version of the Setup project. In most cases, you'll want to create a release version because it's fully optimized and contains no debugging information.

- To change the version of the Setup program that Visual Studio creates, use the Build→Configuration Manager command. Then, use the Configuration drop-down list for the Web Setup project to select the version you want to create.

- To install the web application, copy the Setup.exe and Setup.msi files to a network server or burn them to a CD or DVD. Then, run the Setup program on the server that will host the application.

Figure 26-9   How to create and use a Setup program

Perspective

As you develop a web application, you'll probably find yourself working with both the Web Site Administration Tool and the IIS Management Console. In addition, you'll often find yourself editing the web.config file directly.

As for deployment, you'll probably spend a surprising amount of time developing procedures for deploying even relatively small applications. So for a large application, I recommend that you develop a procedure early in the application's development cycle. Then, you can use this procedure to install the application on multiple servers during testing, and you can use that experience to fine-tune the procedure as you go along. As a side benefit, you may discover installation issues that affect the application's design.

Terms

deployment
XCopy deployment
precompiled deployment
Web Setup project
Setup program

Section 5

Developing reusable code

This section consists of three chapters that show you three different ways to develop reusable code. In chapter 27, you'll learn how to create and use user controls. User controls are easy to develop and are typically reused within a single web application. In chapter 28, you'll learn how to create and use custom server controls. Custom server controls are more difficult to develop and are typically reused within multiple web applications. Finally, in chapter 29, you'll be introduced to web services. Web services allow you to write methods that can be used by any web application, even by web applications that are running under a different web server such as Apache. Web services can also be used by Windows applications.

If you're working in a large development shop, you may never need to develop user controls, custom server controls, or web services. That's because senior developers are usually given the responsibility for developing controls and services that are used across applications. In that case, though, you still need to know how to use these controls and services. And to do that, it never hurts to know what's going on behind the scenes.

27

How to develop user controls

In this chapter, you'll learn how to develop user controls and use them in the web forms you develop. As you'll see, user controls make it possible to group multiple elements into a single user control. Then, instead of recreating these elements on each page that needs them, you can include the user control. Later, if you modify the user control, the changes will be reflected on all pages that contain the user control.

An introduction to user controls **862**
A web page that contains three user controls 862
A procedure for creating and using user controls 862

How to create user controls **864**
How to add a user control to a project 864
How to design a user control 864
How to code a user control 866
How to expose properties, methods, and events 868

How to use user controls **872**
How to add a user control to a web form 872
The aspx code that's generated when you add a user control to a form 874
How to write code that works with properties, methods, and events 876

The ProductDisplay user control **878**
The design 878
The ascx file 878
The code-behind file 878

Perspective **882**

An introduction to user controls

A *user control* is a special type of ASP.NET page that can be added to other pages. In figure 27-1, for example, you can see a web page that contains three user controls, along with a procedure for creating and using user controls.

A web page that contains three user controls

Figure 27-1 presents a new page of the Halloween Store application called the Featured Products page. This page uses three user controls. The first two controls are ProductDisplay controls that contain information about a product. In addition to this information, these controls also include an Add to Cart button that adds the product to the cart and a View Cart button that lets the user view the cart. The third control is a DaysUntil control that displays a message that includes the number of days until Halloween.

As you decide what to include in each user control, keep in mind that the major benefit of user controls is that they are reusable. That means that you want to design a user control so it can be used in two or more places within a web site. For example, the ProductDisplay control is used twice on the Featured Products page. Although it's not shown here, it's also used on the Order page. Similarly, the DaysUntil control could be used on almost any page of the Halloween Store web site.

If you need to, you can change all the pages that contain a user control by changing the user control. In contrast, if you don't use a user control, you have to change each page separately.

A procedure for creating and using user controls

Figure 27-1 also presents a procedure for creating and using user controls. To start, you add a new user control to the web site. Then, you can use the User Control Designer that's displayed to design the control. As you'll see, this designer works much like the Web Forms Designer you use to design web forms.

Next, you add any code that's necessary to implement the control. For instance, the code for the DaysUntil control in this figure must create the message that's displayed. This code is added to the code-behind file for the user control. This works the same as adding code to the code-behind file for a form.

After you create a user control, you can add it to any form in the project. Then, if necessary, you can set its properties, and you can add code for working with the control to the form.

A Featured Products page that contains three user controls

Browser window showing the Halloween Superstore Featured Products page, with callouts pointing to **ProductDisplay.ascx** and **DaysUntil.ascx**.

Concepts

- A *user control* is a special type of ASP.NET web page that has been converted to a control. A user control is stored in a separate file so that it can be added to any form in a project.

- User controls are typically used to develop page elements that can be used in multiple places within a web site.

- Like an ASP.NET web page, a user control can handle Page events such as the Load event. You code the event handlers for those events in the code-behind file for the control.

A procedure for creating and using user controls

1. Add a new user control to the project.
2. Design the user control using the User Control Designer.
3. Add the code to implement the control using the Code Editor.
4. Add the control to any form in the project.
5. If necessary, set any properties of the user control using the Properties window.
6. If necessary, add code to the form that contains the user control using the Code Editor.

Figure 27-1   An introduction to user controls

How to create user controls

Now that you know the basic procedure for creating user controls, the topics that follow present the details. As you'll see, the techniques you use are similar to the techniques you use to create a web form.

How to add a user control to a project

To add a user control to a project, you use the Website→Add New Item command to display the Add New Item dialog box. Then, you select the Web User Control template and enter a name for the control.

After you create a user control, it will appear in the Solution Explorer as shown in figure 27-2. The user control shown here is the DaysUntilHalloween control, which is a simplified version of the DaysUntil control you saw in the previous figure. Note that the file extension for a user control is *ascx*.

This figure also shows the code in the ascx file that Visual Studio generated for the DaysUntilHalloween control. This code begins with a Control directive that's similar to the Page directive for a web form. In particular, it includes a CodeFile attribute that associates the control with its code-behind file. In addition, it includes an Inherits attribute that provides the name of the class in the code-behind file that the control will inherit at runtime.

How to design a user control

After you add a user control to a project, it appears in the *User Control Designer* shown in figure 27-2. Then, you can add ASP.NET controls to the control by dragging them from the Toolbox. In this figure, for example, I added a label to the user control. Then, I set the ID property of the label to lblDaysUntilHalloween, and I set the Text property of the label so it contains some text that approximates what the control will look like at runtime.

You can also add HTML elements to a control by typing the appropriate tags directly into Source view. Note, however, that a user control shouldn't contain a Body or Form element. That's because the control will be added to a form, which already contains these elements.

A user control displayed by the User Control Designer

The ascx code for the user control

```
<%@ Control Language="C#" AutoEventWireup="true"
CodeFile="DaysUntilHalloween.ascx.cs" Inherits="DaysUntilHalloween" %>

<asp:Label ID="lblDaysUntilHalloween" runat="server">
    Today is xx/xx/xxxx. There are only x more days until Halloween.
</asp:Label>
```

Description

- To add a user control to a project, use the Website→Add New Item command to display the Add New Item dialog box. Then, use the Web User Control template to create a user control with the name you specify.

- When you add a user control, it will appear in the Solution Explorer with an extension of *ascx*.

- You can use the *User Control Designer* to add ASP.NET controls and HTML elements to the control. A user control should not include a Body or a Form element.

- The ascx code for a user control begins with a Control directive that's generated by Visual Studio when you create the user control. This directive includes Language, AutoEventWireup, CodeFile, and Inherits attributes just as the Page directive of a page does.

Figure 27-2   How to design a user control

How to code a user control

Before you begin coding user controls, you need to be familiar with the sequence of events that are raised for a page that contains user controls. That way, you can be sure to code the user control appropriately. Figure 27-3 presents this sequence of events.

To start, ASP.NET raises the Load event of the page. Then, it raises the Load event for each user control that the page contains. By default, the Load events for the user controls are raised in the order in which the controls are added to the form. To avoid problems, however, you should code your user controls so they don't depend on other user controls.

After the Load events are raised and processed, ASP.NET raises the control events that result from the user interacting with the page. If the user selects a check box, for example, the CheckedChanged event of that control is raised. Finally, the PreRender event of the page is raised, followed by the PreRender event of each user control.

This figure also presents the code for the DaysUntilHalloween user control. The first thing you should notice here is that the class that defines the control inherits the System.Web.UI.UserControl class. Because this class provides many of the same properties, methods, and events as the System.Web.UI.Page class, the code you use to implement a user control is similar to the code you would use to implement the same function in a web form. For example, you can use the Load event to execute code each time the control is loaded.

You can also use many properties of the UserControl class just as you would use them in the Page class. For example, you can use the Request and Response properties to work with the HttpRequest and HttpResponse objects. You can use the Session property to work with the HttpSessionState object. And you can use the IsPostBack property to determine whether the page that contains the user control is being displayed for the first time or if it's being posted back to the server. The IsPostBack property is illustrated in the Load event handler shown here. As you can see, the code in this event handler is executed only if the page is being displayed for the first time. Then, the label that the user control contains is formatted so that it displays the current date and the number of days until Halloween.

In addition to the properties, methods, and events a user control inherits from the UserControl class, you can add your own properties, methods, and events to a user control. Then, you can access those properties, methods, and events from the page that contains the control. You'll learn how to expose properties, methods, and events in the next figure, and you'll learn how to work with those properties, methods, and events later in this chapter.

The sequence of events that are raised for a page with user controls

1. The Load event for the page.
2. The Load event for each user control.
3. Control events caused by user interaction with the page.
4. The PreRender event for the page.
5. The PreRender event for each user control.

The C# code for the DaysUntilHalloween user control

```csharp
public partial class DaysUntilHalloween : System.Web.UI.UserControl
{
    protected void Page_Load(object sender, EventArgs e)
    {
        if (!IsPostBack)
        {
            lblDaysUntilHalloween.Text = "Today is ";
            lblDaysUntilHalloween.Text += DateTime.Today.ToShortDateString();
            lblDaysUntilHalloween.Text += ". There are only ";
            lblDaysUntilHalloween.Text += this.GetDaysUntilHalloween();
            lblDaysUntilHalloween.Text += " more days until Halloween.";
        }
    }

    private int GetDaysUntilHalloween()
    {
        DateTime halloween = new DateTime(DateTime.Today.Year, 10, 31);
        if (DateTime.Today > halloween)
            halloween = halloween.AddYears(1);
        TimeSpan timeUntil = halloween - DateTime.Today;
        return timeUntil.Days;
    }
}
```

Description

- You can use the Code Editor to add code to the code-behind file that's generated for a user control. The code-behind file should only contain code that's directly related to the user control. It shouldn't contain code that depends on code in other controls.

- You can define properties and methods within a user control and then access them from the page that contains the control. You can also define and raise events within a user control and then respond to them from the page that contains the control. See figures 27-4 and 27-7 for details.

- The class for a user control inherits the System.Web.UI.UserControl class. This class includes many of the same properties as a page, including IsPostBack, Request, Response, Server, and Session. This class also contains a Page property that refers to the Page object that contains the control.

Figure 27-3   How to code a user control

How to expose properties, methods, and events

Figure 27-4 presents the C# code for the DaysUntil user control that you saw in figure 27-1. This control exposes four properties. The first two properties let the developer change the text that's displayed before and after the number of days until a specified date. And the second two properties let the developer specify the date by setting the month and the day. As a result, you could display a message that indicates the number of days until Christmas or any other day of the year. This makes the control more flexible and increases the chance that it will be reused.

The values of the four properties are stored in the private variables that are declared at the beginning of the class. Notice that these variables are assigned default values that are used if the developer doesn't set the corresponding properties. As a result, this control works similarly to the DaysUntilHalloween control by default.

After the variable declarations is the code that declares the four public properties. Each property begins with a *designer attribute* that's coded in square brackets. This attribute determines how the property will be displayed in the Web Forms Designer. In this figure, all four properties include a Category attribute that specifies the category in the Properties window where the property will appear. Here, all four properties will be displayed in the Appearance category.

To use designer attributes like this, a user control must include the System.ComponentModel namespace as shown here. Then, the control can use any of the attributes defined by this namespace. Since you're more likely to use attributes like this with custom server controls, you can learn more about them in the next chapter. Note, however, that these attributes don't always work the same way for user controls as they do for custom server controls.

The C# code for the DaysUntil control   **Page 1**

```csharp
using System.ComponentModel;

public partial class DaysUntil : System.Web.UI.UserControl
{
    private string textBefore = "There are only";
    private string textAfter = "days until Halloween.";
    private int month = 10;
    private int day = 31;

    [Category("Appearance")]
    public string TextBefore
    {
        get
        {
            return textBefore;
        }
        set
        {
            textBefore = value;
        }
    }
    [Category("Appearance")]
    public string TextAfter
    {
        get
        {
            return textAfter;
        }
        set
        {
            textAfter = value;
        }
    }
    [Category("Appearance")]
    public int Month
    {
        get
        {
            return month;
        }
        set
        {
            month = value;
        }
    }
    [Category("Appearance")]
    public int Day
    {
        get
        {
            return day;
        }
        set
        {
            day = value;
        }
    }
```

Figure 27-4   How to expose properties, methods, and events (part 1 of 2)

On page 2 of the code listing for the DaysUntil control, you can see the event handler for the Load event of this control. This event handler creates an appropriate message and assigns it to the Text property of the label named lblDaysUntil. To do that, it uses the four properties declared by the control.

To start, the value of the TextBefore property is assigned to the label, followed by a space. Then, the value returned by the DaysUntilDate method is appended to the label. This method uses the Month and Day properties to get the number of days until the specified date. Finally, a space and the value stored in the TextAfter property are appended to the label.

Although the DaysUntil control only exposes properties, it could also expose methods or events. To expose a method or event, you just code it with the public keyword like any other method or event. You can also expose a field by declaring it with the public keyword. However, you're more likely to use public properties since public fields aren't displayed in the Properties window of the Web Forms Designer.

The C# code for the DaysUntil control   **Page 2**

```csharp
protected void Page_Load(object sender, EventArgs e)
{
    lblDaysUntil.Text = textBefore + " ";
    lblDaysUntil.Text += this.DaysUntilDate();
    lblDaysUntil.Text += " " + textAfter;
}

private int DaysUntilDate()
{
    DateTime targetDate = new DateTime(DateTime.Today.Year, Month, Day);
    if (DateTime.Today > targetDate)
    {
        targetDate = targetDate.AddYears(1);
    }
    TimeSpan timeUntil = targetDate - DateTime.Today;
    return timeUntil.Days;
}
}
```

Description

- A user control can include public properties, methods, and events that you can work with from any page that contains the control.

- If you want to be able to set the properties of a user control at design time, you need to code a *designer attribute* that indicates how the control is used by the Web Forms Designer. Each property of the DaysUntil control includes a Category attribute that indicates the category that the property appears under in the Properties window.

- Although you can also include public fields in a user control, you're more likely to use private fields that can be accessed through public properties of the user control.

Figure 27-4   How to expose properties, methods, and events (part 2 of 2)

How to use user controls

After you design and code a user control, you can add it to any form in the web site that needs it. Then, if necessary, you can use the Web Forms Designer to set the properties for the control, and you can use the Code Editor to add code that works with the control. You'll learn how to do that in the topics that follow. You'll also see the aspx code that's generated for a user control when you add it to a form so you have a better understanding of how user controls are implemented by ASP.NET.

How to add a user control to a web form

Figure 27-5 shows how you add a user control to a web form. To do that, you simply drag the control from the Solution Explorer to the location where you want it displayed on the form. Then, ASP.NET generates a tag that registers the control so it can be used on the form. In addition, it generates a tag that displays the control. You'll see these tags in the next figure.

The form shown here is the Featured Products form. As you can see, it consists of the three user controls you saw back in figure 27-1. In this figure, the DaysUntil control at the bottom of the form is selected, and you can see the custom properties that are exposed by this control in the Properties window. Notice that all four of these properties—Day, Month, TextAfter, and TextBefore—are listed in the Appearance category of this window. That's because "Appearance" was specified for the Category attribute of each property.

In addition to the custom properties for a user control, you can also set some of the properties that are defined by the UserControl class that all user controls inherit. In this figure, for example, you can see the EnableTheming and EnableViewState properties. In addition to these properties, you can set the Visible, ID, and Runat properties.

The Featured Products page with user controls

Description

- To add a user control to an ASP.NET page, drag it from the Solution Explorer onto the page. The Web Forms Designer automatically generates all of the tags necessary to register the user control and insert it into the page.

- To set a public property of a user control, select the control in the Web Forms Designer and use the Properties window to set the property. Any custom properties you have defined for the control appear in this window, along with some of the properties provided by the UserControl class.

Figure 27-5   How to add a user control to a web form

The aspx code that's generated when you add a user control to a form

Figure 27-6 shows an example of the aspx code that's generated by the Web Forms Designer when you add user controls to a web form. This is the code for the Featured Products form you saw in the last figure. As you can see, it starts with two Register directives that register the two user controls. Each Register directive includes three attributes: Src, TagName, and TagPrefix. The Src attribute specifies the name of the ascx file that defines the user control. The TagName attribute associates a name with the control. And the TagPrefix attribute associates a prefix with the control.

The values of the TagPrefix and TagName properties are used in the opening tag for the user control to identify the control. For example, the opening tag for each ProductDisplay user control starts with uc1:ProductDisplay. Each opening tag also includes a Runat attribute and an ID attribute. These attributes work just like they do for standard ASP.NET controls.

The DaysUntil control also includes Day, Month, TextBefore, and TextAfter attributes. These attributes correspond to the properties that are defined by this control and are added when you set the values of these properties.

The aspx code for the Featured Products form that uses user controls

```
<%@ Page Language="C#" AutoEventWireup="true" CodeFile="FeaturedProducts.aspx.cs"
Inherits="FeaturedProducts" %>

<%@ Register Src="ProductDisplay.ascx" TagName="ProductDisplay" TagPrefix="uc1" %>
<%@ Register Src="DaysUntil.ascx" TagName="DaysUntil" TagPrefix="uc2" %>

<!DOCTYPE html PUBLIC "-//W3C//DTD XHTML 1.0 Transitional//EN"
"http://www.w3.org/TR/xhtml1/DTD/xhtml1-transitional.dtd">

<html xmlns="http://www.w3.org/1999/xhtml" >
<head runat="server">
    <title>Chapter 27: Halloween Store</title>
</head>
<body>
    <form id="form1" runat="server">
    <div>
        <asp:Image ID="Image1" runat="server"
            ImageUrl="~/Images/banner.jpg" /><br /><br />
        <h3>Featured Products</h3>
        <uc1:ProductDisplay id="ProductDisplay1" runat="server"
            ProductID="frankc01">
        </uc1:ProductDisplay>
        <uc1:ProductDisplay id="ProductDisplay2" runat="server"
            ProductID="super01">
        </uc1:ProductDisplay>
        <br />
        <asp:Button ID="btnContinue" runat="server"
            PostBackUrl="~/Order.aspx" Text="Continue Shopping" /><br />
        <br />
        <uc2:DaysUntil ID="DaysUntil1" runat="server"
            Day="31" Month="10"
            TextBefore="Hurry! There are only" />
            TextAfter="more shopping days until Halloween."
    </div>
    </form>
</body>
</html>
```

Description

- Visual Studio adds two elements to a page when you add a user control. The Register directive appears before the Html element and registers the user control. The user control element appears within the Form element to place the control on the form.

- The Register directive specifies a tag prefix, which is uc1 by default for the first user control that's added to the form. The number on this tag is incremented by one for each different user control that's added.

- The Register directive also specifies a tag name that corresponds to the class name for the user control.

- The user control element identifies the control by combining the tag prefix and the tag name from the Register directive.

Figure 27-6   The aspx code that's generated when you add a user control to a form

How to write code that works with properties, methods, and events

Figure 27-7 shows how to write code that works with the properties of a user control. The first code example shows how you can use the Load event handler of the page to set a property of a user control. Specifically, it shows how you can set the ProductID property of the ProductDisplay control named ProductDisplay1 to the product ID that's selected in the drop-down list named ddlProducts. (You'll see the code for this user control in just a minute.) This code is used by the Order page of the Halloween Store application. Since the Load event of the page is executed before the Load event of the user control, the Load event handler for the user control can retrieve the appropriate value from this property.

Although this figure only shows a code example for working with properties, the same principles apply to working with methods or events. For example, if the class for a user control defines a public method, you can call it from the Load event handler of the page. In addition, if the class for a user control defines and raises a public event, the page that contains the control can include an event handler to handle that event.

Code that sets a property of the control from the page that contains it

```
protected void Page_Load(object sender, EventArgs e)
{
    if (!IsPostBack)
        ddlProducts.DataBind();
    ProductDisplay1.ProductID = ddlProducts.SelectedValue;
}
```

Description

- You can use code to work with the properties, methods, and events of a user control just as you would the properties, methods, and events of any other control.

- You typically set user control properties from the event handler for the Load event of the page that contains the control. That way, the value will be set before the control's Load event handler is executed.

Figure 27-7   How to write code that works with properties, methods, and events

The ProductDisplay user control

The remaining topics in this chapter present the ProductDisplay user control that you saw in figure 27-1. As you'll see, this control is more complex than the DaysUntil control, but it's still relatively easy to create and use.

The design

Part 1 of figure 27-8 shows the design of the ProductDisplay user control. This control uses a table to align an image control, three label controls, and two button controls. It also includes a SqlDataSource control that's used to get the data that's displayed by the control.

The ascx file

Part 1 of figure 27-8 also shows the ascx code for this control. Notice that the Select statement specified by the data source includes a ProductID parameter that determines what product is retrieved by this statement. Also notice that the Parameter element for this parameter doesn't indicate where the value of this parameter comes from. In a minute, you'll see how this value is set in code.

The code-behind file

Parts 2 and 3 of figure 27-8 present the code-behind file for the ProductDisplay user control. Two private variables are used by this class. The productID variable will hold the product ID of the product that's displayed by the control, and the product variable will hold the Product object for that product.

The property named ProductID provides access to the value that's stored in the productID variable. This property includes a designer attribute that makes this property available to the developer at design time. As a result, the developer can set this property to specify the product that the control should display.

The Page_Load event handler uses the control's GetProduct method to get a Product object from the database. Notice that the first statement in the GetProduct method sets the value of the ProductID parameter to the ProductID property. That way, only the row with that product ID is retrieved. Then, the rest of the method creates the Product object if a row with the specified ID is found.

If the GetProduct method returns a Product object, the data for that object is displayed in the user control. Otherwise, the image and button controls are hidden, and a message that indicates that the product ID was not found is displayed by the labels in the control.

Finally, the btnAdd_Click event handler updates the shopping cart. This code is similar to the code you've seen elsewhere in this book, so you shouldn't have any trouble understanding how it works. The only difference is that a quantity of one is always assumed.

The design of the ProductDisplay user control

The ascx code for the ProductDisplay user control

```
<%@ Control Language="C#" AutoEventWireup="true"
    CodeFile="ProductDisplay.ascx.cs" Inherits="ProductDisplay" %>
<table id="Table1" border="0" cellpadding="5" cellspacing="0"
        style="width: 542px">
    <tr>
        <td rowspan="4" style="width: 123px; height: 140px;" valign="top">
            <asp:Image ID="imgProduct" runat="server" Height="140px" /></td>
        <td style="width: 300px">
            <asp:Label ID="lblShortDesc" runat="server"
                style="font-weight: 700; font-size: medium"></asp:Label></td>
    </tr>
    <tr>
        <td style="width: 300px">
            <asp:Label ID="lblLongDesc" runat="server"></asp:Label></td>
    </tr>
    <tr>
        <td style="width: 300px">
            <asp:Label ID="lblPrice" runat="server"></asp:Label></td>
    </tr>
    <tr>
        <td style="width: 300px">
            <asp:Button ID="btnAdd" runat="server" Text="Add to Cart"
                OnClick="btnAdd_Click" />
            <asp:Button ID="btnViewCart" runat="server" Text="View Cart"
                PostBackUrl="~/Cart.aspx" /></td>
    </tr>
</table>
<asp:SqlDataSource ID="SqlDataSource1" runat="server"
    ConnectionString="<%$ ConnectionStrings:HalloweenConnectionString %>"
    SelectCommand="SELECT [ProductID], [Name], [ShortDescription],
        [LongDescription], [UnitPrice], [ImageFile]
        FROM [Products]
        WHERE ([ProductID] = @ProductID)">
    <SelectParameters>
        <asp:Parameter Name="ProductID" Type="String" />
    </SelectParameters>
</asp:SqlDataSource>
```

Figure 27-8   The ProductDisplay user control (part 1 of 3)

The code-behind file for the ProductDisplay user control   Page 1

```
using System.ComponentModel;

public partial class ProductDisplay : System.Web.UI.UserControl
{
    private string productID;
    private Product product;

    [Category("Appearance")]
    public string ProductID{
        get
        {
            return productID;
        }
        set
        {
            productID = value;
        }
    }

    protected void Page_Load(object sender, EventArgs e){
        product = this.GetProduct();
        if (product == null){
            imgProduct.Visible = false;
            lblShortDesc.Text = "ProductDisplay control";
            lblLongDesc.Text = "ProductID not found.";
            lblPrice.Text = "Make sure to set ProductID property.";
            btnAdd.Visible = false;
            btnViewCart.Visible = false;
        }
        else{
            lblShortDesc.Text = product.ShortDescription;
            lblLongDesc.Text = product.LongDescription;
            lblPrice.Text = "Price: " + product.UnitPrice.ToString("c");
            imgProduct.ImageUrl = "Images/Products/" + product.ImageFile;
        }
    }

    private Product GetProduct(){
        SqlDataSource1.SelectParameters["ProductID"].DefaultValue = ProductID;
        DataView table = (DataView)
            SqlDataSource1.Select(DataSourceSelectArguments.Empty);
        if (table == null)
            return null;
        else{
            DataRowView row = table[0];
            product = new Product();
            product.Name = row["Name"].ToString();
            product.ShortDescription = row["ShortDescription"].ToString();
            product.LongDescription = row["LongDescription"].ToString();
            product.UnitPrice = (decimal) row["UnitPrice"];
            product.ImageFile = row["ImageFile"].ToString();
            return product;
        }
    }
```

Figure 27-8   The ProductDisplay user control (part 2 of 3)

The code-behind file for the ProductDisplay user control   **Page 2**

```
protected void btnAdd_Click(object sender, EventArgs e){
    CartItem item = new CartItem();
    SortedList cart;
    if (Session["Cart"] == null)
        cart = new SortedList();
    else
        cart = (SortedList) Session["Cart"];
    if (cart.ContainsKey(ProductID)){
        item = (CartItem) cart[ProductID];
        item.Quantity += 1;
        cart[ProductID] = item;
    }
    else{
        item.Product = product;
        item.Quantity = 1;
        cart.Add(ProductID, item);
    }
    Session["Cart"] = cart;
    Response.Redirect("Cart.aspx");
    }
}
```

Figure 27-8   The ProductDisplay user control (part 3 of 3)

Perspective

Now that you've completed this chapter, you should be able to develop user controls whenever you need them for your own applications. This is one way to write code once and reuse it on more than one page. Another way to reuse code is to create custom server controls, which you'll learn how to do in the next chapter.

Terms

user control
User Control Designer
designer attribute

28

How to develop custom server controls

In this chapter, you'll learn how to create custom server controls. Custom server controls are similar to user controls, but they're more powerful. They're also more difficult to develop than user controls.

Since custom server controls are an advanced feature, you can't use the Visual Web Developer Express Edition to develop them. As a result, you may want to skip this chapter if you're using this edition.

An overview of custom server controls 884
An introduction to custom server controls 884
How custom server controls compare with user controls 886
Three types of custom server controls 888

How to create a rendered control 890
The default class for a custom server control 890
How to override the Render or RenderContents method for a
custom control 892
The design of the DaysUntil control 894
The code for the DaysUntil control 894

How to create and test a web control library 898
Step 1: Create a web control library 898
Step 2: Create the custom server controls 898
Step 3: Build the web control library 898
Step 4: Add the library to a web site 900
Step 5: Test the controls 900

**Additional programming techniques for custom
controls 902**
How to use the HtmlTextWriter class to render HTML 902
How to use designer attributes 904
How to raise events in a custom control 906

How to create a superclassed control 908
How to code a superclassed control 908
The design of the CaptionedBox control 908
The code for the CaptionedBox control 910

How to create a composite control 914
How to code a composite control 914
The design of the DateDDL control 916
The code for the DateDDL control 916

Perspective 924

An overview of custom server controls

Before I show you how to create and use custom server controls, you need to understand what these controls are and how you work with them. That's what you'll learn in the topics that follow.

An introduction to custom server controls

Figure 28-1 presents an introduction to *custom server controls*. These controls are similar to the server controls that come with ASP.NET. Because you create custom server controls yourself, however, they can include features that aren't available with the standard web server controls.

For example, the form shown at the top of this figure includes four custom server controls. The first two, called CaptionedBox controls, are similar to a TextBox control but include a caption to the left of the text box. The second control, called a DateDDL control, consists of three drop-down lists that let the user select a month, day, and year. Like the CaptionedBox control, the DateDDL control also includes a caption. The third control, called a DaysUntil control, calculates the number of days until a specified date. In addition, text can be displayed before and after the calculated days.

When you create a custom server control, you base it on the WebControl class or a class that's derived from this class. That way, the control inherits the properties, methods, and events of that class. For example, the DaysUntil control is based on the WebControl class. In contrast, the CaptionedBox control is based on the TextBox class so it has access to the additional properties, methods, and events defined by that class. And the DateDDL control is based on the CompositeControl class. You'll learn about this class later in this chapter.

In addition to the properties, methods, and events that are inherited from the base class, a custom server control can define its own custom properties, methods, and events. For example, the DaysUntil control has properties that let you set the month and day that's used in the calculation, as well as properties that let you specify the text that's displayed before and after the calculated number of days. You can also override the properties, methods, and events defined by the base class.

Custom server controls are typically stored in a *web control library*. Then, if you add the web control library to a web site as shown in this figure, the custom server controls become available from the Toolbox. To use a control, you simply drag it to a web form just as you would any other control. When you do, the control is displayed in the Web Forms Designer window.

Although custom server controls are easy to use, they can be difficult to develop. That's because Visual Studio doesn't provide a designer interface to help you create them. Instead, you have to develop custom server controls entirely in code. As a result, you can't see how the control will appear until you build it and add it to a web form.

Four custom server controls displayed in the Web Forms Designer

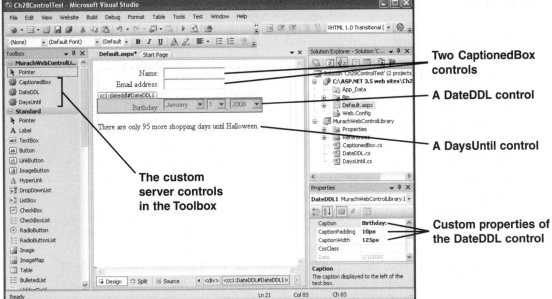

How custom controls are created

- A *custom server control* is a class that inherits the WebControl class or a class that derives from this class.

- Visual Studio doesn't have a designer to help you create custom server controls. As a result, you must create them using code.

- The Professional Edition of Visual Studio includes an ASP.NET Server Control template you can use to create libraries of custom server controls. You can then distribute the library to other developers.

How custom server controls work with designers

- Custom server controls work just like the server controls that come with ASP.NET, but they can be customized with additional features.

- If you add a web control library to a web site, the custom server controls in that library are added to the Toolbox automatically. Then, you can add a custom server control to a web form by dragging it from the Toolbox just like any other server control.

- Custom server controls have a visual interface you can use to work with them when you add them to a web form. For example, you can set the properties of a custom server control by selecting it in the designer and then using the Properties window.

Figure 28-1   An introduction to custom server controls

How custom server controls compare with user controls

In the last chapter, you learned how to create user controls. In some ways, custom server controls are similar to user controls. In other ways, though, they're quite different. To help you understand how these two types of controls compare, figure 28-2 lists their similarities and differences and describes when you should use each type.

The main difference between custom server controls and user controls is that custom server controls are more difficult to develop than user controls. That's because Visual Studio provides a designer that you use to develop user controls, but there's no designer for custom server controls. As a result, to develop custom server controls, you must write C# code that defines the control. However, once you've developed a custom server control, the control behaves more like a standard server control. For example, a custom server control is available from the Toolbox, just like a standard server control.

User controls tend to be application-specific. For example, a typical use of user controls is to define groups of controls that may be reused on multiple pages of a web site. Since you're unlikely to use the same user controls in another application, you usually store them in the same folder as the forms for the rest of the web site.

Custom server controls usually provide more general-purpose functions than user controls. For example, the CaptionedBox and DateDDL user controls shown in the previous figure could be useful in a variety of applications. To make them available to other applications, custom server controls are usually created in a separate web control library. Then, if you add the web control library to a web site, Visual Studio adds the controls in the library to the Toolbox so they're available to all of the forms of the web site.

Custom server controls...

- Are best used to create general-purpose controls you want to reuse in several applications.
- Are more difficult to develop than user controls.
- Are created entirely in code and consist of a single cs class file.
- Are usually created in web control libraries.
- Are available from the Toolbox.

User controls...

- Are best used when you want to create elements you can reuse on several pages within the same application.
- Are easier to develop than custom server controls.
- Are created with the User Control Designer and consist of an ascx file that defines the control's user interface along with a code-behind file.
- Aren't available from the Toolbox.

Figure 28-2   How custom server controls compare with user controls

Three types of custom server controls

Figure 28-3 describes the three basic types of custom server controls. As you'll learn in this chapter, you implement each of these controls using different programming techniques. Keep in mind as you learn these techniques, however, that they're not mutually exclusive. In other words, you can use one or more of these techniques within the same custom server control.

A *rendered control* is a control that contains code that generates all or most of the HTML that's used to render the control. The rendered control shown in this figure is the DaysUntil control you saw in figure 28-1. Rendered controls are usually based on the WebControl class, which provides the basic functionality of an ASP.NET server control. Then, the custom control overrides the Render or RenderContents method of this class to generate its own HTML. You'll see how that works in just a minute.

A *superclassed control* is a control that adds functionality to an existing web server control. The CaptionedBox control you saw in figure 28-1, for example, adds a caption to a TextBox control. Because this control is based on the TextBox class rather than the WebControl class, it has all the properties, methods, and events of a standard TextBox control.

A *composite control* is a control that's made up of two or more web server controls. For example, the DateDDL control consists of three DropDownList controls. Composite controls are based on the CompositeControl class. Then, the *child controls* that make up the control are added to the collection of controls defined by the CompositeControl class.

Note that a control can sometimes be implemented using more than one of the control types. For example, you could implement the DaysUntil control using any three of the control types. To implement it as a superclassed control, you would base it on a Label control. Then, you would calculate the days remaining until the target date and assign the result to the Text property of the control, along with the text you want to display before and after the calculated days. To implement this control as a composite control, you could use three Label controls: one for the text you want to display before the calculated value, one for the calculated value, and one for the text you want to display after the calculated value. Before you create a control, then, you should consider which type will provide the greatest flexibility and ease of use.

A rendered control that calculates the days until a specified date

There are only 95 more shopping days until Halloween.

Two superclassed controls that add a caption to a text box

Name: [   ]
Email address: [   ]

A composite control that consists of three drop-down lists with a caption

Birthday: [January ∨] [1 ∨], [2008 ∨]

Description

- A *rendered control* is a control that inherits the WebControl class and handles the details of rendering its own HTML.

- Rendered controls are the most flexible type of custom control because they aren't bound by the predefined behavior of any existing controls. However, they can also be the most difficult to create.

- A *superclassed control* inherits the class for an existing control, such as a text box, and adds additional features, such as a caption.

- A *composite control* is made up of two or more standard controls. Composite controls inherit the CompositeControl class and add *child controls* to the collection of controls for that class.

- A custom server control can sometimes be implemented as two or more of the control types. In that case, you'll need to decide which type works best.

Figure 28-3   Three types of custom server controls

How to create a rendered control

In the topics that follow, you'll learn how to create a simple rendered control. First, I'll describe the default class that provides a template for creating a custom control. Then, you'll learn how to override the Render or RenderContents method in this class so you can control the HTML that's generated when the control is rendered. Finally, you'll see the design and code for the DaysUntil control.

The default class for a custom server control

When you add a custom server control to a project, Visual Studio creates a class like the one shown in figure 28-4. This class inherits the WebControl class and contains a single property named Text that gets and sets the value of a variable that's stored in the view state of the page. This class also contains a method named RenderContents that overrides the RenderContents method of the WebControl class.

As it is, the default class doesn't provide a useful function. However, it does provide a good starting point for building useful controls. Before you use this class, though, you need to understand how it works. If you've created your own class files using C#, you shouldn't have much trouble understanding most of this code. However, a few of the details might be confusing.

To start, notice the code within the square brackets at the beginning of the class and the property declarations. This code defines *designer attributes* that supply the Web Forms Designer with information about the control when it's used on a web form. You'll learn more about these designer attributes later in this chapter.

Next, notice that the class overrides the RenderContents method of the WebControl class that it inherits. That way, it can generate the HTML needed to display the control. In this case, the RenderContents method uses the Write method of the HtmlTextWriter object that's passed to it to write the value of the Text property to the control's HTML output stream. You'll learn more about the Write method and the other methods of the HtmlTextWriter class later in this chapter too.

You should realize that because the RenderContents method in the default class overrides the RenderContents method of the WebControl class, the properties of the WebControl class that the default class inherits, such as ID, Height, Width, and BorderStyle, never get rendered. To render these properties, you have to call one of the Render methods of the WebControl class. You'll learn how to do that in the next figure.

The starting code for a custom server control

```
using System;
using System.Collections.Generic;
using System.ComponentModel;
using System.Linq;
using System.Text;
using System.Web;
using System.Web.UI;
using System.Web.UI.WebControls;

namespace MurachWebControlLibrary
{
    [DefaultProperty("Text")]
    [ToolboxData
        ("<{0}:WebCustomControl1 runat=server></{0}:WebCustomControl1>")]
    public class WebCustomControl1 : WebControl
    {
        [Bindable(true)]
        [Category("Appearance")]
        [DefaultValue("")]
        [Localizable(true)]
        public string Text
        {
            get
            {
                String s = (String)ViewState["Text"];
                return ((s == null) ? String.Empty : s);
            }

            set
            {
                ViewState["Text"] = value;
            }
        }

        protected override void RenderContents(HtmlTextWriter output)
        {
            output.Write(Text);
        }
    }
}
```

Description

- The code that appears within square brackets before the class and property declarations defines *designer attributes* that specify how the control and its properties work with the Web Forms Designer. See figure 28-11 for more information.

- A class like the one above is created by default when you add a control to a project using the ASP.NET Server Control template or when you create a new ASP.NET Server Control project. It defines a simple rendered control that exposes a property named Text.

- The RenderContents method receives an argument named output that's declared as an HtmlTextWriter object. This object is created by ASP.NET when it receives a request for a page. You can use it to write output to the HTML document for the web page.

Figure 28-4   The default class for a custom server control

How to override the Render or RenderContents method for a custom control

Every web server control has a Render or RenderContents method that's responsible for generating the HTML that's sent to the browser to display the control. In a custom server control, you usually override one of these methods so you can generate the HTML that renders the control. Figure 28-5 shows how you do that.

When ASP.NET receives a request for a web page, it creates an HtmlTextWriter object that's used to write HTML to the output stream. This object is passed to the Render and RenderContents methods, and you can use it within these methods to write the HTML that renders the control.

The first example shows how to override the RenderContents method to add content to the HTML element for the base class. Here, the Write method of the HtmlTextWriter object adds the value of the Text property between the start and end tags that are generated automatically for the base class. The start tag that's generated includes attributes that correspond to any control properties you set as you work with the control in the designer. As a result, you can use the RenderContents method to render the properties the custom control inherits from its base class.

The second example shows how to override the Render method to add content to the HTML element for the base class. The Render method is similar to the RenderContents method, but it renders the start and end tags as well as the content. Because of that, when you override this method to add content to the HTML element, you must use the RenderBeginTag and RenderEndTag methods of the base class to render the start and end tags for the control. To access methods from the base class, you can use the base keyword as illustrated in this example.

The third example shows how to override the Render method to add additional HTML elements before or after the element for the base class. Here, the first statement calls the Write method of the HtmlTextWriter object to add an HTML element before the element for the base class. This statement sends a string that includes an HTML element for the caption to the browser. Then, the second statement calls the Render method of the base class. This method generates the HTML necessary to render the base class, including the start and end tags, and sends it to the browser. In this case, the class is based on the TextBox class. As a result, calling the Render method of the base class renders an HTML element for a text box and sends it to the browser.

Methods of the WebControl class for rendering controls

Method	Description
`RenderContents(output)`	Renders the contents of the control to the specified HtmlTextWriter object, but does not include its start and end tags.
`Render(output)`	Renders the HTML for the control to the specified HtmlTextWriter object, including the start and end tags.
`RenderBeginTag(output)`	Renders the begin tag for the control to the specified HtmlTextWriter object.
`RenderEndTag(output)`	Renders the end tag for the control to the specified HtmlTextWriter object.

A RenderContents method that adds text content to a control

```
protected override void RenderContents(HtmlTextWriter output)
{
    output.Write(Text);
}
```

A Render method that adds text content to a control

```
protected override void Render(HtmlTextWriter output)
{
    base.RenderBeginTag(output);
    output.Write(Text);
    base.RenderEndTag(output);
}
```

A Render method that adds a caption to a superclassed control that's based on a text box

```
protected override void Render(HtmlTextWriter output)
{
    output.Write("Caption");
    base.Render(output);
}
```

Description

- A custom control can inherit the System.Web.UI.WebControls.WebControl class, or a more specific class such as the TextBox class.

- If a custom control inherits the WebControl class and renders a single element, you should override the RenderContents method of the WebControl class. Then, you can use the Write methods of the HtmlTextWriter class to add content between the start and end tags for the element, which are rendered automatically.

- If a custom control renders more than one element, you should override the Render method of the base class. Then, you can use the Write methods of the HtmlTextWriter class to add elements before or after the base class, and you can call the Render method of the base class to render the base class. To add content between the start and end tags for the base class, you can use the RenderBeginTag and RenderEndTag methods of the base class and then write the content between these tags.

- Web controls also have a RenderControl method, but you shouldn't execute this method from your overridden Render or RenderContents method.

Figure 28-5   How to override the Render or RenderContents method

The design of the DaysUntil control

Figure 28-6 presents the design of the DaysUntil control you saw earlier in this chapter. As you'll recall, this control displays the number of days remaining until the target date specified by the Month and Day properties. Note that the default values for the Month and Day properties are 10 and 31, which means that this control displays the number of days until Halloween by default.

In addition to the Month and Day properties, the DaysUntil control includes TextBefore and TextAfter properties. These properties let you specify text that's displayed before and after the number of days. Because these properties don't have default values, no text is displayed by default.

The screen in this figure shows how you could use the DaysUntil control on the Order page of the Halloween Store application. Here, I left the Month and Day properties at their default values so the control will display the number of days until Halloween. In contrast, I set the TextBefore and TextAfter properties so the control appears as shown here.

This figure also shows the aspx code that's generated for the control. This code includes ID and Runat attributes just as it would for any web server control. In addition, the tag for this control uses a prefix of cc1. As you'll see later in this chapter, this is the prefix that's generated by default when you add a custom server control to a web form.

The code for the DaysUntil control

Figure 28-7 presents the complete code for the DaysUntil control. The first thing you should notice is that this control inherits the WebControl class. That means that it can use any of the properties, methods, and events of that class.

This class starts with the four properties of the control. Here, each property consists of simple get and set accessors that retrieve and set the value of a variable that's stored in view state. Notice that the get accessors for the TextBefore and TextAfter properties use the ?: conditional operator. In case you haven't seen this operator before, it returns one of two values based on a Boolean expression. In the code shown here, this operator is used to check if the value of the property is null. If so, an empty string is returned. Otherwise, the value of the property is returned.

This class finishes with the overridden RenderContents method. This method uses the HtmlTextWriter object to write the value of the TextBefore property, followed by the number of days remaining until the target date, followed by the value of the TextAfter property. To calculate the number of days remaining until the target date, the RenderContents method calls the DaysUntilDate method. Because you saw code like this in previous chapters, you shouldn't have any trouble understanding how it works.

The DaysUntil control on the Order page of the Shopping Cart application

The aspx code for the DaysUntil control

```
<cc1:DaysUntil ID="DaysUntil1" runat="server"
    TextAfter="more shopping days until Halloween."
    TextBefore="There are only" />
```

Properties of the DaysUntil control

Property	Description
Month	The target date's month. The default is 10.
Day	The target date's day. The default is 31.
TextBefore	The text that's displayed before the days until the target date.
TextAfter	The text that's displayed after the days until the target date.

Description

- The DaysUntil control is a rendered control that displays the number of days remaining until a target date and, optionally, text before and after the days remaining. The target date is specified by the Month and Day properties.

- By default, the Month and Day properties are set to display the number of days until Halloween. If that's not what you want, you can change these properties after you add the control to a web form.

Figure 28-6   The design of the DaysUntil control

The C# code for the DaysUntil control

```csharp
using System;
using System.Collections.Generic;
using System.ComponentModel;
using System.Linq;
using System.Text;
using System.Web;
using System.Web.UI;
using System.Web.UI.WebControls;

namespace MurachWebControlLibrary
{
    [ToolboxData("<{0}:DaysUntil runat=server></{0}:DaysUntil>")]
    public class DaysUntil : WebControl
    {
        [Bindable(true)] [Category("Appearance")]
        [DefaultValue("")] [Localizable(true)]
        public string TextBefore
        {
            get
            {
                String s = (String) ViewState["TextBefore"];
                return ((s == null) ? String.Empty : s);
            }
            set
            {
                ViewState["TextBefore"] = value;
            }
        }

        [Bindable(true)] [Category("Appearance")]
        [DefaultValue("")] [Localizable(true)]
        public string TextAfter
        {
            get
            {
                String s = (String) ViewState["TextAfter"];
                return ((s == null) ? String.Empty : s);
            }
            set
            {
                ViewState["TextAfter"] = value;
            }
        }
```

Figure 28-7   The code for the DaysUntil control (part 1 of 2)

The C# code for the DaysUntil control

```csharp
[Bindable(true)] [Category("Appearance")]
[DefaultValue("")] [Localizable(true)]
public int Month
{
    get
    {
        String s = (String) ViewState["Month"];
        if (s == null || s.Equals(""))
            return 10;
        else
            return Convert.ToInt32(ViewState["Month"]);
    }
    set
    {
        ViewState["Month"] = value.ToString();
    }
}

[Bindable(true)] [Category("Appearance")]
[DefaultValue("")] [Localizable(true)]
public int Day
{
    get
    {
        String s = (String)ViewState["Day"];
        if (s == null || s.Equals(""))
            return 31;
        else
            return Convert.ToInt32(ViewState["Day"]);
    }
    set
    {
        ViewState["Day"] = value.ToString();
    }
}

protected override void RenderContents(HtmlTextWriter output)
{
    output.Write(TextBefore + " ");
    output.Write(DaysUntilDate());
    output.Write(" " + TextAfter);
}

private int DaysUntilDate()
{
    DateTime targetDate = new DateTime(DateTime.Today.Year,
        Month, Day);
    if (DateTime.Today > targetDate)
        targetDate = targetDate.AddYears(1);
    TimeSpan timeUntil = targetDate - DateTime.Today;
    return timeUntil.Days;
}

    }
}
```

Figure 28-7   The code for the DaysUntil control (part 2 of 2)

How to create and test a web control library

Now that you've seen the basic coding requirements for custom server controls, you're ready to learn how to create and use them in Visual Studio. To do that, you can create a web control library that contains one or more custom server controls. Then, you can add this library to any web site to test these controls.

Figure 28-8 presents a procedure for creating and testing a web control library. You'll learn the details of each step in this procedure in the topics that follow.

Step 1: Create a web control library

The first step for creating a web control library is to create a new ASP.NET Server Control project. To do that, you display the New Project dialog box as described in figure 28-8. Then, you select the ASP.NET Server Control template and enter a name and location for the project. In this figure, for example, you can see a web control library named MurachWebControlLibrary.

When you create an ASP.NET Server Control project, the project is created with a control named WebCustomControl1 by default. This control contains the starting code you saw in figure 28-4.

Step 2: Create the custom server controls

After you create a new ASP.NET Server Control project, the next step is to create the custom server controls you want to include in the library. To create the first control, you can modify the WebCustomControl1.cs file that's generated by default. Alternatively, you can delete this file and add a new file for each custom control.

To add a custom server control to a web control library, right-click on the project and select the Add→New Item command to display the Add New Item dialog box. Then, select the ASP.NET Server Control template that's available from the Web group and enter a name for the control. In figure 28-8, for example, you can see that the library contains the DaysUntil, CaptionedBox, and DateDDL controls.

After you add a new control to a web control library, you need to add the code that implements the control. You'll see examples of that throughout this chapter.

Step 3: Build the web control library

The next step is to build the web control library. To do that, just right-click the project and select the Build command. Then, Visual Studio creates the files you'll need to use the web control library in a web site.

A solution with a Web Control Library project

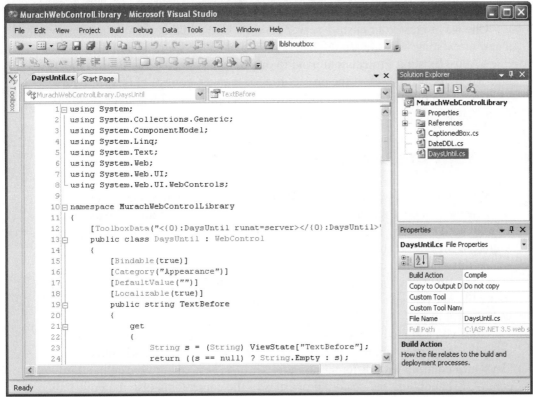

A procedure for creating and testing custom server controls

1. Create a new ASP.NET Server Control project using the ASP.NET Server Control template.
2. Create the custom server controls in the library.
3. Build the web control library.
4. Add the web control library to a solution that contains a web site.
5. Use the Toolbox to add the controls to a web form so you can test them.

Description

- A *web control library* consists of one or more custom server controls. You can build this library into a DLL that you can distribute to other developers.

- To create a project for a web control library, display the New Project dialog box (File→New Project). Then, select the ASP.NET Server Control template that's available from the Web group of the C# group, and enter a name and location for the project. By default, an ASP.NET Server Control project is stored in the Visual Studio projects location directory.

Figure 28-8   How to create a web control library

Step 4: Add the library to a web site

One way to test your custom server controls is to add the web control library to a new or existing web site. To do that, create or open the web site and then use the File→Add→Existing Project command to display the Add Existing Project dialog box. Then, locate and select the project file for the web control library. In figure 28-9, for example, the MurachWebControlLibrary project shown in the previous figure has been added to a web site.

Step 5: Test the controls

When you add a web control library to a web site, Visual Studio automatically adds the custom controls in the library to the Toolbox. The controls are included in a group with the same name as the web control library. This is illustrated by the MurachWebControlLibrary group shown in figure 28-9.

At this point, you can test a control by dragging it from the Toolbox to the form. The first time you add a custom control to a form, Visual Studio creates a Bin folder like the one shown here. This folder contains the dll and pdb files for the web control library.

After you add a custom control to a form, you can set the control properties using the Properties window. In this figure, for example, you can see three DaysUntil controls with different property settings. Note that to create the third control, I set not only the custom properties of the control, but also the Font-Italic property that this control inherits from the WebControl class.

If you find that a control doesn't look or work the way you want it to, you can change its code and then rebuild the web control library that contains it. You may also need to rebuild a form that uses a custom control or refresh the custom controls on a form if you change the code or properties for the control. To rebuild a form, just, right-click on it in the Solution Explorer and select the Build Page command. To refresh a control, right-click on it in the form and select the Refresh command.

When you test your custom controls, you should realize that coding errors sometimes manifest themselves in strange ways. Because of that, they can be difficult to debug. For example, if a control generates invalid HTML, it won't display correctly in the Web Forms Designer. Typically, the designer will simply display the name of the control in brackets. In other cases, the control will appear correctly in the designer, but it won't display properly when you run the application. And in still other cases, the control will throw an exception when you run the application.

Fortunately, you can use the debugger to help you determine the cause of an error. If a control isn't rendered properly, for example, you can set a breakpoint in the Render or RenderContents method. Then, you can review variable values and monitor program execution to determine the cause of the problem.

If the control displays in the browser but doesn't appear or work the way it should, you can also look at the HTML that's generated to be sure it's correct. To do that, use the View→Source command in your browser's menu.

Three instances of the DaysUntil control in the Web Forms Designer

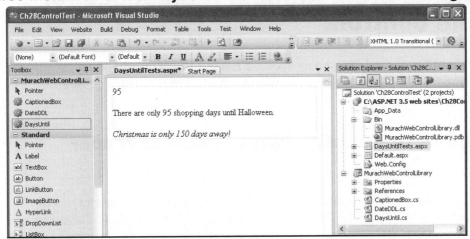

The aspx code for these three controls

```
<%@ Register Assembly="MurachWebControlLibrary"
    Namespace="MurachWebControlLibrary" TagPrefix="cc1" %>
...
<cc1:DaysUntil ID="DaysUntil1" runat="server" /><br /><br />
<cc1:DaysUntil ID="DaysUntil2" runat="server"
    TextAfter="more shopping days until Halloween."
    TextBefore="There are only" /><br /><br />
<cc1:DaysUntil ID="DaysUntil3" runat="server"
    Day="25" Font-Italic="True" Month="12" TextAfter="days away!"
    TextBefore="Christmas is only" />
```

Description

- To test a custom control, just drag it from the Toolbox to a form in your web site. When you do, Visual Studio will generate a Register directive that registers the web control library, and it will generate a tag for the control with a default prefix of cc1.

- After you add the control to a form, you can set its properties in the Properties window to be sure that it appears as it should in the designer. You can also run the project to be sure that the control works properly at runtime.

- If you make changes to a control, make sure to rebuild the control library. To do that, you can right-click on the library in the Solution Explorer and select Build from the resulting menu. Then, the changes are applied to any controls you've added to a web form.

- Because the DaysUntil control inherits the WebControl base class, you can set properties of this class as illustrated by the Font-Italic attribute of the third control shown above.

Note

- If the controls in the web control library aren't added to the Toolbox automatically, you can add them manually. To do that, right-click in the Toolbox, choose Add Tab, and then enter a name for the tab. Then, right-click in the tab and choose Choose Items to display the Choose Toolbox Items dialog box. Click the Browse button in the .NET Framework Components tab, locate and select the dll file for the library, and click the OK button.

Figure 28-9 How to test controls in a web control library

Additional programming techniques for custom controls

Now that you've learned how to create and test a web control library, you're ready to learn some additional programming techniques for creating custom server controls.

How to use the HtmlTextWriter class to render HTML

As you know, the Render and RenderContents methods of a custom server control receive an HtmlTextWriter object as an argument. You use this object to generate the HTML needed to display the control. You've already seen how to use the Write method of this class to write simple text to the output stream. You can use this method to render all of the HTML for a custom server control by carefully constructing the HTML using C#'s string handling features. However, figure 28-10 presents some additional methods of the HtmlTextWriter class that make it easier to generate HTML output.

The methods shown in this figure simplify the process of creating valid HTML. For example, the WriteBeginTag method writes an HTML start tag using the element name you supply. Note, however, that this method doesn't write the closing bracket for the start tag. That way, you can use the WriteAttribute method to add attributes to the tag. Then, you can use the Write method to add the closing bracket for the tag by specifying HtmlTextWriter.TagRightChar for the string value.

You can also use the Write method to add content after the start tag. Then, you can use the WriteEndTag method to write the end tag. This is illustrated in the example in this figure. This code creates a Td element with a Style attribute that specifies the width and alignment of the content between the start and end tags.

If an element doesn't include any content, you can code the start tag as a *self-closing tag*. To do that, you use the HtmlTextWriter.SelfClosingTagEnd field to close the start tag instead of HtmlTextWriter.TagRightChar. This field adds the characters "/>" to the output stream, which indicates the end of the element. Then, you can omit the end tag.

Common methods of the HtmlTextWriter class

Method	Description
Write(string)	Writes the specified string to the HTML output.
WriteBeginTag(tagName)	Writes the start tag for the specified HTML element. This method does not write the closing bracket (>) for the start tag. That way, you can include attributes within the tag.
WriteAttribute(attribute, value)	Writes the specified attribute and assigns the specified value. This method should be coded after the WriteBeginTag method but before the Write method that adds the closing bracket for the start tag.
WriteEndTag(tagName)	Writes the end tag for the specified HTML element.

Common fields of the HtmlTextWriter class

Field	Description
TagRightChar	The closing bracket of an HTML tag (>).
SelfClosingTagEnd	The closing slash and bracket of a self-closing HTML tag (/>).

A method that renders a Td element with text

```
protected override void RenderCaption(HtmlTextWriter output)
{
    output.WriteBeginTag("td");
    string style = "width: " + CaptionWidth.ToString() + ";";
    style += "text-align: right;";
    output.WriteAttribute("Style", style);
    output.Write(HtmlTextWriter.TagRightChar);
    output.Write(Caption);
    output.WriteEndTag("td");
}
```

Description

- You can use the Write methods of the HtmlTextWriter class to create HTML for a custom control.

- To add the closing bracket for a start tag, you use the Write method and specify HtmlTextWriter.TagRightChar.

- If an element doesn't include any content, you can code the start tag as a *self-closing tag*, which ends with the characters />. To add these characters, use the HtmlTextWriter.SelfClosingTagEnd field.

Figure 28-10   How to use the HtmlTextWriter class to render HTML

How to use designer attributes

Figure 28-11 presents some of the designer attributes you can use with custom control classes and properties. The only two *class attributes* you'll typically use are the ones that are added by default to a custom control. As its name implies, the DefaultProperty attribute identifies the default property for the control. This attribute is set to Text by default since this is the only property that's defined for a control when you first create it. If you delete the Text property or change its name, you should delete the DefaultProperty attribute or change it to another property.

The second class attribute, ToolboxData, provides information that Visual Studio uses when you add the control to a form. Specifically, it provides the name of the tag that's used for the control. By default, this is the class name that you specify when you create the web control, which is usually what you want.

The *property attributes* provide the Web Forms Designer with additional information about the custom properties you define. For example, the attributes that are included on the Text property of a custom server control by default specify that the property can be used for binding, that the property should be listed in the Appearance category of the Properties window, that the property has no default value, and that the property can be localized to use a specific user's language and culture. You can modify or delete any of these attributes or add any of the other attributes.

One property attribute you're likely to add is Description. The value you specify for this attribute is displayed in the Description pane at the bottom of the Properties window when you select the control in the designer window and then select the property. In this figure, you can see the description that's specified for the Month property of the DaysUntil control.

Common attributes for custom control classes

Attribute	Description
DefaultProperty(name)	The name of the default property for the control.
ToolboxData(tagName)	The name of the tag that's generated when the control is added to a web form from the Toolbox.

Common attributes for custom control properties

Attribute	Description
Bindable(boolean)	Specifies whether the property is typically used for binding.
Browsable(boolean)	Specifies whether the property should be visible in the Properties window. The default is true.
Category(string)	The category the property should appear under in the Properties window.
DefaultValue(string)	The default value for the property.
Description(string)	A description for the property.
DesignOnly(boolean)	Specifies whether the property is available only at design time. The default is false.
Localizable(boolean)	Specifies whether the property can be localized so that it uses the user's language and culture.

A property definition with property attributes

```
[Bindable(true)] [Category("Appearance")] [DefaultValue("")]
[Description("The month used to determine the target date.")]
public int Month
{
    get
    {
        String s = (String) ViewState["Month"];
        if (s == null || s.Equals(""))
            return 10;
        else
            return Convert.ToInt32(ViewState["Month"]);
    }
    set
    {
        ViewState["Month"] = value.ToString();
    }
}
```

Description

- You can use *class attributes* and *property attributes* to add information to a control class or property that makes the class or property easier to use in the Web Forms Designer.

- Class attributes are coded at the beginning of a class declaration, and property attributes are coded at the beginning of a property declaration. Each attribute consists of an attribute name, followed by a value enclosed in parentheses.

- Each attribute can be coded separately within square brackets as shown above. Alternatively, attributes can be coded in a comma-separated list within a single set of brackets.

Figure 28-11   How to use designer attributes

How to raise events in a custom control

In addition to defining custom properties, a custom server control can raise custom events. For example, the DateDDL control you saw earlier in this chapter raises an event named DateChanged whenever the user selects a different month, day, or year. A web form that uses this control can then include a handler for this event to provide special processing when the user changes the date.

At the top of figure 28-12, for example, you can see a page that includes a DateDDL control that has been named ddExpirationDate. To test the event that has been defined by the DateDDL class, the code for this page includes an event handler that displays a label that contains an appropriate message whenever the DateChanged event occurs. You can see this message on the form.

To define an event, you start by coding an event declaration as shown in this figure. On this declaration, you provide the name of the event and a *delegate* that determines the arguments that will be passed to the event handler. The first statement in this figure, for example, declares a DateChanged event that will use a delegate named EventHandler. This delegate is used with events that don't require any event data. It passes two arguments to the event handler: the object that raised the event and an EventArgs object that contains no event data.

Once you've declared an event, you can raise it by referring to it by name as shown in the second statement in this figure. This statement raises the DateChanged event defined by the first statement. Notice that the this keyword is used as the first argument, which causes the object that raised the event to be passed to the event handler. If the control contains child controls, you can also pass a child control to the event handler. The second argument passes a new EventArgs object to the event handler.

To respond to an event that's raised by a custom control from a page that contains the control, you generate an event handler just as you do for any other control. In this figure, for example, you can see the event handler for the DateChanged event of the ddExpirationDate control. Notice that this event handler accepts the two arguments that will be passed by the DateChanged event. Also notice that the parameters that receive these arguments are named sender and e just as they are in the other event handlers you've seen in this book. Then, within the event handler, you can use the sender parameter to work with the control that was passed to the event handler. In this case, the event handler casts the sender parameter to a WebControl object and then uses the ID property of the control to display its name.

A page that tests the DateChanged event of the ddExpirationDate control

The syntax for declaring an event

```
public event Delegate eventName;
```

The syntax for raising an event

```
eventName(object, EventArgs);
```

Code that defines the DateChanged event in the DateDDL class

```
Public Event EventHandler DateChanged;
```

Code that raises the event in the DateDDL class

```
DateChanged(this, new EventArgs());
```

The event handler for the event in the web form

```
protected void ddExpirationDate_DateChanged(object sender, EventArgs e)
{
    WebControl control = (WebControl) sender;
    lblMessage.Text =
        "The DateChanged event was raised by the "
        + control.ID + " control.";
}
```

Description

- To declare an event for a custom control, you code a public event declaration at the class level. This declaration specifies an event name and a *delegate* that will handle the event.

- The delegate determines what arguments are passed to the method that handles the event. In most cases, you'll use the EventHandler delegate, which passes two arguments: an object that represents the sender of the event, and an EventArgs object.

- To raise an event, you code its name and the arguments required by the delegate. For the EventHandler delegate, you can pass the current object to the event handler by specifying *this* for the first argument. Then, the event handler can use this argument to retrieve information about the control. For the second argument, you can just specify a new EventArgs object since no event data is required.

Figure 28-12   How to raise events in a custom control

How to create a superclassed control

As you know, a superclassed control is a control that inherits a specific web server control rather than the generic WebControl class. The programming techniques for creating a superclassed control are similar to the techniques for creating a rendered control. However, you should be aware of a few coding details.

How to code a superclassed control

Before you create a superclassed control, you should carefully consider which control it inherits. In general, you'll want it to inherit the control that most resembles the appearance and function of the custom control you're creating. For example, if the primary purpose of the custom control is to display text, it should inherit the Label control. On the other hand, if the primary purpose of the control is to accept text input from the user, it should inherit the TextBox control.

When you create a superclassed control, you typically use the Render method to render its HTML. How you code this method depends on how you're extending the base control. If you're simply adding some HTML before or after the control, or if you're just changing some of the base control's property values, your Render method can call the Render method of the base class to render the entire base control. If your enhancements are more substantial, however, you may need to use the RenderBeginTag and RenderEndTag methods so you can render additional HTML between the control's start and end tags.

The design of the CaptionedBox control

To help you understand how superclassed controls work, figure 28-13 presents the design of the CaptionedBox control. This control adds a caption to a standard text box. Because it must provide all the standard features of a text box, it's based on the TextBox class.

To define the caption, this control uses four properties. The Caption property specifies the text to be displayed, the CaptionWidth property specifies the width of the caption, and the RightAlignCaption property determines whether the caption is right-aligned. Finally, the CaptionPadding property specifies how much space appears between the caption and the text box that follows it.

If you take a moment to consider the design for the CaptionedBox control, I think you'll agree that it can be quite useful for aligning text boxes on a form. The web page in this figure illustrates how this works. As you can see, this page contains two CaptionedBox controls. To align the text box portions of these controls, the CaptionWidth and CaptionPadding properties of both controls are set to the same values. In addition, the RightAlign properties of the controls are set to True so that they appear as shown. This can be easier than using tables to align text boxes as you've seen throughout this book. However, as you'll see in a moment, the CaptionedBox control itself uses a table to align its elements.

A web page with two CaptionedBox controls

Properties of the CaptionedBox control

Property	Description
Caption	The text that's displayed to the left of the text box.
CaptionWidth	The width of the control's caption area.
CaptionPadding	The width of the area between the caption and the text box.
RightAlignCaption	Determines whether the caption text is right-aligned. The default is False.

The aspx code for the two CaptionedBox controls

```
<cc1:captionedbox id="CaptionedBox1" runat="server" Caption="Name:"
    CaptionPadding="10px" CaptionWidth="100px" RightAlignCaption="True"
    Width="200px">
</cc1:captionedbox>
<cc1:captionedbox id="CaptionedBox2" runat="server" Caption="Email:"
    CaptionPadding="10px" CaptionWidth="100px" RightAlignCaption="True"
    Width="200px">
</cc1:captionedbox>
```

Description

- The CaptionedBox control is a superclassed control that adds a text caption to the left of a text box. This control makes it easy to align text boxes without using tables.

Figure 28-13   The design of the CaptionedBox control

The code for the CaptionedBox control

Figure 28-14 presents the code for the CaptionedBox control. To start, you can see that the control inherits the TextBox class. In addition, you can see the custom properties that are defined for this class. Notice that, unlike the properties for the DaysUntil control, each of these properties includes a Description attribute that describes the property. In addition, these properties simply get and set the values of class variables. Because that simplifies the code for the properties, we prefer this technique over saving the properties in view state.

Also notice that the CaptionWidth and CaptionPadding properties and the class variables that hold their values are declared with the Unit data type. In case you aren't familiar with this data type, it represents a length measurement that consists of both the length and the unit of measure. By default, the unit of measure is a pixel, which is usually what you want.

The C# code for the CaptionedBox control   **Page 1**

```csharp
using System;
using System.Collections.Generic;
using System.ComponentModel;
using System.Linq;
using System.Text;
using System.Web;
using System.Web.UI;
using System.Web.UI.WebControls;

namespace MurachWebControlLibrary
{
    [DefaultProperty("Text")]
    [ToolboxData("<{0}:CaptionedBox runat=server></{0}:CaptionedBox>")]
    public class CaptionedBox : TextBox
    {
        private string caption;
        private Unit captionWidth;
        private Unit captionPadding;
        private bool rightAlignCaption;

        [Category("Appearance")]
        [Description("The caption displayed to the left of the text box.")]
        public string Caption
        {
            get { return caption; }
            set { caption = value; }
        }

        [Category("Appearance")]
        [Description("The width of the caption.")]
        public Unit CaptionWidth
        {
            get { return captionWidth; }
            set { captionWidth = value; }
        }

        [Category("Appearance")]
        [Description("The space between the caption and the text box.")]
        public Unit CaptionPadding
        {
            get { return captionPadding; }
            set { captionPadding = value; }
        }

        [Category("Appearance")]
        [Description("Determines if the caption is right-aligned.")]
        public bool RightAlignCaption
        {
            get { return rightAlignCaption; }
            set { rightAlignCaption = value; }
        }
```

Figure 28-14   The code for the CaptionedBox control (part 1 of 2)

The overridden Render method uses an HTML table that contains a single row with three columns to align the caption and the text box. To accomplish this, this method uses the Write methods of the HtmlTextWriter object to write the tags and attributes necessary to render the table as HTML. Notice that, within the Table element, the CellPadding and CellSpacing attributes specify 0 pixels of padding and spacing.

Within the Td element for the first column, the Style attribute specifies the width of the caption using the CaptionWidth property. Notice that the ToString method is used to convert the length and unit of measure of this property to a string value. If the caption width is set to 10 pixels, for example, the result is 10px. In addition, if the RightAlignCaption property is set to True, the Style attribute also specifies that the text should be right-aligned. The start tag for the first Td element is followed by its content, which is the value of the Caption property. The content is then followed by an end tag for the Td element.

Next, the Render method renders the Td element for the second column. This Td element creates the space between the caption and the text box. To do that, it includes a Style attribute that specifies the value of the CaptionPadding property as the width of the element.

Finally, the Render method renders the Td element for the third column. This column contains the text box. To render the text box, the shaded statement executes the Render method of the base class. Since this class is based on the TextBox class, this renders the TextBox control.

The C# code for the CaptionedBox control   Page 2

```
protected override void Render(HtmlTextWriter output)
{
    //begin writing table
    output.WriteBeginTag("table");
    output.WriteAttribute("cellpadding", "0");
    output.WriteAttribute("cellspacing", "0");
    output.Write(HtmlTextWriter.TagRightChar);

    //begin writing row
    output.WriteBeginTag("tr");
    output.Write(HtmlTextWriter.TagRightChar);

    //write first column
    output.WriteBeginTag("td");
    string style = "width: "
        + CaptionWidth.ToString() + ";";
    if (RightAlignCaption)
        style += "text-align: right;";
    output.WriteAttribute("Style", style);
    output.Write(HtmlTextWriter.TagRightChar);
    output.Write(Caption);
    output.WriteEndTag("td");

    //write second column
    output.WriteBeginTag("td");
    style = "width: " + CaptionPadding.ToString() + ";";
    output.WriteAttribute("Style", style);
    output.Write(HtmlTextWriter.TagRightChar);
    output.WriteEndTag("td");

    //write third column
    output.WriteBeginTag("td");
    output.Write(HtmlTextWriter.TagRightChar);
    base.Render(output);
    output.WriteEndTag("td");

    //finish writing row
    output.WriteEndTag("tr");

    //finish writing table
    output.WriteEndTag("table");
}
    }
}
```

Figure 28-14   The code for the CaptionedBox control (part 2 of 2)

How to create a composite control

A composite control is a control that includes two or more child controls. Because of that, a composite control can be more difficult to create than rendered controls and superclassed controls. In the topics that follow, you'll learn the basic techniques for creating composite controls, and you'll see the design and code for the DateDDL control.

How to code a composite control

A composite control typically inherits the CompositeControl class, as shown by the first code example in figure 28-15. This class inherits the WebControl class and adds functionality to that class. In particular, it ensures that all the child controls defined by the composite control are created before they're accessed.

The CompositeControl class also implements the INamingContainer interface. In case you're not familiar with interfaces, they define properties, methods, and events just like classes. Unlike classes, however, an interface doesn't include the details of how the properties, methods, and events are implemented. That's left to the classes that use them.

The INamingContainer interface is unusual in that it doesn't define any properties, methods, or events. Instead, it simply identifies a control as a container control, which ensures that its child controls will be unique. That way, you can include two or more instances of the control on the same page.

To work with the collection of child controls in a composite control, you use the Controls property of the CompositeControl class. To add a control to the collection, for example, you can use the Add method of the control collection object, and to remove all of the controls from the collection, you use the Clear method. This is illustrated by the second example in this figure. This method starts by clearing the controls collection. Then, it creates an instance of the Label class and an instance of the TextBox class and adds them both to the controls collection.

Notice that these statements are coded within a method named CreateChildControls. As you can see by the method declaration, this method overrides the CreateChildControls method of the base class. ASP.NET calls this method automatically to create the child controls of the base control, if it has any. To create a composite control, then, you need to override this method to create the child controls you want to include in the composite control.

The last example in this figure shows how to add literal text to the controls collection. To do that, you use a literal control that specifies the text value you want to include. In this example, the literal control contains a single space ( ). Note that when you use a literal control, you can't apply a style to the text it contains. If you need to do that, you'll want to use a Label control instead.

A property and method of the CompositeControl class used with child controls

Property	Description
Controls	Accesses the collection of controls contained by the web control.

Method	Description
CreateChildControls()	Called automatically by ASP.NET when a page is posted back or before it's rendered.

Common methods of control collection objects

Method	Description
Add(control)	Adds the specified child control.
Remove(control)	Removes the specified child control.
Clear()	Removes all child controls.

The start of a class for a typical composite control

```
public class DateDDL : CompositeControl
```

Code that adds a label and a text box to the collection of child controls

```
protected override void CreateChildControls()
{
    Controls.Clear();
    Label lbl = new Label();
    lbl.Text = labelText;
    Controls.Add(lbl);
    TextBox txt = new TextBox();
    Controls.Add(txt);
}
```

Code that adds a literal control with a space to the controls collection

```
Controls.Add(new LiteralControl(" "));
```

Description

- A composite control has two or more child controls that are stored in a ControlCollection object, which you access through the Controls property.
- A composite control inherits the System.Web.UI.WebControls.CompositeControl class, so it has access to all the properties and methods of that class.
- The CompositeControl class inherits the WebControl class and overrides the Render method of that class to ensure that all the child controls are created before they're accessed.
- The CompositeControl class also implements the INamingContainer interface, which ensures that the ID attributes of all the child controls are unique.
- When you create a composite control, you must override the CreateChildControls method to create the child controls it contains.

Figure 28-15   How to code a composite control

The design of the DateDDL control

Figure 28-16 presents the design of the DateDDL control. This control includes three drop-down lists that let the user select a month, day, and year. When the control is displayed, the Month drop-down list is populated with the names of the months, the Day drop-down list is populated with the numbers 1 through 31, and the year drop-down list is populated with the 10 years that begin with the current year. This control also includes a caption just like the CaptionedBox control. In the page that's displayed at the top of this figure, you can see how this control is used to accept an expiration date from the user.

In addition to the Caption, CaptionWidth, CaptionPadding, and RightAlignCaption properties that are used to implement the caption, the DateDDL control has four properties that store date information. The first one, Date, stores the entire date. This property is updated any time the user selects a different month, day, or year. The other properties, Month, Day, and Year, store just the month, day, and year portion of the date and are updated any time the user changes that portion of the date. The last property, AutoPostBack, lets you specify whether the page that contains the control should be posted back to the server when the user selects a different month, day, or year.

The DateDDL control also raises an event named DateChanged whenever the user selects a different month, day, or year. As you'll see, however, the Month, Day, and Year properties for this control are coded so that this event is raised only once each time the page is posted.

The code for the DateDDL control

Figure 28-17 presents the complete source code for the DateDDL control. Because this code is a bit complicated, you may have to study it awhile before you understand how this control works. I'll just describe some of the key portions of the code here.

First, the five child controls that are included in this control are declared at the beginning of the class. Then, this control includes a constructor that wires the SelectedIndexChanged event of each of the three drop-down lists to an event handler. That way, this class can respond to any of these events.

Second, the Date property shown on page 2 of the code listing is a read-only property that consists of just a get accessor. As you can see, this accessor returns a formatted date that's constructed using the Month, Day, and Year properties. Because you can't set the value of this property, it doesn't include any designer attributes.

A web page that uses a DateDDL control

Properties of the DateDDL control

Property	Description
Caption	The text that's displayed to the left of the drop-down lists.
CaptionWidth	The width of the control's caption area.
CaptionPadding	The width of the area between the caption and the drop-down lists.
RightAlignCaption	Determines whether the caption is right-aligned. The default is False.
Date	The date selected by the user.
Month	An integer representing the month (1 to 12).
Day	An integer representing the day of the month (1 to 31).
Year	An integer representing the year.
AutoPostBack	Determines whether the page should be posted when the user selects a different month, day, or year. The default is False.

Event raised by the DateDDL control

Event	Description
DateChanged	Raised when the user selects a different month, day, or year.

The aspx code for the DateDDL control

```
<cc1:DateDDL ID="ddExpirationDate" runat="server" Caption="Expiration Date:"
    CaptionPadding="10px" CaptionWidth="140px"
    OnDateChanged="ddExpirationDate_DateChanged">
</cc1:DateDDL>
```

Description

- The DateDDL control is a composite control. It uses one label to display the caption to the left of the date, another label to provide spacing between the caption and the date, and three drop-down lists to let the user select a date.

Figure 28-16   The design of the DateDDL control

The C# code for the DateDDL control   **Page 1**

```csharp
using System;
using System.Collections.Generic;
using System.ComponentModel;
using System.Linq;
using System.Text;
using System.Web;
using System.Web.UI;
using System.Web.UI.WebControls;

namespace MurachWebControlLibrary
{
    [DefaultProperty("Text")]
    [ToolboxData("<{0}:DateDDL runat=server></{0}:DateDDL>")]
    public class DateDDL : CompositeControl
    {
        private Label lblCaption = new Label();
        private Label lblCaptionPadding = new Label();
        private DropDownList ddlMonth = new DropDownList();
        private DropDownList ddlDay = new DropDownList();
        private DropDownList ddlYear = new DropDownList();

        private string caption;
        private Unit captionWidth;
        private Unit captionPadding;
        private bool rightAlignCaption;

        private int month;
        private int day;
        private int year;
        private bool autoPostBack;
        private bool dateChangedEventRaised = false;

        public event EventHandler DateChanged;

        public DateDDL()
        {
            ddlDay.SelectedIndexChanged
                += new EventHandler(ddlDay_SelectedIndexChanged);
            ddlMonth.SelectedIndexChanged
                += new EventHandler(ddlMonth_SelectedIndexChanged);
            ddlYear.SelectedIndexChanged
                += new EventHandler(ddlYear_SelectedIndexChanged);
        }

        [Category("Appearance")]
        [Description("The caption displayed to the left of the text box.")]
        public string Caption
        {
            get { return caption; }
            set { caption = value; }
        }
```

Figure 28-17   The code for the DateDDL control (part 1 of 5)

The C# code for the DateDDL control   **Page 2**

```csharp
[Category("Appearance")]
[Description("The width of the caption.")]
public Unit CaptionWidth
{
    get { return captionWidth; }
    set { captionWidth = value; }
}

[Category("Appearance")]
[Description("The space between the caption and the text box.")]
public Unit CaptionPadding
{
    get { return captionPadding; }
    set { captionPadding = value; }
}

[Category("Appearance")]
[Description("Determines if the caption is right-aligned.")]
public bool RightAlignCaption
{
    get { return rightAlignCaption; }
    set { rightAlignCaption = value; }
}

public DateTime Date
{
    get { return Convert.ToDateTime(Month + "/" + Day + "/" + Year); }
}

[Category("Misc"), Description("Gets or set the month.")]
public int Month
{
    get
    {
        month = ddlMonth.SelectedIndex + 1;
        return month;
    }
    set
    {
        month = value;
        ddlMonth.SelectedIndex = month - 1;
        if (!dateChangedEventRaised)
        {
            DateChanged(this, new EventArgs());
            dateChangedEventRaised = true;
        }
    }
}
```

Figure 28-17   The code for the DateDDL control (part 2 of 5)

At the bottom of page 3, you can see the Render method for this control. It simply calls the Render method of the base class to render the control and the child controls it contains.

On page 4 of this listing, you can see the overridden CreateChildControls method. This method is responsible for creating the two Label controls and the month, day, and year drop-down lists and adding them to the controls collection. To do that, it starts by executing the private MakeCaption and MakeCaptionPadding methods to initialize the caption and the spacing between the caption and the drop-down lists. Then, it executes the private MakeMonthList, MakeDayList, and MakeYearList methods to initialize the drop-down lists. Next, it clears the controls collection and adds the controls. Notice that literal controls are added between the drop-down lists. Both of these controls contain a space so that these lists don't appear right next to each other when they're displayed. The second literal control also contains a comma that separates the day drop-down list from the year drop-down list.

When the user selects a different month, day, or year from a drop-down list, the event handler for the SelectedIndexChanged event of that control is executed. The code for these event handlers is shown on page 5 of this listing. They simply set the Month, Day, and Year properties to the selection made by the user, and then call the AdjustDay method. If you look at the set accessors for these properties in parts 2 and 3, you can see that they in turn raise the DateChanged event. Notice that a Boolean variable is used to keep track of whether the DateChanged event has already been raised to make sure it isn't raised more than once.

The AdjustDay method that's called by the SelectedIndexChanged event handlers prevents the date from being set to an invalid date. If the user selects April 31, for example, this method adjusts the date to April 30 since April only has 30 days. Or, if the user selects February 29 and it isn't a leap year, this method adjusts the date to February 28 since February only has 29 days in a leap year.

Although this is the simplest solution to the problem, it's probably not the best solution. Another solution would be to post the page any time the user selected a different month and then load the appropriate days for that month into the Day drop-down list. Still another solution would be to raise an event or throw an exception if the user selects an invalid date. These are the types of coding decisions you'll need to make as you design your custom controls.

The C# code for the DateDDL control   **Page 3**

```csharp
[Category("Misc"), Description("Gets or sets the day.")]
public int Day
{
    get
    {
        day = ddlDay.SelectedIndex + 1;
        return day;
    }
    set
    {
        day = value;
        ddlDay.SelectedIndex = day - 1;
        if (!dateChangedEventRaised)
        {
            DateChanged(this, new EventArgs());
            dateChangedEventRaised = true;
        }
    }
}

[Category("Misc"), Description("Gets or sets the year.")]
public int Year
{
    get
    {
        year = Convert.ToInt32(ddlYear.SelectedValue);
        return year;
    }
    set
    {
        year = value;
        ddlYear.SelectedValue = year.ToString();
        if (!dateChangedEventRaised)
        {
            DateChanged(this, new EventArgs());
            dateChangedEventRaised = true;
        }
    }
}

[Category("Misc")]
[Description("Determines whether a postback occurs "
    + "when the selection is changed.")]
[DefaultValue(false)]
public bool AutoPostBack
{
    get { return autoPostBack; }
    set { autoPostBack = value; }
}

protected override void Render(HtmlTextWriter output)
{
    base.Render(output);
}
```

Figure 28-17   The code for the DateDDL control (part 3 of 5)

The C# code for the DateDDL control

```csharp
protected override void CreateChildControls()
{
    this.MakeCaption();
    this.MakeCaptionPadding();
    this.MakeMonthList();
    this.MakeDayList();
    this.MakeYearList();
    Controls.Clear();
    Controls.Add(lblCaption);
    Controls.Add(lblCaptionPadding);
    Controls.Add(ddlMonth);
    Controls.Add(new LiteralControl(" "));
    Controls.Add(ddlDay);
    Controls.Add(new LiteralControl(", "));
    Controls.Add(ddlYear);
}

private void MakeCaption()
{
    lblCaption.Text = Caption;
    lblCaption.Width = CaptionWidth;
    if (RightAlignCaption)
        lblCaption.Style["text-align"] = "right";
}

private void MakeCaptionPadding()
{
    lblCaptionPadding.Width = CaptionPadding;
}

private void MakeMonthList()
{
    ddlMonth.Width = Unit.Pixel(85);
    ddlMonth.Items.Clear();
    ddlMonth.Items.Add("January");
    ddlMonth.Items.Add("February");
    ddlMonth.Items.Add("March");
    ddlMonth.Items.Add("April");
    ddlMonth.Items.Add("May");
    ddlMonth.Items.Add("June");
    ddlMonth.Items.Add("July");
    ddlMonth.Items.Add("August");
    ddlMonth.Items.Add("September");
    ddlMonth.Items.Add("October");
    ddlMonth.Items.Add("November");
    ddlMonth.Items.Add("December");
    ddlMonth.SelectedIndex = Month - 1;
    ddlMonth.AutoPostBack = AutoPostBack;
}
```

Figure 28-17   The code for the DateDDL control (part 4 of 5)

The C# code for the DateDDL control   **Page 5**

```csharp
private void MakeDayList()
{
    ddlDay.Width = Unit.Pixel(40);
    ddlDay.Items.Clear();
    for (int i = 1; i <= 31; i++)
        ddlDay.Items.Add(i.ToString());
    ddlDay.SelectedValue = Day.ToString();
    ddlDay.AutoPostBack = AutoPostBack;
}

private void MakeYearList()
{
    ddlYear.Width = Unit.Pixel(65);
    ddlYear.Items.Clear();
    for (int i = DateTime.Today.Year;
        i <= DateTime.Today.Year + 10; i++)
        ddlYear.Items.Add(i.ToString());
    ddlYear.SelectedValue = Year.ToString();
    ddlYear.AutoPostBack = AutoPostBack;
}

private void ddlMonth_SelectedIndexChanged(object sender, EventArgs e)
{
    this.Month = ddlMonth.SelectedIndex + 1;
    this.AdjustDay();
}

private void ddlDay_SelectedIndexChanged(object sender, EventArgs e)
{
    this.Day = Convert.ToInt32(ddlDay.SelectedValue);
    this.AdjustDay();
}

private void ddlYear_SelectedIndexChanged(object sender, EventArgs e)
{
    this.Year = Convert.ToInt32(ddlYear.SelectedValue);
    this.AdjustDay();
}

private void AdjustDay()
{
    switch (Month)
    {
        case 4:
        case 6:
        case 9:
        case 11:
            if (Day == 31) Day = 30;
            break;
        case 2:
            if (Year % 4 == 0)
                if (Day > 29) Day = 29;
            else
                if (Day > 28) Day = 28;
            break;
    }
}
}
```

Figure 28-17   The code for the DateDDL control (part 5 of 5)

Perspective

In this chapter, you've learned the basics of creating custom server controls. You should realize, however, that there's a lot more to developing custom controls than what's presented in this chapter. For example, if you want to distribute a library of custom server controls that you've developed, you may want to include a bitmap that can be used as the icon for the control when it's displayed in the Toolbox. Or you may want to specify the default prefix that's used for the controls in the library. You may also want to bind data to custom controls, or you may want to create templated controls that work like the GridView control you saw in chapter 14. Although this chapter doesn't show how to accomplish these tasks, the programming techniques you've learned in this chapter should give you a good start toward developing your own custom server controls.

Terms

custom server control
web control library
rendered control
superclassed control
composite control
child control
designer attribute
self-closing tag
class attribute
property attribute
delegate

29

An introduction to web services

In addition to web applications, you can use Visual Studio 2008 to create web services. Web services allow you to store common processing routines on a web server, where they're available to other programmers who need to use the routines in their applications. In other words, web services provide another way to reuse code. In this chapter, you'll learn the basic concepts and skills you need to create and use web services.

Basic concepts and terms **926**
What web services are used for 926
How web services work 926
How to create a web service **928**
How to start a web service web site 928
How to add a web service 928
How to develop the code for a web service 930
The code for the DaysUntilDates web service 932
How to test a web service 934
How to consume a web service **936**
How to add a web reference 936
How to use a web service 938
Perspective **940**

Basic concepts and terms

Simply put, a *web service* is a class that resides on a web server and can be accessed via the Internet or an intranet. As a result, ASP.NET applications or other types of web applications can access the web service from any computer that's connected to the Internet or an intranet.

What web services are used for

Web services are becoming an integral part of web development. One use of web services is to develop *distributed web applications* in which portions of an application can reside on different servers. For example, you might implement the business logic and database processing code for an application as a web service that runs on one server. Then, the user interface portion of the application can run on another server and call on the web service whenever business logic or database features are needed. It's even possible to provide two interfaces to the same web service: a web interface provided by an ASP.NET application that can be run from any computer that has a browser and Internet access, and a Windows interface provided by a Windows application that's installed on the user's computer.

Another use for web services is to allow applications developed by different companies or organizations to interact with one another. For example, the United States Postal Service has web services that let you calculate shipping rates, correct addresses, and track packages. You can use web services like these to incorporate the features they provide into your applications. Similarly, the popular search site Google offers web services that let you incorporate Google searches into your applications. As more companies create web services and publish them on the Internet, applications that use these services will become more popular.

How web services work

Figure 29-1 illustrates how web services work. As you can see, the web service is accessed from a web page running on a web server. In this example, the web service and the application's web pages reside on two different web servers. Although that doesn't have to be the case, this arrangement illustrates how web services can be used to create distributed applications. The server that hosts the web service must have both IIS and the .NET Framework installed.

Notice that the web page and the web service communicate using XML. Actually, web services use a rather complicated collection of protocols that are built on XML. These protocols include *WSDL*, which stands for *Web Services Description Language,* and *SOAP*, which stands for *Simple Object Access Protocol*. Fortunately, all of this is taken care of for you when you create and use a web service. As a result, you don't usually have to deal directly with XML, WSDL, or SOAP.

The operation of a distributed ASP.NET web application

Description

- A *web service* is a class that resides on a web server and can be accessed by web applications or other web services to implement distributed ASP.NET web applications. A web service can also be accessed by Windows applications.

- Web services typically contain business logic that's coded as a collection of public methods.

- Like ASP.NET web applications, ASP.NET web services typically reside on a web server with IIS. Although they can reside on the same server as the web applications that use them, they can also reside on a separate server.

- Information is passed between a web page and a web service using XML. Each web service must contain an XML document written in the *Web Services Description Language* (*WSDL*) that describes how the web service works and how clients can interact with it.

- If the web page and web service reside on the same server, the XML is passed as part of an HTTP request or response. If the web service resides on a different web server, the *Simple Object Access Protocol*, or *SOAP*, is used to facilitate the HTTP request and response.

- Since web services use a standard XML protocol to pass data between servers, they allow different types of servers to be able to communicate with each other. For example, a web application that's running on an IIS web server can use a web service that's running on an Apache web server. Conversely, a web application that's running on an Apache web server can use a web service that's running on an IIS web server.

Figure 29-1   How web services work

How to create a web service

To create a web service, you start by creating a web service web site. Then, you add each web service you want to create to this web site. Finally, you use the Code Editor to develop the public and private code for each web service. The following topics show you how.

How to start a web service web site

Figure 29-2 shows the New Web Site dialog box for creating a web service web site. From this dialog box, you identify the location of the web server and the name of the directory where the web service web site will reside just as you do for a regular web site. Then, all of the files for the web site are stored in that directory on the web server, and the solution file is stored in a directory with the same name within the projects location for Visual Studio directory.

How to add a web service

When you first start a web service web site, it contains a single web service named Service. In most cases, you'll want to delete this web service and add your own. In the next figure, for example, you'll see a web site with a web service named DaysUntilDates. To add a web service like this, you use the Add New Item dialog box shown in figure 29-2.

The New Web Site and Add New Item dialog boxes

Description

- To start a web service web site, display the New Web Site dialog box and select the ASP.NET Web Service template. Then, select HTTP from the Location drop-down list and identify the IIS server and the directory where you want the web site stored. Visual Studio creates this directory in the Inetpub\wwwroot directory of the IIS server by default.

- Visual Studio also creates a directory with the name you specify in the projects location for Visual Studio and stores the solution file there.

- By default, a web service web site consists of a single web service named Service. In most cases, you'll delete this web service and add your own. To add a web service, display the Add New Item dialog box, select the Web Service template, and enter a name.

Figure 29-2   How to start a web service web site and add a web service

How to develop the code for a web service

When you create a web service, two files are added to the web site. The first one has an extension of *asmx* and is the file you use to call the methods that you add to the web service. Like the aspx extension that's used for web pages, the asmx extension tells IIS that the file should be processed by ASP.NET.

The second file for a web service has a *cs* extension and is stored in the App_Code folder. This file contains the methods and other code that define the web service. The starting code in this file is displayed by default when you create a web service. You can see this code in figure 29-3.

You'll want to note several things about the code in this figure. First, like everything else that's built on the .NET Framework, a web service is implemented as a class. In this case, the class inherits the WebService class, which provides the web service with access to the ASP.NET objects commonly used by web services.

Second, notice the WebService *attribute* that precedes the class definition. An attribute is similar to a keyword (like public or private) that provides information as to how the code should be used. In this case, the WebService attribute identifies the namespace that will contain the web service. The default is tempuri.org, which is a temporary namespace that you can use during development of a web service. If you publish a web service so it's available to other users, however, you'll want to change this name to something unique. That way, if someone else publishes a web service with the same name, the two can be distinguished by the namespace that contains them.

The WebService attribute can also contain a description of the web service. If you publish a web service, you'll want to include this information to provide potential users of the service with information about what it does. You'll see an example of how you code this information in the next figure.

To code a method that's accessible from outside the web service, you use the public keyword, and you precede the method with the WebMethod attribute. This is illustrated by the HelloWorld method that's included in the starting code for a web service. As its name implies, the WebMethod attribute identifies a public method as a *web method*. Aside from the WebMethod attribute, you code a web method just as you would any other method. In addition, you can include private variables and methods that are used by the web method.

One key difference between a web service and a regular C# class is that a web service can't have properties. You can define public variables, but those variables aren't accessible to clients that use the web service. As a result, web methods are the only interface a client has to a web service.

You can still implement the equivalent of properties using web methods, though. For example, to retrieve the value of a property, use a web method that returns the value of the variable for the property. And to set the value of a property, use a method that accepts the value of the property and assigns it to a variable.

The starting code for a web service

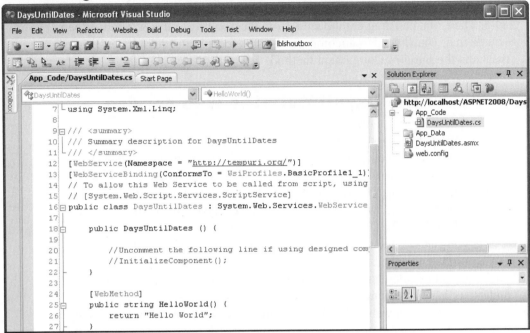

Description

- A web service is made up of two files. The file with the *asmx* extension is the file that you use to call the web service methods. The file with the *cs* extension in the App_Code folder contains the code for the web service.

- A web service is implemented as a class that inherits the WebService class of the System.Web.Services namespace. This class provides the basic functionality for all web services.

- You develop the code for a web service by coding *web methods*. A web method is a public method with the WebMethod *attribute* ([WebMethod]). A web service can also include private code that's not available from outside the service.

- Web services don't support property declarations or public variables. Instead, you can use public methods to get and set the values of private variables.

- You can use the WebService attribute ([WebService]) to identify the namespace for a web service. The default namespace is http://tempuri.org. If a web service is made public, it must have a unique namespace to distinguish it from other web services with the same name.

- The WebService attribute can also include a description of the web service. This description is displayed on the help and service description pages for the service.

- If you need to add a component such as a dataset to a web service, you can do that by dragging the component from the Toolbox to the Component Designer window. To display the Component Designer window, highlight the code file and then click the View Designer button at the top of the Solution Explorer.

Figure 29-3   How to develop the code for a web service

By the way, you can also add components such as datasets to a web service. To do that, you display the Component Designer window as described in figure 29-3. Then, you can drag components from the Toolbox to this window. When you do that, you'll need to uncomment the statement in the default constructor that calls the InitializeComponent method.

The code for the DaysUntilDates web service

To illustrate how you can use a web service, figure 29-4 presents the code for a web service named DaysUntilDates. This service contains three web methods that calculate the days remaining until a specified date. The first method, named simply DaysUntil, accepts the target date as a parameter. The other methods, named DaysUntilHalloween and DaysUntilChristmas, assume 10/31 and 12/25 as the target date.

As you can see, the web methods use a private method named DaysUntilDate to calculate the days remaining until the target date. Since you've seen this calculation earlier in this book, you shouldn't have any trouble understanding how it works.

Notice that each web method starts with a WebMethod attribute. Although this attribute isn't required, it can improve the readability of a web service that contains private methods in addition to web methods. So we recommend that you use this format for all your web services.

You should also notice the WebService attribute at the beginning of the web service. This attribute identifies the namespace for the web service as

`http://murach.com/`

This namespace is used to uniquely identify the web service. Although it isn't required, it is common practice to use an Internet domain name to help ensure that the namespace is unique.

The WebService attribute in this example also includes a brief description of the web service. You'll see one way this information is used in the next figure.

The C# code for the DaysUntilDates web service

```csharp
using System;
using System.Collections;
using System.Linq;
using System.Web;
using System.Web.Services;
using System.Web.Services.Protocols;
using System.Xml.Linq;


/// <summary>
/// Summary description for DaysUntilDates
/// </summary>
[WebService(Namespace = "http://murach.com/",
    Description="Calculates the number of days until a given date.")]
[WebServiceBinding(ConformsTo = WsiProfiles.BasicProfile1_1)]
public class DaysUntilDates : System.Web.Services.WebService
{

    [WebMethod]
    public int DaysUntil(DateTime date)
    {
        return DaysUntilDate(date.Month, date.Day);
    }

    [WebMethod]
    public int DaysUntilHalloween()
    {
        return DaysUntilDate(10, 31);
    }

    [WebMethod]
    public int DaysUntilChristmas()
    {
        return DaysUntilDate(12, 25);
    }

    private int DaysUntilDate(int month, int day)
    {
        DateTime targetDate;
        targetDate = DateTime.Parse(month.ToString() + "/"
                + day.ToString() + "/"
                + DateTime.Today.Year);
        if (DateTime.Today > targetDate)
        {
            targetDate = targetDate.AddYears(1);
        }
        TimeSpan timeUntil = targetDate - DateTime.Today;
        return timeUntil.Days;
    }
}
```

Figure 29-4　The code for the DaysUntilDates web service

How to test a web service

After you develop a web service, you can test it without having to create a client program that uses it. To do that, you simply build and run the web service in your default browser or in a Browse window just as you would a web application. When you do that, a *Web Service help page* like the first one shown in figure 29-5 is displayed.

The Web Service help page identifies the web service and displays the description you specified in the WebService attribute. It also includes a link to the *service description* for the web service. This is the XML document you learned about in figure 29-1 that contains the Web Services Description Language (WSDL) that describes the web service. If you're interested in what this document looks like, you can click on this link to display it.

Finally, the Web Service help page lists the web methods that are available from the web service. If you click on the link for one of these methods, a help page for that method is displayed. The second screen in this figure, for example, is the help page for the DaysUntil method.

If a method requires parameters, the help page for that method lists them by name and lets you enter values for them. Then, when you click the Invoke button, the method is executed and the XML that's generated as a result is displayed. In this figure, for example, you can see the XML that's generated when the DaysUntil method is executed using 10-17 as the value of the date parameter. If you're familiar with XML, you can see that the actual result of the calculation is contained within <int> and </int> tags. These tags are generated based on the return type of the method.

Although you can't see it in this figure, the help page for a method also contains sample SOAP and HTTP requests and responses. If you're interested in what this code looks like, you may want to scroll down so you can see it. In general, though, you don't need to worry about how it works.

When you test a web service in your browser as shown in this figure, you can use the Visual Studio debugging tools you learned about in chapter 4 to debug it. To do that, just set one or more breakpoints before you run the web service. Then, the web service will enter break mode before it executes a statement that has a breakpoint, and you can use the tools that are available from break mode to debug the web service.

Help pages for the DaysUntilDates web service

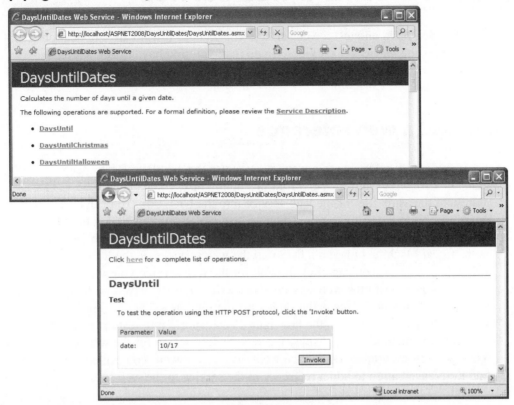

XML output for the DaysUntil web method

Description

- To test a web service in your default browser, click the Start button in the Standard toolbar. A *Web Service help page* like the first one shown above is displayed.

- To test a web method, click the link for that method. Then, enter any required parameters in the help page that's displayed and click the Invoke button. A page that shows the XML output for the method is displayed.

- When you use your browser to test a web service, you can set breakpoints and debug the web service just as you do for a web application.

Figure 29-5   How to test a web service

How to consume a web service

After you build and test a web service, you can use it from any application that requires the services it provides. To do that, you first have to add a reference to the web service. Then, you can create an instance of it and use it like any other class.

How to add a web reference

To add a web reference to a web site, you use the Add Web Reference dialog box shown in figure 29-6. From this dialog box, you can enter the address of the asmx file for the web service into the URL box. You can also locate a web service using the links that are available from this dialog box. If the service is on your local server, for example, you can click the Web Services on the Local Machine link and a list of all the web services on the local server will be listed. Then, you can click the link for the web service you want to add.

After you identify the web service, its description is displayed in the left pane of the dialog box. This is the same information that's displayed in the Web Service help page you saw in the last figure. You can use it to test or review the available web methods or to display the service description for the web service. When you're sure you've located the web service you want, you can click the Add Reference button to add a reference to the service to the web site.

The dialog box for adding a web reference

Description

- To add a reference to a web service to a web site, right-click the web site in the Solution Explorer and select the Add Web Reference command from the shortcut menu to display the Add Web Reference dialog box.

- To locate a web service, enter the address of its asmx file in the URL box and press Enter, or select the URL from the drop-down list. Then, information about the service is displayed, and you can click the Add Reference button to add a reference to the web service to your web site.

- You can also use the links in the Add Web Reference dialog box to locate web services in the current solution, on your local machine, or on a local network.

Figure 29-6   How to add a web reference

How to use a web service

After you add a reference to a web service, it appears in a folder that has the same name as the server that contains the web service. This folder is subordinate to the App_WebReferences folder, which is added automatically if it doesn't already exist. You can see these folders and the three files that make up the DaysUntilDates web service in the Solution Explorer shown in figure 29-7.

The first two files for the web service, DaysUntilDates.discomap and DaysUntilDates.disco, contain information about the location of the web service that let other users "discover" the web service. The third file, DaysUntilDates.wsdl, is an XML document that describes the web service and contains information on how a client can interact with it. This file can be helpful for figuring out how to interact with a web service if you find that the documentation for the service is incomplete or confusing.

To use a web service, you create an instance of it and assign it to an object variable as shown in the first statement in this figure. Notice that when you name the web service, you must qualify it with the name of the server where it's located. In this case, because the web service resides on the local server, the server name is localhost.

After you assign an instance of the web service to an object variable, you can refer to any web method defined by the service using standard techniques. The second statement in this figure, for example, shows how you refer to the DaysUntilHalloween method defined by the DaysUntilDates web service.

The Solution Explorer with a web service reference

A statement that creates an instance of the DaysUntilDates web service

```
localhost.DaysUntilDates daysUntilDates = new localhost.DaysUntilDates();
```

A statement that executes the DaysUntilHalloween method of this web service

```
daysUntilHalloween = daysUntilDates.DaysUntilHalloween();
```

Description

- When you add a reference to a web service to a web site, a folder with the name of the server where the web service is located is created under the App_WebReferences folder in the Solution Explorer.

- Three files are included for the web service. The *disco* and *discomap* files contain information about the location of the web service. The *wsdl* file contains a description of the web service.

- To use a web service in an application, you can create an instance of it using a declaration statement with the new keyword like the one shown above. The reference to the web service must include the name of the server where it resides.

- After you create an instance of a web service, you can execute its web methods using the same techniques you use to execute a method of any object.

Figure 29-7   How to use a web service

Perspective

Although the web service presented in this chapter is trivial, it demonstrates the techniques you can use to develop more substantial web services. As a result, the basic skills you've learned here are enough to get you started developing your own web services. In addition, you'll be prepared to learn the more complicated aspects of web services programming when the need arises.

* * *

In this book, we've done our best to present all of the skills that you need for developing e-commerce web applications. Now, if you've read all 29 chapters of this book, we hope you feel that you're adequately prepared for doing that. You should also feel like you have the concepts, skills, and perspective to learn whatever else you need to know as you develop web applications. If that's the case, this book has done its job. And we thank you for reading it.

Terms

web service
distributed web application
WSDL (Web Services Description Language)
SOAP (Simple Object Access Protocol)
attribute
web method
Web Service help page
service description

Appendix A

How to install and use the software and downloadable files

To develop ASP.NET 3.5 applications, you need to have Visual Studio 2008 or Visual Web Developer 2008 Express Edition installed on your PC. Both of these products include a development web server that you can use to run your applications. However, because of the limitations of this server, you'll also want to test your applications using IIS. The easiest way to do that is to install IIS on your own PC.

If you're going to develop applications that use databases that are stored on your own PC rather than on a remote server, you also need to install SQL Server on your PC. The easiest way to do that is to install SQL Server 2005 Express Edition. In fact, this edition of SQL Server is installed by default when you install most editions of Visual Studio 2008.

This appendix shows you how to install both Visual Studio and IIS. In addition, it shows you how to install SQL Server 2005 Express Edition and how to attach the database that's used in this book to this database server. But first, it describes the files for this book that are available for download from our web site and shows you how to download, install, and use them. We recommend you read these topics before you start developing your first web application so you can be sure that you have all the software and files you need.

How to download and install the files for this book 942
How to install IIS under Windows XP 944
How to install IIS under Windows Vista 946
How to install Visual Studio 2008 948
How to install and use SQL Server 2005 Express 950
How to attach the database for this book to the database server 952
How to use the downloaded web applications 954

How to download and install the files for this book

Throughout this book, you'll see complete applications that illustrate the material presented in each chapter. To help you understand how these applications work, you can download the source code and databases for these applications from our web site at www.murach.com. Then, you can open and run them in Visual Studio. These files come in a single download, as summarized in figure A-1. This figure also describes how you download and install these files.

When you download the single install file and execute it, it will install all of the files for this book in the Murach\ASP.NET 3.5 C# directory on your C drive. Within this directory, you'll find a directory named Book Applications that contains all the applications in this book. You can open and run these applications in Visual Studio as file-system applications as described in figure A-7. The exception is the application for chapter 19, which must be run under IIS because it requires a digital secure certificate. The procedure for running a file-system web site under IIS is also presented in figure A-7. For more information on digital secure certificates, see chapter 19.

The download also includes Access and SQL Server Express versions of the Halloween database used by many of the applications. Since the Access database is small, we've included it in the App_Data folder of each application that uses it so you can run these applications without any trouble. The SQL Server database is stored in the Database and Database Backup directories. The Database directory also contains files that you can use to attach this database to a SQL Server Express database server, detach this database from the server, restore the original database, and grant ASP.NET access to the database. Figure A-6 describes how to use these files.

To help you get started right, we've included exercises at the end of the first four chapters of this book. These exercises guide you through the process of running the application in chapter 1 and the process of designing, coding, and testing the applications in chapters 2 and 3. That should get you comfortable with Visual Studio 2008 and ASP.NET 3.5 web programming.

To help you with these exercises, we've included the application you'll need for the chapter 1 exercise and some of the files you'll need for the chapter 2 and 3 exercises in the download. These files and application are installed in the Exercise Starts subdirectory of the C:\Murach\ASP.NET 3.5 C# directory. When you execute the install file, the subdirectory and file in the Exercise Starts subdirectory are copied to the C:\ASP.NET 3.5 C# directory. That will make it easy for you to locate them as you work through the exercises.

We've also included the solutions for the exercises for chapters 2 and 3. That way, when you complete the exercises, you can compare them with the solutions we provide. Or, if you have trouble doing the exercises on your own, you can review our solutions to see how they work.

What the downloadable application file for this book contains

- The source code for all of the applications presented in the book
- Access and SQL Server Express versions of the Halloween database used in these applications
- Files you can use to work with the SQL Server Express version of the Halloween database
- The starting points and solutions for the exercises in this book

How to download and install the files for this book

1. Go to www.murach.com, and go to the page for *Murach's ASP.NET 3.5 Web Programming with C# 2008.*
2. Click on the link for "FREE download of the book applications." Then, download "All book files." This will download one file named acs8_allfiles.exe to your C drive.
3. Use Windows Explorer to find the downloaded file on your C drive. Then, double-click on this file and respond to the dialog boxes that follow. This installs the files in directories that start with C:\Murach\ASP.NET 3.5 C#.

How your system is prepared for doing the exercises

- One of the exercises for chapter 1 has you open and run an existing web application. In addition, some of the exercises for chapters 2 and 3 have you copy existing files to the applications you create. These files and application are installed in the C:\Murach\ASP.NET 3.5 C#\Exercise Starts directory. Then, a batch file named exercise_starts_setup.bat copies the subdirectory and file in the Exercises Starts directory to the C:\ASP.NET 3.5 C# directory. This is the directory you'll use for the exercises.

How to prepare your system for using the database

- To use the database that comes with this book on your PC, you need to make sure that SQL Server 2005 Express is installed as described in figure A-5, and you need to attach the database to SQL Server Express as described in figure A-6.

Description

- You can download the sample applications, databases, and exercise solutions for this book from www.murach.com.
- The Access version of the Halloween database is included in the App_Data folder of each application that uses it.

Figure A-1   How to download and install the files for this book

How to install IIS under Windows XP

When you run an ASP.NET web application from Visual Studio, it runs under the built-in development server by default. Because of that, you don't have to have IIS installed to develop the applications in this book or to run the applications that you download from our web site (with the exception noted in the previous topic). Keep in mind, however, that the built-in server has some limitations, which you'll learn about in chapter 4. Because of that, you'll want to install IIS so that you can thoroughly test the applications you develop. (Note that you can't install IIS if you're using Windows XP Home Edition. In that case, IIS isn't available to you, and you'll have to use the development server or you'll have to have access to a separate web server.)

Figure A-2 shows how to install IIS under Windows XP. To start, you display the Add/Remove Programs dialog box and then click the Add/Remove Windows Components button at the left side of the dialog box that's displayed. When you do, the Windows Components Wizard starts and the first dialog box shown in this figure is displayed. This dialog box lists all the available Windows components. The components that are currently installed have a check mark in front of them. To install another component (in this case, IIS), just check it, click the Next button, and complete the dialog boxes that are displayed.

In chapter 4, you'll learn how to create remote IIS web sites, and you'll learn how to use IIS as an FTP server. To use either of these features, you must install components of IIS that aren't installed by default. To install these components, select IIS in the Windows Components Wizard and then click the Details button to display the Internet Information Services (IIS) dialog box shown here. Then, if you want to use IIS as an FTP server, select the File Transfer Protocol (FTP) Service component. And, if you want to create remote IIS web sites, select the FrontPage 2000 Server Extensions component. When you're done, click OK and then continue with the Windows Components Wizard.

The Windows Components Wizard

How to install IIS

1. Double-click Add or Remove Programs in the Control Panel. Then, click on Add/Remove Windows Components to display the Windows Components Wizard, and select Internet Information Services (IIS) from the list of components that are displayed.

2. If you want to install FPSE, or if you want to configure IIS as an FTP Server, click the Details button, select the appropriate options from the Internet Information Services (IIS) dialog box that's displayed, and click OK.

3. Click the Next button to complete the installation.

Description

- If you want to run applications from a local IIS server, install IIS before you install Visual Studio.

- To create or access an IIS web site on a remote computer, that computer must have FPSE installed. To use IIS as an FTP server, the FTP Service must be installed.

Figure A-2   How to install IIS under Windows XP

How to install IIS under Windows Vista

If you want to be able to test the web applications you develop under IIS on a Windows Vista machine, you'll need to use the procedure in figure A-3 to install IIS. (Note that IIS doesn't come with the Home Basic Edition or the Starter Edition of Windows Vista. Because of that, you'll have to use the development server that comes with ASP.NET to test your applications, or you'll need to have access to a separate web server.) To start, you display the Control Panel and then click the Turn Windows Features on or off link at the left side of the window. When you do, the Windows Features dialog box shown in this figure is displayed. This dialog box lists all the available Windows components. If all of the features of a component are installed, the check box in front of the component will have a check mark in it. If only some of the features are installed, the check box for the component will be shaded.

To install the default components of IIS, you simply check its box and then click the OK button. If you want to install features other than the defaults, you can expand the Internet Information Services node and any of its subordinate nodes to select the features you want. For example, if you want to use IIS as an FTP server as described in chapter 4, you can select the FTP Publishing Service feature.

Note that the version of IIS that comes with Vista (IIS 7.0) doesn't include FrontPage Server Extensions (FPSE). Because of that, you can't work with web sites on a remote server. Since the release of Vista, however, an edition of FPSE that works with IIS 7.0 has become available. You can download this product from the IIS web site as described in this figure.

The Windows Features dialog box

How to install IIS

1. Display the Control Panel and make sure it's in Classic View. Then, click the Turn Windows Features on or off link to display the Windows Features dialog box.
2. Select Internet Information Services from the list of components that are displayed.
3. If you want to configure IIS as an FTP Server, expand the Internet Information Services node and select the FTP Publishing Service component.
4. Click the OK button to complete the installation.

Description

- If you want to run applications from a local IIS server, install IIS before you install Visual Studio.
- Windows Vista comes with IIS 7.0, which doesn't include FPSE. If you want to create or access a web site on a remote computer, then, you'll need to download FPSE from the IIS web site. To do that, go to www.iis.net/downloads, click the link for the Administration category, and then click the link for FrontPage 2002 Server Extensions for IIS 7.0.
- If the check box for a component is shaded, it means that only some of the features of that component are installed. To see a list of the individual features, you can expand the component.

Figure A-3   How to install IIS under Windows Vista

How to install Visual Studio 2008

If you've installed Windows applications before, you shouldn't have any trouble installing Visual Studio 2008. You simply insert the DVD or the first CD and the setup program starts automatically. This setup program will lead you through the steps for installing Visual Studio as summarized in figure A-4.

When you click the Install Visual Studio 2008 link, the setup program starts loading the installation components it needs. Then, after you click the Next button and accept the license agreement, the program lets you select the type of installation. In most cases, you'll perform a default installation so the most commonly used features are installed, including the .NET Framework, Visual Studio, C#, the development web server, and SQL Server Express.

After you install Visual Studio, you can install the documentation for Visual Studio and all of the products that come with it. To do that, just click the Install Product Documentation link.

If you're using the Visual Web Developer 2008 Express Edition, you have to download and install Web Developer 2008 and SQL Server Express separately. But if you follow the directions on the Microsoft web site when you download these products, you shouldn't have any trouble installing them.

The final setup step is to apply any updates that have become available since the product was released. If you don't perform this step, though, you can check for updates from within Visual Studio by using the Help→Check for Updates command. In fact, you should use this command periodically to be sure that Visual Studio is up-to-date.

By the way, the first time you start Visual Studio, you'll be asked to select the default environment settings. Then, you can choose Web Development Settings so your menus will look like the ones in this book.

The Visual Studio 2008 Setup program

How to install Visual Studio 2008

1. Insert the DVD or Disc 1 of the installation CDs. The setup program will start automatically.
2. Click the Install Visual Studio 2008 link and follow the instructions. When the Options page is displayed, you can accept the Default option unless you have special requirements.
3. To install the documentation for Visual Studio and the related products (C#, ASP.NET, etc.), click the Install Product Documentation link.
4. To install any updates that are available, click the Check for Service Releases link.

How to install Visual Web Developer 2008 Express Edition

1. Go to the page on Microsoft's web site for the download of Visual Web Developer 2008 Express Edition and follow the instructions to download the setup program.
2. Run the setup program. It works similarly to the setup program for Visual Studio 2008, but fewer options are available.

Description

*   The Visual Studio 2008 Setup program installs not only Visual Studio, but also the .NET Framework, the development web server, and SQL Server Express.
*   The setup program for Visual Web Developer 2008 Express Edition does not install SQL Server 2005 Express. As a result, if you want to use SQL Server 2005 Express to work with databases, you'll need to download and install it as described in figure A-5.

Figure A-4   How to install Visual Studio 2008

How to install and use SQL Server 2005 Express

SQL Server 2005 Express Edition is a free, lightweight version of SQL Server 2005 that you can install on your PC to test database applications. If SQL Server Express isn't installed when you install Visual Studio, you can download and install it from Microsoft's web site. Figure A-5 describes the procedure for installing SQL Server Express.

After you install SQL Server Express, you can use the SQL Server Configuration Manager shown at the top of this figure to work with the server. In particular, you can use it to start, continue, pause, or stop the SQL Server engine. By default, SQL Server is started each time you start your PC. If that's not what you want, you can display the Properties dialog box for the server, click the Services tab, and then select Manual for the Start Mode option. Then, you can start SQL Server whenever you need it using the Configuration Manager.

Although you don't need to know much about how SQL Server Express works to use it, you should know that when you run the setup program, it creates a copy of SQL Server with the same name as your computer appended with SQLEXPRESS. For example, the copy of SQL Server on my system is named MMA-DSK-001\SQLEXPRESS. After this server is installed and started, you can attach databases to it. Then, you can create connections to those databases that you can use in your ASP.NET applications.

The SQL Server Configuration Manager

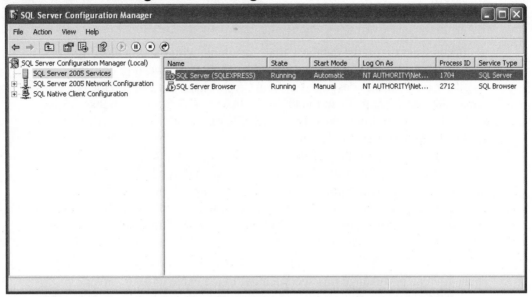

How to install SQL Server 2005 Express

- If you're using Visual Studio 2008, SQL Server 2005 Express is installed when you install Visual Studio as described in figure A-4.
- If you're using Visual Web Developer 2008 Express Edition, you can download the setup file for SQL Server 2005 Express Edition from Microsoft's web site for free. Then, you can run the setup file to install SQL Server Express.

How to use SQL Server Express

- After you install SQL Server Express, it will start automatically each time you start your PC. To start or stop this service or change its start mode, start the SQL Server Configuration Manager (Start→All Programs→Microsoft SQL Server 2005→Configuration Tools→SQL Server Configuration Manager), select the server in the right pane, and use the buttons in the toolbar.
- The setup program creates a copy of SQL Server with a name that consists of your computer name followed by \SqlExpress. You can use this name to define connections to the databases that you use with this server.

Note

- When SQL Server 2008 Express Edition becomes available, you'll be able to download and install it just as you would SQL Server 2005 Express Edition.

Figure A-5   How to install and use SQL Server 2005 Express

How to attach the database for this book to the database server

If you want to use the database that's available with the download for this book, you can do that without much trouble. First, you'll need to download and install the book files as described in figure A-1. Then, you can run the batch file named db_attach.bat that's in the C:\Murach\ASP.NET 3.5 C#\Database directory as described in figure A-6. This batch file runs a SQL Server script named db_attach.sql that attaches the data files for the database to the SQL Server Express database server that's running on your computer.

Note, however, that if the database server on your system has a name other than the computer name appended with SQLEXPRESS, the batch file we provide won't work. But you can easily change it so it will work. To do that, just open the file in a text editor such as NotePad. When you do, you'll see a single command with this server specification:

```
sqlcmd -S localhost\SQLExpress -E /i db_attach.sql
```

Then, you can just change this specification to the name of your server.

Another problem can arise if you try to attach the database by running the db_attach.bat file under the Windows Vista operating system. Specifically, you may get an error like this:

```
CREATE DATABASE permission denied in database master
```

This is due to the fact that under Vista, you aren't automatically given administrator privileges even if you're logged on as an administrator, and you need to have administrator privileges to attach the database. Normally, Vista will notify you when administrator privileges are required to perform a task, but this doesn't happen when you run a batch file.

To get around this problem, you'll need to turn off a feature of Vista called User Account Control as described in this figure. Then, after you restart your system, you should be able to attach the database without any problem. Be sure to turn User Account Control back on when you're done as it provides added security for your system.

You'll also need to turn User Account Control off to run the db_detach.bat and db_restore.bat files in the Database directory. These files provide for detaching the database and restoring the original database from the Database Backup directory. Note that if you detach the database and then move the mdf and ldf files, you'll need to use an edited version of the db_attach.sql file to reattach them.

If you're using Windows XP, you'll also need to grant ASP.NET access to the database. To do that, you can run the db_grant_access.bat file in the Database directory. But first, you must modify the db_grant_access.sql file that this batch file runs so it uses the name of your computer. To do that, open the file in a text editor, and replace each occurrence of [machineName] with the name of your computer. Then, save and close this file, and run the db_grant_access.bat file to grant ASP.NET access to the Halloween database.

The dialog box for turning User Account Control on and off under Vista

How to attach the database for this book to SQL Server Express

- If you're going to use the SQL Server version of the Halloween database that's used by some of the applications in this book on your own PC, you need to attach it to SQL Server Express. To do that, you can use one of the batch files and SQL scripts that are downloaded and installed along with the other files for this book.

- To attach the database to SQL Server Express, run the db_attach.bat file. To do that, you can use the Windows Explorer to navigate to the C:\Murach\ASP.NET 3.5 C#\Database directory and double-click the db_attach.bat file.

How to detach the database and restore the original database

- To detach the database from the server, run the db_detach.bat file.

- To restore the original database, run the db_restore.bat file. This detaches the database, copies the original database files in the Database Backup directory over the current files in the Database directory, and reattaches the database.

How to work with the database under Windows Vista

- To use the batch files we provide to attach, detach, or restore the MMABooks database under Windows Vista, you will need to temporarily turn a feature of Vista called User Account Control off.

- To access User Account Control, display the Control Panel and make sure it's in Classic View. Next, double-click on User Accounts and click on the Turn User Account Control on or off link. Then, remove the check mark from the Use User Account Control option, click the OK button, and restart your system when instructed.

Figure A-6   How to attach the database for this book to the database server

How to use the downloaded web applications

You can use two techniques to run the downloaded web applications for this book. First, you can open the applications in Visual Studio and then run them using the built-in development server. Second, you can run them under a local IIS server. Figure A-7 describes both of these techniques.

Before you can run an application with a local IIS server, you must create a virtual directory for the application within IIS. A virtual directory is a directory that contains a pointer to the directory that actually contains the files for a web site. To create a virtual directory, you can use the procedure shown in this figure. Then, you can run the application from within Visual Studio just as you would a file-system application.

Once you create a virtual directory for a web application, you can also run the application from outside of Visual Studio. To do that, open a browser window and specify //localhost/ followed by the virtual directory name and the starting page. For example, if the virtual directory name is Ch03Cart and the starting page is Order.aspx, you can run the application by entering //localhost/Ch03Cart/Order.aspx in the browser's address bar.

The dialog box for working with a local IIS web site

How to run a file-system web site under the development web server

1. Start Visual Studio and open the web site using the File→Open Web Site command.
2. Right-click the starting page for the application and select Set As Start Page.
3. Run the application using the Debug→Start Debugging command.

How to run a file-system web site under IIS

1. Start Visual Studio and display the New Web Site dialog box using the File→New Web Site command.
2. Select HTTP for the location, then click the Browse button to display the Choose Location dialog box.
3. Select the Local IIS button at the left side of the dialog box, select the Default Web Site node (or a directory that's subordinate to that node) from the tree that's displayed, and then click the Create New Virtual Directory button near the upper right corner of the dialog box. This displays the New Virtual Directory dialog box.
4. Enter the name for the virtual directory you want to create, enter the path where the files for the web site are stored, and click OK to return to the Choose Location dialog box.
5. Select the virtual directory you just created, and click Open to return to the New Web Site dialog box.
6. Click OK. A warning will be displayed indicating that there is already a web site at the location you specified. Select the Open the Existing Web Site option, and click OK.
7. Right-click the starting page for the application and select Set As Start Page.
8. Run the application using the Debug→Start Debugging command.

Figure A-7   How to use the downloaded web applications

Appendix B

How to work with web applications using IIS under Windows XP

In several places throughout this book, we've indicated that you can perform certain operations on a web application using IIS. You'll learn how to perform those operations under Windows XP in the topics that follow. Then, in appendix C, you'll learn how to perform the same operations under Windows Vista.

Please note that you don't need to understand the material in these topics to develop web applications as described in this book. But as a professional programmer, you'll probably need these skills. So if you're using Windows XP, we recommend that you read these topics when we refer to them in the book or after you've completed the book.

How to create a virtual directory 958
How to set the default page for a web site 960
How to force a page to use a secure connection 962

How to create a virtual directory

In appendix A, you learned how to create a virtual directory for a file-system web site from within Visual Studio. But if you prefer, you can create a virtual directory from the IIS Management Console. In figure B-1, for example, you can see two of the dialog boxes for creating a virtual directory named Ch03Cart that points to the web site stored in the C:\ASP.NET 3.5 web sites\Ch03Cart directory.

After you create a virtual directory, it will appear under the Default Web Site node in the IIS Management Console. Then, you can use Visual Studio to open the web site from this directory so you can run the application under IIS. You can also run the application from outside of Visual Studio. Note that you can also create a virtual directory in a subdirectory of the Default Web Site node. In the illustration in this figure, for example, the virtual directory is being created in the ASPNET2008 directory.

The dialog boxes for creating a virtual directory in IIS

How to create a virtual directory for a file-system web site

1. Open the Control Panel, and make sure it's displayed in Classic View rather than Category View. Then, double-click Administrative Tools, and double-click Internet Information Services to open the IIS Management Console.

2. Use the tree to locate the Default Web Site node, right-click Default Web Site (or a directory that's subordinate to that node), and choose New➔Virtual Directory to start the Virtual Directory Creation Wizard.

3. Enter the name you want to use for the virtual directory on the Virtual Directory Alias page of the wizard, enter the path for the directory that contains the web site on the Web Site Content Directory page, and accept the defaults on the Access Permissions page.

Description

- In chapter 4, you can learn how to create a virtual directory for a new or existing web site using Visual Studio. You can also create a virtual directory for a web site from IIS. Then, you can use Visual Studio to open the web site from the virtual directory, and you can run the web site under IIS.

Figure B-1   How to create a virtual directory

How to set the default page for a web site

To run a web application from outside of Visual Studio, you typically enter the URL of the application and the starting page in a browser. If you don't enter a starting page, however, IIS will look for a page with a name in the default document list for the application. By default, this list doesn't include a document with the aspx extension. Because of that, you'll need to add the name of the page you want to be displayed by default to this list if you want the users of the application to be able to omit the starting page from the URL for the application. Figure B-2 shows how you do that.

The dialog box in this figure shows the default document list for the Ch03Cart application after I added the document named Order.aspx. Note that when you add a document to the list, it's displayed at the end of the list. Because IIS will check for documents in the order that they appear in the list, you'll usually want to move the document you add to the beginning of the list. To do that, you use the up arrow button to the left of the list. Alternatively, you can remove all the other documents from the list.

When you start a new web site, Visual Studio creates a page named Default.aspx. In most cases, you'll change the name of this page to something more meaningful, or you'll delete this page and then add pages with the names you want. If you use Default.aspx as the default page for your applications, though, you can add this page to the default document list for all your web sites rather than for each individual web site. To do that, you use the same technique shown in this figure, but you change the list for the Default Web Site node instead of for a specific web site.

The Documents tab of the Properties dialog box

How to work with the list of default documents for a web site

- To display the list of default documents for a web site, display the IIS Management Console, and locate the web site. Then, right-click on the web site, select Properties from the shortcut menu, and click the Documents tab in the Properties dialog box that's displayed.

- To add a document to the list of default documents, click the Add button, enter the document name in the dialog box that's displayed, and click OK.

- To change the order in which IIS looks for the documents, use the up and down arrow buttons to the left of the document list.

- To remove a document from the list, select the document and click the Remove button.

Description

- By default, if you run a web application from a browser outside of Visual Studio and you don't include the name of the page you want to display in the URL, IIS looks for a document with the name Default.htm, Default.asp, index.htm, or iisstart.asp. If you want IIS to look for a document with a different name, you can use the procedure above to add that document to the list of default documents.

- You can also add a document to the list of default documents for all your web sites. To do that, use the procedure above, but right-click the Default Web Site node instead of a specific web site. For example, you might want to add Default.aspx to the list since this is the file that's created by default when you start a new web site in Visual Studio.

Figure B-2   How to set the default page for a web site

How to force a page to use a secure connection

In chapter 19, you can learn how to secure a web application. One aspect of securing an application that's covered in that chapter is how to be sure that a page that should always use a secure connection can't be displayed without one. The technique shown in that chapter involves adding code to the Load event of the page. That way, if a user tries to bypass the navigation features provided by an application and access a page directly, the page will still be secured. Another way to provide that security is to use the IIS Management Console as shown in figure B-3.

In most cases, you'll only secure the pages of a web site that contain confidential information. If you need to, however, you can secure all the pages in a folder within the web site or all of the pages within the web site. To do that, you use the same technique shown in this figure, but you display the properties of the folder or the web site.

The dialog boxes for securing a web page

How to set the security for a web page

1. Display the IIS Management Console, locate the web site that contains the page you want to secure, and select the web site or the folder within the web site that contains the page.

2. Right-click the page (.aspx) in the right pane of the IIS Management Console, select the Properties command from the shortcut menu, and display the File Security tab of the Properties dialog box that's displayed.

3. Click the Edit button in the Secure Communications section to display the Secure Communications dialog box. Then, select the Require Secure Channel (SSL) option. If you want the page to be displayed only if 128-bit encryption is used, select the Require 128-bit Encryption option.

Description

*   In chapter 19, you can learn how to add C# code to a page to be sure that it uses a secure connection. Another way to do that is to set IIS security properties for the page.

*   You can also set the security for all the pages within a folder of a web site or for all the pages of a web site. To do that, display the properties for the folder or web site, display the Directory Security tab, and then set the appropriate options.

Figure B-3   How to force a page to use a secure connection

Appendix C

How to work with web applications using IIS under Windows Vista

If you'll be developing your ASP.NET applications under Windows Vista, you should know that this operating system comes with the newest version of IIS, IIS 7.0. As you'll see in this appendix, the IIS Management Console for IIS 7.0 is quite different from the IIS Management Console that came with previous versions of IIS. So even if you've used a previous version of IIS, you'll want to review the material in this appendix to learn some basic skills for working with the IIS Management Console under Windows Vista.

In several places throughout this book, we've indicated that you can perform certain operations on a web application using IIS. Although you don't need to know how to use IIS to perform these operations to develop web applications as described in this book, you'll probably need these skills as a professional programmer. So if you're using Windows Vista, we recommend that you read these topics when we refer to them in the book or after you've completed the book.

How to create an IIS virtual directory or application 966

How to set the default page for a web site 968

How to force a page to use a secure connection 970

How to create an IIS virtual directory or application

In appendix A, you learned how to create a virtual directory for a file-system web site from within Visual Studio. But if you prefer, you can create a virtual directory from the IIS Management Console. In figure C-1, for example, you can see the dialog box for creating a virtual directory named Ch03Cart that points to the web site stored in the C:\ASP.NET 3.5 web sites\Ch03Cart directory. Notice in this figure that the virtual directory is being created in the ASPNET2008 directory of the Default Web Site node. You can also create a virtual directory directly under the Default Web Site node.

After you create a virtual directory, you can use Visual Studio to open the web site from this directory. When you do that, Visual Studio will display a dialog box indicating that the directory is a virtual directory and asking you if you want to open it. After you do that, you can run the application under IIS. But first, Visual Studio will display a dialog box that asks you if you want to convert the virtual directory to an application. Since this is necessary to run the application under IIS, you'll want to click Yes when this dialog box is displayed.

If you want to run the application from outside of Visual Studio, you'll need to convert the virtual directory to an application from the IIS Management Console as described in this figure. Alternatively, you can create an application without first creating a virtual directory. The technique for doing that is also presented in this figure.

When you run an application under IIS, you may run into a problem that's caused by insufficient permissions for the directory that contains the web site. In that case, you can use Windows Explorer to add the required permissions. To do that, right-click on the directory, choose Properties to display the Properties dialog box, and then display the Security tab. Then, review the list of groups and users to see if it includes Users (<computer name>\Users) and IIS_IUSRS (<computer name>\IIS_IUSRS) where <computer name> is the name of your computer. If not, you will need to add these two groups.

To add these groups, click the Edit button and then the Add button. In the dialog box that's displayed, enter the group name, including the computer name. For example, if the name of your computer is VistaPC, you would enter VistaPC\Users to add the Users group. To be sure you've entered the name correctly, click the Check Names button. Then, click the OK button and make sure that the Read & Execute, List Folder Contents, and Read permissions are selected. Repeat this process for the IIS_IUSRS group.

The dialog box for creating a virtual directory in IIS

How to create an IIS virtual directory for a file-system web site

1. Open the Control Panel, and make sure it's displayed in Classic View. Then, double-click Administrative Tools, and double-click Internet Information Services to open the IIS Management Console.

2. Use the tree to locate the Default Web Site node, right-click Default Web Site (or a directory that's subordinate to that node), and choose Add Virtual Directory to display the Add Virtual Directory dialog box.

3. Enter the name you want to use for the virtual directory, enter the path for the directory that contains the web site, and click the OK button.

Two ways to create an IIS application for a file-system web site

- If a virtual directory already exists for the web site, right-click on it, select Convert to Application, and then click OK in the Add Application dialog box that's displayed.

- If a virtual directory doesn't exist for the web site, use the procedure above for creating a virtual directory, but choose Add Application to display the Add Application dialog box.

Description

- In chapter 4, you can learn how to create a virtual directory for a new or existing web site using Visual Studio. When you do that, the directory is automatically configured as an IIS application. You can also create a virtual directory or application for a web site from IIS. Then, you can use Visual Studio to open the web site from the virtual directory or application, and you can run the web site under IIS.

Figure C-1   How to create a virtual directory

How to set the default page for a web site

To run a web application from outside of Visual Studio, you typically enter the URL of the application and the starting page in a browser. If you don't enter a starting page, however, IIS will look for a page with a name in the default document list for the application. Figure C-2 shows the file names that are in this list by default.

The last file name in the default document list, default.aspx, is the name of the page that's created when you start a new ASP.NET web site from Visual Studio. If you don't change the name of this page, you don't need to change the default document list. However, you may want to move the default.aspx file to the beginning of the list so IIS looks for it first. Alternatively, you can delete the other files from the list.

In most cases, you'll change the name of the Default.aspx page that's created for a new web site to something more meaningful, or you'll delete this page and then add pages with the names you want. Then, you can add the name of the first page to be displayed to the default document list for the application. That way, the users of the application will be able to omit the starting page from the URL for the application.

The Default Document window of the IIS Management Console

How to work with the list of default documents for a web site

- To display the list of default documents for a web site, display the IIS Management Console, and locate and select the web site. Then, double-click Default Document in the IIS group on the Home page for the web site to display the Default Document page.

- The Default Document page displays a list of file names that it looks for by default when you run a web application. You can add names to this list, remove names from the list, or change the order of the names in the list.

Description

- By default, if you run a web application from a browser outside of Visual Studio and you don't include the name of the page you want to display in the URL, IIS looks for a file with the name Default.htm, Default.asp, index.htm, index.html, iisstart.asp, or default.aspx. If you want IIS to look for a file with a different name, you can use the procedure above to add that file name to the list of default file names.

- You can also add a file to the list of default file names for all your web sites. To do that, use the procedure above, but select the Default Web Site node instead of a specific web site.

Figure C-2   How to set the default page for a web site

How to force a page to use a secure connection

In chapter 19, you can learn how to secure a web application. One aspect of securing an application that's covered in that chapter is how to be sure that a page that should always use a secure connection can't be displayed without one. The technique shown in that chapter involves adding code to the Load event of the page. That way, if a user tries to bypass the navigation features provided by an application and access a page directly, the page will still be secured. Another way to provide that security is to use the IIS Management Console as shown in figure C-3.

In most cases, you'll only secure the pages of a web site that contain confidential information. If you need to, however, you can secure all the pages in a folder within the web site or all of the pages within the web site. To do that, you just display the SSL Settings window shown in this figure for the web site or folder.

Two IIS windows for securing a web page

How to set the security for a web page

1. Display the IIS Management Console, and then locate and select the web site that contains the page you want to secure.

2. Click the Content View tab on the Home page for the web site, select the page you want to secure, and then click the Switch to Features View link in the Actions pane.

3. Double-click SSL Settings in the IIS group of the Home page to display the SSL Settings page. Then, select the Require SSL option. If you want the page to be displayed only if 128-bit encryption is used, select the Require 128-bit SSL option.

Description

- In chapter 19, you can learn how to add C# code to a page to be sure that it uses a secure connection. Another way to do that is to use the IIS Management Console.

- You can also set the security for all the pages within a folder of a web site or for all the pages of a web site. To do that, select the folder or web site, display the SSL Settings window, and then set the appropriate options.

Figure C-3   How to force a page to use a secure connection

Index

 , 42, 43, 162, 164
?: operator, 892
.NET data provider, 380, 381
.NET data type (profile property), 694, 695
.NET Framework, 16, 17
.NET Framework Class Library, 16, 17
.NET Framework version (for new web site), 32, 33
~ operator, 88, 89, 90, 91
3-layer architecture, 546, 547
3-tier architecture, 548

A

A (Anchor) element, 174, 175
A tags (query strings), 296, 297
Absolute URL, 90, 91
Accelerator key, 208
Access data source
    configuring, 94, 95
    creating, 92, 93
Access key, 208, 209
Access rules, 652, 653
    Authentication application, 672, 673
AccessDataSource control, 74, 75, 92, 93
AccessKey attribute, 208, 209
Activate event (View control), 728, 729
Active class, 182, 183
Active mode (FTP), 126, 127
ActiveStepChanged event (Wizard control), 738, 739
ActiveStepIndex property (Wizard control), 734, 735, 738, 739
ActiveViewChanged event (MultiView control), 728, 729
ActiveViewIndex attribute (MultiView control), 720, 721, 728, 729
Add method
    ControlCollection class, 914, 915
    HttpApplicationState class, 287
    HttpCookieCollection class, 292, 293
    HttpSessionState class, 102, 103

Add method (continued)
    ListItemCollection class, 226, 227
    StateBag class, 275
AddUserToRole method (Roles class), 682, 683
ADO.NET 3.5 (ActiveX Data Objects), 380, 381
    classes, 386-389
AffectedRows property (e argument), 446, 447, 570, 571
Aggregate column (LINQ data source), 608, 609
AJAX, 805-837
    architecture, 808, 809
    ASP.NET architecture, 810, 811
    extension controls, 202, 203
    server controls, 810, 811, 814, 815
Alias, 608, 609
Align attribute (Td element), 197
Allow element (Authorization element), 674, 675
AllowAnonymous attribute (profile property), 688, 689, 702, 703
AllowCustomSqlDatabase attribute (sessionState element), 282, 283
AllowPaging attribute
    DetailsView control, 469, 470
    GridView control, 436, 437
AllowReturn property (WizardStep control), 738, 739
AllowSorting attribute (GridView control), 434, 435
AlternateText attribute
    image button, 210, 211
    image control, 236, 237
AlternatingItemStyle element (DataList control), 415
AlternatingItemTemplate element
    DataList control, 412, 413
    DetailsView control, 483
    GridView control, 459
    ListView control, 507, 509, 512
AlternatingRowStyle element
    DetailsView control, 469
    GridView control, 433

Anchor (A) element, 174, 175

Anonymous identification (profiles), 688, 689, 702, 703, 705

Anonymous type, 598, 599

Anonymous user (LoginView control), 666, 667

AnonymousId property (ProfileMigrateEventsArg class), 704, 705

AnonymousIdentification element (web.config file), 688, 689, 702, 703

AnonymousIdentificationModule class, 704, 705

Apache HTTP Server, 6, 927

App_Code folder, 20, 21, 26, 27, 78, 79, 80, 81
   data access class, 546
   web service, 930, 931

App_Data folder, 78, 79, 654

App_Themes folder, 78, 79, 344, 345

App_WebReferences folder, 938, 839

AppearanceEditorPart class, 801

AppearanceEditorPart control, 794

Application, 284, 285

Application events, 288, 289

Application execution (controlling), 144, 145

Application mappings, 10, 11

Application object, 284, 285

Application path (storing in web.config file), 630, 631

Application property
   HttpContext class, 286, 287
   page, 286, 287, 289

Application server, 10, 11

Application state, 12, 13, 284-289
   common uses, 284, 285

Application state object, 12, 13, 284-287

Application_End event, 288, 289

Application_Error event handler, 756, 757, 758, 759

Application_Start event, 288, 289

Apply Styles window, 190, 191

AppSettings property (ConfigurationManager class), 630, 631

AppSettings section (web.config file), 630, 631

Asp tag, 22, 50, 51

ASP.NET AJAX, 810-827
   architecture, 810, 811
   server controls, 810, 811, 814, 815

ASP.NET AJAX Control Toolkit, 810, 811, 816, 817

ASP.NET Development Server, 18, 19, 66, 67

ASP.NET runtime, 26, 27

ASP.NET Server Control project, 891, 898, 899

ASP.NET Server Control template, 885, 898, 899

ASP.NET Web Service template, 929

aspnet_compiler command, 846, 847, 852, 853

AspNetDb.mdf database, 654, 655
   profile provider, 690, 691
   profiles, 686
   web parts, 778, 779

AspNetSqlMembershipProvider, 654

AspNetSqlProfileProvider, 690, 691

AspNetSqlProvider, 654, 655

AspNetSqlRoleProvider, 654

AspNetWindowsTokenRoleProvider, 654

Aspx code, 20, 50, 51

Assembly, 26, 27

AssociatedControlID attribute (label), 208, 209

AssociatedUpdatePanelID attribute (UpdateProgress control), 826, 827

Association (entity classes), 596, 597

Asynchronous JavaScript and XML, *see AJAX*

Asynchronous postback, 810, 811, 822, 823

AsyncPostBackTimeout attribute (ScriptManager control), 818, 819

Attachment (email), 752, 753

Attachment class, 752, 753

Attachments property (MailMessage class), 749, 752, 753

Attribute, 22
   data access class, 564, 565
   HTML element, 162, 163
   modifying in Source view, 165
   server control, 50, 51

Authenticated user
   LoginView control, 666, 667
   profiles, 688, 689, 692-701

Authentication, 621, 640, 641
   application, 668-675
   web parts, 778, 779

Authentication element (web.config file), 674, 675

Authentication ticket, 642, 643
   FormsAuthentication class, 680

Authorization, 640, 641

Authorization element (web.config file), 674, 675

AutoEventWireup attribute
　　Control directive, 865
　　Page directive, 170, 171
AutoGenerateColumns attribute (GridView control), 428, 429
AutoGenerateDeleteButton attribute (DetailsView control), 475
AutoGenerateEditButton attribute (DetailsView control), 475
AutoGenerateInsertButton attribute (DetailsView control), 475
AutoGenerateRows attribute (DetailsView control), 468, 469
AutoHide button, 35
AutoPage attribute (LinqDataSource control), 599, 600
AutoPostBack property
　　drop-down list, 20, 21, 22
　　web server control, 48, 49, 62, 63
Autos window, 142, 146, 147
AutoSort attribute (LinqDataSource control), 599, 600

B

B element, 173
Back-button problem, 766-771
BannerBitMap property (User Interface Editor), 854
Base64 format, 752, 753
Bcc property (MailMessage class), 748, 749
BehaviorEditorPart class, 801
BehaviorEditorPart control, 794
Bin folder, 78, 79
　　web control library, 900, 901
Bind method, 418, 419
　　FormView control, 494, 495
　　GridView template field, 458
　　ListView control, 534, 535
Bindable attribute (property declaration), 905
Binding (for HTTPS protocol), 628, 629
Binding expression (FormView control), 492, 494, 495, 496, 497
Body element, 168, 169
Body property (MailMessage class), 748, 749, 755
Body tag, 22
Border attribute (Table element), 196, 197
BorderColor attribute (calendar control), 242, 243

BorderStyle attribute (calendar control), 242, 243
Bottom attribute (RectangleHotSpot element), 240
BoundField element
　　DetailsView control, 466, 467, 468, 469
　　GridView control, 428, 432, 433
Br element, 42, 43, 172, 173
Bread crumbs, 336
Break All command, 144, 145
Break mode, 136-139, 142, 143
Breakpoint, 138, 139
Breakpoints window, 138, 139
Browsable attribute (property declaration), 905
Browse display mode (web parts), 790, 791
Browse location, 130
　　FTP web site, 130
Browse window, 130, 131
Browser (adding), 130, 131
Browser page caching (disabling), 768, 769
Bulleted list, 232, 233
Bulleted list control, 205, 232, 233, 417
BulletImageUrl attribute (bullet list), 233
BulletStyle attribute (bulleted list), 232, 233
Business class, 20, 21
　　object data source, 576, 577, 578
Business object, 550
　　using with object data sources, 576, 577
Business object class, 546
Button control, 40, 41, 205, 210, 211
ButtonCount attribute (numeric pager), 519
ButtonField element
　　DetailsView control, 469
　　GridView control, 433
ButtonType attribute
　　CommandField element (GridView control), 445
　　next/previous pager, 519
　　numeric pager, 519

C

CacheDuration attribute (SqlDataSource control), 424, 425
CacheExpiration attribute (SqlDataSource control), 425
CacheKeyDependency attribute (SqlDataSource control), 425
Caching data, 424, 425

Calculated column, 374, 375

Calendar control, 205, 242, 243

Cancel button (Wizard control), 734, 735

Cancel property (e argument), 446, 447, 478

CancelButtonClick event (Wizard control), 734, 735, 738, 739

CancelButtonStyle element (Wizard control), 741

CancelDestinationPageUrl attribute (ChangePassword control), 664, 665

CancelImage attribute (CommandField element), 445

CancelText attribute (CommandField element), 445

CaptionedBox custom server control, 908-913

Cart Profile application, 706-715

CartItem class, 104, 105

Cascading style sheets (CSS), 176, 342, 344, 345, 348, 349
   with AJAX, 808, 809

Catalog display mode, 792, 793

CatalogPart control, 792, 793

CatalogZone class, 801

CatalogZone control, 792, 793
   formatting, 798

Category attribute
   property declaration, 905
   user control property, 868, 869, 871

Category class (business object version, Category Maintenance application), 580, 581

Category Maintenance application
   business objects with ObjectDataSource control version, 578-583
   Grid View version, 450-457
   GridView with templates version, 460-463
   ListView version, 536-543
   ObjectDataSource control version, 566-575

CategoryDB class, 572, 573
   business object version (Category Maintenance application), 580, 582-583

CausesValidation attribute
   button, 211, 261
   CommandField element (GridView control), 444, 445

CausesValidation property
   button, 56, 57, 58
   web server control, 48, 49

CC property (MailMessage class), 748, 749

Cellpadding attribute (Table element), 196, 197

Cells (table), 44, 45, 194, 195

Cellspacing attribute (Table element), 196, 197

Certification authority (CA), 622, 623

Chained root certificate, 622, 623

ChangePassword control, 664, 665
   compatibility issues with AJAX, 822, 823

ChangePassword method (MembershipUser class), 678, 679

ChangePasswordQuestionAndAnswer method (MembershipUser class), 679

Character class (regular expression), 264, 265

Check box control, 205, 218, 219

Check box list control, 205, 230, 231
   binding, 417

Check constraint, 370, 371

CheckBoxField element
   DetailsView control, 469
   GridView control, 433

Checked attribute (check box and radio button), 218, 219

Checked property (check box and radio button), 220, 221

CheckedChanged event, 207
   radio button and check box, 62, 63, 220, 221

Checkout application
   MultiView control version, 718, 719
   Wizard control version, 730, 731

Child control, 888, 889

Child element, 168, 169

Child elements (DetailsView control), 468, 469

Child master page, 316, 317

ChildrenAsTriggers attribute (UpdatePanel control), 822, 823

Chrome, 796, 797

CircleHotSpot element, 241

Class, 16, 17
   adding, 80, 81
   style sheet, 182, 183

Class attribute (HTML element), 180, 181, 182, 183, 348, 349

Class attributes (custom server control), 904, 905

Class declaration, 24
   custom server control, 890, 891
   designer attributes, 905

Class library, 80, 81
Class template, 80, 81
Classes (ADO.NET 3.5), 386-389
Clear method
  ControlCollection class, 914, 915
  HttpApplicationState class, 287
  HttpCookieCollection class, 293
  HttpSessionState class, 103
  ListItemCollection class, 227
  StateBag class, 275
ClearError method (HttpServerUtility class), 758, 759
Click event, 207
  button, 62, 63, 210, 211
Client, 6, 7
Client certificate, 621
Client/server application, 6, 7
Client-side script, 57
Client-side validation, 56, 250
Close method (SqlConnection class), 387, 389
CLR, 16, 17
Code (adding to a form), 60-63
Code Editor, 34, 35, 60, 61
Code-behind file, 20, 21
CodeFile attribute
  Control directive, 864, 865
  Master page directive, 305
  Page directive, 22, 170, 171
Colors, 197
Colspan attribute (Td element), 196, 197
Column
  database table, 366, 367
  HTML table, 44, 45, 194, 195
Column Name property (database table), 370, 371
Columns attribute (text box), 216, 217
Columns element (GridView control), 428, 432, 433
Command, 380, 381, 384, 385, 386, 387
  executing directly, 384, 385
Command buttons
  DetailsView control, 475, 476, 477
  FormView control, 494
Command event, 207
  button, 210, 211, 214, 215
Command fields (GridView control), 444, 445

CommandArgument attribute
  button, 211, 514, 515
  MultiView control, 724, 725, 728, 729
CommandArgument property (CommandEventArgs class), 214, 215
CommandEventArgs class, 214, 215
CommandField element
  DetailsView control, 469, 476, 477
  GridView control, 428, 433, 444, 445
CommandName attribute
  button, 211, 514, 515
  button in a ListView control, 532, 533, 534, 535
  MultiView control, 720, 721, 724, 725, 728, 729
CommandName property (CommandEventArgs class), 214, 215
CommandRowStyle element (DetailsView control), 469
CommandText property (SqlCommand class), 386, 387
CommandType property (SqlCommand class), 386, 387
Comment
  HTML, 162, 163
  skin, 351
Common Language Runtime (CLR), 16, 17
Common Type System, 16, 17
Compare validator, 247, 254, 255
Compiling an application, 26, 27
Completion step (Wizard control), 736, 737
Component Designer window, 930, 931
Composite control, 888, 889, 914-923
Composite primary key, 366, 367
CompositeControl class, 884, 888, 889, 914, 915
Concurrency, 134, 382, 383
Concurrency control, 382, 383
Concurrency error, 134, 135
  DetailsView control, 478, 479
  GridView control, 447
  ObjectDataSource control, 570
Concurrency exception, 382, 383
Configure Data Source wizard, *see also Data Source Configuration Wizard*
  configuring an Access data source, 94, 95
  creating an Access data source, 92, 93

Configuring ASP.NET applications
　IIS Management Console (Windows Vista),
　　844, 845
　IIS Management Console (Windows XP), 842,
　　843
　Web Site Administration Tool, 840, 841
ConflictDetection attribute (ObjectDataSource
　control), 548, 549, 576
Connection, 380, 381, 384, 385, 386, 387
　defining, 396, 397
　secure, 618, 619, 630- 633
Connection property (SqlCommand class), 386,
　387
Connection string, 386
　saving in web.config file, 398, 399
ConnectionString attribute (SqlDataSource
　control), 395, 398, 399
ConnectionString property (SqlConnection class),
　386, 387
ConnectionStrings element (web.config file), 398
ConnectionsZone class, 801
Content (HTML element), 162, 163
Content element (content page), 310, 311
Content page, 300, 301, 310-313
Content placeholder, 300, 301, 302, 303
ContentLength property (HttpPostedFile class),
　239
ContentPlaceHolder control, 302, 303, 304, 305
ContextTypeName attribute (LinqDataSource
　control), 598, 599
ContinueDestinationPageUrl attribute
　(ChangePassword control), 664, 665
Control
　accessing from content page, 320, 321
　adding to a view, 722, 723
　exposing from a master page, 318, 319
Control directive (user control), 864, 865
Control events, 62, 63
　handling, 206, 207
　master and content pages, 306, 309
Control parameter, 404, 405
ControlID attribute (ControlParameter element),
　405
ControlParameter element
　ObjectDataSource control, 560, 561
　SqlDataSource control, 404, 405

Controls
　AJAX, 814, 815
　ASP.NET AJAX Control Toolkit, 816, 817
　binding in a template, 418, 419
　used as web parts, 780, 781
Controls property (CompositeControl class), 914,
　915
ControlToCompare property (compare validator),
　254, 255
ControlToValidate property (validator), 58, 59,
　248, 249
ConvertEmptyStringToNull property (GridView
　field), 430, 431
Cookie-based session tracking, 281, 282
Cookieless attribute
　anonymousIdentification element, 702, 703
　sessionState element, 282, 283
Cookieless session tracking, 281, 282
CookieName attribute (anonymousIdentification
　element), 702, 703
CookieParameter element, 405
Cookies, 100, 101, 290-295
　anonymous identification, 702, 703
　authentication ticket, 642, 643
　enabling or disabling, 294, 295
　FormsAuthentication class, 680
Cookies property
　HttpCookieCollection class, 293
　HttpRequest class, 292, 293
　HttpResponse class, 292, 293
　HttpSessionState class, 103
　ListItemCollection class, 226, 227
　SelectedDates collection, 242, 243
　StateBag class, 275
CookieTimeout attribute (anonymousIdentification
　element), 702, 703
Coordinates attribute (PolygonHotSpot element),
　240
Copy Web Site command, 846, 847, 848, 849
Count property (HttpApplicationState class), 287
CreateChildControls method (CompositeControl
　class), 914, 915
CreateRole method (Roles class), 683
CreateUser method (Membership class), 677
CreateUserWizard control, 660, 661
　compatibility issues with AJAX, 822, 823

CreationDate property (MembershipUser class), 679

Credit card validation, 268, 269

Cross-page posting, 88, 89

CSS, *see Cascading style sheets*

CSS Outline window, 188, 189

CSS Properties window, 192, 193

CssClass attribute (server control), 348, 349

Current property (HttpContext class), 102, 103, 155, 276, 277, 286, 287

Custom Actions Editor (web setup project), 854

Custom type (profile property), 694, 695, 700, 701

Custom error handling, 756-765

Custom error page, 756, 757
  code, 762, 763

Custom membership provider, 654

Custom mode (session state), 280, 281

Custom profile provider, 690, 691

Custom server controls, 883-923
  compared to user controls, 886, 887
  starting code, 890, 891

Custom validator, 247, 266, 267

Custom WebPart control, 780, 781, 802, 803

CustomErrors element (web.config file), 756, 757, 764, 765

Customization theme, 360, 361

CustomProvider attribute (sessionState element), 283

D

Data access class, 546, 547, 551
  attributes, 564, 565
  creating, 558-565
  for paging, 586, 587

Data access methods (that use business objects), 576, 577

Data adapter, 380, 381, 388, 389

Data component, 550

Data controls, 202, 203

Data group (Toolbox), 92, 93, 395, 414, 415, 429, 493

Data list, 410, 411

Data object, 550

Data object class, 546

Data provider, 654, 655

Data reader, 384, 385, 388, 389
  select method, 560, 561

Data source, 92
  updatable, 422, 423

Data Source Configuration Wizard
  binding a drop-down list, 96, 97
  binding a list control, 416, 417
  LinqDataSource control, 600, 601, 608, 609
  ObjectDataSource control, 550, 551
  SiteMapDataSource control, 332, 333
  SqlDataSource control, 394, 395

Data source mode, 424, 425

Data table, 380, 381

Data tip, 142, 143

Data Type property (database table), 370, 371

Data types
  profile properties, 694, 695
  SQL Server, 371

Database exception
  DetailsView control, 478, 479
  ObjectDataSource control, 570

Database layer, 546, 547

Database management system, 6, 7

DataBind method, 478, 479
  drop-down list, 24

DataBinder class, 418

DataBound event (DetailsView control), 479

DataContext class, 592, 594
  selecting, 600, 601

DataField property (GridView field), 430, 431

DataFormatString property (GridView field), 430, 431, 434

DataKeyNames attribute
  DetailsView control, 468, 469
  GridView control, 429
  ListView control, 507

DataList control, 410-415

DataObject attribute, 556, 565

DataObjectMethod attribute, 556, 565

DataObjectTypeName attribute (ObjectDataSource control), 548, 549, 577, 578

DataPager control, 508, 509, 516-519

DataRowView class, 98, 99

Dataset, 380, 381
  select method, 560, 561

DataSourceID attribute
  DataList control, 411
  DetailsView control, 466, 467, 469
  GridView control, 429

DataSourceID attribute (continued)
list control, 416, 417
ListView control, 507
Menu control, 335
TreeView control, 330, 331
DataSourceMode attribute (SqlDataSource control), 424, 425, 514, 515
DataTable (select method), 560, 561
DataTextField attribute (list control), 416, 417
DataTextField property (drop-down list), 96, 97
DataTextFormatString attribute (list control), 417
DataValueField attribute (list control), 416, 417
DataValueField property (drop-down list), 96, 97
DataView class, 98, 99
DateDDL custom server control, 916-923
DaysUntil custom server control, 894-897
DaysUntil user control, 868-871
DaysUntilDates web service, 932, 933
DaysUntilHalloween user control, 867
DBMS, 6, 7
Dd element, 831, 832
Deactivate event (View control), 728, 729
Debug menu, 144, 145
Debug toolbar, 144, 145
Debug version, 856, 857
Debugger, 138-149
DeclarativeCatalogPart class, 801
DeclarativeCatalogPart control, 792, 793
Default browser, 128, 129
Default button, 208, 209
Default group, 260, 261
Default page
setting under Windows Vista, 966, 967
setting under Windows XP, 960, 961
Default skin, 350, 351
Default value, 370, 371
profile property, 698, 699
DefaultButton attribute (form), 208, 209
DefaultDocument property (File System Editor), 854
DefaultFocus attribute (form), 208, 209
DefaultMode attribute (DetailsView control), 469
DefaultProperty attribute (class declaration), 904, 905
DefaultRedirect attribute (customErrors element), 764, 765

DefaultValue attribute
profile property, 698, 699
property declaration, 905
DefaultValue property (Parameter class), 449
Delegate (event), 906, 907
Delete method
data access class, 558, 559, 562, 563
data access class with business objects, 576, 577
SqlDataSource control, 444
Delete statement
SQL, 95, 378, 379
SqlDataSource control, 400
DeleteCommand attribute (SqlDataSource control), 422, 423
DeleteCommand property (SqlDataAdapter class), 388, 389
DeleteImage attribute (CommandField element), 445
DeleteMethod attribute (ObjectDataSource control), 548, 549, 558
DeleteParameters element (SqlDataSource control), 422, 423
DeleteRole method (Roles class), 683
DeleteText attribute (CommandField element), 445
DeleteUser method (Membership class), 677
Deny element (Authorization element), 674, 675
Deploying ASP.NET applications, 846, 847
Description attribute
property declaration, 904, 905
siteMapNode element, 327
Design display mode (web parts), 790, 791
Design view, 34, 40-49
Designer attributes
custom server control, 890, 891, 904, 905
user control property, 868, 869, 871
DesignOnly attribute (property declaration), 905
DetailsView control, 466-491
adding command field, 476, 477
compared to FormView control, 492, 493
compatibility issues with AJAX, 822, 823
updating, 474-481
Development server, 18, 19, 66, 67
limitations, 132, 133
DHTML, 52, 56, 250, 251
with AJAX, 808, 809
Diagram pane (Query Builder), 406, 407

Digital secure certificate, 620, 621
    working with in Windows Vista, 628, 629
    working with in Windows XP, 626, 627
Directive block, 170
Directory structure (Authentication application), 672, 673
disco file, 938, 939
discomap file, 938, 939
Disconnected data architecture, 380, 381
    disadvantages, 382, 383
Display property (validator), 58, 59, 248, 249, 258, 259
DisplayAfter attribute (UpdateProgress control), 826, 827
DisplayCancelButton property (Wizard control), 734, 735, 738, 739
DisplayMode attribute (bulleted list), 232, 233
DisplayMode property
    validation summary control, 258, 259
    WebPartManager class, 790, 791
DisplayRememberMe attribute (Login control), 657
DisplaySideBar property (Wizard control), 738, 739
Distributed web application, 926
Div element, 168, 169
Div tag, 22, 54
Dl element, 830, 831
dll file (web control library), 900
DOCTYPE declaration, 22, 168, 169, 170, 171
Document Object Model, *see DOM*
DOM
    with AJAX, 808, 809
    with ASP.NET AJAX, 810, 811
Domain name, 8, 9
DOS XCopy command, 846, 847
Downloaded applications (running), 954, 955
Drop-down list control, 20, 40, 41, 205, 222, 223
    binding, 96, 97, 417
Dt element, 830, 831, 832
Dynamic HTML, *see DHTML*
Dynamic menu, 334
Dynamic pseudo-class, 182, 183
Dynamic web page, 10, 11
DynamicLayout attribute (UpdateProgress control), 826, 827

E

e argument
    Click event, 210, 211
    Command event, 214, 215
    image button, 212, 213
Edit and Continue feature, 142
Edit display mode, 794, 795, 797
Edit mode
    DetailsView control, 466, 467
    FormView control, 497
    GridView control, 444
    ListView control, 532, 533
EditImage attribute (CommandField element), 445
EditItemTemplate element
    DetailsView control, 482, 483
    FormView control, 492, 496, 497
    GridView control, 458, 459
    ListView control, 507, 508, 509, 532, 534, 535
EditorPart control, 794, 797
EditorZone class, 801
EditorZone control, 794, 797
    formatting, 798
EditRowStyle element
    DetailsView control, 469
    GridView control, 433, 444
EditText attribute (CommandField element), 444, 445
Element-based style, 180
Email, 744-755
Email message
    creating, 748, 749
    sending, 750, 751
Email property (MembershipUser class), 678, 679
EmptyDataRowStyle element
    DetailsView control, 469
    GridView control, 433
EmptyDataTemplate element
    DetailsView control, 469
    FormView control, 492
    ListView control, 507
EmptyItemTemplate element (ListView control), 507
EnableCaching attribute
    ObjectDataSource control, 560
    SqlDataSource control, 424, 425

EnableClientScript property (validator), 248, 249, 250, 251

Enabled attribute
   AnonymousIdentification element, 688, 689, 702, 703
   Timer control, 824, 825

Enabled property
   binding, 418, 419
   validator, 248, 249
   web server control, 49

EnableDelete attribute (LinqDataSource control), 598, 599, 606, 607

EnableInsert attribute (LinqDataSource control), 598, 599, 606, 607

EnablePageMethods attribute (ScriptManager control), 819

EnablePaging attribute (ObjectDataSource control), 584, 585

EnableScriptGlobalization (ScriptManager control), 819

EnableScriptLocalization (ScriptManager control), 819

EnableTheming property (server control), 358, 359

EnableUpdate attribute (LinqDataSource control), 598, 599, 606, 607

EnableViewState property
   control, 48, 49, 273
   page, 273

End tag, 162, 163

Ending an application, 129

Entity class, 595, 596, 597

Error, 66, 67

Error element (custom error), 764, 765

Error handling (custom), 756-765

Error List window, 66, 67

ErrorMessage property (validator), 56, 58, 59, 248, 249, 258, 259

Escape character (regular expression), 264, 265

Eval method, 418, 419
   FormView control, 494, 495
   ListView control, 512, 513, 534, 535

Event attribute, 60, 61, 206, 207

Event declaration, 906, 907

Event handler, 60, 61, 206, 207

EventHandler delegate, 906, 907

Events
   application, 288, 289
   control, 62, 63

Events (continued)
   custom server control, 906, 907
   declaring, 906, 907
   DetailsView control, 478, 479
   GridView control, 446, 447
   ListView control, 534
   MultiView control, 728, 729
   page, 62, 63
   raising, 906, 907
   sequence for pages with user controls, 866, 867
   View control, 728, 729

Exception, 136, 137

Exception Assistant, 136, 137

Exception object
   custom error handling, 757, 758, 759
   saving in session state, 760, 761

Exception property (e argument), 446, 447, 478, 479, 570

ExceptionHandled property (e argument), 446, 447, 479, 570

ExecuteNonQuery method (SqlCommand class), 386, 387, 388

ExecuteReader method (SqlCommand class), 386, 387

ExecuteScalar method (SqlCommand class), 386, 387

Execution (controlling), 144, 145

ExpandDepth attribute (TreeView control), 330, 331

Expires property (HttpCookie class), 290, 291, 292, 293

Exposing members of a user control, 868, 869

Extensible Markup Language, *see XML*

External style sheet, 186, 187

F

FailureText attribute (Login control), 657

Field (database), 366, 367

FieldCount property (SqlDataReader class), 389

Fields (GridView control), 430, 431

Fields element
   DataPager control, 516, 517
   DetailsView control, 466, 467, 468, 469

File (adding to a web site), 36, 37

File System Editor (web setup project), 854

File Transfer Protocol (FTP), 18, 19

File Types Editor (web setup project), 854

File-system web site, 32, 66
    testing with IIS, 132, 133
FileName property (file upload control), 238, 239
FileUpload control, 205, 238, 239
    compatibility issues with AJAX, 822, 823
Fill method (SqlDataAdapter class), 388, 389
Filter expression, 98
FindByText method (ListItemCollection class), 227
FindByValue method (ListItemCollection class), 227
FindControl method (Page class), 88, 89
FinishButtonClick event (Wizard control), 736, 737, 738, 739
FinishCompleteButtonStyle element (Wizard control), 741
FinishNavigationTemplate element (Wizard control), 741
FinishPreviousButtonStyle element (Wizard control), 741
Firefox, 6, 7, 14, 134, 135
FirstBulletNumber (bullet list), 233
FirstPageImageUrl attribute (PagerSettings element), 438, 439
FirstPageText attribute (PagerSettings element), 438, 439
Flow layout, 42, 43
Focus, 208, 209
Focus class, 182, 183
Focus method (web server control), 208, 209
Folders
    adding to a web site, 36, 37
    ASP.NET, 78, 79
FooterStyle element
    DataList control, 415
    DetailsView control, 469
    GridView control, 433
FooterTemplate element
    DataList control, 413
    DetailsView control, 469
    GridView control, 459
ForeColor attribute (NextPrevStyle element), 242
ForeColor property (validator), 249
Foreign key, 368, 369
Foreign key table, 369
Form, *see Web form*
Form element, 168, 169
Form tag, 22, 50

FormatString attribute (LoginName control), 658, 659
FormParameter element, 405
Forms-based authentication, 640-643
    enabling, 646, 647
FormsAuthentication class, 680, 681
FormView control, 492-503
    compared to DetailsView control, 492, 493
FPSE, 14, 15, 18, 19, 125
From attribute (MailDefinition element), 660, 661
From clause (Select statement), 374, 375
from keyword (C#), 590, 591
From property (MailMessage class), 748, 749
FrontPage Server Extensions (FPSE), 14, 15, 18, 19, 125
FTP, 18, 19
FTP Server, 18, 19, 126, 127
FTP web site
    creating, 126, 127
    running, 130
Future Value form
    aspx code, 54, 55
    C# code, 64, 65
    design, 40, 41
    HTML, 69
    validation controls, 57

G

Generics feature (C#), 560, 561
GenericWebPart class, 780, 781, 782, 785, 801
GetAllRoles method (Roles class), 683
GetAllUsers method (Membership class), 677
GetLastError method (Server class), 758, 759
GetPassword method (MembershipUser class), 679
GetProfile method (ProfileCommon class), 704, 705
GetRolesForUser method (Roles class), 683
GetUser method (Membership class), 677
GetUserNameByEmail method (Membership class), 677
GetUsersInRole method (Roles class), 683
GIF (Graphic Interchange format) file, 236, 237
Global Application Class template, 289
Global.asax file, 285, 288, 289
    custom error handling, 756, 757
    Profile_MigrateAnonymous event, 704, 705
Grid pane (Query Builder), 406, 407

GridView control, 427-463
  compatibility issues with AJAX, 822, 823
  events, 446, 447
  inserting a row, 448, 449
  template fields, 458, 459
  updating, 444-449
group keyword (C#), 591
Group element (profile properties), 696, 697
Group placeholder (ListView control), 526
GroupBy attribute (LinqDataSource control), 598, 599, 609
Grouping profile properties, 696, 697
GroupItemCount attribute (ListView control), 526, 527
GroupName attribute (radio button), 218, 219
GroupPlaceholderID attribute (ListView control), 526
GroupSeparatorTemplate element (ListView control), 507
GroupTemplate element (ListView control), 507, 526, 527

H

H1 element, 172, 173
H2 element, 172, 173
H3 element, 172, 173
Halloween database, 372, 373
  attaching to SQL Server Express, 952, 953
  granting ASP.NET access, 952
Halloween Store application (SSL version), 634-637
Halloween Store master page, 301, 306, 307, 308
HasFile property (file upload control), 238, 239
Head element, 168, 169
Head tag, 22, 50, 54
HeaderStyle element
  DataList control, 414, 415
  DetailsView control, 469
  GridView control, 433
  Wizard control, 741
HeaderTemplate element
  DataList control, 412, 413
  DetailsView control, 469, 483
  GridView control, 459
  Wizard control, 740, 741

HeaderText attribute
  CatalogZone control, 792, 793
  WebPartZone control, 784, 785
HeaderText property
  GridView field, 430, 431
  validation summary control, 258, 259
Height attribute (image control), 236, 237
Height property (web server control), 46, 47, 49
Help documentation, 234, 235
Help page (web service), 934, 935
Horizontal menu, 334, 335
Hot spot, 240, 241
HotSpotMode attribute (image map), 240, 241
Hover class, 182, 183
Href attribute
  A element, 174, 175
  Link element, 186, 187
HTML, 7, 8
  reviewing, 68, 69
HTML controls, 202, 203
  adding to form, 46
HTML document, 8, 9, 162, 163
  coding, 168-175
  structure, 168, 169
HTML Editor, 50, 164
HTML element, 162, 163, 168, 169
  changing, 50, 51
HTML group (Toolbox), 46, 47
HTML image control (adding to a form), 46, 47
HTML message, 754, 755
HTML server control, 40, 41, 202, 203
Html tag, 22, 50, 51
HtmlTextWriter class, 902, 903
HtmlTextWriter object (custom server control), 890, 891, 892, 893
HTTP, 6, 7
HTTP errors, 764, 765
HTTP output stream, 154, 155
HTTP protocol, 618, 619, 630, 631
HTTP redirect message, 83, 86
HTTP request, 8, 9
  AJAX, 808, 809
HTTP response, 8, 9, 100, 101
HttpApplication class, 284, 285
HttpApplicationState class, 284, 285

HttpCookie class, 290, 291
HttpCookieCollection class, 292, 293
HttpRequest class, 632, 633
HTTPS protocol, 618, 619, 630, 631, 632, 633
HttpSessionState class, 102, 103, 276, 277
HttpUnhandledException, 758, 759
Hyperlink control, 205, 236, 237
    with query strings, 296, 297
HyperlinkField element
    DetailsView control, 469
    GridView control, 433
Hypertext Markup Language, *see HTML*
Hypertext Transfer Protocol (HTTP), 6, 7

I

I element, 173
ID attribute
    content placeholder, 305
    DataList control, 411
    DataPager control, 519
    DetailsView control, 469
    GridView control, 429
    LinqDataSource control, 599
    ListView control, 507
    Menu control, 335
    ObjectDataSource control, 548, 549
    SiteMapPath control, 337
    SqlDataSource control, 395
    TreeView control, 330, 331
    user control, 874, 875
ID property (web server control), 48, 49
IDE, 34, 35
Identity column, 370, 371
Identity Increment property (column), 370
Identity property (column), 370
Identity Seed property (column), 370
IEnumerable interface, 591
    select method, 560, 561
IEnumerable type, 98, 99
IEnumerable<T> interface, 590, 591
IIS, 6, 7
    configuring an application (Windows Vista),
      844, 845
    configuring an application (Windows XP), 842,
      843

IIS (continued)
    creating an application (Windows Vista), 966,
      967
    creating a virtual directory (Windows Vista),
      966, 967
    creating a virtual directory (Windows XP), 958,
      959
    forcing a secure connection (Windows Vista),
      970, 971
    forcing a secure connection (Windows XP),
      962, 963
    installing (Windows Vista), 946, 947
    installing (Windows XP), 944, 945
    setting the default page (Windows Vista), 968,
      969
    setting the default page (Windows XP), 960,
      961
    working with certificates (Windows Vista), 628,
      629
IIS 7.0 (working with certificates), 628, 629
IIS Certificate Wizard, 626, 627
IIS Management Console
    Windows Vista, 628, 629, 844, 845, 946, 947,
      966-969, 970, 971
    Windows XP, 842, 843, 944, 945, 960-963, 958,
      959
Image button control, 205, 210, 211
Image control, 205, 236, 237
    adding to a form, 46, 47
Image map, 240, 241
Image map control, 205, 240, 241
ImageAlign attribute (image control), 236, 237
ImageClickEventArgs class, 213
ImageField element
    DetailsView control, 469
    GridView control, 433
Images
    in an email message, 754, 755
    with themes, 344, 345, 354, 355
ImageUrl attribute
    hyperlink control, 236, 237
    image button control, 210, 211
    image control, 236, 237
    image map control, 241
Immediate window, 148, 149
ImportCatalogPart class, 801
ImportCatalogPart control, 793

In-process mode (session state), 280, 281

INamingContainer interface, 914, 915

Index, 366, 367

Index property (e argument), 232

Indexer

   DataRowView class, 99

   DataView class, 99

   HttpApplicationState class, 287

   HttpCookieCollection class, 292, 293

   HttpSessionState class, 102, 103, 277

   ListItemCollection class, 226, 227

   SqlDataReader class, 389

   StateBag class, 275

Inherits attribute

   Control directive, 864, 865

   Master page directive, 305

   Page directive, 22, 170, 171

Init event (page), 62, 63

InitialValue property (required field validator), 252, 253

Inline styles, 176, 177

Inner join, 376, 377

InnerException property (Exception class), 570, 758, 759

Input element (HTML), 166, 167

Insert method

   data access class, 558, 559, 562, 563

   data access class with business objects, 576, 577

   ListItemCollection class, 227

   SqlDataSource control, 448, 449

Insert mode

   DetailsView control, 466, 467, 474

   FormView control, 497

Insert statement

   SQL, 95, 378, 379

   SqlDataSource control, 400

InsertCommand attribute (SqlDataSource control), 422, 423, 449

InsertCommand property (SqlDataAdapter class), 388, 389

InsertItemPosition attribute (ListView control), 506, 507, 509

InsertItemTemplate element

   DetailsView control, 482, 483

   FormView control, 492, 496, 497

   ListView control, 507, 508, 509, 534, 535

InsertMethod attribute (ObjectDataSource control), 548, 549, 558

InsertParameters element (SqlDataSource control), 422, 423

InsertParameters property (SqlDataSource control), 449

InsertRowStyle element (DetailsView control), 469

Instance of a page, 26, 27

Integrated Development Environment (IDE), 34, 35

Intermediate Language (IL), 16, 17

Internal style sheet, 180, 181

Internal styles (content page), 314, 315

Internal Web Browser, 130, 131

Internet Explorer, 6, 7

Internet Information Services, *see IIS*

Interval attribute (Timer control), 824, 825

Intranet, 6, 7

Invoices By Date application (LINQ data source with groups), 610-613

IPageableItemContainer interface, 518

IQueryable<T> interface, 591

IsApproved property (MembershipUser class), 678, 679

IsBodyHtml property (MailMessage class), 749, 754, 755

IsEnabled property (TraceContext class), 152, 153

IsInAsyncPostBack attribute (ScriptManager control), 818, 819

IsPostBack property

   page, 24

   UserControl class, 866, 867

   view state, 273

IsSecureConnection property (HttpRequest class), 632, 633

IsUserInRole method (Roles class), 683

IsValid property

   page, 56, 57, 248, 250, 251

   ServerValidateEventArgs class, 266, 267

   validator, 56, 248, 249, 250

Item placeholder (ListView control), 510, 511, 526

ItemCommand event

   DetailsView control, 479

   ListView control, 533

ItemCreated event (DetailsView control), 479

ItemDeleted event
   DetailsView control, 478, 479
   ListView control, 534
ItemDeleting event
   DetailsView control, 478, 479
   ListView control, 534
ItemInserted event
   DetailsView control, 479
   ListView control, 534
ItemInserting event
   DetailsView control, 479
   ListView control, 534
ItemPlaceholderID attribute (ListView control), 511
Items property
   list box and drop-down list, 224, 225, 226
   list control, 48, 49
   radio button list and check box list, 230, 231
ItemSeparatorTemplate element (ListView control), 507
ItemStyle element
   DataList control, 415
   GridView control, 428, 432, 433
ItemStyle.Width property (GridView field), 430, 431
ItemTemplate element
   DataList control, 412, 413
   DetailsView control, 482, 483
   FormView control, 492, 494, 495
   GridView control, 458, 459
   ListView control, 506, 507, 508, 509, 512, 513
ItemUpdated event
   DetailsView control, 478, 479
   ListView control, 534
ItemUpdating event
   DetailsView control, 478, 479
   ListView control, 534
ItemWrap attribute (Menu control), 335

J

JavaScript, 810, 811
   with AJAX, 808, 809
JavaScript code
   loading with ScriptManager control, 818, 819
   loading with ScriptManagerProxy control, 820, 821

JavaScript Object Notation (JSON), 808, 809
Join, 376, 377
join keyword (C#), 591
JPEG (Joint Photographic Experts Group) file, 236, 237
JSON, 808, 809

K

KeepInEditMode property (e argument), 446, 447, 479, 570
KeepInInsertMode property (e argument), 479
Keys property (StateBag class), 275

L

Label control, 40, 41, 205, 216, 217
LAN (local area network), 6, 7, 18, 19
Language attribute
   Control directive, 865
   Master page directive, 305
   Page directive, 22, 170, 171
Language-Integreted Query, *see LINQ*
Last in wins, 382, 383
LastActivityDate property (MembershipUser class), 679
LastLoginDate property (MembershipUser class), 679
LastPageImageUrl attribute (PagerSettings element), 438, 439
LastPageText attribute (PagerSettings element), 438, 439
Launch Conditions Editor (web setup project), 854
LayoutEditorPart class, 801
LayoutEditorPart control, 794
LayoutOrientation attribute (WebPartZone control), 784
LayoutTemplate element
   ListView control, 506, 507, 510, 511
   ListView control with grouping, 526, 527
Left attribute (RectangleHotSpot element), 240
Line break, 42, 43
Link, 174, 175
Link button control, 205, 210, 211
Link class, 182, 183
Link element, 186, 187
Linking table, 368

LINQ, 590, 591
   using with SQL Server database, 592, 593
LINQ data sources, 589-613
LINQ to Objects, 591, 592
LINQ to SQL, 592, 593
LinqDataSource control, 598-613
   configuring, 600, 601
   configuring for updates, 606, 607
   grouping data, 608-613
List box control, 205, 222-233
   binding, 416, 417
List item, 224, 225
List Members feature, 60
ListControl class, 417
ListItem Collection Editor, 228, 229
ListItem object, 224, 225, 227, 230, 231, 232, 233
ListItemCollection object, 225, 227
ListView control, 505-543
   configuring, 508, 509
   embedded in another ListView control, 610-613
ListView data
   grouping, 526-531
   updating, 532-535
Literal text, 43
   adding to a controls collection, 914, 915
   adding to a table, 44, 45
   formatting, 172, 173, 178
Load event
   page, 24, 62, 63
   retrieving session state data, 278, 279
   user controls, 866, 867
LoadScriptsBeforeUI attribute (ScriptManager
   control), 818, 819
Local IIS web site
   creating, 122, 123
   running in a browser, 134, 135
Localizable attribute (property declaration), 905
Locals window, 146, 147
Lock method (HttpApplicationState class), 287
Login control, 656, 657
   compatibility issues with AJAX, 822, 823
Login controls, 202, 203, 656-667
Login group (Toolbox), 656
Login page, 656, 657
LoginName control, 658, 659
LoginStatus control, 658, 659

LoginText attribute (LoginStatus control), 658, 659
LoginView control, 666, 667
LogoutText attribute (LoginStatus control), 658, 659

M

Machine.config file
   membership provider, 654, 655
   profile provider, 690
Mail client, 744, 745
Mail server, 744, 745
MailAddress class, 748, 749
MailDefinition element (PasswordRecovery
   control), 660, 661
MailMessage class, 748, 749
Manage Styles window, 190
Many-to-many relationship, 368, 369
Master directive, 304, 305
Master page
   aspx code, 304, 305
   code-behind file, 306, 309
   specifying in Page_PreInit event handler, 311, 312
   specifying in web.config file, 311, 312
Master Page template, 302, 303
Master pages, 299-315, 318-321
   nesting, 316, 317
Master property (content page), 320, 321
Master/Detail page, 472, 473
MasterPageFile attribute
   page, 312
   Page directive, 310, 311
   Pages element, 312
MasterType directive (content page), 320, 321
MaxDepthDataBind attribute (TreeView control), 330, 331
Maximum property (range validator), 58, 59, 256, 257
MaximumDynamicDisplay attribute (Menu
   control), 334, 335
MaximumRowsParameterName attribute
   (ObjectDataSource control), 584, 585
MaxLength attribute (text box), 216, 217
Membership class, 676, 677
Membership element (machine.config file), 654
Membership provider, 654, 655

MembershipCreateUserException, 676
MembershipProvider class, 654
MembershipUser class, 676, 678, 679
Menu control, 324, 325, 334, 335
    compatibility issues with AJAX, 822, 823
Message property (Exception class), 758, 759
Methods
    coding, 60, 61
    data access class, 558, 559
Microsoft AJAX Library, 810, 811, 812, 813
Microsoft Certificate Services, 624, 625
Microsoft Intermediate Language (MSIL), 17
Microsoft Passport, 640, 641
Microsoft SharePoint, 778
Middle layer, 546, 547
Migrating data from anonymous to authenticated
    user, 704, 705
MIME (Multipurpose Internet Mail Extension),
    744, 745
Minimum property (range validator), 58, 59, 256,
    257
MinRequiredNonAlphanumericCharacters attribute
    (membership provider), 654, 655
MinRequiredPasswordLength attribute (member-
    ship provider), 654, 655
Mode attribute
    Authentication element, 674, 675
    customErrors element, 765
    PagerSettings element, 438, 439
    sessionState element, 282, 283
Mozilla Firefox, 6, 7, 14, 134, 135
MultiView control, 718-729

N

Name attribute
    ControlParameter element, 404, 405
    Group element, 696, 697
    profile property, 688, 689, 692, 693
Name property (HttpCookie class), 291
Named skin, 350, 351
Namespace, 16, 17
Navigate views, 724, 725
NavigateUrl attribute
    hot spot, 240, 241
    hyperlink control, 236, 237
Navigation application, 338, 339
    web.sitemap file, 328, 329

Navigation controls, 202, 203, 324, 325
NavigationButtonStyle element (Wizard control),
    741
NavigationStyle element (Wizard control), 740,
    741
Nested master pages, 316, 317
Next/previous pager, 516, 517
NextButtonClick event (Wizard control), 739
NextPageImageUrl attribute (PagerSettings
    element), 438, 439
NextPageText attribute (PagerSettings element),
    438, 439
NextPrevStyle element (calendar control), 242
NodeIndent attribute (TreeView control), 330, 331
NodeWrap attribute (TreeView control), 330, 331
Non-primary key, 366, 367
NullDisplayText property (GridView field), 430,
    431
Nulls, 370, 371
    optimistic concurrency bug, 480, 481
Numbered list, 232, 233
Numeric pager, 516, 517

O

O/R Designer, 594-597
Object data sources, 545-575
    and business objects, 576, 577
Object model, 592, 593, 594, 595
Object Relational Designer, 593, 594-597
ObjectDataSource control, 546, 547
    configuring, 550, 551
    paging, 584-587
OldValuesParameterFormatString attribute
    ObjectDataSource control, 562, 563, 564, 576
    SqlDataSource control, 452
OnClick attribute (button), 22, 23
One-to-many relationship, 368, 369
One-to-one relationship, 368, 369
Open method (SqlConnection class), 387
Opera, 6, 7, 14
Operator property (compare validator), 254, 255
Optimistic concurrency, 382, 383, 422, 423
    affect on parameters, 562, 563, 564
    bug, 480, 481
    GridView control, 446, 447
    LinqDataSource control, 606, 607

Optimistic concurrency (continued)
　　with update method that uses business objects, 576, 577
Oracle, 6
Order By clause (Select statement), 374, 375
Order content page, 314, 315
Order form (Shopping Cart application), 20-25
OrderBy attribute (LinqDataSource control), 598, 599
orderby keyword (C#), 590, 591
OrderGroupsBy attribute (LinqDataSource control), 598, 599, 609
Orientation attribute (Menu control), 334, 335
Output window, 140, 141

P

P element, 172, 173
Page, 40
Page caching (browser), 768, 769
Page class, 24
Page directive, 22, 168, 169, 170, 171
　　content page, 310, 311
Page events, 62, 63
　　master and content pages, 306, 309
Page layout, 198, 199
Page property (UserControl class), 866, 867
Page_Error event handler, 756-759
PageButtonCount attribute (PagerSettings element), 438, 439
PageCatalogPart class, 801
PageCatalogPart control, 792, 793
PagedControlID attribute (DataPager control), 518, 519
PageIndexChanged event (DetailsView control), 479
PagerSettings element
　　DetailsView control, 469, 470
　　GridView control, 437, 438, 439
PagerStyle element
　　DetailsView control, 469, 470
　　GridView control, 433, 436, 437
PagerTemplate element (DetailsView control), 469, 470
Pages element (web.config file), 312, 346, 347
PageSize attribute
　　DataPager control, 518, 519
　　GridView control, 439

Paging
　　DetailsView control, 470, 471
　　GridView control, 436-439
　　ListView control, 508, 509, 516-519
　　object data source, 584-587
Panel class, 780, 781
Parameter class, 449
Parameter sources, 408, 409
Parameterless constructor (data access class), 558
ParameterName property (SqlParameter class), 387
Parameters, 387, 388
　　defining, 408, 409
　　for data access methods that use business objects, 576, 577
　　for update, delete, and insert methods, 562, 563
　　passing to select method, 560
Parameters property (SqlCommand class), 387
Parent element, 168, 169
Parent master page, 316, 317
ParentLevelsDisplayed attribute (SiteMapPath control), 337
Part class, 780, 781
PartChromeStyle element, 796
Partial class, 24, 26, 27
partial keyword (class declaration), 24
Passive mode (FTP), 126, 127
Passport authentication, 640, 641
PasswordQuestion property (MembershipUser class), 679
PasswordRecovery control, 662, 663, 750
　　compatibility issues with AJAX, 822, 823
PathDirection attribute (SiteMapPath control), 337
PathSeparator attribute (SiteMapPath control), 337
pdb file (web control library), 900
Permissions (directory), 966
Persistent cookies, 290, 291
　　authentication ticket, 642, 643
Personalization feature, 686
Personalization provider, 778, 779
Placeholder (ListView control), 510, 511
PolygonHotSpot element (image map), 240, 241
POP (Post Office Protocol), 744, 745
Portals, 774, 779
Position attribute (PagerSettings element), 438, 439
Postback, 10, 11

PostBackUrl attribute
   button, 22, 88, 89, 210, 211
   query string, 296, 297
PostBackUrl property (Continue button,
      CreateUserWizard control), 660, 661
PostBackValue attribute (hot spot), 240, 241
PostedFile property (file upload control), 239
PostedFile.ContentLength property (file upload
      control), 238
Precompiled deployment, 846, 847-853, 850
PreInit event (page), 356, 357, 358, 359
PreRender event
   page, 62, 63
   saving session state data, 278, 279
   user control, 866, 867
Presentation layer, 546, 547
PreviousButtonClick event (Wizard control), 739
PreviousPage property (Page class), 88, 89
PreviousPageImageUrl attribute (PagerSettings
      element), 438, 439
PreviousPageText attribute (PagerSettings ele-
      ment), 438, 439
Primary key, 366, 367
   affect on parameters, 562, 563, 564
Primary key table, 369
Product class, 104, 105
Product List application
   AJAX-enabled version, 828-837
   GridView control version, 440-443
   LinqDataSource control version, 602-605
   ListView control version, 520-525
   ListView control with groups version, 528-531
   ObjectDataSource control version, 552-557
   SqlDataSource control version, 392, 393, 420,
      421
Product Maintenance application, 484-491
ProductDB class, 556, 557
ProductDisplay user control, 878-881
Profile element (web.config file), 688, 689, 692,
      693
Profile feature, 12, 13, 686, 687
Profile properties
   defining, 692, 693
   grouping, 696, 697
Profile property (HttpContext class), 688, 689,
      692, 693
Profile provider, 686, 687, 690, 691

Profile_MigrateAnonymous event, 704, 705
ProfileCommon class, 686, 687, 690, 691
ProfileManager class, 704, 705
ProfileParameter element, 405
ProfileProvider class, 690
Profiles, 685-715
   anonymous users, 702-705
   authenticated users, 692-701
   compared to session state, 686, 687
Project, 32
Properties (changing from Source view), 50, 51
Properties element (profile), 688, 689, 692, 693
Properties window, 34, 35, 46, 47
Property attributes (custom server control), 904,
      905
Property declaration
   custom server control, 890, 891
   designer attributes, 905
Property names (for business class used with object
      data source), 577, 578
PropertyGridEditorPart class, 801
PropertyGridEditorPart control, 794
PropertyName attribute
   ControlParameter element, 405
   SqlDataSource control, 395
Pseudo-class, 182, 183
Public attribute (Doctype declaration), 171
Publish Web Site command, 846, 847, 850, 851

Q

Quantifier (regular expression), 264, 265
Query Builder, 406-409
Query expression, 590, 591
Query operators, 591
Query string, 296, 297, 404
Query variable, 590, 591
Querying a table, 374, 375
QueryString property (HttpRequest class), 296,
      297
QueryStringParameter element, 404, 405

R

Radio button control, 205, 218, 219
Radio button list control, 205, 230, 231
   binding, 417
Radius attribute (CircleHotSpot element), 240

Range validator, 56, 58, 59, 247, 256, 257
Read method (SqlDataReader class), 389
Read-only properties (profiles), 698, 699
ReadOnly attribute
   profile property, 698, 699
   text box, 216, 217
ReadOnly mode
   DetailsView control, 466, 467
   FormView control, 495
ReadOnly property (GridView field), 430, 431
Record, 366, 367
RectangleHotSpot element, 241
Redirect attribute (Error element), 765
Redirect method
   custom error handling, 760, 761
   HttpResponse class, 24, 83, 86
   query strings, 296, 297
   secure connections, 630, 632
RedirectFromLoginPage method
     (FormsAuthentication class), 680, 681
Reference-type variable, 278, 279
Reflection, 550, 558, 559, 562
Refresh-button problem, 770
Register a custom WebPart control, 802, 803
Register directive
   custom server control, 901
   custom WebPart control, 802, 803
   user control, 788, 789, 874, 875
Registration Authority (RA), 622, 623
Registry Editor (web setup project), 854
Regular class, 182, 183
Regular expression, 264, 265
Regular expression validator, 247, 262, 263
Rel attribute (Link element), 186, 187
Relational database, 366, 367
Relative URL, 90, 91
Release version, 856, 857
RememberMeSet attribute (Login control), 657
RememberMeText attribute (Login control), 657
Remote Debug Monitor, 128
Remote IIS web site
   creating, 124, 125
   running in a browser, 134, 135
Remove method
   ControlCollection class, 915
   HttpApplicationState class, 287
   HttpCookieCollection class, 293

Remove method (continued)
   HttpSessionState class, 102, 103
   ListItemCollection class, 227
   StateBag class, 275
RemoveAt method (ListItemCollection class), 227
RemoveUserFromRole method (Roles class), 683
Render method (WebControl class)
   overriding, 892, 893
   superclassed control, 908
RenderBeginTag method (WebControl class), 892, 893
   superclassed control, 908
RenderContents method (WebControl class)
   custom server control, 890, 891
   custom WebPart control, 802, 803
   overriding, 892, 893
RenderCurrentNodeAsLink attribute (SiteMapPath control), 337
Rendered control, 888-897
RenderEndTag method (WebControl class), 892, 893
   superclassed control, 908
Rendering controls, 22, 166, 167
RepeatColumns attribute (radio button list and check box list), 230, 231
RepeatDirection attribute (radio button list and check box list), 230, 231
Repeater control, 410
RepeatLayout attribute (radio button list and check box list), 230, 231
Request property
   page, 292, 293, 297
   UserControl class, 866, 867
Required field validator, 56, 58, 59, 247, 252, 253
RequiresQuestionAndAnswer attribute (membership provider), 676
ResetPassword method (MembershipUser class), 679
Response property
   HttpContext class, 155
   page, 24, 83, 86, 155
   UserControl class, 866, 867
Response.AppendHeader method, 769
Response.Cache.SetCacheability method, 769
Response.Cache.SetExpires method, 769
Response.Cache.SetNoStore method, 769
Restart command, 145

Result set, 374, 375

Result table, 374, 375

ReturnValue property (e argument), 570

Rich internet application (RIA), 806, 807

Right attribute (RectangleHotSpot element), 240

Role provider, 654, 655

RoleProvider class, 654

Roles, 648, 649

Roles class, 682, 683

Root element, 168, 169

Round trip, 10, 11

Row
  database table, 366, 367
  HTML table, 44, 45, 194, 195
  inserting in GridView control, 448, 449

Row property (text box), 217

RowCancelingEdit event (GridView control), 447

RowDataBound event (GridView control), 447

RowDeleted event (GridView control), 446, 447

RowDeleting event (GridView control), 446, 447

RowEditing event (GridView control), 447

RowFilter property (DataView class), 98, 99

Rows property (list box and drop-down list), 224, 225

Rowspan attribute (Td element), 196, 197

RowStyle element
  DetailsView control, 469
  GridView control, 433

RowUpdated event (GridView control), 447

RowUpdating event (GridView control), 446, 447

Run To Cursor command, 144, 145

Runat attribute
  content placeholder, 305
  DataList control, 411
  DataPager control, 519
  DetailsView control, 469
  GridView control, 429
  HTML element, 202
  LayoutTemplate element (ListView control), 510, 511
  LinqDataSource control, 599
  ListView control, 507
  Menu control, 335
  ObjectDataSource control, 548, 549
  SiteMapPath control, 337
  SqlDataSource control, 395

Runat attribute (continued)
  user control, 874, 875
  web server control, 22, 48, 49

Running an application, 26, 27, 66, 67, 129

S

Sales Portal page, 774-777, 779

SaveAs method (file upload control), 238, 239

ScriptManager control, 814, 815, 818, 819

ScriptManagerProxy control, 814, 815, 820, 821

Secure connection, 618, 619, 630-633
  forcing under Windows Vista, 970, 971
  forcing under Windows XP, 962, 963
  login page, 656

Secure property (HttpCookie class), 291

Security, 617-627, 630-637

Security Setup Wizard, 644

Select attribute (LinqDataSource control), 598, 599

Select clause (Select statement), 374, 375

select keyword (C#), 590, 591

Select method
  AccessDataSource class, 98, 99
  data access class, 558-561

Select parameter, 404, 405

Select statement (SQL), 94, 95, 374-377
  configuring, 400, 401
  creating with Query Builder, 406, 407

SelectCommand attribute (SqlDataSource control), 395

SelectCommand property (SqlDataAdapter class), 388, 389

SelectCountMethod attribute (ObjectDataSource control), 584, 585

Selected property
  list item, 224, 225, 232, 233
  radio button list and check box list, 230

SelectedDate property (calendar control), 242

SelectedDates property (calendar control), 242

SelectedIndex property
  GridView control, 429, 444
  list box and drop-down list, 224, 225, 226
  list control, 49
  radio button list and check box list, 230, 231

SelectedIndexChanged event, 207
  GridView control, 447
  list box and drop-down list, 224, 225
  list control, 62, 63

SelectedIndexChanging event (GridView control), 447

SelectedItem property
   list box and drop-down list, 224, 225
   list control, 49
   radio button list and check box list, 230, 231

SelectedItemTemplate element (ListView control), 507, 532

SelectedRow property (GridView control), 444

SelectedRowStyle element (GridView control), 433, 444

SelectedValue property
   drop-down list, 96, 97, 224, 225
   list box, 224, 225
   list control, 48, 49, 416, 417
   radio button list and check box list, 230, 231

SelectImage attribute (CommandField element), 445

SelectionChanged event (calendar control), 242

SelectionMode property
   calendar control, 242, 243
   list box and drop-down list, 224, 225

SelectMethod attribute (ObjectDataSource control), 548, 549, 550, 558

SelectParameters element
   ObjectDataSource control, 560, 561
   SqlDataSource control, 404, 405

SelectText attribute (CommandField element), 445

Self-closing tag, 172

Self-signed certificate, 628, 629

SelfClosingTagEnd field (HtmlTextWriter class), 902, 903

Send method (SmtpClient class), 750, 751

Sender argument (Click event), 210, 211

SeparatorStyle element (DataList control), 415

SeparatorTemplate element (DataList control), 413

Serializable attribute (custom data type), 700, 701

SerializeAs attribute (profile property), 700, 701

Server, 6, 7

Server certificate, 621

Server controls, 10, 11, 40
   adding, 46, 47, 165
   setting properties, 46, 47
   types, 202, 203
   UserControl class, 867

Server Error page, 137

Server property (page), 83, 86, 758

ServerValidate event (custom validator), 266, 267

Service description (web service), 934

Session cookie, 290, 291
   authentication ticket, 642, 643

Session ID, 12, 13, 100, 101, 276, 277
   tracking, 280, 281, 282

Session property
   HttpContext class, 102, 103, 276, 277
   page, 24, 103, 276, 277
   UserControl class, 866, 867

Session state, 12, 13, 74, 100-103, 276-283
   compared to profiles, 686, 687
   uses, 100, 101
   with custom error handling, 760, 761
   with the back-button problem, 770, 771

Session state object, 12, 13, 24, 100, 101, 102, 103, 276, 277

Session state store provider, 280, 281

Session_End event, 289

Session_Start event, 288, 289

SessionID property (HttpSessionState class), 103

SessionParameter element, 405

SessionState element (web.config file), 282, 283

Set Next Statement command, 144, 145

Setup program, 846, 847, 854-857

Setup.exe file, 856, 857

Setup.msi file, 856, 857

Shopping Cart application
   basic version, 74-79, 104-115
   files, 20, 21
   FormView control version, 498-503
   master page version, 301

ShoutBox application, 828-837

ShoutItem class, 830, 831

ShoutItemList class, 830, 831

Show Next Statement command, 144, 145

ShowCancelButton attribute (CommandField element), 445

ShowDeleteButton attribute (CommandField element), 445

ShowEditButton attribute (CommandField element), 444, 445

ShowExpandCollapse attribute (TreeView control), 330, 331

ShowFirstPageButton attribute (next/previous pager), 519

ShowHeader property (GridView field), 430, 431

ShowLastPageButton attribute (next/previous pager), 519

ShowLines attribute (TreeView control), 330, 331

ShowMessageBox property (validation summary control), 258, 259

ShowNextPageButton attribute (next/previous pager), 519

ShowPreviousPageButton attribute (next/previous pager), 519

ShowSelectButton attribute (CommandField element), 445

ShowStartingNode attribute (SiteMapDataSource control), 332, 333

ShowSummary property (validation summary control), 258, 259

Side bar (Wizard control), 730

SideBarButtonClick event (Wizard control), 739

SideBarButtonStyle element (Wizard control), 741

SideBarStyle element (Wizard control), 740, 741

SideBarTemplate element (Wizard control), 740, 741

SignOut method (FormsAuthentication class), 680, 681

Single root certificate, 622, 623

Site map data source, 332

Site Map template, 326, 327

Site navigation, 323-339

SiteMap element (web.sitemap), 326

SiteMapDataSource control, 324, 325, 332, 333

SiteMapNode element (web.sitemap), 326, 327

SiteMapPath control, 324, 325, 336, 337

Skin (WebPartZone control), 798, 799

Skin File template, 351

SkinID attribute (skin), 350, 351, 356, 357

SkinID property (server control), 356, 357

Skins, 344, 345, 350, 351
    applying to controls, 356, 357
    storing in separate files, 352, 353

Smart tag (syntax error), 66, 67

Smart tag menu, 47, 48

SMTP (Simple Mail Transfer Protocol), 744, 745

Smtp section (web.config file), 750

SMTP service (IIS), 746, 747

SMTP settings, 750, 751

SmtpClient class, 750, 751

SOAP (Simple Object Access Protocol), 926, 927

Software requirements, 14, 15

Solution Explorer, 20, 21, 34, 35
    adding items, 36, 37

Solution file, 32, 33

SortExpression attribute (GridView column), 434, 435

Sorting
    GridView control, 434, 435
    ListView control, 514, 515

Source property (Exception class), 758, 759

Source view, 34, 50, 51, 54, 55, 164, 165

Span element, 42, 43, 178, 179

Split view, 34, 52, 53, 164

SQL data source, 392

SQL dialect, 374

SQL pane (Query Builder), 407

SQL Server, 6, 7, 14, 15, 365

SQL Server 2005 Express Edition, 14, 15, 18, 365
    installing, 950, 951

SQL Server Configuration Manager, 950, 951

SQL Server data types, 371

SQL Server mode (session state), 280, 281

SqlCommand class, 386, 387

SqlConnection class, 386, 387

SqlConnectionString attribute (sessionState element), 282, 283

SqlDataAdapter class, 388, 389

SqlDataReader class, 388, 389

SqlDataSource control, 392, 393
    creating, 394, 395

SqlDbType property (SqlParameter class), 387

SqlParameter class, 387, 388

Src attribute (Register directive), 874, 875

SSL (Secure Sockets Layer), 618, 619

SSL client authentication, 620

SSL server authentication, 620

SSL strength, 622, 623

Stack trace, 137

Standalone environment, 18, 19

Standard controls, 202, 203

Standard group (Toolbox), 46, 47

Standard toolbar, 34, 35

Start tag, 162, 163

Start/Continue command, 145

StartFromCurrentNode attribute (SiteMapDataSource control), 332, 333

StartingNodeUrl attribute (SiteMapDataSource control), 332, 333

StartNavigationTemplate element (Wizard control), 740, 741

StartNextButtonStyle element (Wizard control), 741

StartRowIndexParameterName attribute (ObjectDataSource control), 584, 585

State, 12, 13

State server mode (session state), 280, 281

StateBag class, 274, 275

StateConnectionString attribute (sessionState element), 282, 283

Stateless protocol, 12, 13

Statement completion feature, 164, 165

Static menu, 334

Static web pages, 8, 9

StaticDisplayLevels attribute (Menu control), 335

StaticEnableDefaultPopOutImage attribute (Menu control), 335

StatusCode attribute (Error element), 765

Step Into command, 144, 145

Step Out command, 144, 145

Step Over command, 144, 145

StepNavigationTemplate element (Wizard control), 741

StepNextButtonStyle element (Wizard control), 741

StepPreviousButtonStyle element (Wizard control), 741

Steps (Wizard control), 730, 731
  adding or removing, 732, 733

StepType attribute (WizardStep control), 736, 737, 738, 739

Stop Debugging command, 145

Stored procedure (SqlDataSource control), 400

Strong element, 42, 43

Strongly-typed collection (select method), 560, 561

Style Application toolbar, 190

Style attribute, 176, 177
  Span element, 42, 43, 179

Style Builder, 349

Style class, 178, 180, 181, 182, 183

Style element, 178, 180, 181
  master page, 306, 307

Style elements (DataList control), 414, 415

Style properties, 176, 177
  adding to style rule, 188, 189
  tables, 196, 197

Style rule, 180, 181, 186, 187
  adding, 184, 185, 188, 189
  applying to document, 192, 193
  modifying, 184, 185

Style sheet, 188, 189

Style Sheet template, 188, 189, 349

Style sheet themes, 360, 361

Style tag, 22

Styles, 176-179, 182-189
  applying to document, 190, 191
  inline, 176, 177
  Wizard control, 740, 741

StyleSheetTheme attribute (Pages element), 360, 361

StyleSheetTheme property (page), 360, 361

Subject property (MailMessage class), 748, 749

Superclassed control, 888, 889, 908-913

Syntax error (HTML), 164, 165

System data type, 370

System.ComponentModel namespace, 565, 868

System.Data namespace, 363

System.Net.Mail namespace, 749, 751

System.web element (web.config file), 282, 692, 693

System.Web.Security namespace, 677, 679, 681, 683

System.Web.Services namespace, 931

T

TabIndex property (web server control), 49

Table element, 194, 195

Table tag, 50

TableName attribute (LinqDataSource control), 598, 599

Tables (database), 366, 367
  joining, 376, 377
  querying, 374, 375

Tables (HTML), 44, 45, 194-199
  controlling page layout, 198, 199

Tag
  custom server control, 901
  custom WebPart control, 802, 803
  HTML, 162, 163
  self-closing, 172
  user control, 874, 875

TagName attribute (Register directive), 874, 875

TagPrefix attribute (Register directive), 874, 875

TagRightCharacter field (HtmlTextWriter class), 902, 903
Target framework, 32
Td element, 194, 195, 196
Template fields
    DetailsView control, 482, 483
    GridView control, 458, 459
Template-editing mode
    DataList control, 392, 413
    FormView control, 492, 493
    Wizard control, 740, 741
TemplateField element
    DetailsView control, 469, 483
    GridView control, 433, 458, 459
Templates, 410, 411
    DataList control, 412, 413
    FormView control, 492, 493
    ListView control, 506, 507
    Wizard control, 740, 741
Testing applications, 128-135
    file-system web sites with IIS, 132, 133
    from outside Visual Studio, 134, 135
    with a browser other than the default, 130, 131
    with the default browser, 128, 129
Text attribute
    button and link button, 210, 211
    check box and radio button, 218, 219
    hyperlink control, 236, 237
Text box control, 40, 41, 205, 216, 217
Text Editor toolbar, 60, 61
Text Editor window, 188
Text formatting elements, 172, 173
Text property
    binding, 418, 419
    custom server control, 890, 891
    label, 216, 217, 220
    list item, 224, 225, 226, 227, 228, 229
    text box, 217, 220
    validator, 248, 249, 258, 259
    web server control, 48, 49
TextChanged event (text box), 62, 63, 207
TextMode attribute (text box), 216, 217
Th element, 510, 511
Theme attribute
    Page directive, 356, 357, 358, 359
    Pages element, 346, 347, 358, 359

Theme property (page), 356, 357, 358, 359
Themes, 341-361
    applying to a page, 356, 357
    applying to an application, 346, 347
    making available to an application, 346, 347
    removing, 358, 359
Tilde operator, 88, 89, 90, 91
Timeout attribute (sessionState element), 282, 283
Timer control, 814, 815, 824, 825
Timestamps (using to avoid the back-button problem), 770, 771
Title (form), 54
    modifying, 50, 51
Title attribute
    Page directive, 310
    Part class, 782, 785
    siteMapNode element, 327
Title element, 168, 169
Title property (custom WebPart control), 802, 803
Title tag, 22
TitleStyle element (calendar control), 242
To property (MailMessage class), 748, 749
TodayDayStyle element (calendar control), 242
Toolbox, 34, 35
ToolboxData attribute (class declaration), 904, 905
ToolTip property (web server control), 49
Top attribute (RectangleHotSpot element), 240
Tr element, 194, 195
Trace attribute (Page directive), 150, 151, 170, 171
Trace feature, 150-153
    size of view state, 272, 273
Trace messages (custom), 152, 153
Trace output, 150, 151
Trace property (page), 152, 153
Tracepoint, 140, 141
Transact-SQL, 374
Transfer method
    HttpServerUtility class, 83, 86
    query strings, 296, 297
TreeView control, 324, 325, 330, 331
    compatibility issues with AJAX, 822, 823
Trial certificate, 624, 625
Trigger (UpdatePanel control), 822, 823
try-catch statement (custom error handling), 756, 757, 758, 759
Two-way binding, 418, 419, 458

Type attribute
  ControlParameter element, 405
  Input element, 166, 167
  Link element, 186, 187
  profile property, 688, 689, 694, 695
  Style element, 180
Type property
  compare validator, 254, 255
  range validator, 58, 59, 256, 257
TypeName attribute (ObjectDataSource control),
  548, 549, 550

U

Uniform Resource Locator, *see URL*
Unique constraint, 366
Unique key, 366, 367
Unique key constraint, 366, 367
Unlock method (HttpApplicationState class), 287
Update method
  data access class, 558, 559, 562, 563
  data access class with business objects, 576, 577
  data source control, 444
  SqlDataAdapter class, 388, 389
Update statement
  SQL, 95, 378, 379
  SqlDataSource control, 400
UpdateCheck property (entity class column), 606,
  607
UpdateCommand attribute (SqlDataSource
  control), 422, 423
UpdateCommand property (SqlDataAdapter class),
  388, 389
UpdateImage attribute (CommandField element),
  445
UpdateMethod attribute (ObjectDataSource
  control), 548, 549, 558
UpdateMode attribute (UpdatePanel control), 822,
  823, 824
UpdatePanel control, 814, 815, 822, 823
UpdateParameters element (SqlDataSource
  control), 422, 423
UpdateProgress control, 814, 815, 826, 827
UpdateText attribute (CommandField element),
  445
UpdateUser method (Membership class), 677, 678
URL, 8, 9
  coding, 90, 91

Url attribute (siteMapNode element), 327
URL encoding, 296, 297
Url property (HttpRequest class), 632, 633
User Account Control (Windows Vista), 952, 953
User Control Designer, 864, 865
User controls, 861-881
  adding to web forms, 872, 873
  adding to web part zones, 786, 787
  compared to custom server controls, 886, 887
  creating, 864-871
  working with from web form, 876, 877
User Interface Editor (web setup project), 854
UserControl class, 866, 867
Username property (MembershipUser class), 679
Users, 650, 651
Users attribute (Deny and Allow elements), 674,
  675
using statement, 77
UUEncode format, 752, 753

V

Validate method (page), 249, 260, 261
ValidateUser method (Membership class), 676,
  677, 680
Validation controls, 40, 56-59, 202, 203, 245-269
Validation group, 260, 261
  Toolbox, 56
Validation summary control, 246, 247, 258, 259
ValidationExpression property (regular expression
  validator), 262, 263
ValidationGroup attribute
  button, 260, 261
  CommandField element, 445
ValidationGroup property (validator), 249
Validators, 56, 246, 247
Valign attribute (Td and Tr elements), 197
Value attribute (bulleted list), 232, 233
Value property
  HttpCookie class, 290, 291
  list item, 224, 225, 226, 227, 228, 229
  ServerValidateEventArgs class, 266, 267
  SqlParameter class, 387
Value-type variable, 278, 279
Values property (StateBag class), 275
ValueToCompare property (compare validator),
  254, 255

Verb (web part), 792
Vertical menu, 334, 335
View control, 720, 721
View state, 12, 13, 272-275
    MultiView control, 726, 727
    using to avoid the back-button problem, 770,
        771
    when to disable, 272, 273
    Wizard control, 736
View state data, 68, 69
View state object, 274, 275
Views (MultiView control), 718, 719
    adding, 720, 721
    navigating, 724, 725
Views property (MultiView control), 728, 729
ViewState property (page), 274, 275
Virtual directory (IIS)
    creating from Visual Studio, 122, 123
    creating under Windows Vista, 966, 967
    creating under Windows XP, 958, 959
Virtual root, 126
VirtualDirectory property (File System Editor),
    854
Visible attribute
    calendar control, 242
    CloseVerb element, 792, 793
    HeaderCloseVerb element, 792, 793
    PagerSettings element, 438, 439
Visible property
    binding, 418, 419
    web server control, 49
Visited class, 182, 183
Visual Studio 2008
    editions, 14, 15
    installing, 948, 949
Visual Web Developer 2008 Express Edition, 14,
    15
    installing, 948, 949

W

Warn method (TraceContext class), 152, 153
Watch expression, 147
Watch window, 146, 147
Web application, 4
    compiling, 26, 27
    ending, 66, 67

Web application (continued)
    running, 26, 27, 66, 67
    testing, 66, 67, 128-135
Web application project, 33
Web browser, 6, 7
Web Configuration File template, 282
Web control library, 884, 885, 886, 887
    creating, 898, 899
    testing, 900, 901
Web Custom Control template, 891
Web form, 4, 7, 34, 35
    adding, 82, 83
    modifying title, 50, 51
    renaming, 84, 85
    starting, 84, 85
Web Form template, 82, 83
Web Forms Designer, 20, 21, 34, 35
Web method, 930, 931
Web page, 4, 7
    linking to a style sheet, 189
Web part controls, 202, 203
Web part zone, 776, 779
Web parts, 773-803
    formatting, 798, 799
Web project, 33, 34
Web reference, 936, 937
Web server, 6, 7
Web server controls, 40, 41, 202, 203, 204, 205
    rendering, 166, 167
Web Service help page, 934, 935
Web service proxy, 818, 819
Web Service template, 929
Web services, 925-939
    consuming, 936-939
    creating, 928-933
    registering with ScriptManager control, 818,
        819
    registering with ScriptManagerProxy control,
        820, 821
    testing, 934-935
Web Setup project, 846, 847, 854-857
Web site, 32, 33
    closing, 38, 39
    opening, 38, 39
    starting, 32, 33
Web Site Administration Tool
    configuring an application, 840, 841

Web Site Administration Tool (continued)
  security, 644-653
  SMTP settings, 750, 751
Web User Control template, 864, 865
Web.config file, 33, 78, 79
  adding, 693
  application path, 630, 631
  HTTP errors, 764, 765
  profile properties, 686, 687
  themes, 346, 347
Web.config files (Authentication application), 674, 675
Web.sitemap file, 324, 325, 326, 327
  Navigation application, 328, 329
WebControl class (custom server controls), 884, 885, 888, 889, 890
WebMethod attribute, 930, 931
WebPart class, 780, 781, 801, 802, 803
WebPart control (custom), 802, 803
WebPart hierarchy, 780, 781
WebPartManager class, 800, 801
WebPartManager control, 782, 783, 785
WebParts group (Toolbox), 782, 783
WebPartsTemplate element (web parts catalog), 792, 793
WebPartVerb class, 801
WebPartZone class, 801
WebPartZone control, 782, 783, 785
  formatting, 798, 799
WebService attribute, 930, 931
WebService class, 930, 931
Where attribute (LinqDataSource control), 598, 599
Where clause (Select statement), 374, 375
  creating for SqlDataSource control, 402, 403
where keyword (C#), 590, 591
White space (HTML), 162, 164
Whitespace character (regular expression), 264, 265
Width attribute (image control), 236, 237
Width property (web server control), 49
Windows-based authentication, 640, 641
Wizard control, 730-741
WizardStep Collection Editor, 732, 733
WizardStep control, 738, 739
WizardStep tag, 732, 733

WizardSteps tag, 732, 733
Word character (regular expression), 264, 265
Wrap attribute (text box), 216, 217
Write method
  HtmlTextWriter class, 890, 891, 892, 893, 902, 903
  HttpResponse class, 154, 155
  TraceContext class, 152, 153
WriteAttribute method (HtmlTextWriter class), 902, 903
WriteBeginTag method (HtmlTextWriter class), 902, 903
WriteEndTag method (HtmlTextWriter class), 902, 903
WSDL (Web Services Description Language), 926, 927, 934
wsdl file, 938, 939

X

X attribute (CircleHotSpot element), 240
X property (ImageClickEventArgs class), 212, 213
XCopy deployment, 846-849
XHTML version 1.0 Transitional, 170, 171
XML
  web service, 926, 927, 934
  with AJAX, 808, 809
XMLHttpRequest object, 808, 809, 810

Y

Y attribute (CircleHotSpot element), 240
Y property (ImageClickEventArgs class), 212, 213

Z

ZoneTemplate element (WebPartZone control), 782, 783, 785

What software you need for this book

- Any full edition of Microsoft Visual Studio 2008 or the free Visual Web Developer Express Edition.

- These editions include everything you need for developing ASP.NET 3.5 applications, including .NET Framework 3.5, ASP.NET 3.5, C# 2008, a built-in web server, and a scaled-back version of SQL Server called SQL Server Express.

- If you want to use IIS (Internet Information Services) instead of the built-in web server to run web applications on your own PC, you also need to install IIS. You need to do this to test some aspects of web applications, and IIS comes with Windows XP (except the Home Edition) and Windows Vista (except the Home Basic Edition and the Starter Edition).

- To learn more about installing these products, please read appendix A.

The downloadable files for this book

- The source code for all the applications presented in this book.

- Access and SQL Server Express versions of the Halloween database used by these applications.

- Files you can use to work with the SQL Server Express version of the Halloween database.

- The application and files you'll need to do the exercises at the end of chapters 1 through 4.

- Solutions for the exercises for chapters 2 and 3 so you can see how they work.

- To learn more about downloading and installing these applications and databases, please read appendix A.

The Visual Basic edition of this book

- If this book looks interesting but you're a Visual Basic developer, please see *Murach's ASP.NET 3.5 Web Programming with VB 2008*. It covers all of the same features but uses Visual Basic coding examples.

www.murach.com